FIGHTS

ONE BOY'S TRIUMPH OVER VIOLENCE

AN ONI PRESS PUBLICATION

DESIGNED BY **SONJA SYNAK**
EDITED BY **ANDREA COLVIN** WITH **SHAWNA GORE**

PUBLISHED BY **ONI PRESS, INC.**
FOUNDER & CHIEF FINANCIAL OFFICER **JOE NOZEMACK**
PUBLISHER **JAMES LUCAS JONES**
EDITOR IN CHIEF **SARAH GAYDOS**
E.V.P. OF CREATIVE & BUSINESS DEVELOPMENT **CHARLIE CHU**
DIRECTOR OF OPERATIONS **BRAD ROOKS**
DIRECTOR OF SALES **MARGOT WOOD**
SPECIAL PROJECTS MANAGER **AMBER O'NEILL**
DIRECTOR OF DESIGN & PRODUCTION **TROY LOOK**
DIGITAL PREPRESS LEAD **ANGIE KNOWLES**
SENIOR GRAPHIC DESIGNER **KATE Z. STONE**
GRAPHIC DESIGNER **SONJA SYNAK**
SENIOR EDITOR **ROBIN HERRERA**
EXECUTIVE ASSISTANT **MICHELLE NGUYEN**
LOGISTICS COORDINATOR **JUNG LEE**

ONIPRESS.COM
FACEBOOK.COM/ONIPRESS
TWITTER.COM/ONIPRESS
ONIPRESS.TUMBLR.COM
INSTAGRAM.COM/ONIPRESS

INSTAGRAM.COM/JOELCHRISTIANGILL
TWITTER.COM/JCG007

1319 SE Martin Luther King, Jr. Blvd.
Suite 240
Portland, OR 97214

First Edition: January 2020
ISBN 978-1-5493-0335-7
eISBN 978-1-62010-713-3

Printing numbers:
1 2 3 4 5 6 7 8 9 10

Printed in China

Library of Congress Control Number: 2019945918

FIGHTS

ONE BOY'S TRIUMPH OVER VIOLENCE

WORDS AND PICTURES
JOEL CHRISTIAN GILL
COLORS **SHANNON SCOTT**
PRODUCTION ASSISTANCE **JADE RODRIGUEZ**

For my **mother:**
She gave me life.

For my **wife:**
She saved my life.

For **Aerial, Victoria,
Mary-Catherine,**
and **Christian:**
They are my life.

*"Society must accept some
things as real; but he must always know
that visible reality hides a deeper one,
and that all our action and achievement
rest on things unseen."*

—JAMES BALDWIN

PROLOGUE

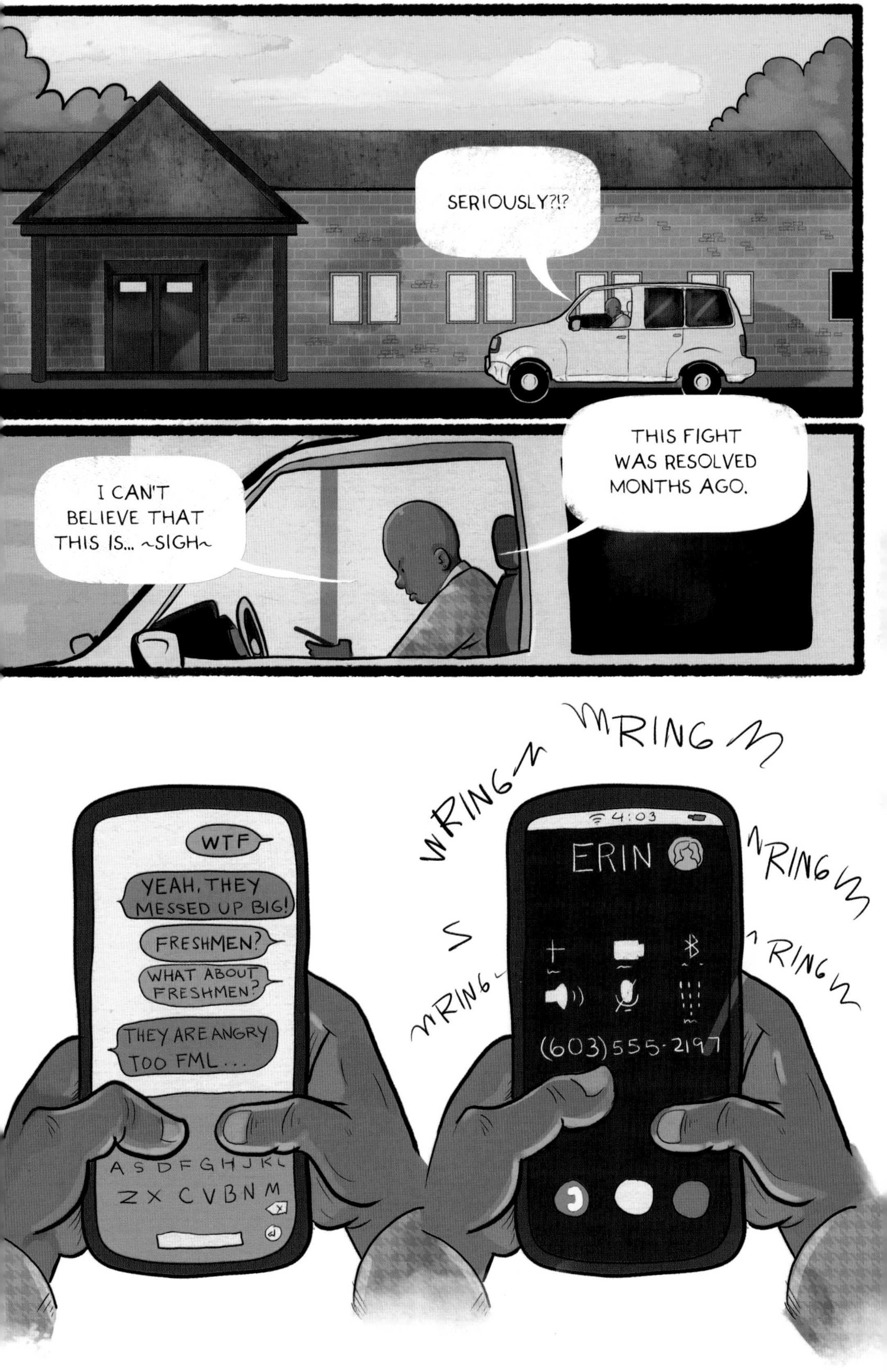
SERIOUSLY?!?
I CAN'T BELIEVE THAT THIS IS... ~SIGH~
THIS FIGHT WAS RESOLVED MONTHS AGO.
WTF
YEAH, THEY MESSED UP BIG!
FRESHMEN?
WHAT ABOUT FRESHMEN?
THEY ARE ANGRY TOO FML...
ASDFGHJKL
ZXCVBNM
RING
RING
RING
RING
RING
4:03
ERIN
(603)555-2197

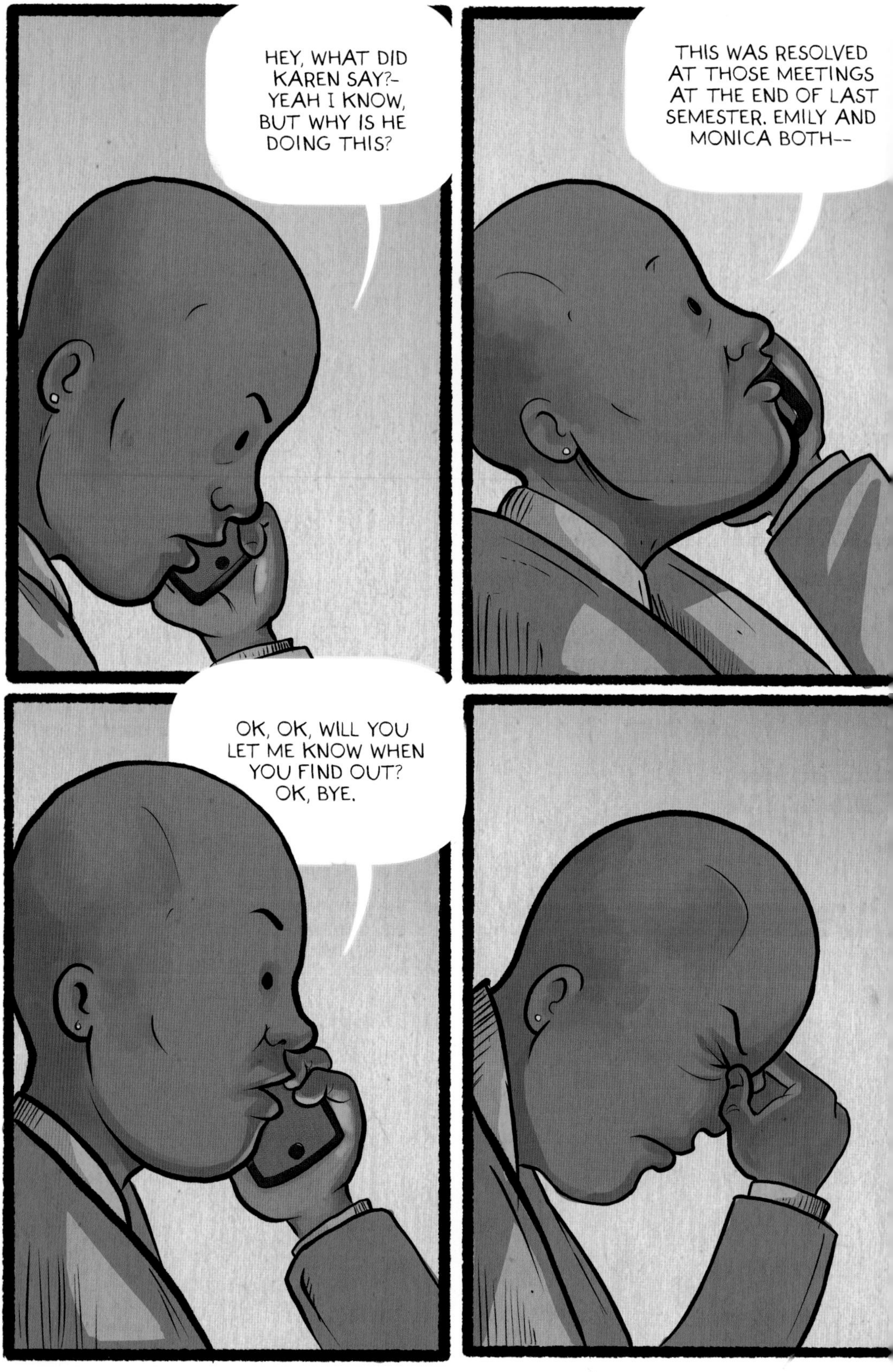
HEY, WHAT DID KAREN SAY?- YEAH I KNOW, BUT WHY IS HE DOING THIS?
THIS WAS RESOLVED AT THOSE MEETINGS AT THE END OF LAST SEMESTER. EMILY AND MONICA BOTH--
OK, OK, WILL YOU LET ME KNOW WHEN YOU FIND OUT? OK, BYE.

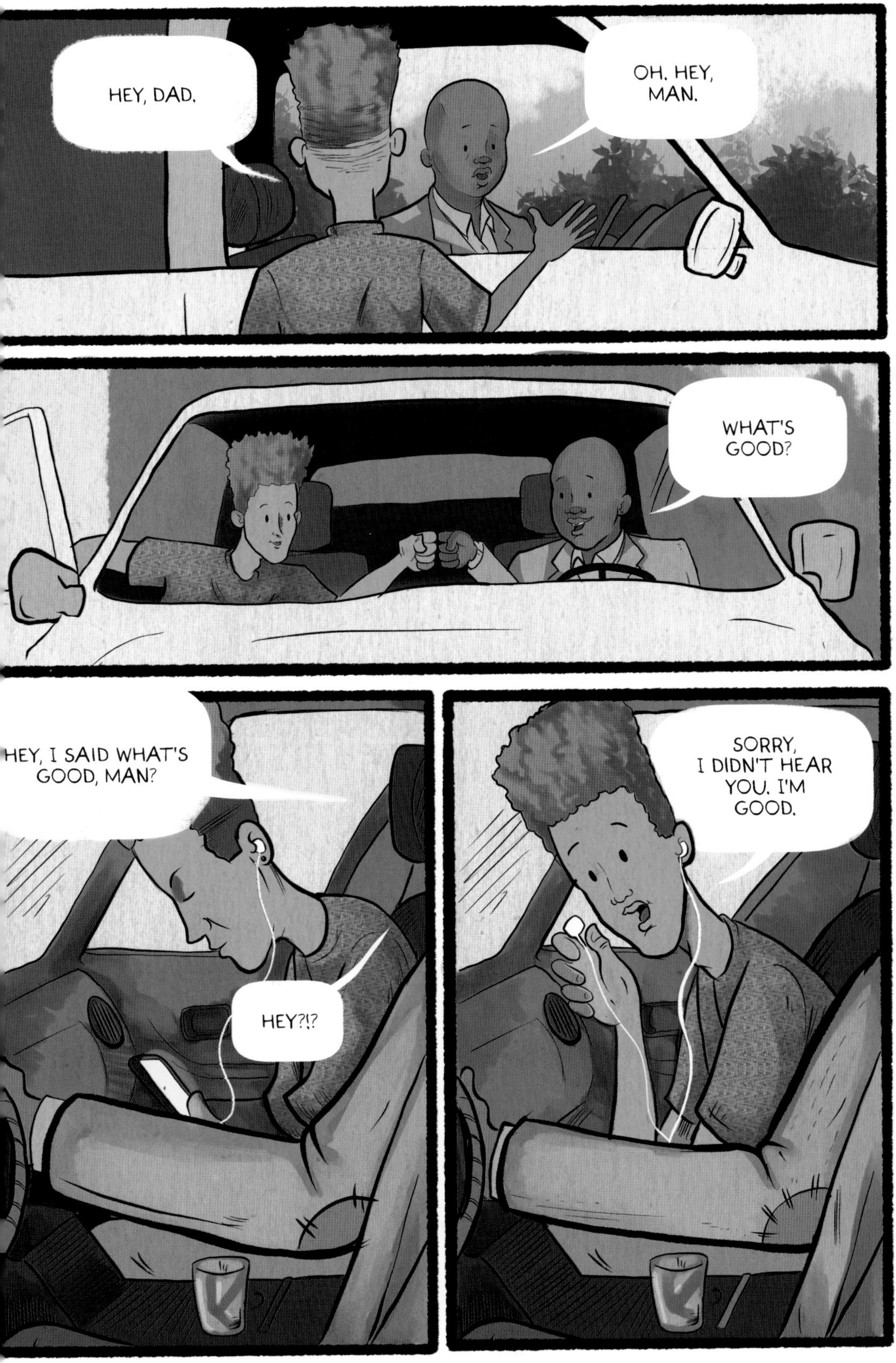
HEY, DAD.
OH. HEY, MAN.
WHAT'S GOOD?
HEY, I SAID WHAT'S GOOD, MAN?
HEY?!?
SORRY, I DIDN'T HEAR YOU. I'M GOOD.

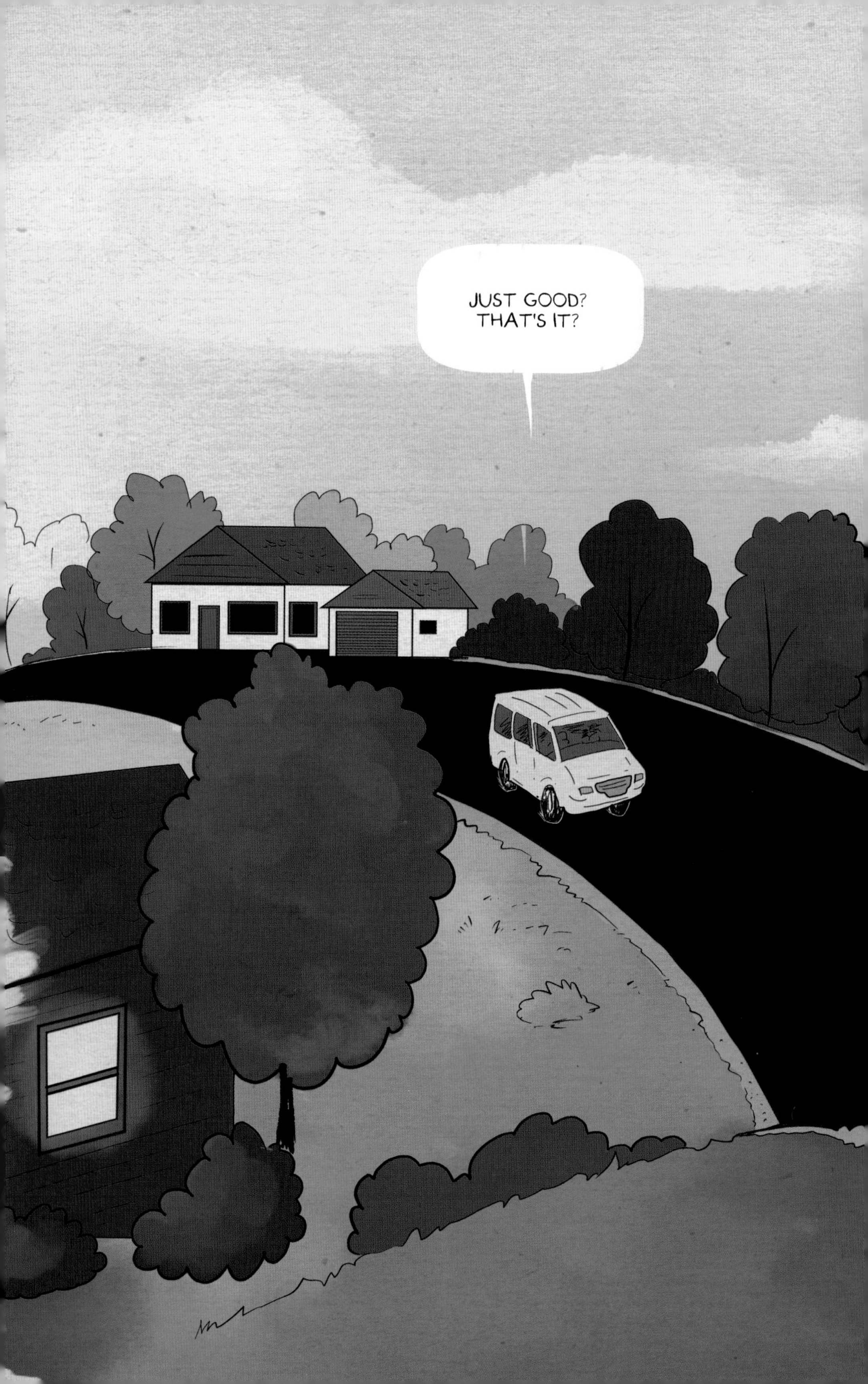
JUST GOOD? THAT'S IT?

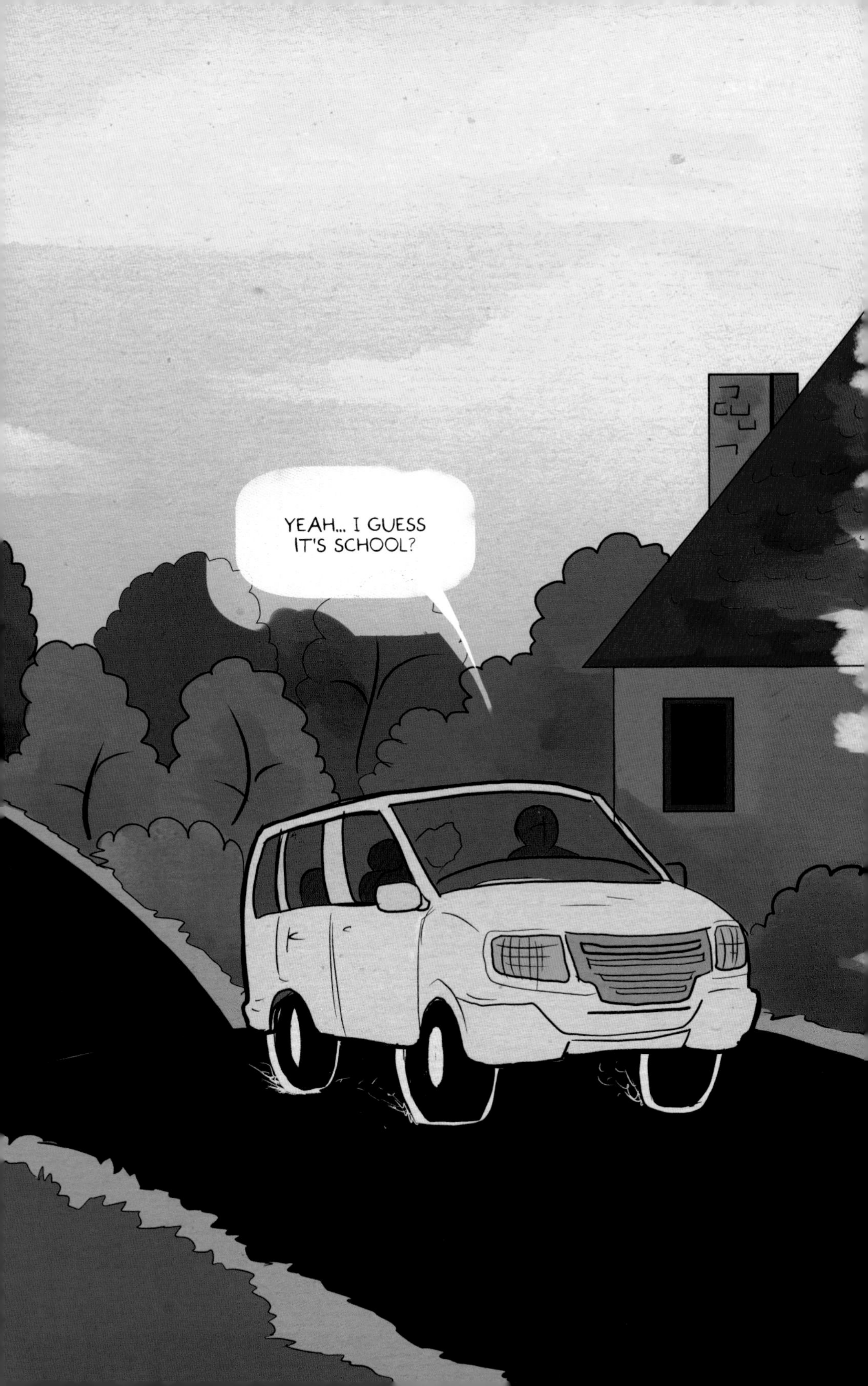
YEAH... I GUESS IT'S SCHOOL?

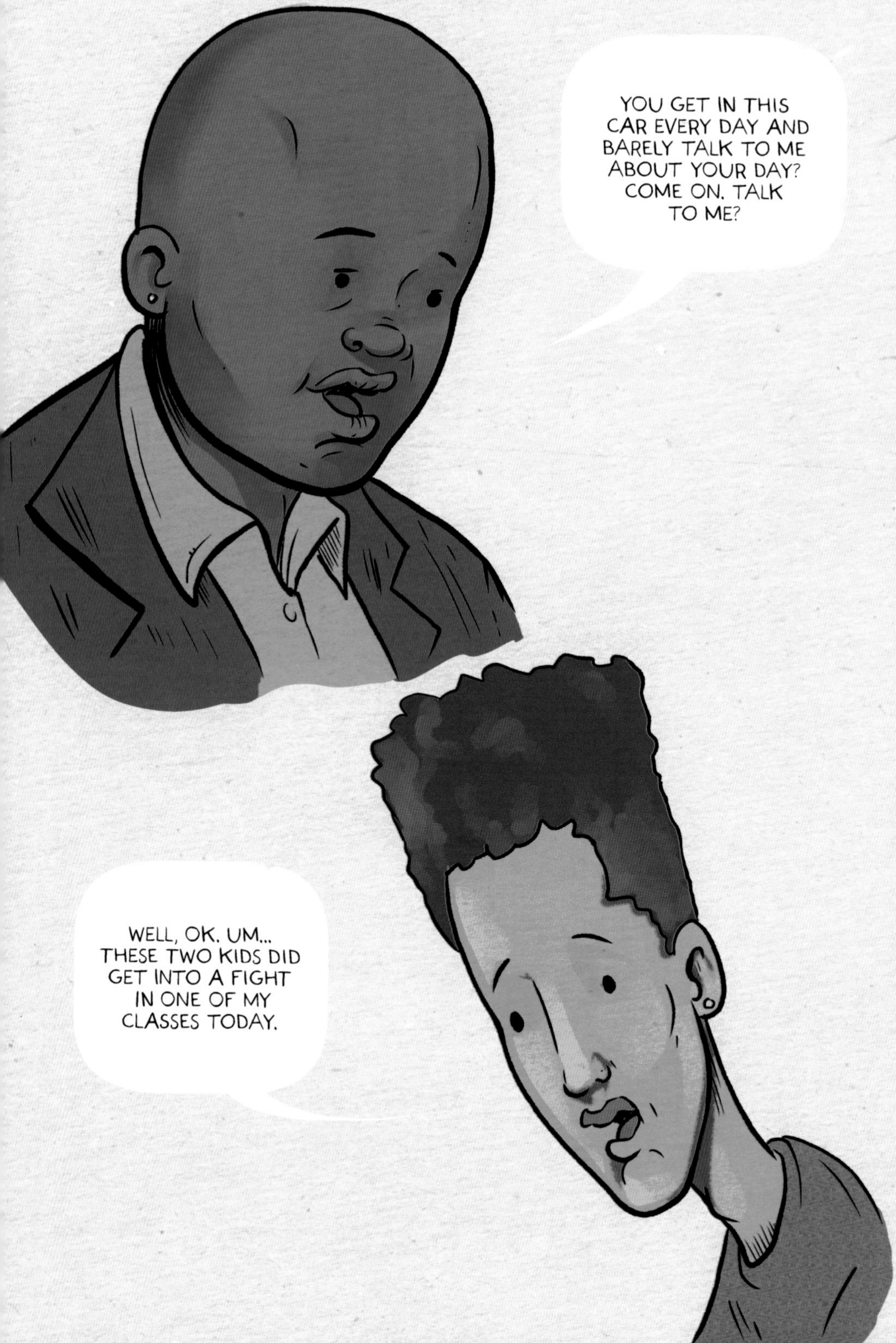
YOU GET IN THIS CAR EVERY DAY AND BARELY TALK TO ME ABOUT YOUR DAY? COME ON. TALK TO ME?
WELL, OK. UM... THESE TWO KIDS DID GET INTO A FIGHT IN ONE OF MY CLASSES TODAY.

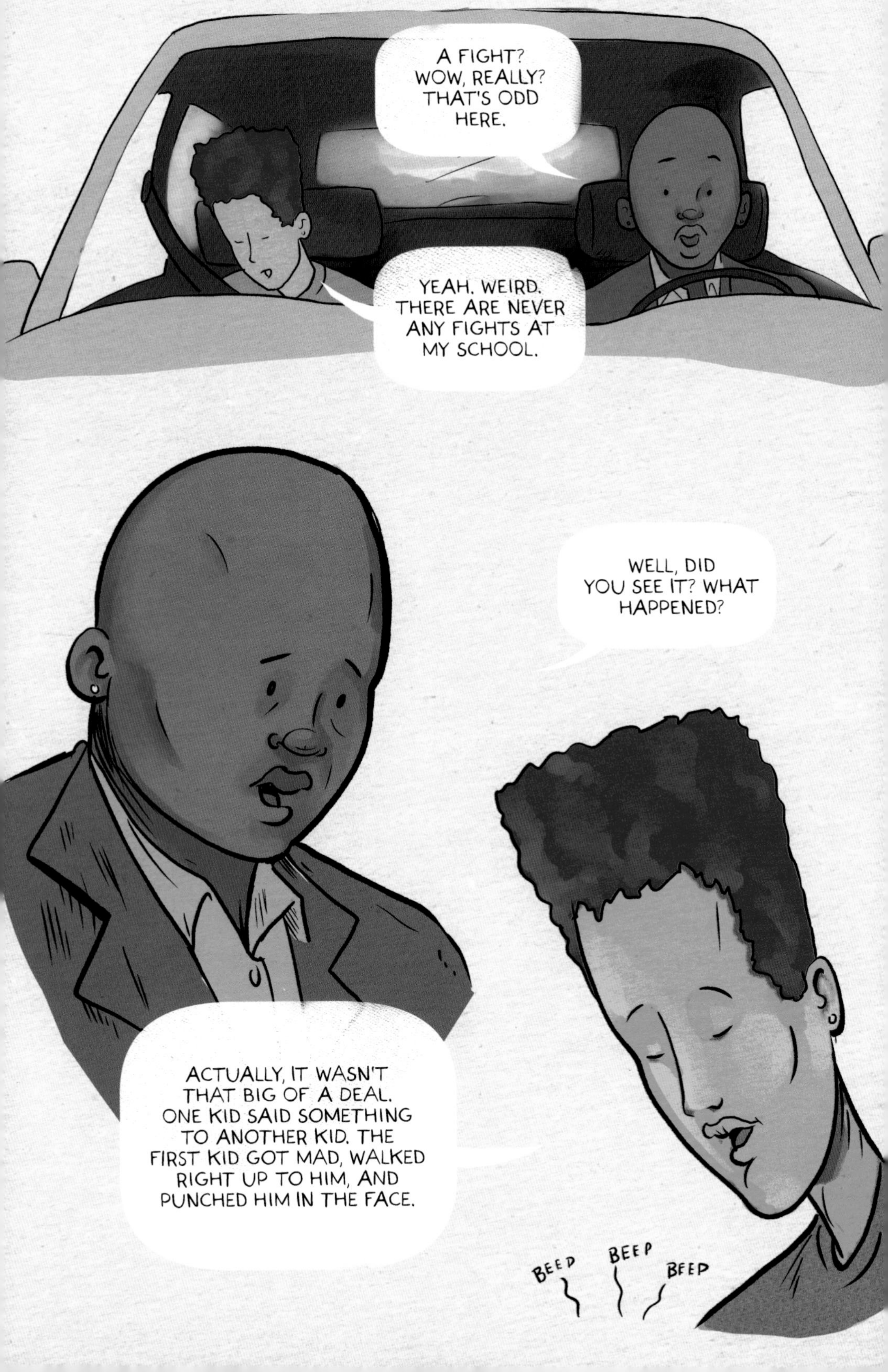
A FIGHT? WOW, REALLY? THAT'S ODD HERE.
YEAH. WEIRD. THERE ARE NEVER ANY FIGHTS AT MY SCHOOL.
WELL, DID YOU SEE IT? WHAT HAPPENED?
ACTUALLY, IT WASN'T THAT BIG OF A DEAL. ONE KID SAID SOMETHING TO ANOTHER KID. THE FIRST KID GOT MAD, WALKED RIGHT UP TO HIM, AND PUNCHED HIM IN THE FACE.
BEEP
BEEP
BEEP

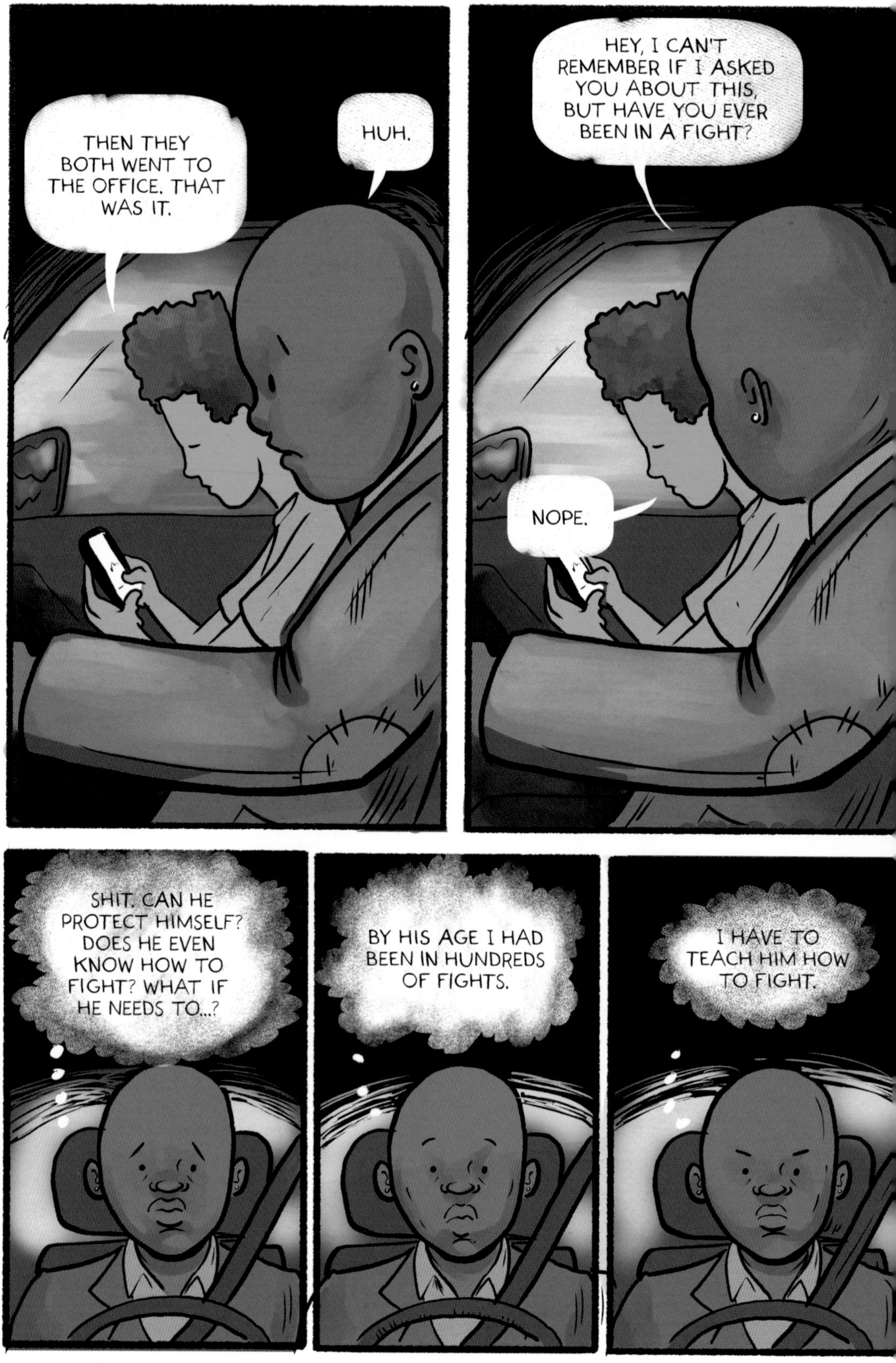
THEN THEY BOTH WENT TO THE OFFICE. THAT WAS IT.
HUH.
HEY, I CAN'T REMEMBER IF I ASKED YOU ABOUT THIS, BUT HAVE YOU EVER BEEN IN A FIGHT?
NOPE.
SHIT. CAN HE PROTECT HIMSELF? DOES HE EVEN KNOW HOW TO FIGHT? WHAT IF HE NEEDS TO...?
BY HIS AGE I HAD BEEN IN HUNDREDS OF FIGHTS.
I HAVE TO TEACH HIM HOW TO FIGHT.

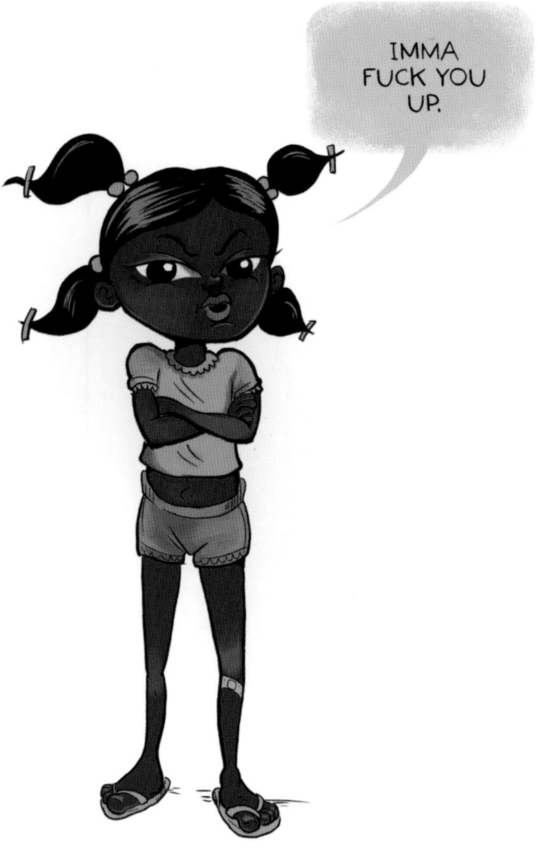
IMMA FUCK YOU UP.

CHAPTER ONE

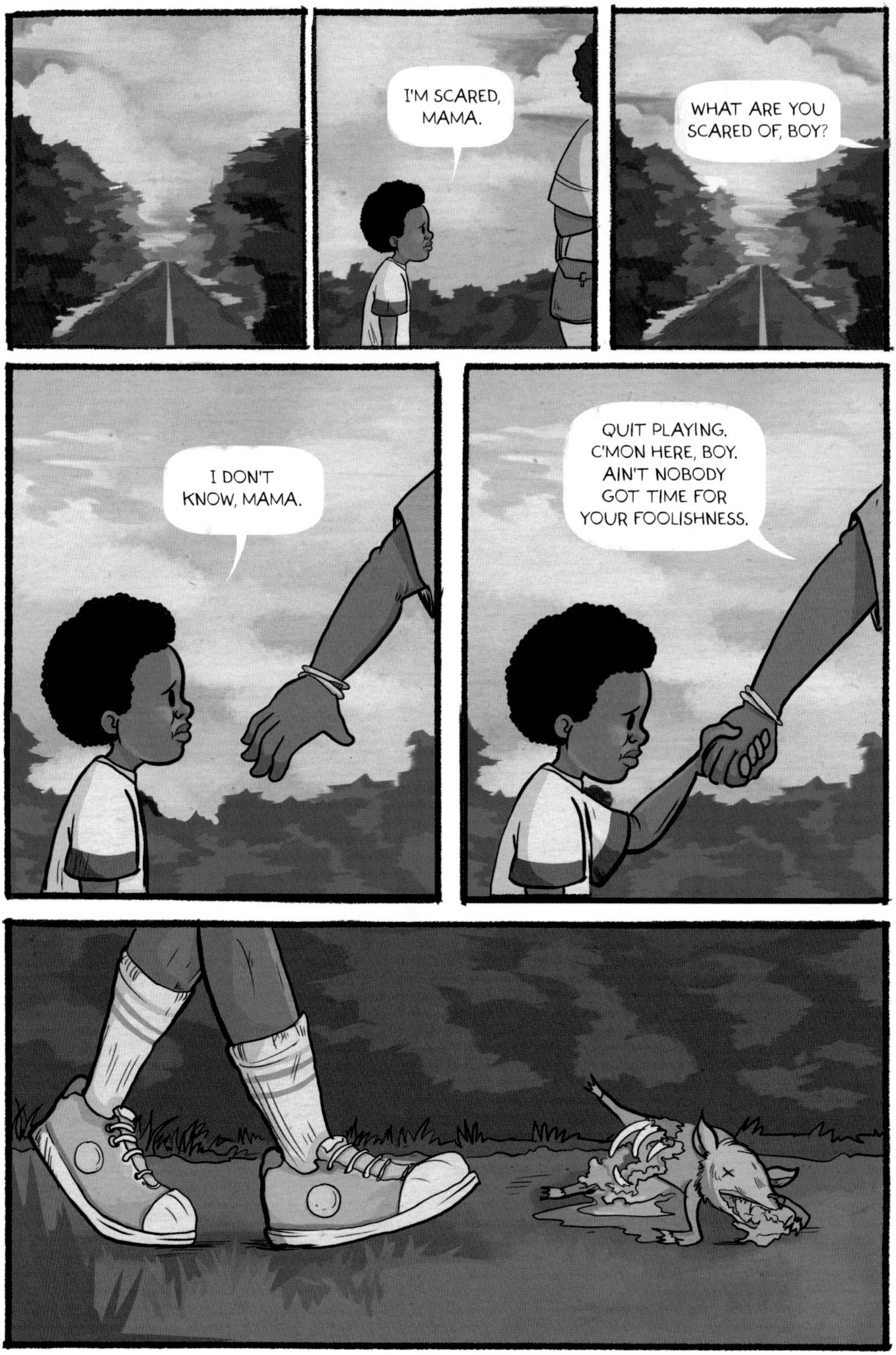
I'M SCARED, MAMA.
WHAT ARE YOU SCARED OF, BOY?
I DON'T KNOW, MAMA.
QUIT PLAYING. C'MON HERE, BOY. AIN'T NOBODY GOT TIME FOR YOUR FOOLISHNESS.

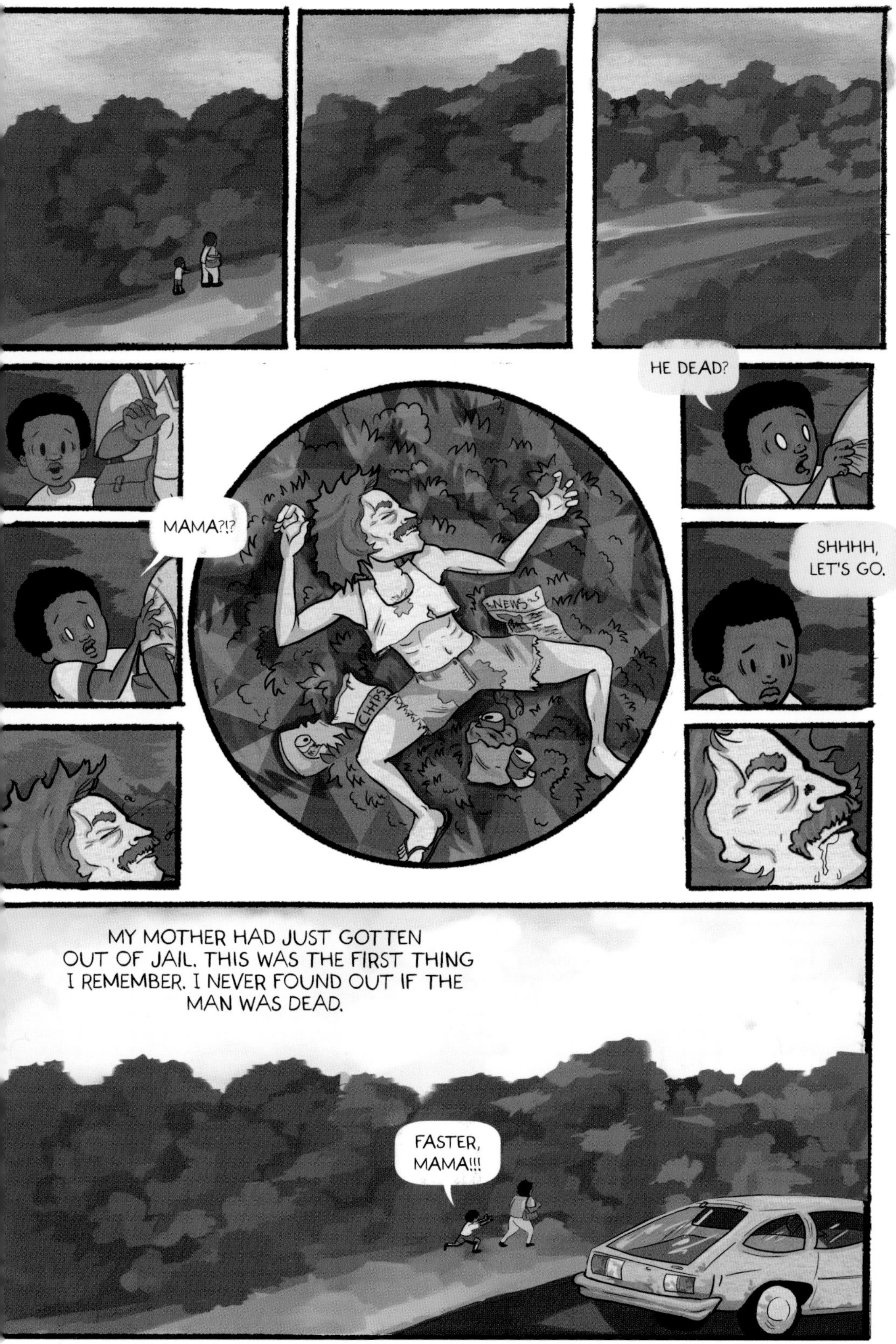
MAMA?!?
HE DEAD?
SHHHH, LET'S GO.
NEWS
CHIPS
MY MOTHER HAD JUST GOTTEN OUT OF JAIL. THIS WAS THE FIRST THING I REMEMBER. I NEVER FOUND OUT IF THE MAN WAS DEAD.
FASTER, MAMA!!!

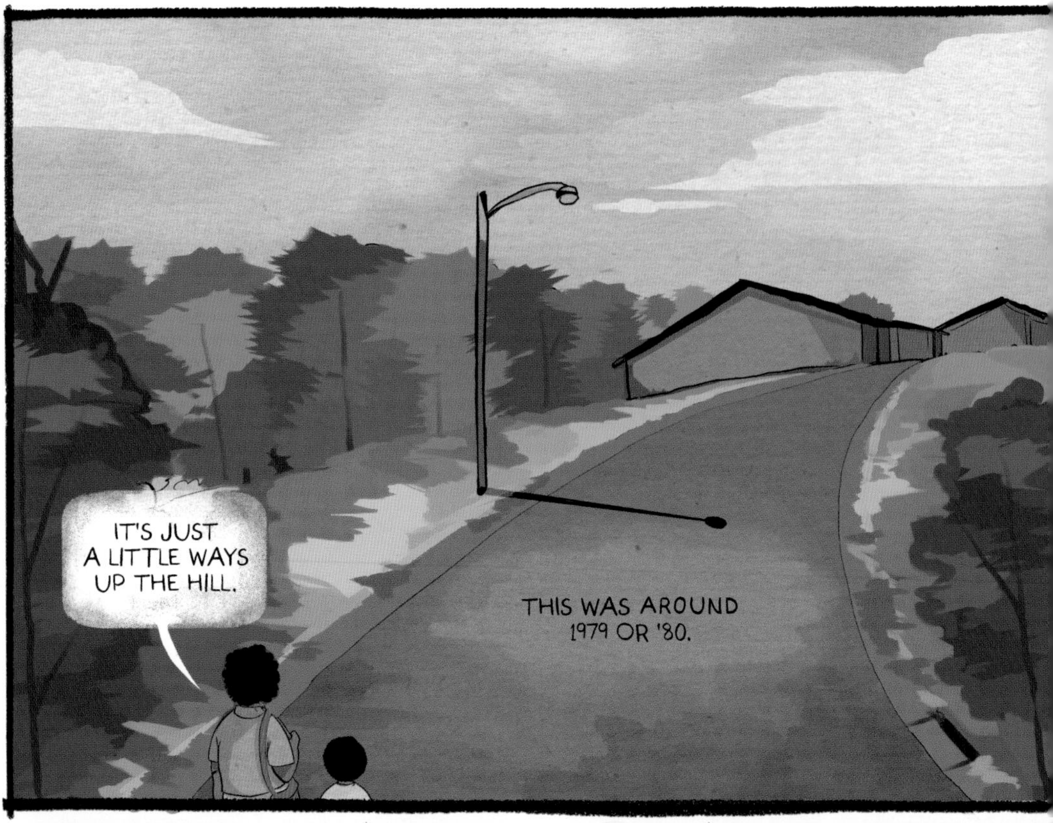
IT'S JUST A LITTLE WAYS UP THE HILL.
THIS WAS AROUND 1979 OR '80.
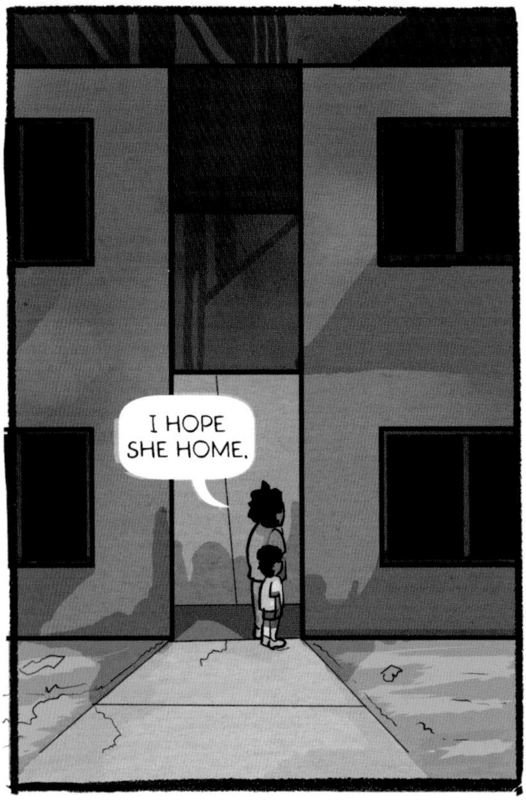
I HOPE SHE HOME.
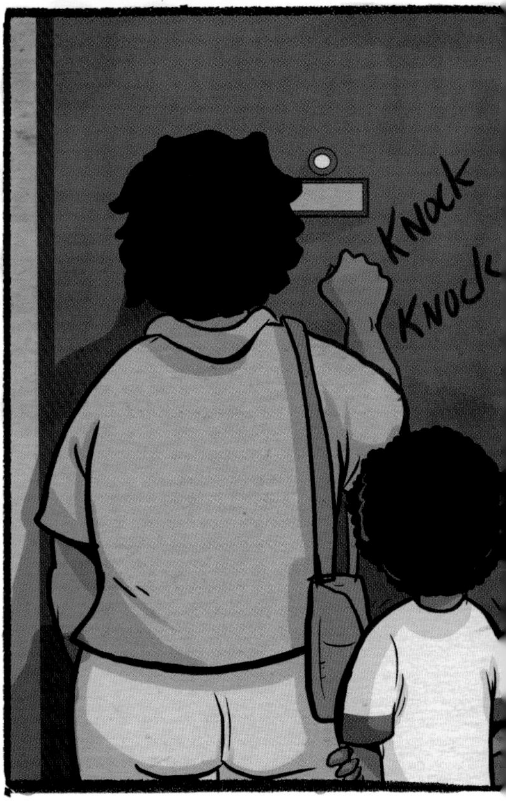
Knock Knock

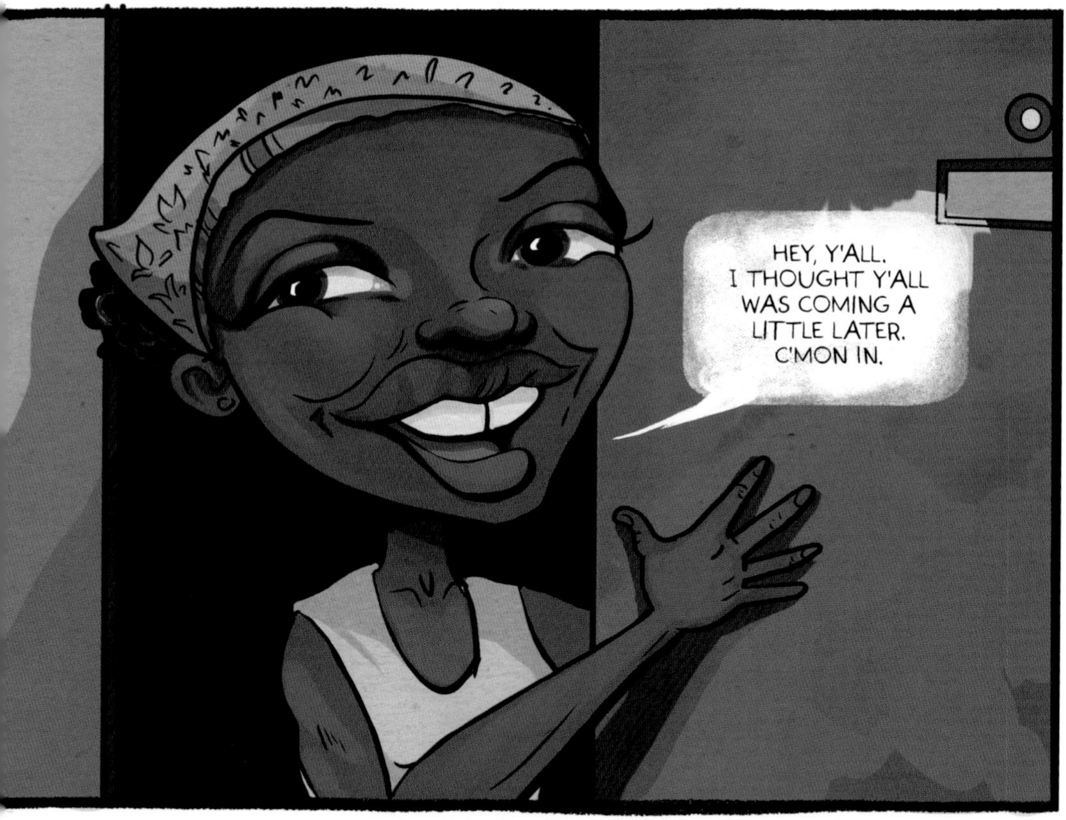
HEY, Y'ALL. I THOUGHT Y'ALL WAS COMING A LITTLE LATER. C'MON IN.

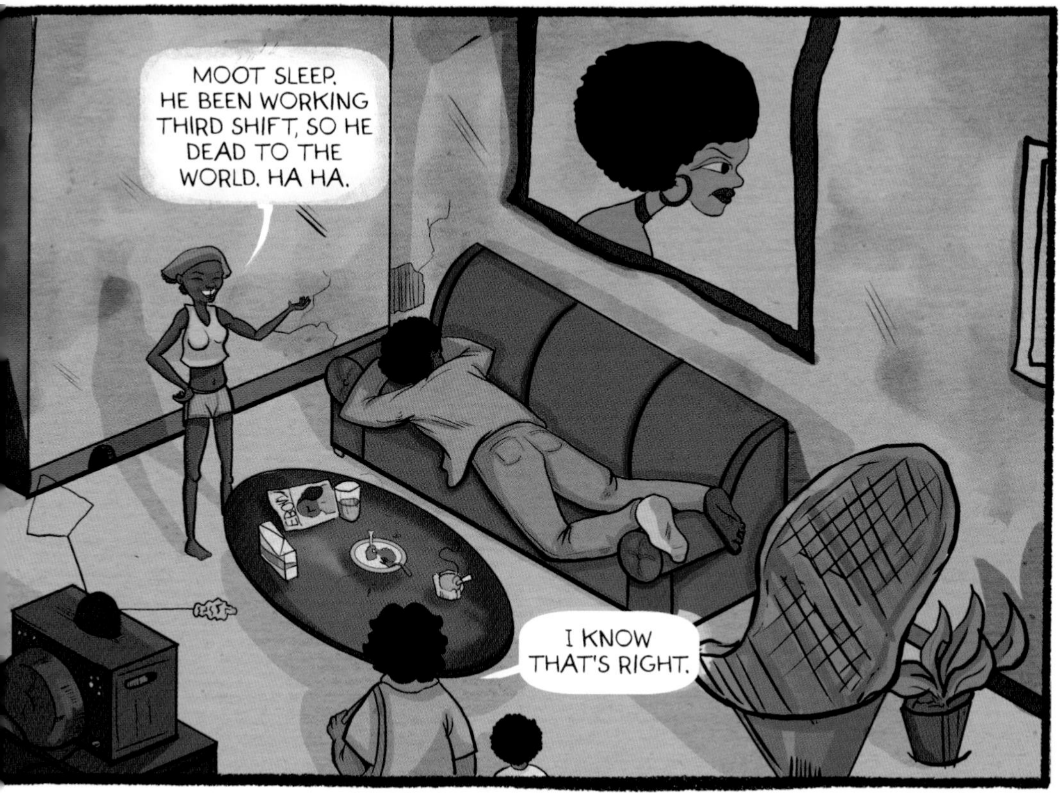
MOOT SLEEP. HE BEEN WORKING THIRD SHIFT, SO HE DEAD TO THE WORLD. HA HA.
EBONY
I KNOW THAT'S RIGHT.

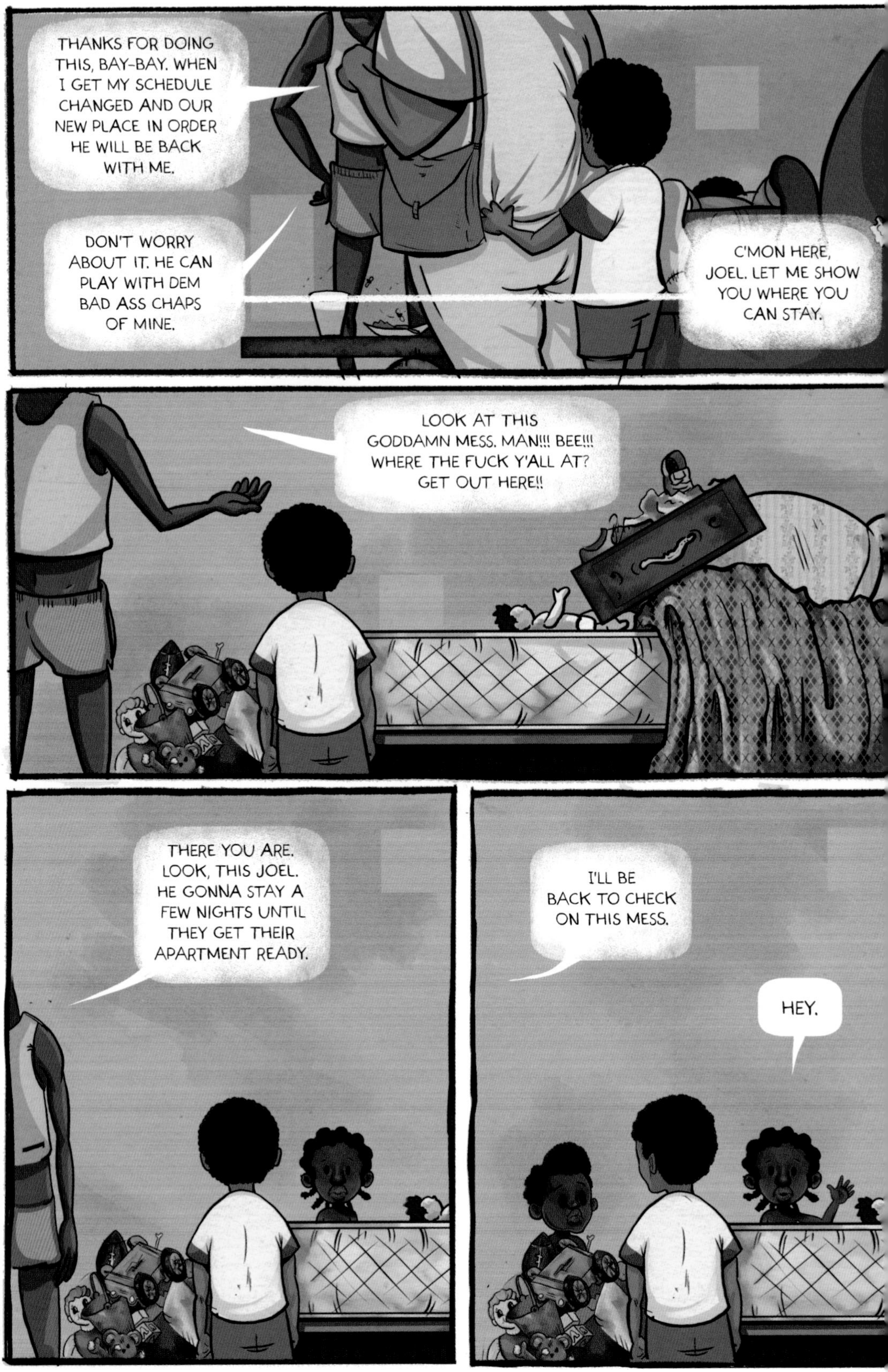
THANKS FOR DOING THIS, BAY-BAY. WHEN I GET MY SCHEDULE CHANGED AND OUR NEW PLACE IN ORDER HE WILL BE BACK WITH ME.
DON'T WORRY ABOUT IT. HE CAN PLAY WITH DEM BAD ASS CHAPS OF MINE.
C'MON HERE, JOEL. LET ME SHOW YOU WHERE YOU CAN STAY.
LOOK AT THIS GODDAMN MESS. MAN!!! BEE!!! WHERE THE FUCK Y'ALL AT? GET OUT HERE!!
THERE YOU ARE. LOOK, THIS JOEL. HE GONNA STAY A FEW NIGHTS UNTIL THEY GET THEIR APARTMENT READY.
I'LL BE BACK TO CHECK ON THIS MESS.
HEY.

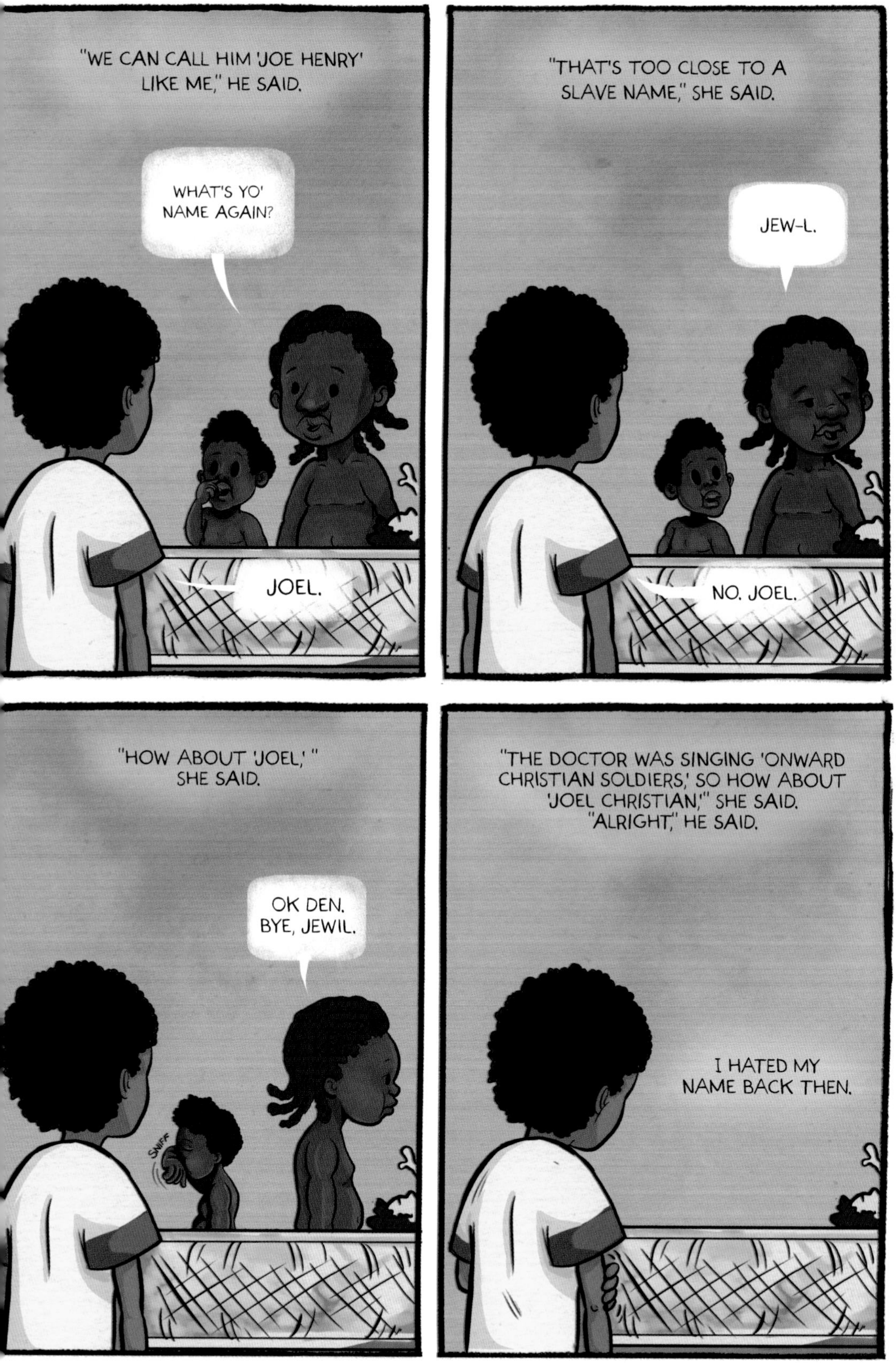
"WE CAN CALL HIM 'JOE HENRY' LIKE ME," HE SAID.
WHAT'S YO' NAME AGAIN?
JOEL.
"THAT'S TOO CLOSE TO A SLAVE NAME," SHE SAID.
JEW-L.
NO. JOEL.
"HOW ABOUT 'JOEL,' " SHE SAID.
OK DEN. BYE, JEWIL.
SNIFF
"THE DOCTOR WAS SINGING 'ONWARD CHRISTIAN SOLDIERS,' SO HOW ABOUT 'JOEL CHRISTIAN,'" SHE SAID. "ALRIGHT," HE SAID.
I HATED MY NAME BACK THEN.

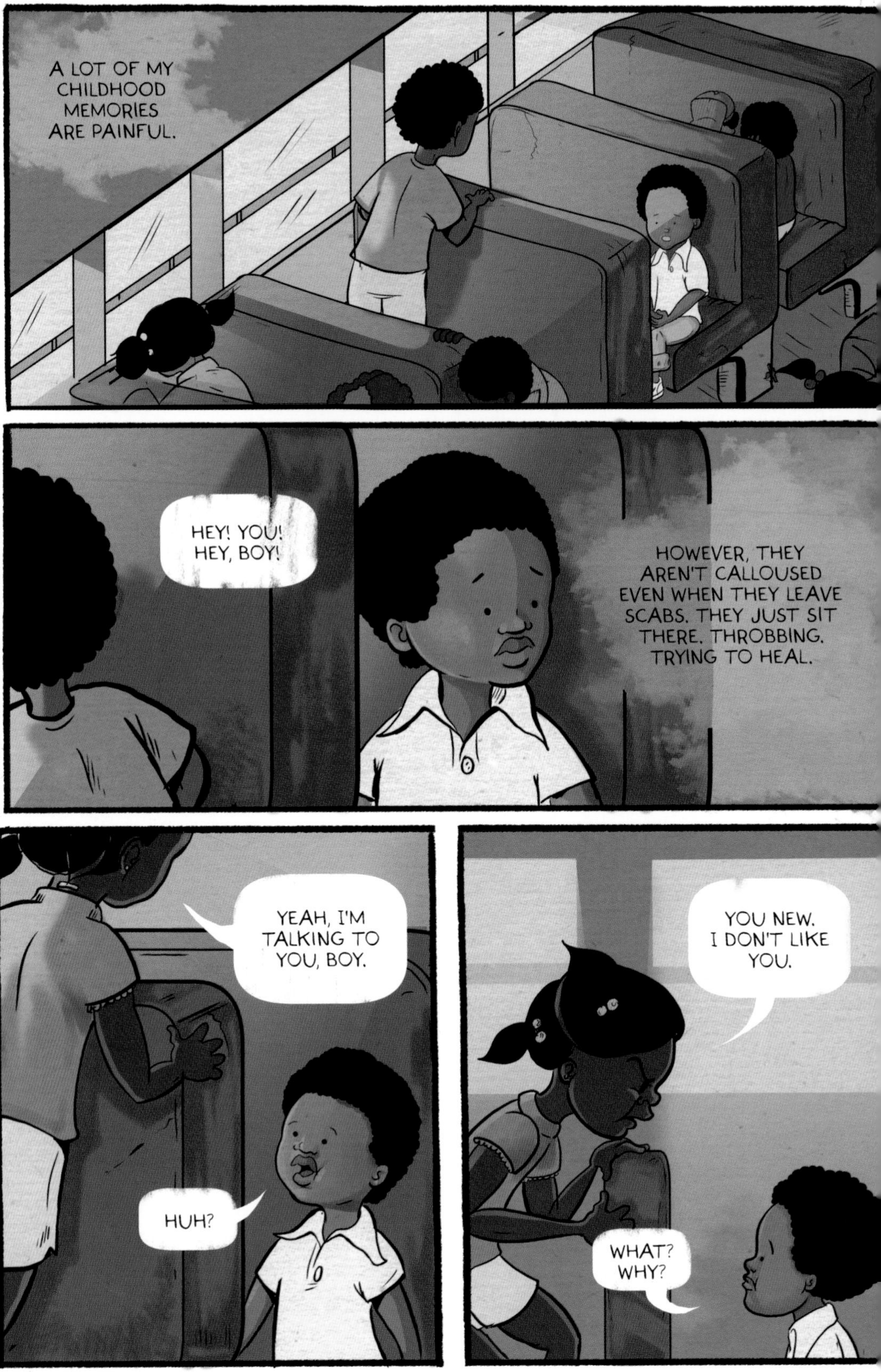
A LOT OF MY CHILDHOOD MEMORIES ARE PAINFUL.
HEY! YOU! HEY, BOY!
HOWEVER, THEY AREN'T CALLOUSED EVEN WHEN THEY LEAVE SCABS. THEY JUST SIT THERE. THROBBING. TRYING TO HEAL.
YEAH, I'M TALKING TO YOU, BOY.
HUH?
YOU NEW. I DON'T LIKE YOU.
WHAT? WHY?

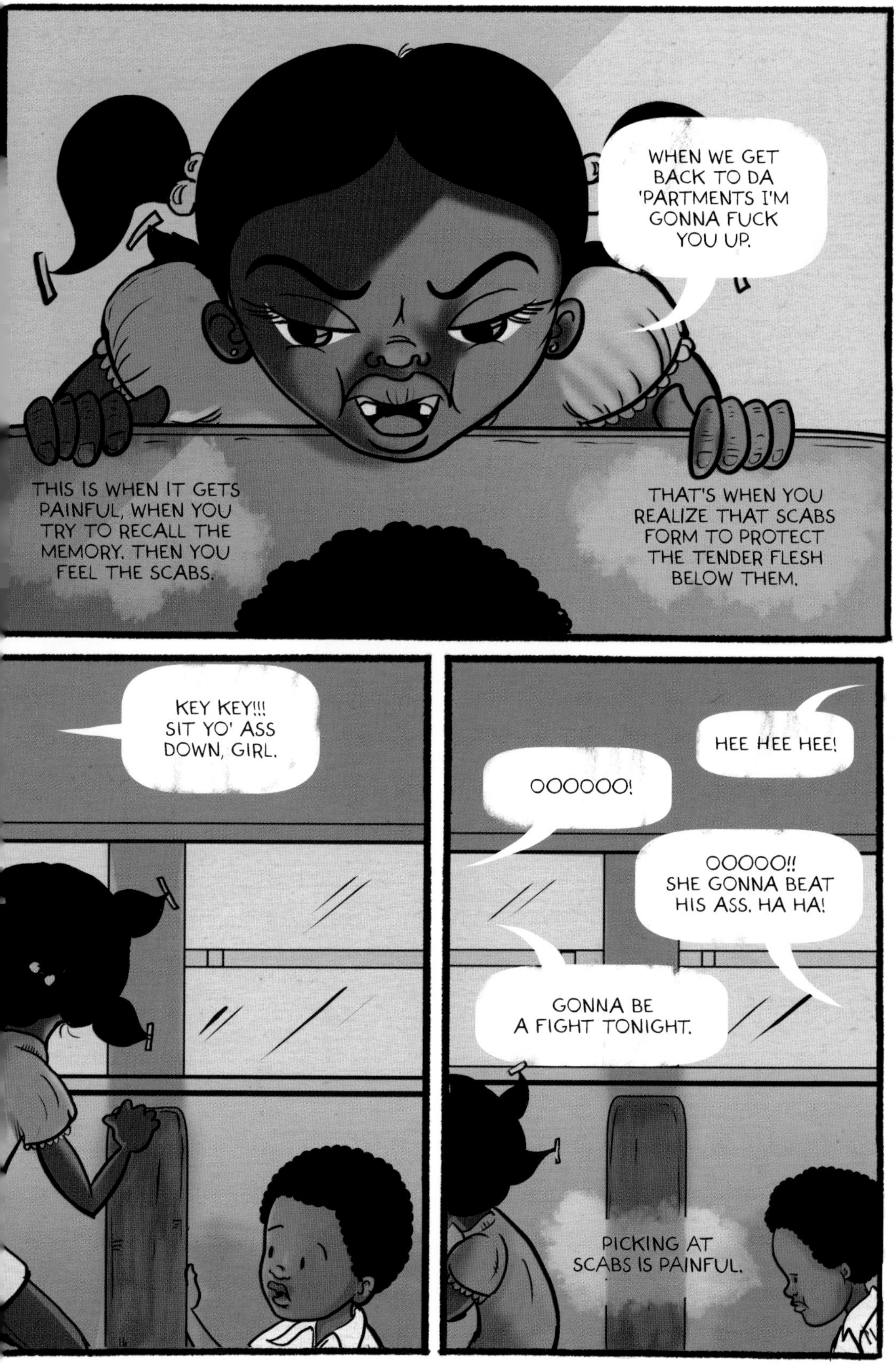
WHEN WE GET BACK TO DA 'PARTMENTS I'M GONNA FUCK YOU UP.
THIS IS WHEN IT GETS PAINFUL, WHEN YOU TRY TO RECALL THE MEMORY. THEN YOU FEEL THE SCABS.
THAT'S WHEN YOU REALIZE THAT SCABS FORM TO PROTECT THE TENDER FLESH BELOW THEM.
KEY KEY!!! SIT YO' ASS DOWN, GIRL.
HEE HEE HEE!
OOOOOO!
OOOOO!! SHE GONNA BEAT HIS ASS. HA HA!
GONNA BE A FIGHT TONIGHT.
PICKING AT SCABS IS PAINFUL.

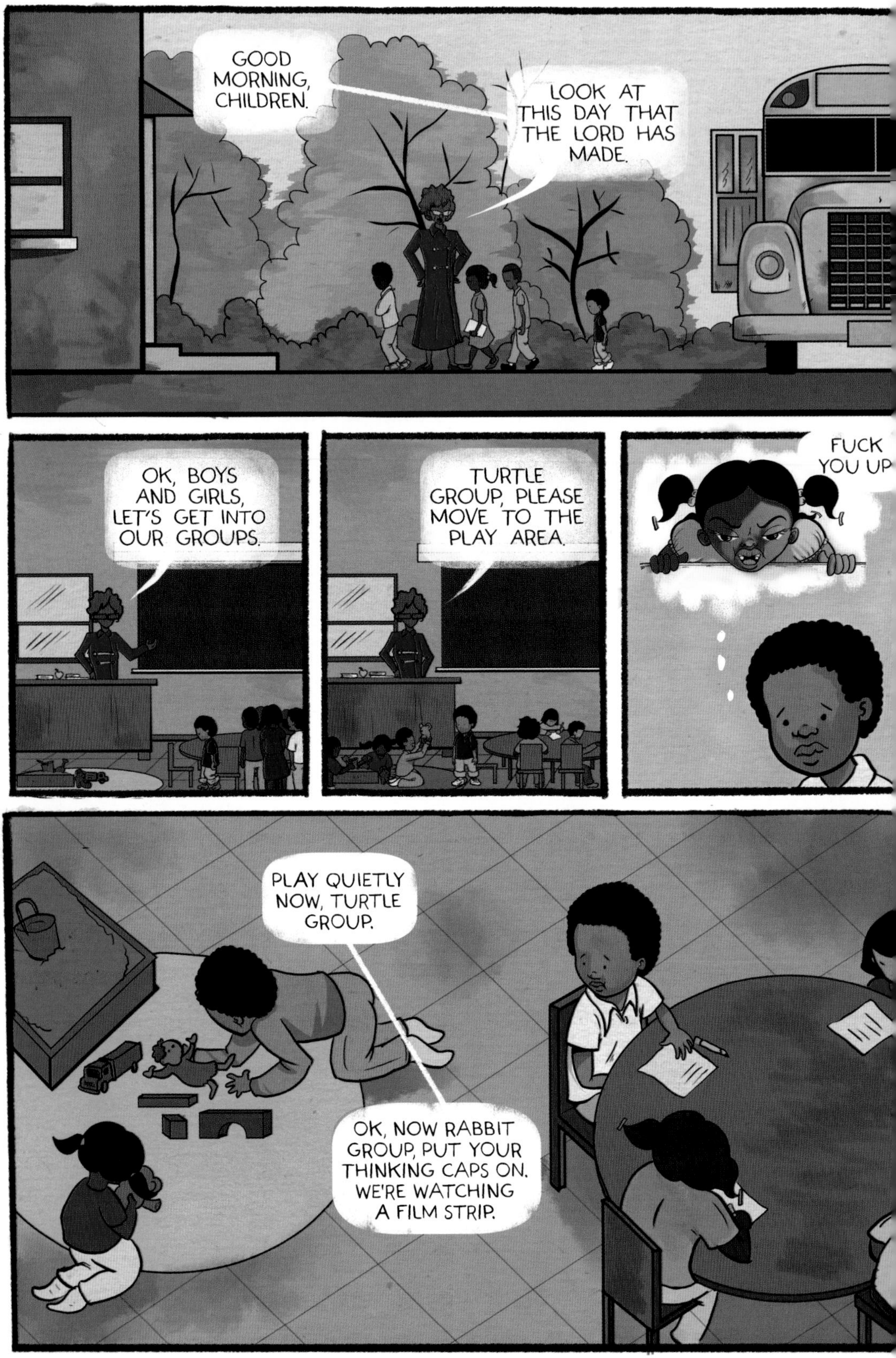
GOOD MORNING, CHILDREN.
LOOK AT THIS DAY THAT THE LORD HAS MADE.
OK, BOYS AND GIRLS, LET'S GET INTO OUR GROUPS.
TURTLE GROUP, PLEASE MOVE TO THE PLAY AREA.
FUCK YOU UP
PLAY QUIETLY NOW, TURTLE GROUP.
OK, NOW RABBIT GROUP, PUT YOUR THINKING CAPS ON. WE'RE WATCHING A FILM STRIP.

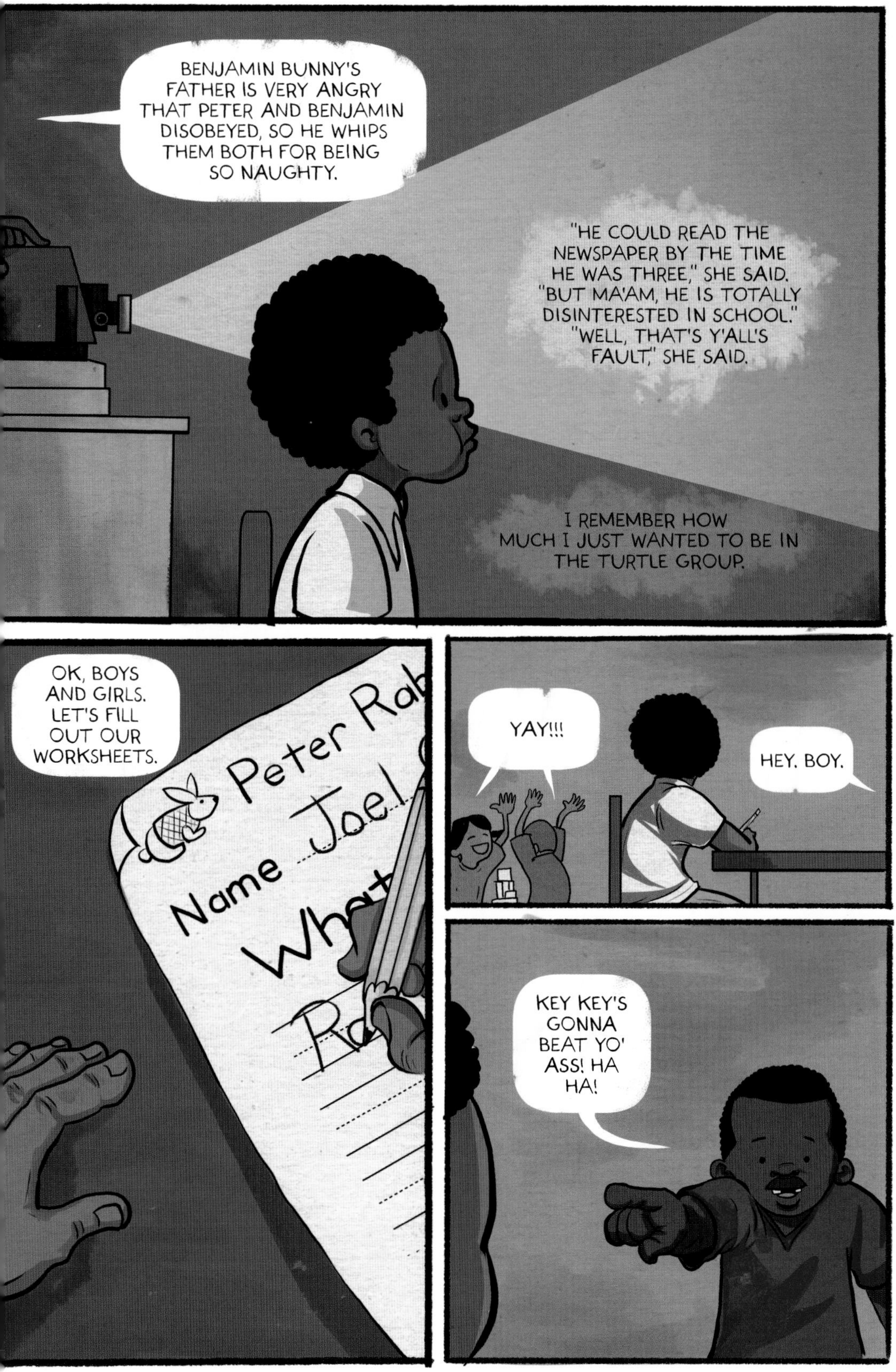
BENJAMIN BUNNY'S FATHER IS VERY ANGRY THAT PETER AND BENJAMIN DISOBEYED, SO HE WHIPS THEM BOTH FOR BEING SO NAUGHTY.
"HE COULD READ THE NEWSPAPER BY THE TIME HE WAS THREE," SHE SAID. "BUT MA'AM, HE IS TOTALLY DISINTERESTED IN SCHOOL." "WELL, THAT'S Y'ALL'S FAULT," SHE SAID.
I REMEMBER HOW MUCH I JUST WANTED TO BE IN THE TURTLE GROUP.
OK, BOYS AND GIRLS. LET'S FILL OUT OUR WORKSHEETS.
Peter Rab
Name Joel
YAY!!!
HEY. BOY.
KEY KEY'S GONNA BEAT YO' ASS! HA HA!

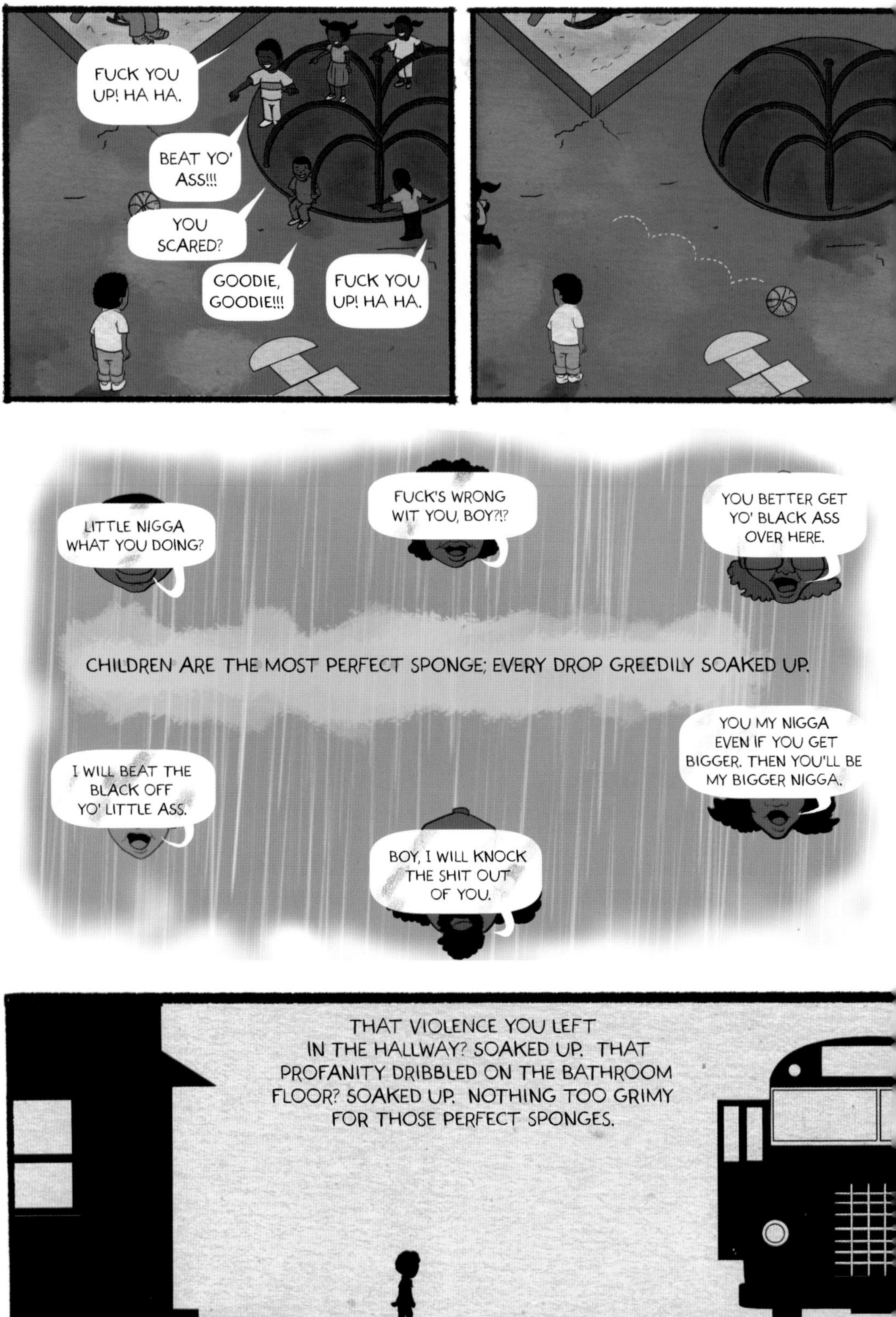
FUCK YOU UP! HA HA.
BEAT YO' ASS!!!
YOU SCARED?
GOODIE, GOODIE!!!
FUCK YOU UP! HA HA.
LITTLE NIGGA WHAT YOU DOING?
FUCK'S WRONG WIT YOU, BOY?!?
YOU BETTER GET YO' BLACK ASS OVER HERE.
CHILDREN ARE THE MOST PERFECT SPONGE; EVERY DROP GREEDILY SOAKED UP.
I WILL BEAT THE BLACK OFF YO' LITTLE ASS.
YOU MY NIGGA EVEN IF YOU GET BIGGER. THEN YOU'LL BE MY BIGGER NIGGA.
BOY, I WILL KNOCK THE SHIT OUT OF YOU.
THAT VIOLENCE YOU LEFT IN THE HALLWAY? SOAKED UP. THAT PROFANITY DRIBBLED ON THE BATHROOM FLOOR? SOAKED UP. NOTHING TOO GRIMY FOR THOSE PERFECT SPONGES.

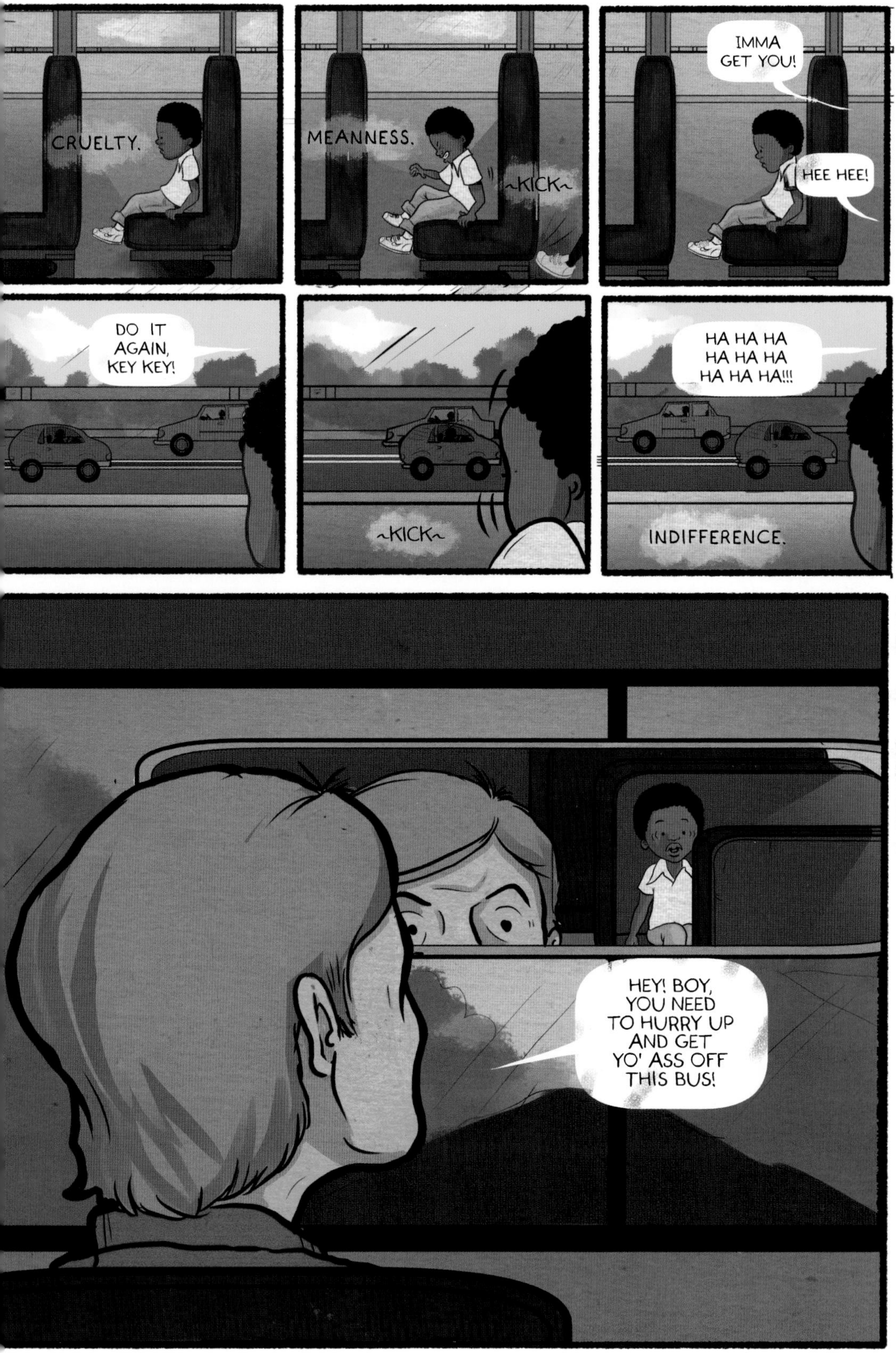
CRUELTY.
MEANNESS.
~KICK~
IMMA GET YOU!
HEE HEE!
DO IT AGAIN, KEY KEY!
~KICK~
HA HA HA HA HA HA HA HA HA!!!
INDIFFERENCE.
HEY! BOY, YOU NEED TO HURRY UP AND GET YO' ASS OFF THIS BUS!

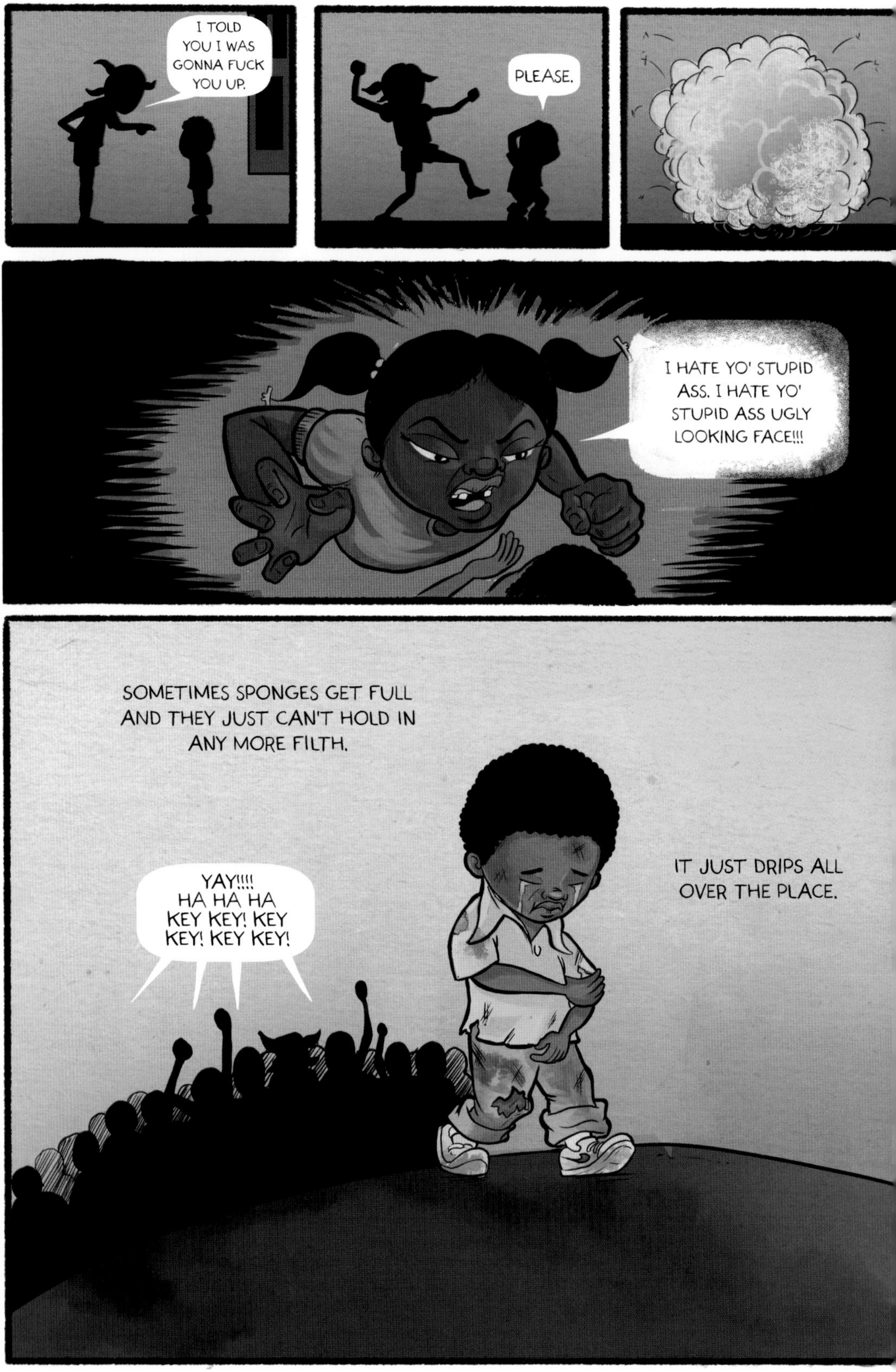
I TOLD YOU I WAS GONNA FUCK YOU UP.
PLEASE.
I HATE YO' STUPID ASS. I HATE YO' STUPID ASS UGLY LOOKING FACE!!!
SOMETIMES SPONGES GET FULL AND THEY JUST CAN'T HOLD IN ANY MORE FILTH.
YAY!!!! HA HA HA KEY KEY! KEY KEY! KEY KEY!
IT JUST DRIPS ALL OVER THE PLACE.

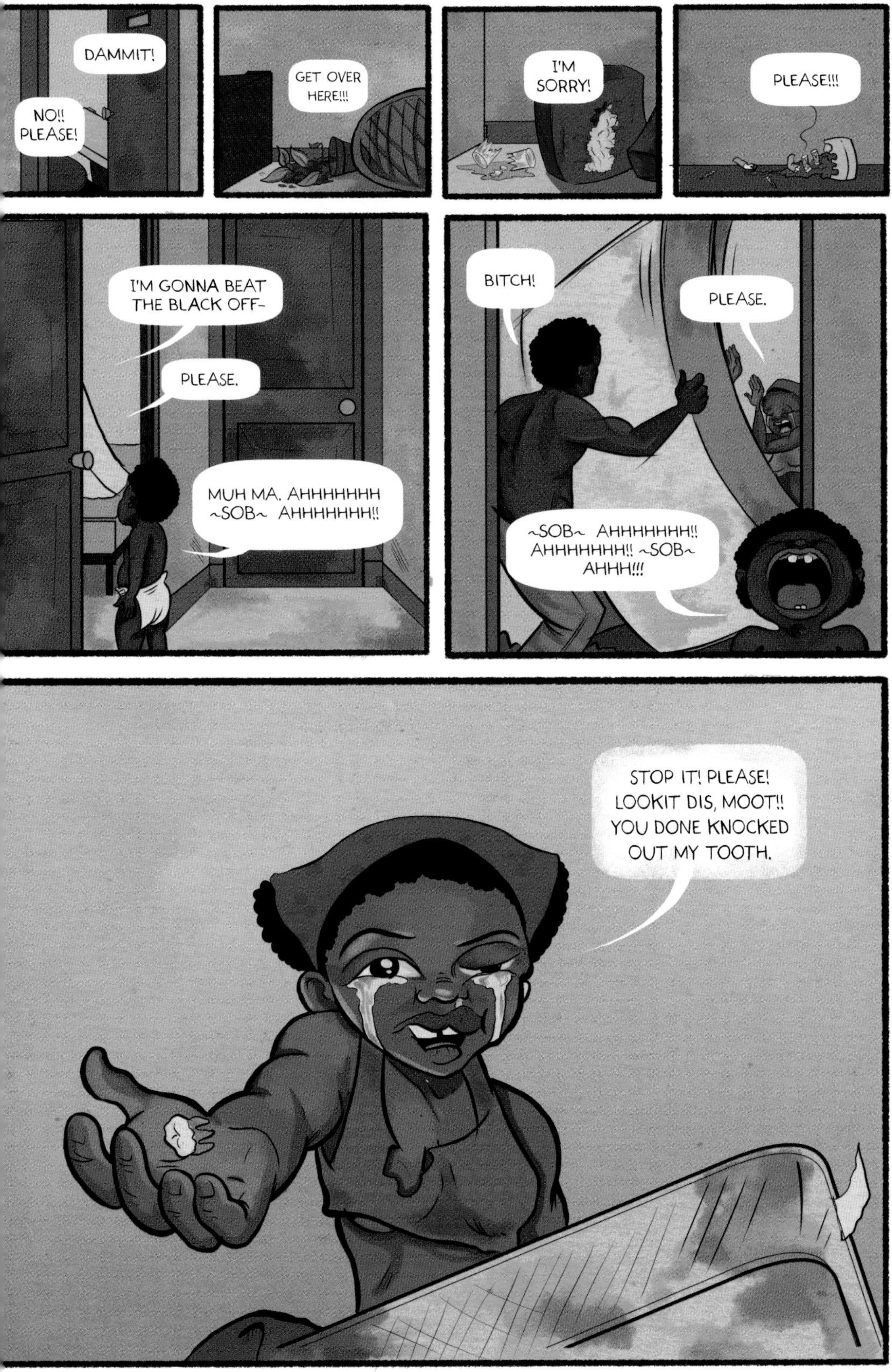
DAMMIT!
NO!! PLEASE!
GET OVER HERE!!!
I'M SORRY!
PLEASE!!!
I'M GONNA BEAT THE BLACK OFF-
PLEASE.
MUH MA. AHHHHHHH ~SOB~ AHHHHHHH!!
BITCH!
PLEASE.
~SOB~ AHHHHHHH!! AHHHHHHH!! ~SOB~ AHHH!!!
STOP IT! PLEASE! LOOKIT DIS, MOOT!! YOU DONE KNOCKED OUT MY TOOTH.

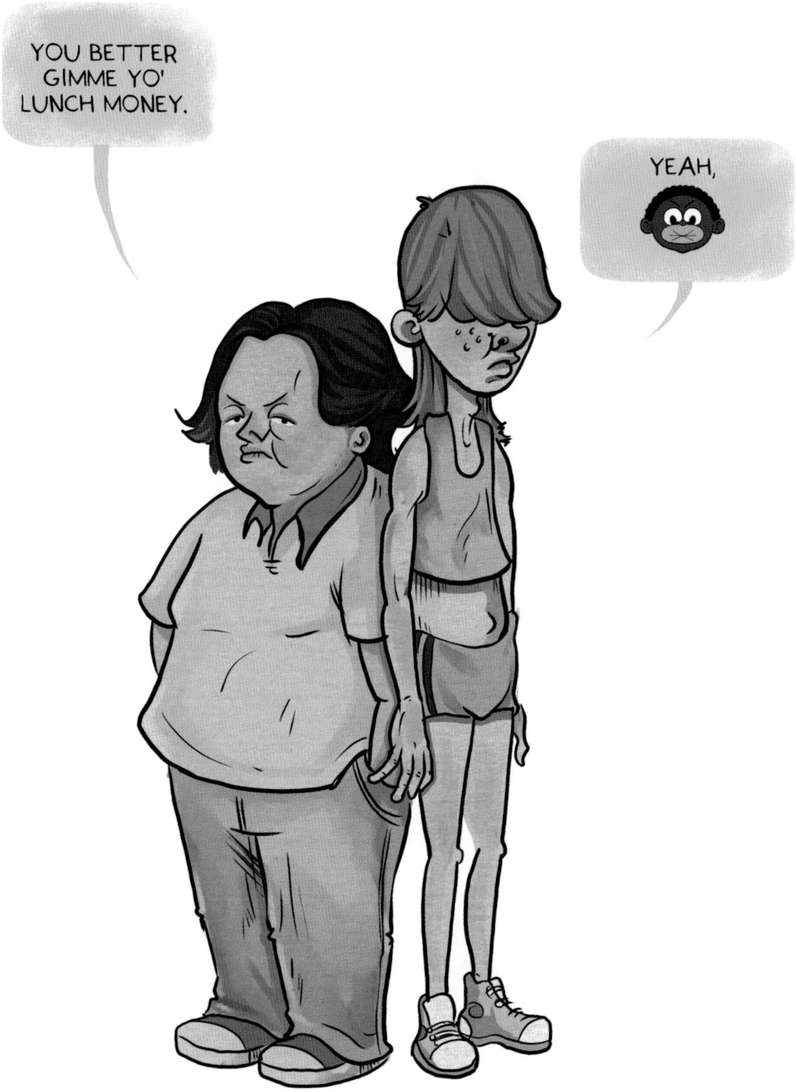
YOU BETTER GIMME YO' LUNCH MONEY.
YEAH,

CHAPTER TWO

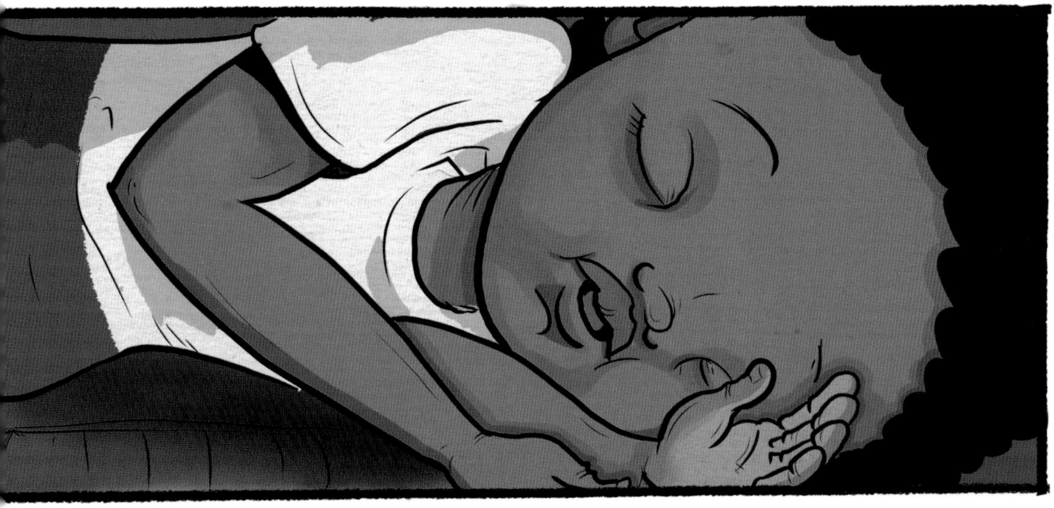

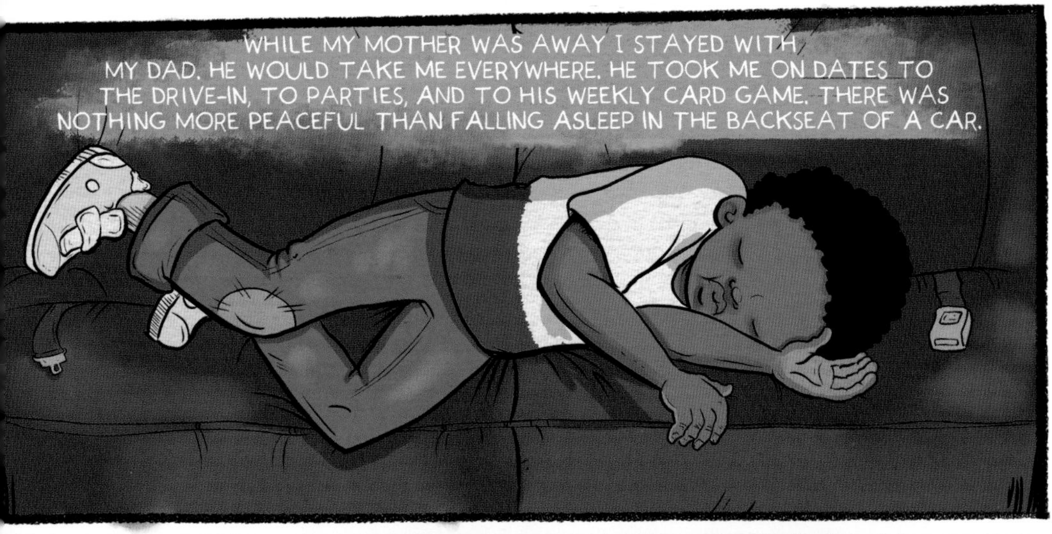
WHILE MY MOTHER WAS AWAY I STAYED WITH MY DAD. HE WOULD TAKE ME EVERYWHERE. HE TOOK ME ON DATES TO THE DRIVE-IN, TO PARTIES, AND TO HIS WEEKLY CARD GAME. THERE WAS NOTHING MORE PEACEFUL THAN FALLING ASLEEP IN THE BACKSEAT OF A CAR.

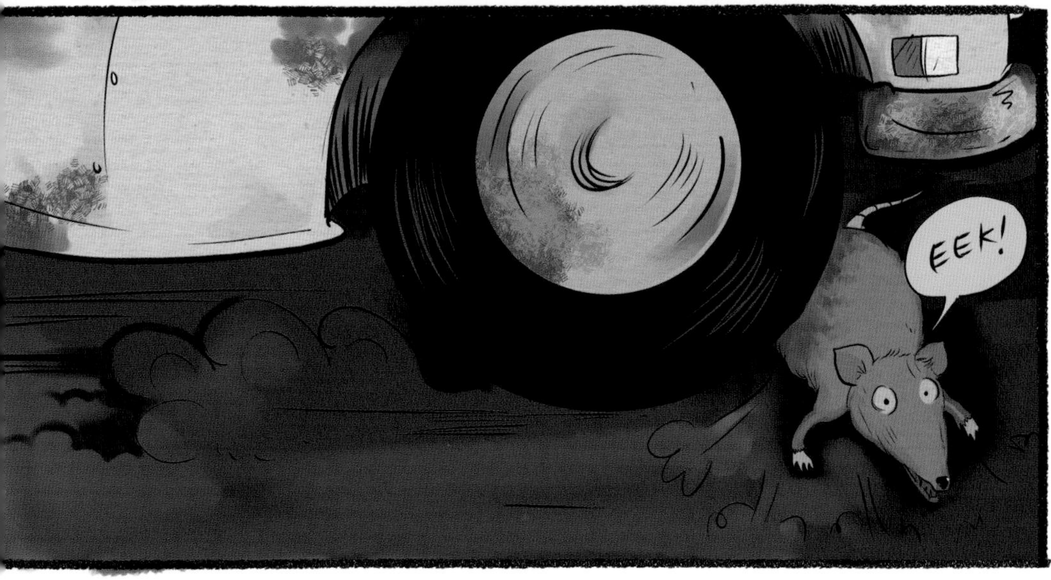
EEK!

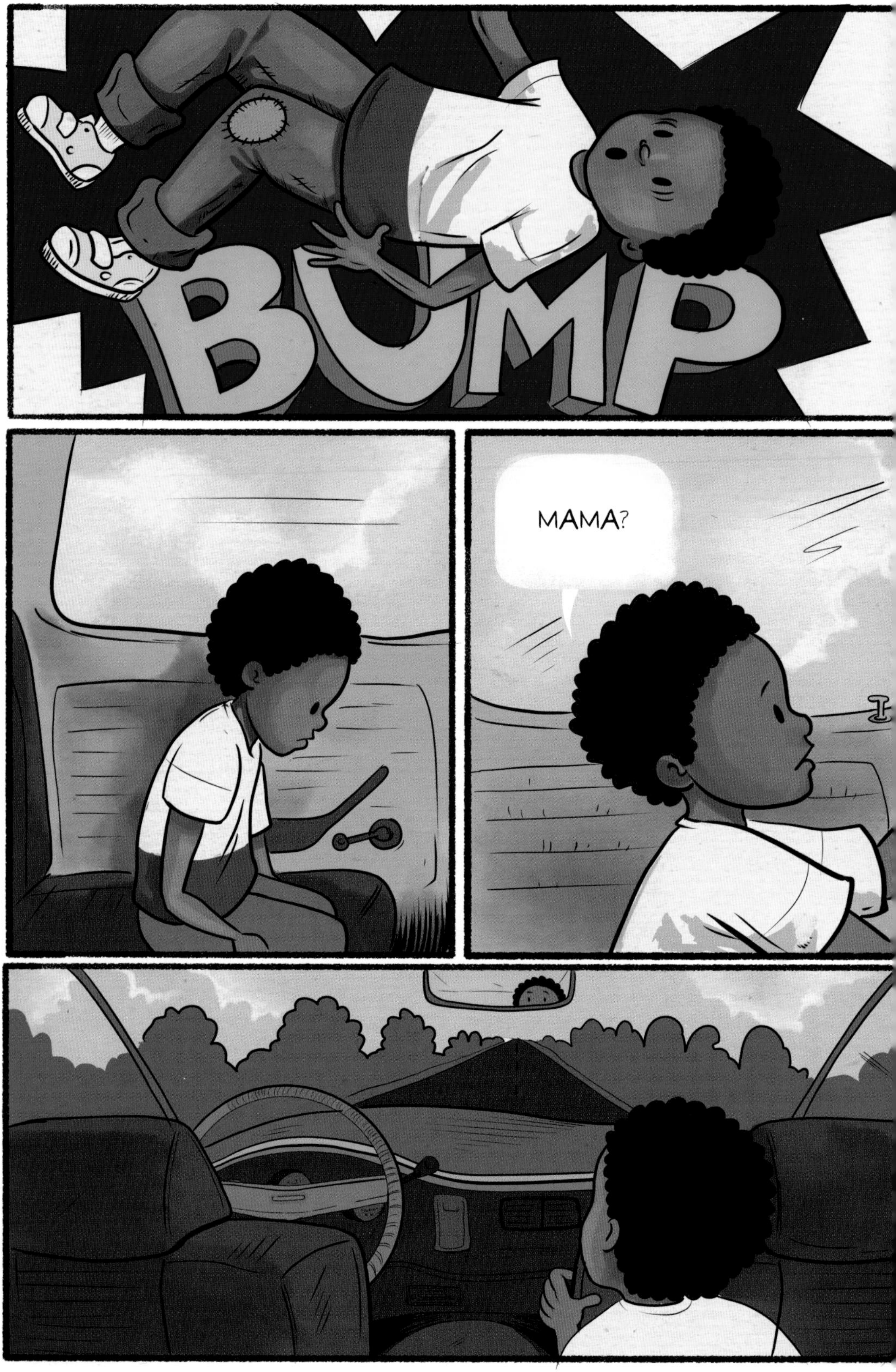
BUMP
MAMA?

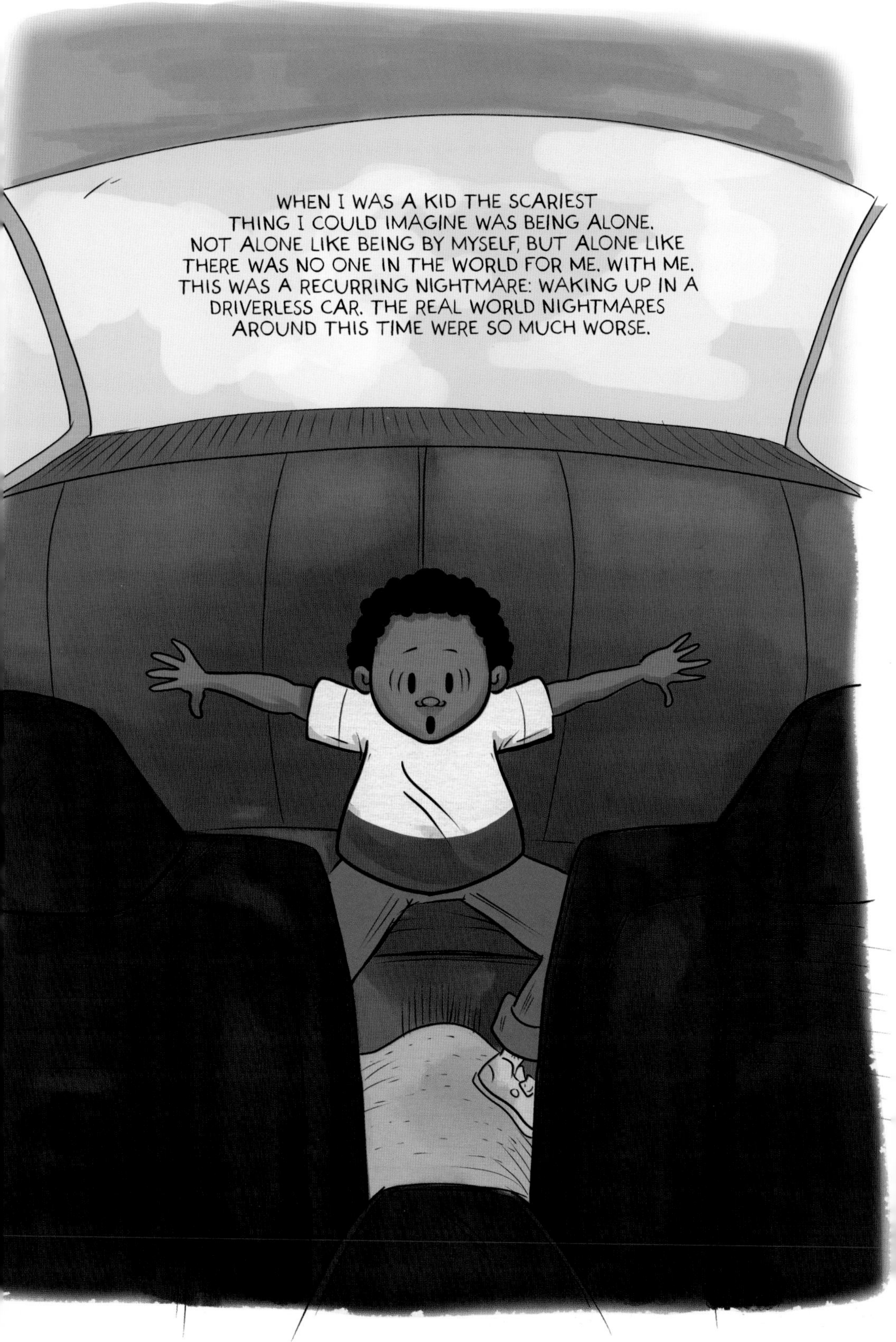
WHEN I WAS A KID THE SCARIEST THING I COULD IMAGINE WAS BEING ALONE. NOT ALONE LIKE BEING BY MYSELF, BUT ALONE LIKE THERE WAS NO ONE IN THE WORLD FOR ME. WITH ME. THIS WAS A RECURRING NIGHTMARE: WAKING UP IN A DRIVERLESS CAR. THE REAL WORLD NIGHTMARES AROUND THIS TIME WERE SO MUCH WORSE.

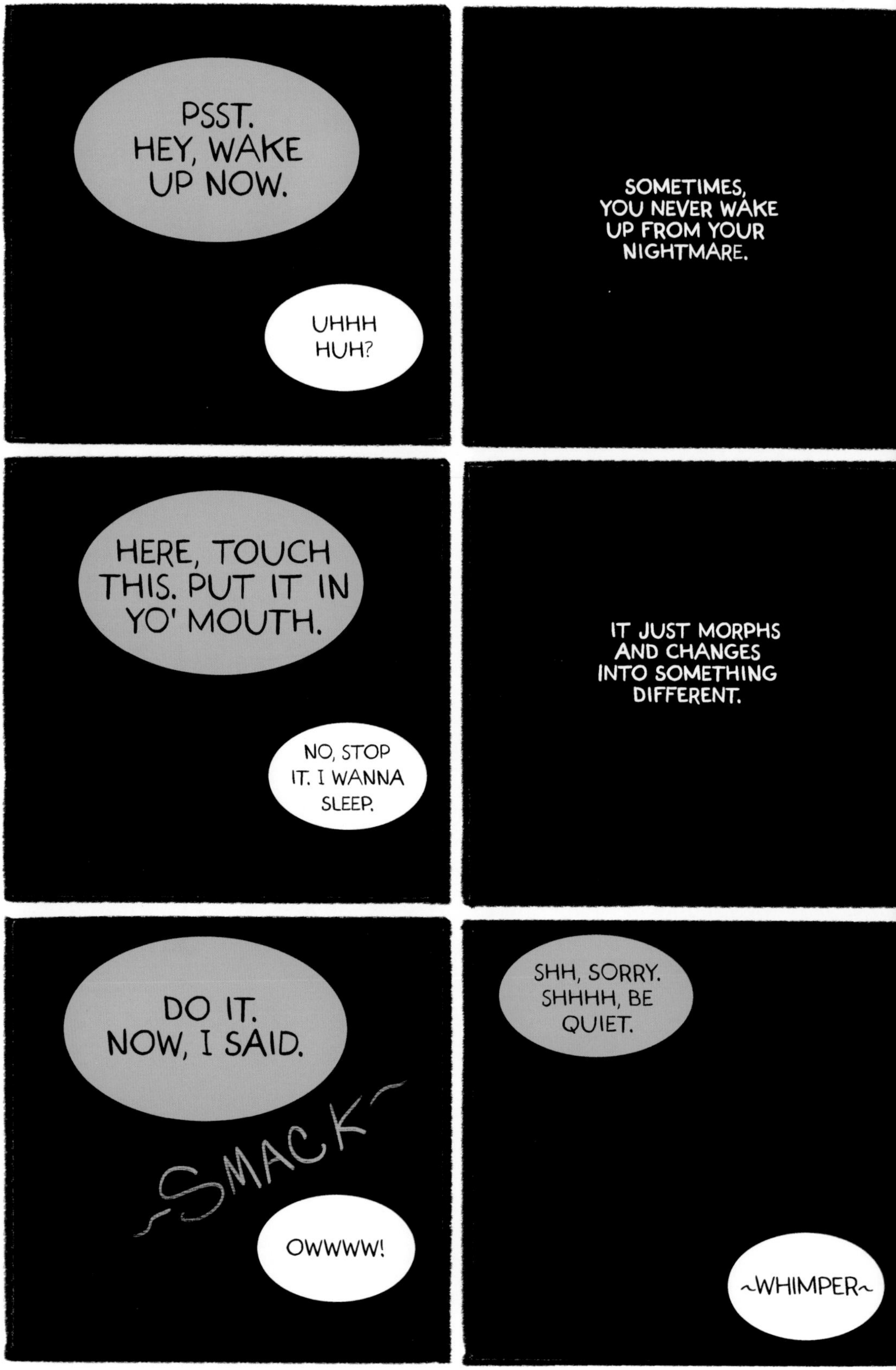
PSST.
HEY, WAKE UP NOW.
UHHH HUH?
SOMETIMES, YOU NEVER WAKE UP FROM YOUR NIGHTMARE.
HERE, TOUCH THIS. PUT IT IN YO' MOUTH.
NO, STOP IT. I WANNA SLEEP.
IT JUST MORPHS AND CHANGES INTO SOMETHING DIFFERENT.
DO IT. NOW, I SAID.
~SMACK~
OWWWW!
SHH, SORRY. SHHHH, BE QUIET.
~WHIMPER~

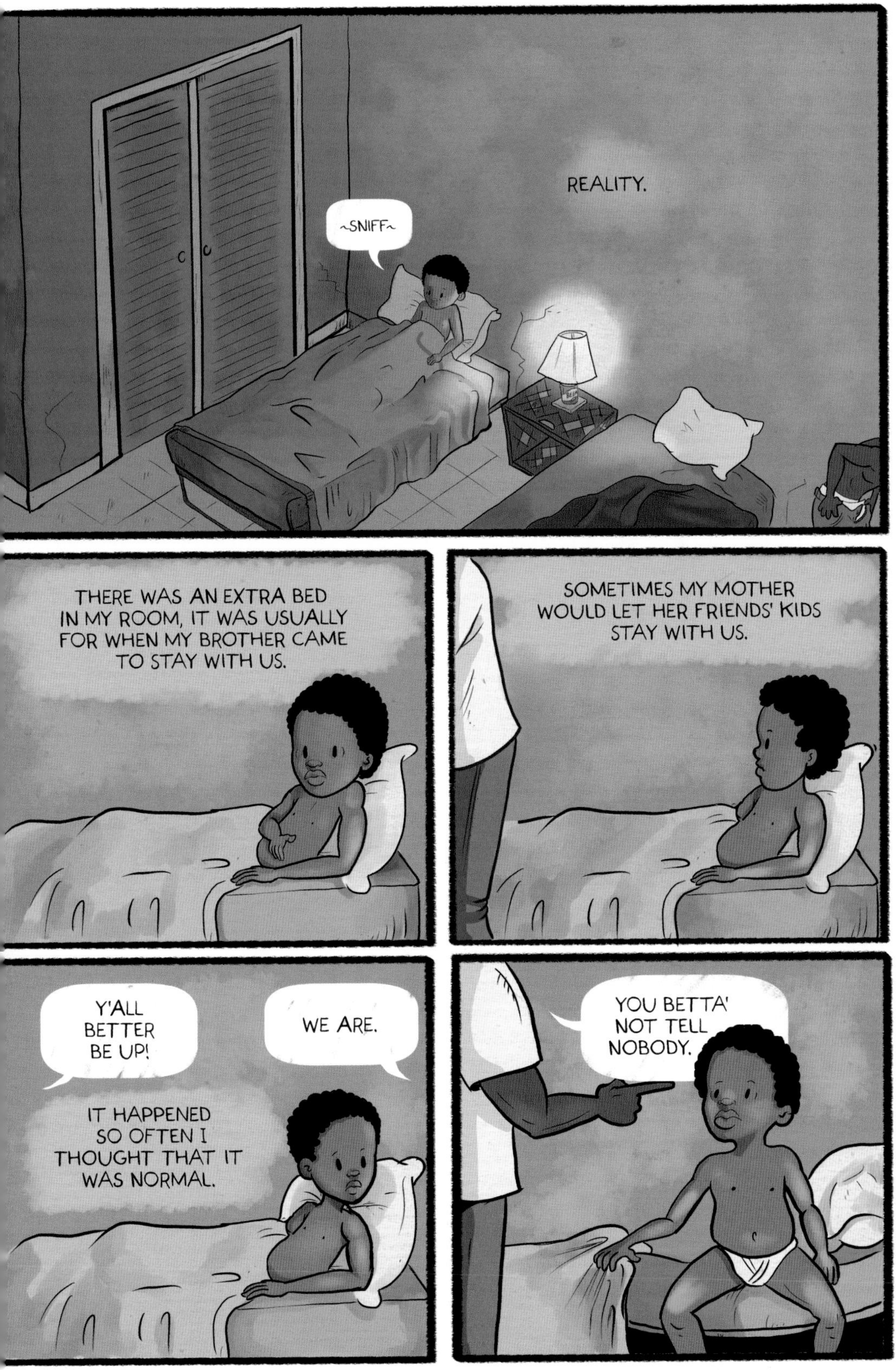
REALITY.
~SNIFF~
THERE WAS AN EXTRA BED IN MY ROOM, IT WAS USUALLY FOR WHEN MY BROTHER CAME TO STAY WITH US.
SOMETIMES MY MOTHER WOULD LET HER FRIENDS' KIDS STAY WITH US.
Y'ALL BETTER BE UP!
WE ARE.
IT HAPPENED SO OFTEN I THOUGHT THAT IT WAS NORMAL.
YOU BETTA' NOT TELL NOBODY.

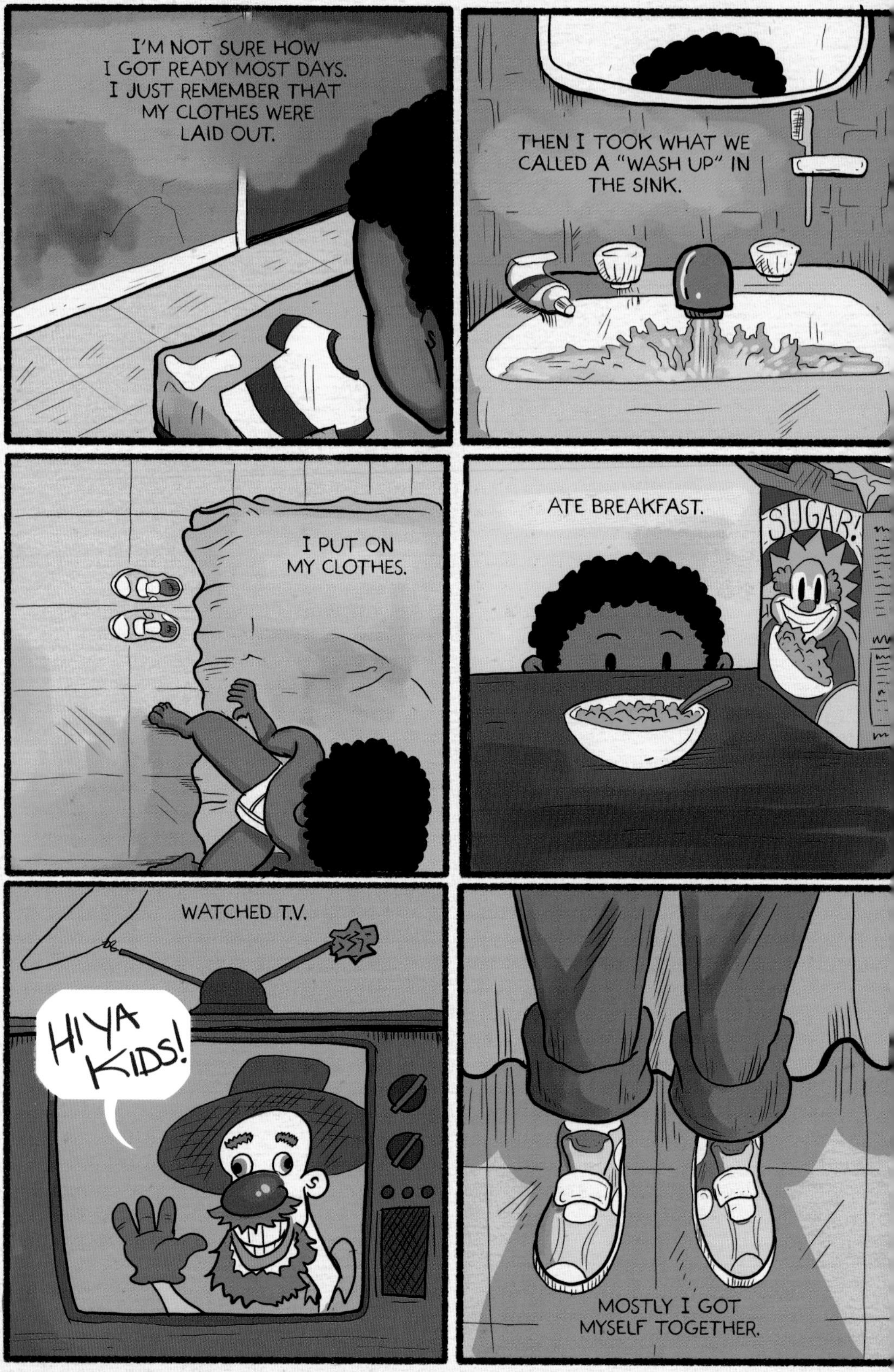
I'M NOT SURE HOW I GOT READY MOST DAYS. I JUST REMEMBER THAT MY CLOTHES WERE LAID OUT.
THEN I TOOK WHAT WE CALLED A "WASH UP" IN THE SINK.
I PUT ON MY CLOTHES.
ATE BREAKFAST.
SUGAR!
WATCHED T.V.
HIYA KIDS!
MOSTLY I GOT MYSELF TOGETHER.

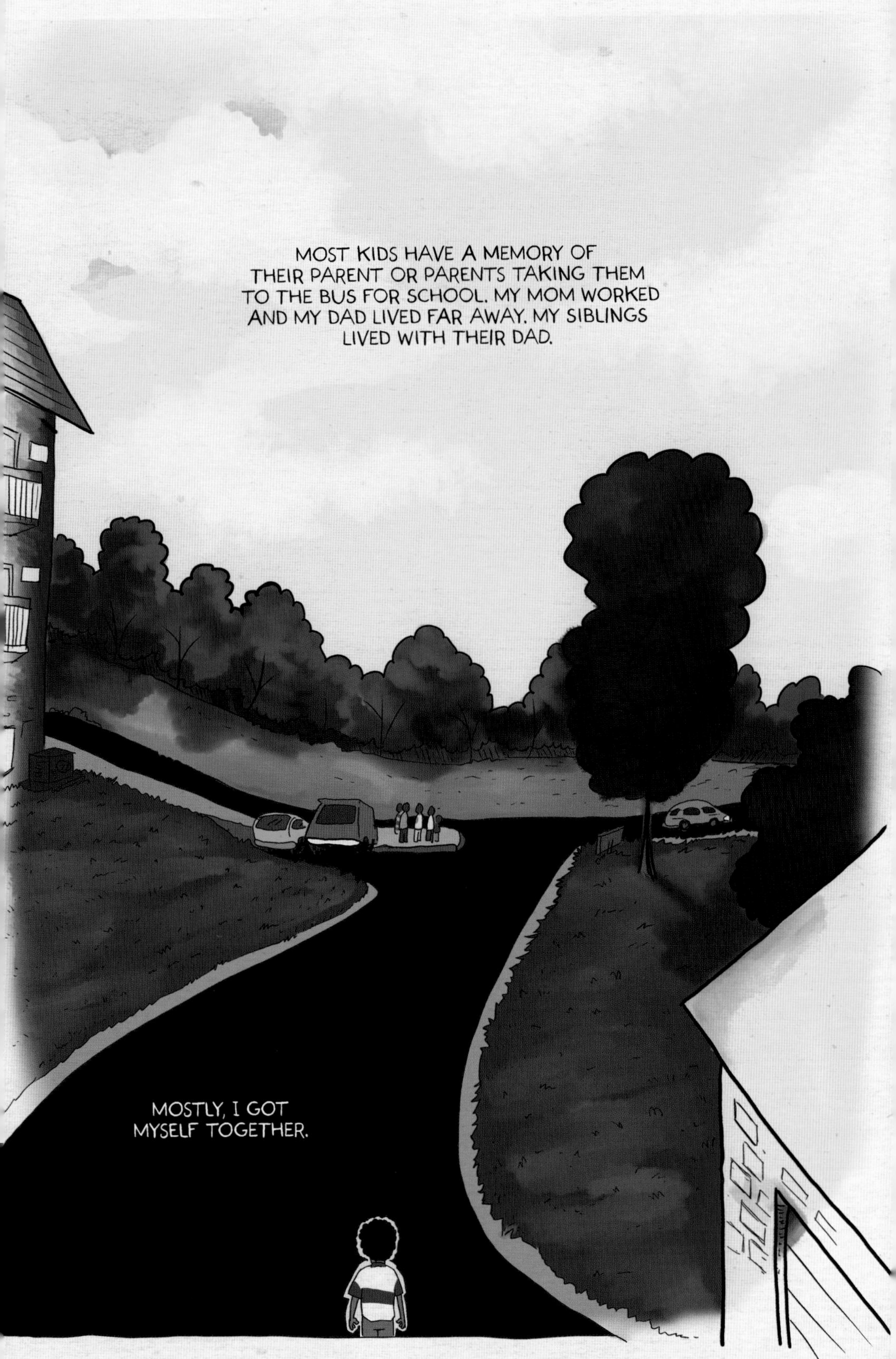
MOST KIDS HAVE A MEMORY OF THEIR PARENT OR PARENTS TAKING THEM TO THE BUS FOR SCHOOL. MY MOM WORKED AND MY DAD LIVED FAR AWAY. MY SIBLINGS LIVED WITH THEIR DAD.
MOSTLY, I GOT MYSELF TOGETHER.

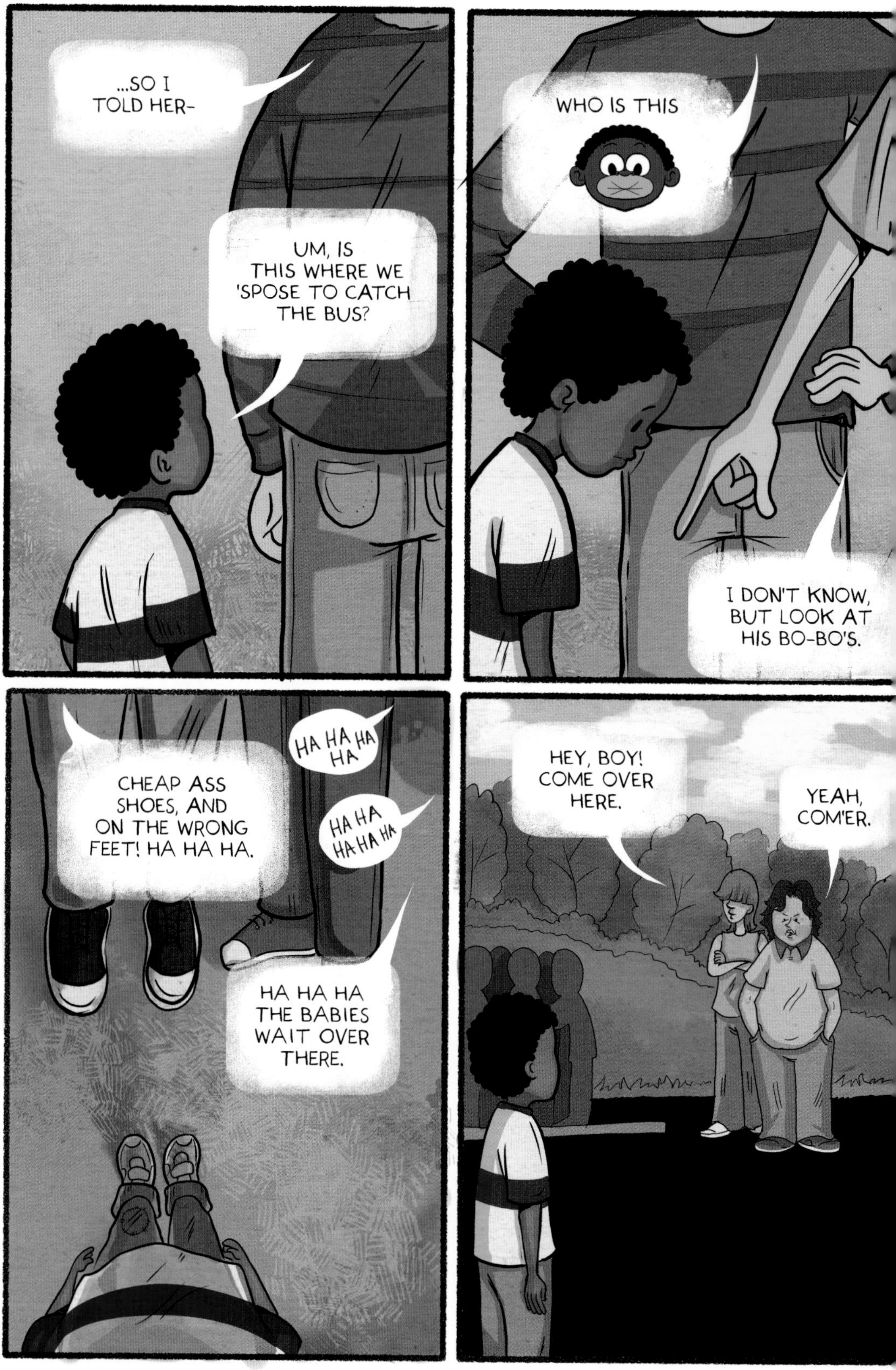

...SO I TOLD HER-
UM, IS THIS WHERE WE 'SPOSE TO CATCH THE BUS?
WHO IS THIS
I DON'T KNOW, BUT LOOK AT HIS BO-BO'S.
CHEAP ASS SHOES, AND ON THE WRONG FEET! HA HA HA.
HA HA HA HA
HA HA HA HA HA
HA HA HA THE BABIES WAIT OVER THERE.
HEY, BOY! COME OVER HERE.
YEAH, COM'ER.

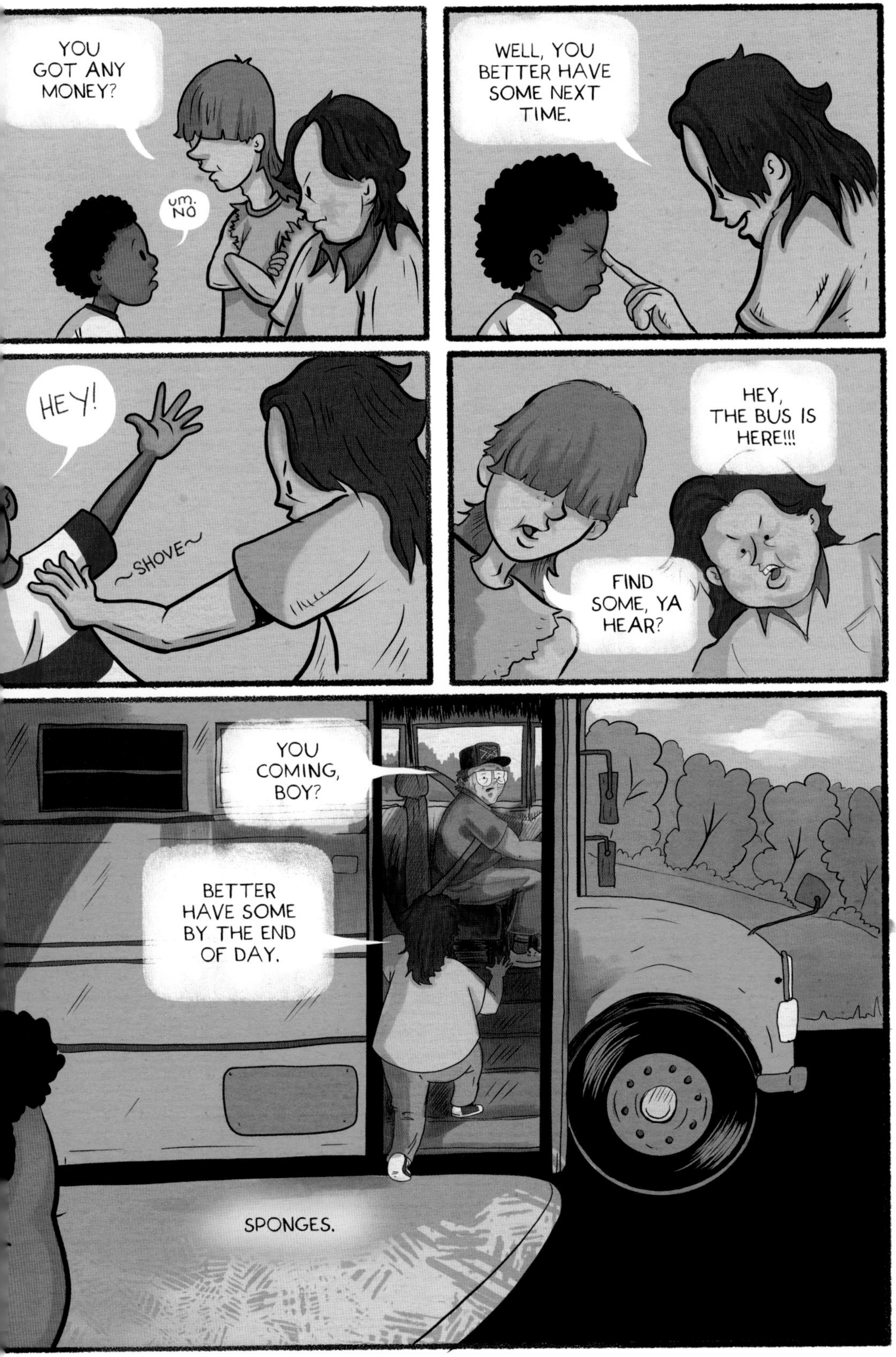
YOU GOT ANY MONEY?
um. NO
WELL, YOU BETTER HAVE SOME NEXT TIME.
HEY!
~SHOVE~
HEY, THE BUS IS HERE!!!
FIND SOME, YA HEAR?
YOU COMING, BOY?
BETTER HAVE SOME BY THE END OF DAY.
SPONGES.

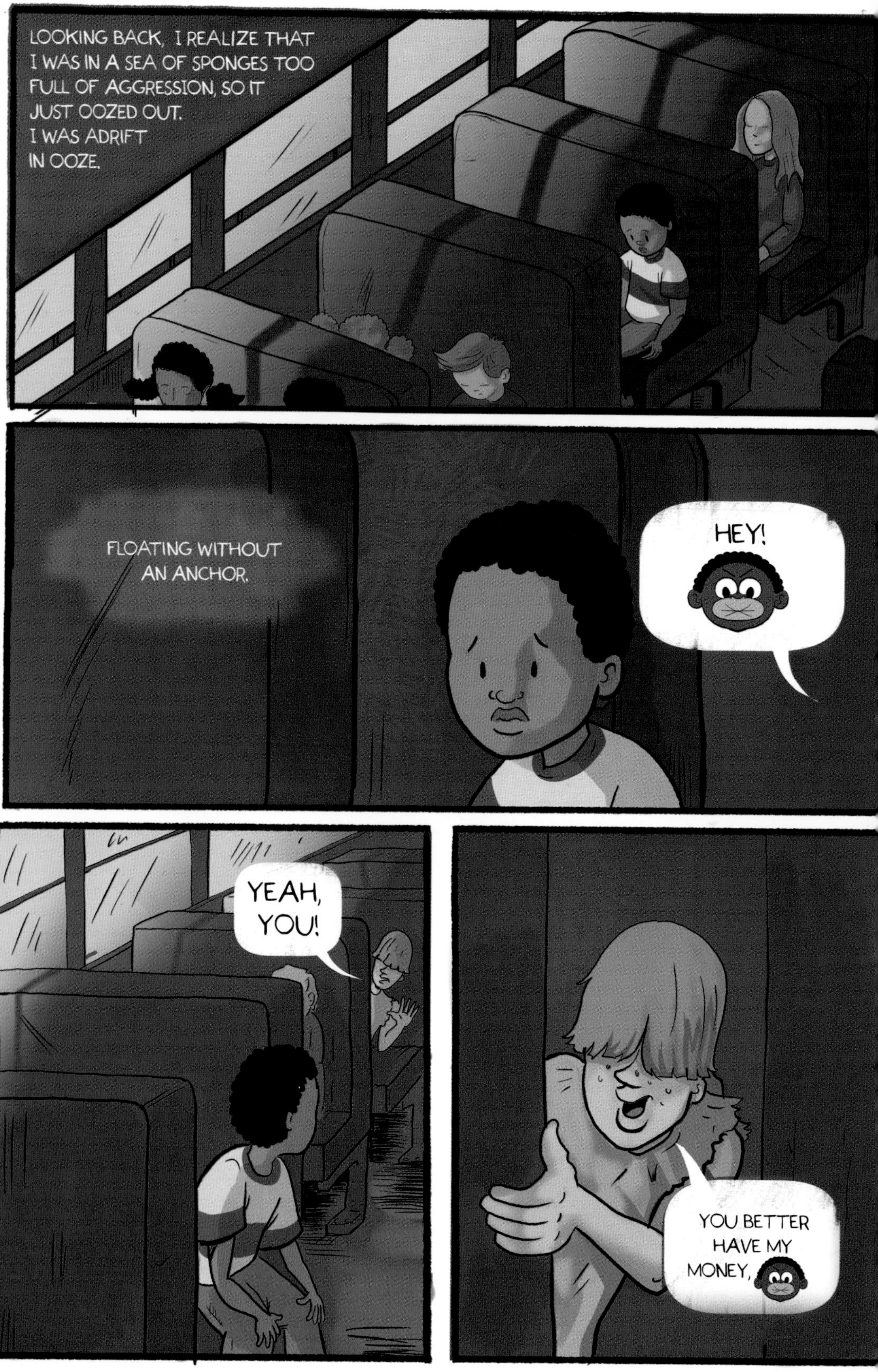
LOOKING BACK, I REALIZE THAT I WAS IN A SEA OF SPONGES TOO FULL OF AGGRESSION, SO IT JUST OOZED OUT. I WAS ADRIFT IN OOZE.
FLOATING WITHOUT AN ANCHOR.
HEY!
YEAH, YOU!
YOU BETTER HAVE MY MONEY,

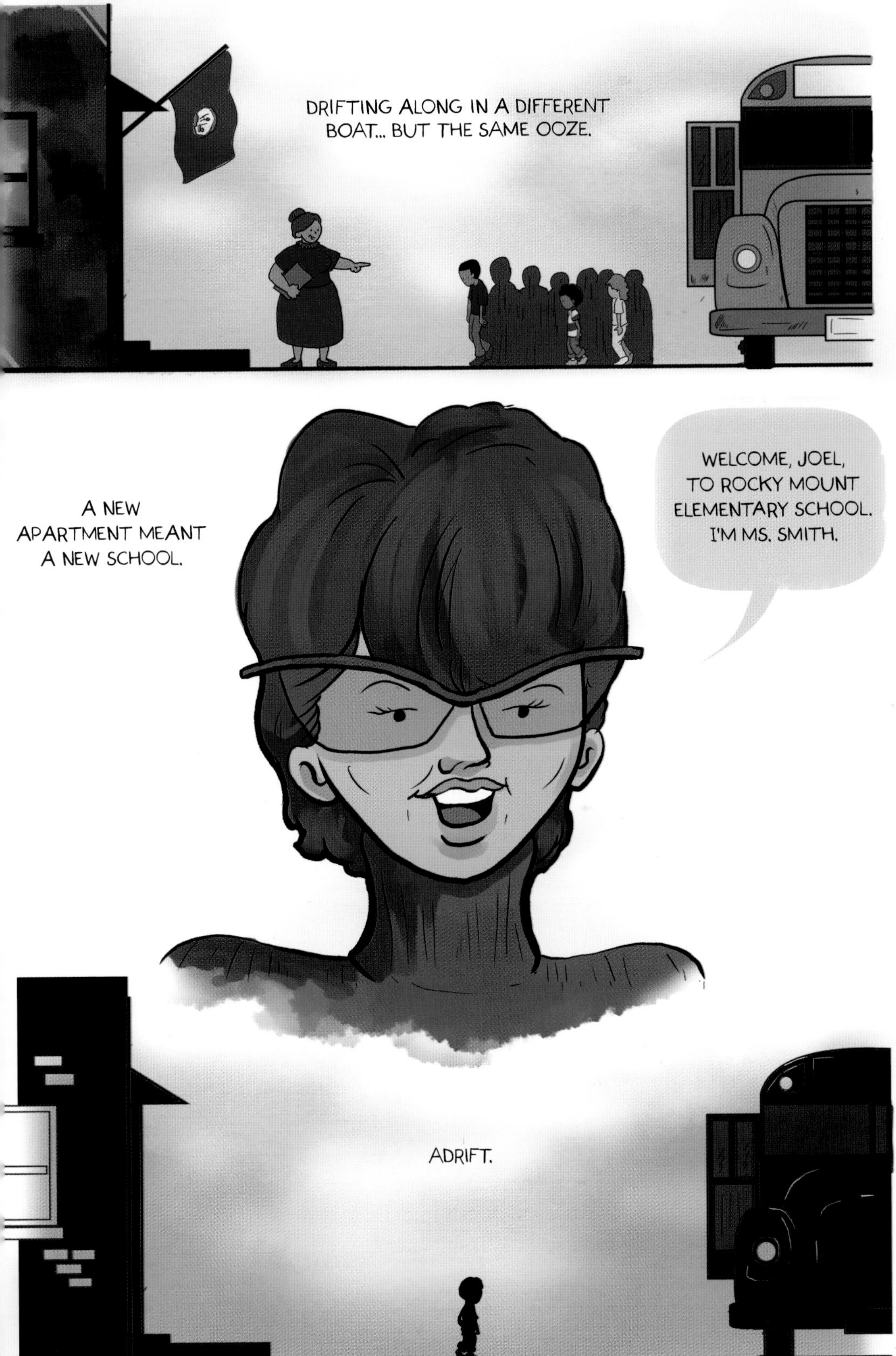
DRIFTING ALONG IN A DIFFERENT BOAT... BUT THE SAME OOZE.
A NEW APARTMENT MEANT A NEW SCHOOL.
WELCOME, JOEL, TO ROCKY MOUNT ELEMENTARY SCHOOL. I'M MS. SMITH.
ADRIFT.

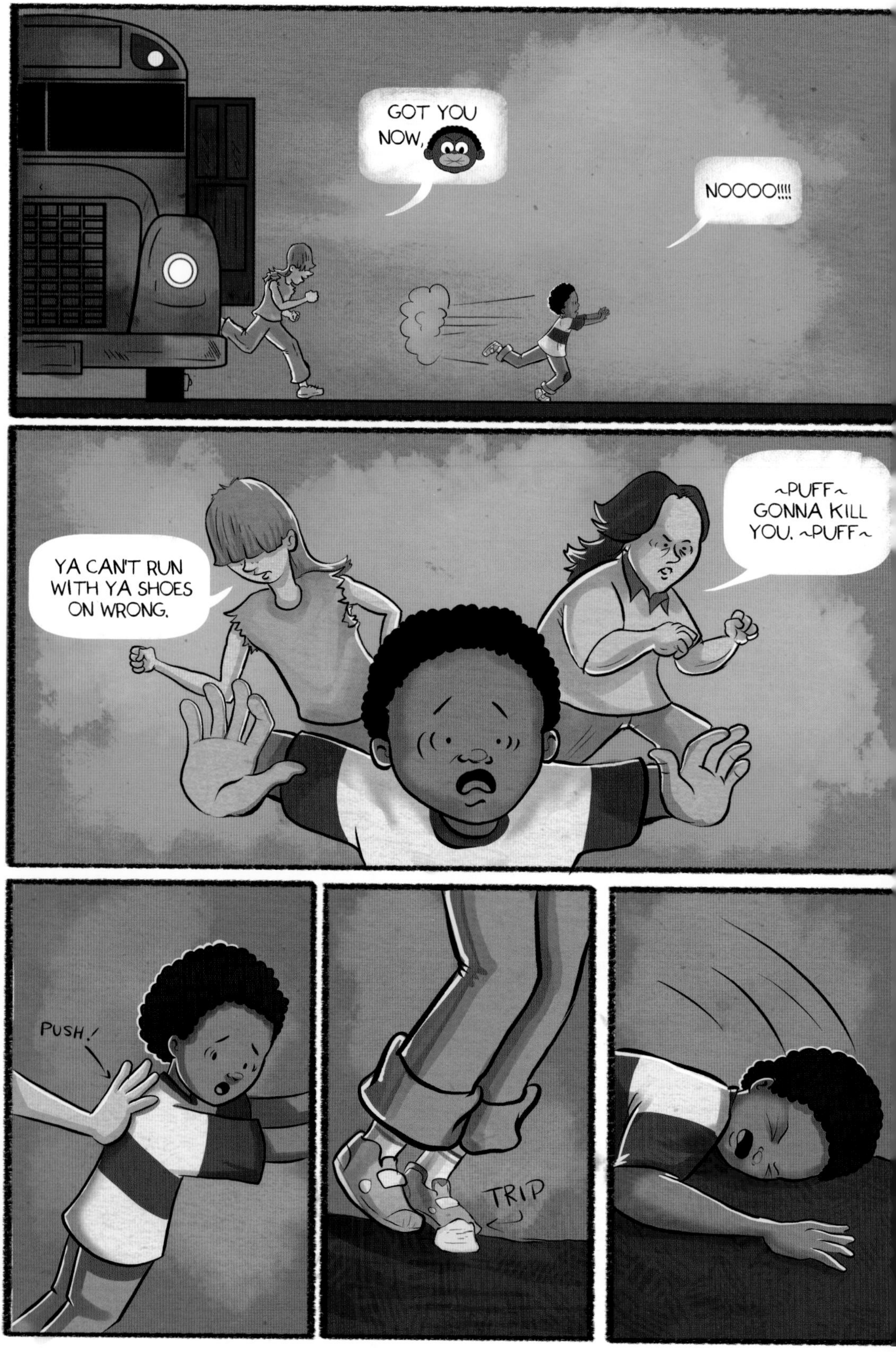
GOT YOU NOW,
NOOOO!!!!
YA CAN'T RUN WITH YA SHOES ON WRONG.
~PUFF~ GONNA KILL YOU. ~PUFF~
PUSH!
TRIP

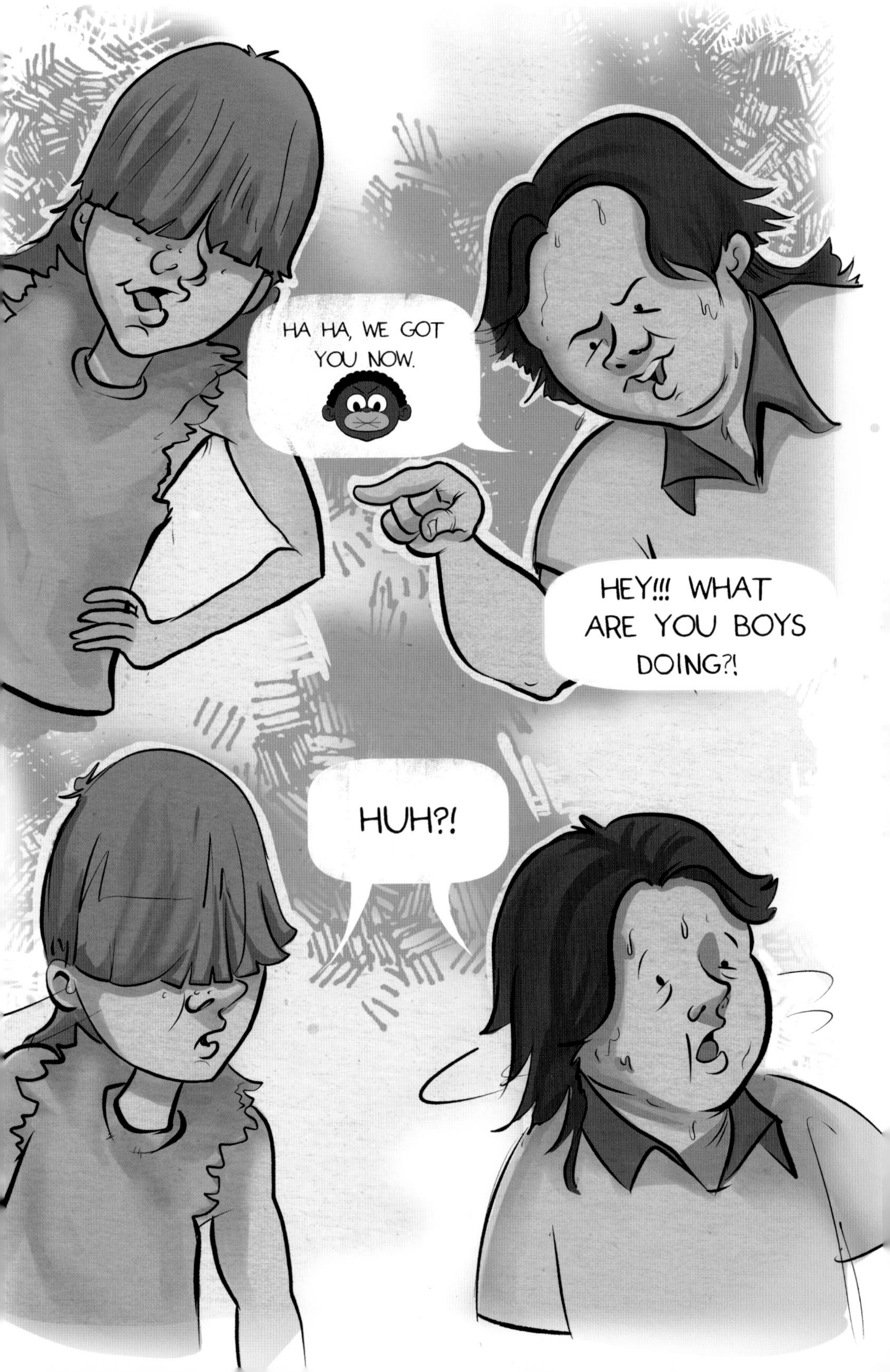
HA HA, WE GOT YOU NOW.
HEY!!! WHAT ARE YOU BOYS DOING?!
HUH?!

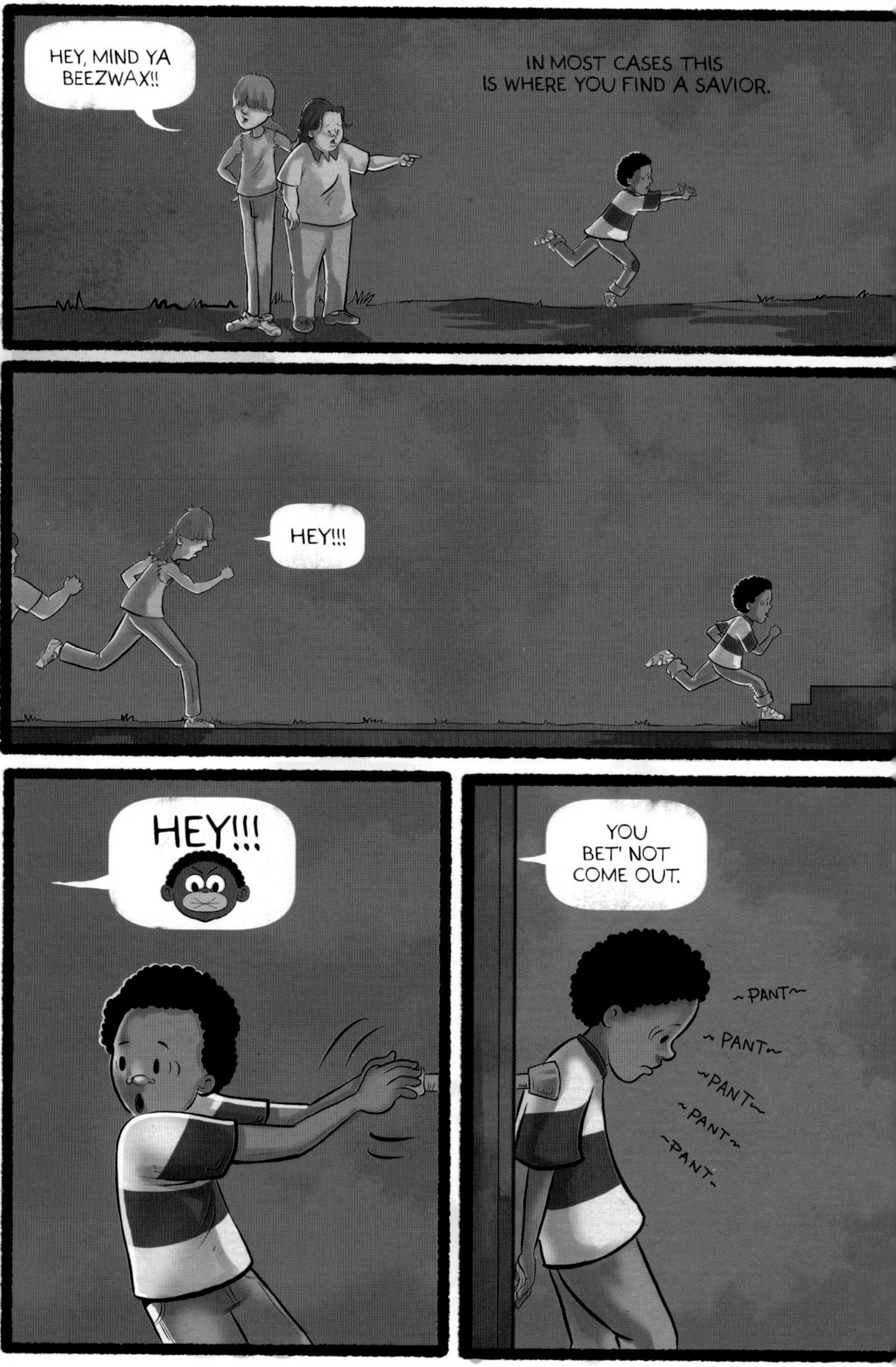
HEY, MIND YA BEEZWAX!!
IN MOST CASES THIS IS WHERE YOU FIND A SAVIOR.
HEY!!!
HEY!!!
YOU BET' NOT COME OUT.
~PANT~
~PANT~
~PANT~
~PANT~
~PANT~

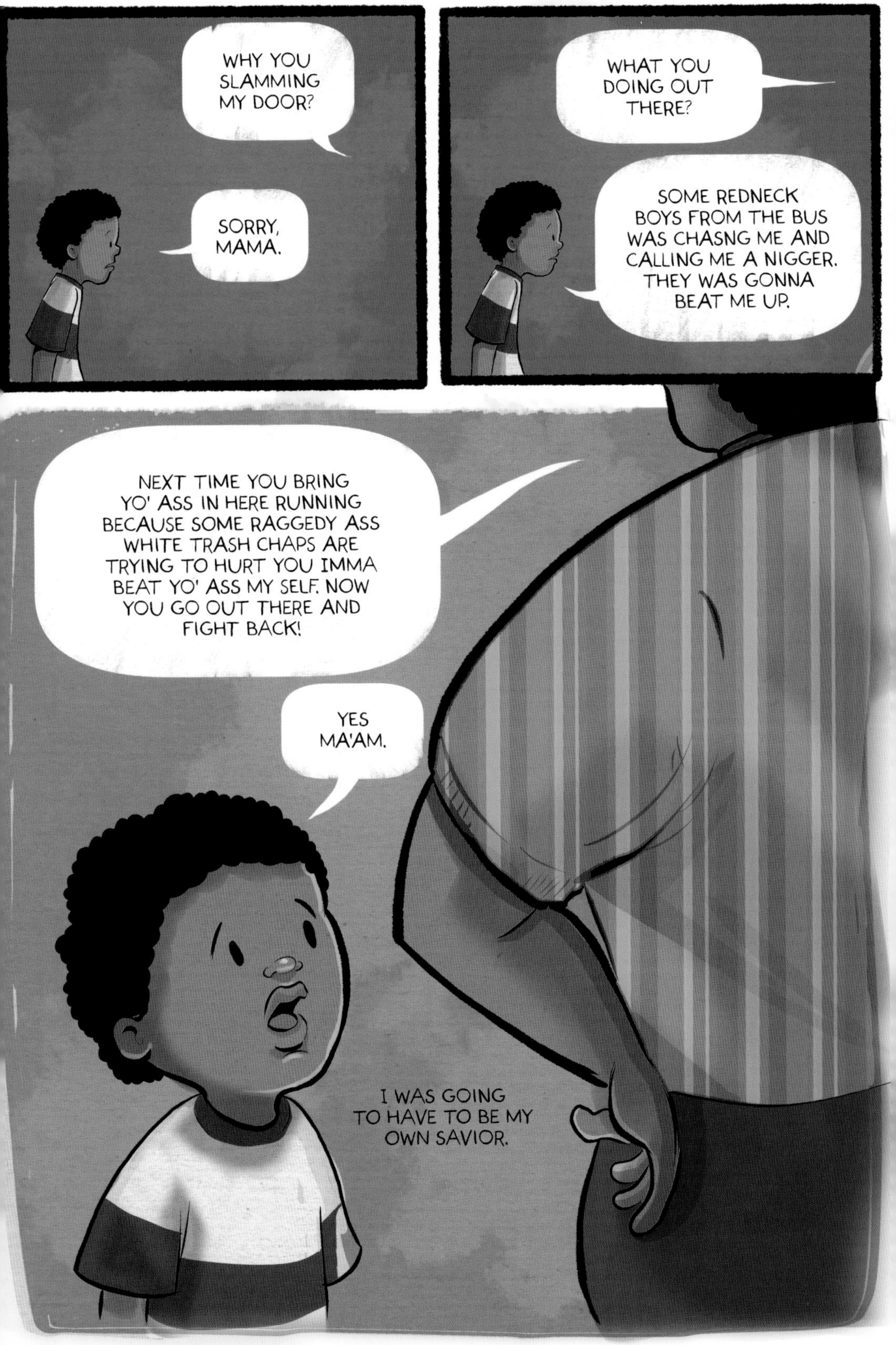
WHY YOU SLAMMING MY DOOR?
SORRY, MAMA.
WHAT YOU DOING OUT THERE?
SOME REDNECK BOYS FROM THE BUS WAS CHASNG ME AND CALLING ME A NIGGER. THEY WAS GONNA BEAT ME UP.
NEXT TIME YOU BRING YO' ASS IN HERE RUNNING BECAUSE SOME RAGGEDY ASS WHITE TRASH CHAPS ARE TRYING TO HURT YOU IMMA BEAT YO' ASS MY SELF. NOW YOU GO OUT THERE AND FIGHT BACK!
YES MA'AM.
I WAS GOING TO HAVE TO BE MY OWN SAVIOR.

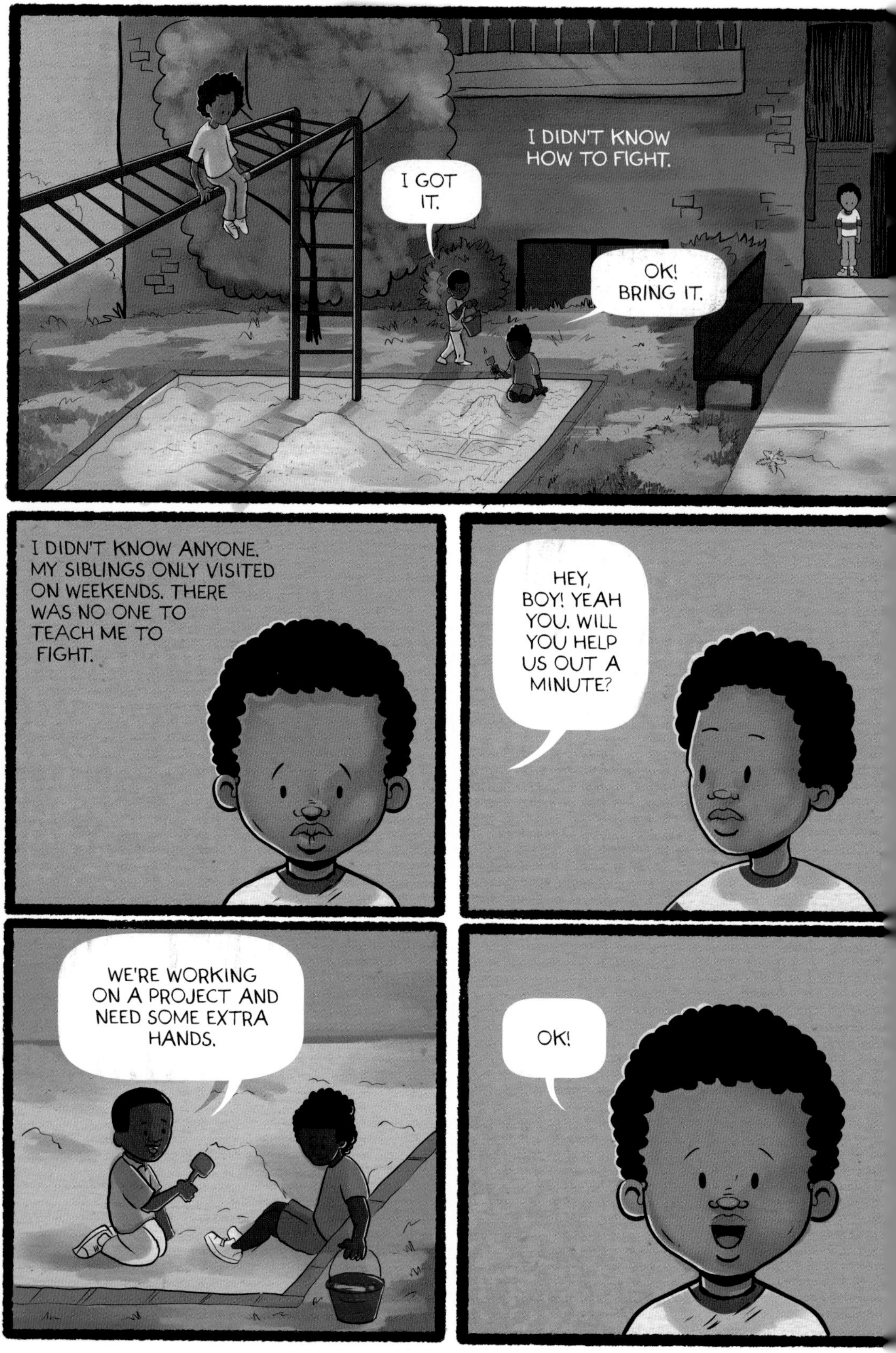

I DIDN'T KNOW HOW TO FIGHT.
I GOT IT.
OK! BRING IT.
I DIDN'T KNOW ANYONE. MY SIBLINGS ONLY VISITED ON WEEKENDS. THERE WAS NO ONE TO TEACH ME TO FIGHT.
HEY, BOY! YEAH YOU. WILL YOU HELP US OUT A MINUTE?
WE'RE WORKING ON A PROJECT AND NEED SOME EXTRA HANDS.
OK!

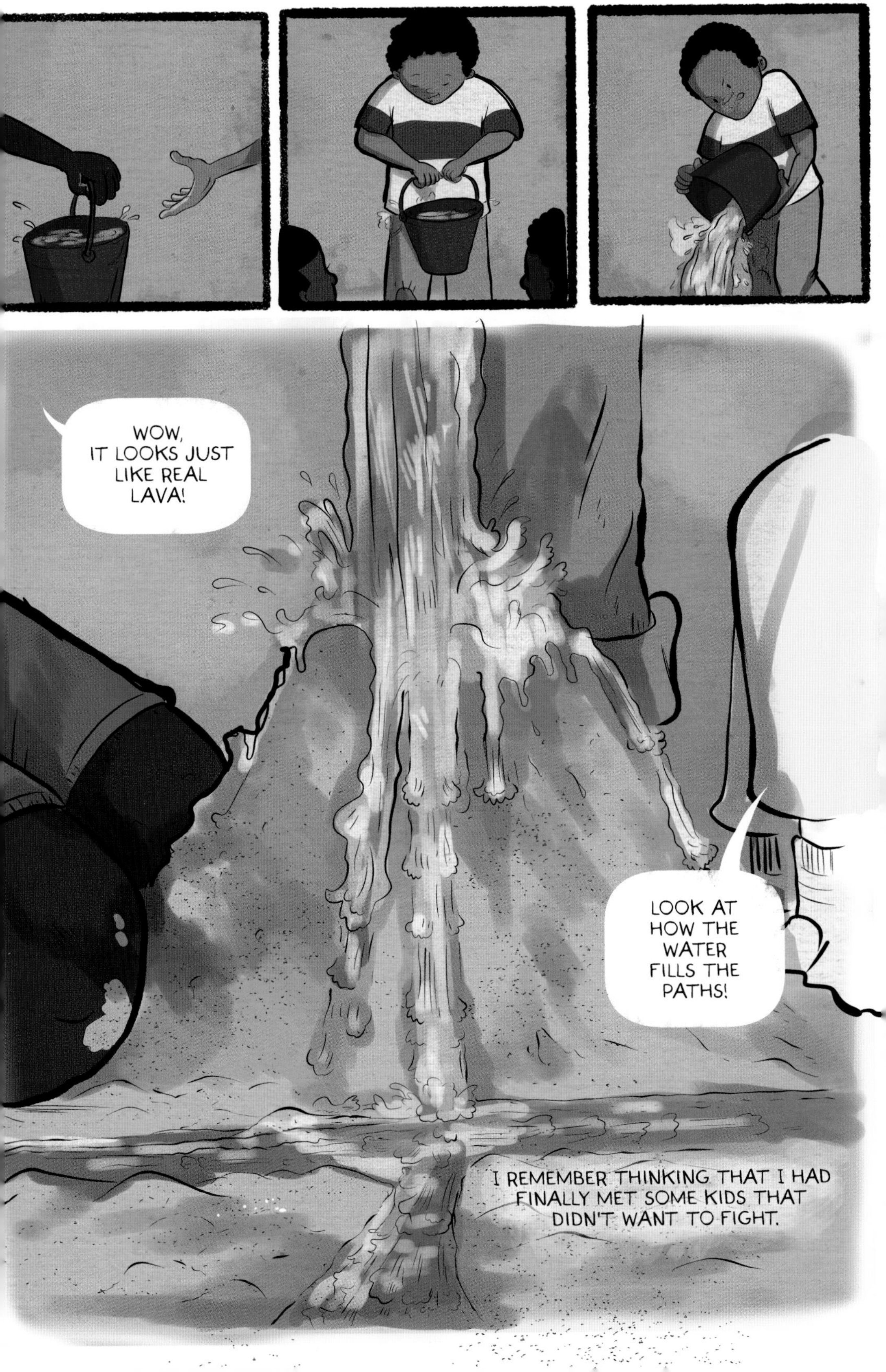
WOW, IT LOOKS JUST LIKE REAL LAVA!
LOOK AT HOW THE WATER FILLS THE PATHS!
I REMEMBER THINKING THAT I HAD FINALLY MET SOME KIDS THAT DIDN'T WANT TO FIGHT.

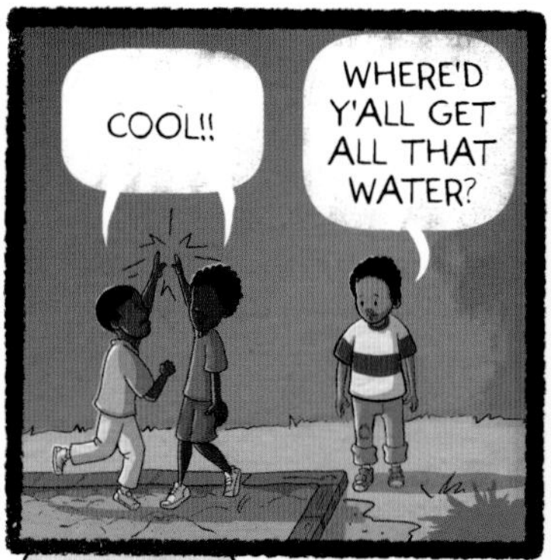
COOL!!
WHERE'D Y'ALL GET ALL THAT WATER?

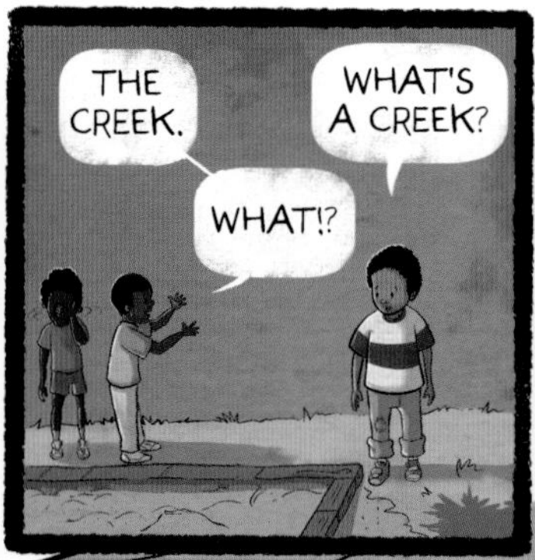
THE CREEK.
WHAT'S A CREEK?
WHAT!?

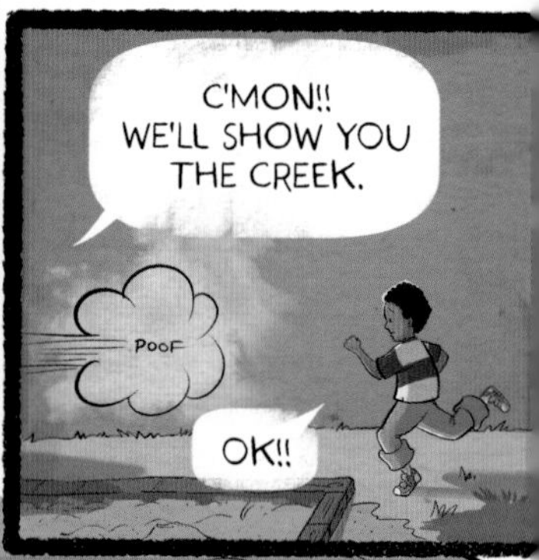
C'MON!! WE'LL SHOW YOU THE CREEK.
POOF
OK!!

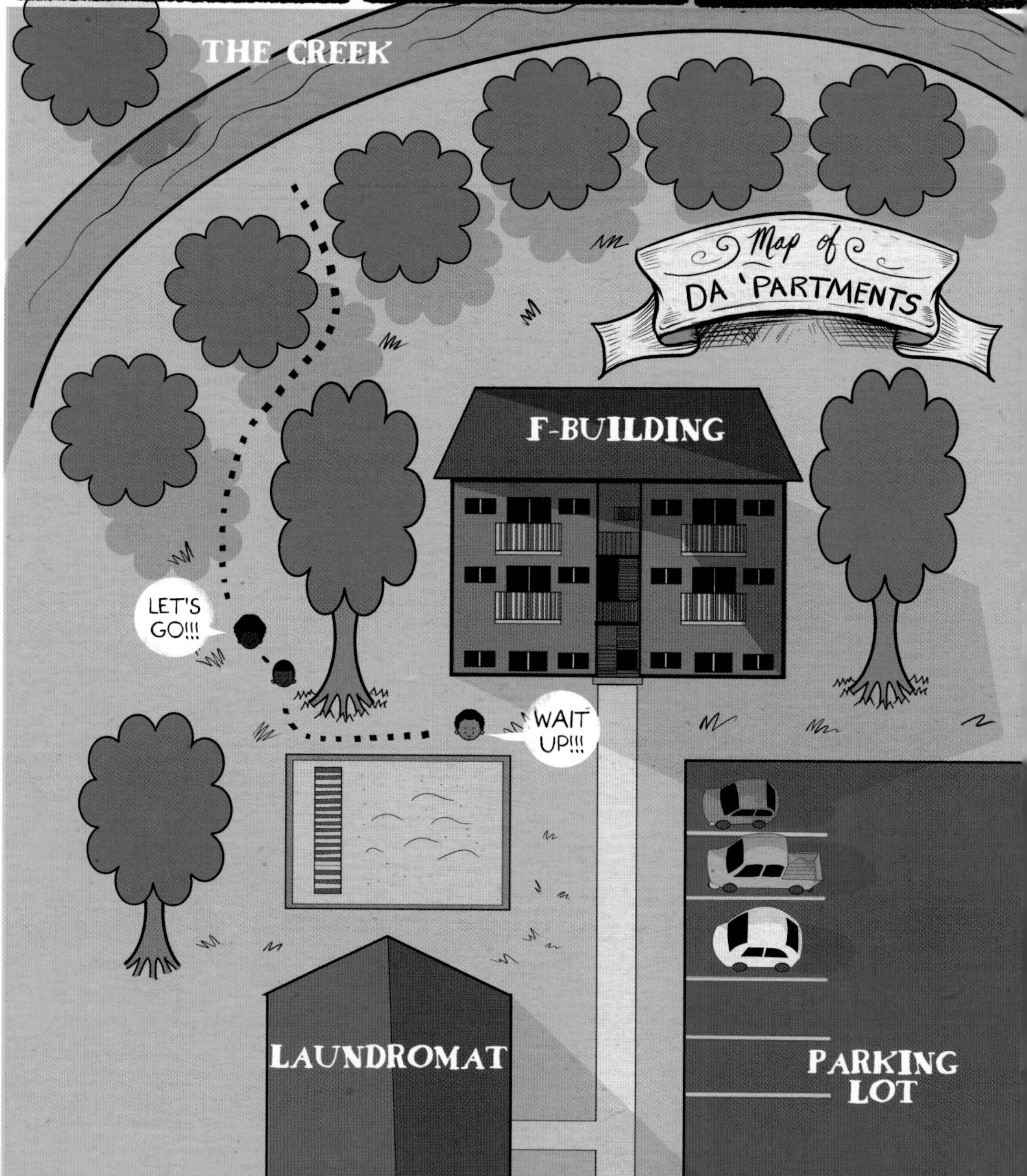
THE CREEK
Map of DA 'PARTMENTS
F-BUILDING
LET'S GO!!!
WAIT UP!!!
LAUNDROMAT
PARKING LOT

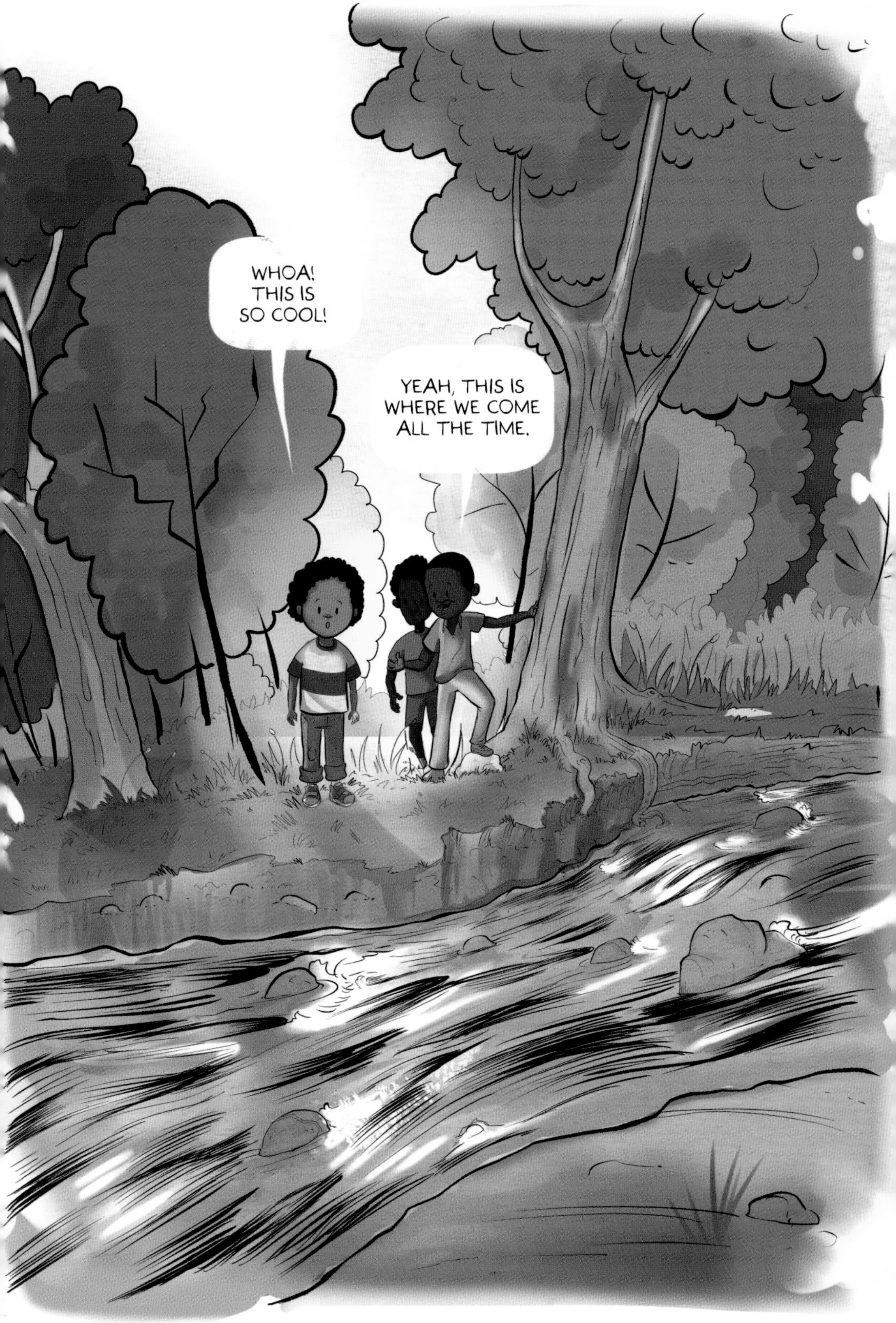
WHOA! THIS IS SO COOL!
YEAH, THIS IS WHERE WE COME ALL THE TIME.

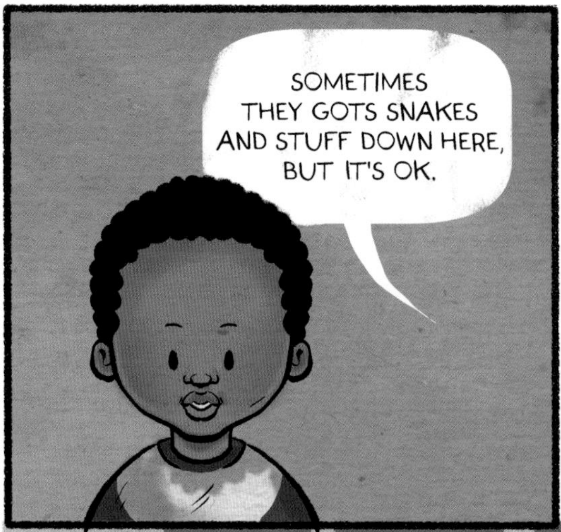
SOMETIMES THEY GOTS SNAKES AND STUFF DOWN HERE, BUT IT'S OK.

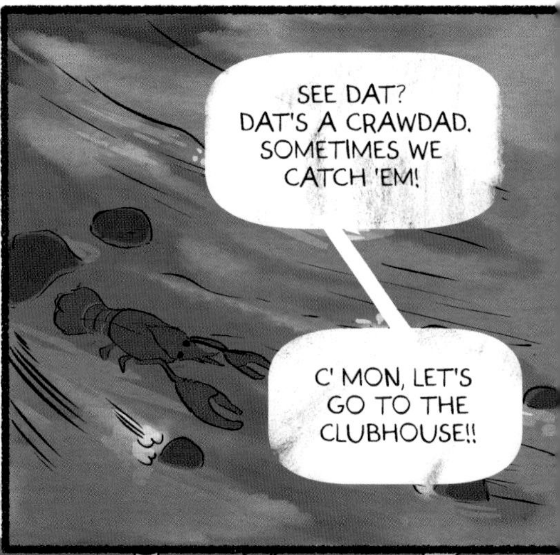
SEE DAT? DAT'S A CRAWDAD. SOMETIMES WE CATCH 'EM!
C' MON, LET'S GO TO THE CLUBHOUSE!!

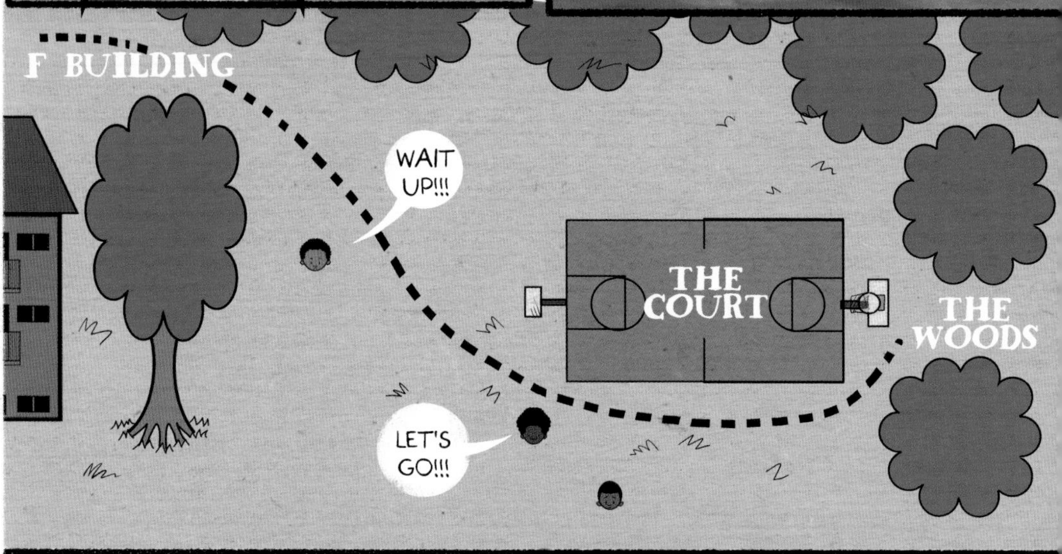
F BUILDING
WAIT UP!!!
THE COURT
THE WOODS
LET'S GO!!!

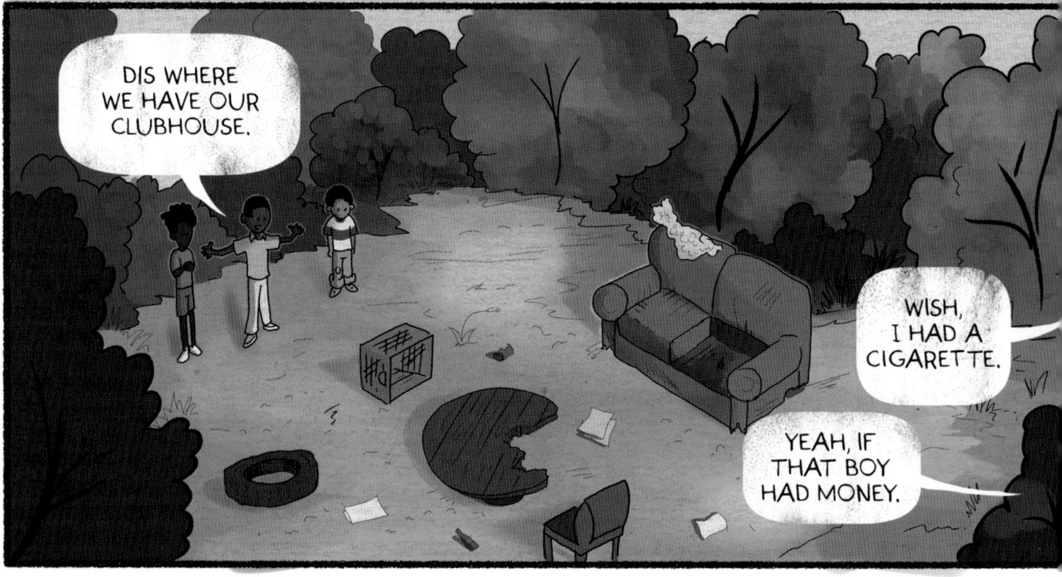
DIS WHERE WE HAVE OUR CLUBHOUSE.
WISH, I HAD A CIGARETTE.
YEAH, IF THAT BOY HAD MONEY.

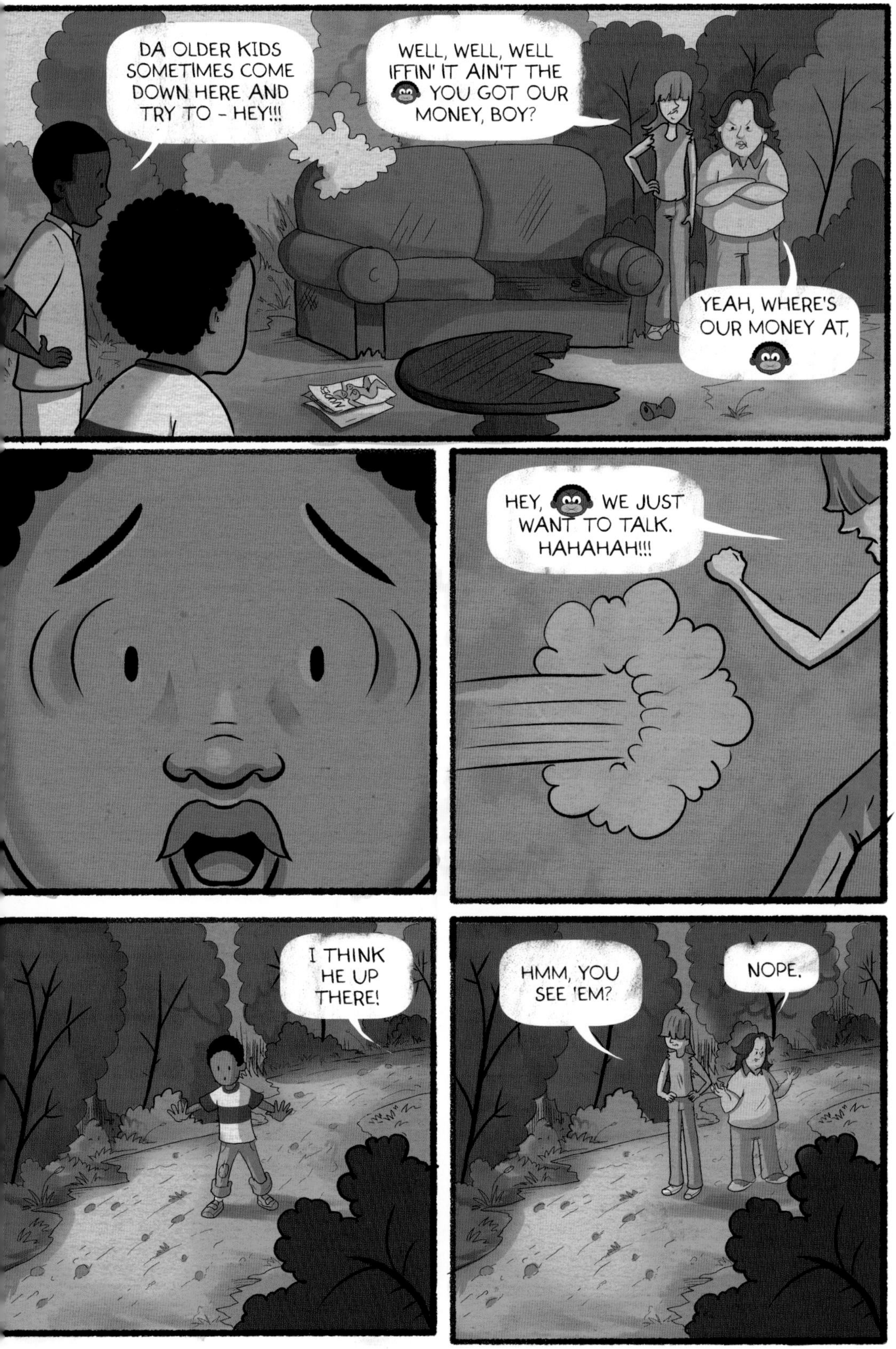
DA OLDER KIDS SOMETIMES COME DOWN HERE AND TRY TO - HEY!!!
WELL, WELL, WELL IFFIN' IT AIN'T THE YOU GOT OUR MONEY, BOY?
YEAH, WHERE'S OUR MONEY AT,
HEY, WE JUST WANT TO TALK. HAHAHAH!!!
I THINK HE UP THERE!
HMM, YOU SEE 'EM?
NOPE.

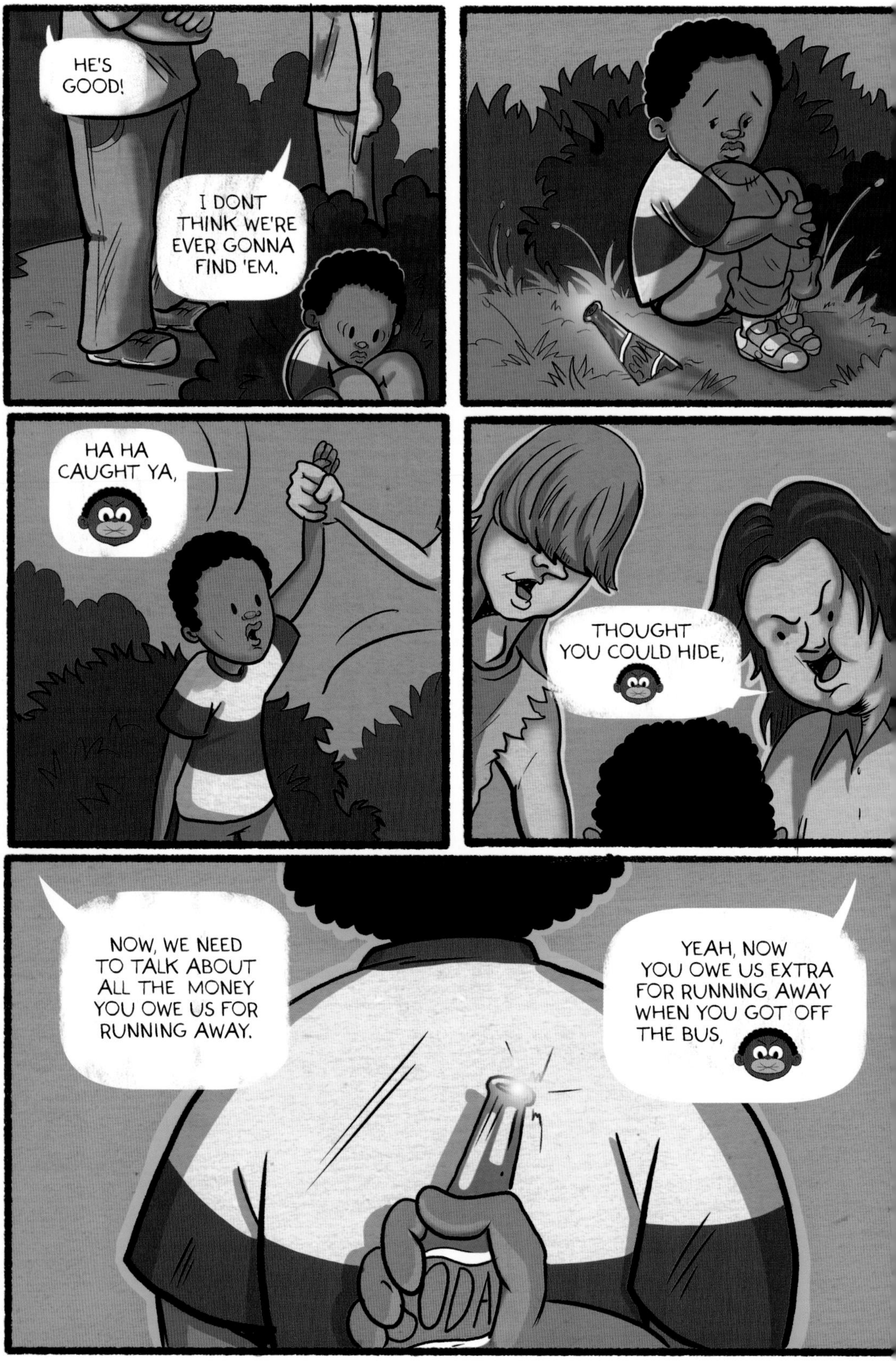
HE'S GOOD!
I DONT THINK WE'RE EVER GONNA FIND 'EM.
HA HA CAUGHT YA,
THOUGHT YOU COULD HIDE,
NOW, WE NEED TO TALK ABOUT ALL THE MONEY YOU OWE US FOR RUNNING AWAY.
YEAH, NOW YOU OWE US EXTRA FOR RUNNING AWAY WHEN YOU GOT OFF THE BUS,
SODA

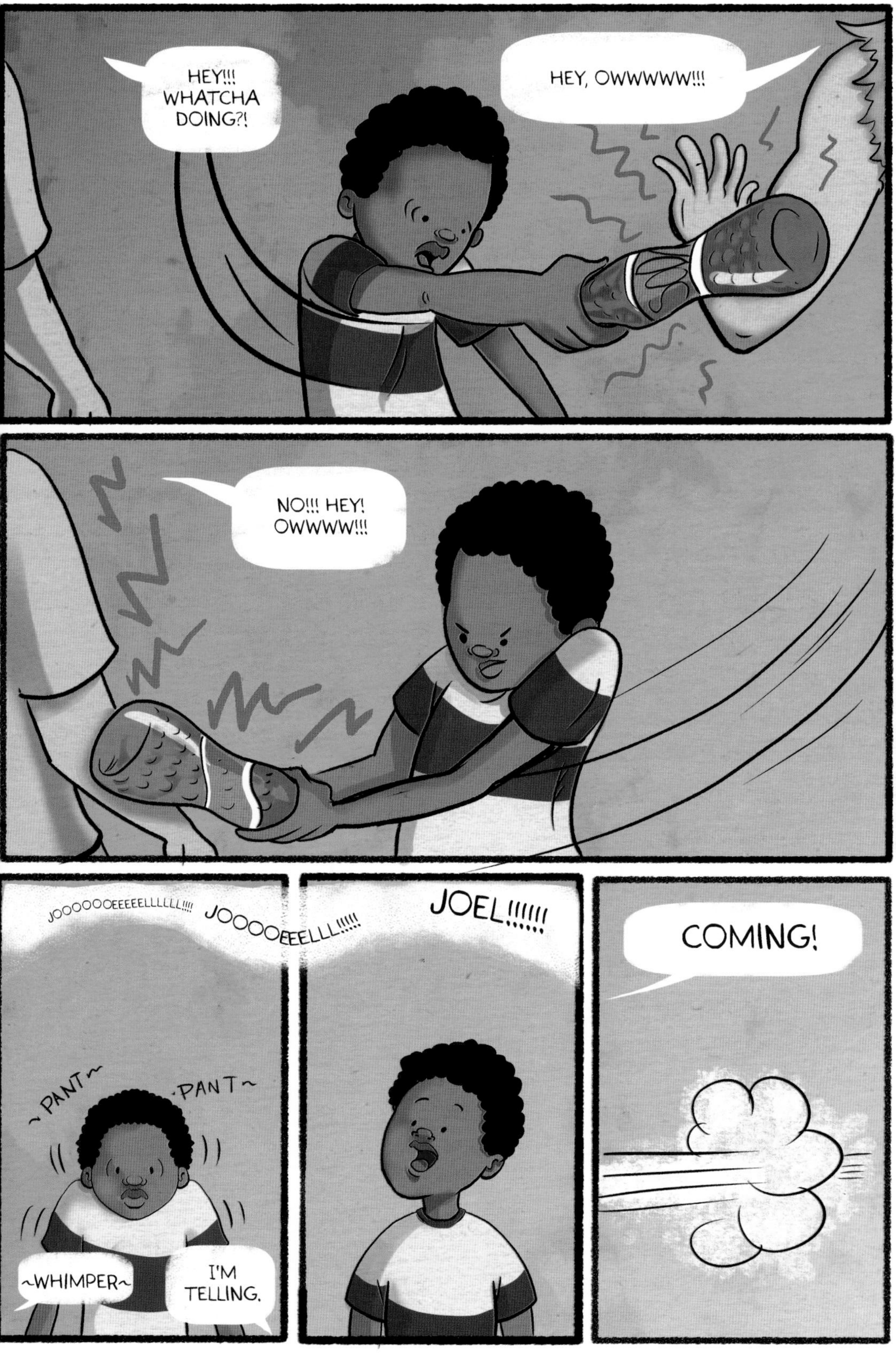
HEY!!! WHATCHA DOING?!
HEY, OWWWWW!!!
NO!!! HEY! OWWWW!!!
JOOOOOOEEEEELLLLLL!!!!
~PANT~
~PANT~
~WHIMPER~
I'M TELLING.
JOOOOEEELLL!!!!!
JOEL!!!!!!
COMING!

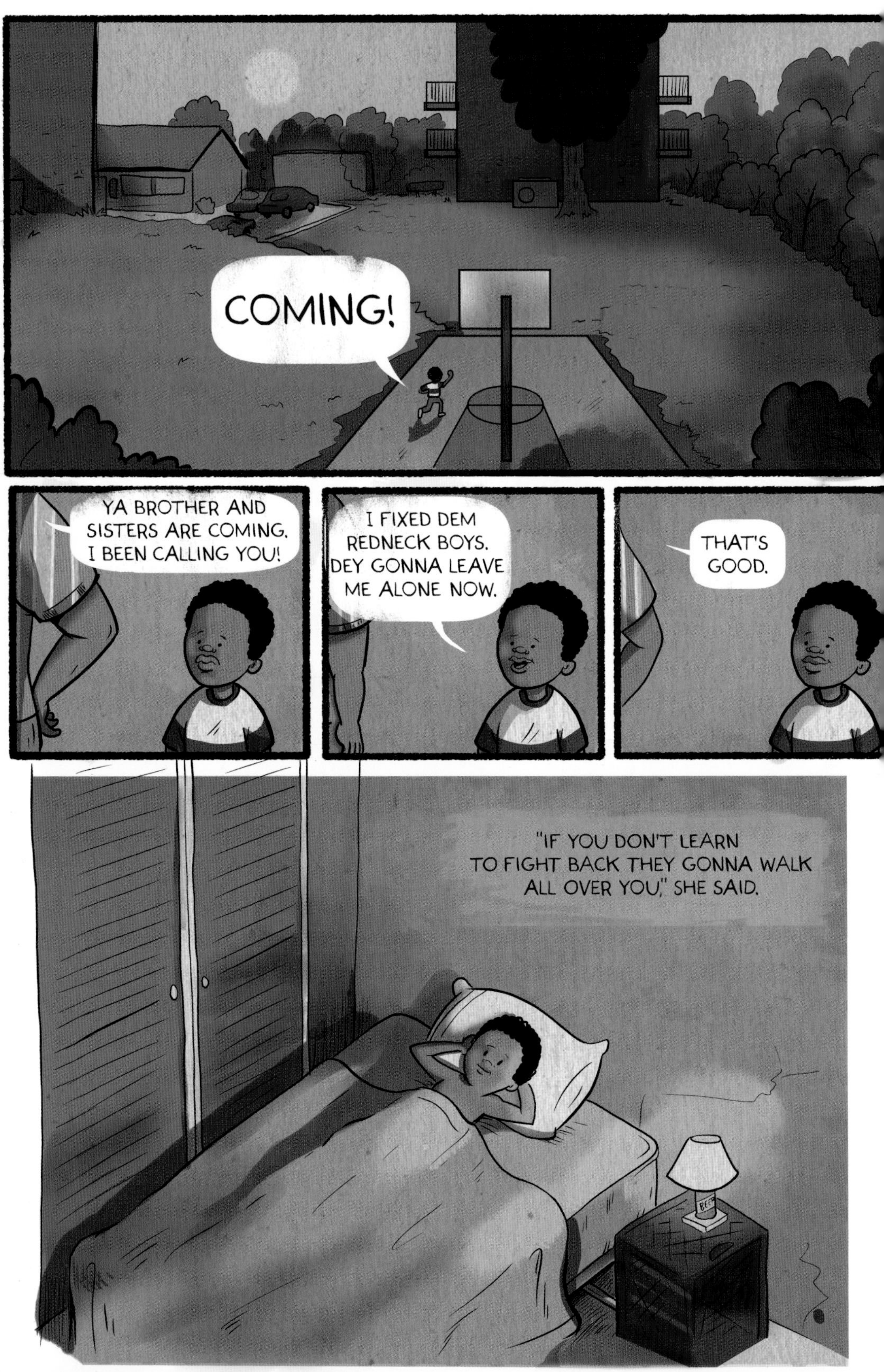
COMING!
YA BROTHER AND SISTERS ARE COMING. I BEEN CALLING YOU!
I FIXED DEM REDNECK BOYS. DEY GONNA LEAVE ME ALONE NOW.
THAT'S GOOD.
"IF YOU DON'T LEARN TO FIGHT BACK THEY GONNA WALK ALL OVER YOU," SHE SAID.

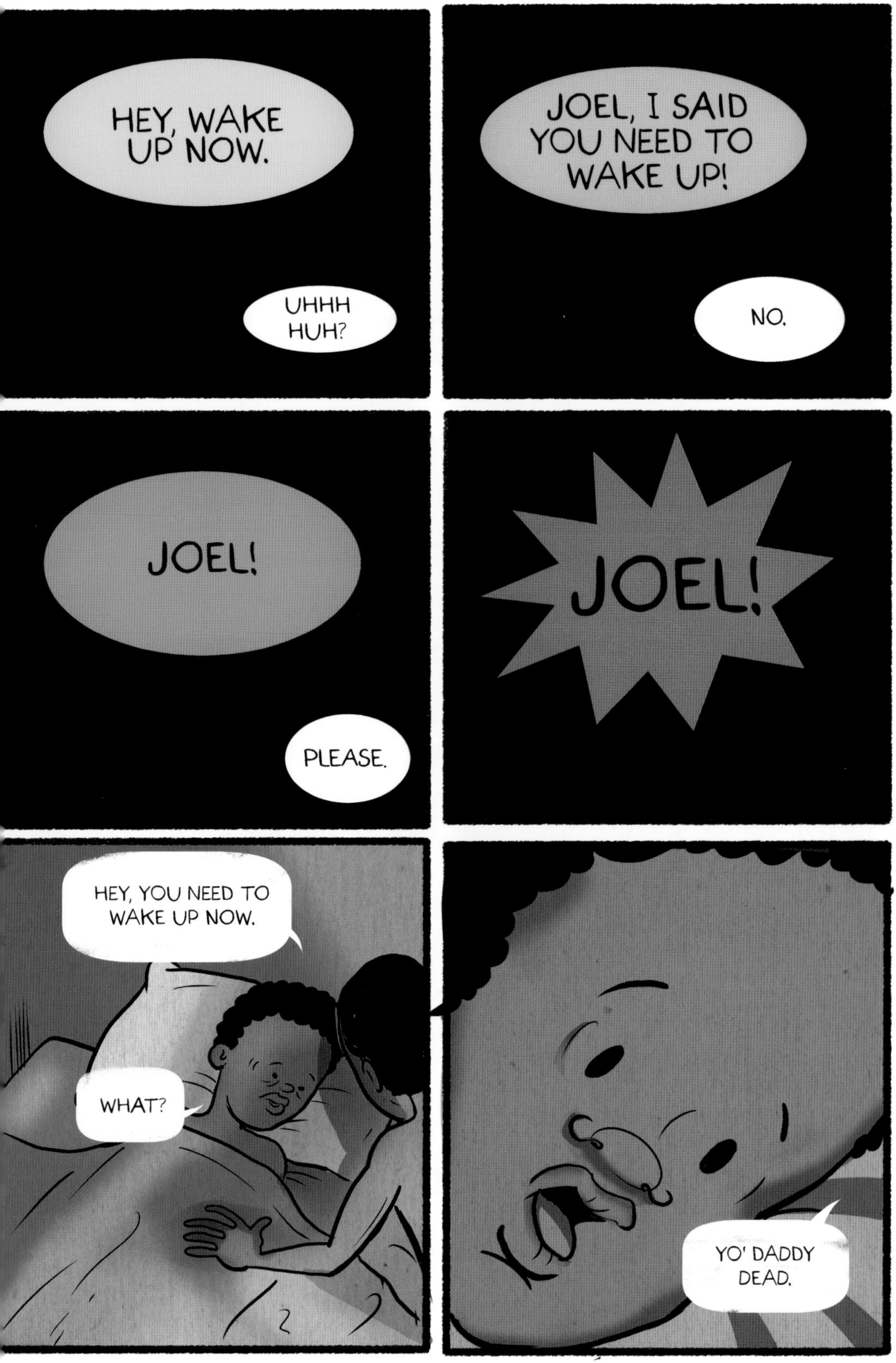
HEY, WAKE UP NOW.
UHHH HUH?
JOEL, I SAID YOU NEED TO WAKE UP!
NO.
JOEL!
PLEASE.
JOEL!
HEY, YOU NEED TO WAKE UP NOW.
WHAT?
YO' DADDY DEAD.

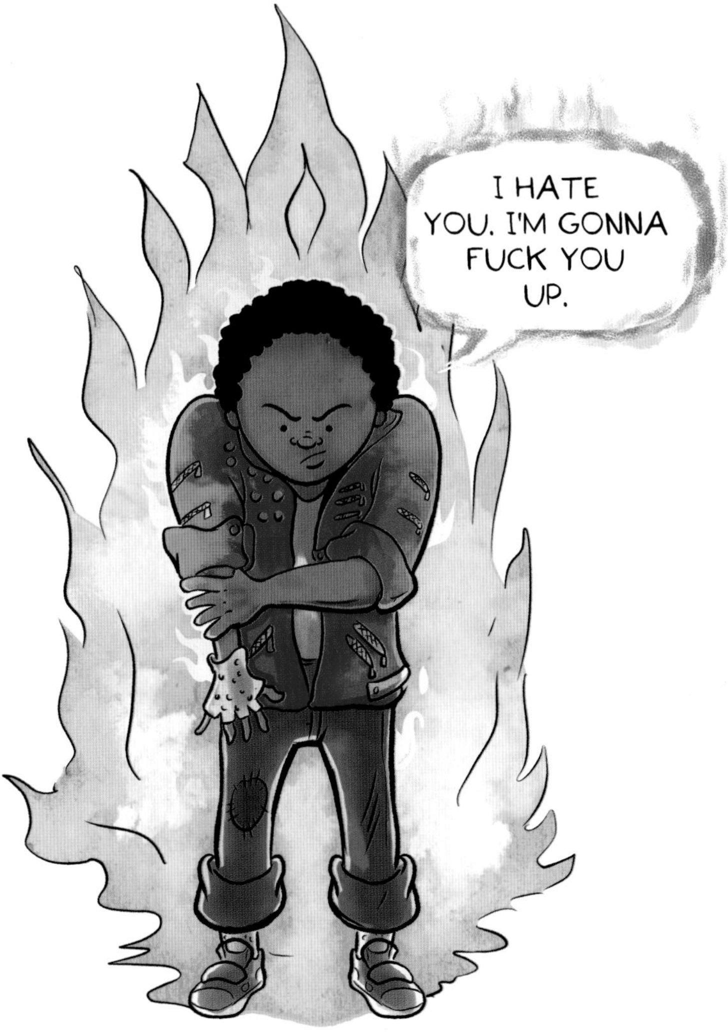
I HATE YOU. I'M GONNA FUCK YOU UP.

CHAPTER THREE

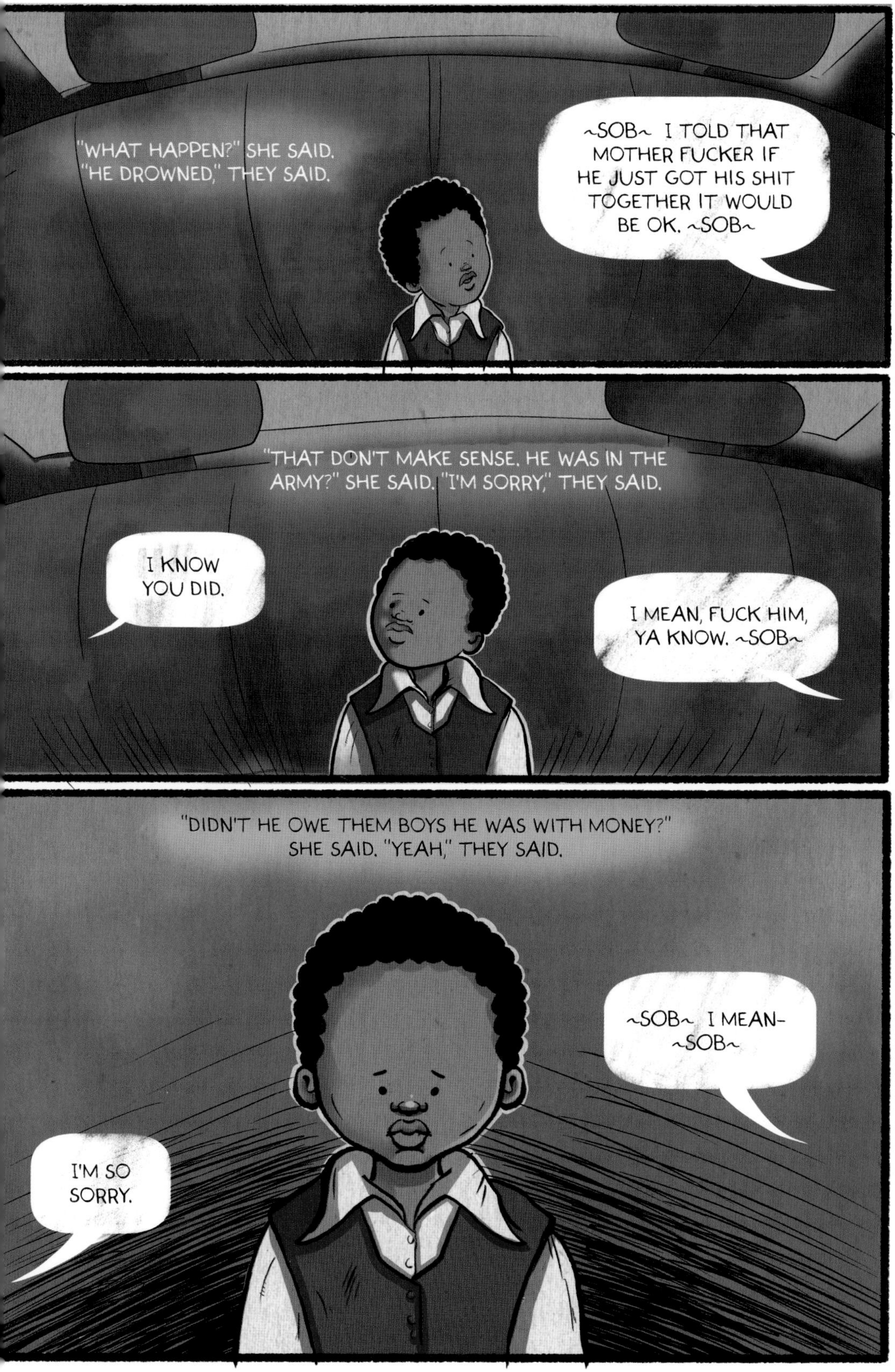
"WHAT HAPPEN?" SHE SAID. "HE DROWNED," THEY SAID.
~SOB~ I TOLD THAT MOTHER FUCKER IF HE JUST GOT HIS SHIT TOGETHER IT WOULD BE OK. ~SOB~
"THAT DON'T MAKE SENSE. HE WAS IN THE ARMY?" SHE SAID. "I'M SORRY," THEY SAID.
I KNOW YOU DID.
I MEAN, FUCK HIM, YA KNOW. ~SOB~
"DIDN'T HE OWE THEM BOYS HE WAS WITH MONEY?" SHE SAID. "YEAH," THEY SAID.
~SOB~ I MEAN- ~SOB~
I'M SO SORRY.

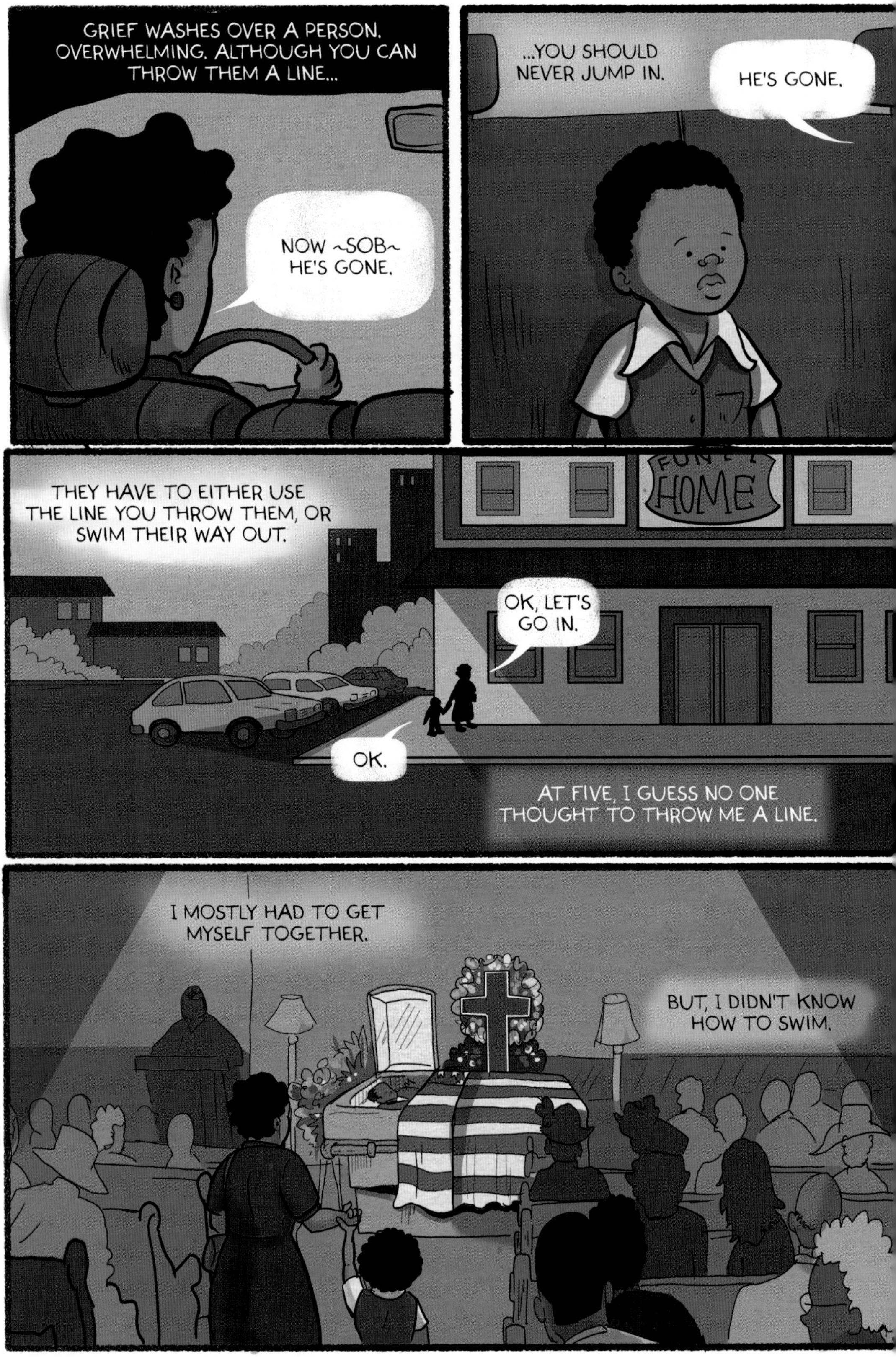
GRIEF WASHES OVER A PERSON. OVERWHELMING. ALTHOUGH YOU CAN THROW THEM A LINE...
NOW ~SOB~ HE'S GONE.
...YOU SHOULD NEVER JUMP IN.
HE'S GONE.
THEY HAVE TO EITHER USE THE LINE YOU THROW THEM, OR SWIM THEIR WAY OUT.
HOME
OK, LET'S GO IN.
OK.
AT FIVE, I GUESS NO ONE THOUGHT TO THROW ME A LINE.
I MOSTLY HAD TO GET MYSELF TOGETHER.
BUT, I DIDN'T KNOW HOW TO SWIM.

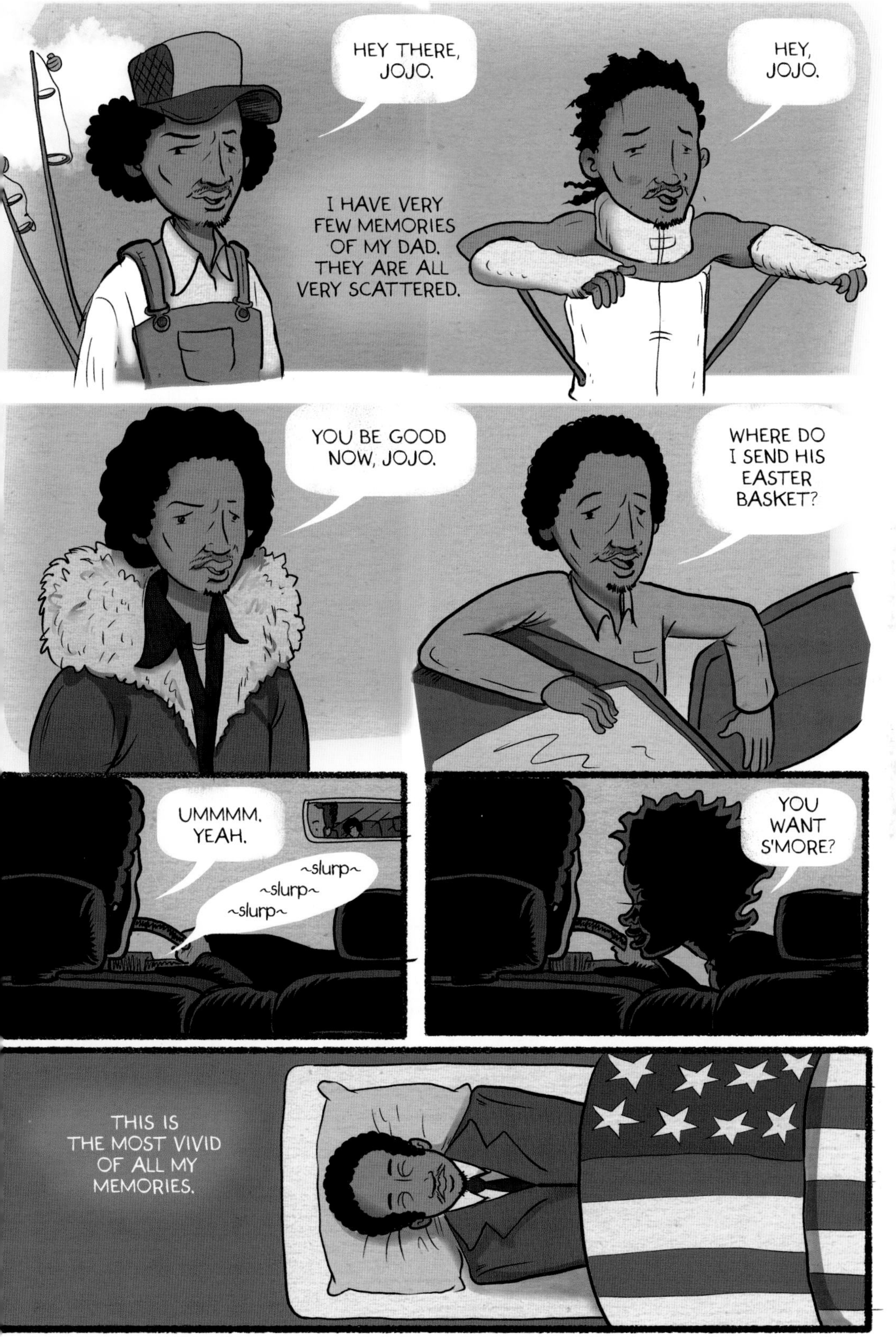
HEY THERE, JOJO.
I HAVE VERY FEW MEMORIES OF MY DAD. THEY ARE ALL VERY SCATTERED.
HEY, JOJO.
YOU BE GOOD NOW, JOJO.
WHERE DO I SEND HIS EASTER BASKET?
UMMMM. YEAH.
~slurp~
~slurp~
~slurp~
YOU WANT S'MORE?
THIS IS THE MOST VIVID OF ALL MY MEMORIES.

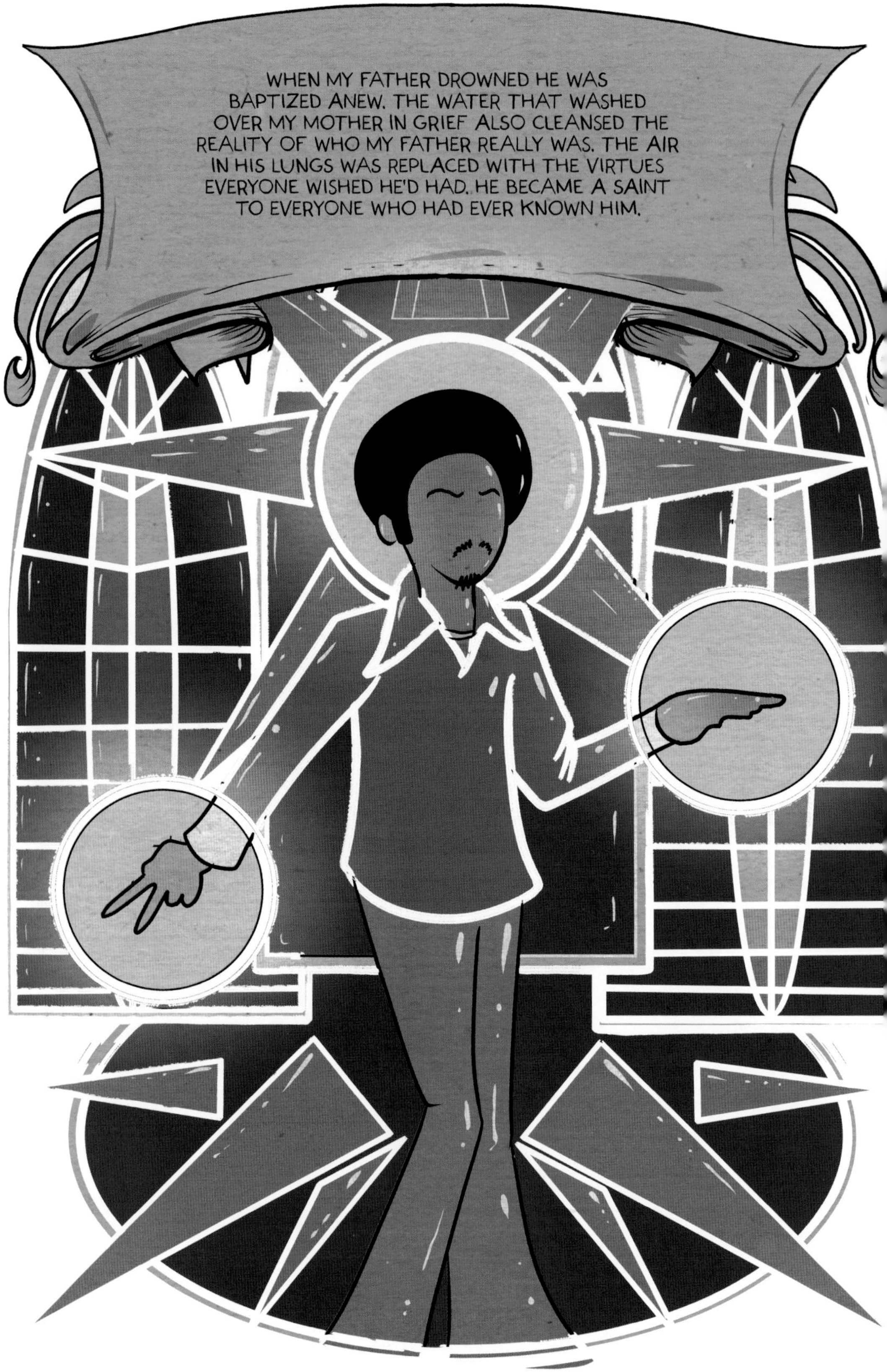
WHEN MY FATHER DROWNED HE WAS BAPTIZED ANEW. THE WATER THAT WASHED OVER MY MOTHER IN GRIEF ALSO CLEANSED THE REALITY OF WHO MY FATHER REALLY WAS. THE AIR IN HIS LUNGS WAS REPLACED WITH THE VIRTUES EVERYONE WISHED HE'D HAD. HE BECAME A SAINT TO EVERYONE WHO HAD EVER KNOWN HIM.

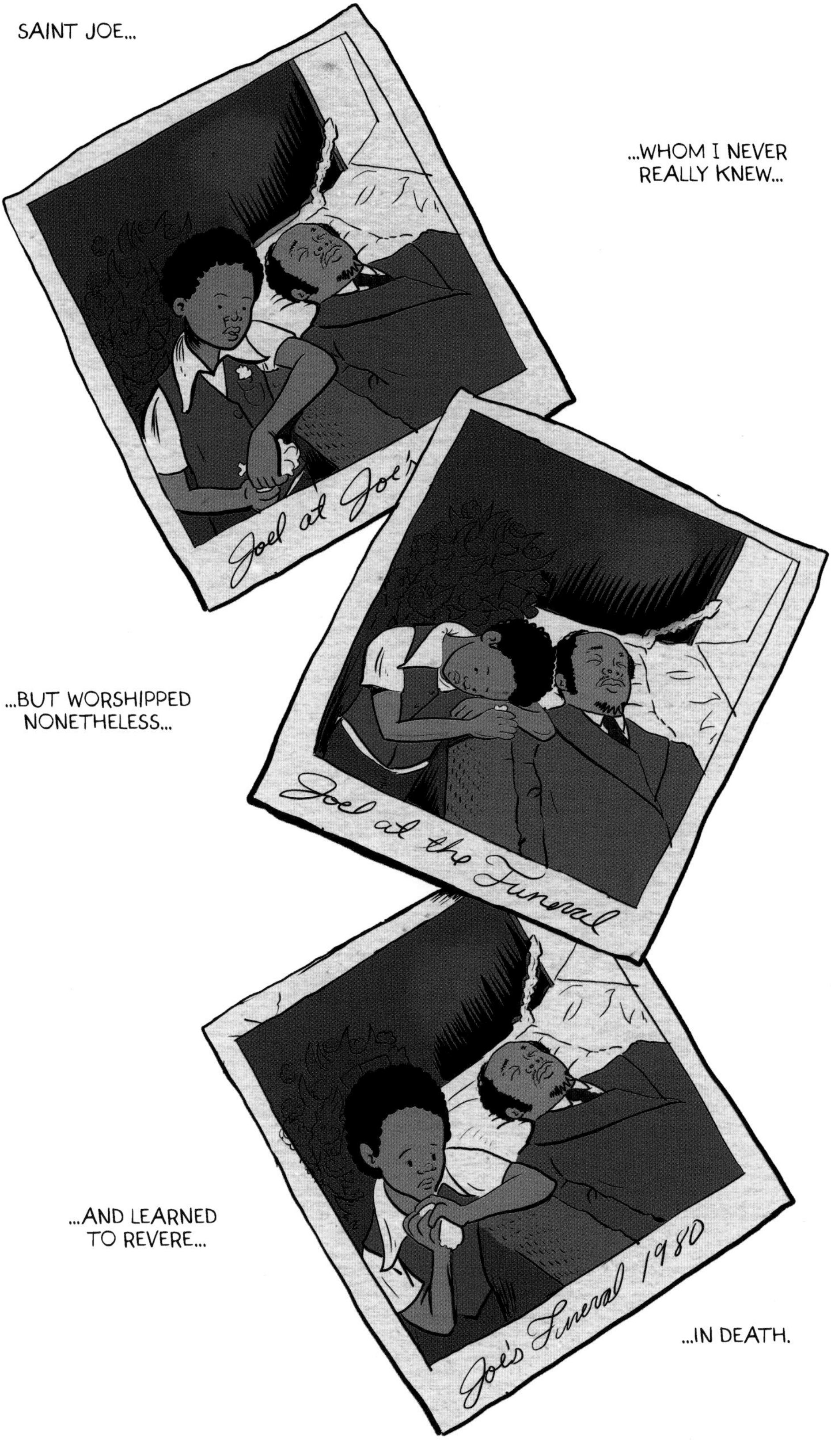
SAINT JOE...
...WHOM I NEVER REALLY KNEW...
Joel at Joe'
...BUT WORSHIPPED NONETHELESS...
Joel at the Funeral
...AND LEARNED TO REVERE...
Joe's Funeral 1980
...IN DEATH.

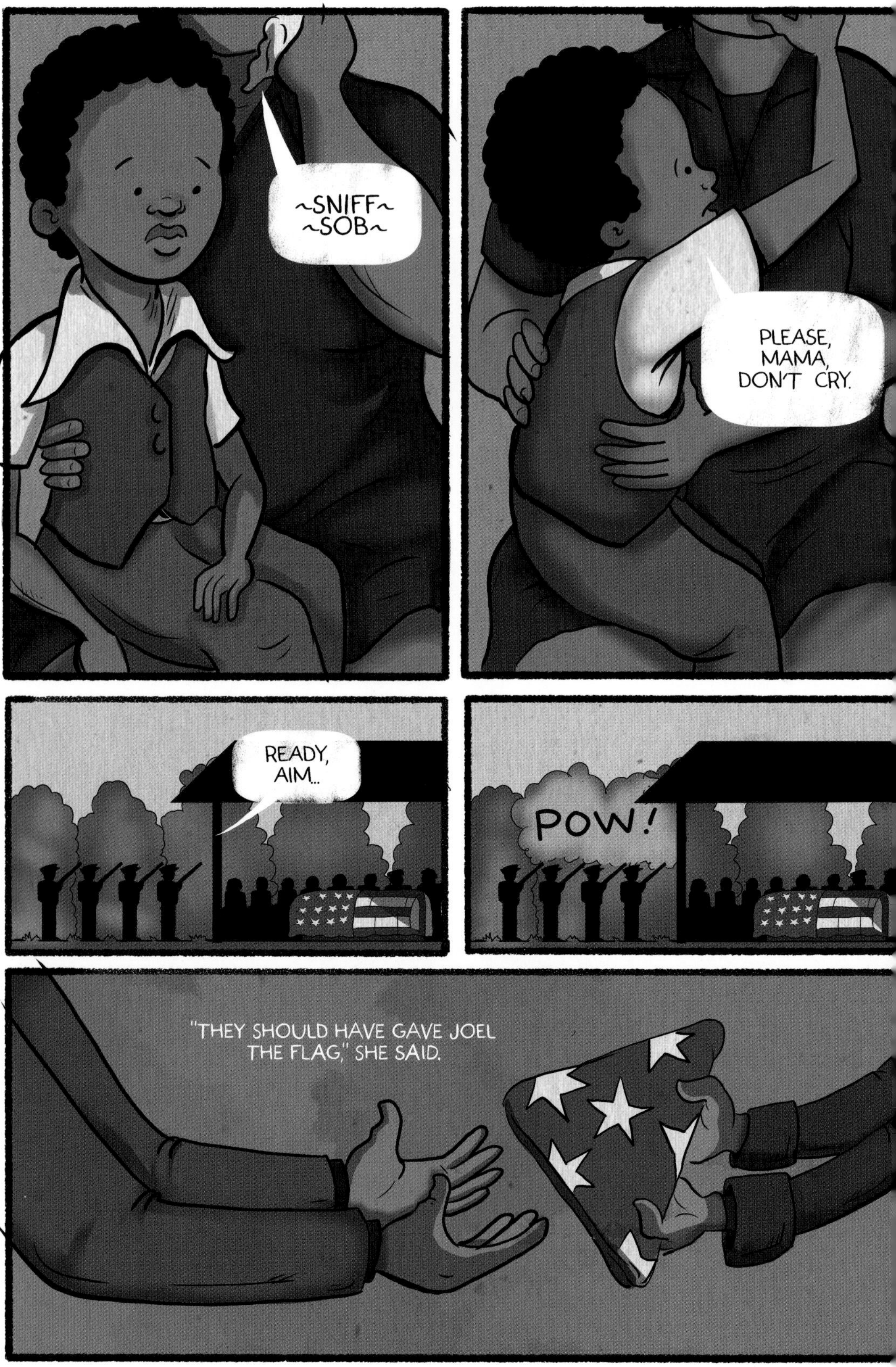
~SNIFF~
~SOB~
PLEASE, MAMA, DON'T CRY.
READY, AIM...
POW!
"THEY SHOULD HAVE GAVE JOEL THE FLAG," SHE SAID.

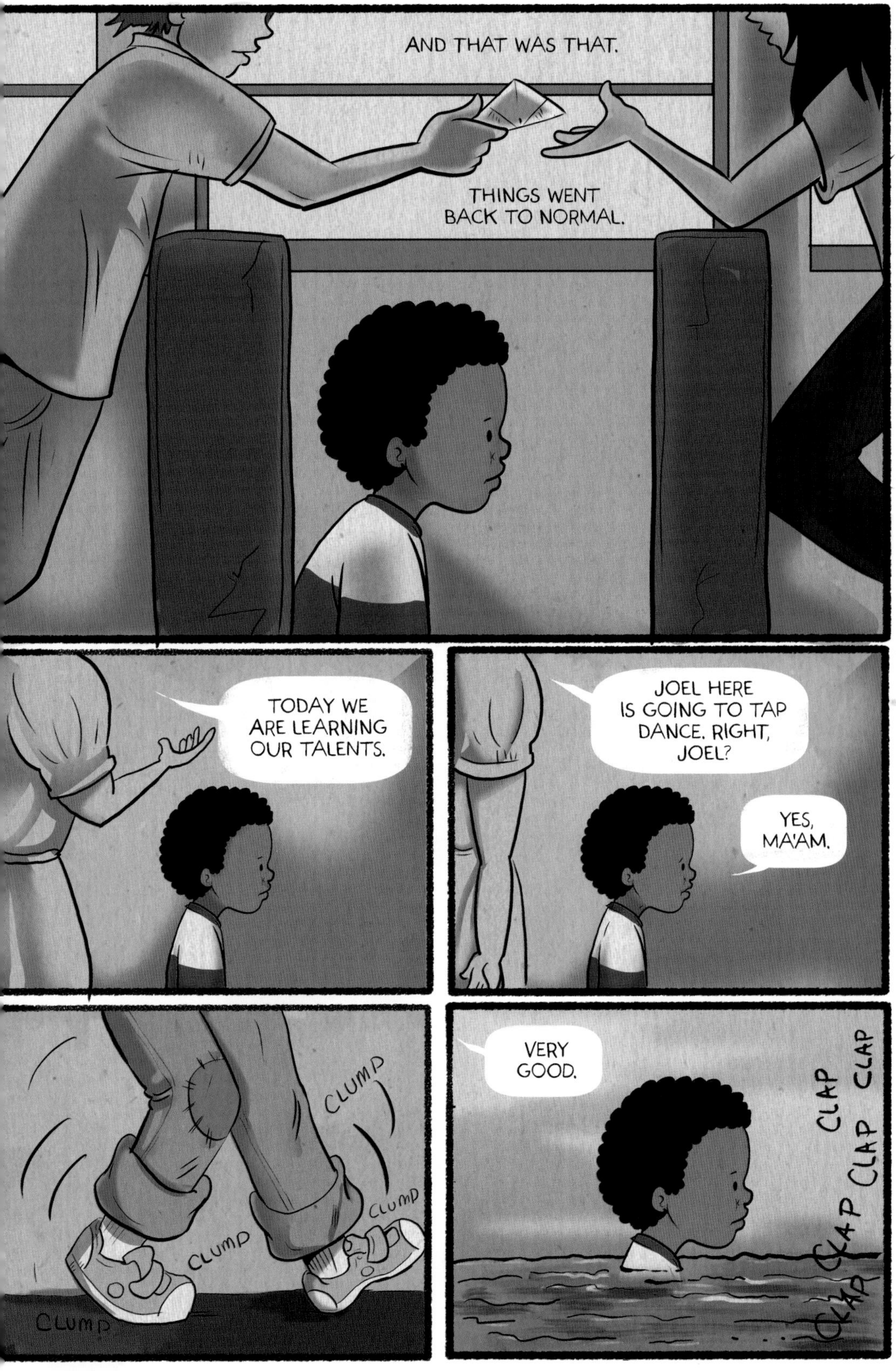
AND THAT WAS THAT.
THINGS WENT BACK TO NORMAL.
TODAY WE ARE LEARNING OUR TALENTS.
JOEL HERE IS GOING TO TAP DANCE. RIGHT, JOEL?
YES, MA'AM.
CLUMP
CLUMP
CLUMP
CLUMP
VERY GOOD.
CLAP CLAP
CLAP CLAP
CLAP CLAP

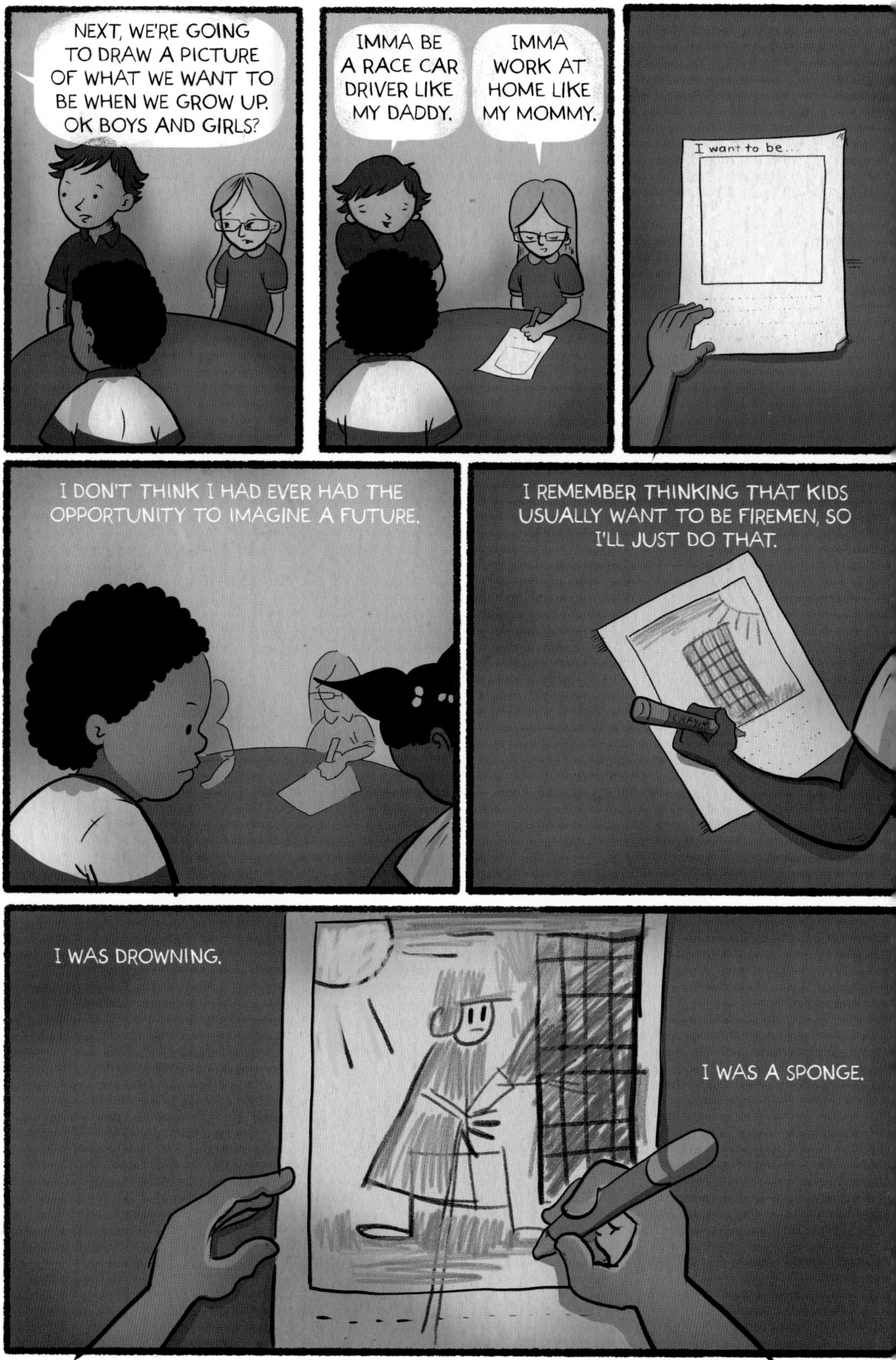
NEXT, WE'RE GOING TO DRAW A PICTURE OF WHAT WE WANT TO BE WHEN WE GROW UP. OK BOYS AND GIRLS?
IMMA BE A RACE CAR DRIVER LIKE MY DADDY.
IMMA WORK AT HOME LIKE MY MOMMY.
I want to be...
I DON'T THINK I HAD EVER HAD THE OPPORTUNITY TO IMAGINE A FUTURE.
I REMEMBER THINKING THAT KIDS USUALLY WANT TO BE FIREMEN, SO I'LL JUST DO THAT.
I WAS DROWNING.
I WAS A SPONGE.

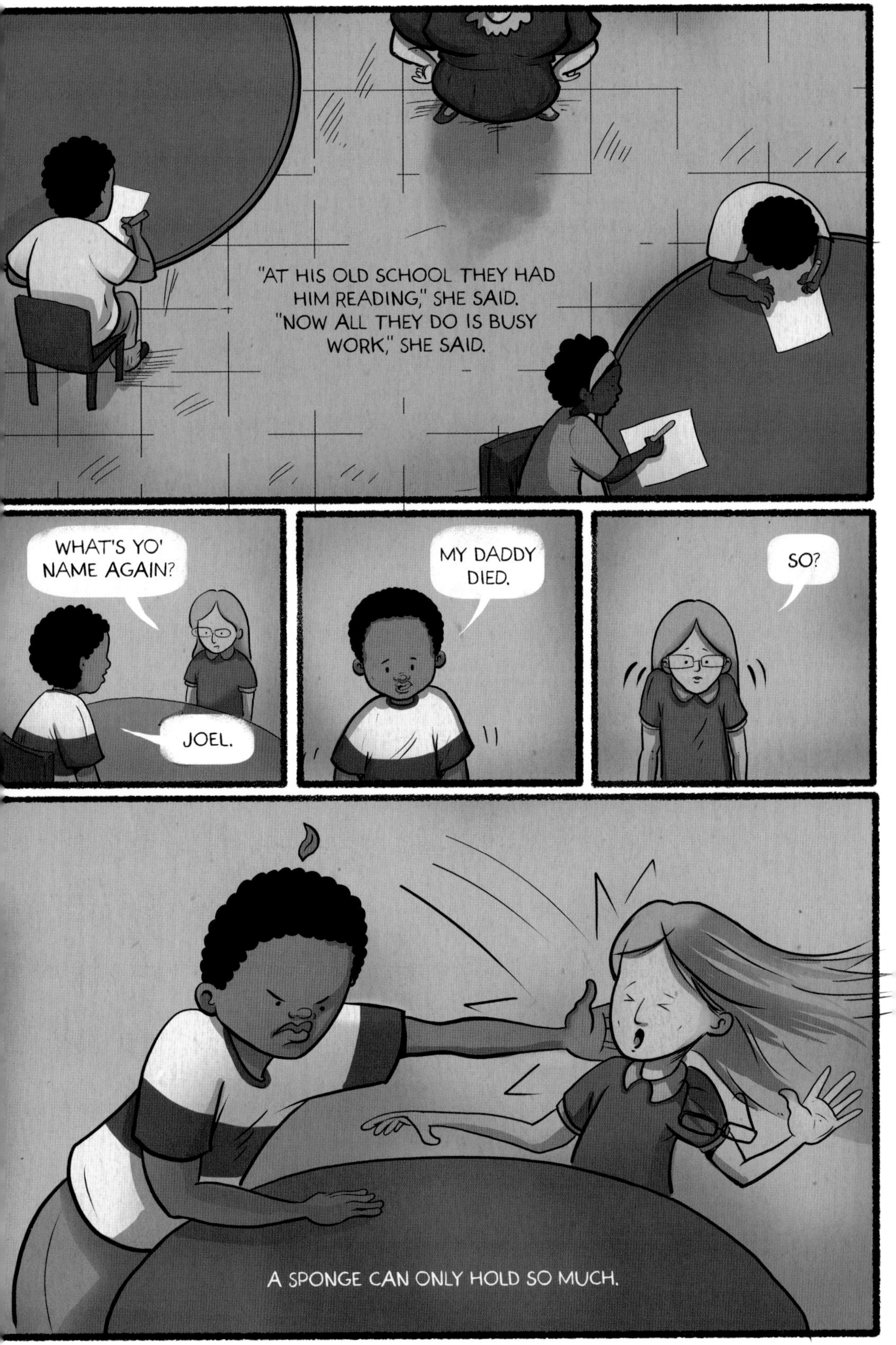
"AT HIS OLD SCHOOL THEY HAD HIM READING," SHE SAID. "NOW ALL THEY DO IS BUSY WORK," SHE SAID.
WHAT'S YO' NAME AGAIN?
JOEL.
MY DADDY DIED.
SO?
A SPONGE CAN ONLY HOLD SO MUCH.

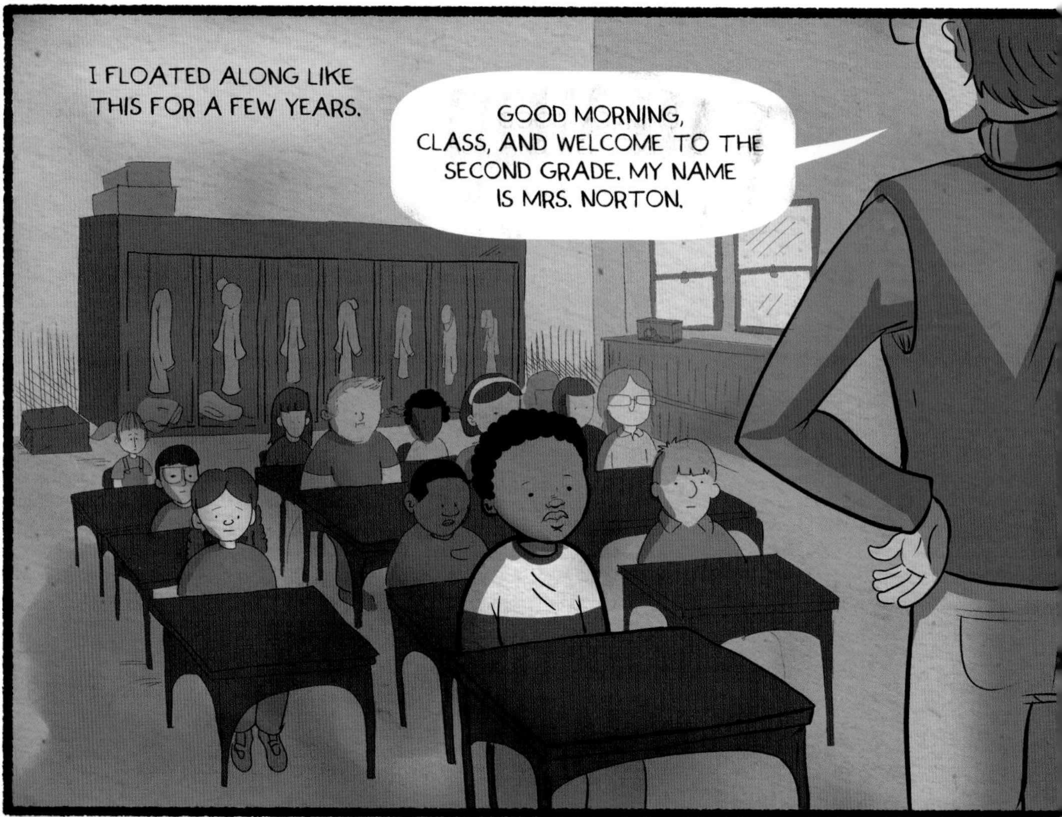
I FLOATED ALONG LIKE THIS FOR A FEW YEARS.
GOOD MORNING, CLASS, AND WELCOME TO THE SECOND GRADE. MY NAME IS MRS. NORTON.
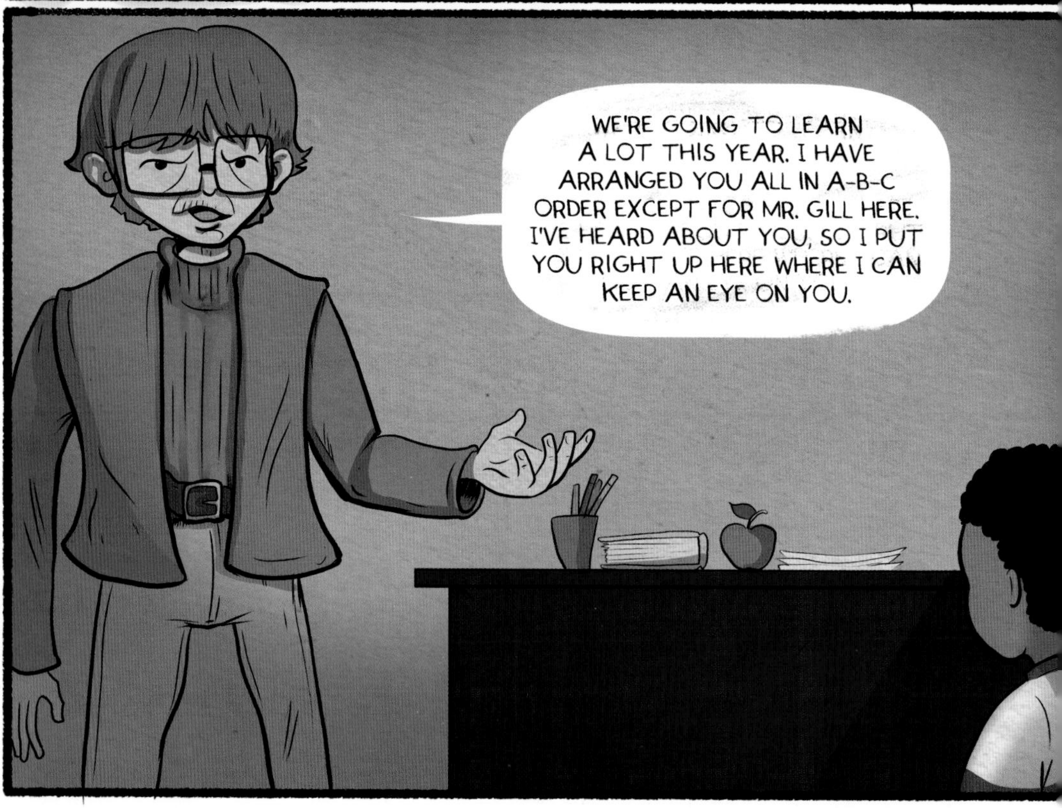
WE'RE GOING TO LEARN A LOT THIS YEAR. I HAVE ARRANGED YOU ALL IN A-B-C ORDER EXCEPT FOR MR. GILL HERE. I'VE HEARD ABOUT YOU, SO I PUT YOU RIGHT UP HERE WHERE I CAN KEEP AN EYE ON YOU.

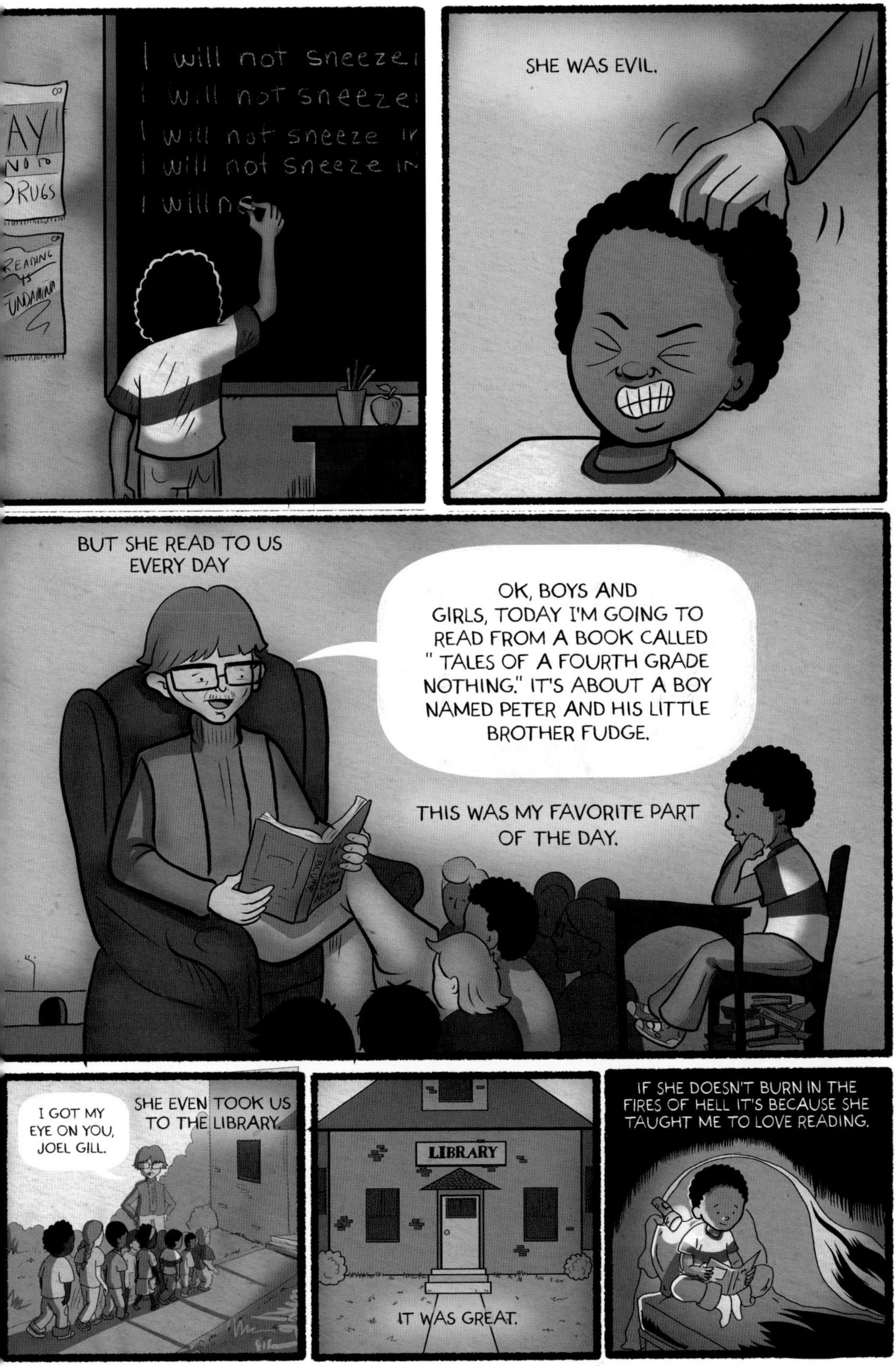
I will not sneeze
I will not sneeze
I will not sneeze ir
I will not sneeze in
I will ns
AY
NO TO
DRUGS
READING
IS
FUNDAMENTAL
SHE WAS EVIL.
BUT SHE READ TO US EVERY DAY
OK, BOYS AND GIRLS, TODAY I'M GOING TO READ FROM A BOOK CALLED " TALES OF A FOURTH GRADE NOTHING." IT'S ABOUT A BOY NAMED PETER AND HIS LITTLE BROTHER FUDGE.
THIS WAS MY FAVORITE PART OF THE DAY.
I GOT MY EYE ON YOU, JOEL GILL.
SHE EVEN TOOK US TO THE LIBRARY.
LIBRARY
IT WAS GREAT.
IF SHE DOESN'T BURN IN THE FIRES OF HELL IT'S BECAUSE SHE TAUGHT ME TO LOVE READING.

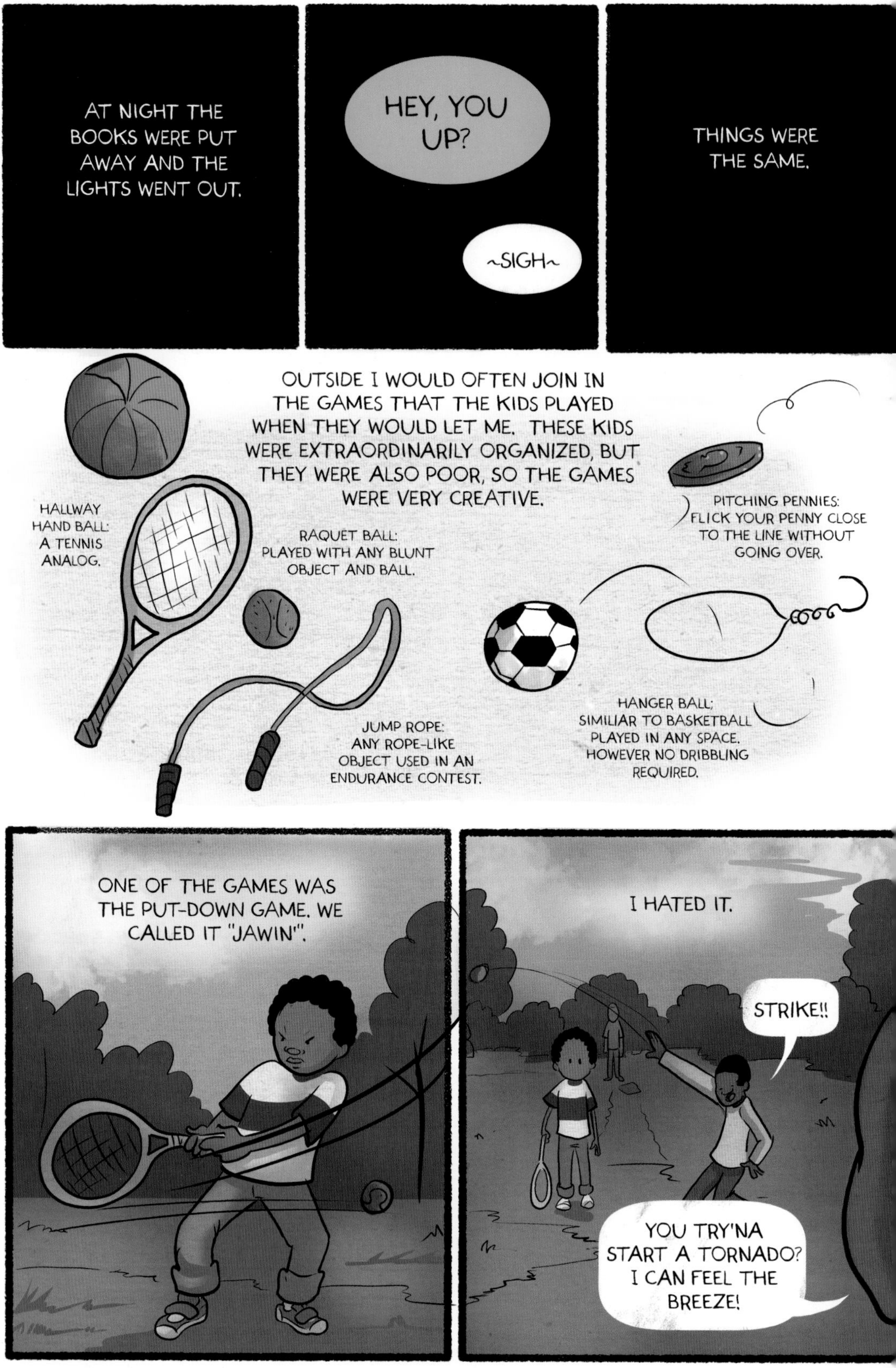
AT NIGHT THE BOOKS WERE PUT AWAY AND THE LIGHTS WENT OUT.
HEY, YOU UP?
~SIGH~
THINGS WERE THE SAME.
OUTSIDE I WOULD OFTEN JOIN IN THE GAMES THAT THE KIDS PLAYED WHEN THEY WOULD LET ME. THESE KIDS WERE EXTRAORDINARILY ORGANIZED, BUT THEY WERE ALSO POOR, SO THE GAMES WERE VERY CREATIVE.
HALLWAY HAND BALL: A TENNIS ANALOG.
RAQUET BALL: PLAYED WITH ANY BLUNT OBJECT AND BALL.
PITCHING PENNIES: FLICK YOUR PENNY CLOSE TO THE LINE WITHOUT GOING OVER.
JUMP ROPE: ANY ROPE-LIKE OBJECT USED IN AN ENDURANCE CONTEST.
HANGER BALL; SIMILIAR TO BASKETBALL PLAYED IN ANY SPACE. HOWEVER NO DRIBBLING REQUIRED.
ONE OF THE GAMES WAS THE PUT-DOWN GAME. WE CALLED IT "JAWIN".
I HATED IT.
STRIKE!!
YOU TRY'NA START A TORNADO? I CAN FEEL THE BREEZE!

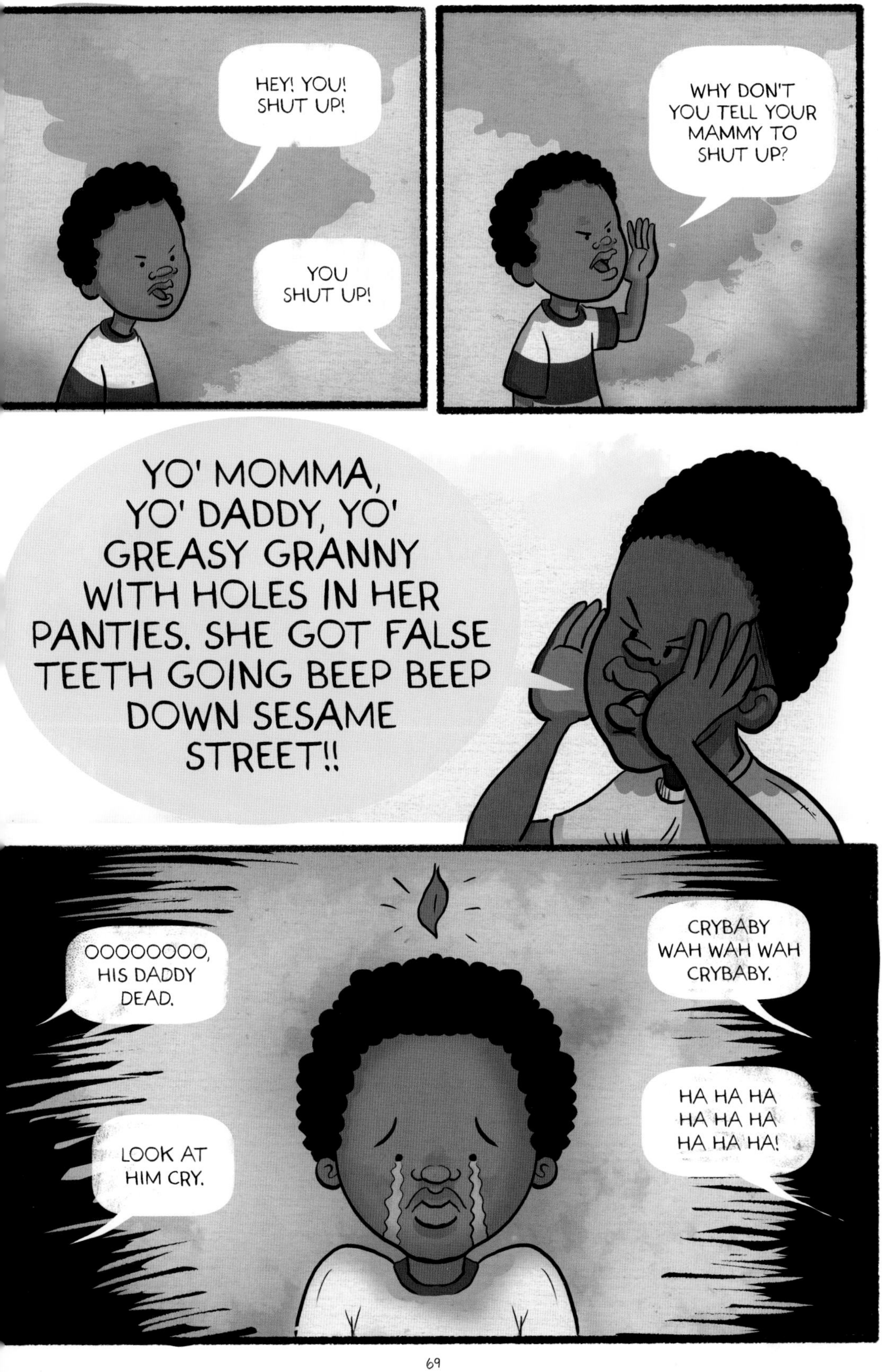
HEY! YOU! SHUT UP!
YOU SHUT UP!
WHY DON'T YOU TELL YOUR MAMMY TO SHUT UP?
YO' MOMMA, YO' DADDY, YO' GREASY GRANNY WITH HOLES IN HER PANTIES. SHE GOT FALSE TEETH GOING BEEP BEEP DOWN SESAME STREET!!
OOOOOOOO, HIS DADDY DEAD.
CRYBABY WAH WAH WAH CRYBABY.
LOOK AT HIM CRY.
HA HA HA HA HA HA HA HA HA!

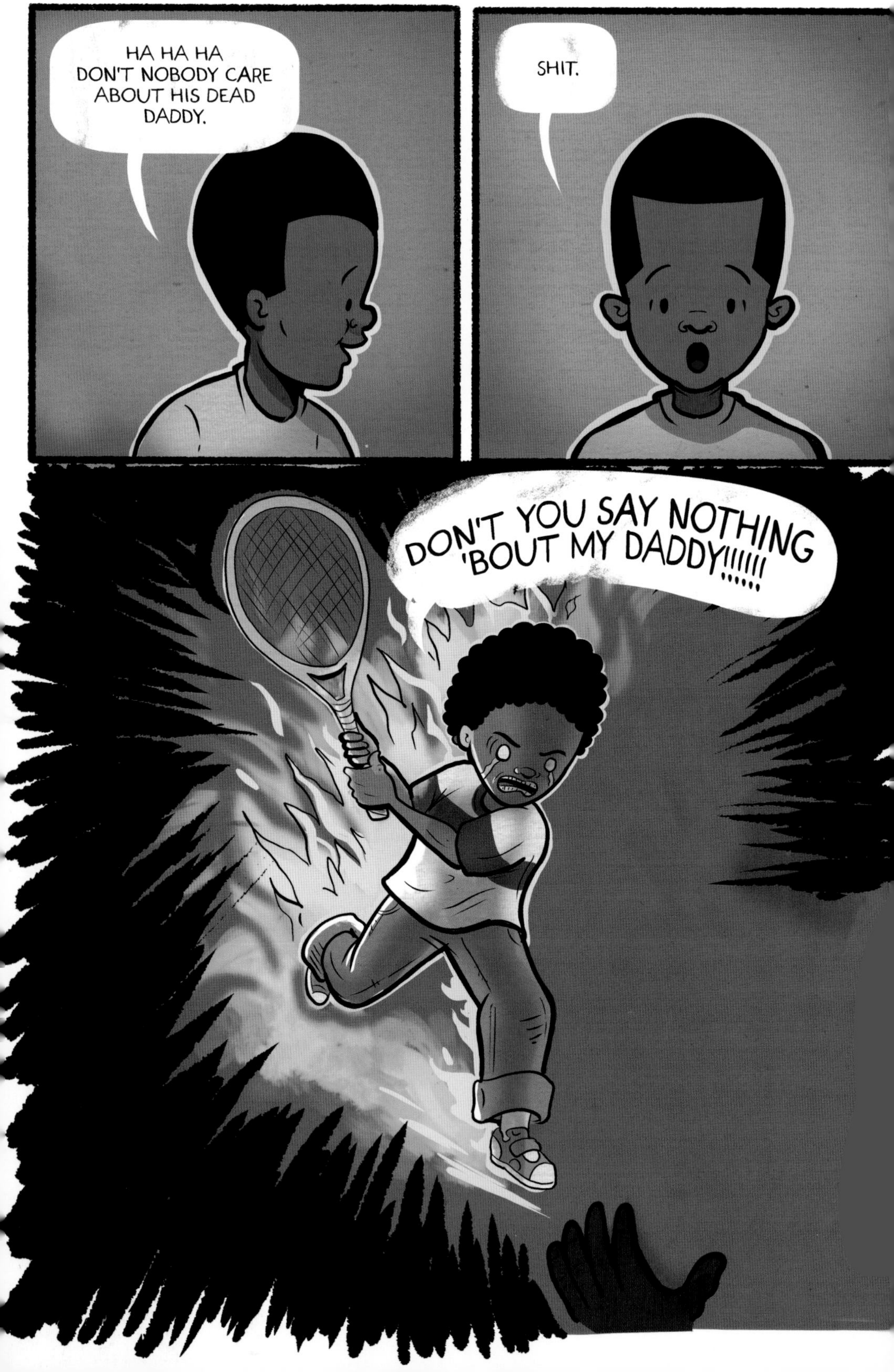
HA HA HA DON'T NOBODY CARE ABOUT HIS DEAD DADDY.
SHIT.
DON'T YOU SAY NOTHING 'BOUT MY DADDY!!!!!!

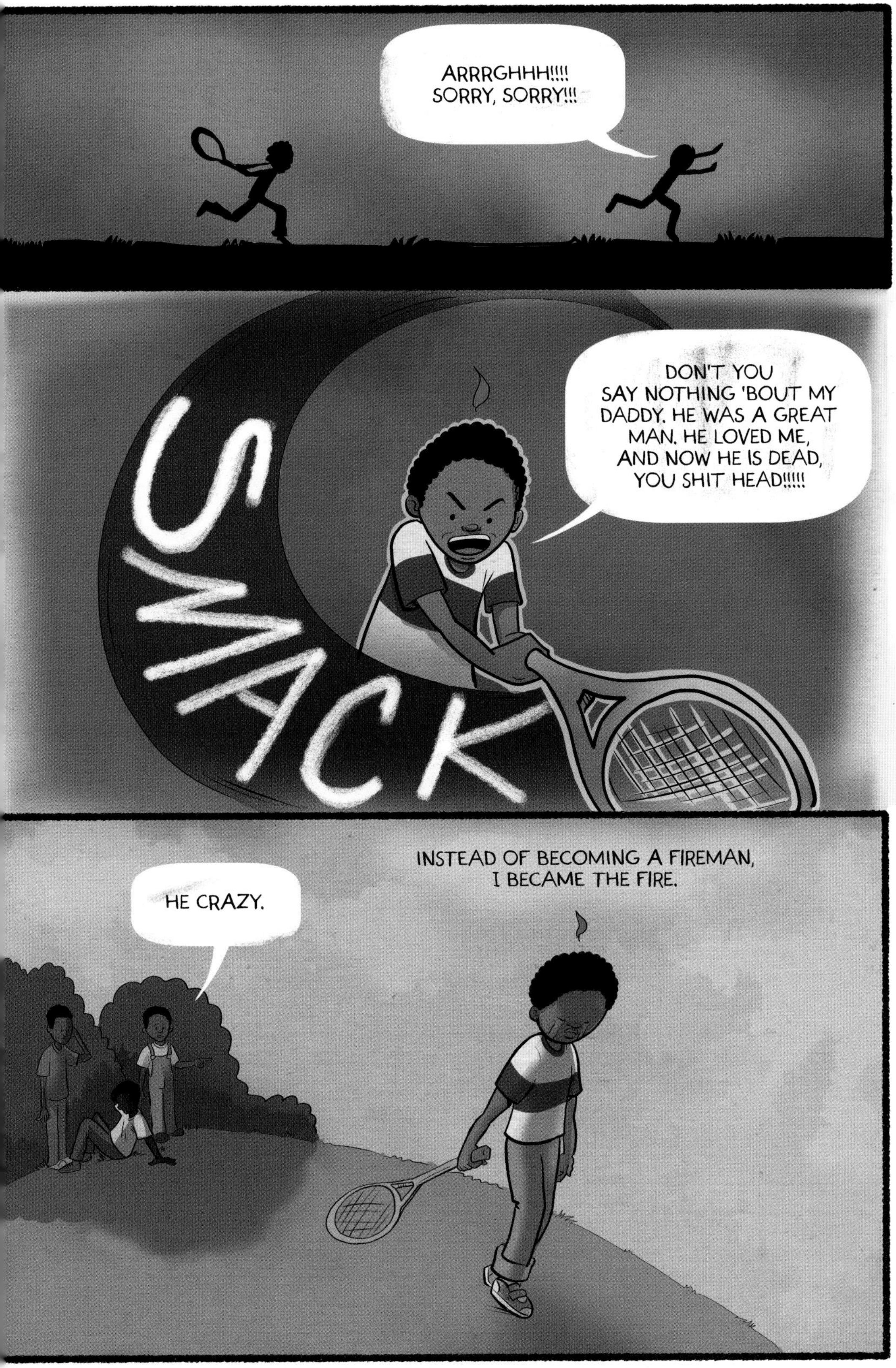
ARRRGHHH!!!!
SORRY, SORRY!!!
SMACK
DON'T YOU SAY NOTHING 'BOUT MY DADDY. HE WAS A GREAT MAN. HE LOVED ME, AND NOW HE IS DEAD, YOU SHIT HEAD!!!!!
HE CRAZY.
INSTEAD OF BECOMING A FIREMAN, I BECAME THE FIRE.

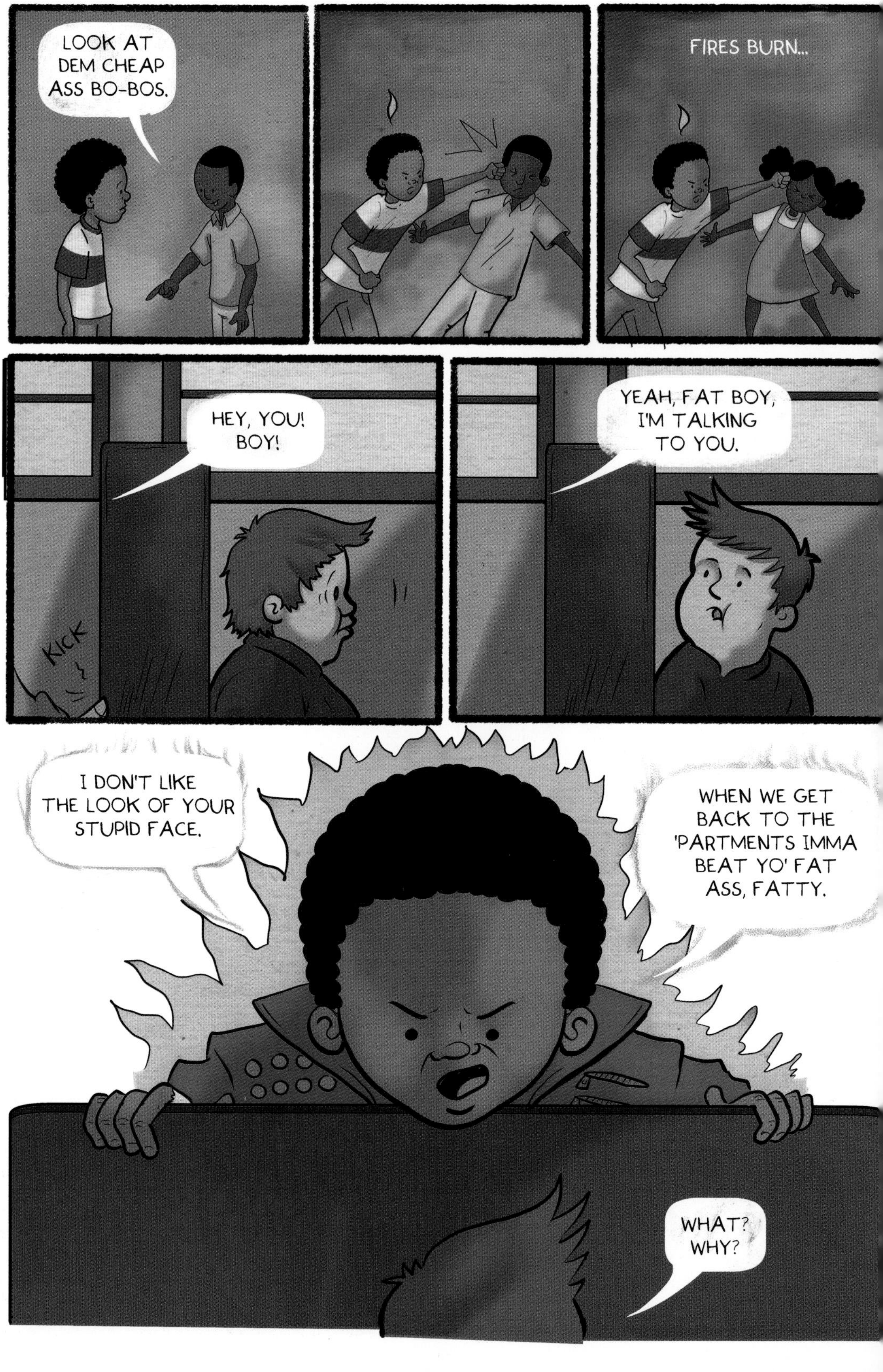
LOOK AT DEM CHEAP ASS BO-BOS.
FIRES BURN...
HEY, YOU! BOY!
KICK
YEAH, FAT BOY, I'M TALKING TO YOU.
I DON'T LIKE THE LOOK OF YOUR STUPID FACE.
WHEN WE GET BACK TO THE 'PARTMENTS IMMA BEAT YO' FAT ASS, FATTY.
WHAT? WHY?

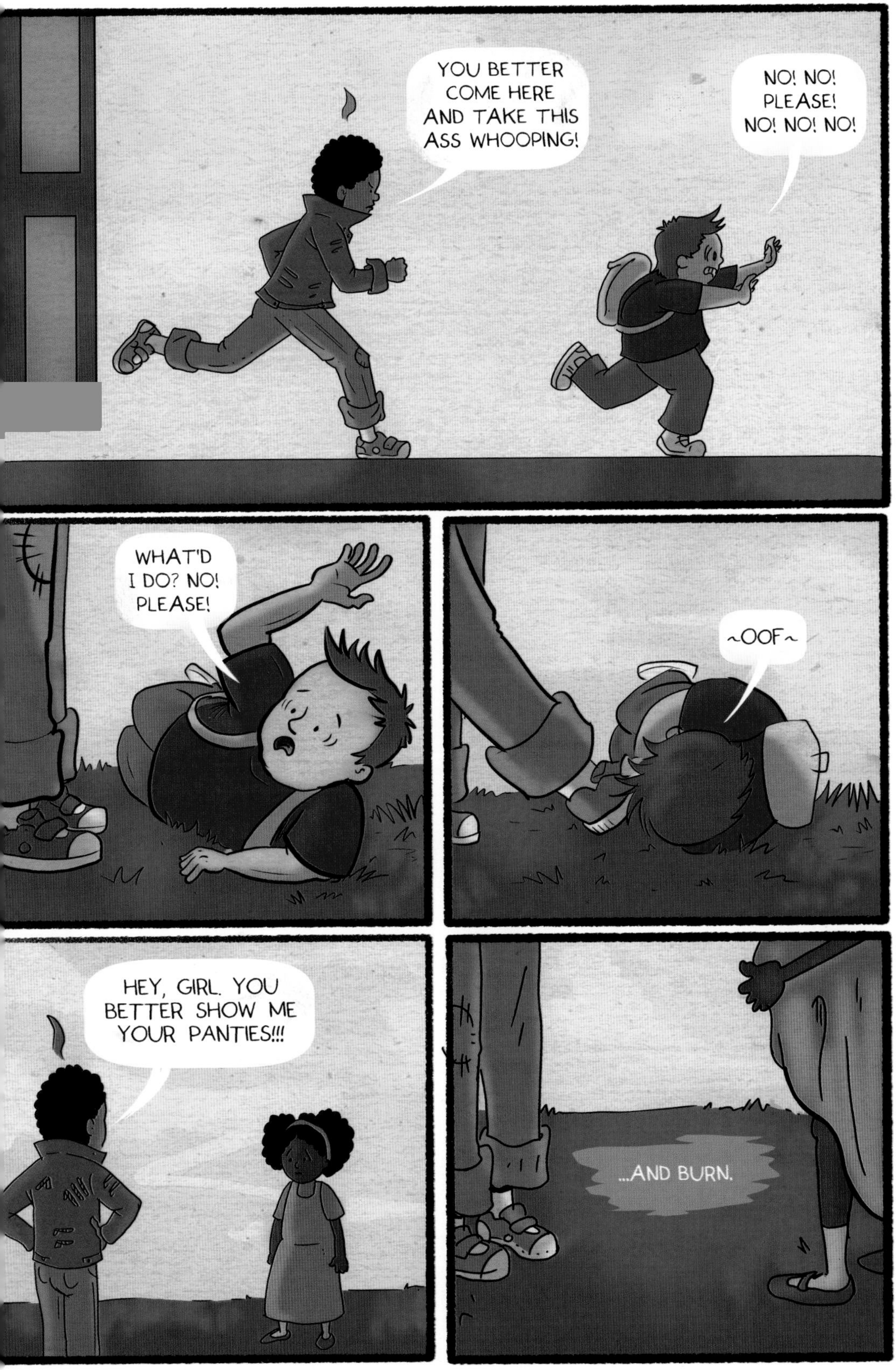
YOU BETTER COME HERE AND TAKE THIS ASS WHOOPING!
NO! NO! PLEASE! NO! NO! NO!
WHAT'D I DO? NO! PLEASE!
~OOF~
HEY, GIRL. YOU BETTER SHOW ME YOUR PANTIES!!!
...AND BURN.

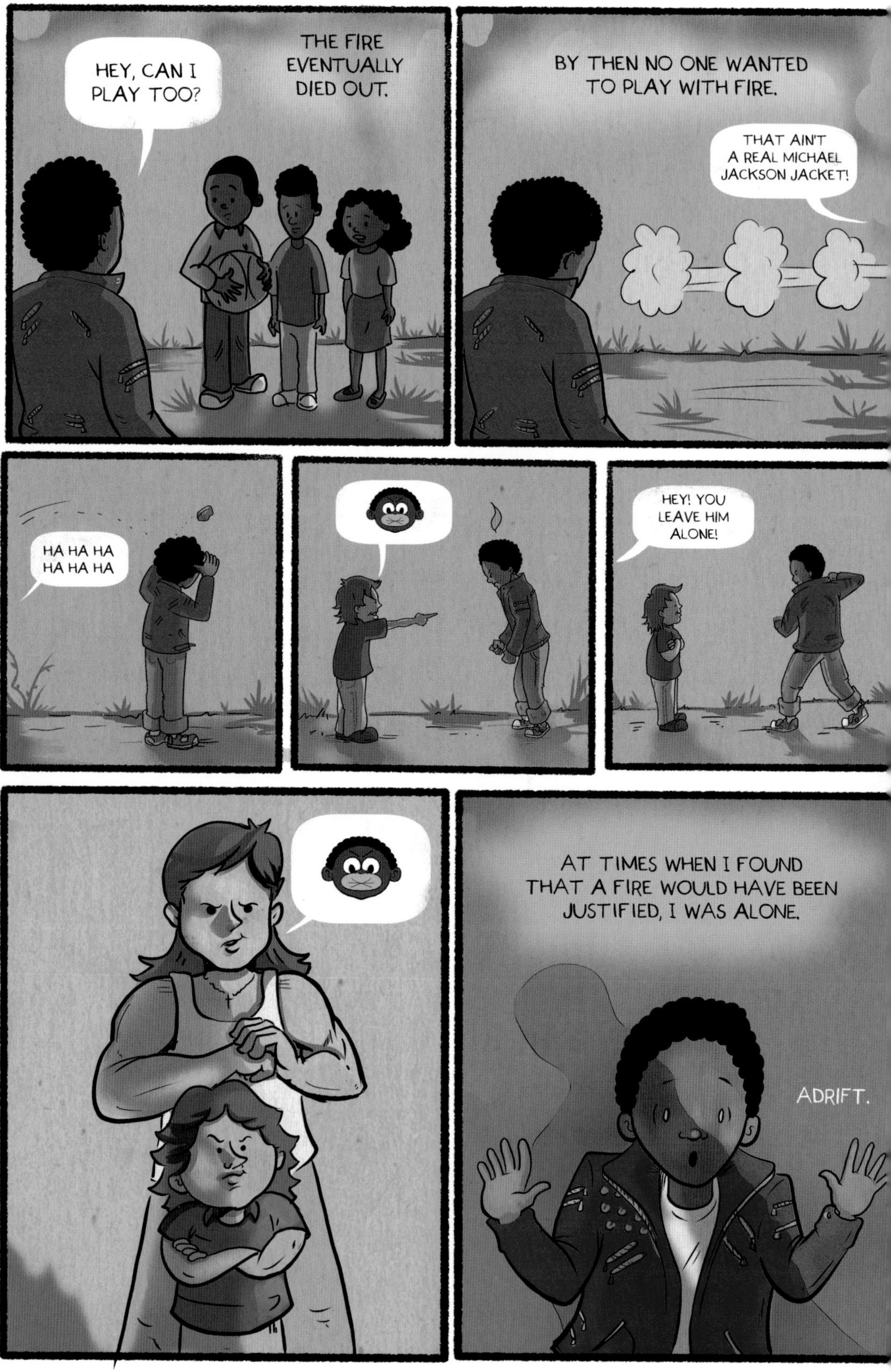
THE FIRE EVENTUALLY DIED OUT.
HEY, CAN I PLAY TOO?
BY THEN NO ONE WANTED TO PLAY WITH FIRE.
THAT AIN'T A REAL MICHAEL JACKSON JACKET!
HA HA HA HA HA HA
HEY! YOU LEAVE HIM ALONE!
AT TIMES WHEN I FOUND THAT A FIRE WOULD HAVE BEEN JUSTIFIED, I WAS ALONE.
ADRIFT.

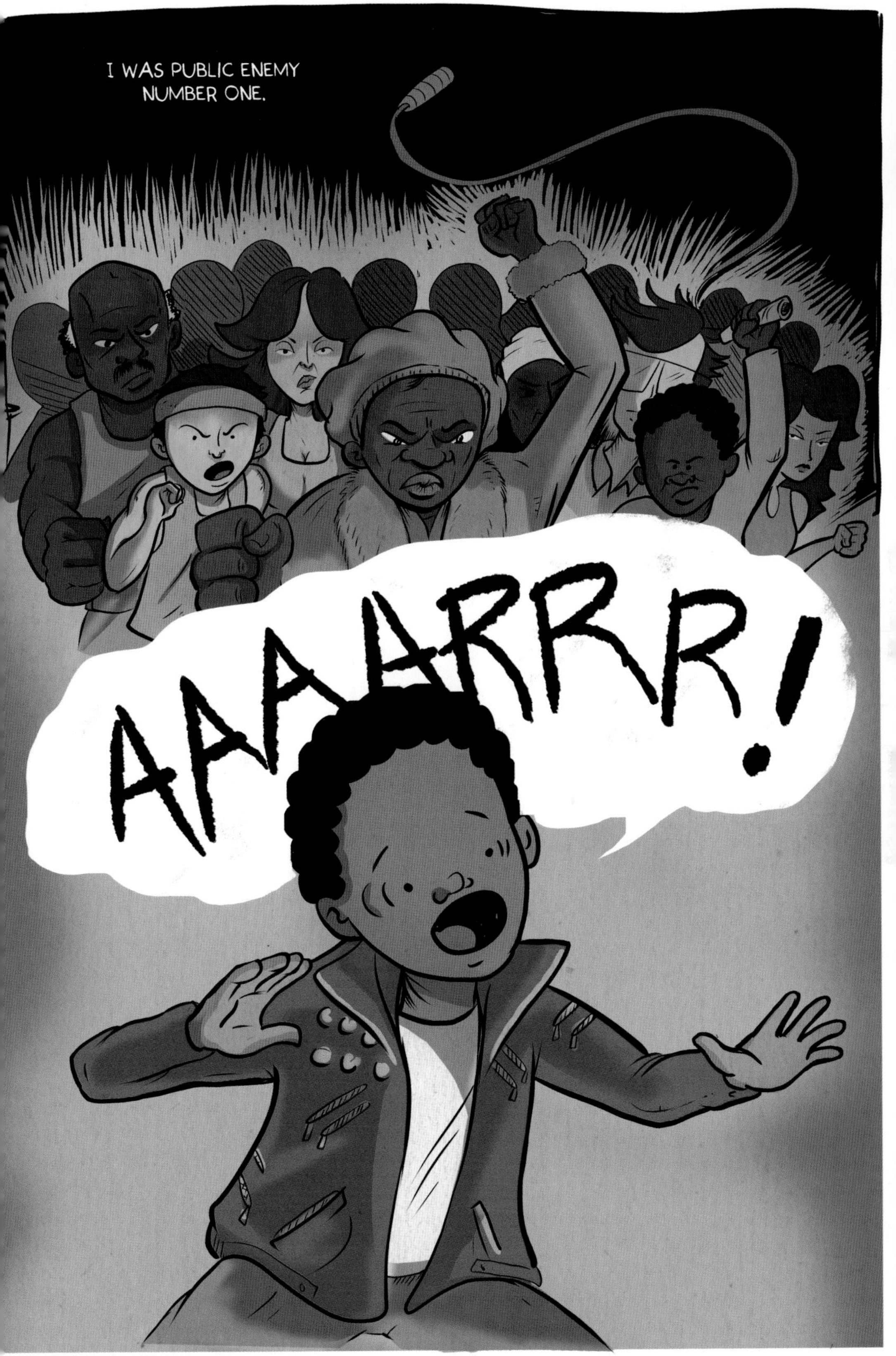
I WAS PUBLIC ENEMY NUMBER ONE.
AAAARRRR!

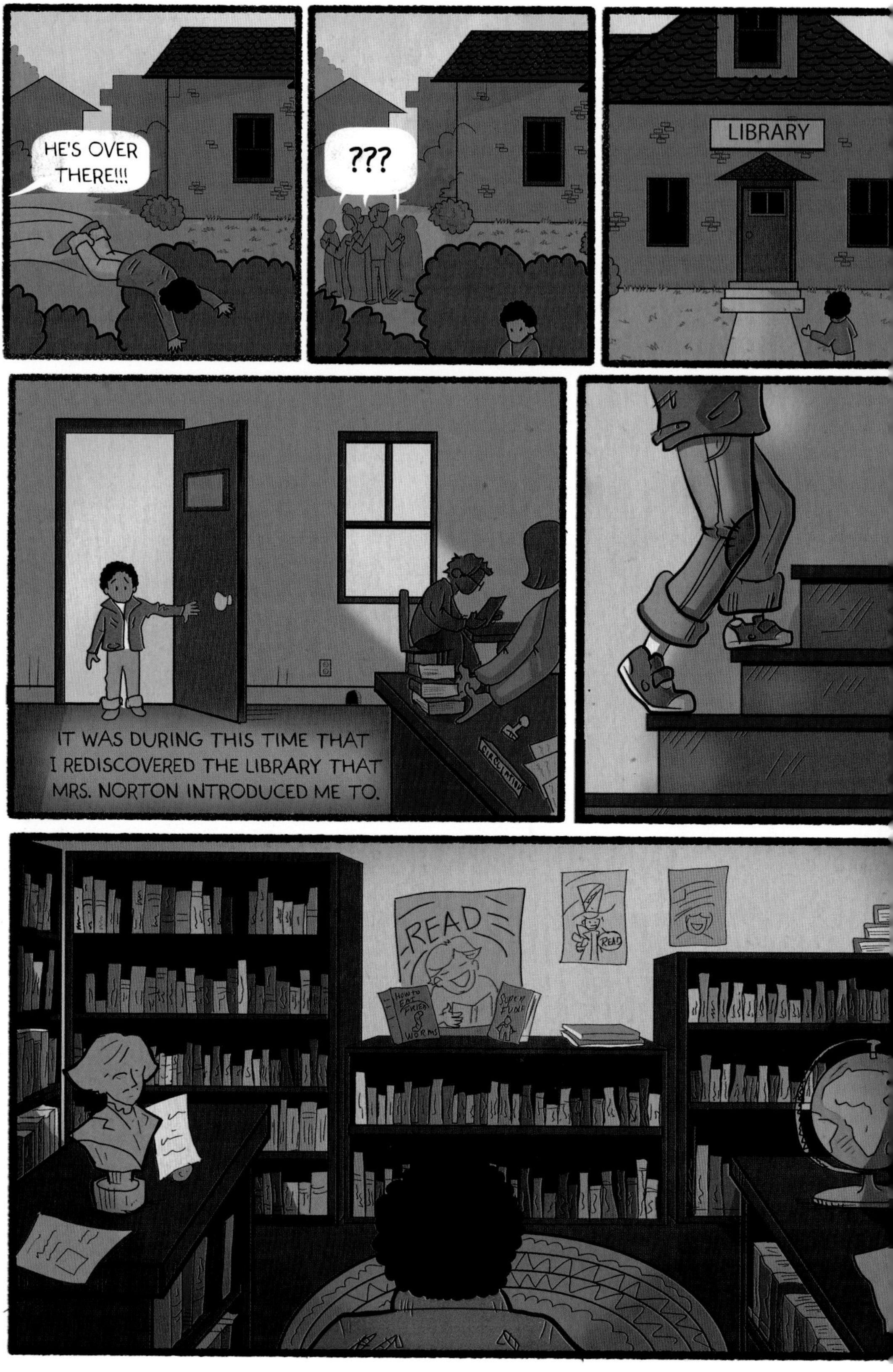
HE'S OVER THERE!!!
???
LIBRARY
IT WAS DURING THIS TIME THAT I REDISCOVERED THE LIBRARY THAT MRS. NORTON INTRODUCED ME TO.
CIRCULATION
READ
HOW TO EAT FRIED WORMS
SUPER FUNK
READ

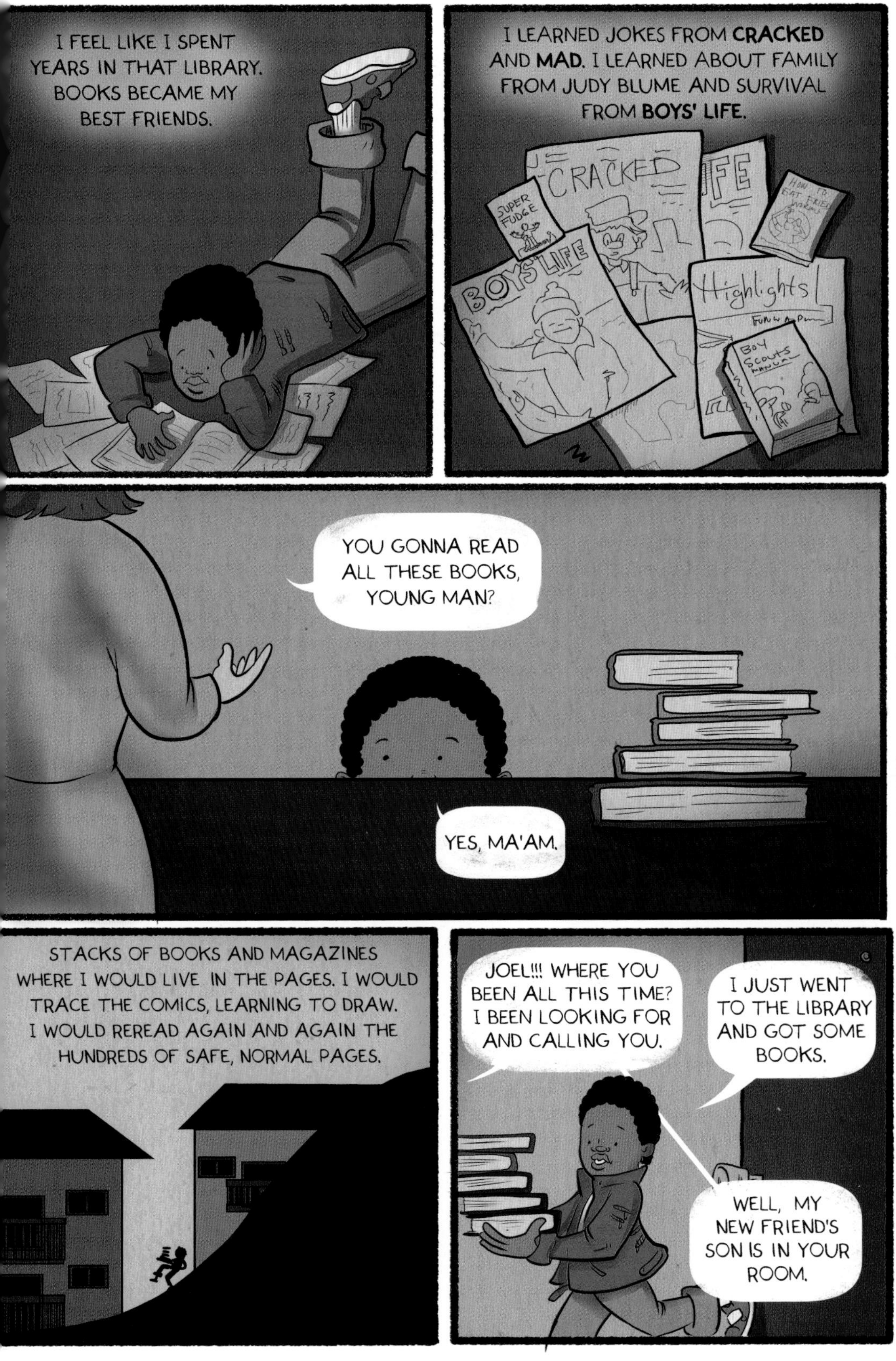
I FEEL LIKE I SPENT YEARS IN THAT LIBRARY. BOOKS BECAME MY BEST FRIENDS.
I LEARNED JOKES FROM **CRACKED** AND **MAD**. I LEARNED ABOUT FAMILY FROM JUDY BLUME AND SURVIVAL FROM **BOYS' LIFE**.
CRACKED
SUPER FUDGE
BOYS' LIFE
Highlights
BOY SCOUTS MANUAL
YOU GONNA READ ALL THESE BOOKS, YOUNG MAN?
YES, MA'AM.
STACKS OF BOOKS AND MAGAZINES WHERE I WOULD LIVE IN THE PAGES. I WOULD TRACE THE COMICS, LEARNING TO DRAW. I WOULD REREAD AGAIN AND AGAIN THE HUNDREDS OF SAFE, NORMAL PAGES.
JOEL!!! WHERE YOU BEEN ALL THIS TIME? I BEEN LOOKING FOR AND CALLING YOU.
I JUST WENT TO THE LIBRARY AND GOT SOME BOOKS.
WELL, MY NEW FRIEND'S SON IS IN YOUR ROOM.

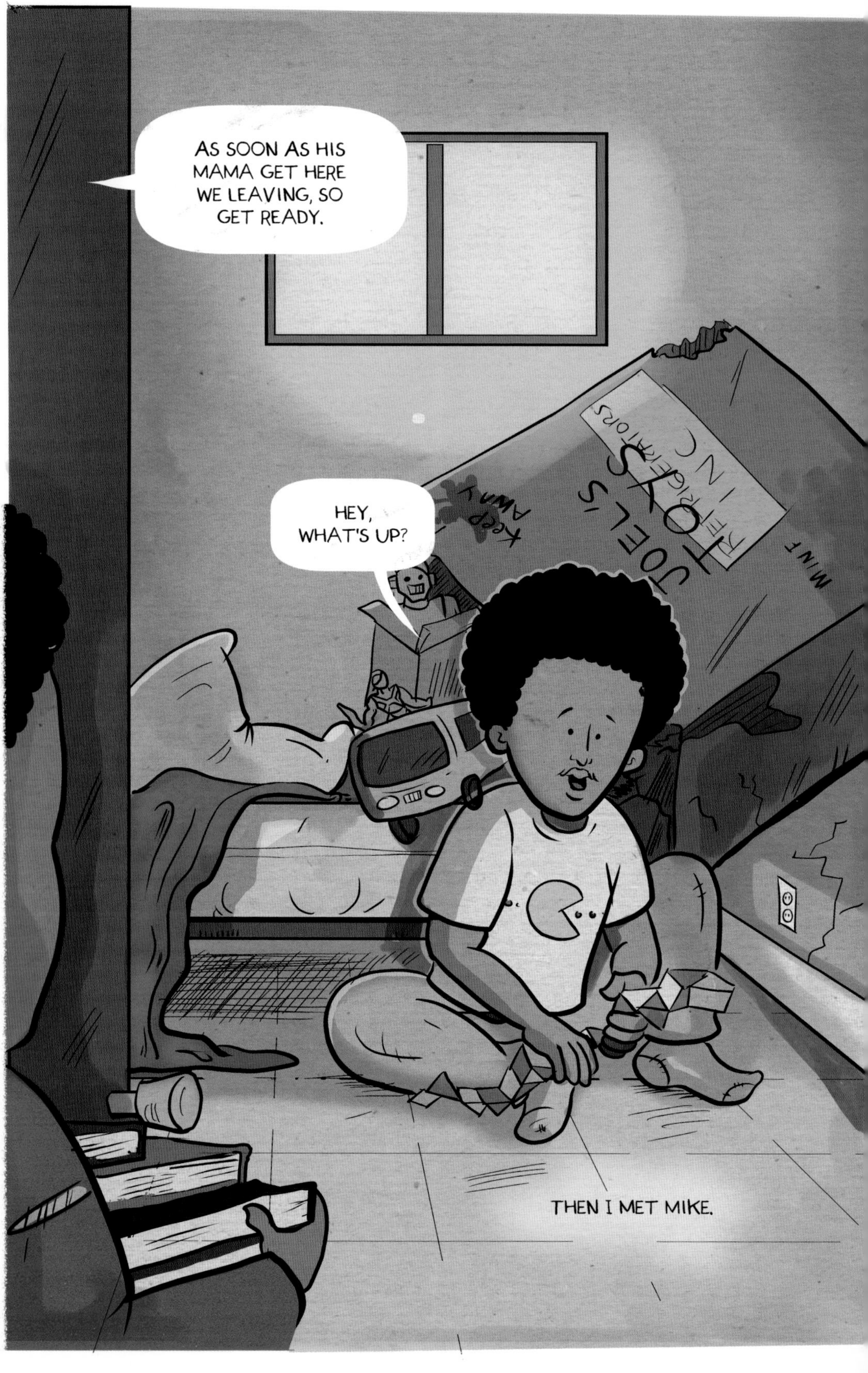
AS SOON AS HIS MAMA GET HERE WE LEAVING, SO GET READY.
HEY, WHAT'S UP?
THEN I MET MIKE.

CHAPTER FOUR

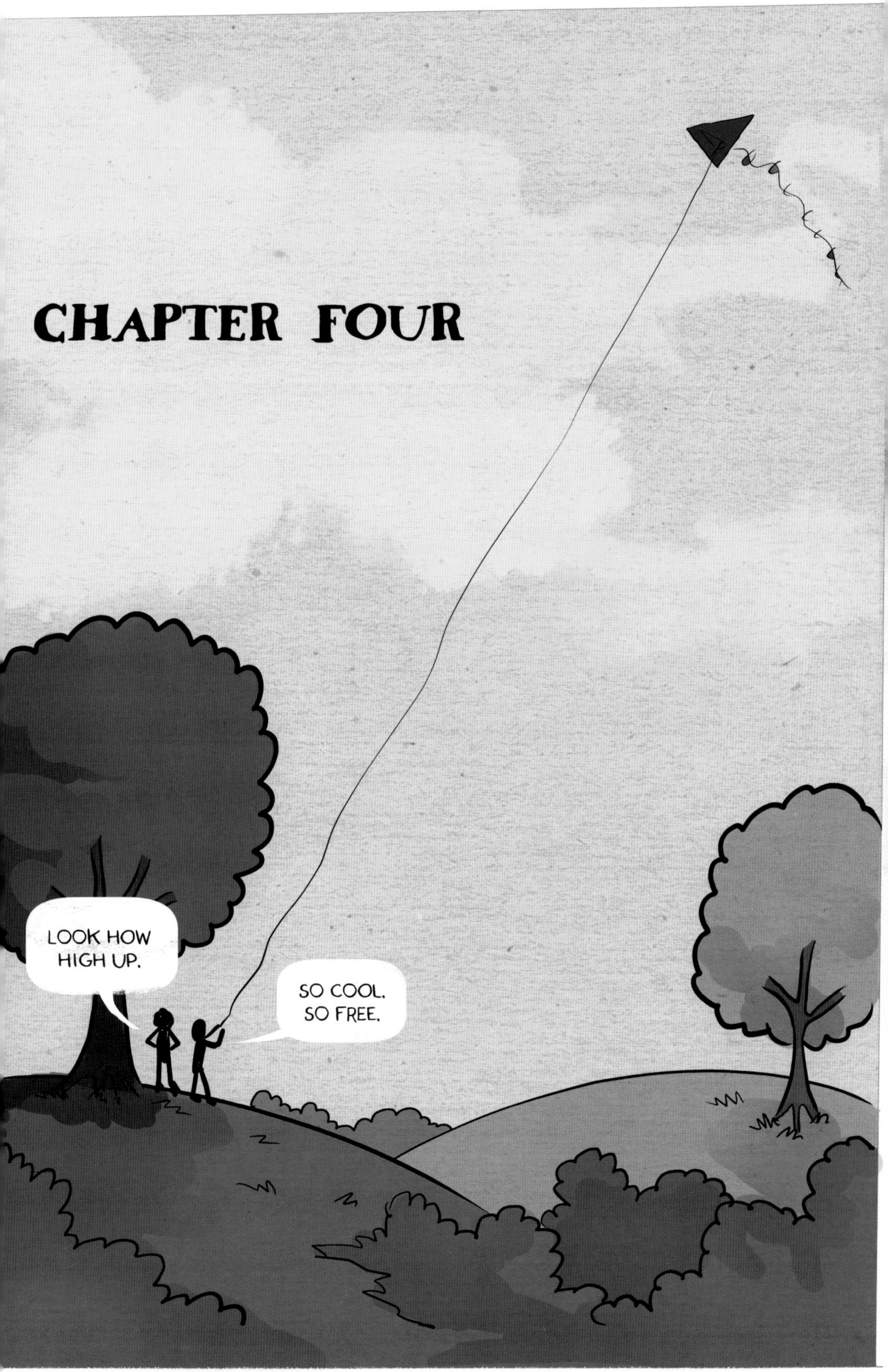

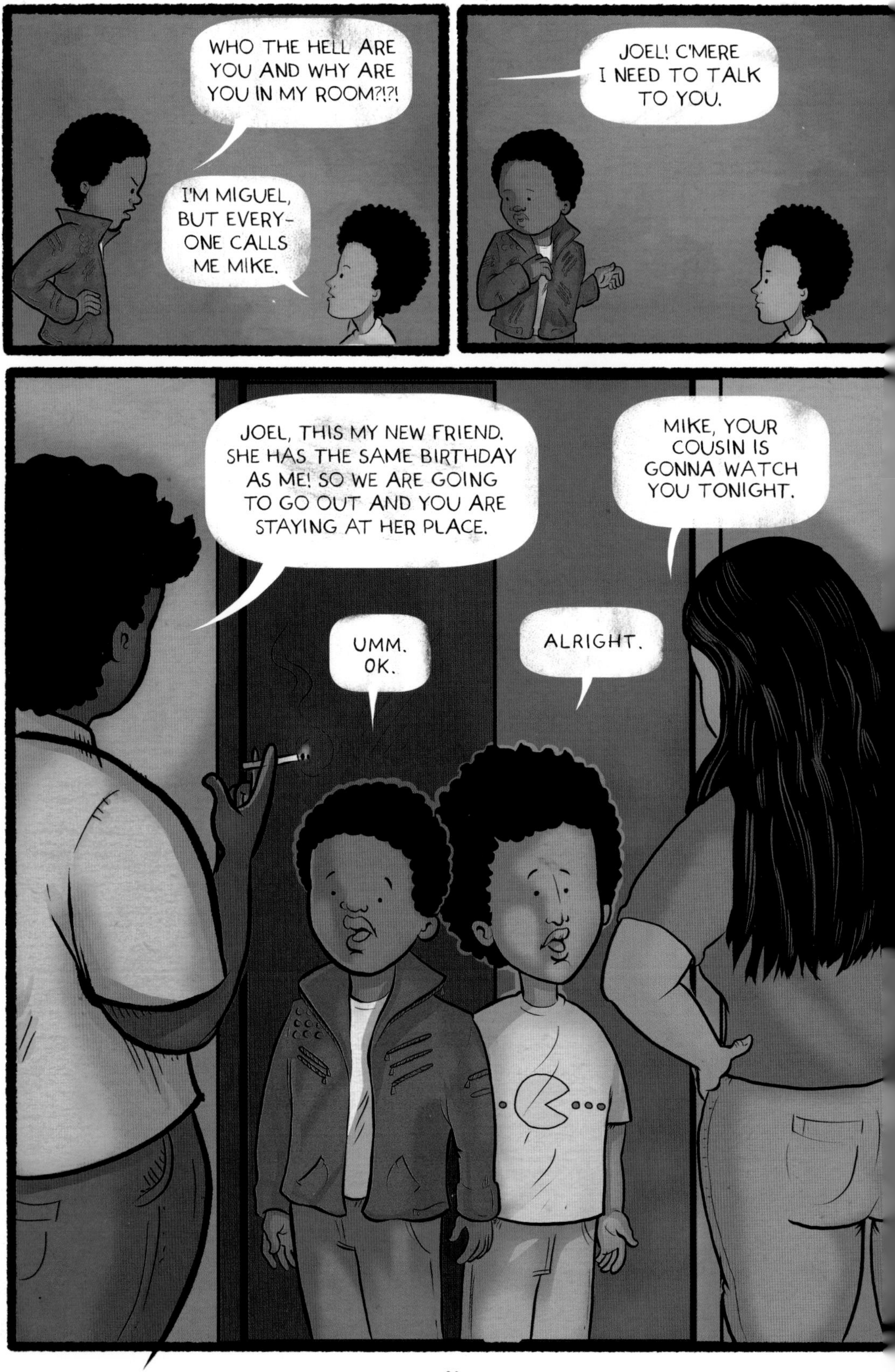
WHO THE HELL ARE YOU AND WHY ARE YOU IN MY ROOM?!?!
I'M MIGUEL, BUT EVERY-ONE CALLS ME MIKE.
JOEL! C'MERE I NEED TO TALK TO YOU.
JOEL, THIS MY NEW FRIEND. SHE HAS THE SAME BIRTHDAY AS ME! SO WE ARE GOING TO GO OUT AND YOU ARE STAYING AT HER PLACE.
MIKE, YOUR COUSIN IS GONNA WATCH YOU TONIGHT.
UMM. OK.
ALRIGHT.

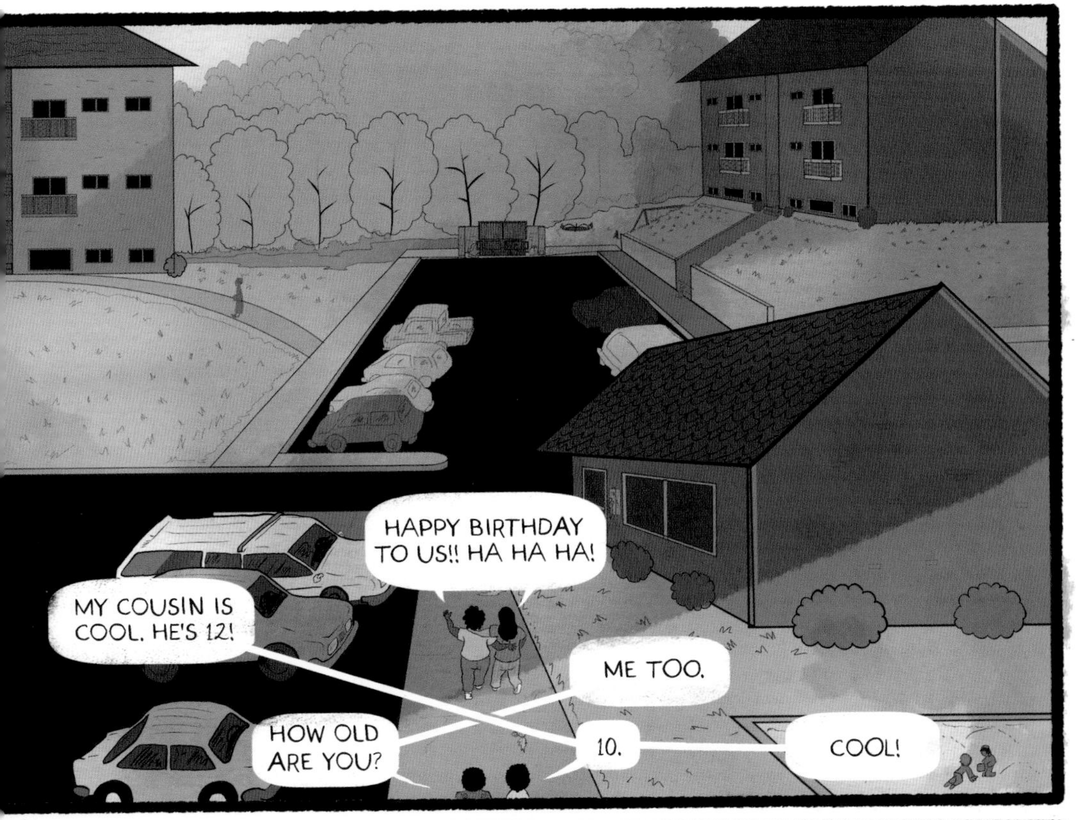
HAPPY BIRTHDAY TO US!! HA HA HA!
MY COUSIN IS COOL. HE'S 12!
ME TOO.
HOW OLD ARE YOU?
10.
COOL!
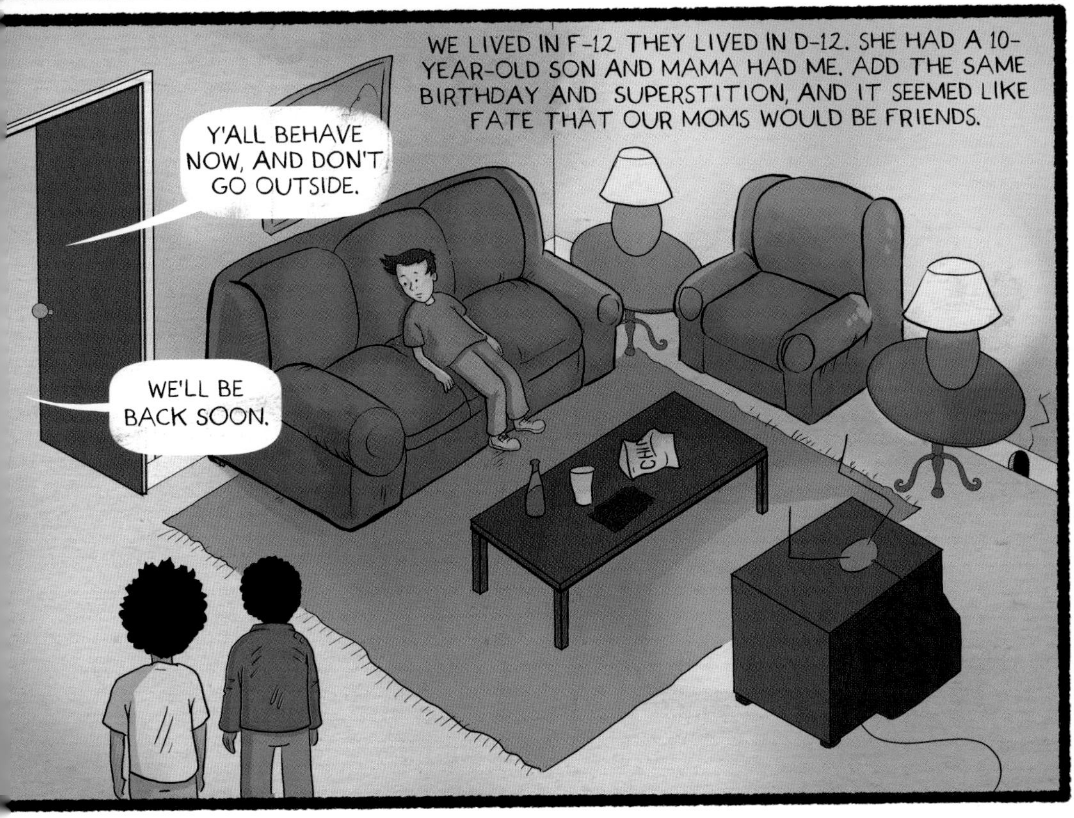
WE LIVED IN F-12 THEY LIVED IN D-12. SHE HAD A 10-YEAR-OLD SON AND MAMA HAD ME. ADD THE SAME BIRTHDAY AND SUPERSTITION, AND IT SEEMED LIKE FATE THAT OUR MOMS WOULD BE FRIENDS.
Y'ALL BEHAVE NOW, AND DON'T GO OUTSIDE.
WE'LL BE BACK SOON.

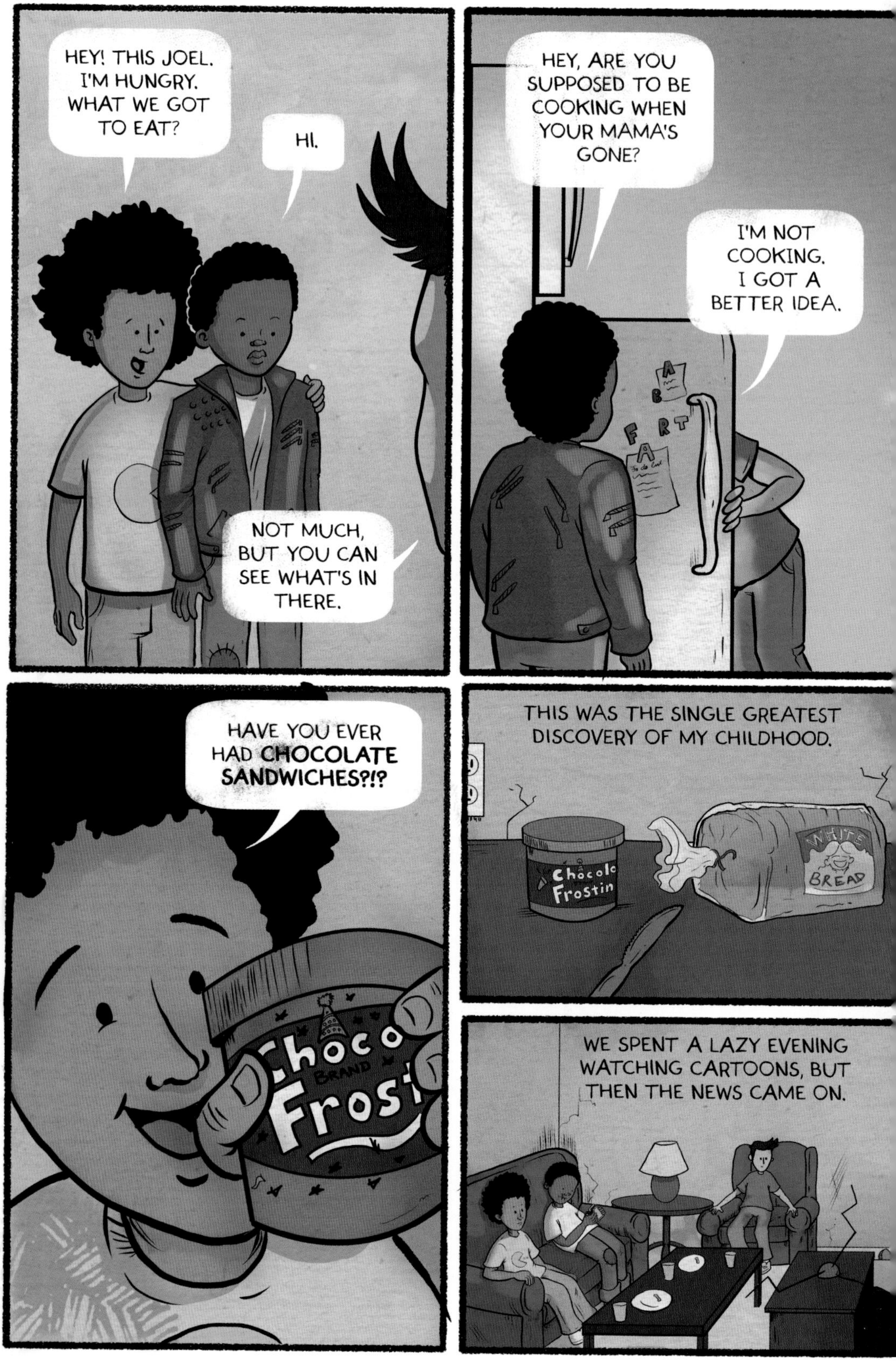
HEY! THIS JOEL. I'M HUNGRY. WHAT WE GOT TO EAT?
HI.
NOT MUCH, BUT YOU CAN SEE WHAT'S IN THERE.
HEY, ARE YOU SUPPOSED TO BE COOKING WHEN YOUR MAMA'S GONE?
I'M NOT COOKING. I GOT A BETTER IDEA.
HAVE YOU EVER HAD **CHOCOLATE SANDWICHES?!?**
Choco BRAND Frost
THIS WAS THE SINGLE GREATEST DISCOVERY OF MY CHILDHOOD.
Chocolo Frostin
WHITE BREAD
WE SPENT A LAZY EVENING WATCHING CARTOONS, BUT THEN THE NEWS CAME ON.

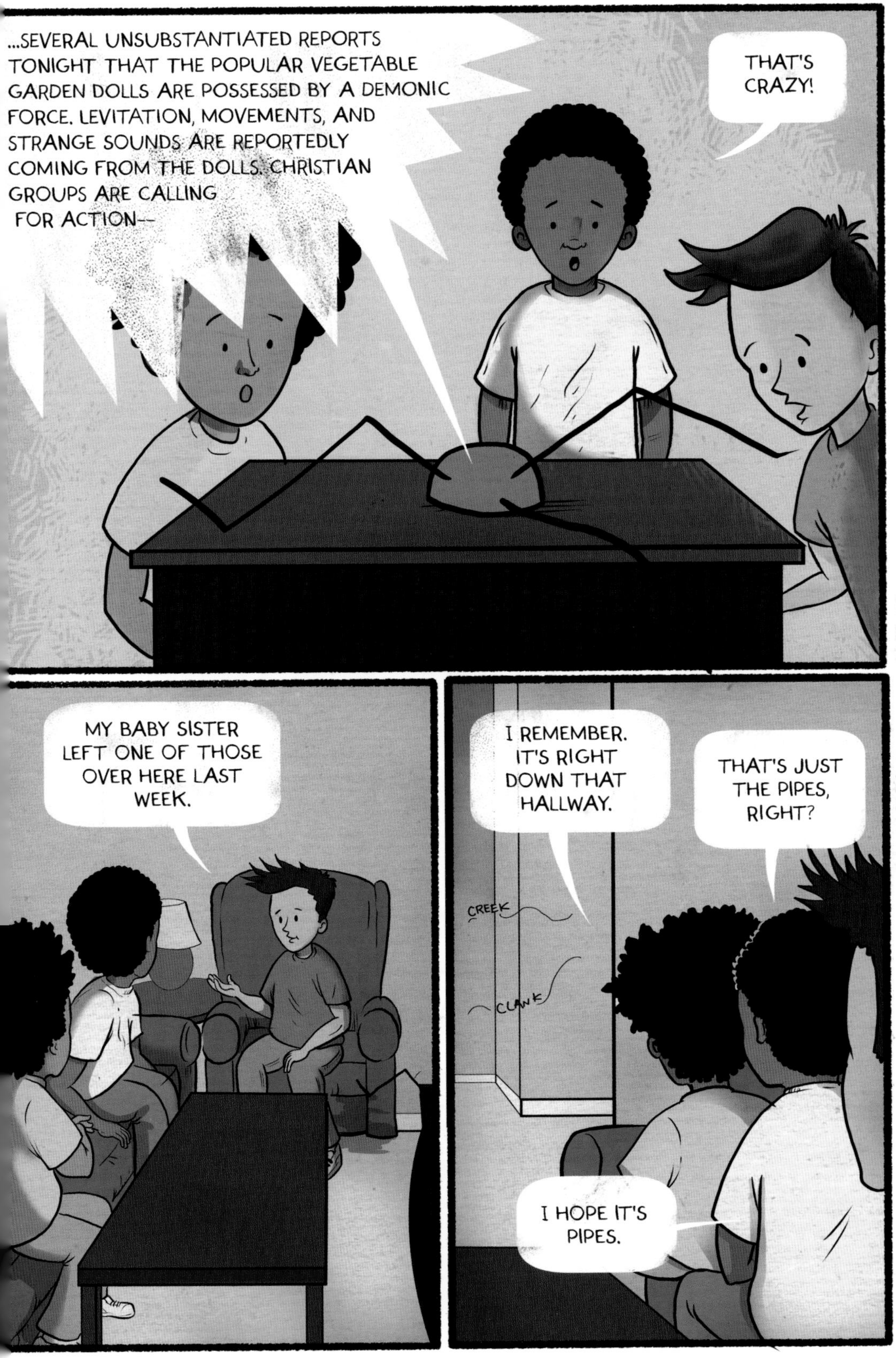
...SEVERAL UNSUBSTANTIATED REPORTS TONIGHT THAT THE POPULAR VEGETABLE GARDEN DOLLS ARE POSSESSED BY A DEMONIC FORCE. LEVITATION, MOVEMENTS, AND STRANGE SOUNDS ARE REPORTEDLY COMING FROM THE DOLLS. CHRISTIAN GROUPS ARE CALLING FOR ACTION--
THAT'S CRAZY!
MY BABY SISTER LEFT ONE OF THOSE OVER HERE LAST WEEK.
I REMEMBER. IT'S RIGHT DOWN THAT HALLWAY.
THAT'S JUST THE PIPES, RIGHT?
CREEK
CLANK
I HOPE IT'S PIPES.

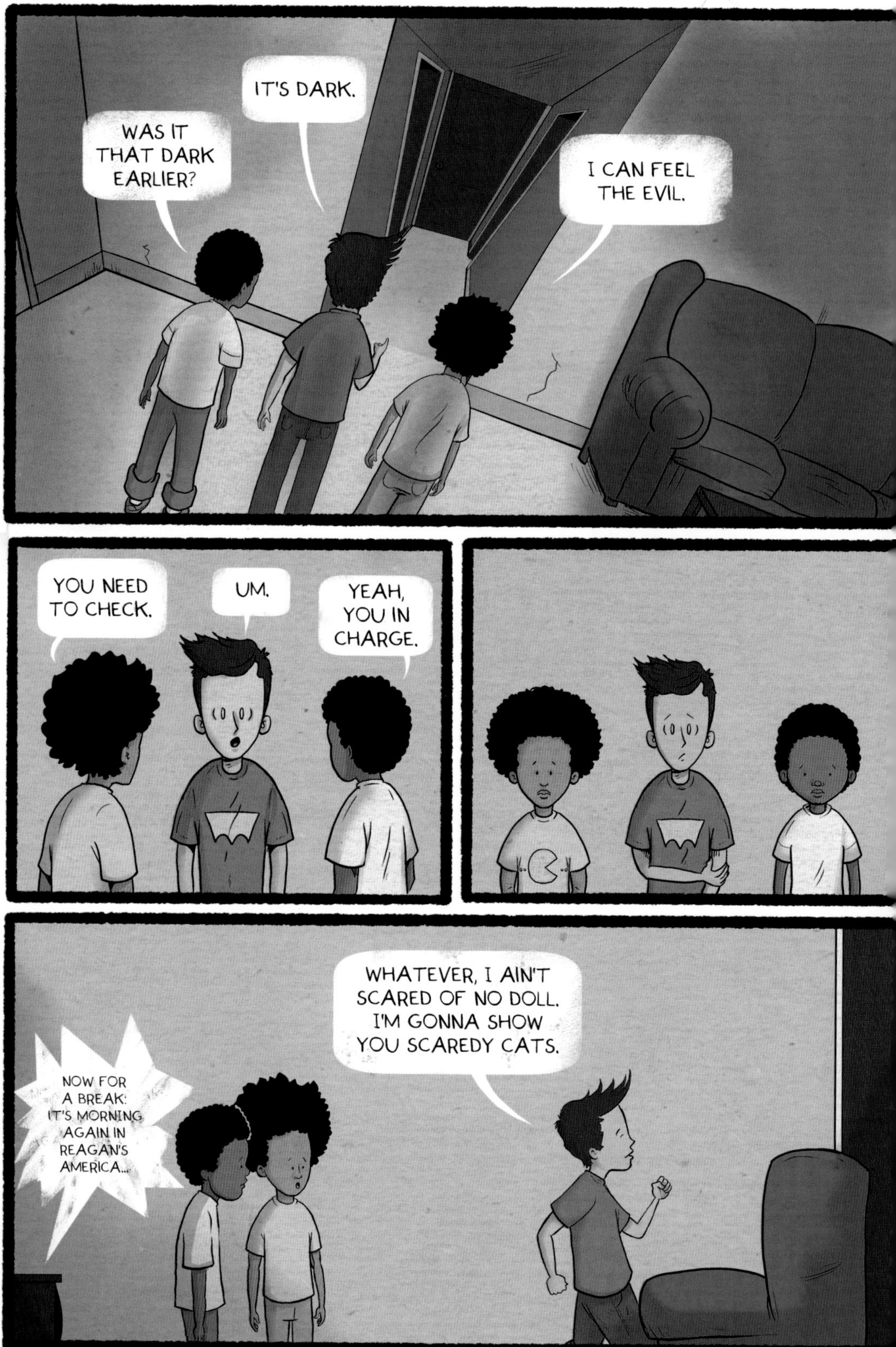
WAS IT THAT DARK EARLIER?
IT'S DARK.
I CAN FEEL THE EVIL.
YOU NEED TO CHECK.
UM.
YEAH, YOU IN CHARGE.
NOW FOR A BREAK: IT'S MORNING AGAIN IN REAGAN'S AMERICA...
WHATEVER, I AIN'T SCARED OF NO DOLL. I'M GONNA SHOW YOU SCAREDY CATS.

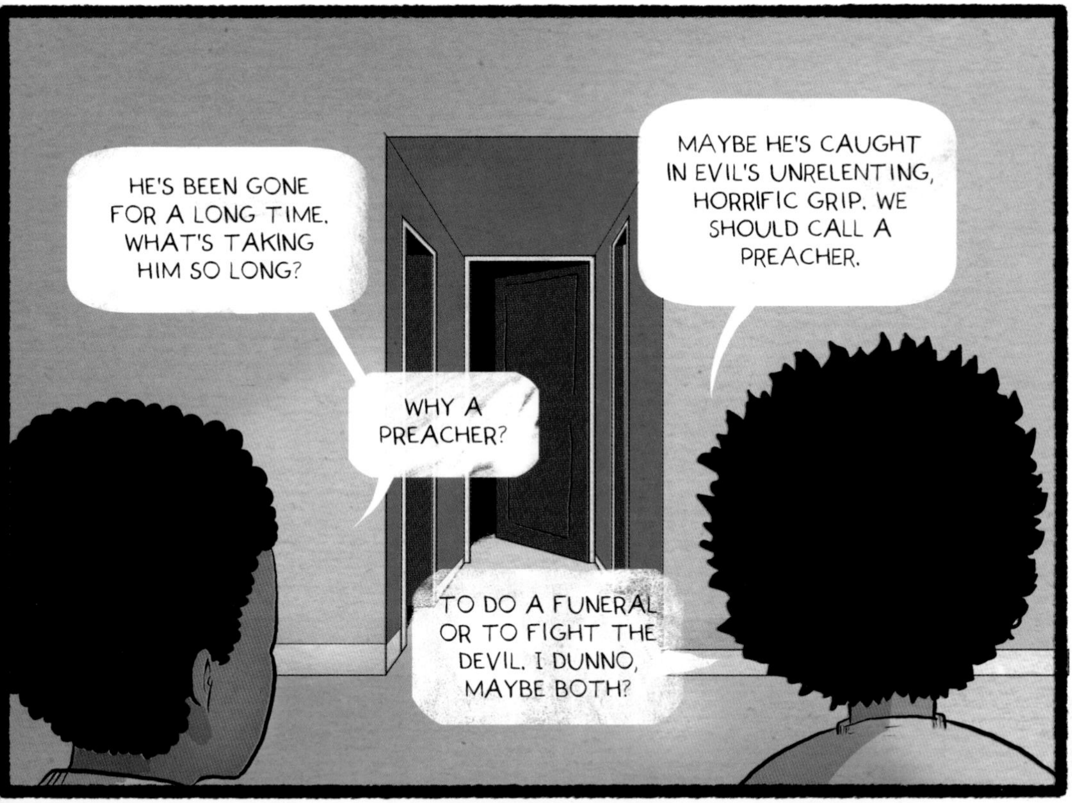
HE'S BEEN GONE FOR A LONG TIME. WHAT'S TAKING HIM SO LONG?
WHY A PREACHER?
MAYBE HE'S CAUGHT IN EVIL'S UNRELENTING, HORRIFIC GRIP. WE SHOULD CALL A PREACHER.
TO DO A FUNERAL OR TO FIGHT THE DEVIL. I DUNNO, MAYBE BOTH?

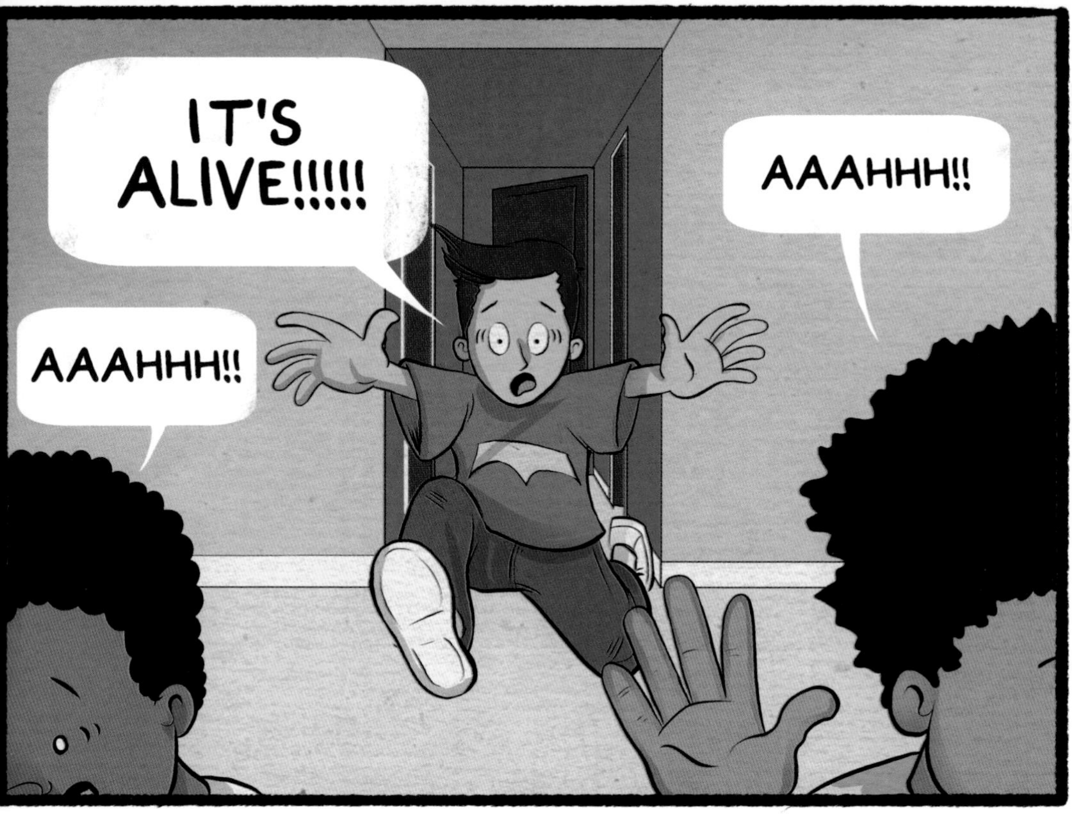
IT'S ALIVE!!!!!
AAAHHH!!
AAAHHH!!

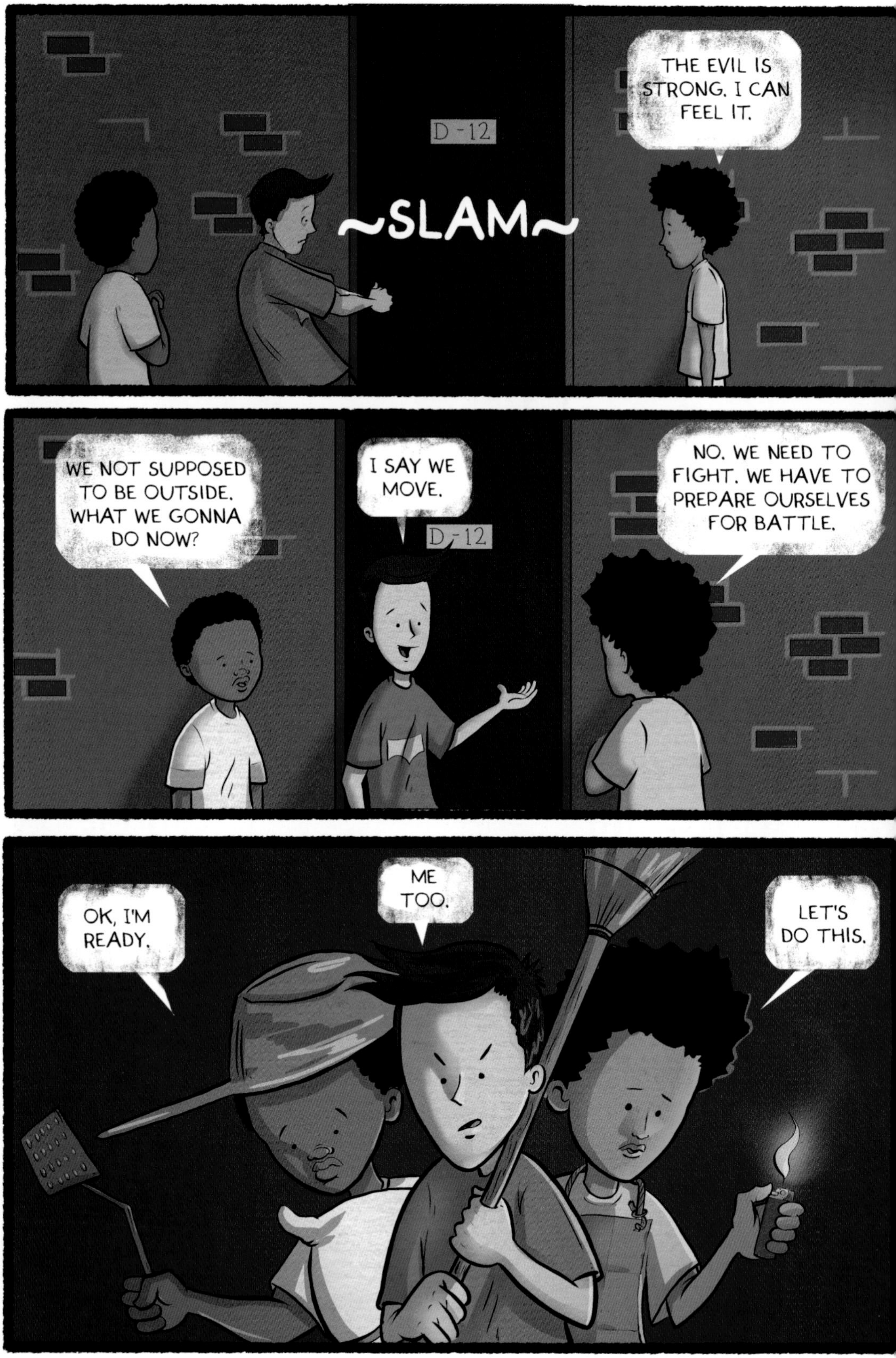

D-12
~SLAM~
THE EVIL IS STRONG. I CAN FEEL IT.
WE NOT SUPPOSED TO BE OUTSIDE. WHAT WE GONNA DO NOW?
I SAY WE MOVE.
D-12
NO. WE NEED TO FIGHT. WE HAVE TO PREPARE OURSELVES FOR BATTLE.
OK, I'M READY.
ME TOO.
LET'S DO THIS.

~CLICK~

LOOK! THERE IT IS!

IT WAS ON THE FLOOR BEFORE.

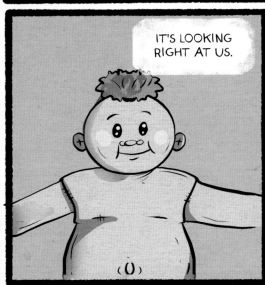

IT'S LOOKING RIGHT AT US.

IT'S PURE EVIL!

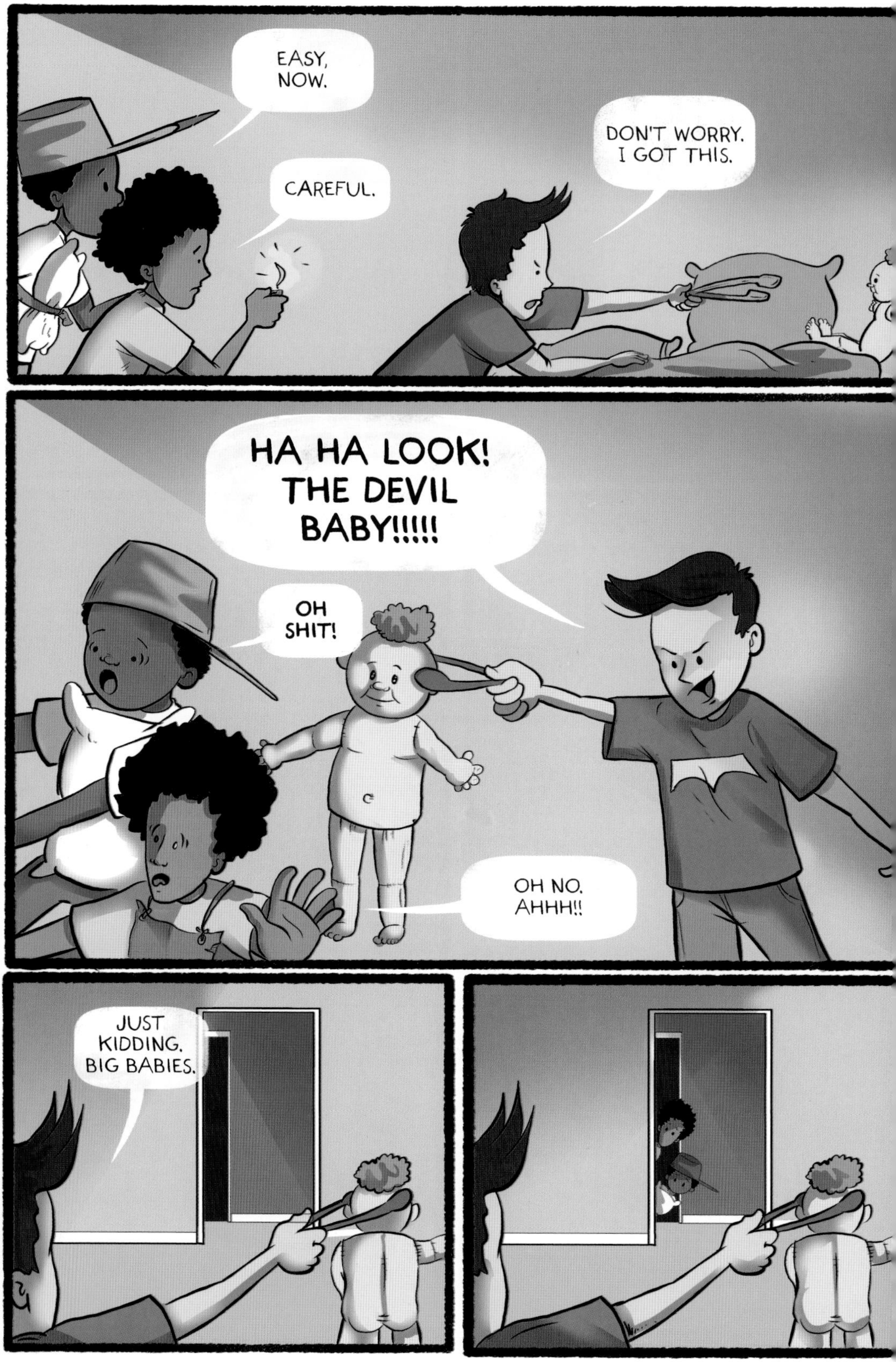
EASY, NOW.
CAREFUL.
DON'T WORRY. I GOT THIS.
HA HA LOOK! THE DEVIL BABY!!!!!
OH SHIT!
OH NO. AHHH!!
JUST KIDDING. BIG BABIES.

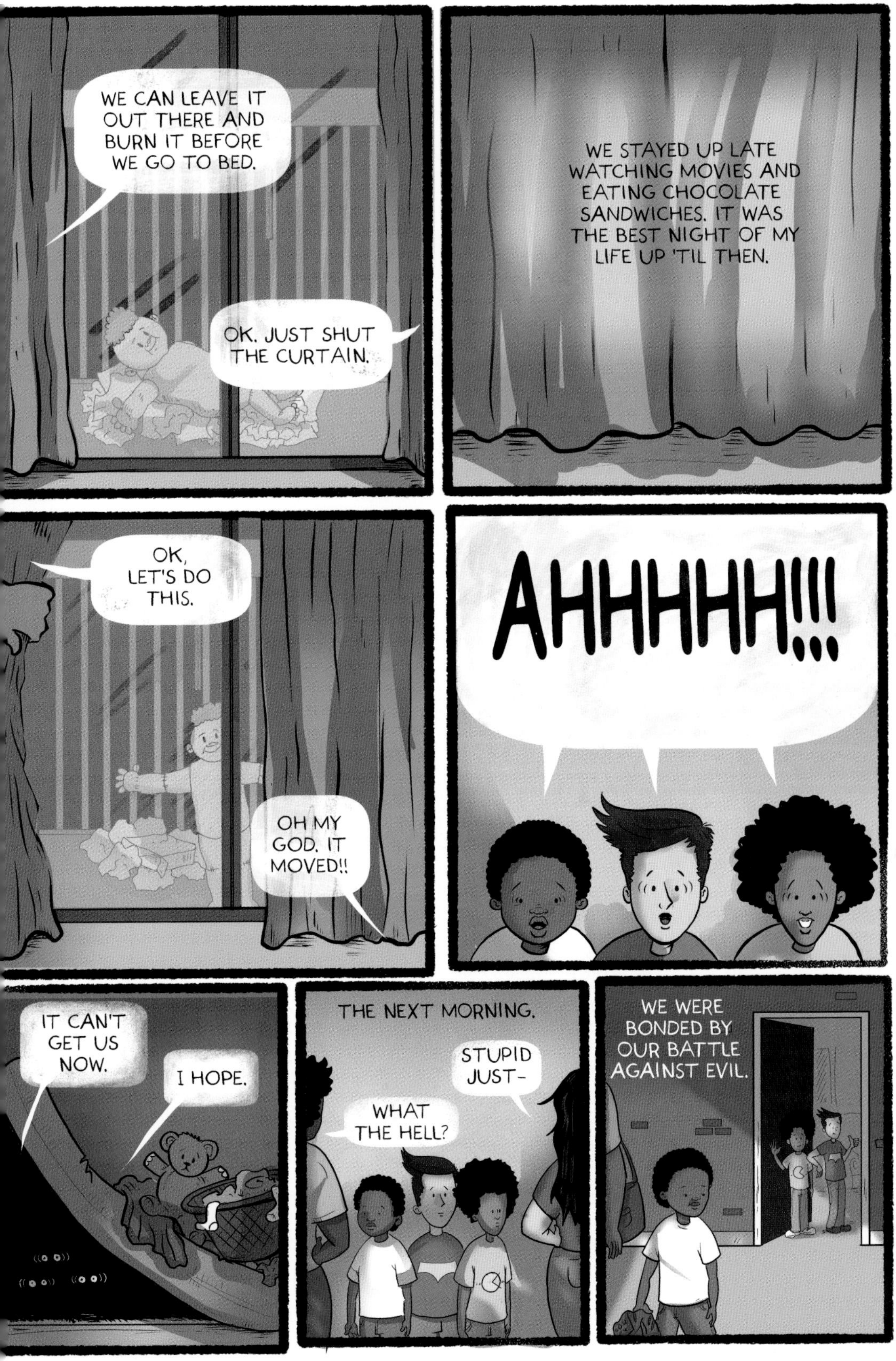
WE CAN LEAVE IT OUT THERE AND BURN IT BEFORE WE GO TO BED.
OK. JUST SHUT THE CURTAIN.
WE STAYED UP LATE WATCHING MOVIES AND EATING CHOCOLATE SANDWICHES. IT WAS THE BEST NIGHT OF MY LIFE UP 'TIL THEN.
OK, LET'S DO THIS.
OH MY GOD. IT MOVED!!
AHHHHH!!!
IT CAN'T GET US NOW.
I HOPE.
THE NEXT MORNING.
STUPID JUST-
WHAT THE HELL?
WE WERE BONDED BY OUR BATTLE AGAINST EVIL.

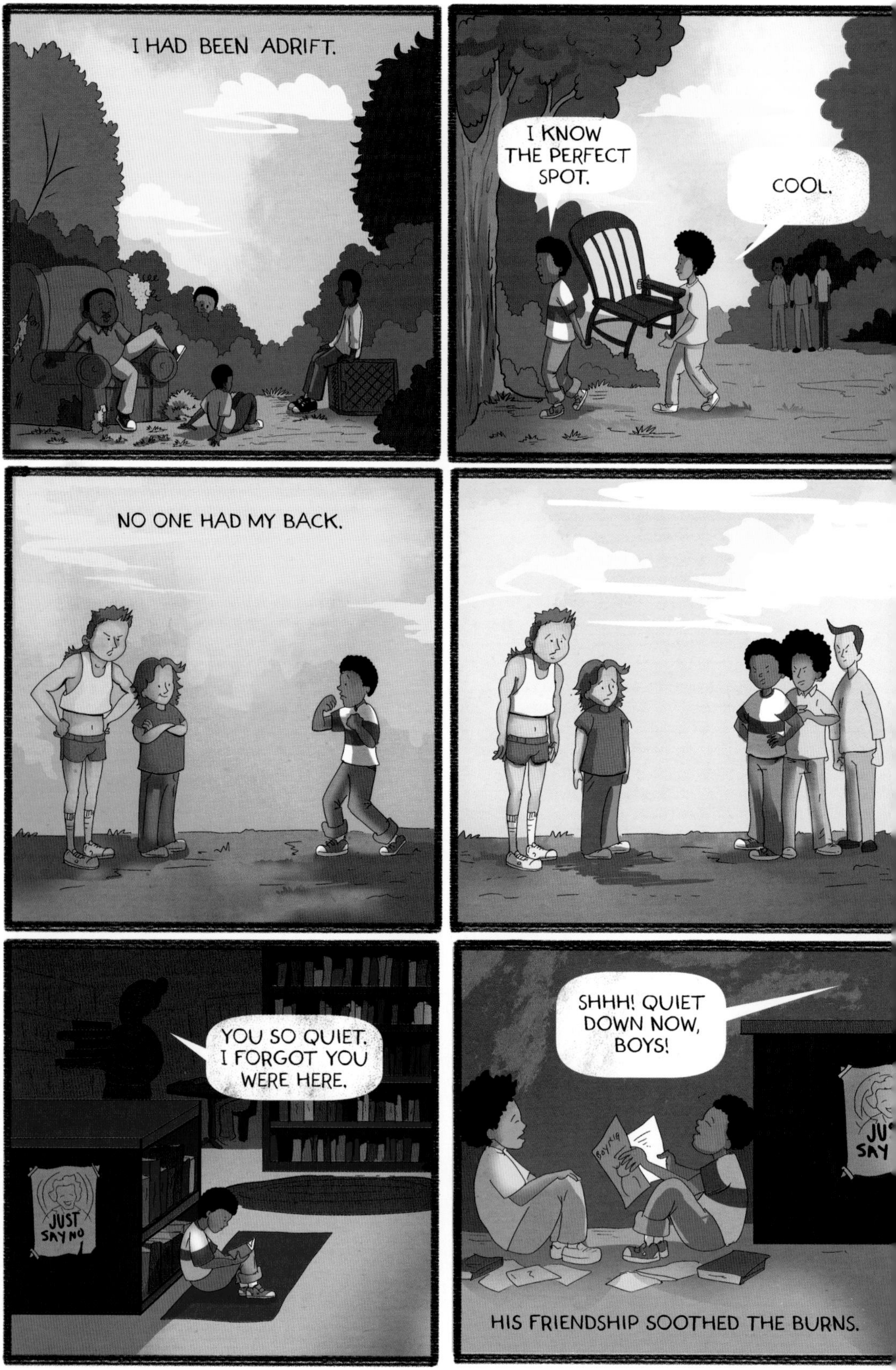
I HAD BEEN ADRIFT.
I KNOW THE PERFECT SPOT.
COOL.
NO ONE HAD MY BACK.
YOU SO QUIET. I FORGOT YOU WERE HERE.
JUST SAY NO
SHHH! QUIET DOWN NOW, BOYS!
HIS FRIENDSHIP SOOTHED THE BURNS.

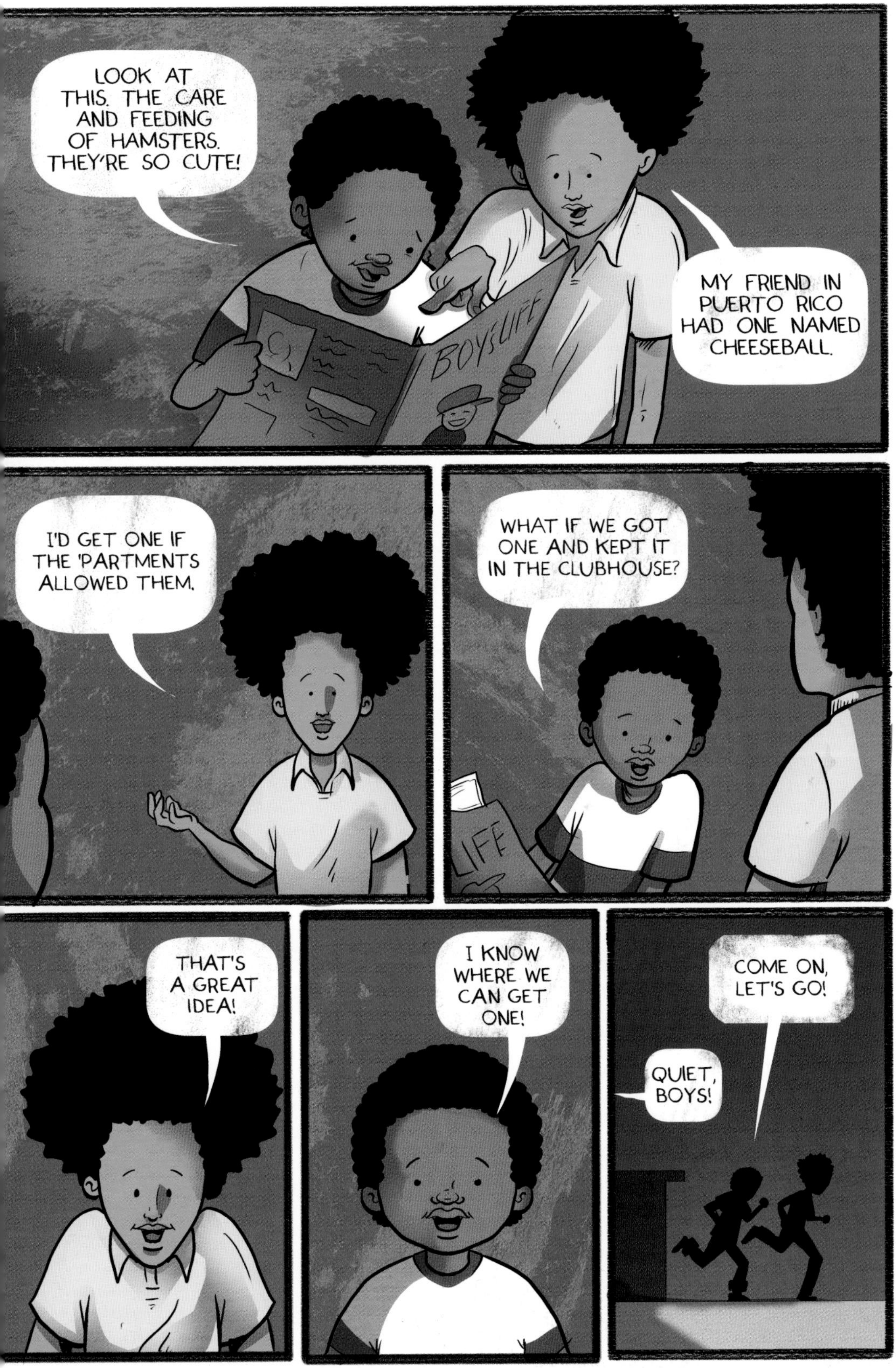
LOOK AT THIS. THE CARE AND FEEDING OF HAMSTERS. THEY'RE SO CUTE!
MY FRIEND IN PUERTO RICO HAD ONE NAMED CHEESEBALL.
BOYS' LIFE
I'D GET ONE IF THE 'PARTMENTS ALLOWED THEM.
WHAT IF WE GOT ONE AND KEPT IT IN THE CLUBHOUSE?
LIFE
THAT'S A GREAT IDEA!
I KNOW WHERE WE CAN GET ONE!
COME ON, LET'S GO!
QUIET, BOYS!

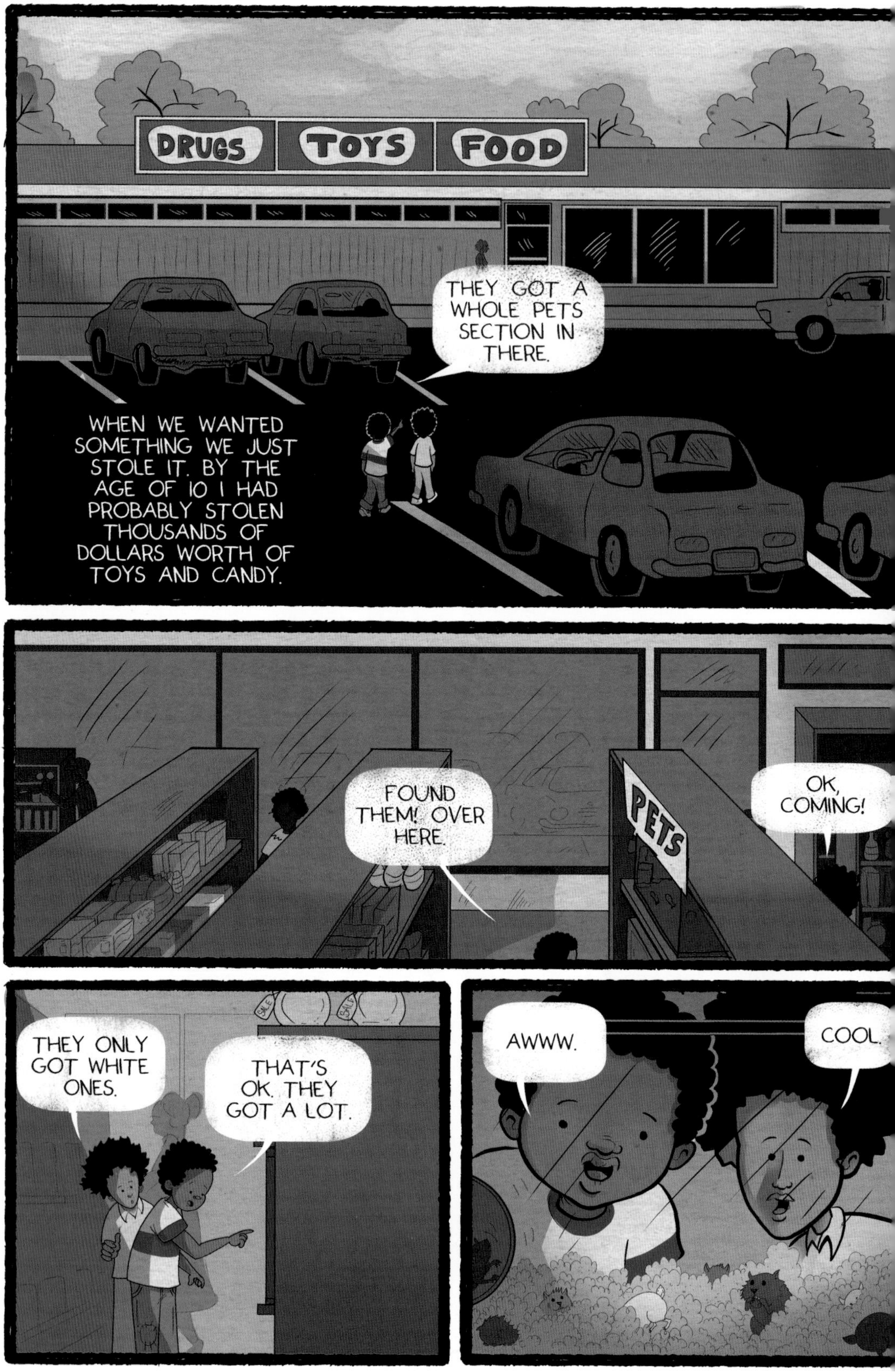
DRUGS
TOYS
FOOD
THEY GOT A WHOLE PETS SECTION IN THERE.
WHEN WE WANTED SOMETHING WE JUST STOLE IT. BY THE AGE OF 10 I HAD PROBABLY STOLEN THOUSANDS OF DOLLARS WORTH OF TOYS AND CANDY.
FOUND THEM! OVER HERE.
PETS
OK, COMING!
SALE
SALE
THEY ONLY GOT WHITE ONES.
THAT'S OK. THEY GOT A LOT.
AWWW.
COOL.

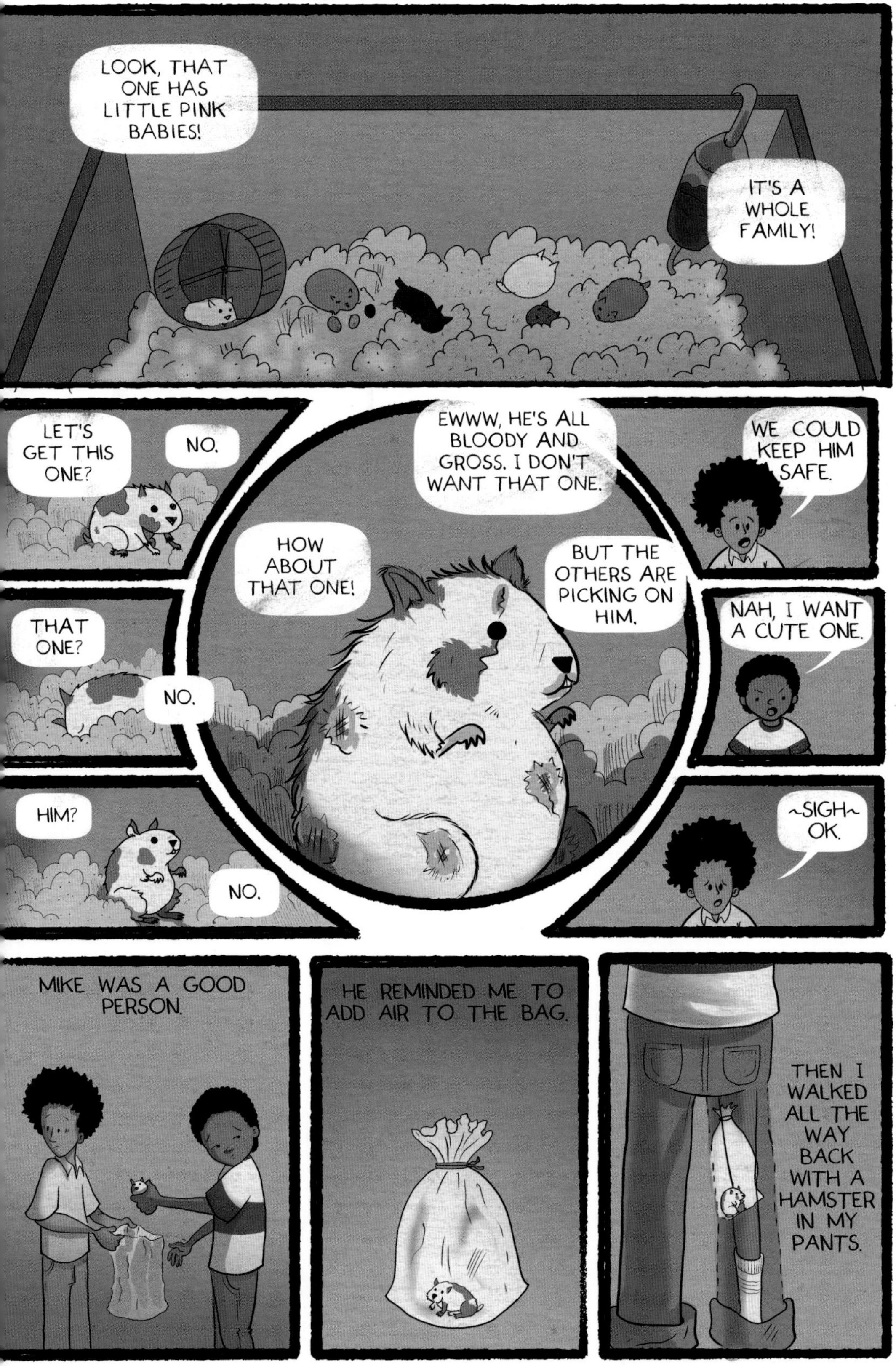
LOOK, THAT ONE HAS LITTLE PINK BABIES!
IT'S A WHOLE FAMILY!
LET'S GET THIS ONE?
NO.
THAT ONE?
NO.
HIM?
NO.
HOW ABOUT THAT ONE!
EWWW, HE'S ALL BLOODY AND GROSS. I DON'T WANT THAT ONE.
BUT THE OTHERS ARE PICKING ON HIM.
WE COULD KEEP HIM SAFE.
NAH, I WANT A CUTE ONE.
~SIGH~ OK.
MIKE WAS A GOOD PERSON.
HE REMINDED ME TO ADD AIR TO THE BAG.
THEN I WALKED ALL THE WAY BACK WITH A HAMSTER IN MY PANTS.

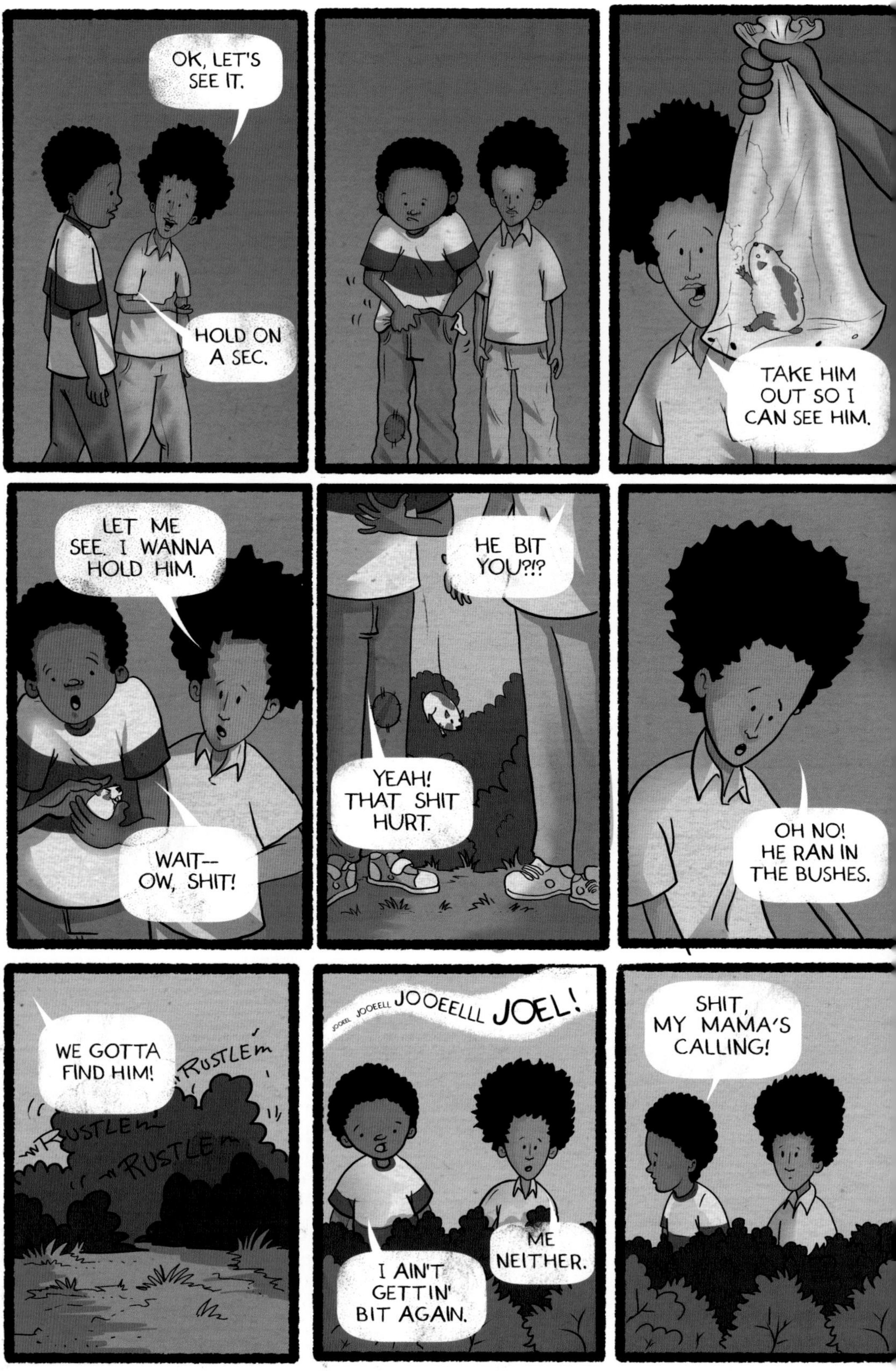
OK, LET'S SEE IT.
HOLD ON A SEC.
TAKE HIM OUT SO I CAN SEE HIM.
LET ME SEE. I WANNA HOLD HIM.
WAIT-- OW, SHIT!
HE BIT YOU?!?
YEAH! THAT SHIT HURT.
OH NO! HE RAN IN THE BUSHES.
WE GOTTA FIND HIM!
RUSTLE
RUSTLE
RUSTLE
JOOEL JOOEELL JOOEELLL JOEL!
I AIN'T GETTIN' BIT AGAIN.
ME NEITHER.
SHIT, MY MAMA'S CALLING!

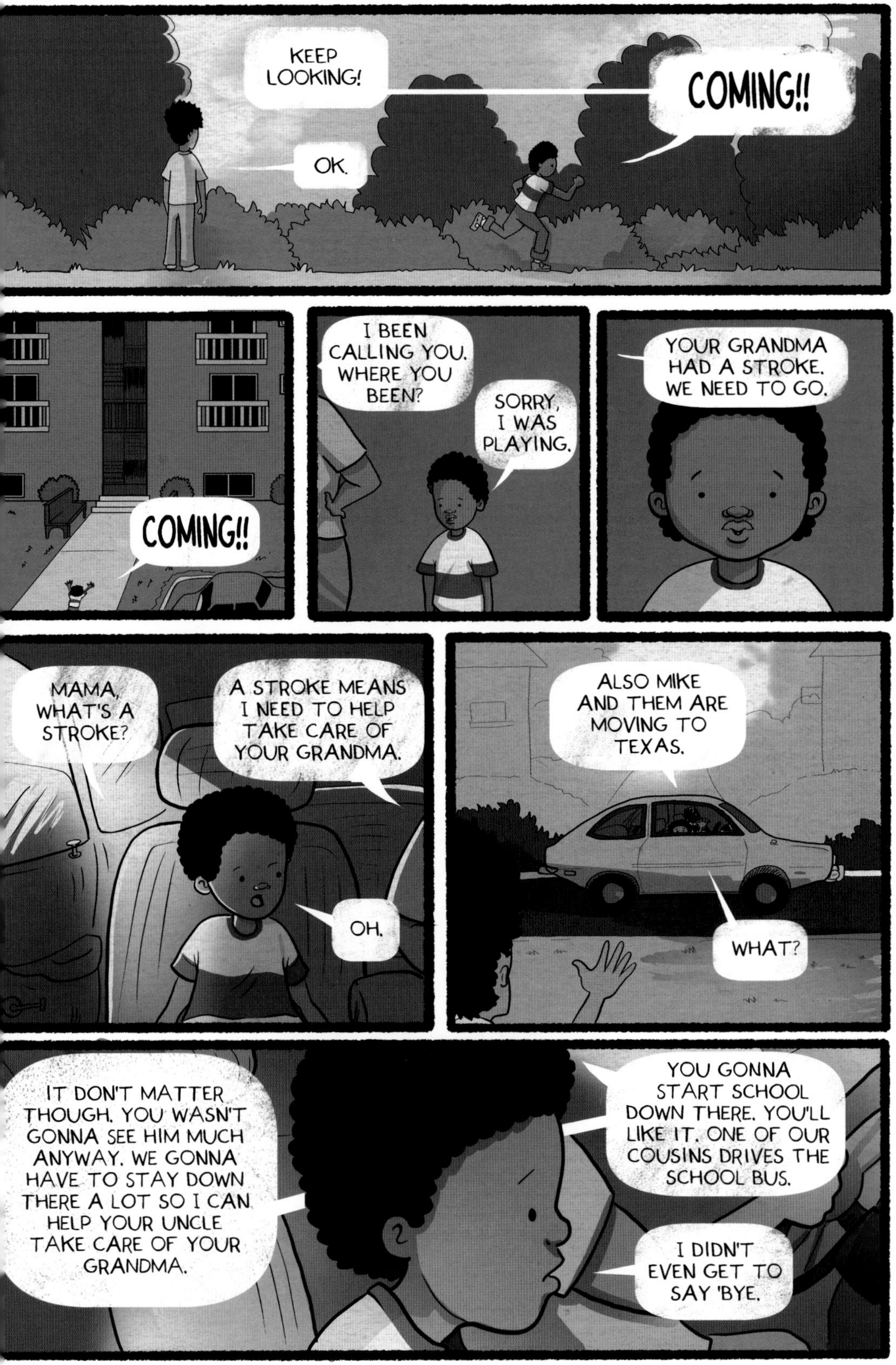
KEEP LOOKING!
OK.
COMING!!
COMING!!
I BEEN CALLING YOU. WHERE YOU BEEN?
SORRY, I WAS PLAYING.
YOUR GRANDMA HAD A STROKE. WE NEED TO GO.
MAMA, WHAT'S A STROKE?
A STROKE MEANS I NEED TO HELP TAKE CARE OF YOUR GRANDMA.
OH.
ALSO MIKE AND THEM ARE MOVING TO TEXAS.
WHAT?
IT DON'T MATTER THOUGH. YOU WASN'T GONNA SEE HIM MUCH ANYWAY. WE GONNA HAVE TO STAY DOWN THERE A LOT SO I CAN HELP YOUR UNCLE TAKE CARE OF YOUR GRANDMA.
YOU GONNA START SCHOOL DOWN THERE. YOU'LL LIKE IT. ONE OF OUR COUSINS DRIVES THE SCHOOL BUS.
I DIDN'T EVEN GET TO SAY 'BYE.

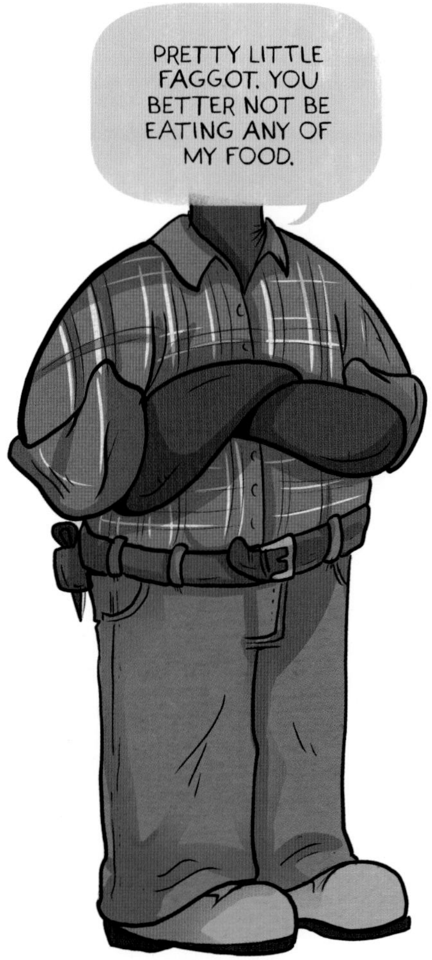
PRETTY LITTLE FAGGOT. YOU BETTER NOT BE EATING ANY OF MY FOOD.

CHAPTER FIVE

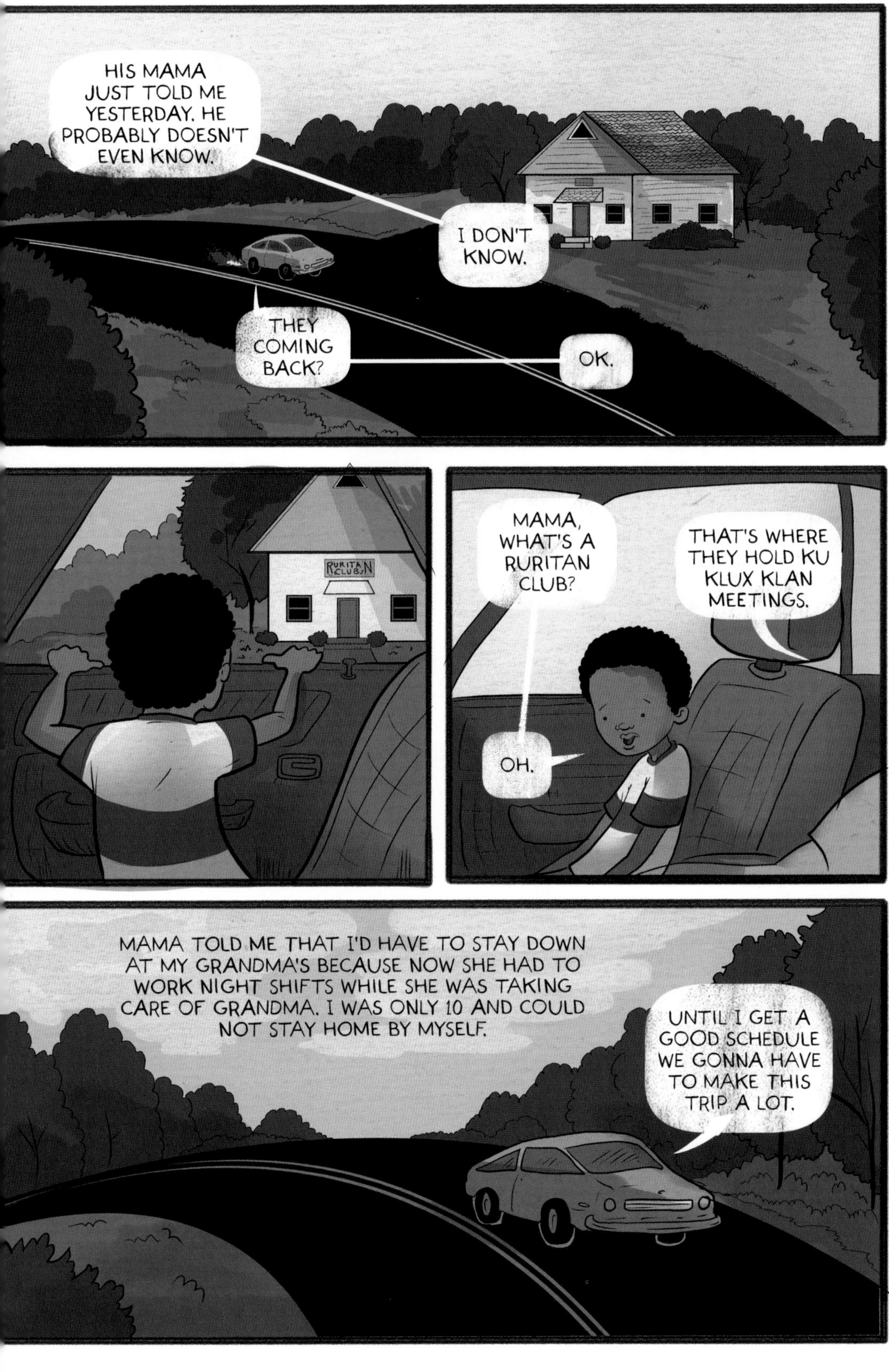
HIS MAMA JUST TOLD ME YESTERDAY. HE PROBABLY DOESN'T EVEN KNOW.
I DON'T KNOW.
THEY COMING BACK?
OK.
RURITAN CLUB
MAMA, WHAT'S A RURITAN CLUB?
THAT'S WHERE THEY HOLD KU KLUX KLAN MEETINGS.
OH.
MAMA TOLD ME THAT I'D HAVE TO STAY DOWN AT MY GRANDMA'S BECAUSE NOW SHE HAD TO WORK NIGHT SHIFTS WHILE SHE WAS TAKING CARE OF GRANDMA. I WAS ONLY 10 AND COULD NOT STAY HOME BY MYSELF.
UNTIL I GET A GOOD SCHEDULE WE GONNA HAVE TO MAKE THIS TRIP A LOT.

MY GRANDPARENTS WERE AT ONE POINT THE WEALTHY PEOPLE IN THE COUNTY. WHAT I HAD ALWAYS CALLED GRANDMA'S HOUSE WAS A COLLECTION OF HOUSES ON THE DEFUNCT FAMILY FARM.

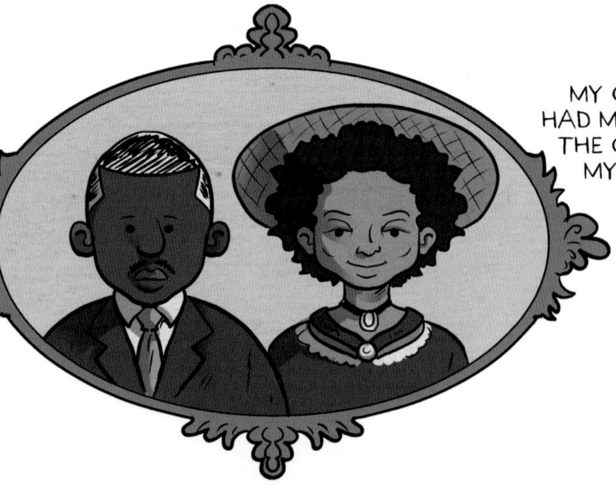

MY GRANDPARENT
HAD MOVED BACK T
THE COUNTY AFTE
MY GRANDFATHE
LOST A LE
IN A MININ
ACCIDEN
IN WES
VIRGINI

FAMILY LORE IS THAT MY GRANDFATHER TOOK A SETTLEMENT OF $500 FOR THE LOSS OF HIS LEG AND USED THAT MONEY TO BUY 300 ACRES OF LAND FOR $1 AN ACRE.

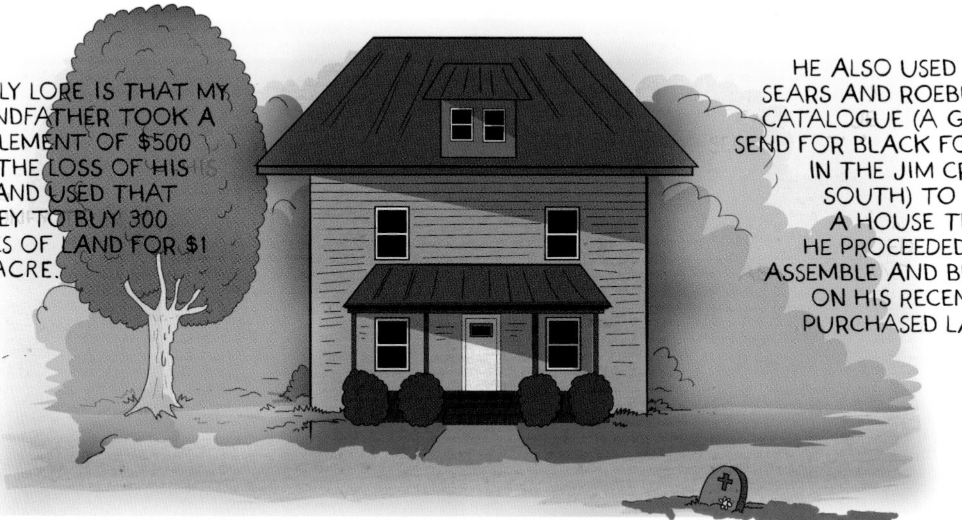

HE ALSO USED TH
SEARS AND ROEBUC
CATALOGUE (A GOD
SEND FOR BLACK FOLK
IN THE JIM CRO
SOUTH) TO BU
A HOUSE THA
HE PROCEEDED T
ASSEMBLE AND BUIL
ON HIS RECENTL
PURCHASED LAN

HE WAS KILLED WHEN A TOBACCO DRYER EXPLODED 12 YEARS BEFORE I WAS BORN.

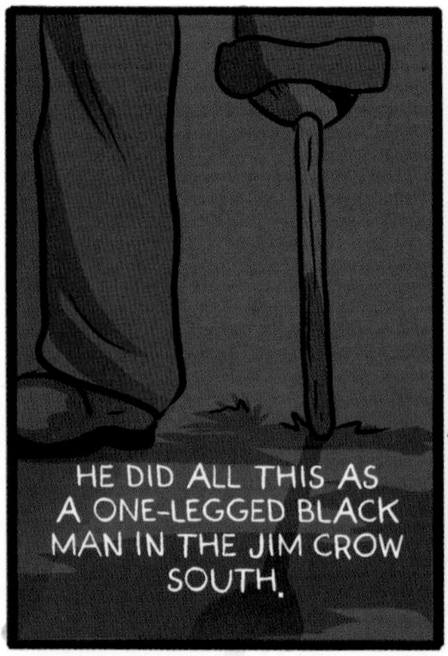
HE DID ALL THIS AS A ONE-LEGGED BLACK MAN IN THE JIM CROW SOUTH.

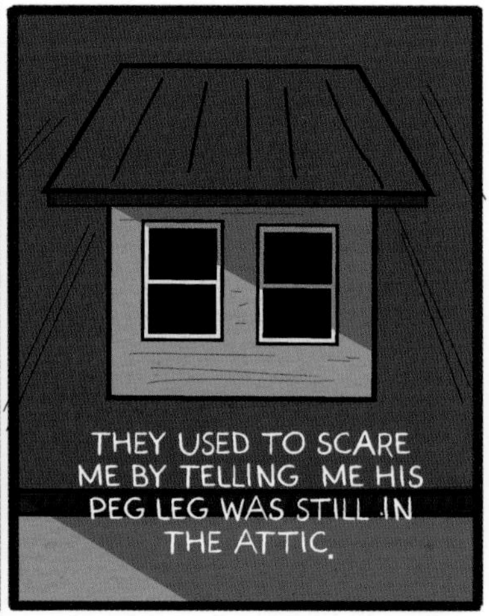
THEY USED TO SCARE ME BY TELLING ME HIS PEG LEG WAS STILL IN THE ATTIC.

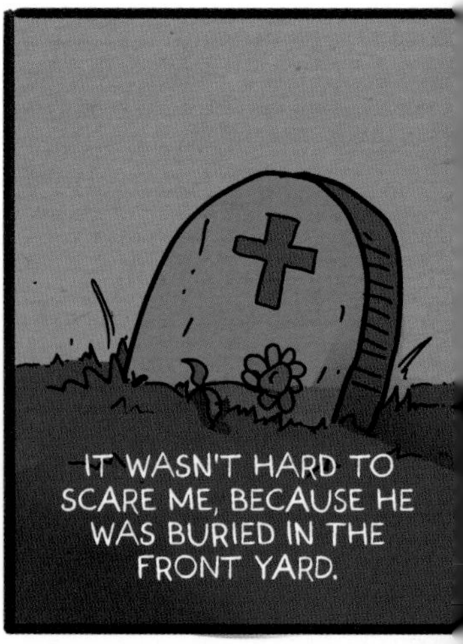
IT WASN'T HARD TO SCARE ME, BECAUSE HE WAS BURIED IN THE FRONT YARD.

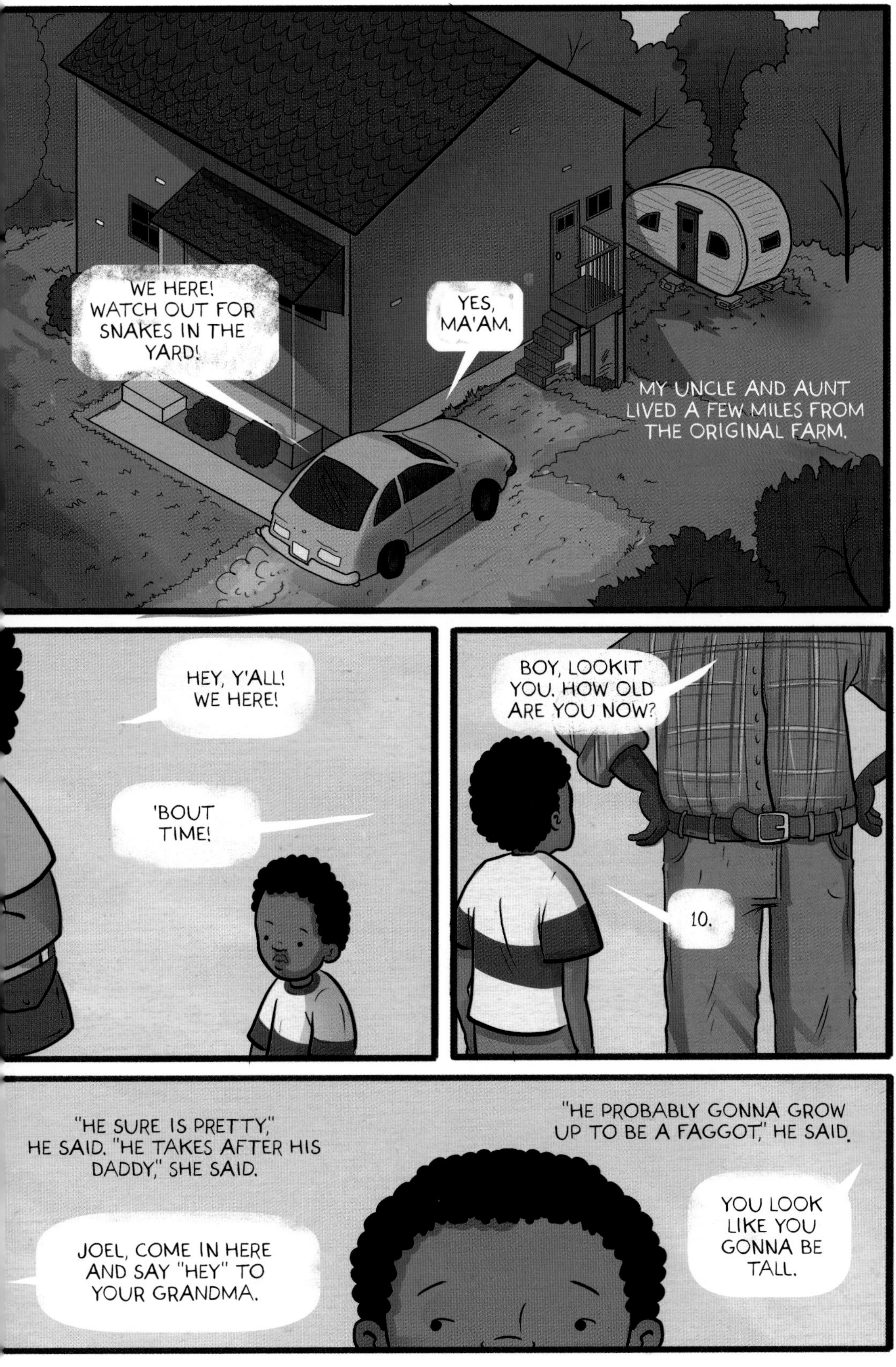
WE HERE! WATCH OUT FOR SNAKES IN THE YARD!
YES, MA'AM.
MY UNCLE AND AUNT LIVED A FEW MILES FROM THE ORIGINAL FARM.
HEY, Y'ALL! WE HERE!
'BOUT TIME!
BOY, LOOKIT YOU. HOW OLD ARE YOU NOW?
10.
"HE SURE IS PRETTY," HE SAID. "HE TAKES AFTER HIS DADDY," SHE SAID.
"HE PROBABLY GONNA GROW UP TO BE A FAGGOT," HE SAID.
JOEL, COME IN HERE AND SAY "HEY" TO YOUR GRANDMA.
YOU LOOK LIKE YOU GONNA BE TALL.

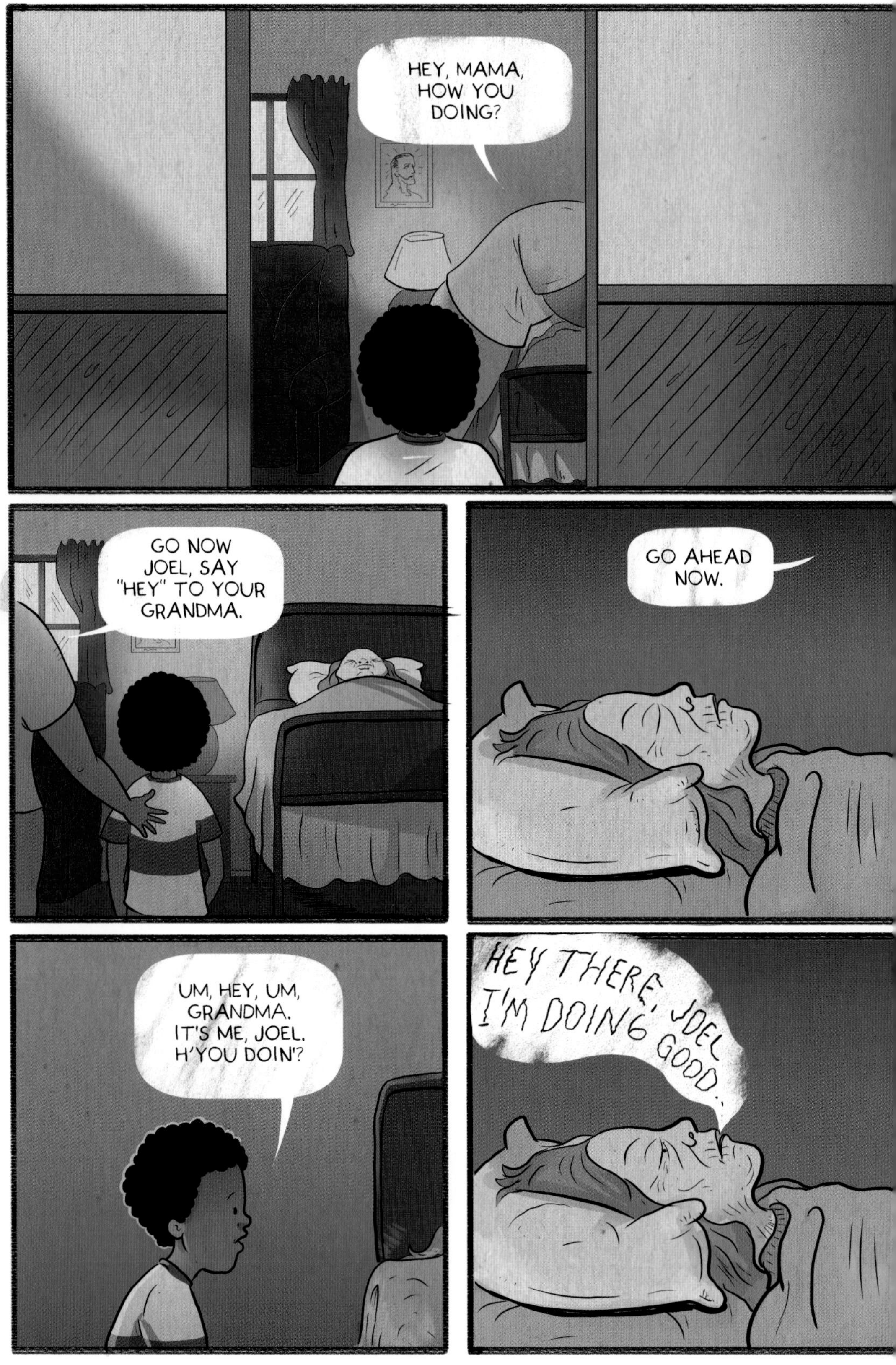
HEY, MAMA, HOW YOU DOING?
GO NOW JOEL, SAY "HEY" TO YOUR GRANDMA.
GO AHEAD NOW.
UM, HEY, UM, GRANDMA. IT'S ME, JOEL. H'YOU DOIN'?
HEY THERE, JOEL I'M DOING GOOD...

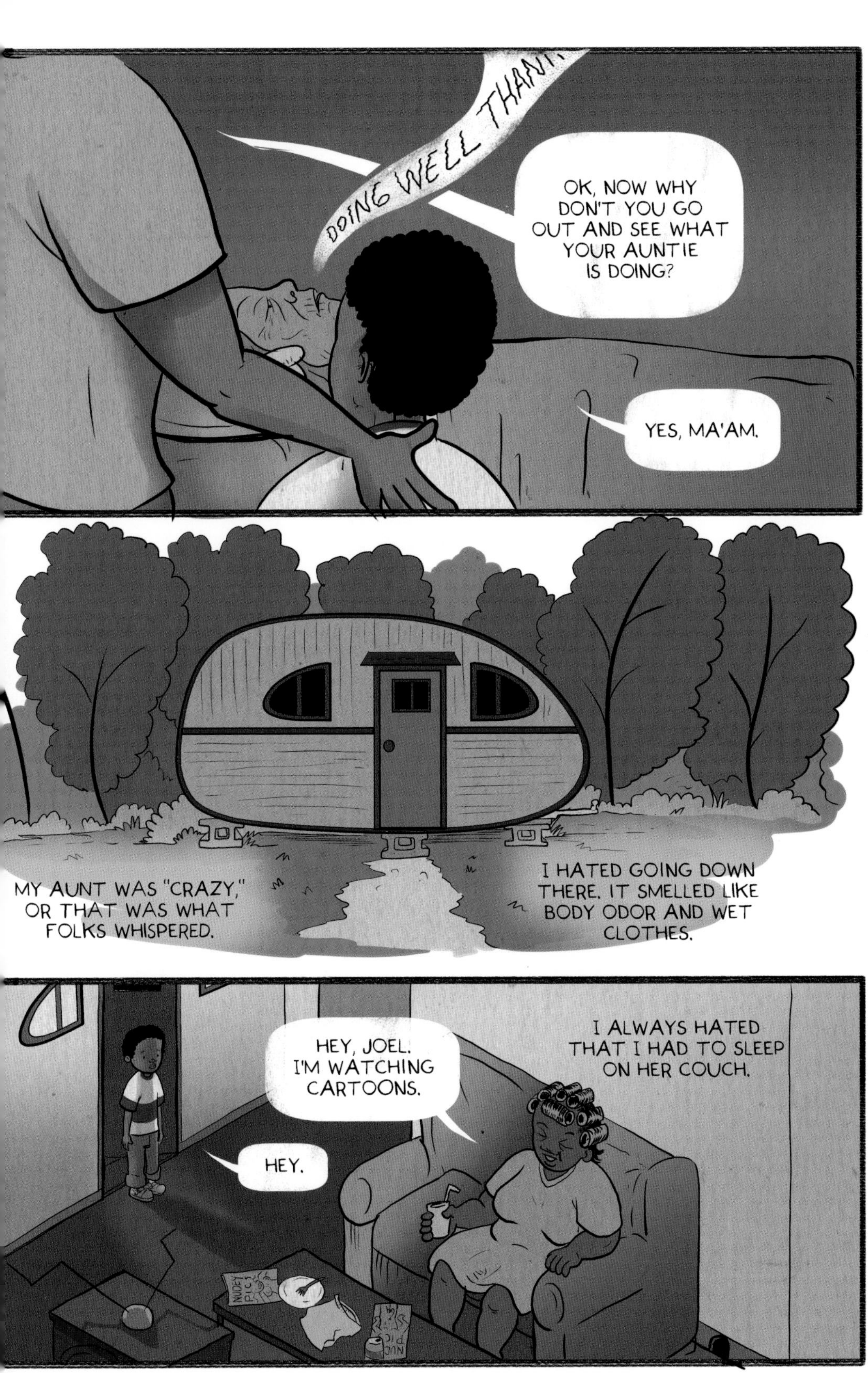
DOING WELL THAN
OK, NOW WHY DON'T YOU GO OUT AND SEE WHAT YOUR AUNTIE IS DOING?
YES, MA'AM.
MY AUNT WAS "CRAZY," OR THAT WAS WHAT FOLKS WHISPERED.
I HATED GOING DOWN THERE. IT SMELLED LIKE BODY ODOR AND WET CLOTHES.
I ALWAYS HATED THAT I HAD TO SLEEP ON HER COUCH.
HEY, JOEL. I'M WATCHING CARTOONS.
HEY.
NUDEY PICS
NUD PIC

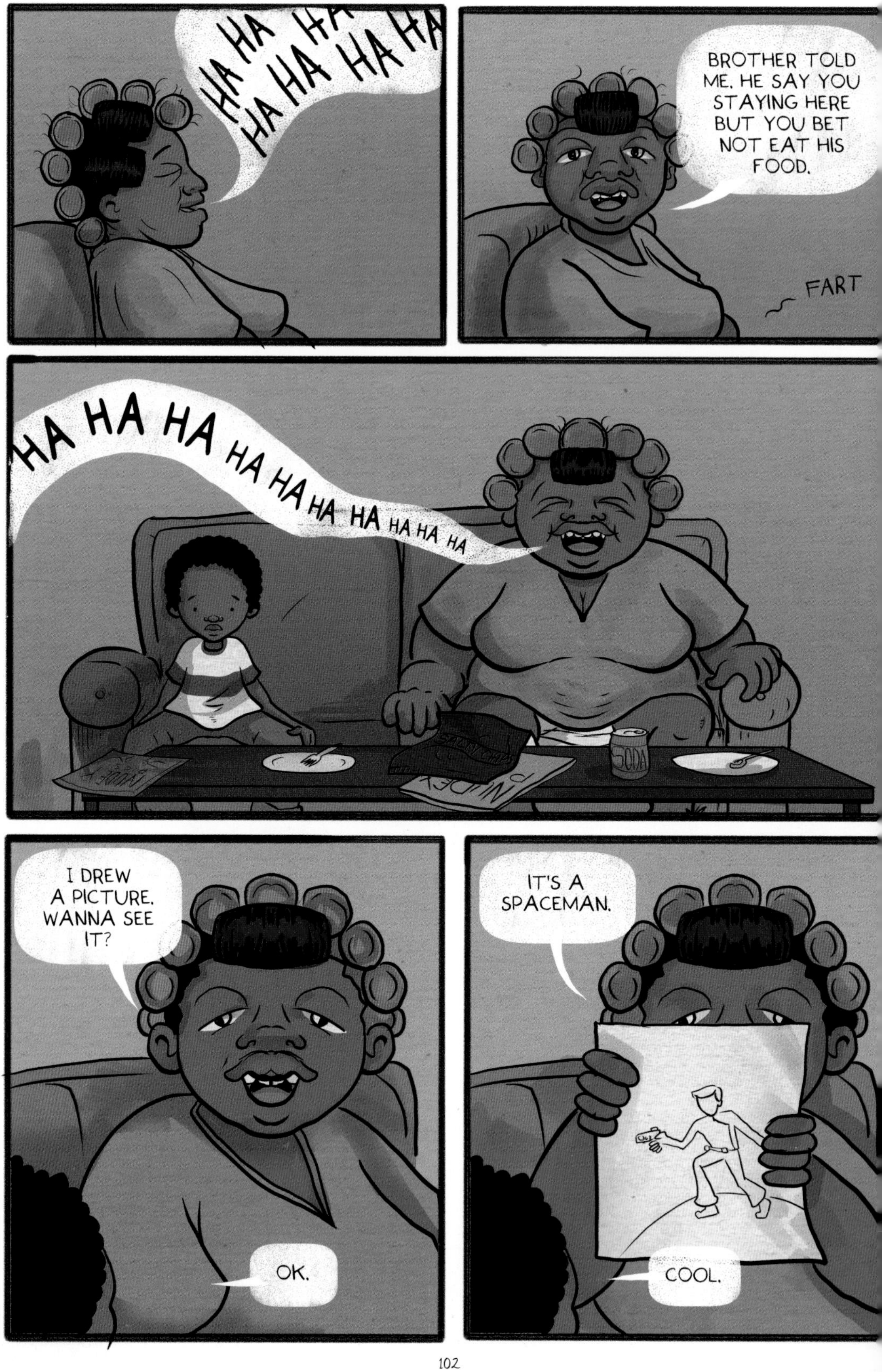
HA HA HA HA HA HA HA
BROTHER TOLD ME. HE SAY YOU STAYING HERE BUT YOU BET NOT EAT HIS FOOD.
FART
HA HA HA HA HA HA HA HA HA HA HA
SODA
I DREW A PICTURE. WANNA SEE IT?
OK.
IT'S A SPACEMAN.
COOL.

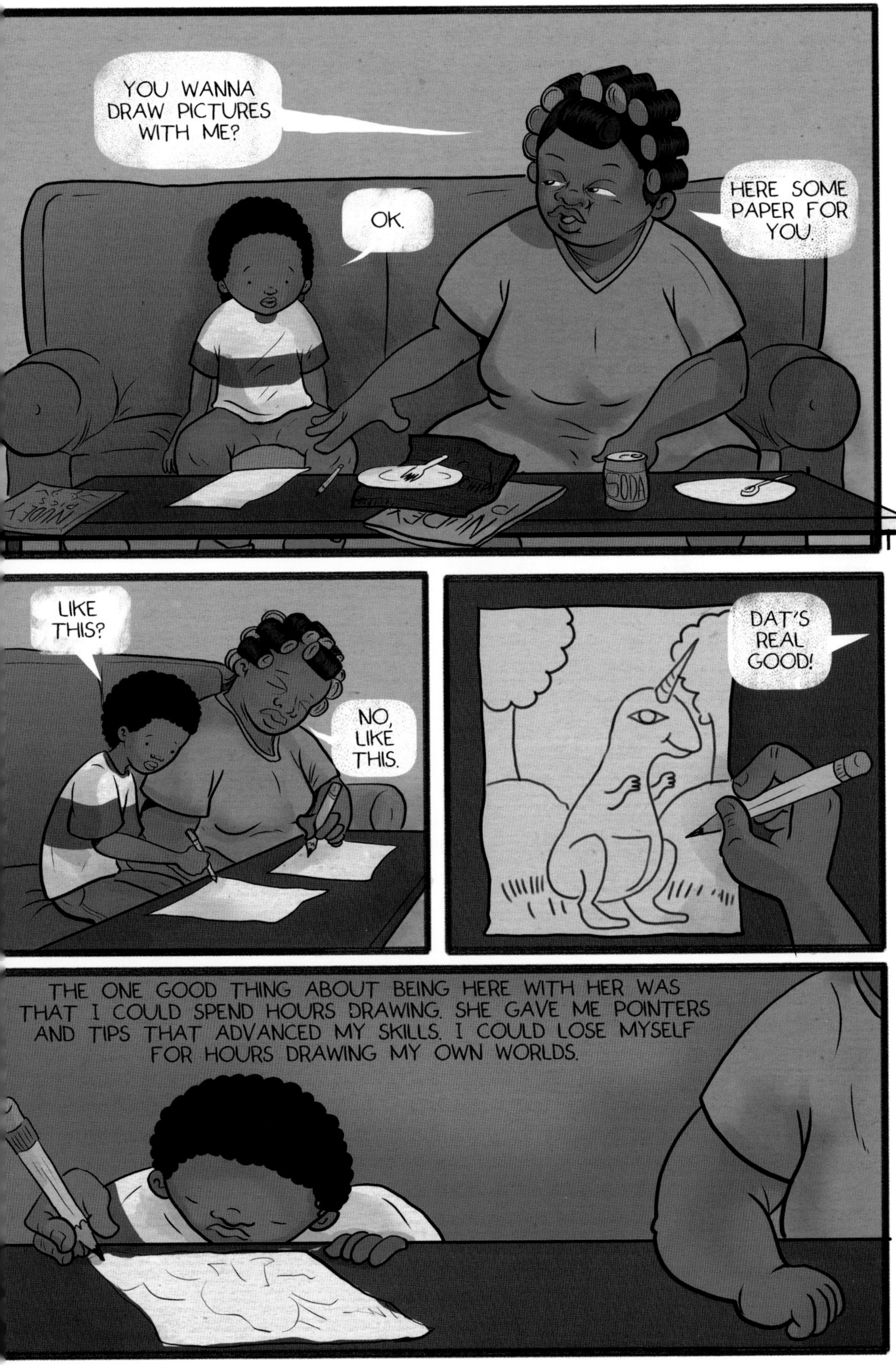
YOU WANNA DRAW PICTURES WITH ME?
OK.
HERE SOME PAPER FOR YOU.
SODA
LIKE THIS?
NO, LIKE THIS.
DAT'S REAL GOOD!
THE ONE GOOD THING ABOUT BEING HERE WITH HER WAS THAT I COULD SPEND HOURS DRAWING. SHE GAVE ME POINTERS AND TIPS THAT ADVANCED MY SKILLS. I COULD LOSE MYSELF FOR HOURS DRAWING MY OWN WORLDS.

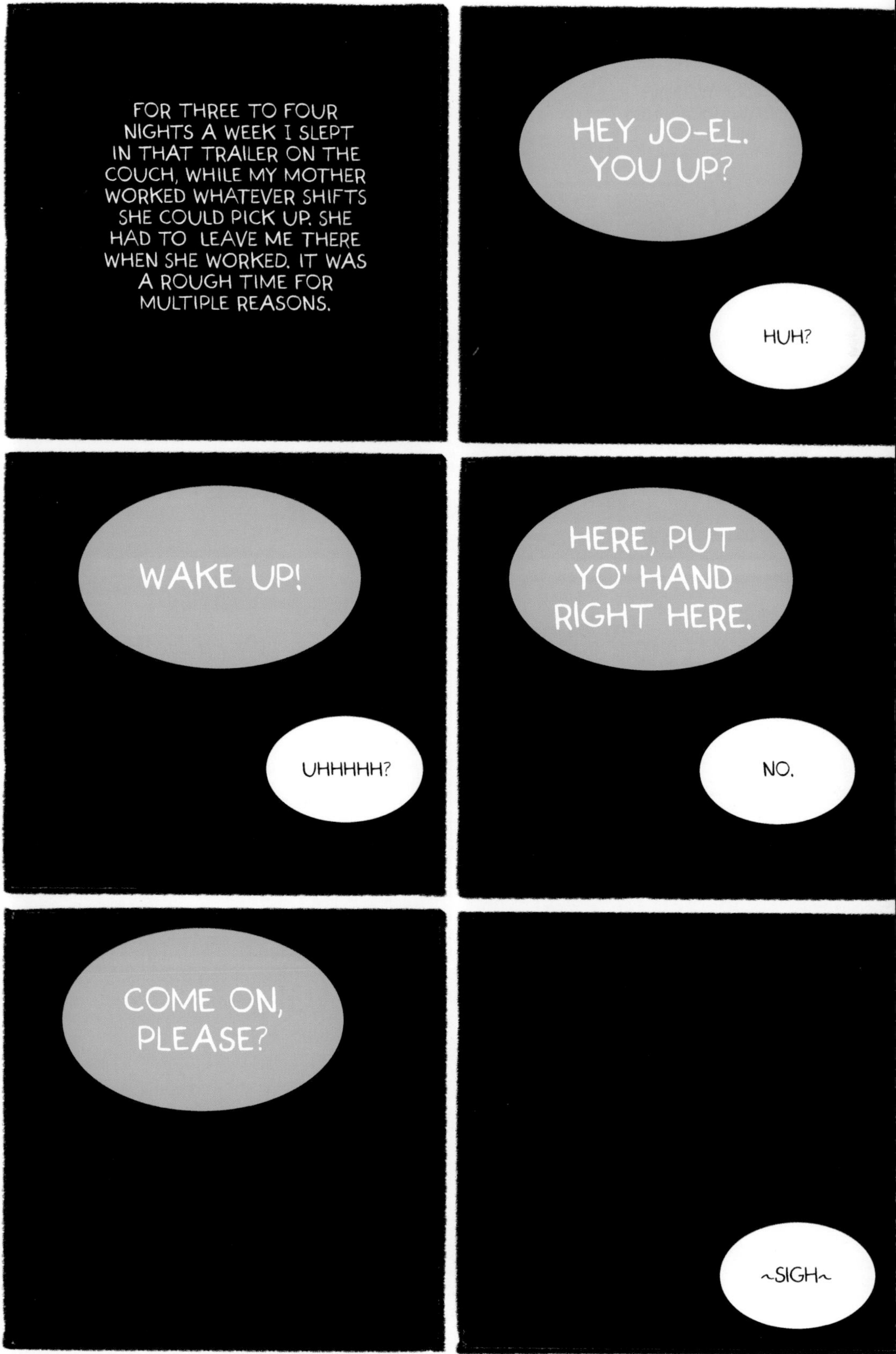
FOR THREE TO FOUR NIGHTS A WEEK I SLEPT IN THAT TRAILER ON THE COUCH, WHILE MY MOTHER WORKED WHATEVER SHIFTS SHE COULD PICK UP. SHE HAD TO LEAVE ME THERE WHEN SHE WORKED. IT WAS A ROUGH TIME FOR MULTIPLE REASONS.
HEY JO-EL. YOU UP?
HUH?
WAKE UP!
UHHHHH?
HERE, PUT YO' HAND RIGHT HERE.
NO.
COME ON, PLEASE?
~SIGH~

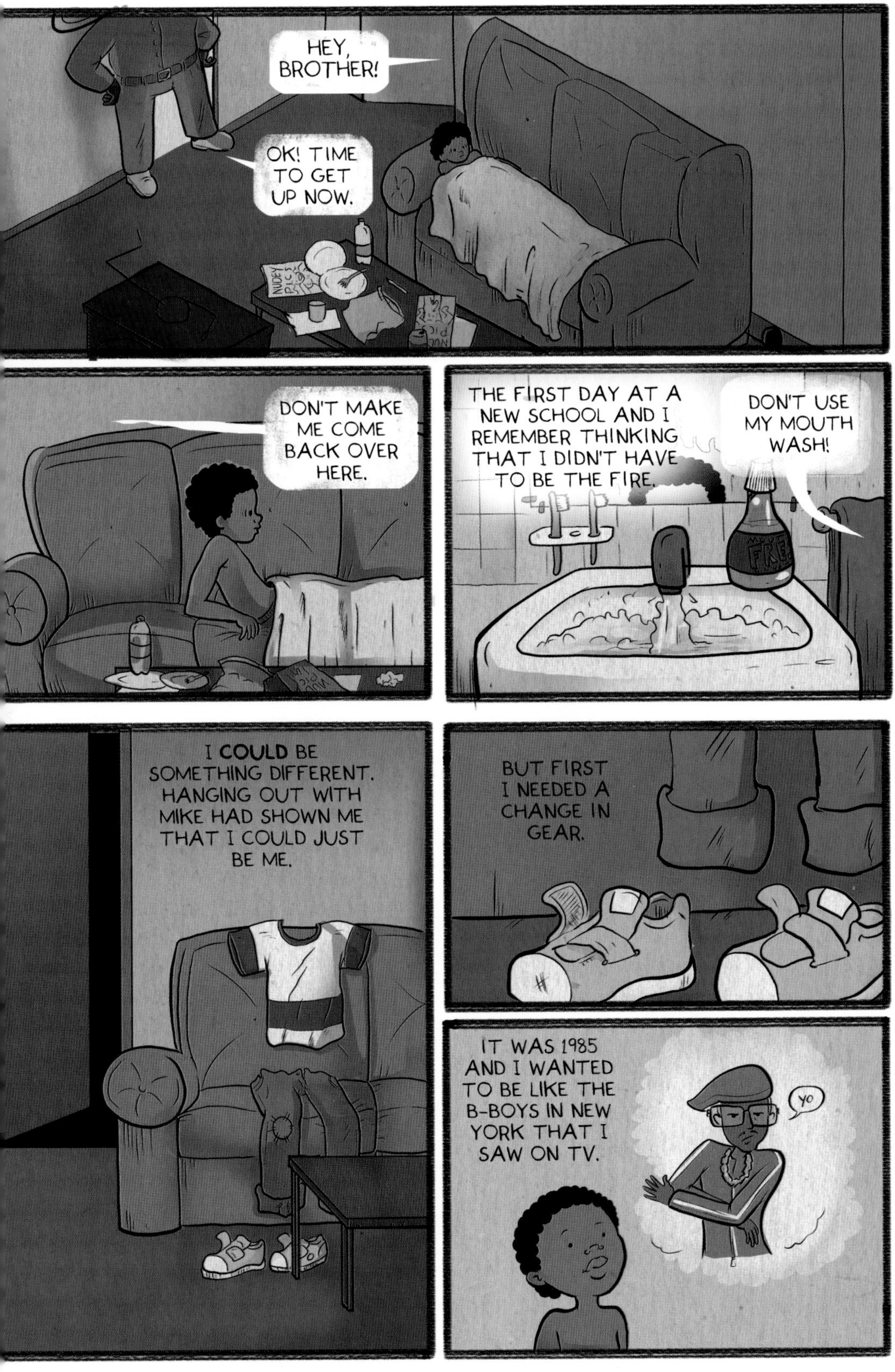
HEY, BROTHER!
OK! TIME TO GET UP NOW.
DON'T MAKE ME COME BACK OVER HERE.
THE FIRST DAY AT A NEW SCHOOL AND I REMEMBER THINKING THAT I DIDN'T HAVE TO BE THE FIRE.
DON'T USE MY MOUTH WASH!
I **COULD** BE SOMETHING DIFFERENT. HANGING OUT WITH MIKE HAD SHOWN ME THAT I COULD JUST BE ME.
BUT FIRST I NEEDED A CHANGE IN GEAR.
IT WAS 1985 AND I WANTED TO BE LIKE THE B-BOYS IN NEW YORK THAT I SAW ON TV.
YO

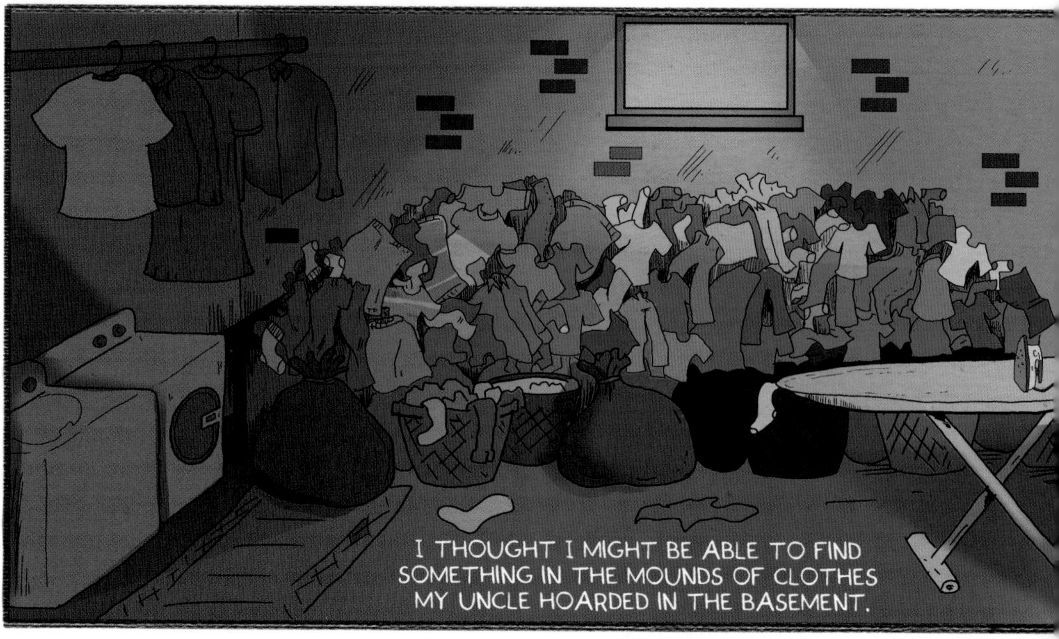
I THOUGHT I MIGHT BE ABLE TO FIND SOMETHING IN THE MOUNDS OF CLOTHES MY UNCLE HOARDED IN THE BASEMENT.

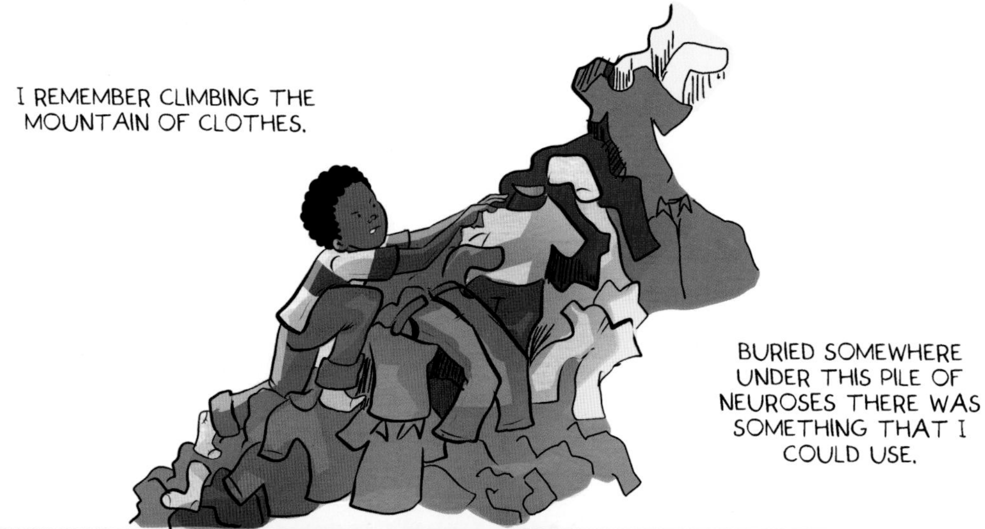
I REMEMBER CLIMBING THE MOUNTAIN OF CLOTHES.
BURIED SOMEWHERE UNDER THIS PILE OF NEUROSES THERE WAS SOMETHING THAT I COULD USE.

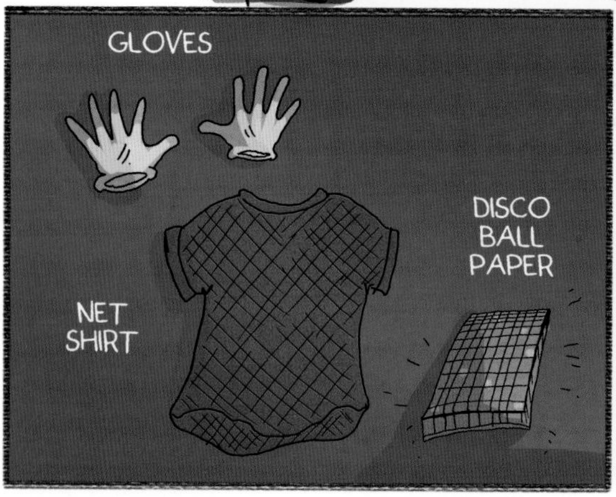
GLOVES
DISCO BALL PAPER
NET SHIRT

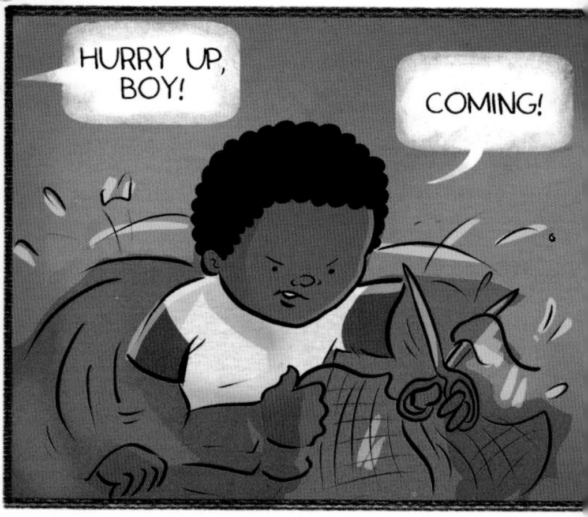
HURRY UP, BOY!
COMING!

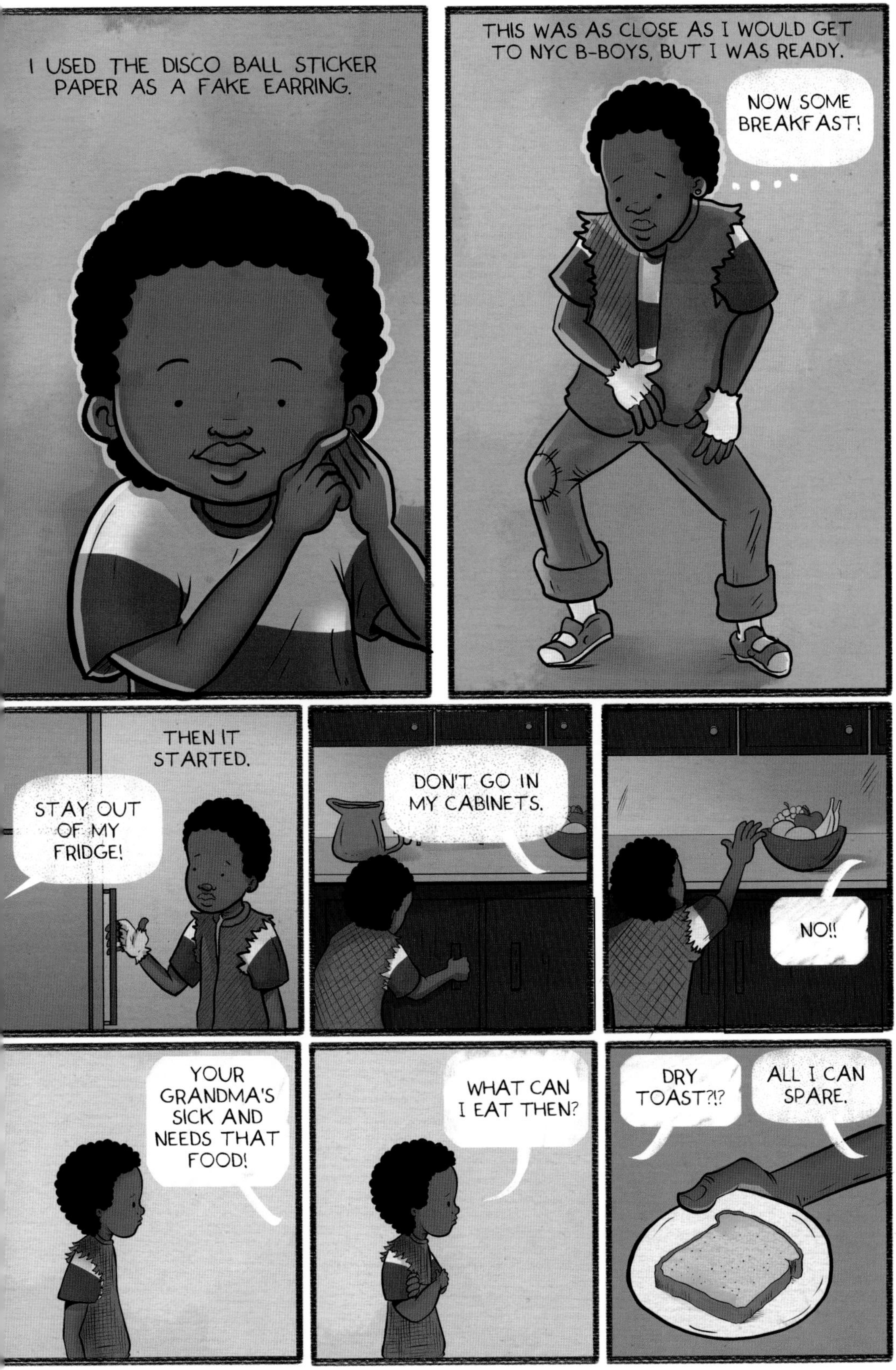
I USED THE DISCO BALL STICKER PAPER AS A FAKE EARRING.
THIS WAS AS CLOSE AS I WOULD GET TO NYC B-BOYS, BUT I WAS READY.
NOW SOME BREAKFAST!
THEN IT STARTED.
STAY OUT OF MY FRIDGE!
DON'T GO IN MY CABINETS.
NO!!
YOUR GRANDMA'S SICK AND NEEDS THAT FOOD!
WHAT CAN I EAT THEN?
DRY TOAST?!?
ALL I CAN SPARE.

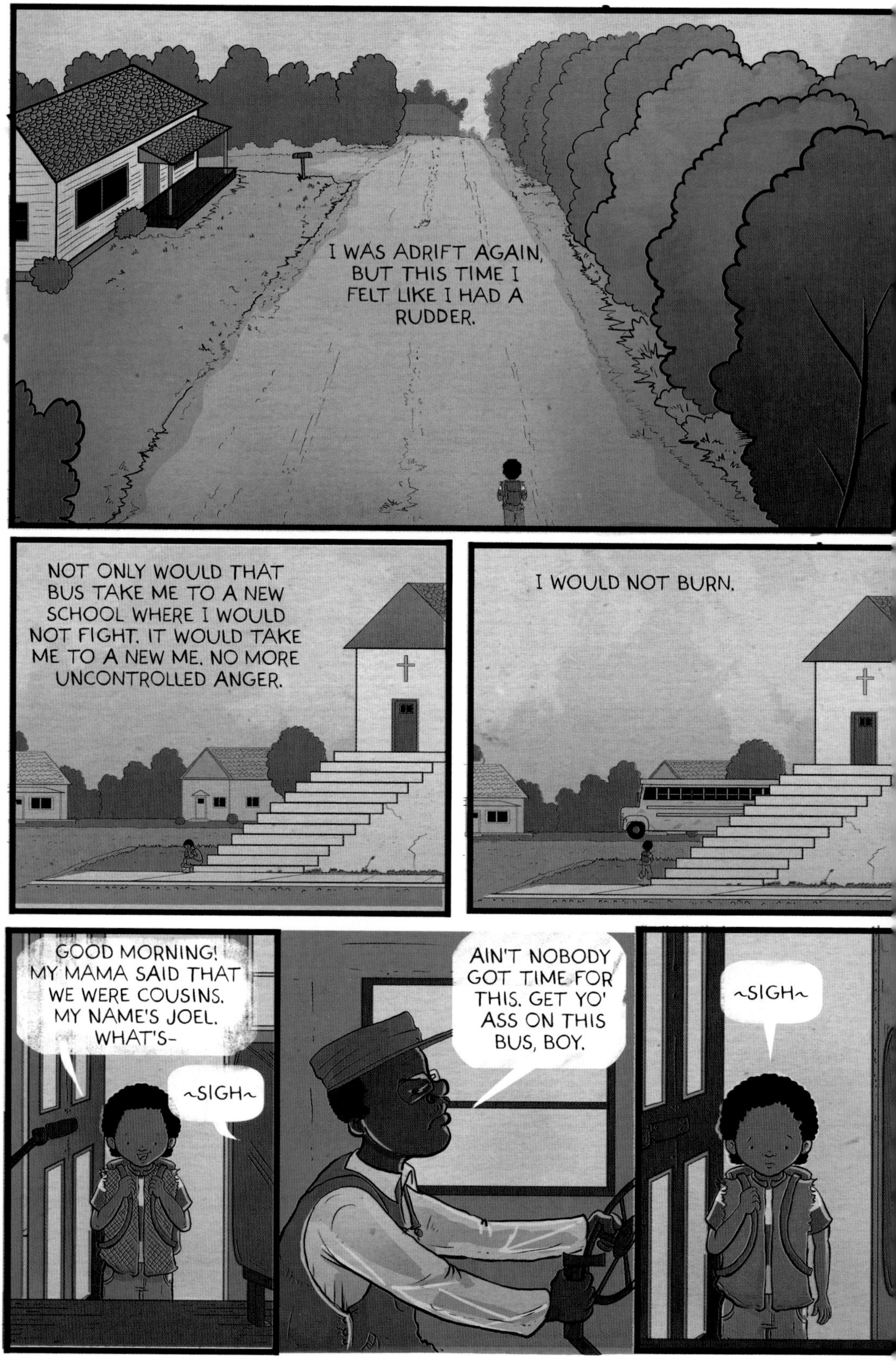
I WAS ADRIFT AGAIN, BUT THIS TIME I FELT LIKE I HAD A RUDDER.
NOT ONLY WOULD THAT BUS TAKE ME TO A NEW SCHOOL WHERE I WOULD NOT FIGHT. IT WOULD TAKE ME TO A NEW ME. NO MORE UNCONTROLLED ANGER.
I WOULD NOT BURN.
GOOD MORNING! MY MAMA SAID THAT WE WERE COUSINS. MY NAME'S JOEL. WHAT'S-
~SIGH~
AIN'T NOBODY GOT TIME FOR THIS. GET YO' ASS ON THIS BUS, BOY.
~SIGH~

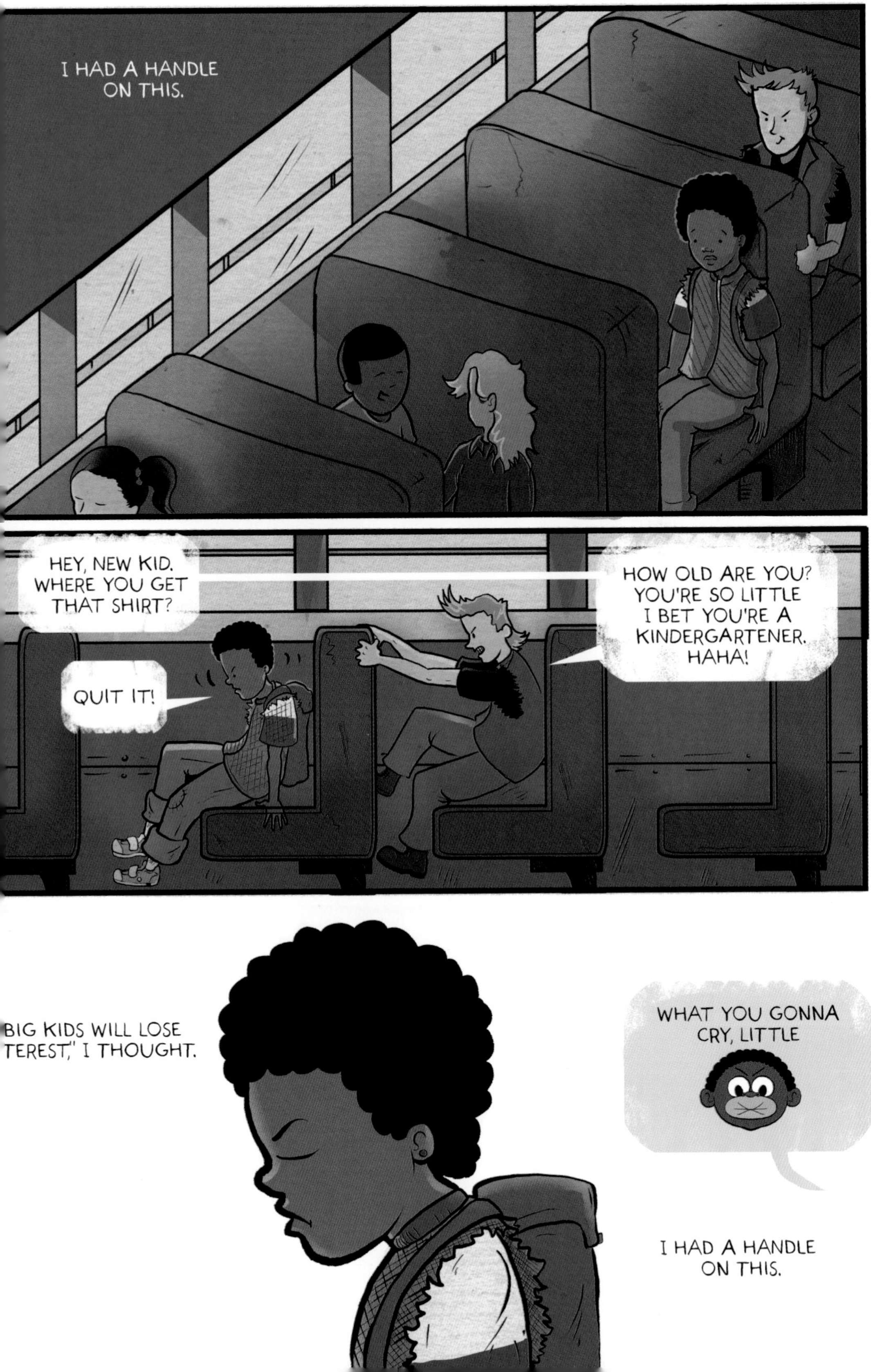
I HAD A HANDLE ON THIS.
HEY, NEW KID. WHERE YOU GET THAT SHIRT?
HOW OLD ARE YOU? YOU'RE SO LITTLE I BET YOU'RE A KINDERGARTENER. HAHA!
QUIT IT!
BIG KIDS WILL LOSE
TEREST," I THOUGHT.
WHAT YOU GONNA CRY, LITTLE
I HAD A HANDLE ON THIS.

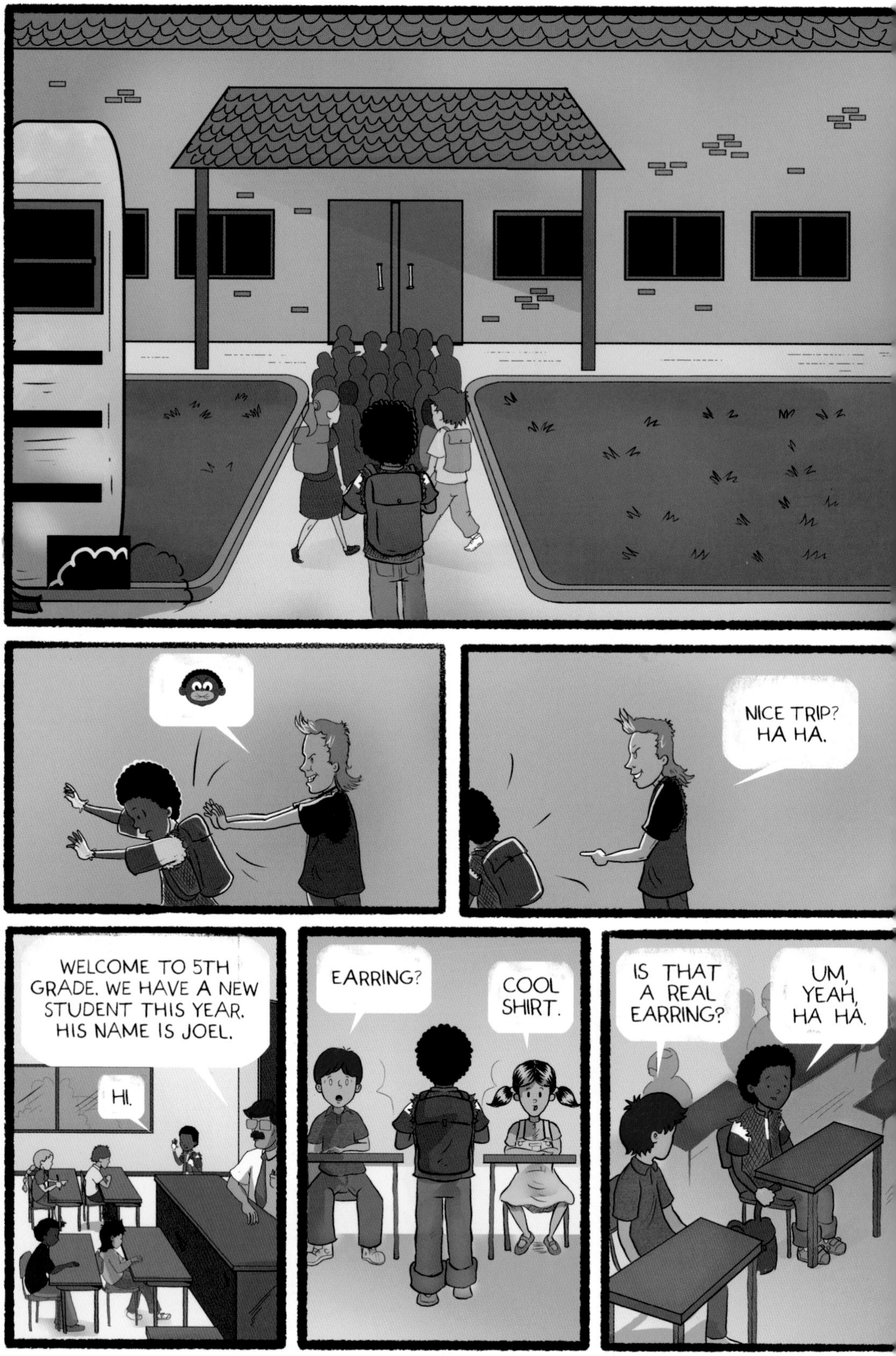
NICE TRIP? HA HA.
WELCOME TO 5TH GRADE. WE HAVE A NEW STUDENT THIS YEAR. HIS NAME IS JOEL.
HI.
EARRING?
COOL SHIRT.
IS THAT A REAL EARRING?
UM, YEAH, HA HA.

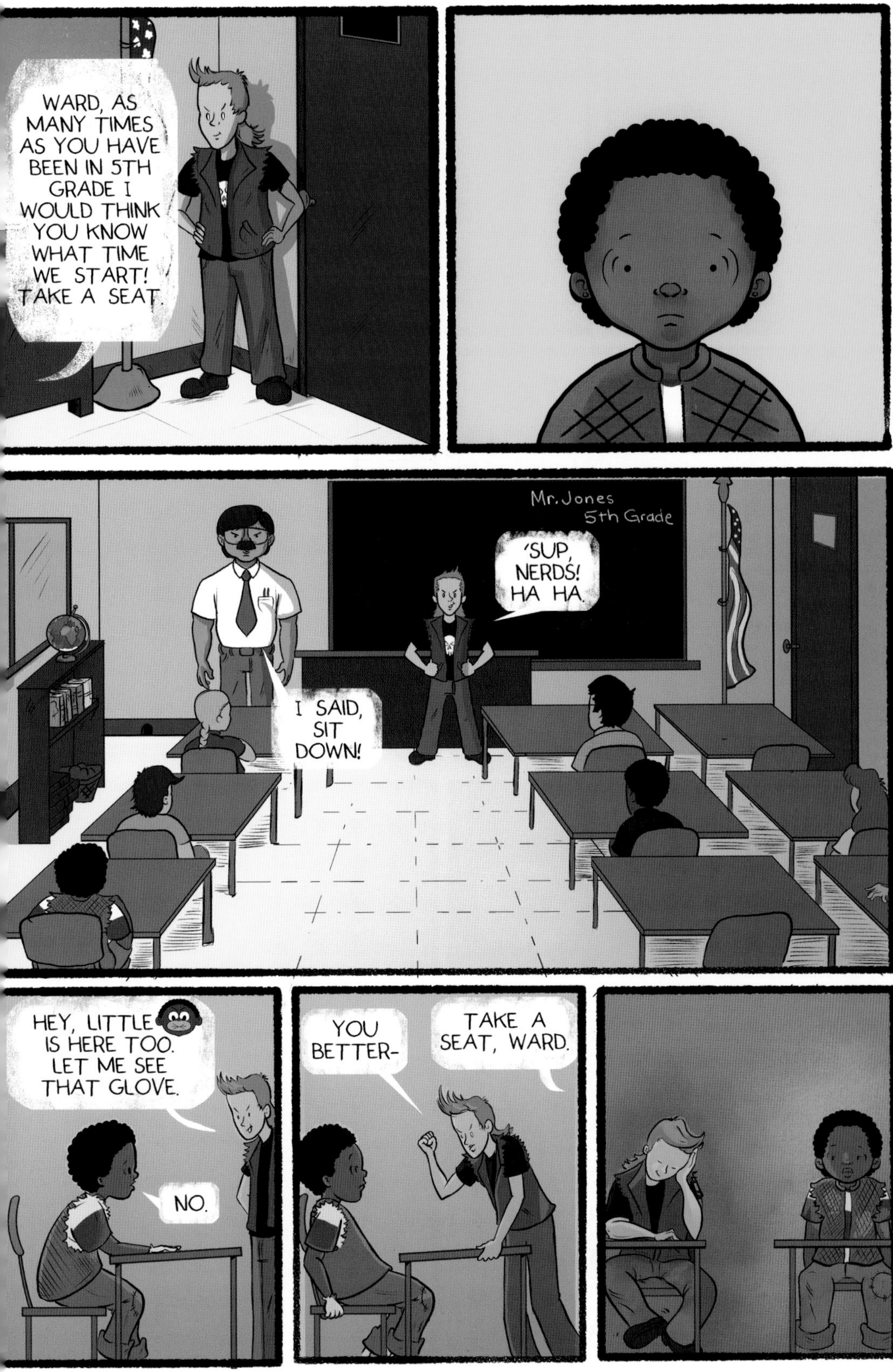
WARD, AS MANY TIMES AS YOU HAVE BEEN IN 5TH GRADE I WOULD THINK YOU KNOW WHAT TIME WE START! TAKE A SEAT.
Mr. Jones 5th Grade
'SUP, NERDS! HA HA.
I SAID, SIT DOWN!
HEY, LITTLE IS HERE TOO. LET ME SEE THAT GLOVE.
NO.
YOU BETTER-
TAKE A SEAT, WARD.

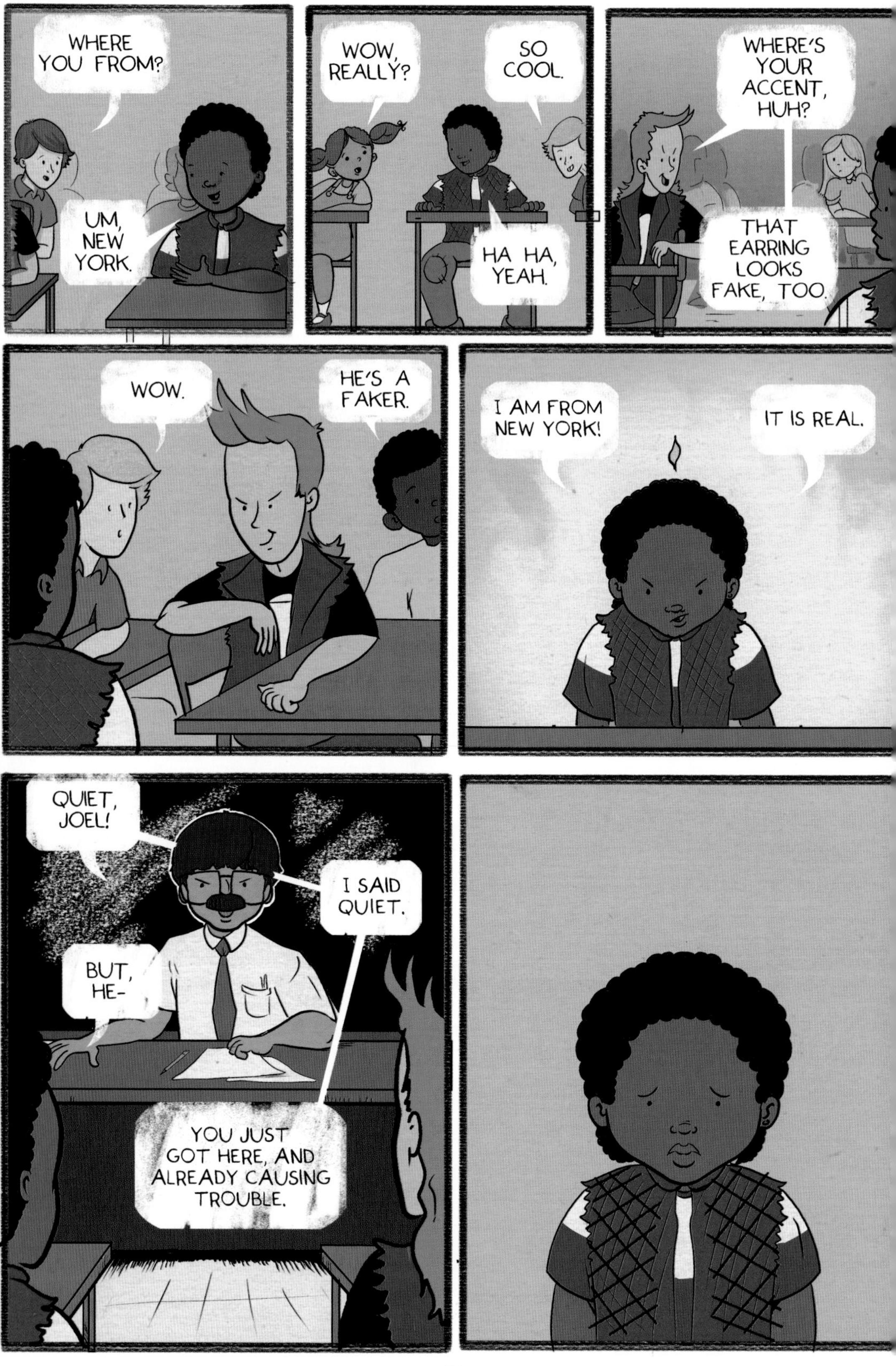
WHERE YOU FROM?
UM, NEW YORK.
WOW, REALLY?
SO COOL.
HA HA, YEAH.
WHERE'S YOUR ACCENT, HUH?
THAT EARRING LOOKS FAKE, TOO.
WOW.
HE'S A FAKER.
I AM FROM NEW YORK!
IT IS REAL.
QUIET, JOEL!
I SAID QUIET.
BUT, HE-
YOU JUST GOT HERE, AND ALREADY CAUSING TROUBLE.

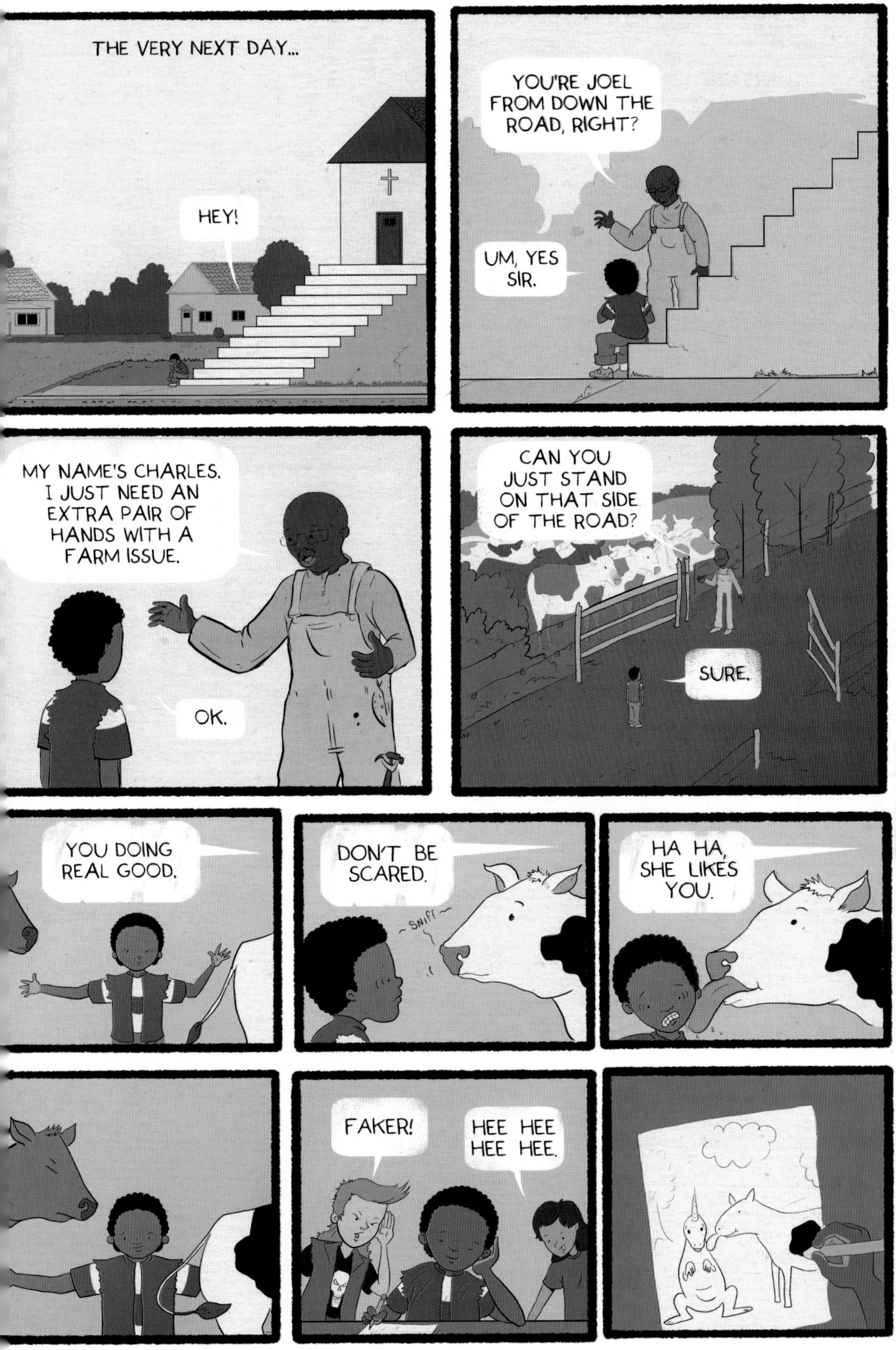
THE VERY NEXT DAY...
HEY!
YOU'RE JOEL FROM DOWN THE ROAD, RIGHT?
UM, YES SIR.
MY NAME'S CHARLES. I JUST NEED AN EXTRA PAIR OF HANDS WITH A FARM ISSUE.
OK.
CAN YOU JUST STAND ON THAT SIDE OF THE ROAD?
SURE.
YOU DOING REAL GOOD.
DON'T BE SCARED.
~SNIFF~
HA HA, SHE LIKES YOU.
FAKER!
HEE HEE HEE HEE.

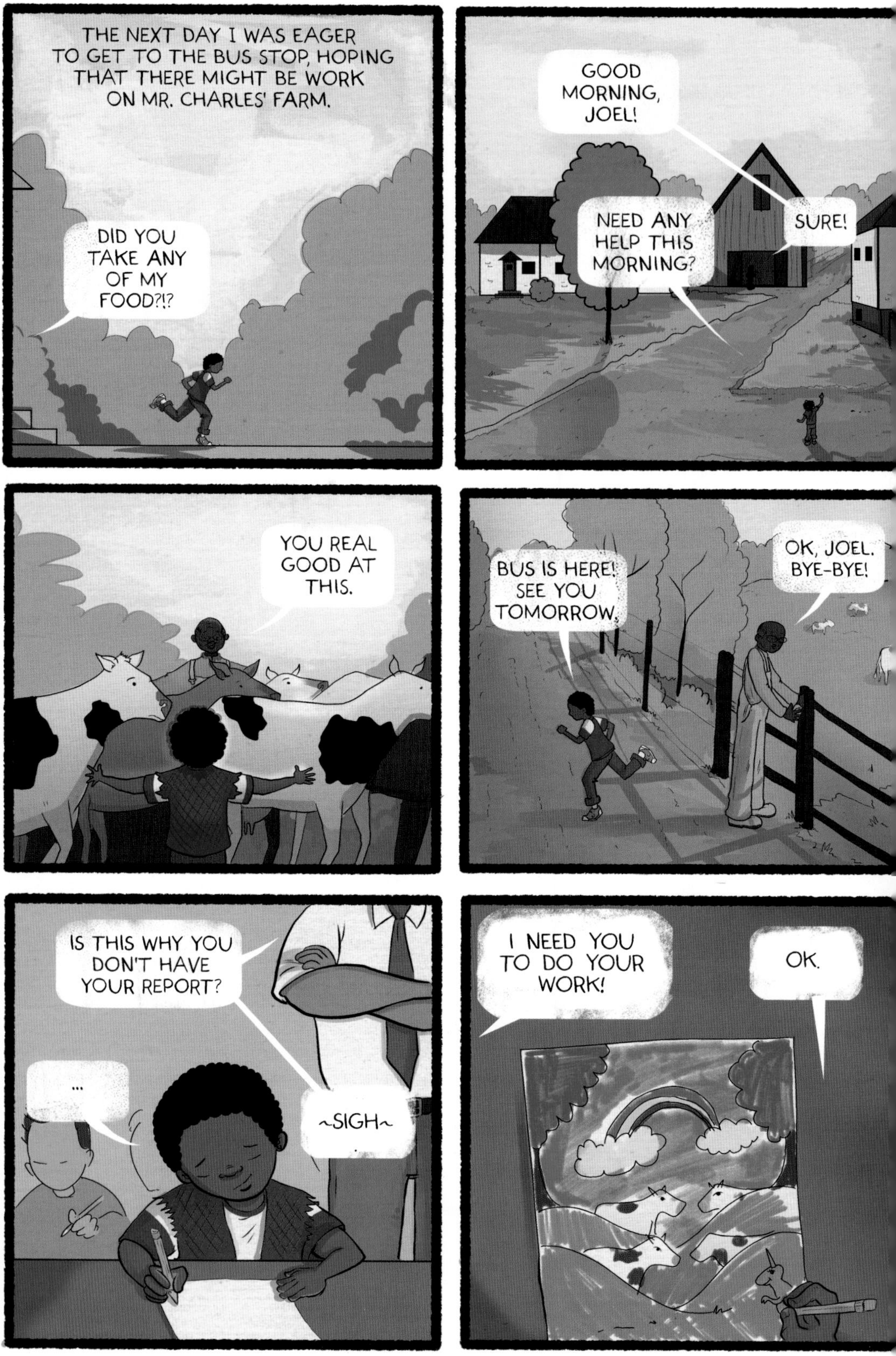
THE NEXT DAY I WAS EAGER TO GET TO THE BUS STOP, HOPING THAT THERE MIGHT BE WORK ON MR. CHARLES' FARM.
DID YOU TAKE ANY OF MY FOOD?!?
GOOD MORNING, JOEL!
NEED ANY HELP THIS MORNING?
SURE!
YOU REAL GOOD AT THIS.
BUS IS HERE! SEE YOU TOMORROW.
OK, JOEL. BYE-BYE!
IS THIS WHY YOU DON'T HAVE YOUR REPORT?
...
~SIGH~
I NEED YOU TO DO YOUR WORK!
OK.

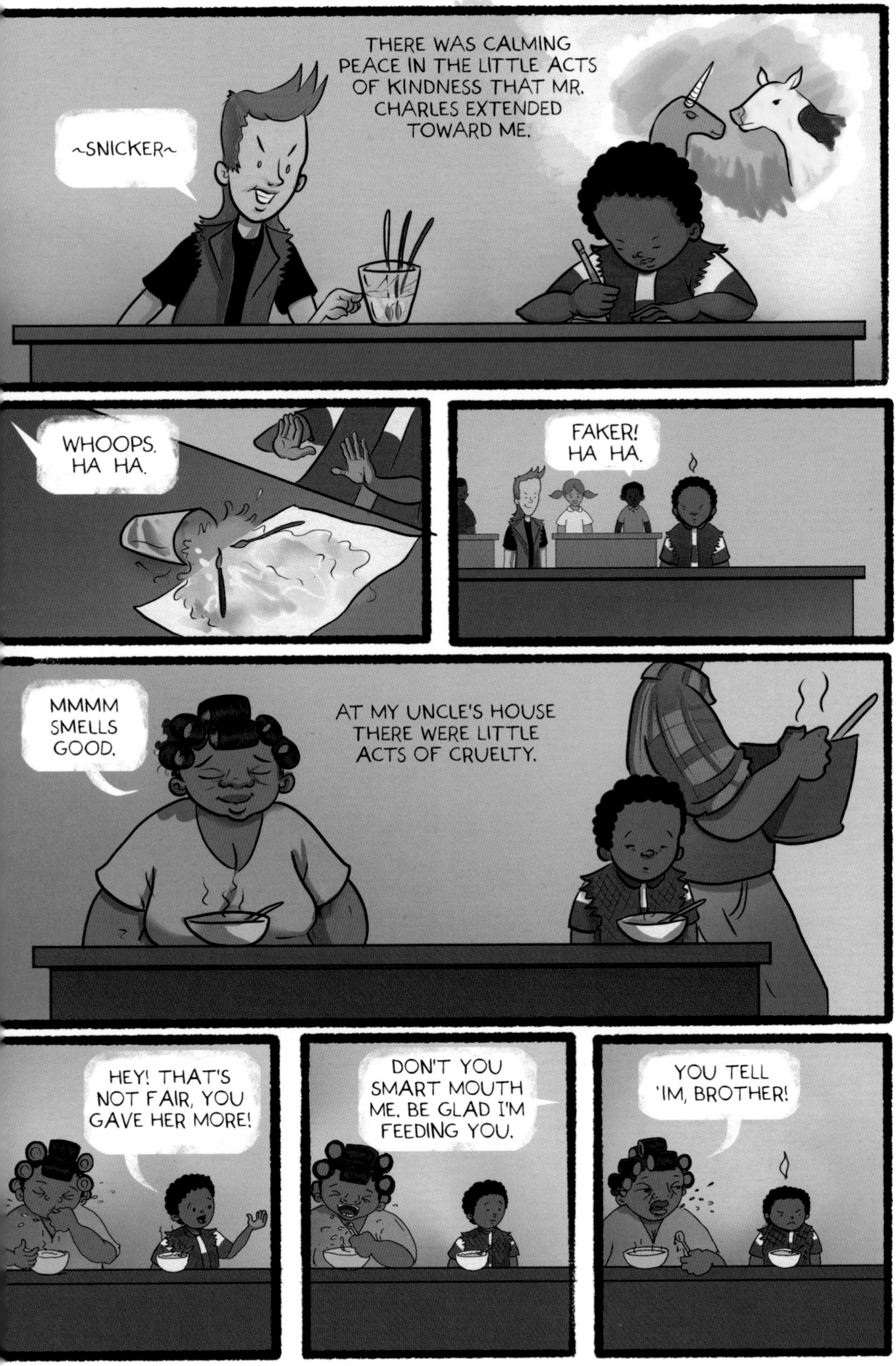

THERE WAS CALMING PEACE IN THE LITTLE ACTS OF KINDNESS THAT MR. CHARLES EXTENDED TOWARD ME.
~SNICKER~
WHOOPS. HA HA.
FAKER! HA HA.
MMMM SMELLS GOOD.
AT MY UNCLE'S HOUSE THERE WERE LITTLE ACTS OF CRUELTY.
HEY! THAT'S NOT FAIR, YOU GAVE HER MORE!
DON'T YOU SMART MOUTH ME. BE GLAD I'M FEEDING YOU.
YOU TELL 'IM, BROTHER!

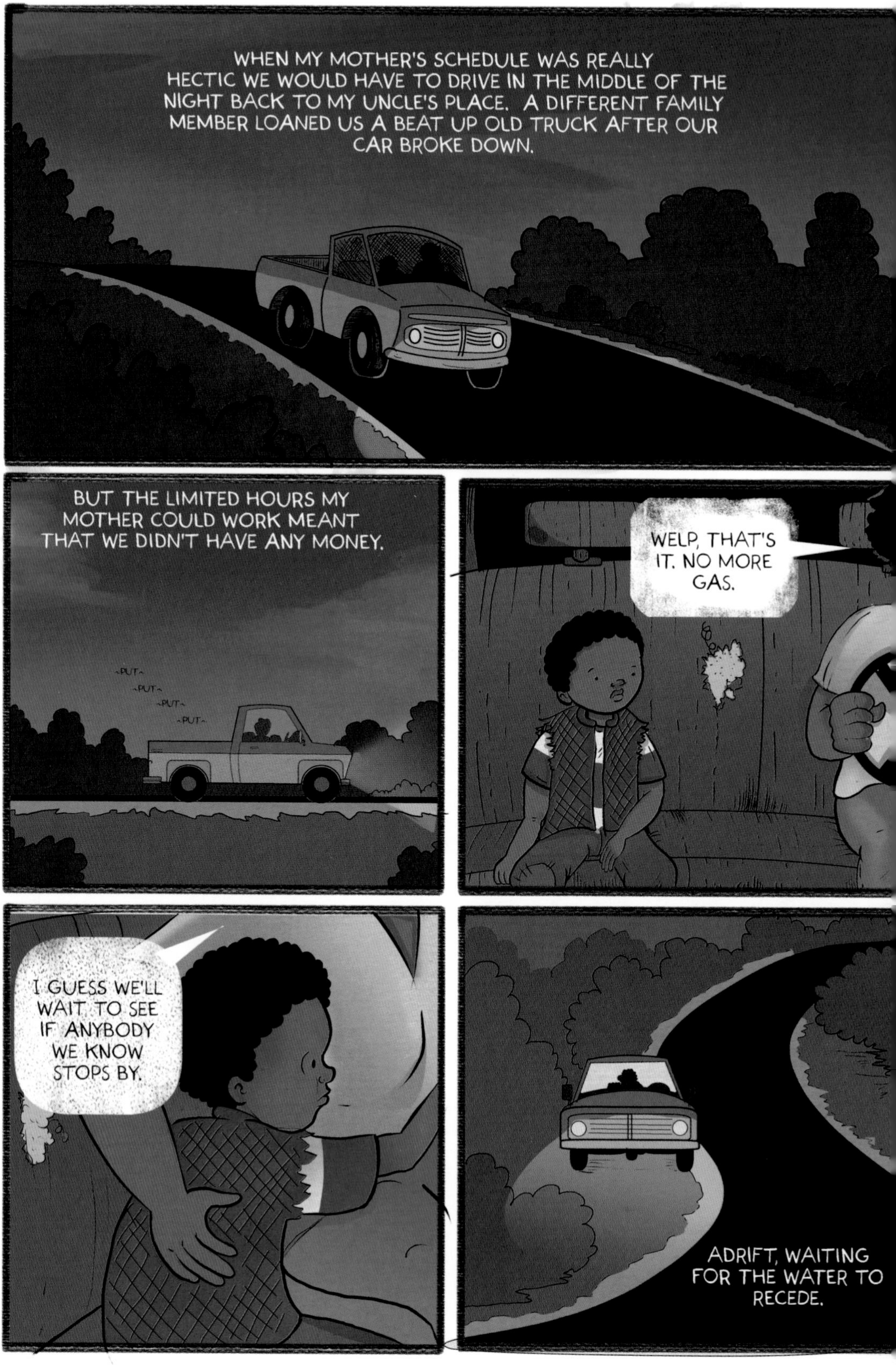
WHEN MY MOTHER'S SCHEDULE WAS REALLY HECTIC WE WOULD HAVE TO DRIVE IN THE MIDDLE OF THE NIGHT BACK TO MY UNCLE'S PLACE. A DIFFERENT FAMILY MEMBER LOANED US A BEAT UP OLD TRUCK AFTER OUR CAR BROKE DOWN.
BUT THE LIMITED HOURS MY MOTHER COULD WORK MEANT THAT WE DIDN'T HAVE ANY MONEY.
~PUT~
~PUT~
~PUT~
~PUT~
WELP, THAT'S IT. NO MORE GAS.
I GUESS WE'LL WAIT TO SEE IF ANYBODY WE KNOW STOPS BY.
ADRIFT, WAITING FOR THE WATER TO RECEDE.

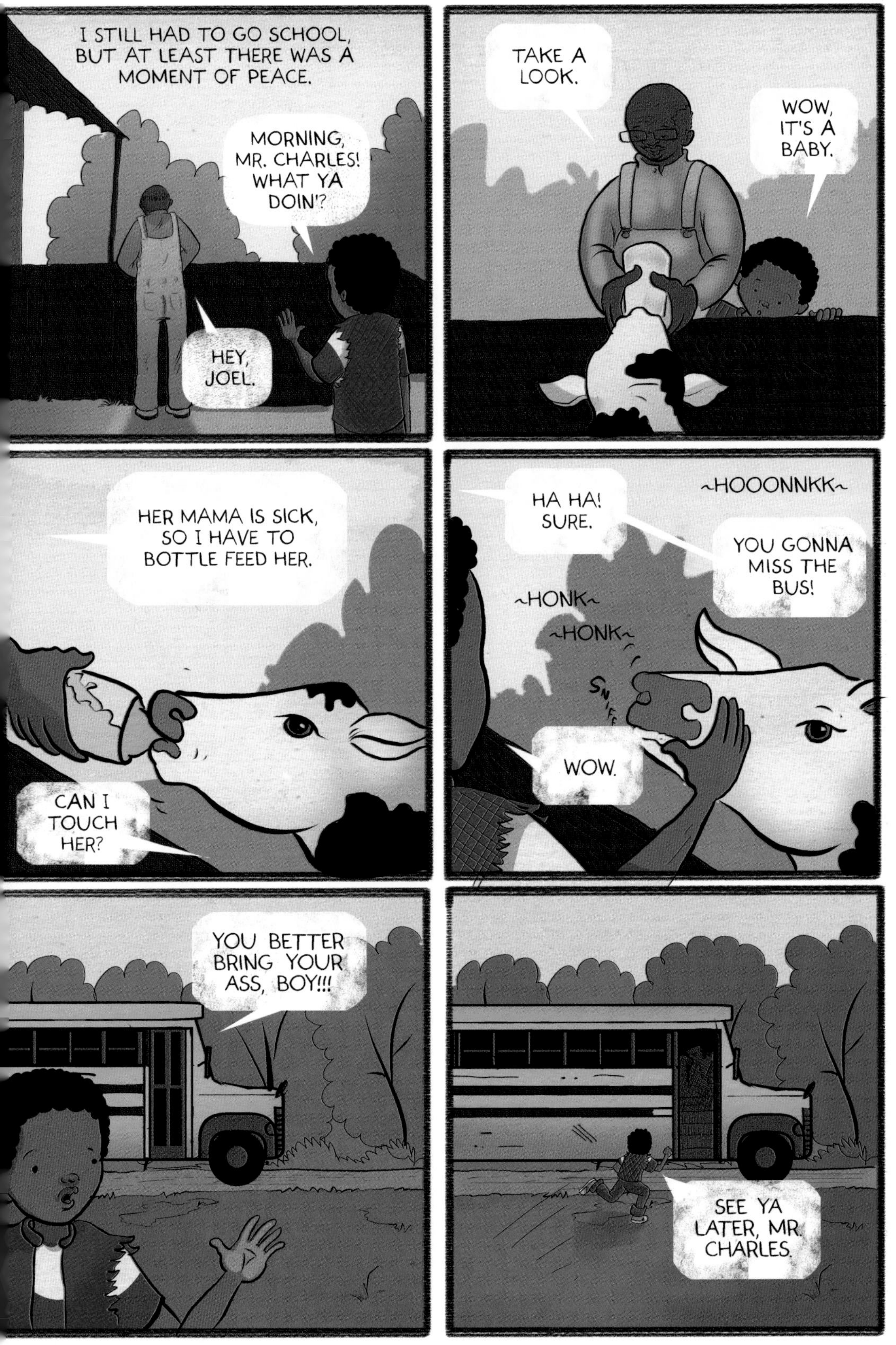
I STILL HAD TO GO SCHOOL, BUT AT LEAST THERE WAS A MOMENT OF PEACE.
MORNING, MR. CHARLES! WHAT YA DOIN'?
HEY, JOEL.
TAKE A LOOK.
WOW, IT'S A BABY.
HER MAMA IS SICK, SO I HAVE TO BOTTLE FEED HER.
CAN I TOUCH HER?
HA HA! SURE.
~HOOONNKK~
YOU GONNA MISS THE BUS!
~HONK~
~HONK~
SNIFF
WOW.
YOU BETTER BRING YOUR ASS, BOY!!!
SEE YA LATER, MR. CHARLES.

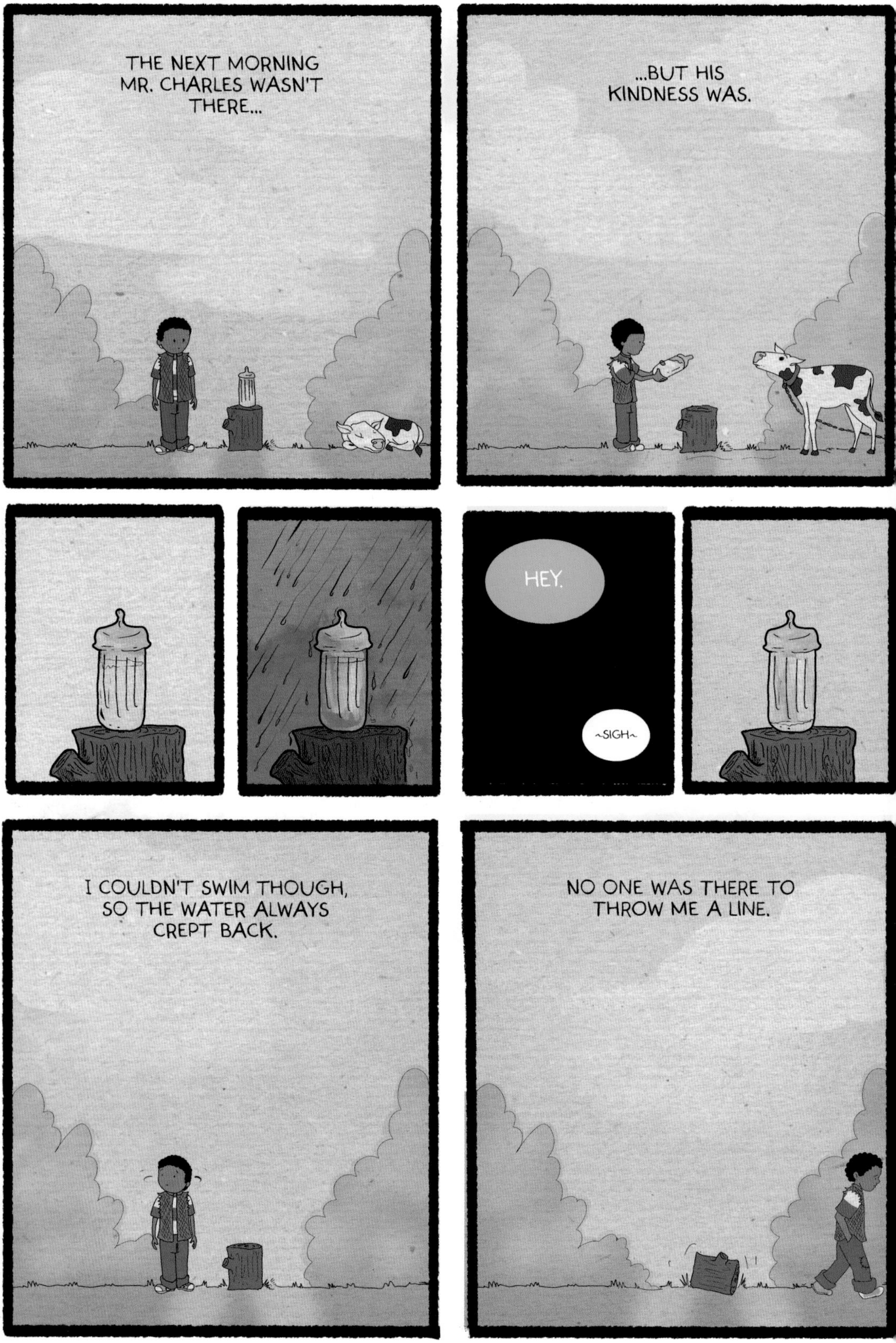
THE NEXT MORNING MR. CHARLES WASN'T THERE...
...BUT HIS KINDNESS WAS.
HEY.
~SIGH~
I COULDN'T SWIM THOUGH, SO THE WATER ALWAYS CREPT BACK.
NO ONE WAS THERE TO THROW ME A LINE.

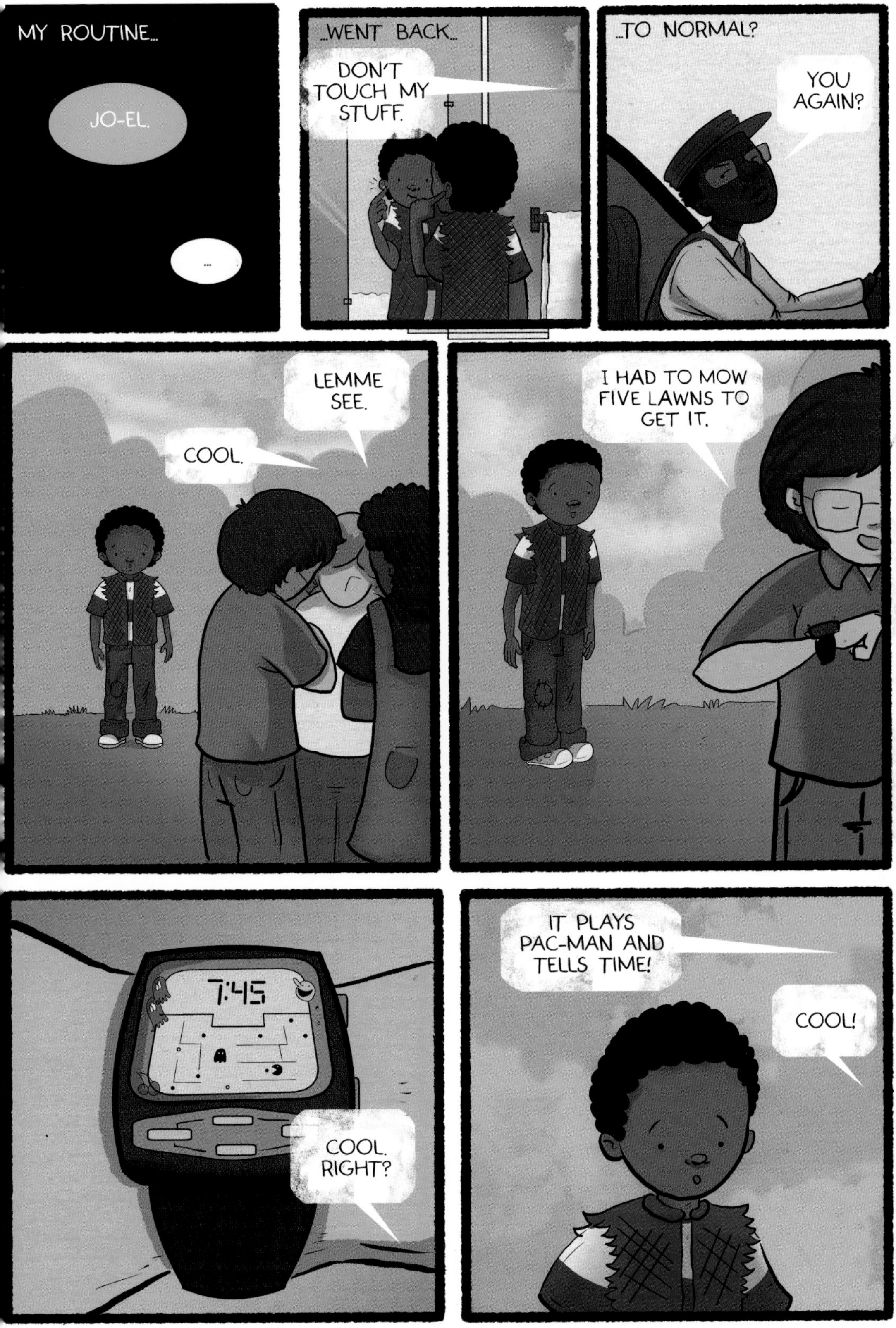
MY ROUTINE...
JO-EL.
...
...WENT BACK...
DON'T TOUCH MY STUFF.
...TO NORMAL?
YOU AGAIN?
COOL.
LEMME SEE.
I HAD TO MOW FIVE LAWNS TO GET IT.
7:45
COOL. RIGHT?
IT PLAYS PAC-MAN AND TELLS TIME!
COOL!

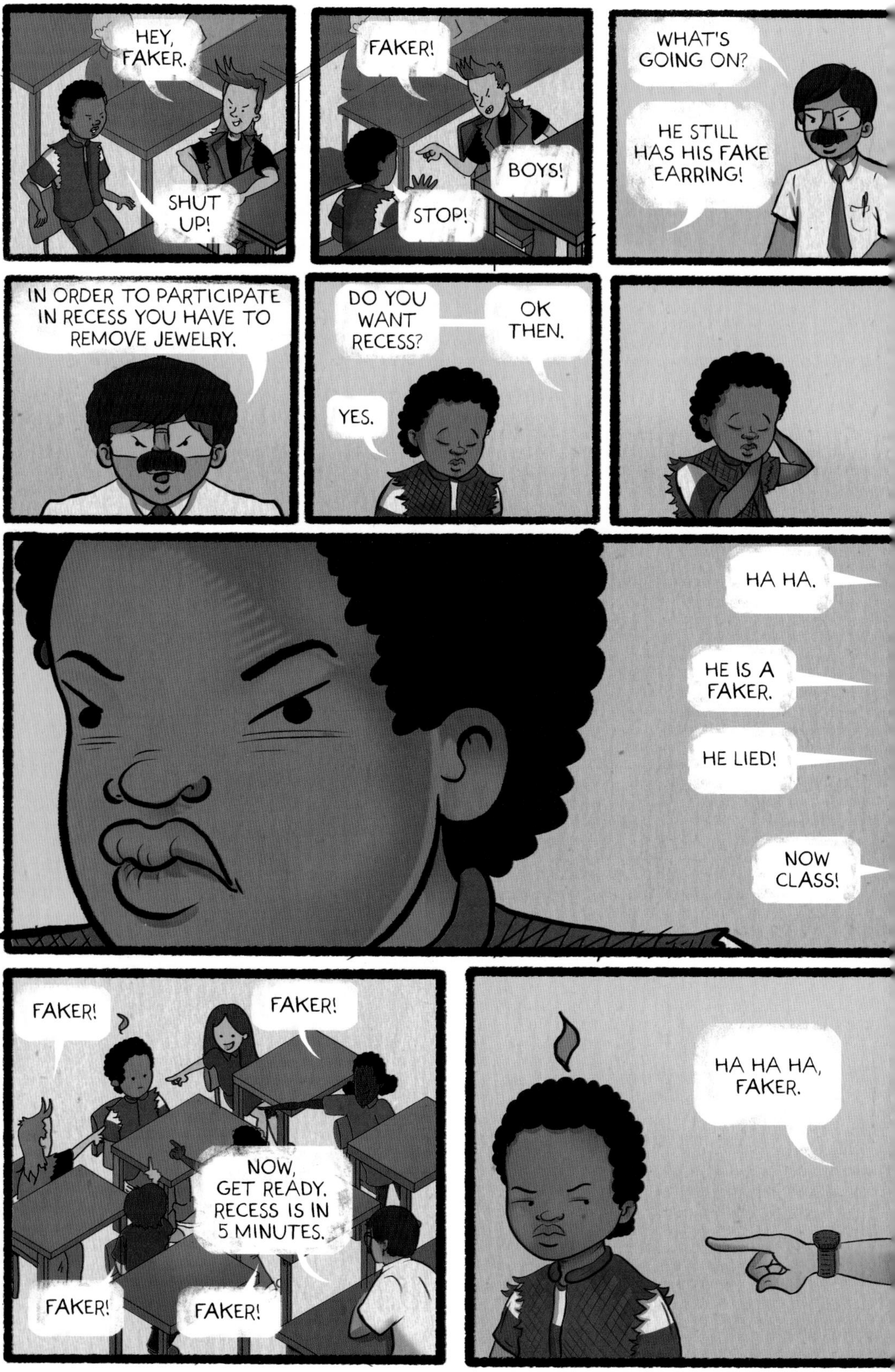
HEY, FAKER.
SHUT UP!
FAKER!
BOYS!
STOP!
WHAT'S GOING ON?
HE STILL HAS HIS FAKE EARRING!
IN ORDER TO PARTICIPATE IN RECESS YOU HAVE TO REMOVE JEWELRY.
DO YOU WANT RECESS?
OK THEN.
YES.
HA HA.
HE IS A FAKER.
HE LIED!
NOW CLASS!
FAKER!
FAKER!
NOW, GET READY. RECESS IS IN 5 MINUTES.
FAKER!
FAKER!
HA HA HA, FAKER.

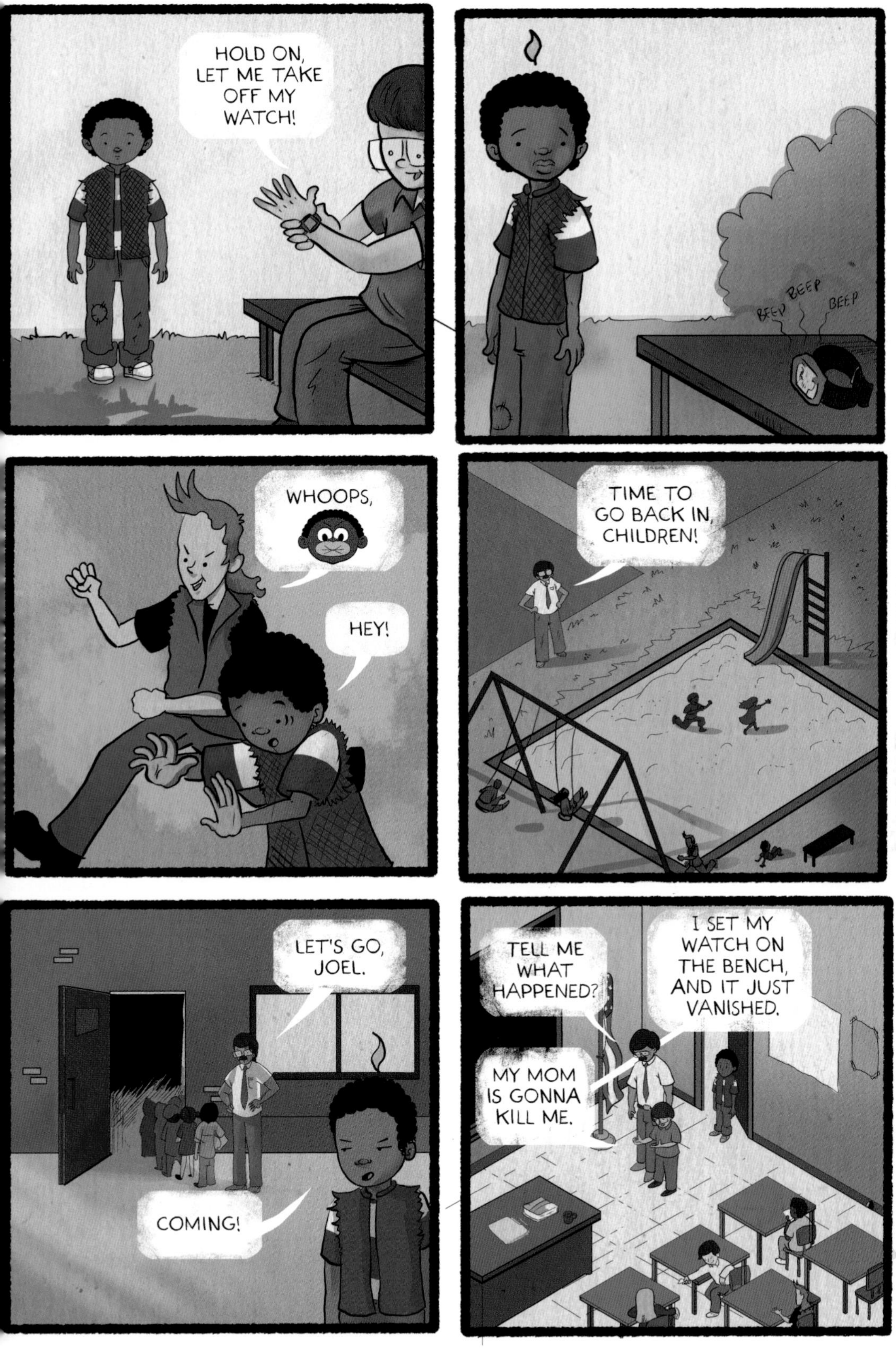
HOLD ON, LET ME TAKE OFF MY WATCH!
BEEP BEEP BEEP
WHOOPS,
HEY!
TIME TO GO BACK IN, CHILDREN!
LET'S GO, JOEL.
COMING!
TELL ME WHAT HAPPENED?
I SET MY WATCH ON THE BENCH, AND IT JUST VANISHED.
MY MOM IS GONNA KILL ME.

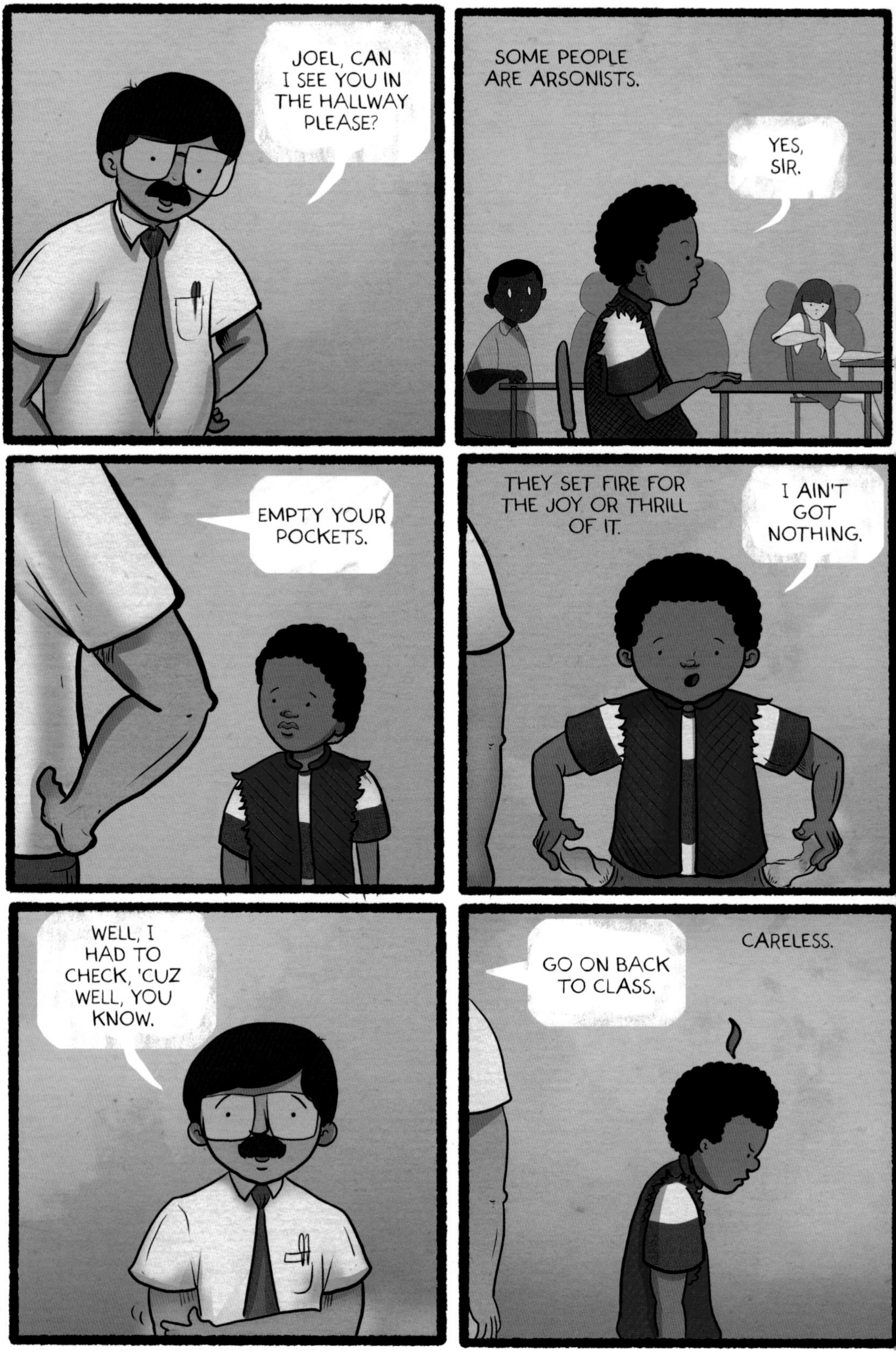
JOEL, CAN I SEE YOU IN THE HALLWAY PLEASE?
SOME PEOPLE ARE ARSONISTS.
YES, SIR.
EMPTY YOUR POCKETS.
THEY SET FIRE FOR THE JOY OR THRILL OF IT.
I AIN'T GOT NOTHING.
WELL, I HAD TO CHECK, 'CUZ WELL, YOU KNOW.
GO ON BACK TO CLASS.
CARELESS.

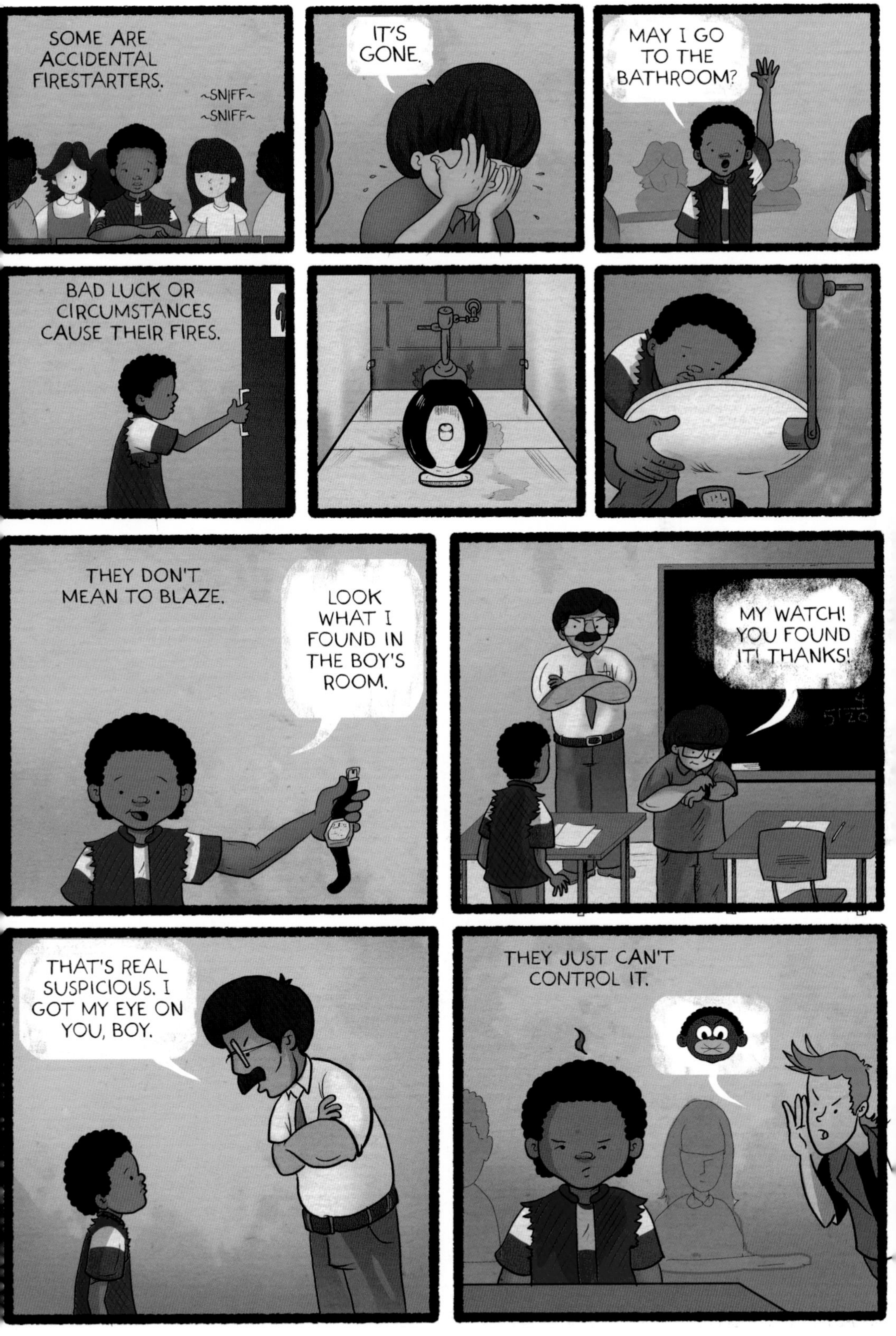
SOME ARE ACCIDENTAL FIRESTARTERS.
~SNIFF~
~SNIFF~
IT'S GONE.
MAY I GO TO THE BATHROOM?
BAD LUCK OR CIRCUMSTANCES CAUSE THEIR FIRES.
THEY DON'T MEAN TO BLAZE.
LOOK WHAT I FOUND IN THE BOY'S ROOM.
MY WATCH! YOU FOUND IT! THANKS!
THAT'S REAL SUSPICIOUS. I GOT MY EYE ON YOU, BOY.
THEY JUST CAN'T CONTROL IT.

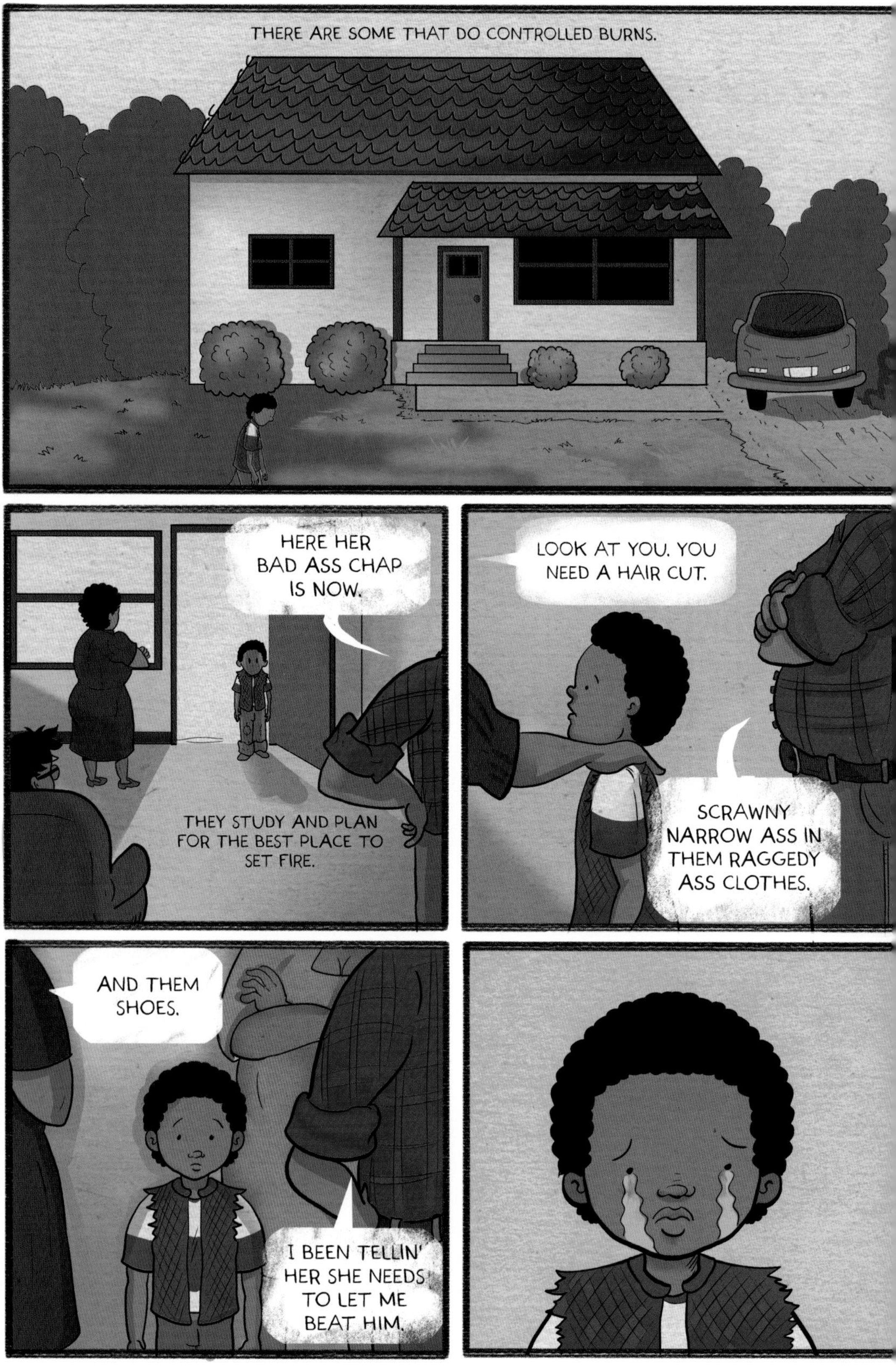
THERE ARE SOME THAT DO CONTROLLED BURNS.
HERE HER BAD ASS CHAP IS NOW.
THEY STUDY AND PLAN FOR THE BEST PLACE TO SET FIRE.
LOOK AT YOU. YOU NEED A HAIR CUT.
SCRAWNY NARROW ASS IN THEM RAGGEDY ASS CLOTHES.
AND THEM SHOES.
I BEEN TELLIN' HER SHE NEEDS TO LET ME BEAT HIM.

IF THEY DO IT JUST RIGHT AND BURN IN THE PROPER PLACES THEY MIGHT BE ABLE TO AVERT A DISASTER.

SLAM

IT WAS AT THIS POINT THAT I RAN AWAY.

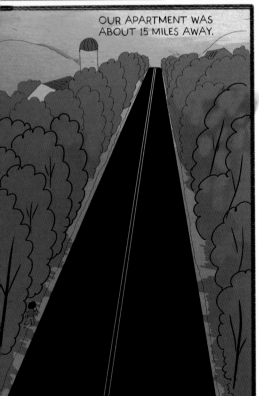

OUR APARTMENT WAS ABOUT 15 MILES AWAY.

BUT I REMEMBER THINKING THAT I HAD TO DO SOMETHING.

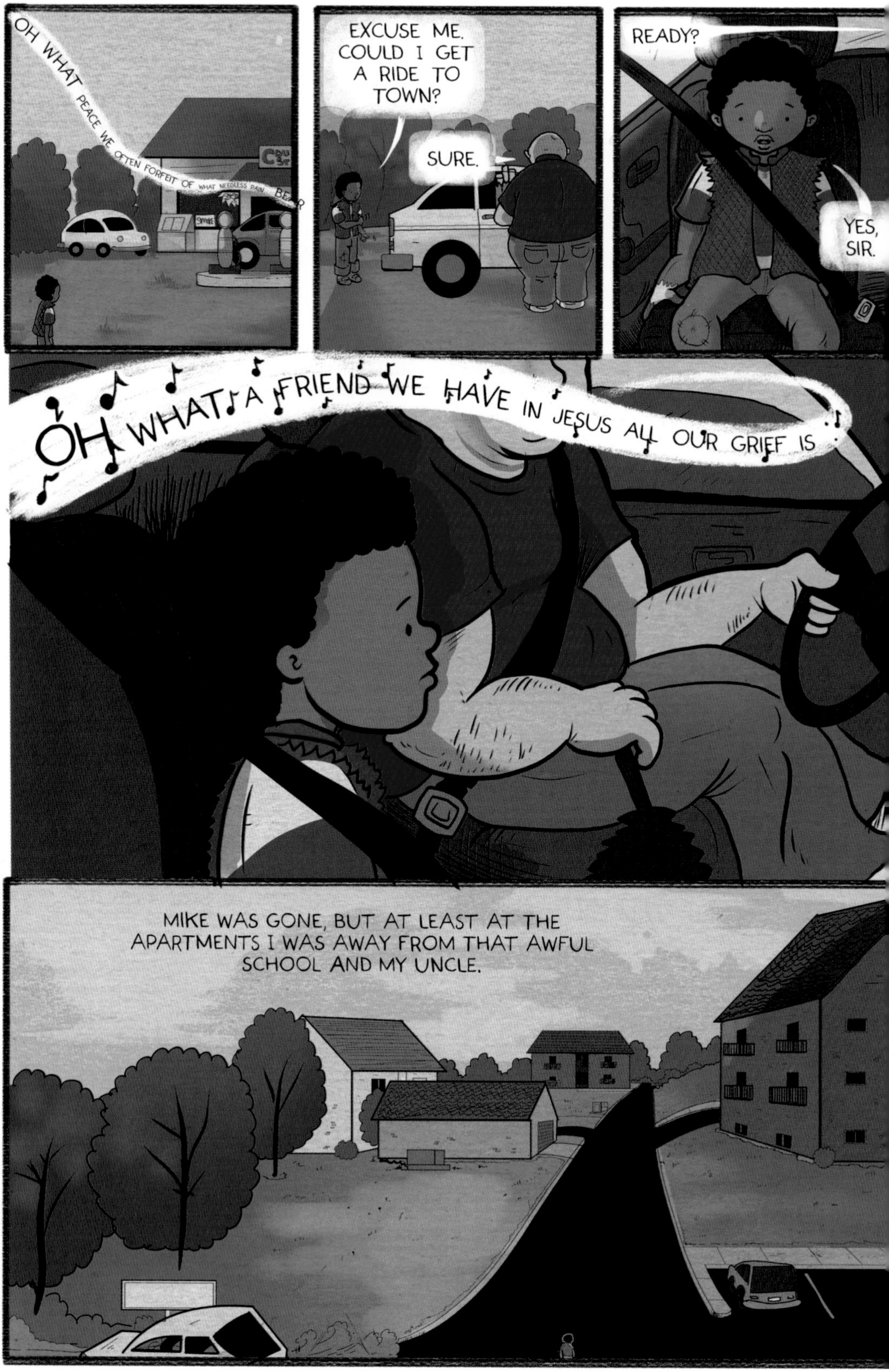

OH WHAT PEACE WE OFTEN FORFEIT OF WHAT NEEDLESS PAIN BEAR
EXCUSE ME. COULD I GET A RIDE TO TOWN?
SURE.
READY?
YES, SIR.
OH WHAT A FRIEND WE HAVE IN JESUS ALL OUR GRIEF IS
MIKE WAS GONE, BUT AT LEAST AT THE APARTMENTS I WAS AWAY FROM THAT AWFUL SCHOOL AND MY UNCLE.

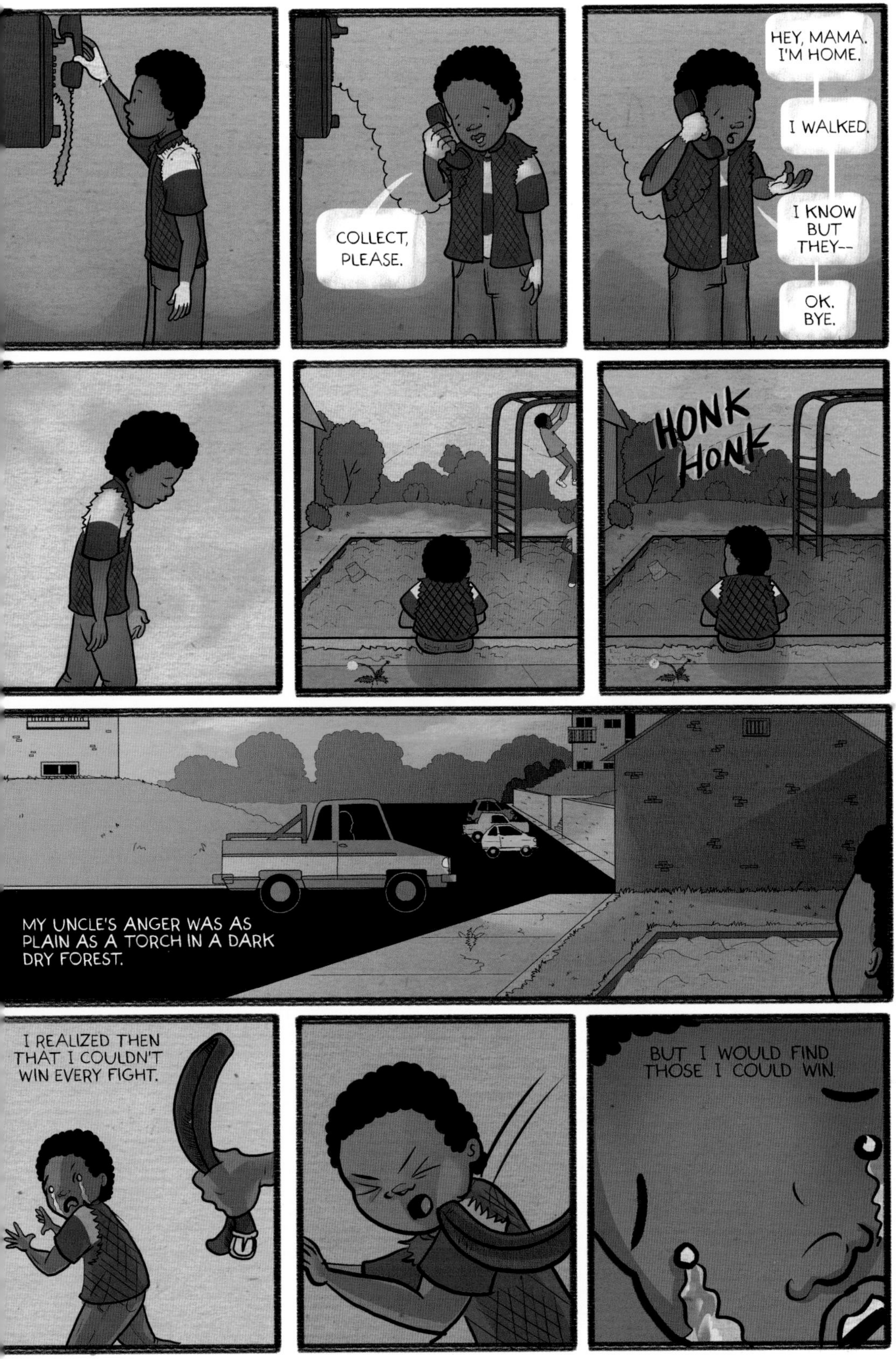
COLLECT, PLEASE.
HEY, MAMA. I'M HOME.
I WALKED.
I KNOW BUT THEY--
OK. BYE.
HONK HONK
MY UNCLE'S ANGER WAS AS PLAIN AS A TORCH IN A DARK DRY FOREST.
I REALIZED THEN THAT I COULDN'T WIN EVERY FIGHT.
BUT I WOULD FIND THOSE I COULD WIN.

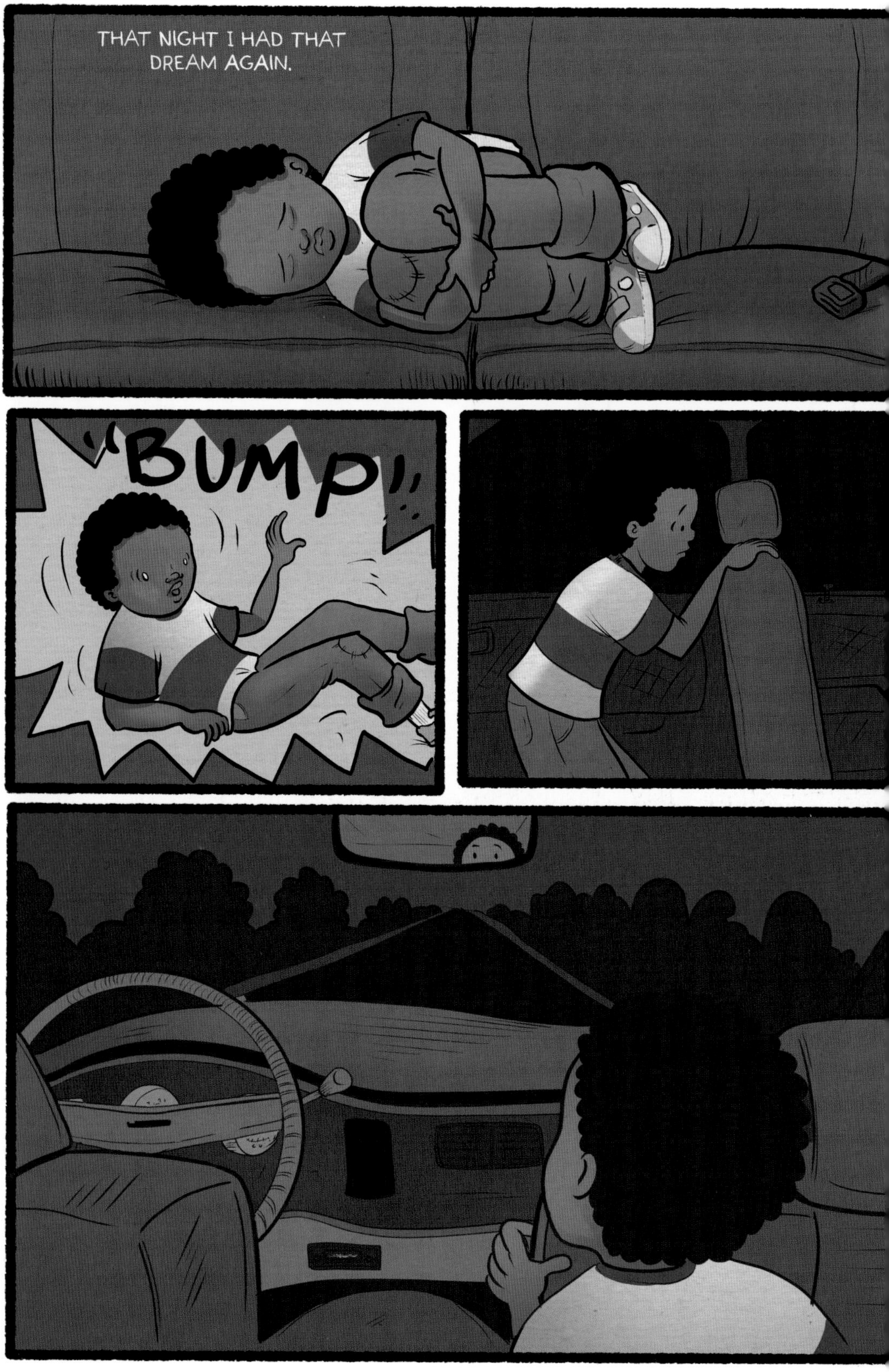
THAT NIGHT I HAD THAT DREAM AGAIN.
"BUMP"

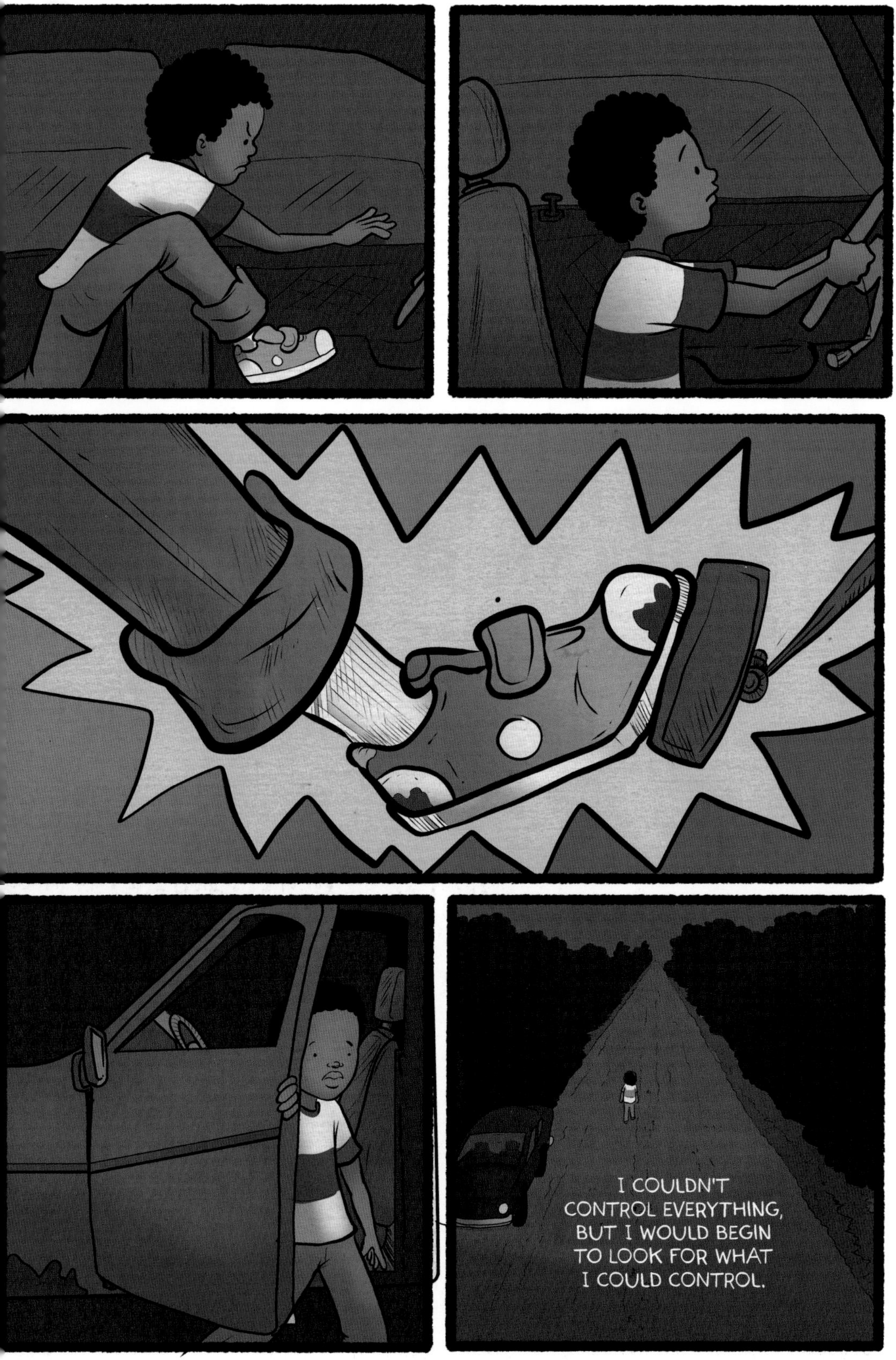
I COULDN'T
CONTROL EVERYTHING,
BUT I WOULD BEGIN
TO LOOK FOR WHAT
I COULD CONTROL.

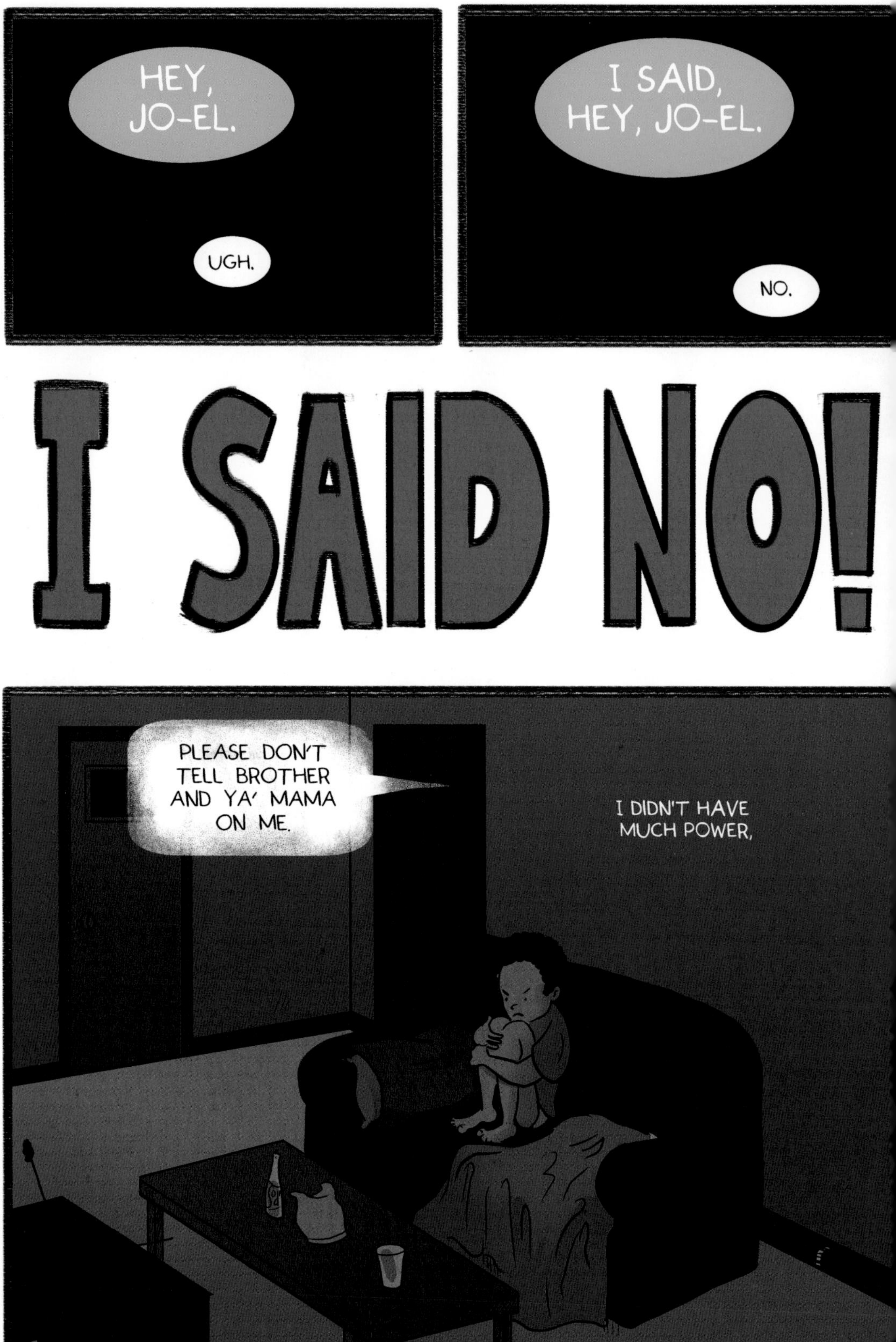
HEY, JO-EL.
UGH.
I SAID, HEY, JO-EL.
NO.
I SAID NO!
PLEASE DON'T TELL BROTHER AND YA' MAMA ON ME.
I DIDN'T HAVE MUCH POWER,

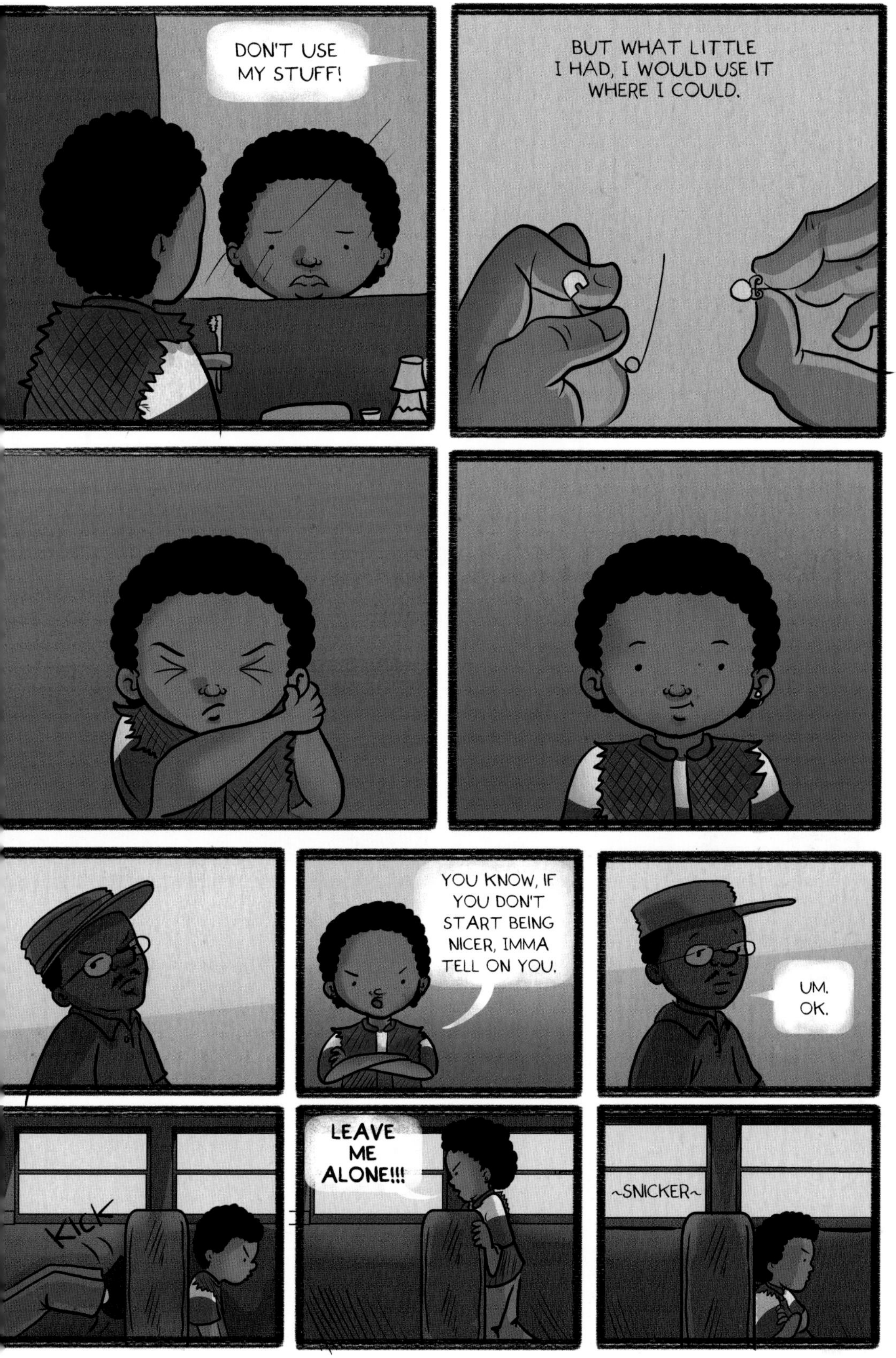
DON'T USE MY STUFF!
BUT WHAT LITTLE I HAD, I WOULD USE IT WHERE I COULD.
YOU KNOW, IF YOU DON'T START BEING NICER, IMMA TELL ON YOU.
UM. OK.
KICK
LEAVE ME ALONE!!!
~SNICKER~

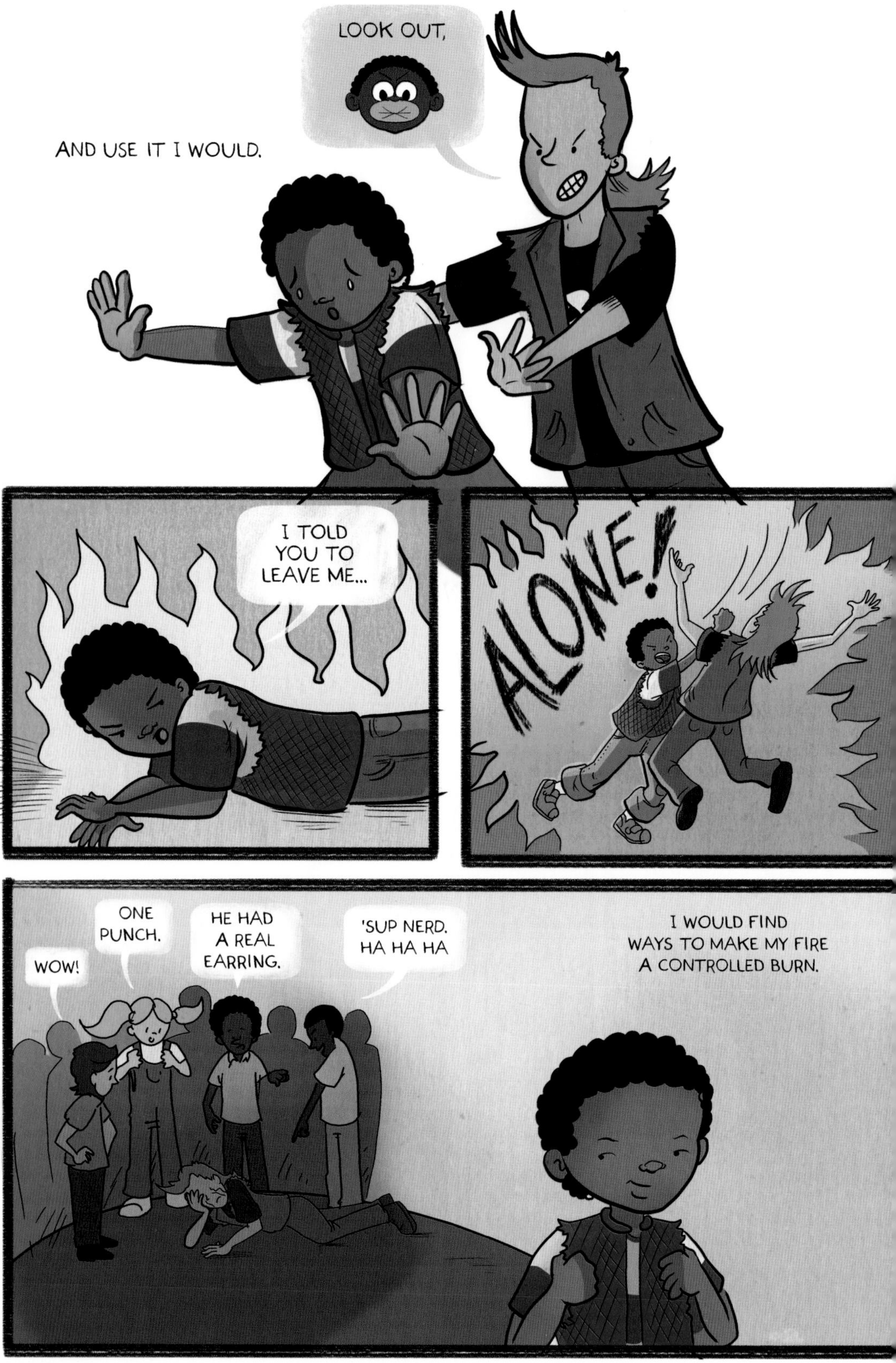
AND USE IT I WOULD.
LOOK OUT,
I TOLD YOU TO LEAVE ME...
ALONE!
WOW!
ONE PUNCH.
HE HAD A REAL EARRING.
'SUP NERD. HA HA HA
I WOULD FIND WAYS TO MAKE MY FIRE A CONTROLLED BURN.

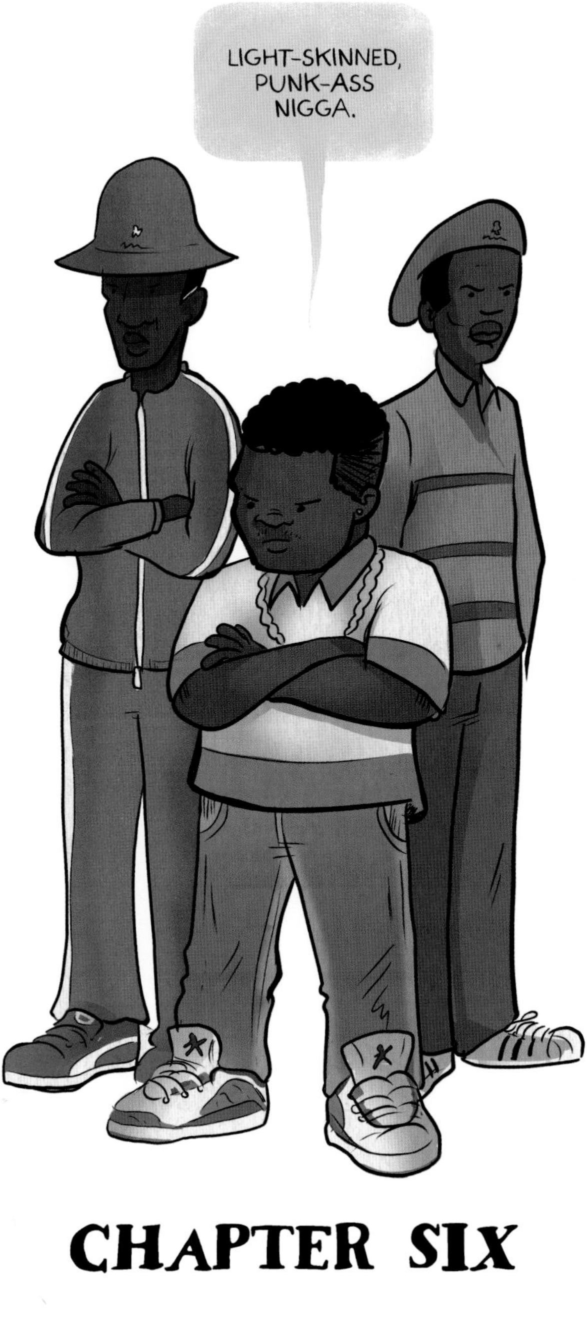
LIGHT-SKINNED, PUNK-ASS NIGGA.

CHAPTER SIX

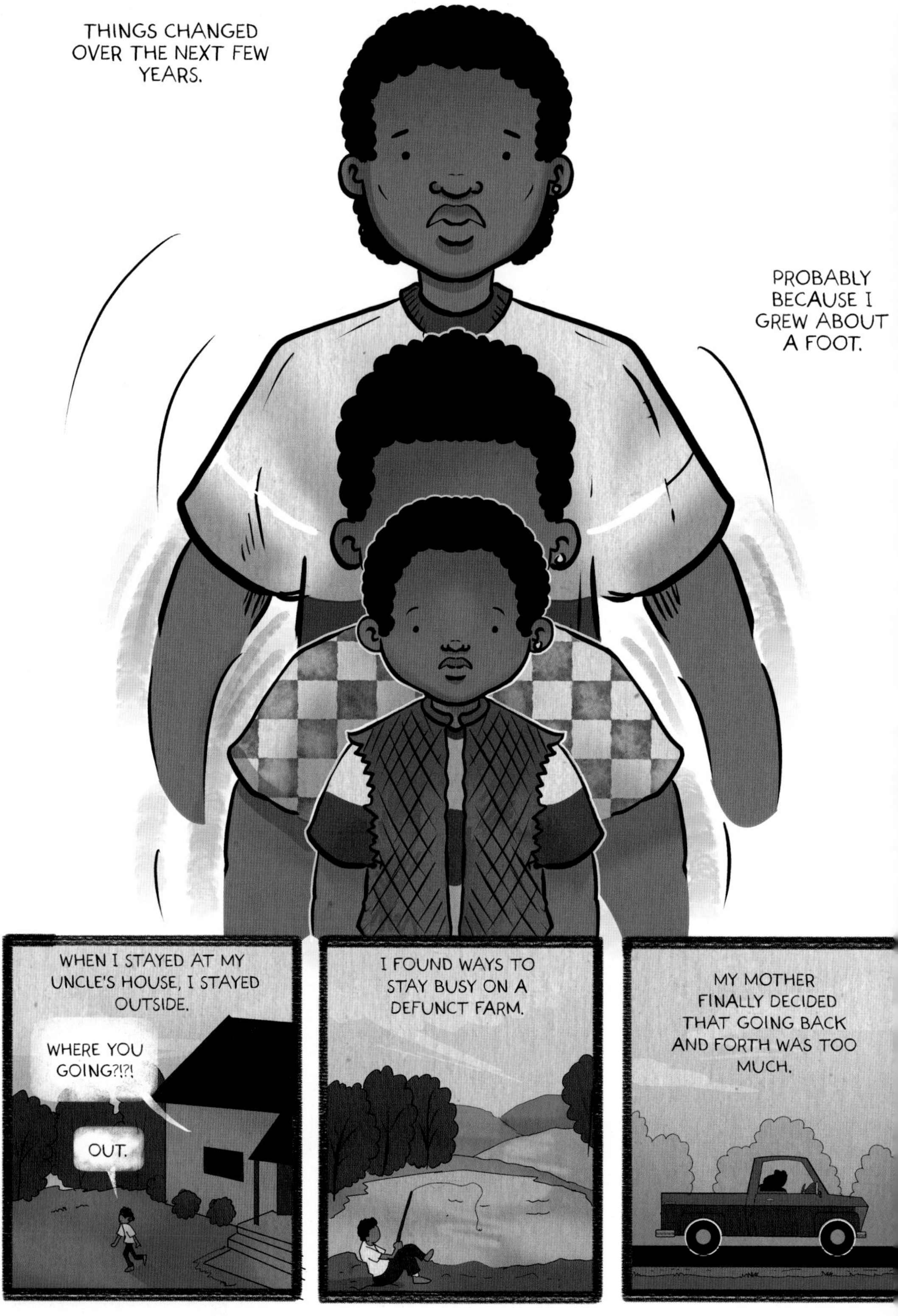
THINGS CHANGED OVER THE NEXT FEW YEARS.
PROBABLY BECAUSE I GREW ABOUT A FOOT.
WHEN I STAYED AT MY UNCLE'S HOUSE, I STAYED OUTSIDE.
WHERE YOU GOING?!?!
OUT.
I FOUND WAYS TO STAY BUSY ON A DEFUNCT FARM.
MY MOTHER FINALLY DECIDED THAT GOING BACK AND FORTH WAS TOO MUCH.

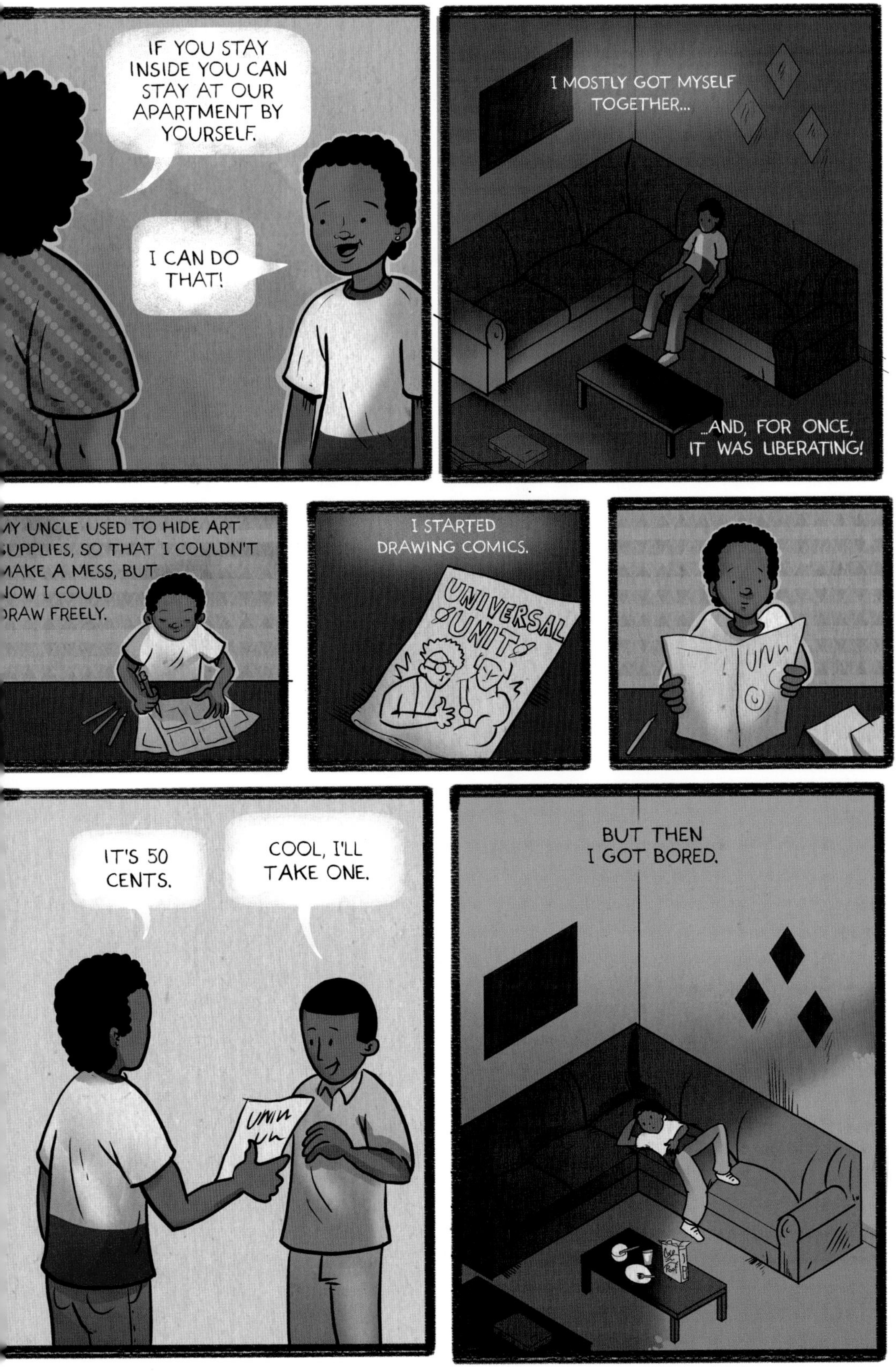
IF YOU STAY INSIDE YOU CAN STAY AT OUR APARTMENT BY YOURSELF.
I CAN DO THAT!
I MOSTLY GOT MYSELF TOGETHER...
...AND, FOR ONCE, IT WAS LIBERATING!
MY UNCLE USED TO HIDE ART SUPPLIES, SO THAT I COULDN'T MAKE A MESS, BUT NOW I COULD DRAW FREELY.
I STARTED DRAWING COMICS.
UNIVERSAL UNIT
IT'S 50 CENTS.
COOL, I'LL TAKE ONE.
BUT THEN I GOT BORED.

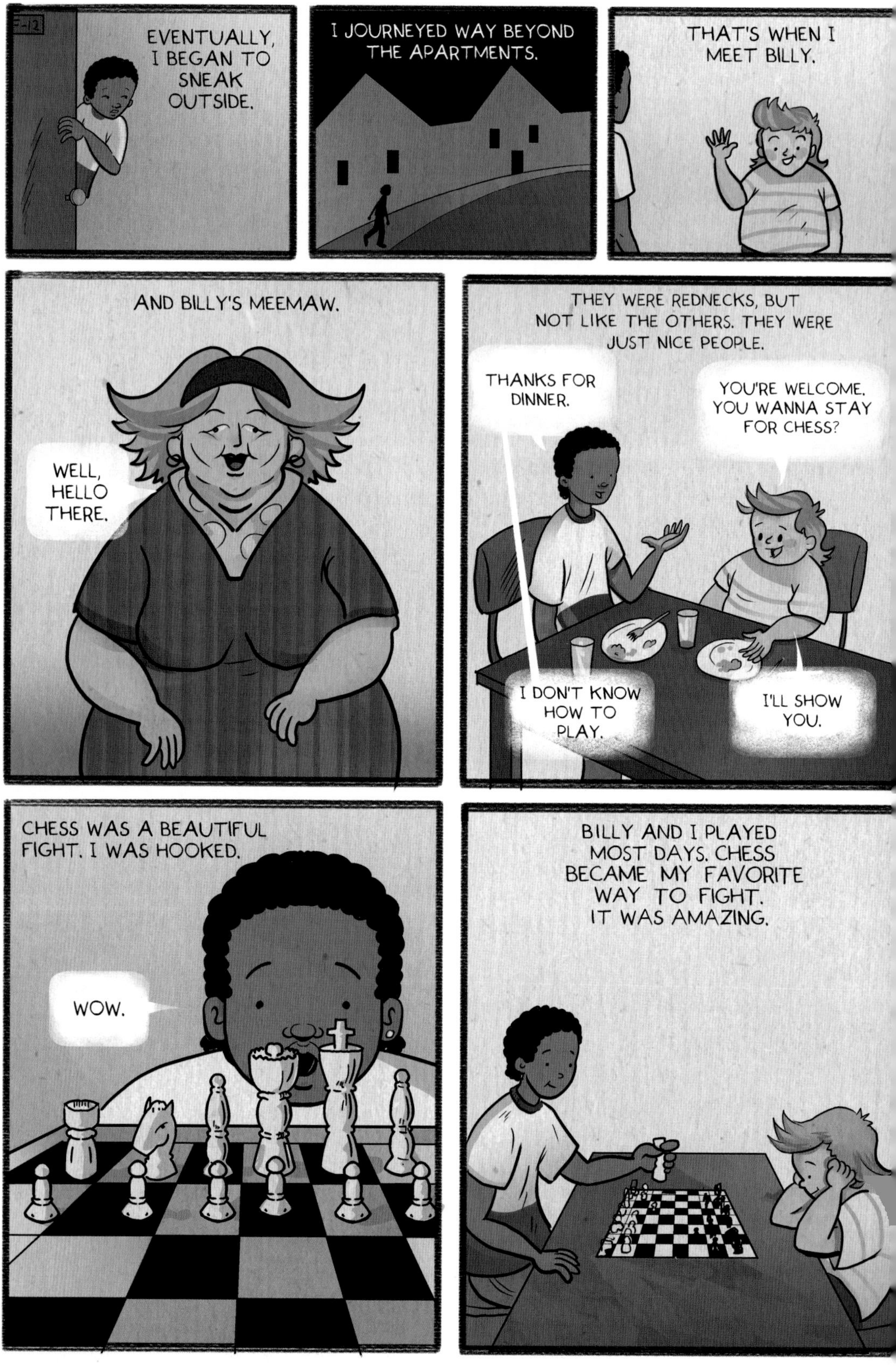
F-12
EVENTUALLY, I BEGAN TO SNEAK OUTSIDE.
I JOURNEYED WAY BEYOND THE APARTMENTS.
THAT'S WHEN I MEET BILLY.
AND BILLY'S MEEMAW.
WELL, HELLO THERE.
THEY WERE REDNECKS, BUT NOT LIKE THE OTHERS. THEY WERE JUST NICE PEOPLE.
THANKS FOR DINNER.
YOU'RE WELCOME. YOU WANNA STAY FOR CHESS?
I DON'T KNOW HOW TO PLAY.
I'LL SHOW YOU.
CHESS WAS A BEAUTIFUL FIGHT. I WAS HOOKED.
WOW.
BILLY AND I PLAYED MOST DAYS. CHESS BECAME MY FAVORITE WAY TO FIGHT. IT WAS AMAZING.

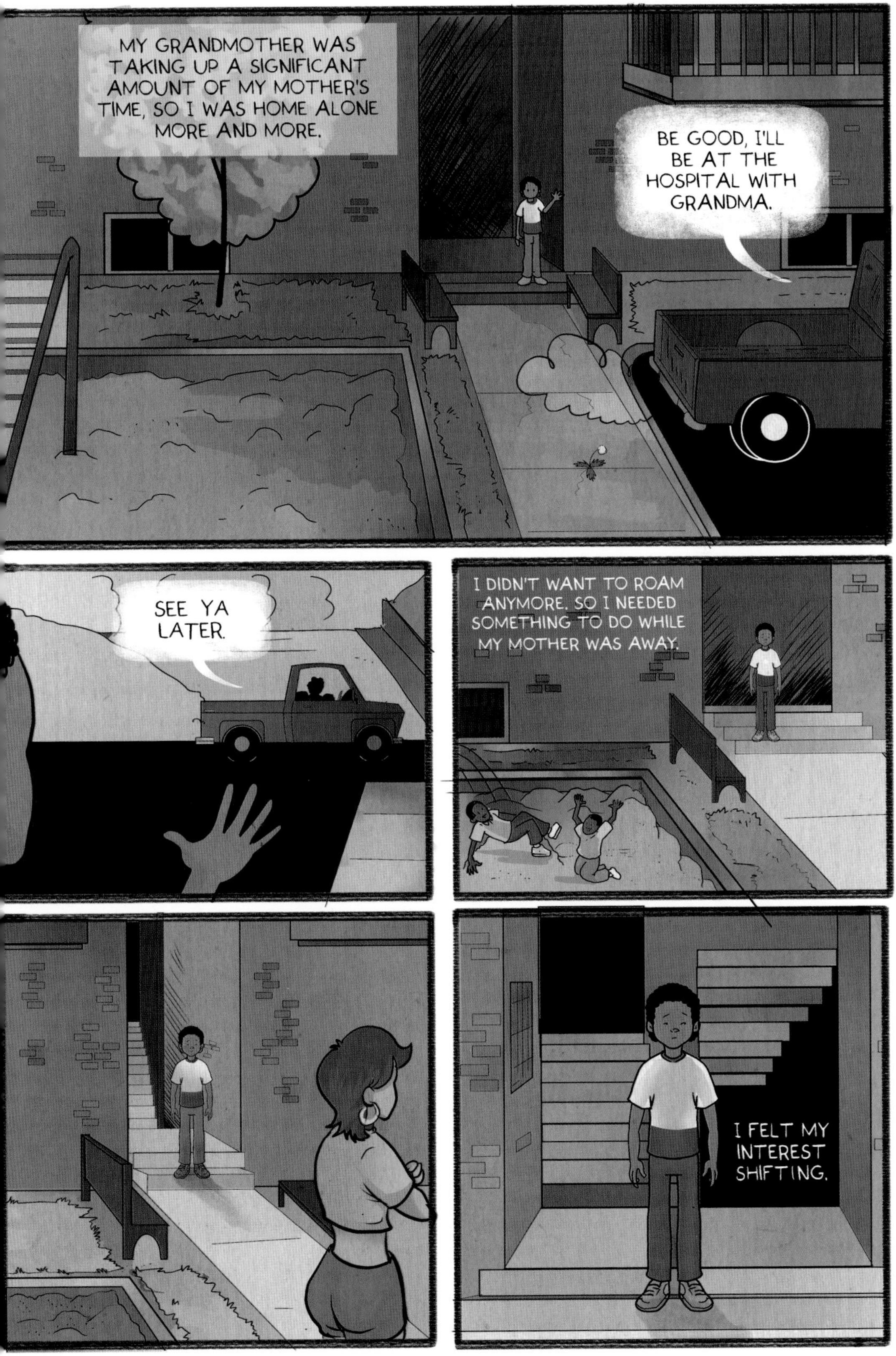
MY GRANDMOTHER WAS TAKING UP A SIGNIFICANT AMOUNT OF MY MOTHER'S TIME, SO I WAS HOME ALONE MORE AND MORE.
BE GOOD, I'LL BE AT THE HOSPITAL WITH GRANDMA.
SEE YA LATER.
I DIDN'T WANT TO ROAM ANYMORE. SO I NEEDED SOMETHING TO DO WHILE MY MOTHER WAS AWAY.
I FELT MY INTEREST SHIFTING.

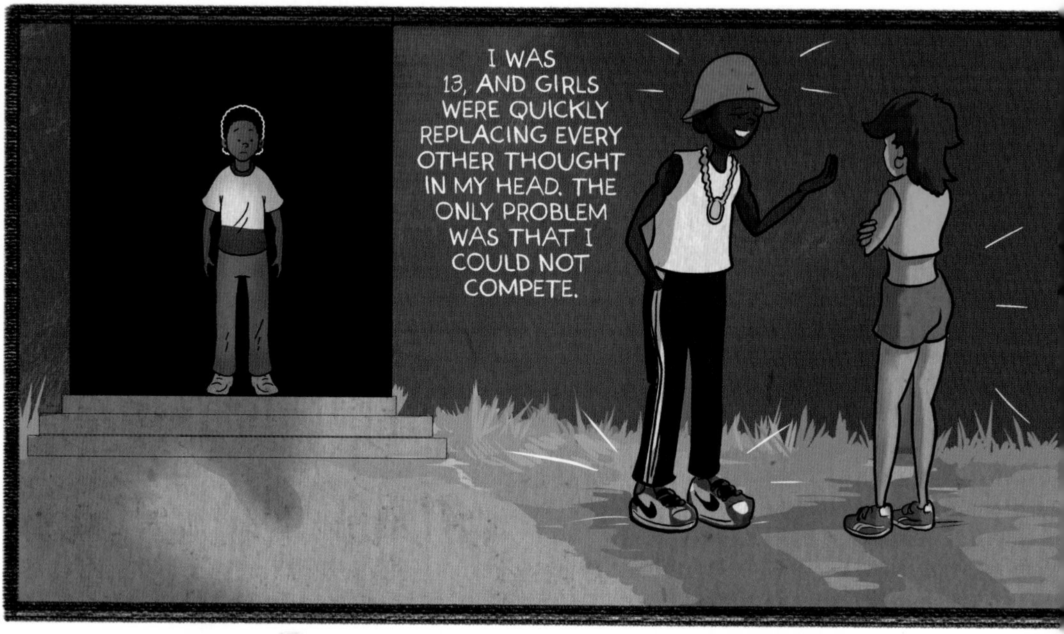
I WAS 13, AND GIRLS WERE QUICKLY REPLACING EVERY OTHER THOUGHT IN MY HEAD. THE ONLY PROBLEM WAS THAT I COULD NOT COMPETE.

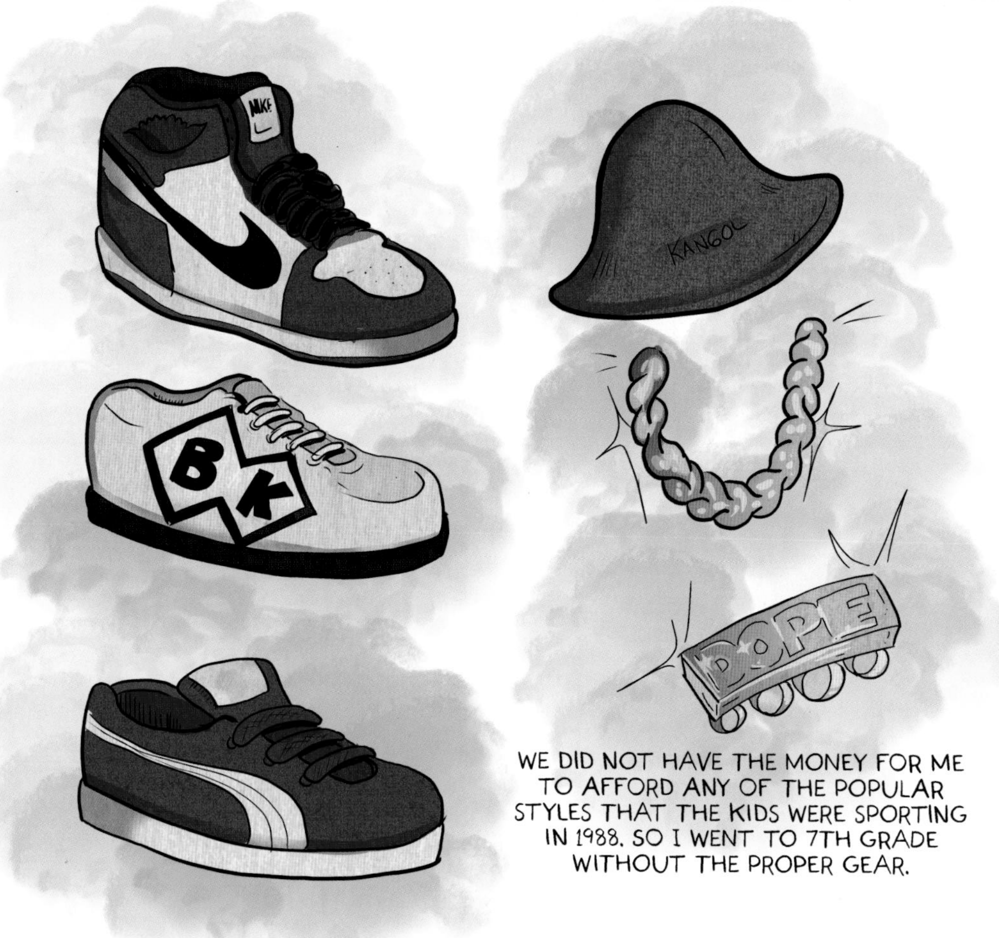
KANGOL
BK
DOPE
WE DID NOT HAVE THE MONEY FOR ME TO AFFORD ANY OF THE POPULAR STYLES THAT THE KIDS WERE SPORTING IN 1988, SO I WENT TO 7TH GRADE WITHOUT THE PROPER GEAR.

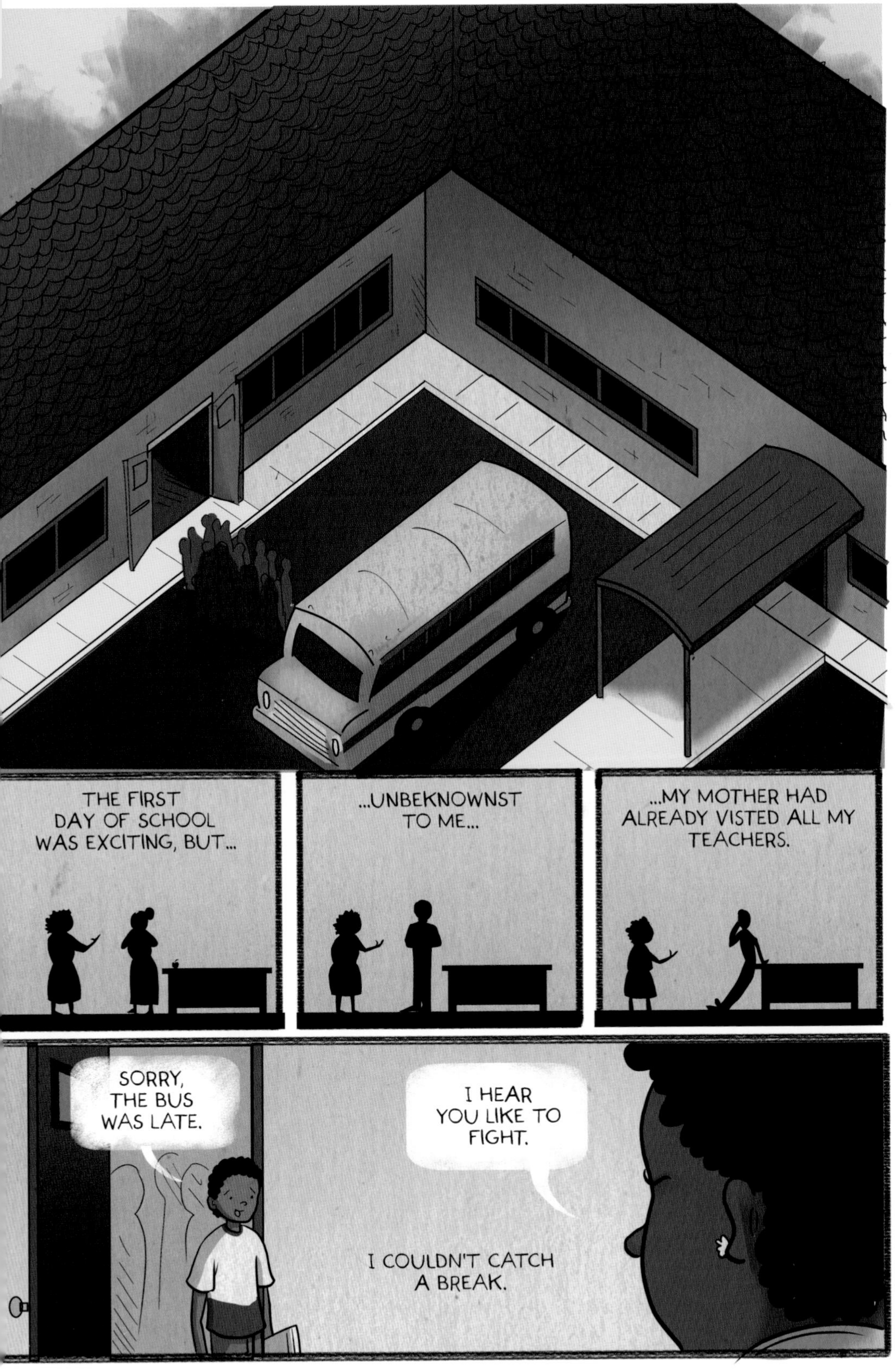
THE FIRST DAY OF SCHOOL WAS EXCITING, BUT...
...UNBEKNOWNST TO ME...
...MY MOTHER HAD ALREADY VISTED ALL MY TEACHERS.
SORRY, THE BUS WAS LATE.
I HEAR YOU LIKE TO FIGHT.
I COULDN'T CATCH A BREAK.

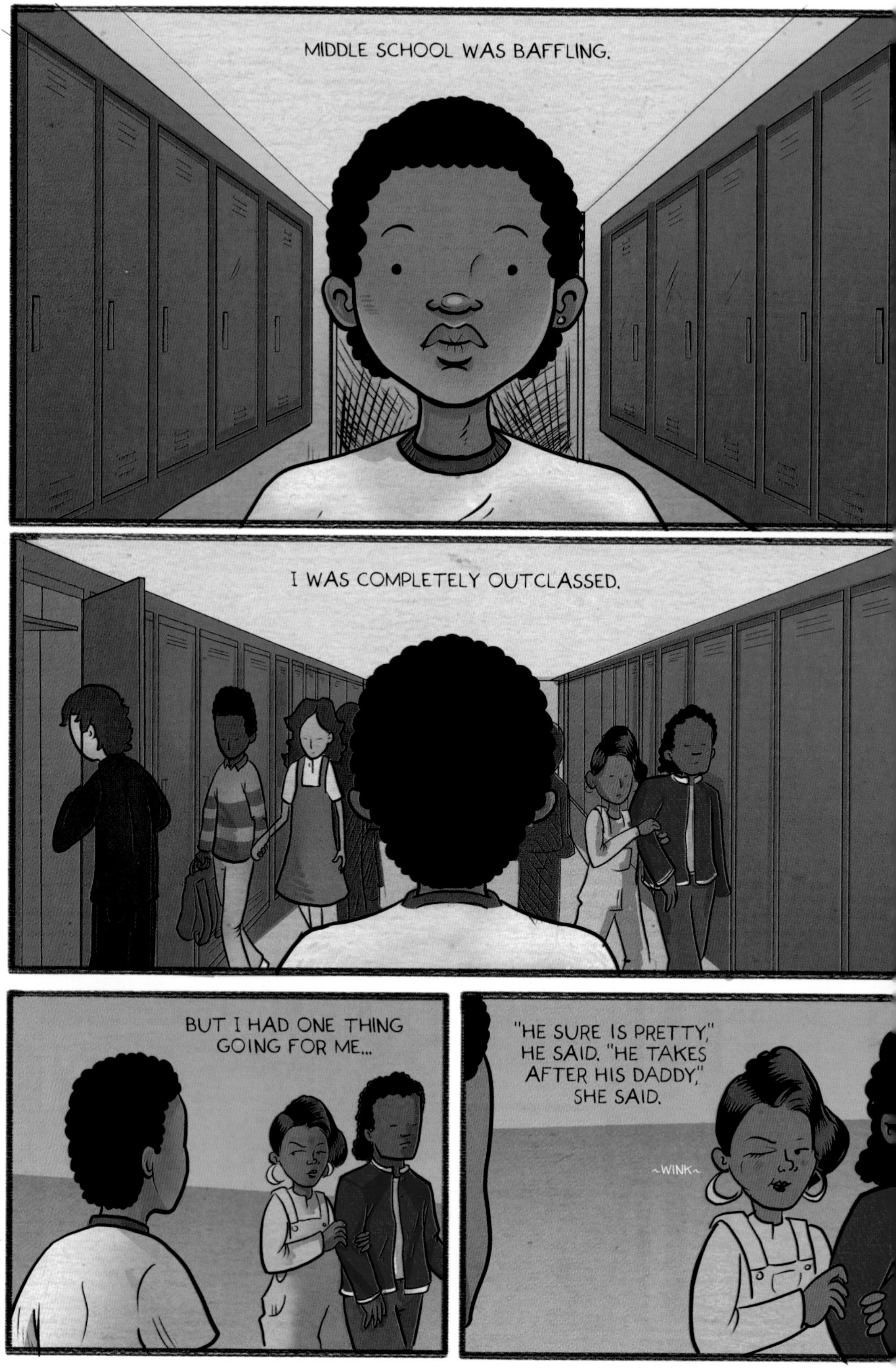
MIDDLE SCHOOL WAS BAFFLING.
I WAS COMPLETELY OUTCLASSED.
BUT I HAD ONE THING GOING FOR ME...
"HE SURE IS PRETTY," HE SAID. "HE TAKES AFTER HIS DADDY," SHE SAID.
~WINK~

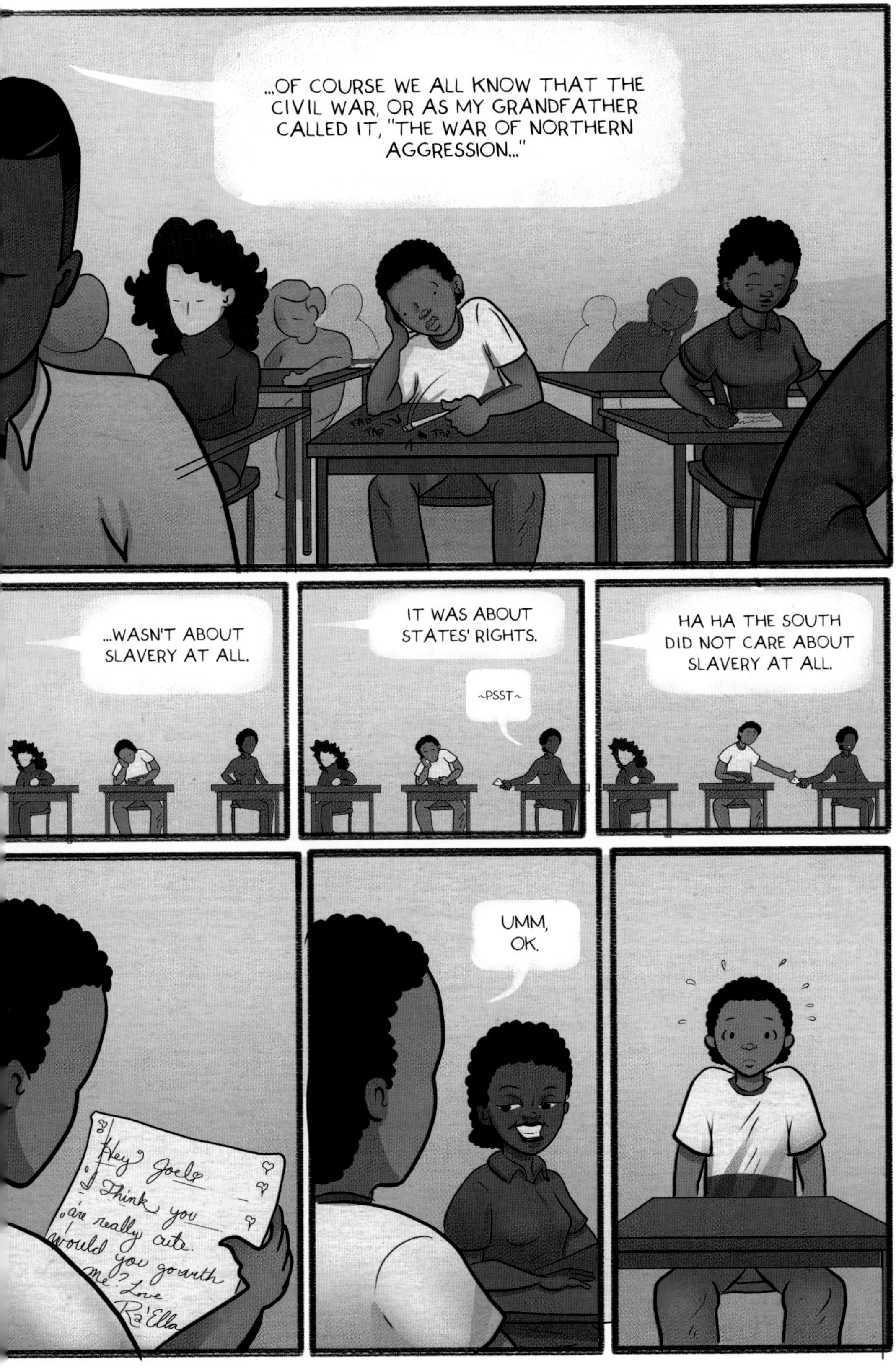

...OF COURSE WE ALL KNOW THAT THE CIVIL WAR, OR AS MY GRANDFATHER CALLED IT, "THE WAR OF NORTHERN AGGRESSION..."
TAP TAP TAP
...WASN'T ABOUT SLAVERY AT ALL.
IT WAS ABOUT STATES' RIGHTS.
~PSST~
HA HA THE SOUTH DID NOT CARE ABOUT SLAVERY AT ALL.
Hey Joel
I Think you
are really cute.
would you go with
me? Love
Ra'Ella
UMM, OK.

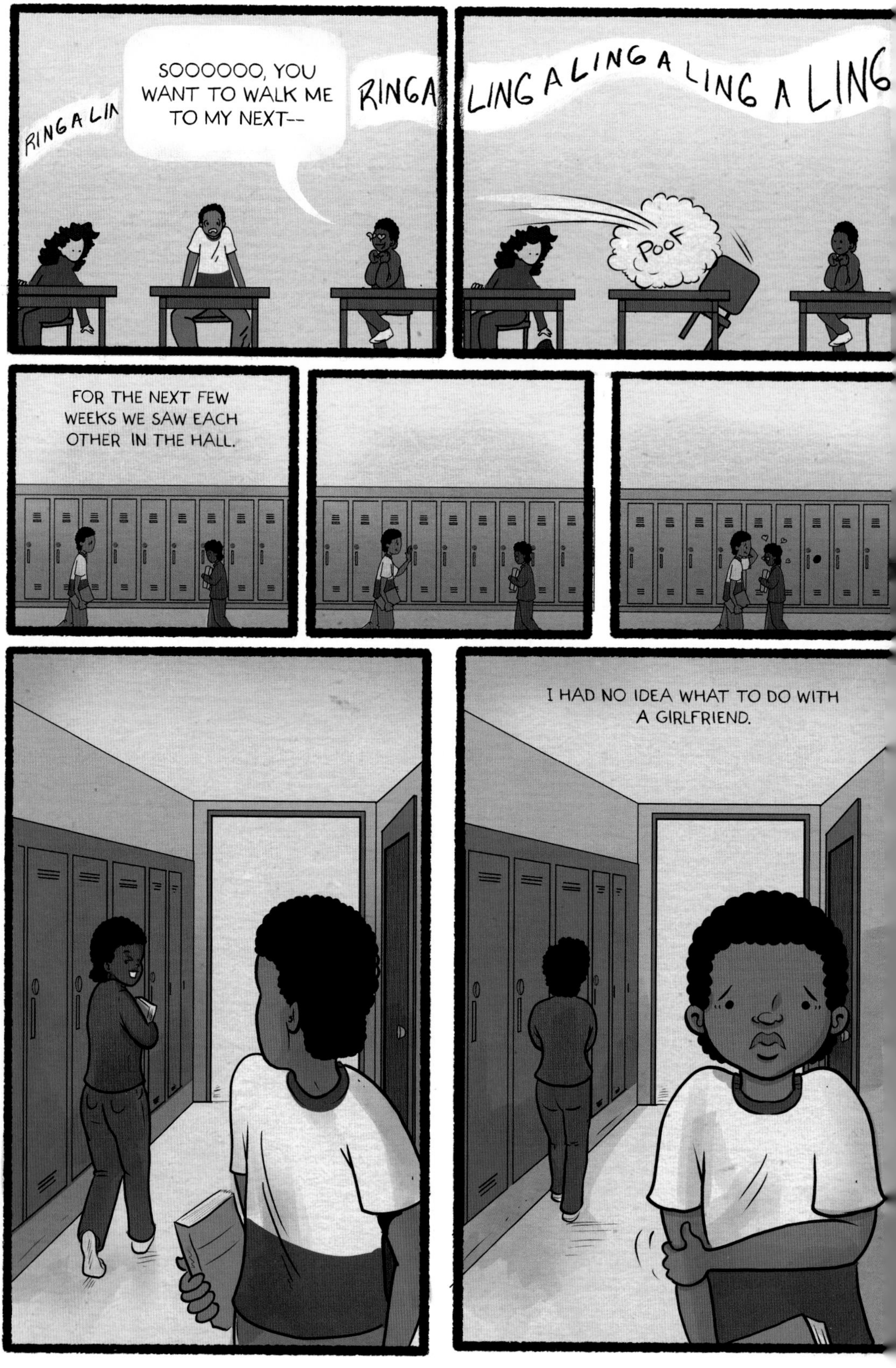
RINGALIN
SOOOOOO, YOU WANT TO WALK ME TO MY NEXT--
RINGA
LING A LING A LING A LING
POOF
FOR THE NEXT FEW WEEKS WE SAW EACH OTHER IN THE HALL.
I HAD NO IDEA WHAT TO DO WITH A GIRLFRIEND.

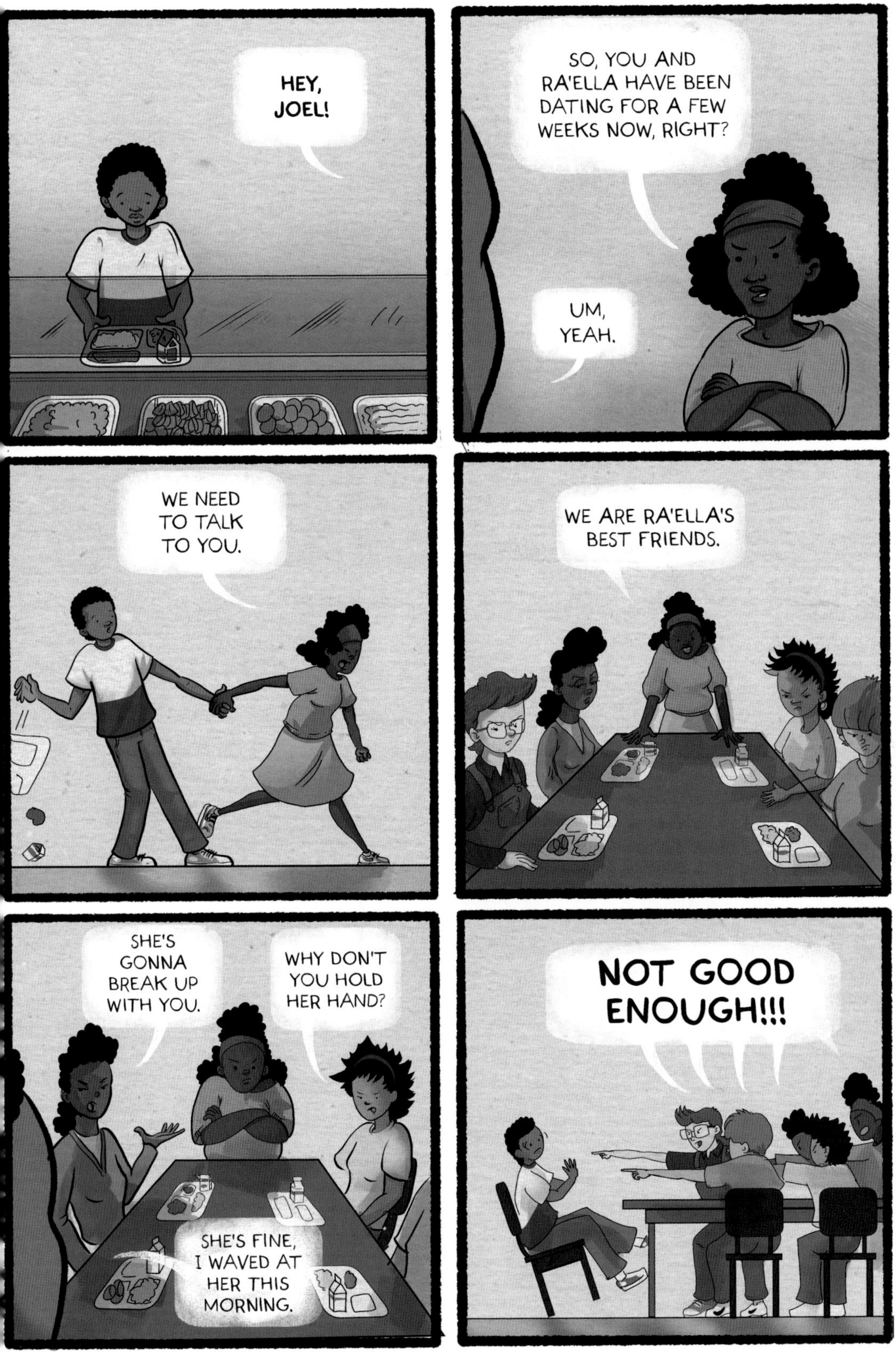
HEY, JOEL!
SO, YOU AND RA'ELLA HAVE BEEN DATING FOR A FEW WEEKS NOW, RIGHT?
UM, YEAH.
WE NEED TO TALK TO YOU.
WE ARE RA'ELLA'S BEST FRIENDS.
SHE'S GONNA BREAK UP WITH YOU.
WHY DON'T YOU HOLD HER HAND?
SHE'S FINE, I WAVED AT HER THIS MORNING.
NOT GOOD ENOUGH!!!

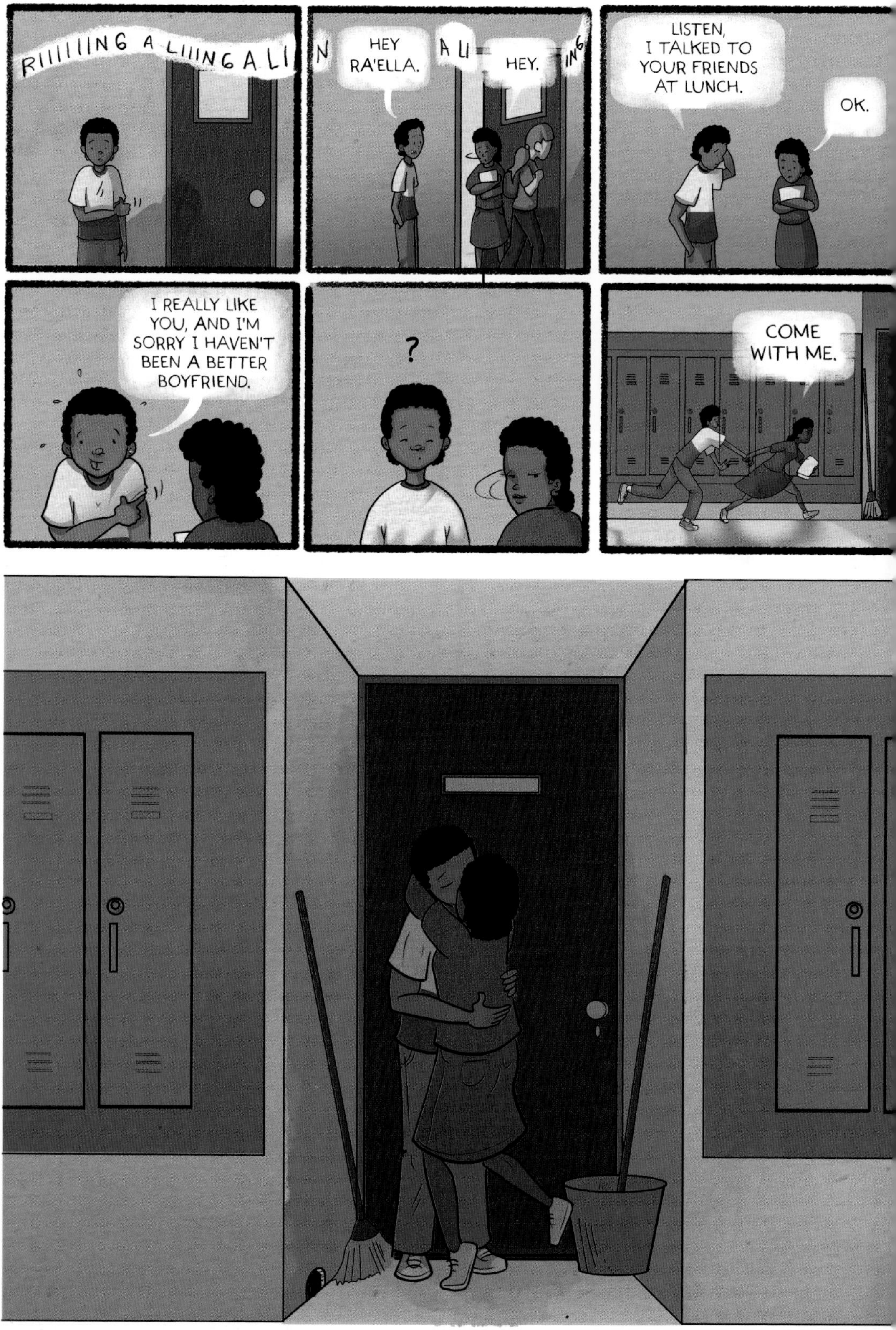

RIIIIIING A LIIING A LI
N
HEY RA'ELLA.
A LI
HEY.
ING
LISTEN, I TALKED TO YOUR FRIENDS AT LUNCH.
OK.
I REALLY LIKE YOU, AND I'M SORRY I HAVEN'T BEEN A BETTER BOYFRIEND.
?
COME WITH ME.

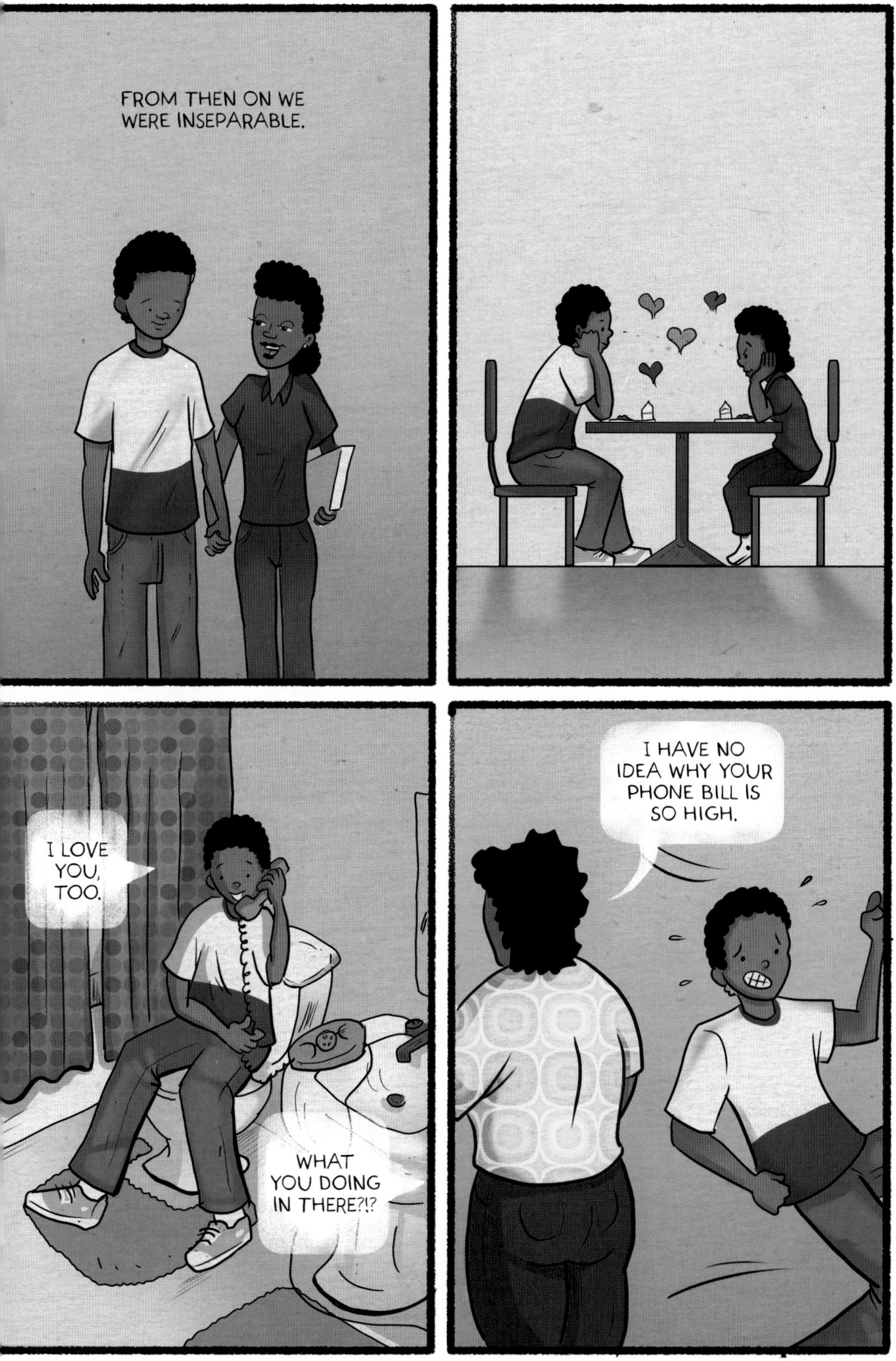
FROM THEN ON WE WERE INSEPARABLE.
I LOVE YOU, TOO.
WHAT YOU DOING IN THERE?!?
I HAVE NO IDEA WHY YOUR PHONE BILL IS SO HIGH.

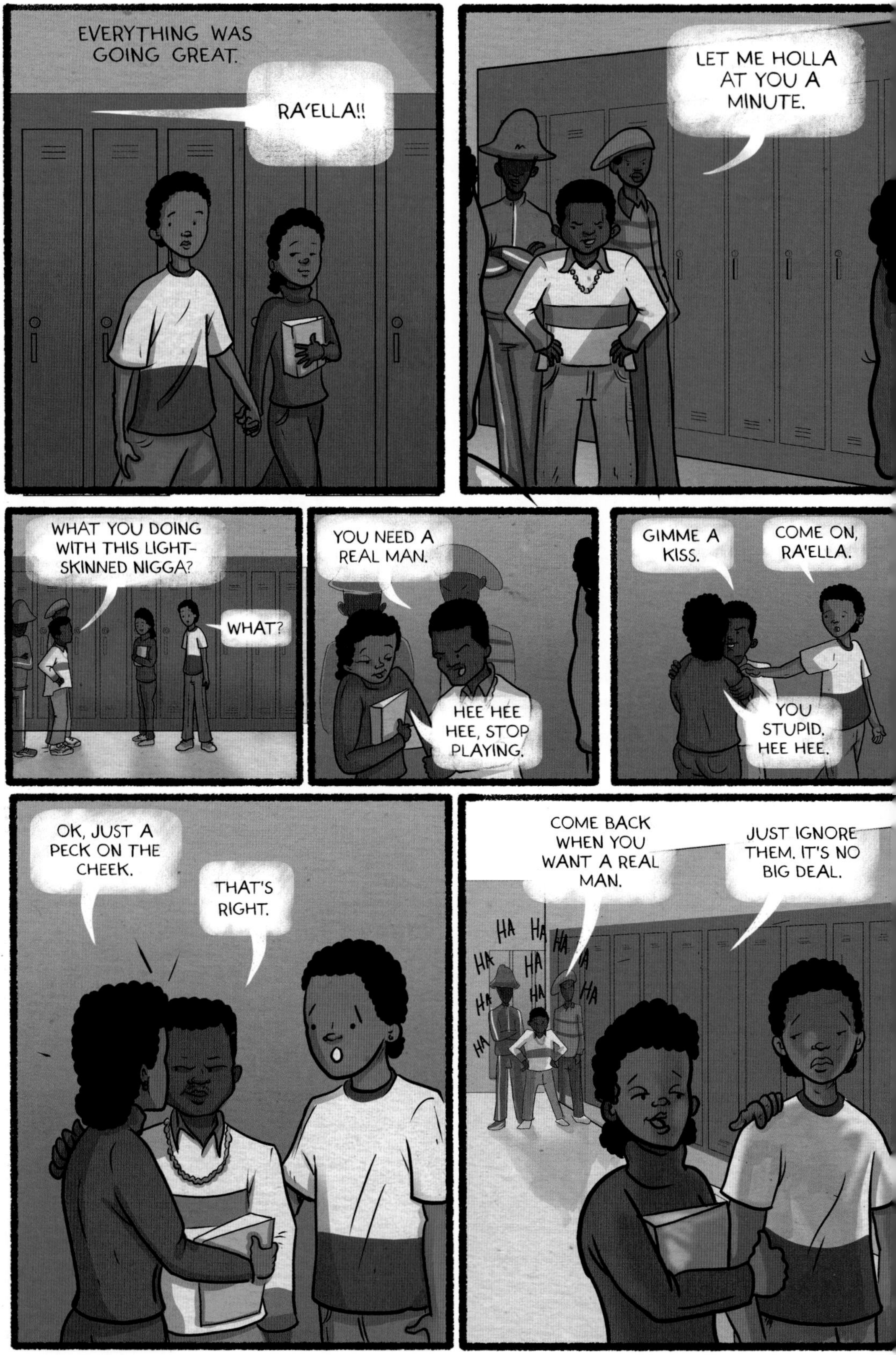
EVERYTHING WAS GOING GREAT.
RA'ELLA!!
LET ME HOLLA AT YOU A MINUTE.
WHAT YOU DOING WITH THIS LIGHT-SKINNED NIGGA?
WHAT?
YOU NEED A REAL MAN.
HEE HEE HEE, STOP PLAYING.
GIMME A KISS.
COME ON, RA'ELLA.
YOU STUPID. HEE HEE.
OK, JUST A PECK ON THE CHEEK.
THAT'S RIGHT.
COME BACK WHEN YOU WANT A REAL MAN.
HA HA HA HA HA HA HA HA HA HA
JUST IGNORE THEM. IT'S NO BIG DEAL.

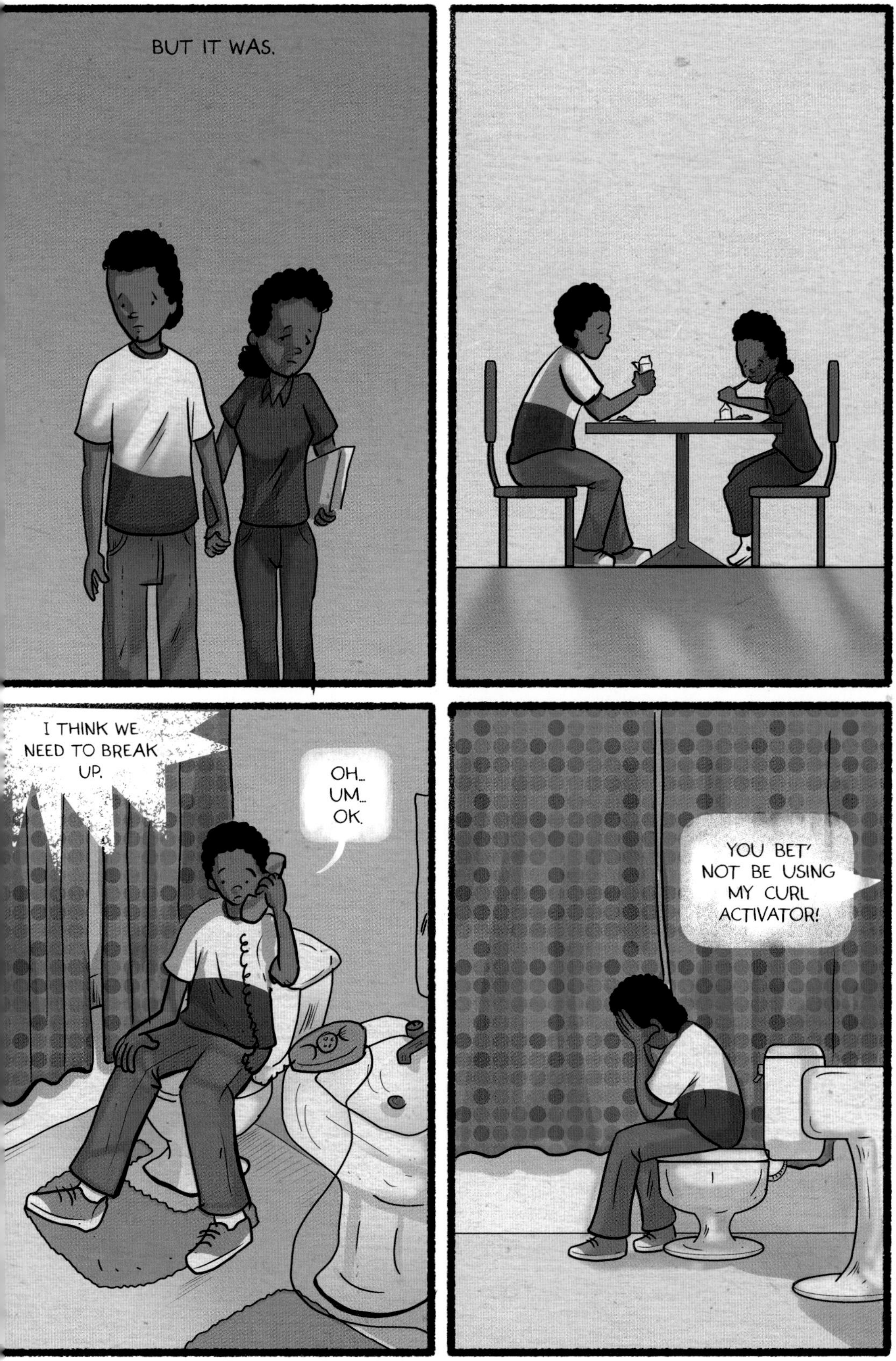
BUT IT WAS.
I THINK WE NEED TO BREAK UP.
OH... UM... OK.
YOU BET' NOT BE USING MY CURL ACTIVATOR!

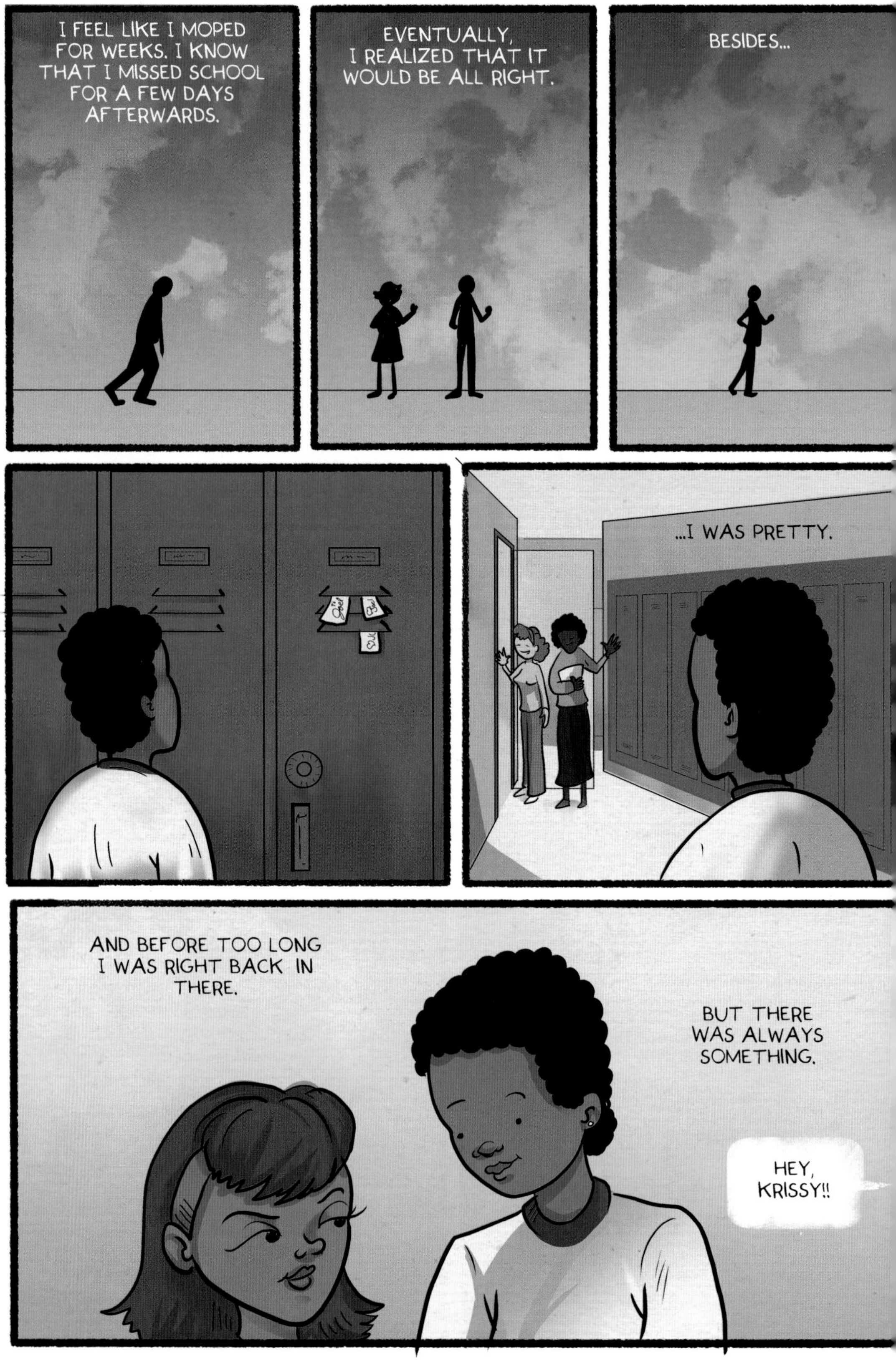
I FEEL LIKE I MOPED FOR WEEKS. I KNOW THAT I MISSED SCHOOL FOR A FEW DAYS AFTERWARDS.
EVENTUALLY, I REALIZED THAT IT WOULD BE ALL RIGHT.
BESIDES...
...I WAS PRETTY.
AND BEFORE TOO LONG I WAS RIGHT BACK IN THERE.
BUT THERE WAS ALWAYS SOMETHING.
HEY, KRISSY!!

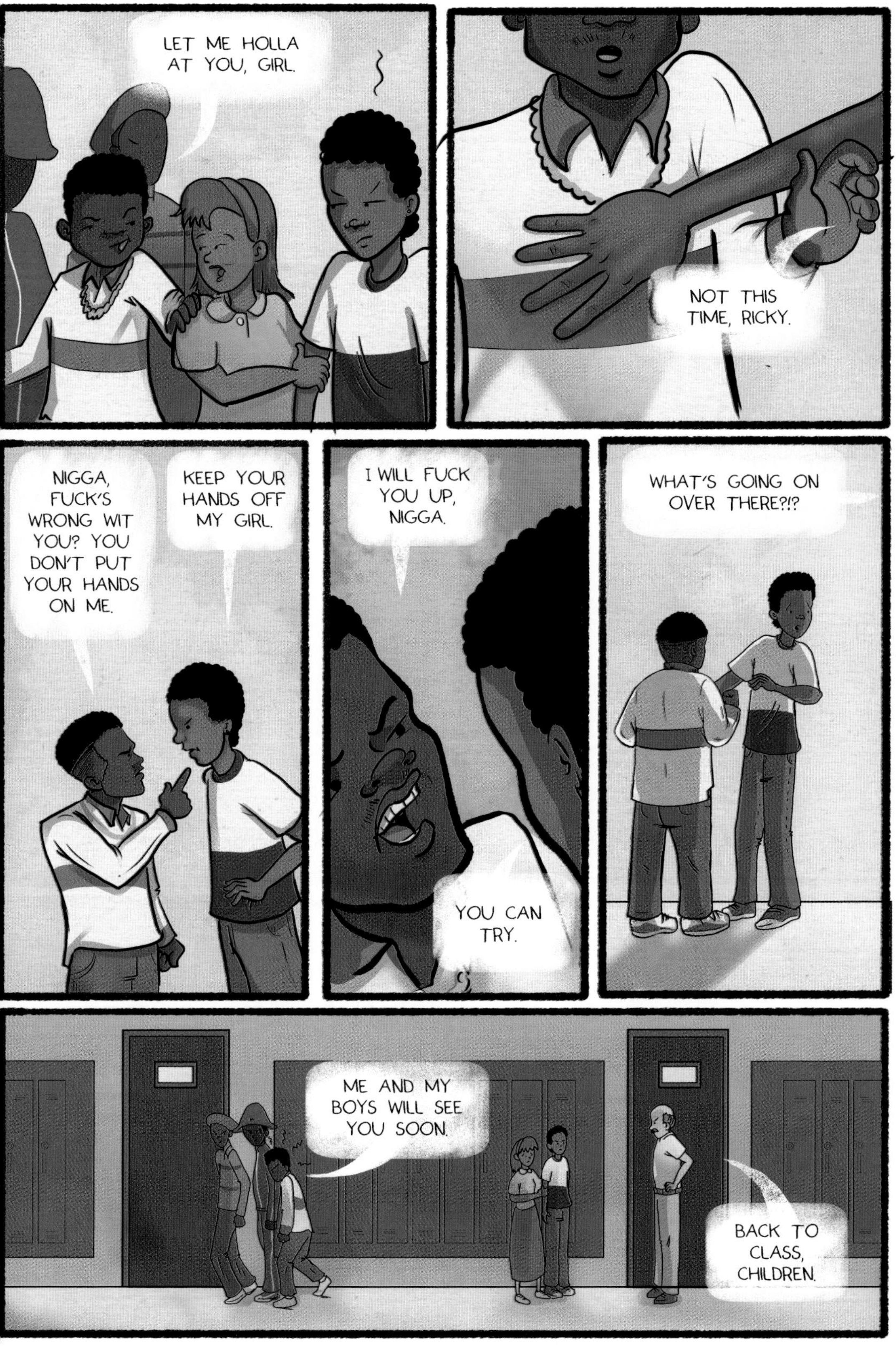
LET ME HOLLA AT YOU, GIRL.
NOT THIS TIME, RICKY.
NIGGA, FUCK'S WRONG WIT YOU? YOU DON'T PUT YOUR HANDS ON ME.
KEEP YOUR HANDS OFF MY GIRL.
I WILL FUCK YOU UP, NIGGA.
YOU CAN TRY.
WHAT'S GOING ON OVER THERE?!?
ME AND MY BOYS WILL SEE YOU SOON.
BACK TO CLASS, CHILDREN.

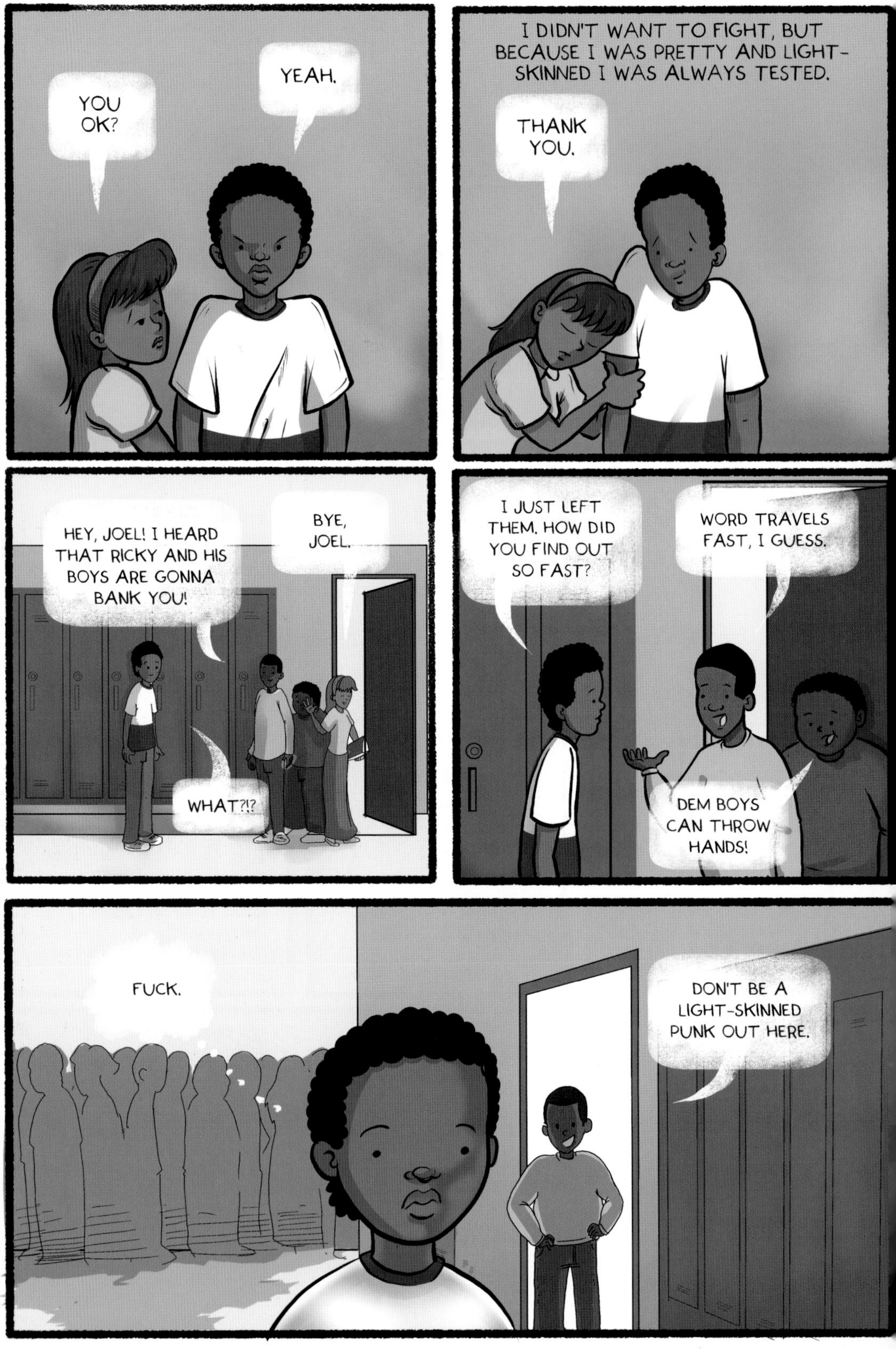
YOU OK?
YEAH.
I DIDN'T WANT TO FIGHT, BUT BECAUSE I WAS PRETTY AND LIGHT-SKINNED I WAS ALWAYS TESTED.
THANK YOU.
HEY, JOEL! I HEARD THAT RICKY AND HIS BOYS ARE GONNA BANK YOU!
BYE, JOEL.
WHAT?!?
I JUST LEFT THEM. HOW DID YOU FIND OUT SO FAST?
WORD TRAVELS FAST, I GUESS.
DEM BOYS CAN THROW HANDS!
FUCK.
DON'T BE A LIGHT-SKINNED PUNK OUT HERE.

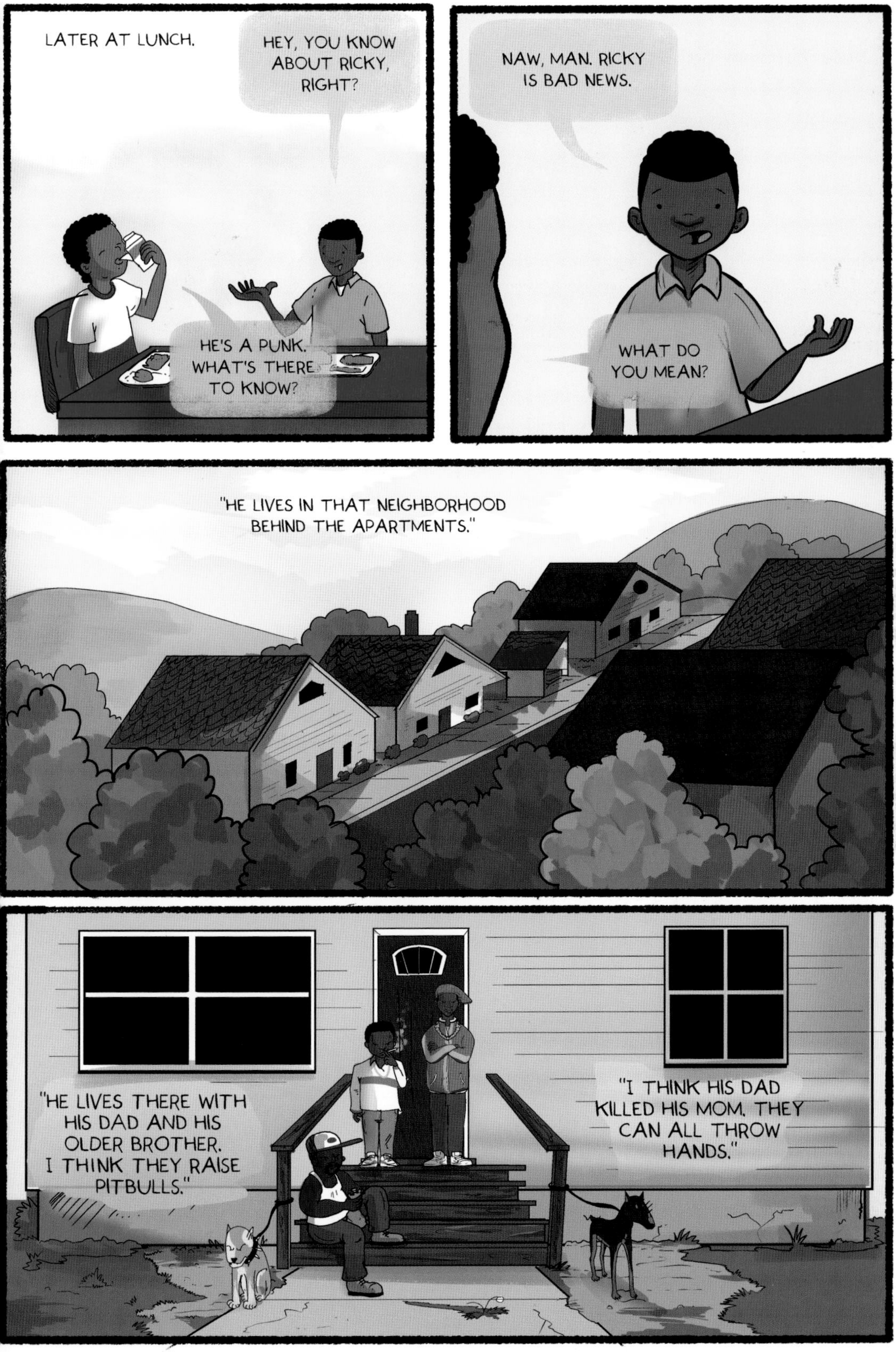
LATER AT LUNCH.
HEY, YOU KNOW ABOUT RICKY, RIGHT?
HE'S A PUNK. WHAT'S THERE TO KNOW?
NAW, MAN. RICKY IS BAD NEWS.
WHAT DO YOU MEAN?
"HE LIVES IN THAT NEIGHBORHOOD BEHIND THE APARTMENTS."
"HE LIVES THERE WITH HIS DAD AND HIS OLDER BROTHER. I THINK THEY RAISE PITBULLS."
"I THINK HIS DAD KILLED HIS MOM. THEY CAN ALL THROW HANDS."

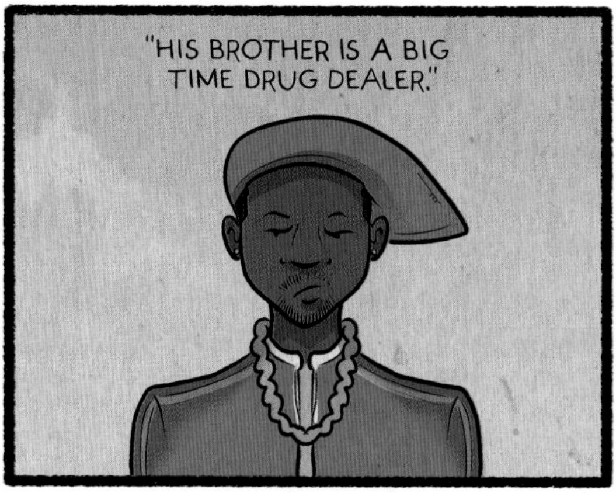
"HIS BROTHER IS A BIG TIME DRUG DEALER."

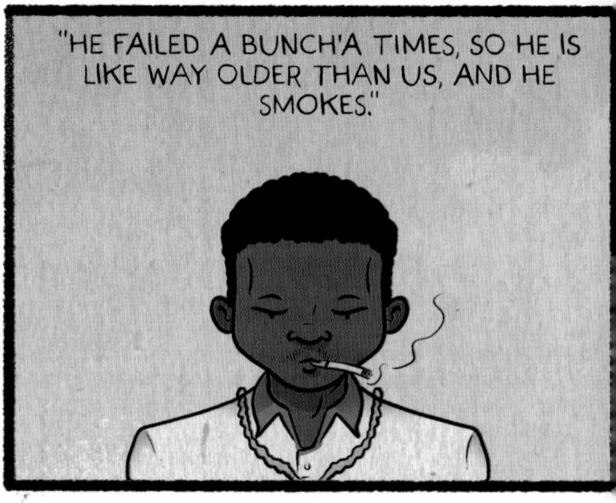
"HE FAILED A BUNCH'A TIMES, SO HE IS LIKE WAY OLDER THAN US, AND HE SMOKES."

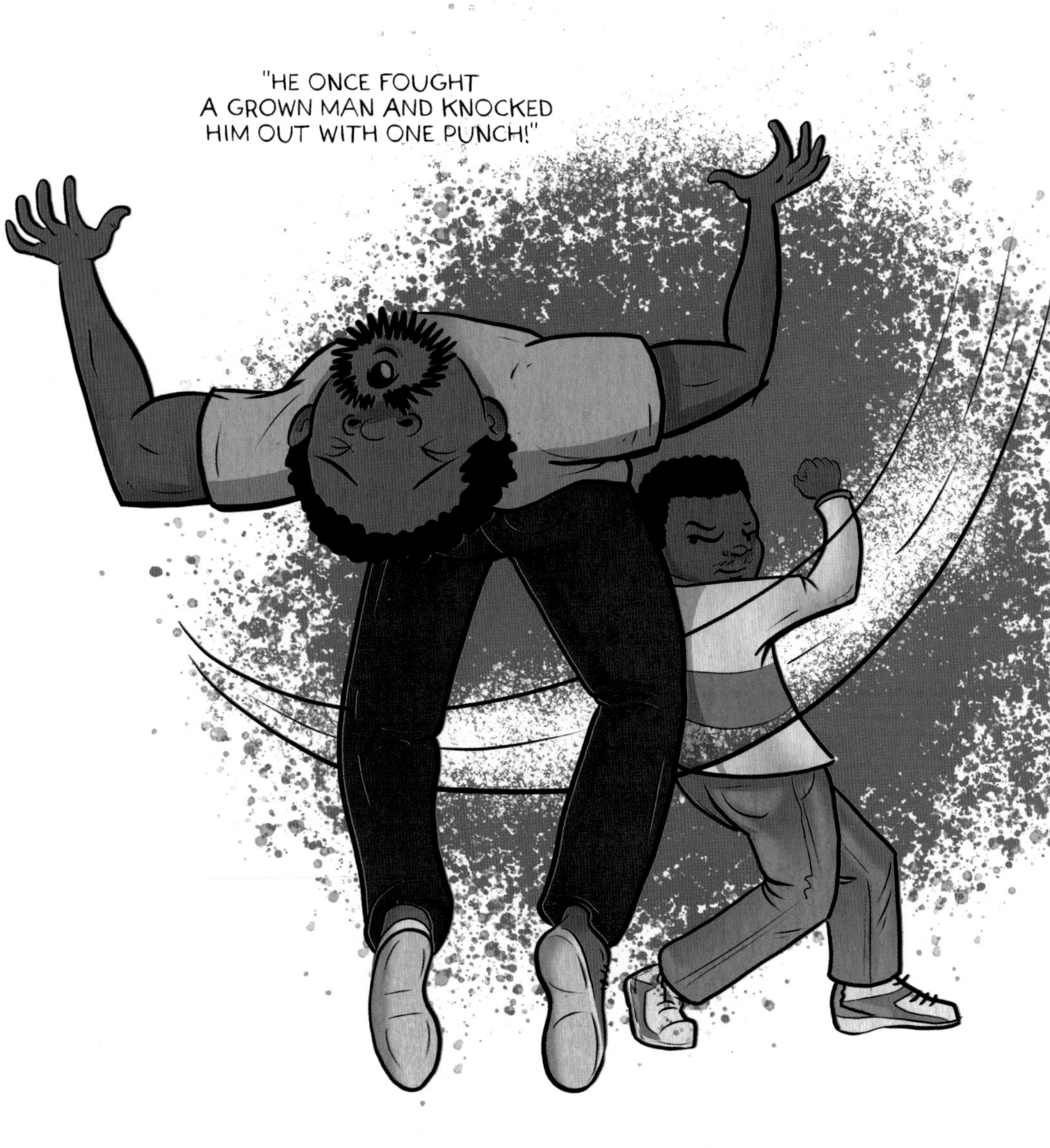
"HE ONCE FOUGHT A GROWN MAN AND KNOCKED HIM OUT WITH ONE PUNCH!"

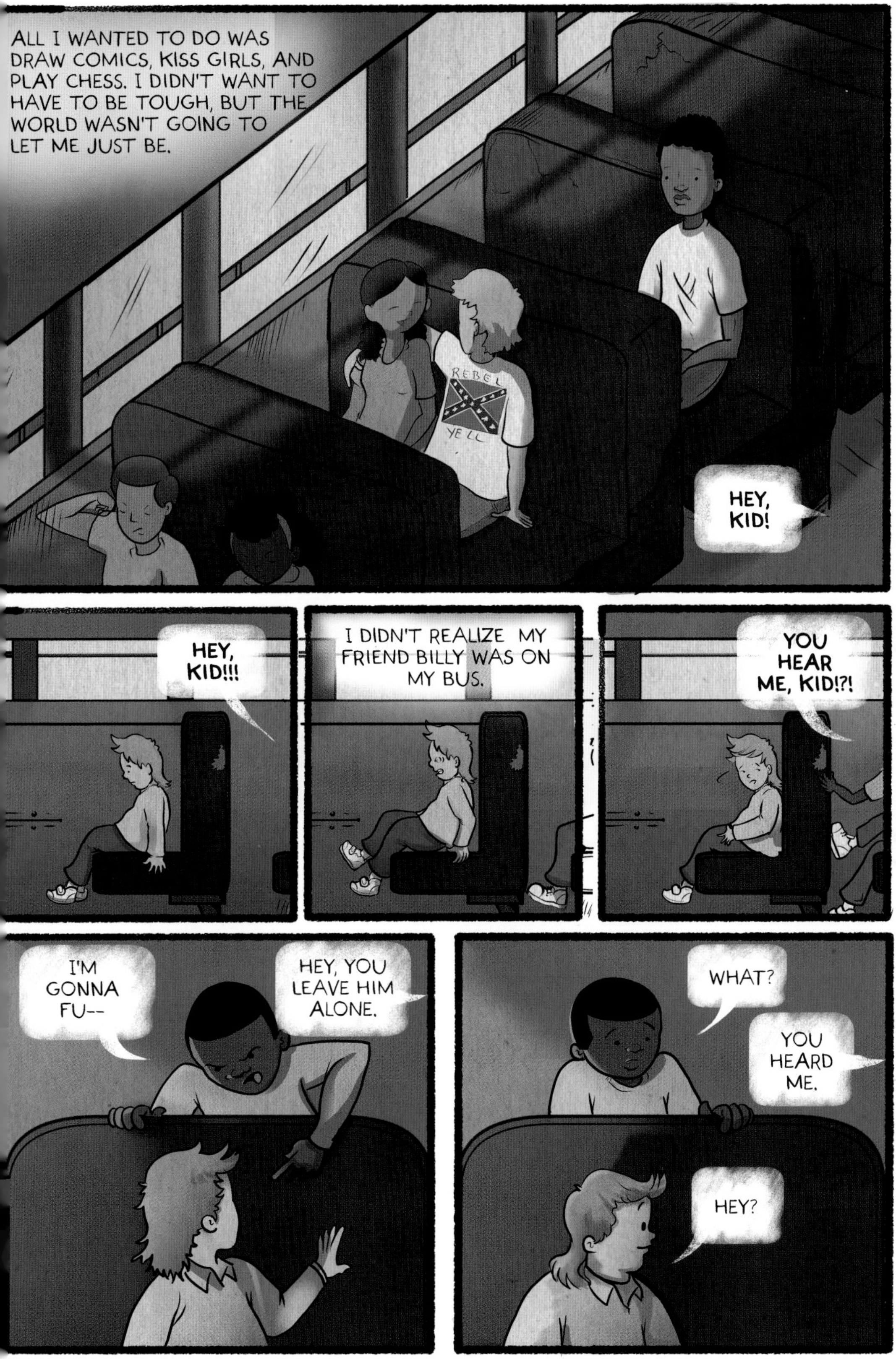
ALL I WANTED TO DO WAS DRAW COMICS, KISS GIRLS, AND PLAY CHESS. I DIDN'T WANT TO HAVE TO BE TOUGH, BUT THE WORLD WASN'T GOING TO LET ME JUST BE.
REBEL YELL
HEY, KID!
HEY, KID!!!
I DIDN'T REALIZE MY FRIEND BILLY WAS ON MY BUS.
YOU HEAR ME, KID!?!
I'M GONNA FU--
HEY, YOU LEAVE HIM ALONE.
WHAT?
YOU HEARD ME.
HEY?

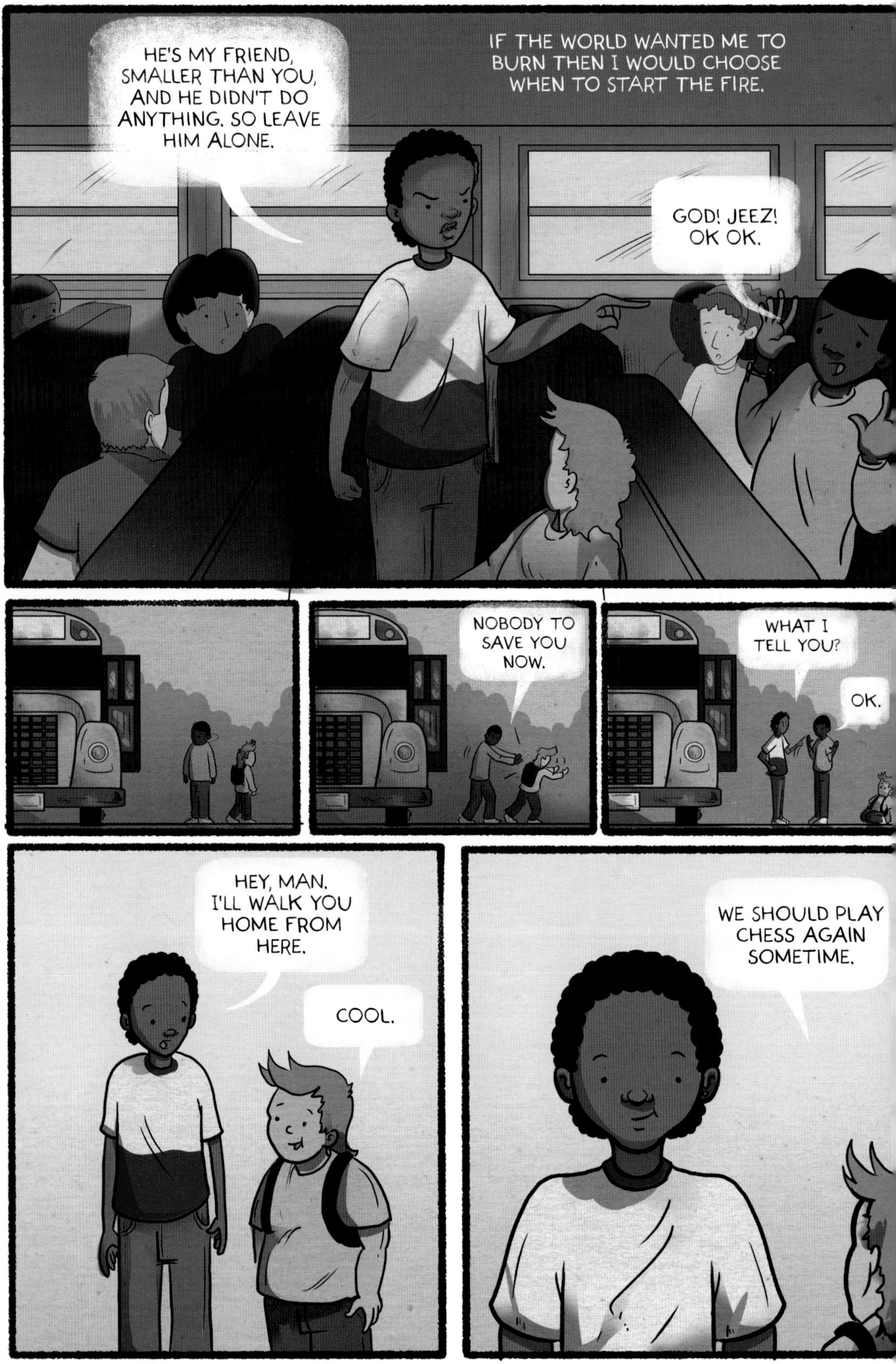
HE'S MY FRIEND, SMALLER THAN YOU, AND HE DIDN'T DO ANYTHING. SO LEAVE HIM ALONE.
IF THE WORLD WANTED ME TO BURN THEN I WOULD CHOOSE WHEN TO START THE FIRE.
GOD! JEEZ! OK OK.
NOBODY TO SAVE YOU NOW.
WHAT I TELL YOU?
OK.
HEY, MAN. I'LL WALK YOU HOME FROM HERE.
COOL.
WE SHOULD PLAY CHESS AGAIN SOMETIME.

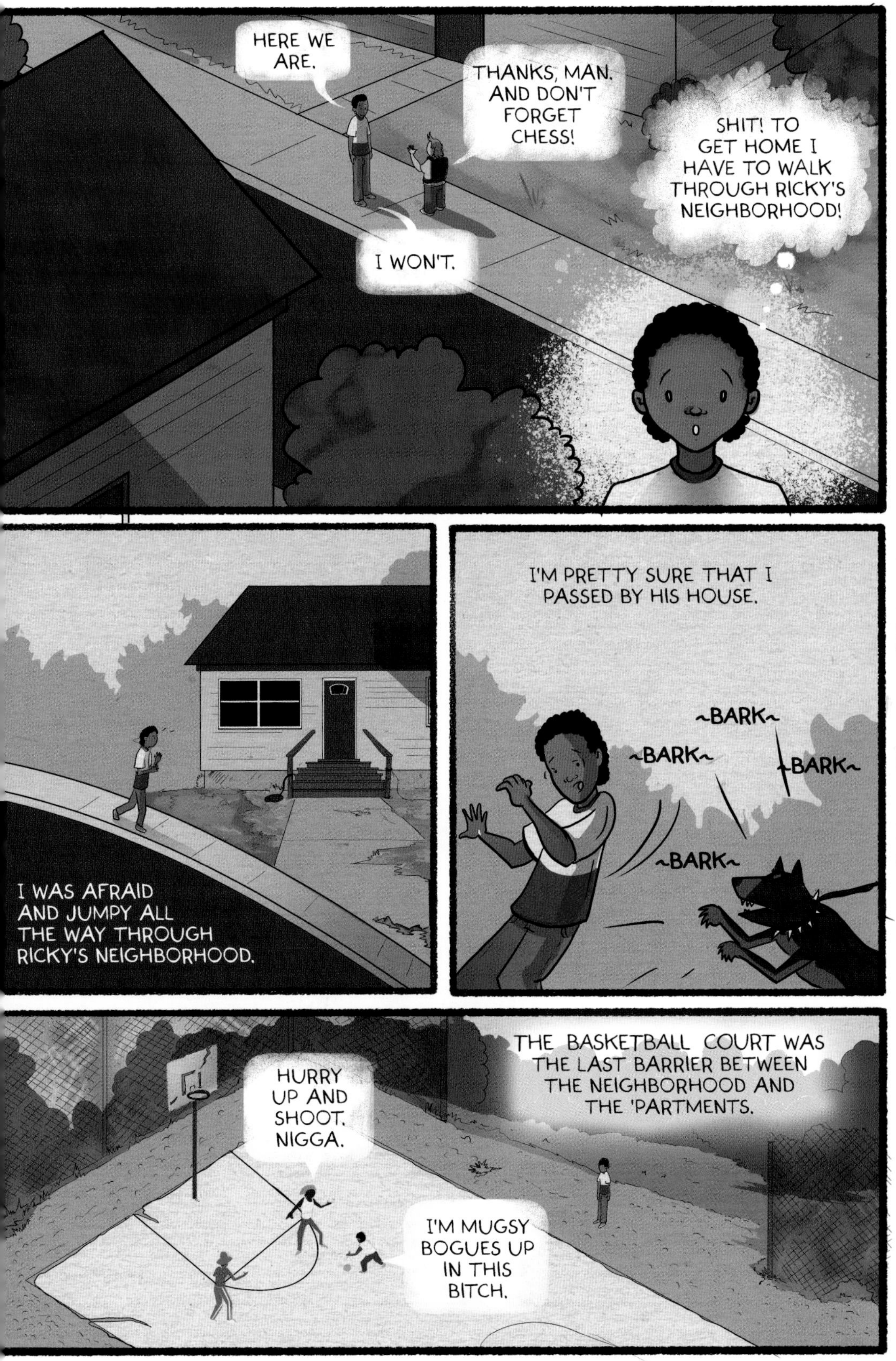
HERE WE ARE.
THANKS, MAN. AND DON'T FORGET CHESS!
I WON'T.
SHIT! TO GET HOME I HAVE TO WALK THROUGH RICKY'S NEIGHBORHOOD!
I WAS AFRAID AND JUMPY ALL THE WAY THROUGH RICKY'S NEIGHBORHOOD.
I'M PRETTY SURE THAT I PASSED BY HIS HOUSE.
~BARK~
~BARK~
~BARK~
~BARK~
THE BASKETBALL COURT WAS THE LAST BARRIER BETWEEN THE NEIGHBORHOOD AND THE 'PARTMENTS.
HURRY UP AND SHOOT, NIGGA.
I'M MUGSY BOGUES UP IN THIS BITCH.

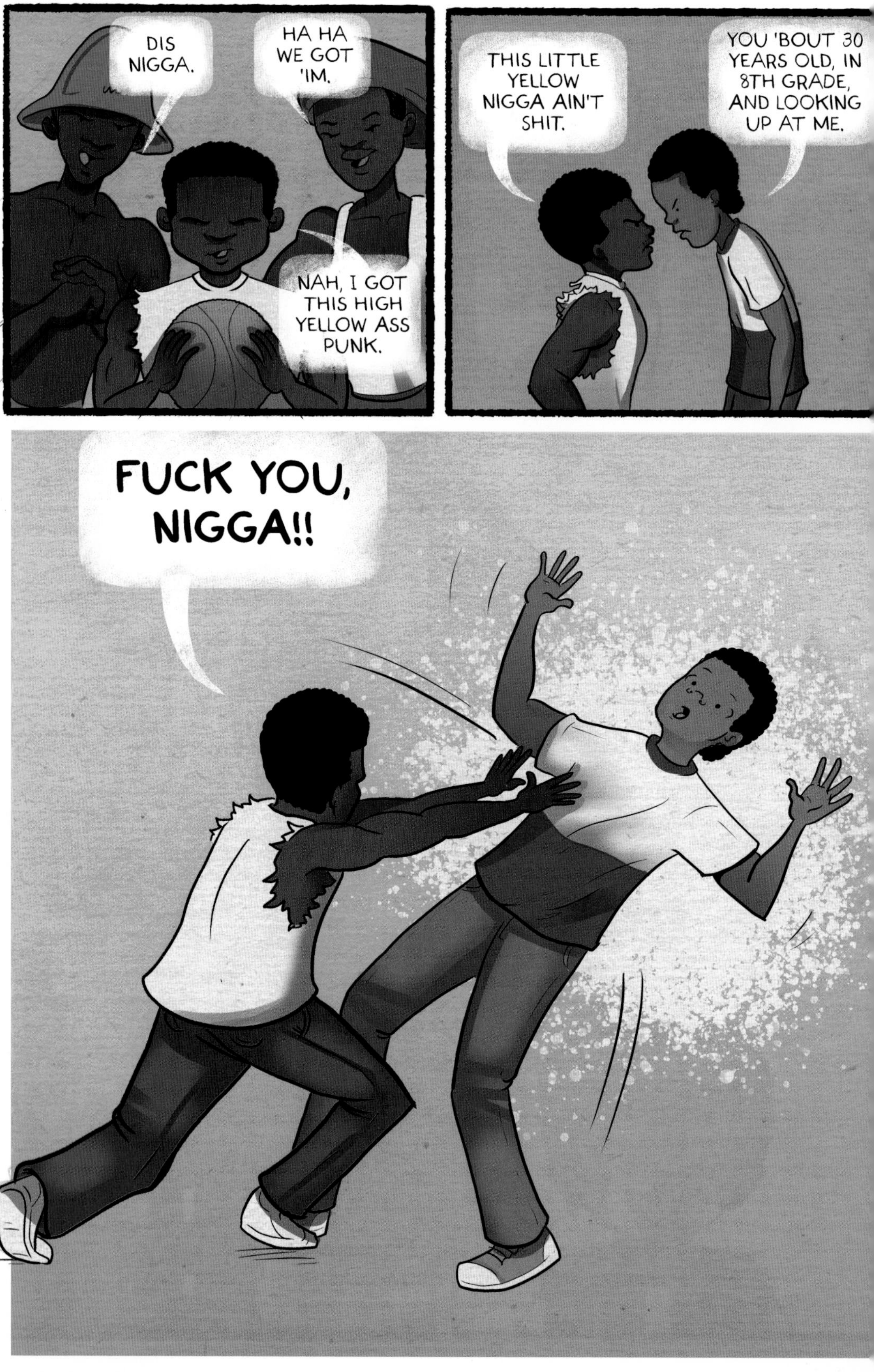
DIS NIGGA.
HA HA WE GOT 'IM.
NAH, I GOT THIS HIGH YELLOW ASS PUNK.
THIS LITTLE YELLOW NIGGA AIN'T SHIT.
YOU 'BOUT 30 YEARS OLD, IN 8TH GRADE, AND LOOKING UP AT ME.
FUCK YOU, NIGGA!!

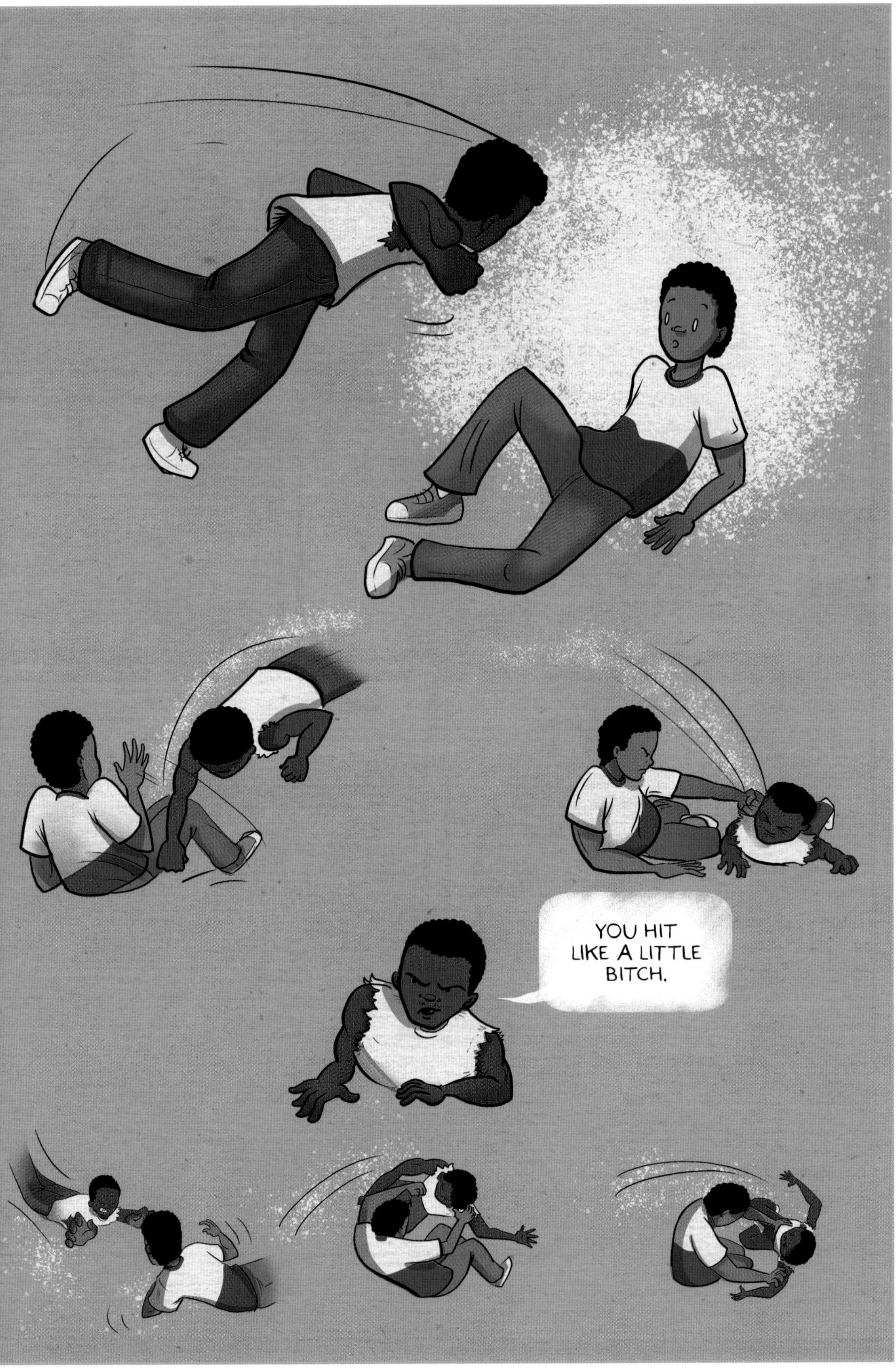
YOU HIT LIKE A LITTLE BITCH.

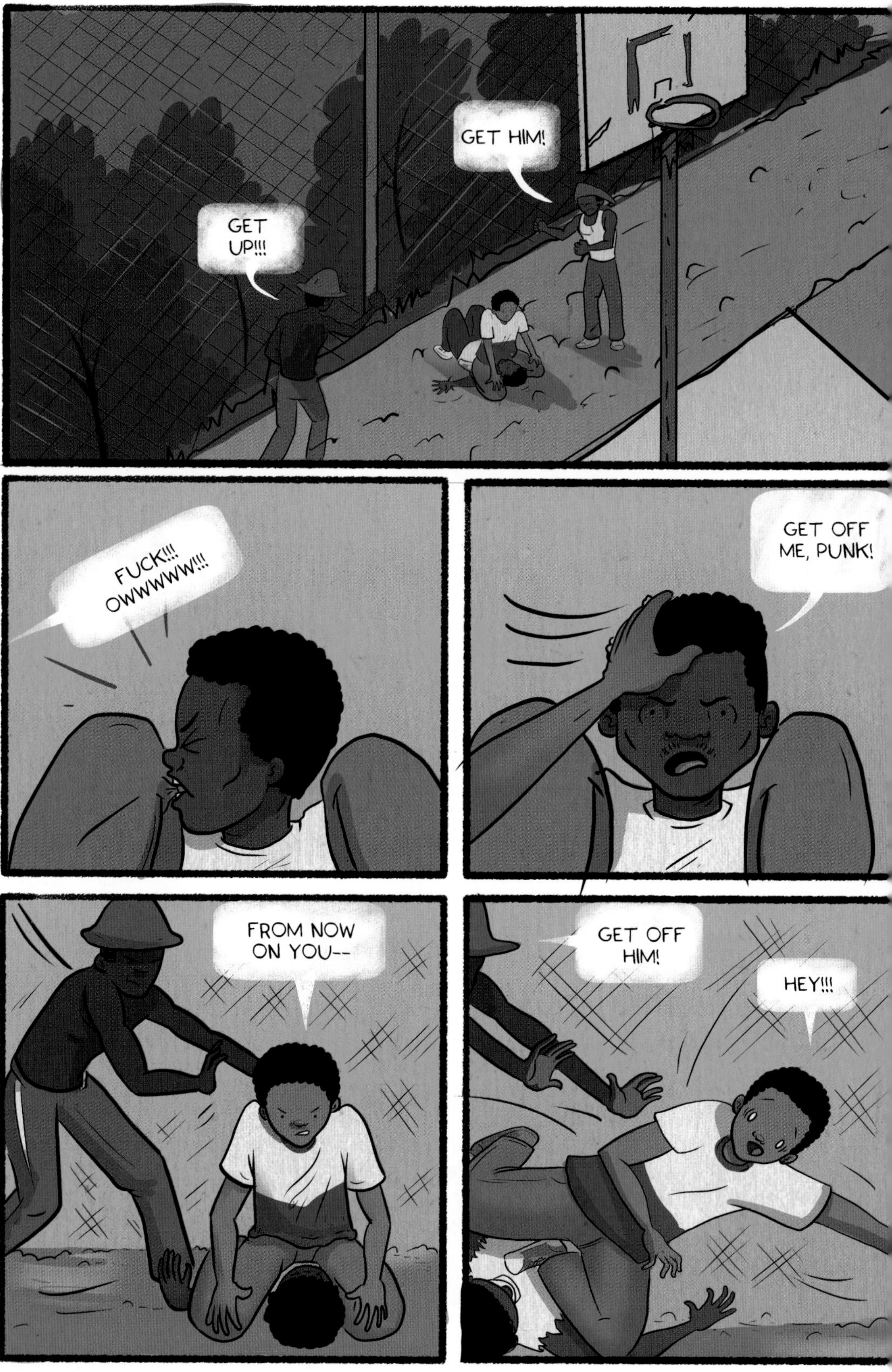
GET UP!!!
GET HIM!
FUCK!!! OWWWWW!!!
GET OFF ME, PUNK!
FROM NOW ON YOU--
GET OFF HIM!
HEY!!!

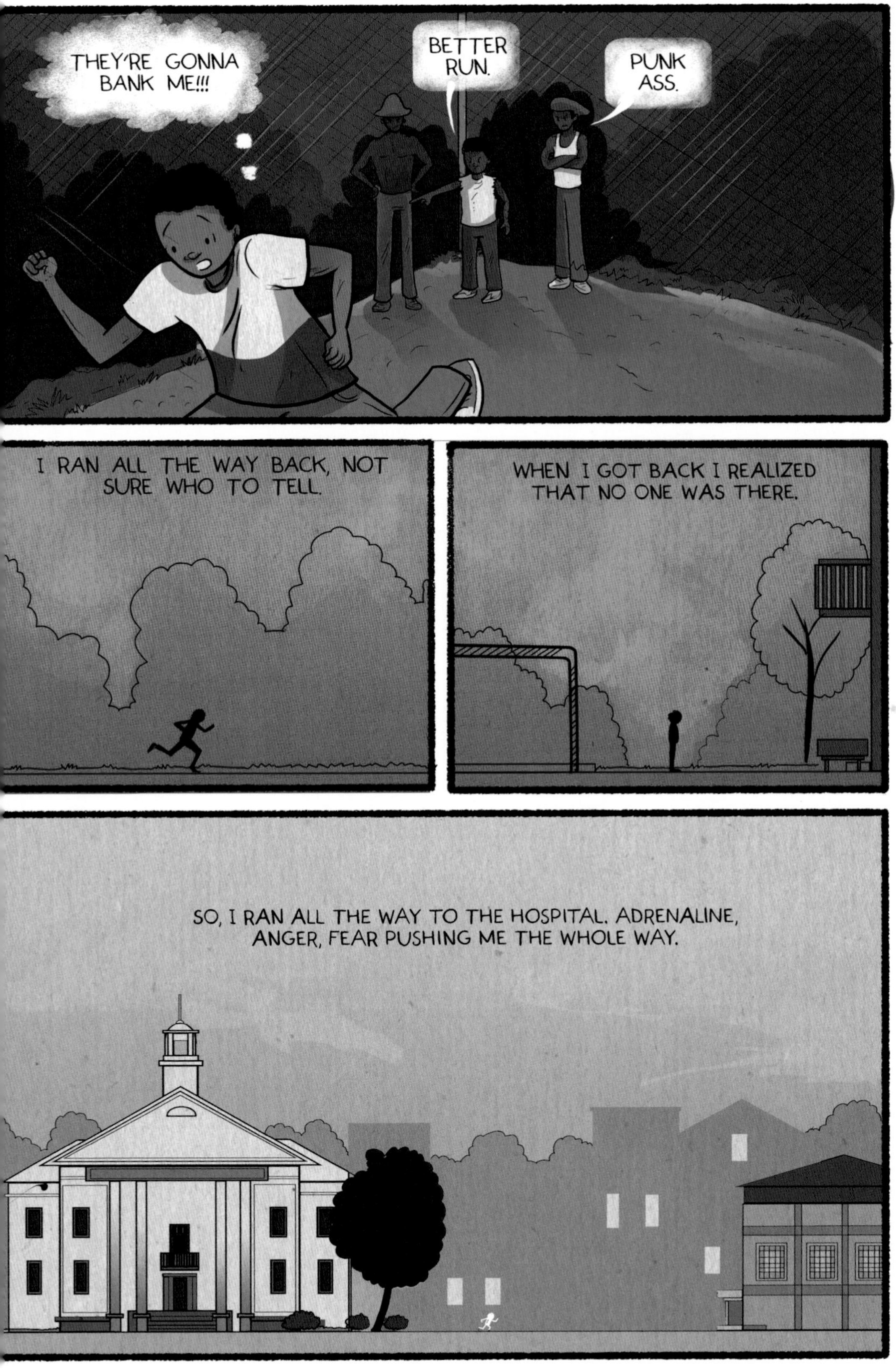
THEY'RE GONNA BANK ME!!!
BETTER RUN.
PUNK ASS.
I RAN ALL THE WAY BACK, NOT SURE WHO TO TELL.
WHEN I GOT BACK I REALIZED THAT NO ONE WAS THERE.
SO, I RAN ALL THE WAY TO THE HOSPITAL. ADRENALINE, ANGER, FEAR PUSHING ME THE WHOLE WAY.

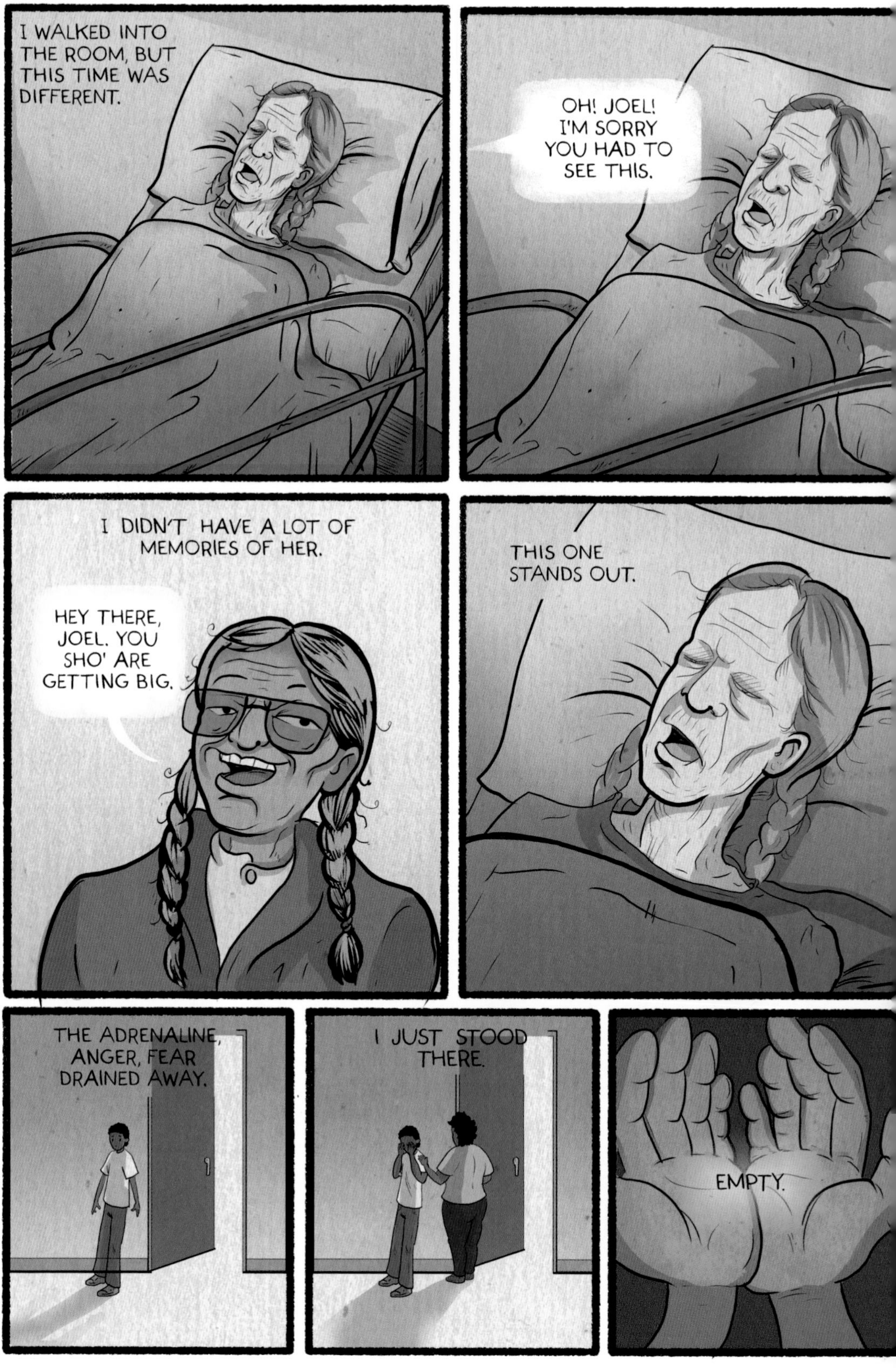

I WALKED INTO THE ROOM, BUT THIS TIME WAS DIFFERENT.
OH! JOEL! I'M SORRY YOU HAD TO SEE THIS.
I DIDN'T HAVE A LOT OF MEMORIES OF HER.
HEY THERE, JOEL. YOU SHO' ARE GETTING BIG.
THIS ONE STANDS OUT.
THE ADRENALINE, ANGER, FEAR DRAINED AWAY.
I JUST STOOD THERE.
EMPTY.

MY GRANDMOTHER WAS A BIG PART OF THE COMMUNITY, SO HER FUNERAL WAS A HUGE EVENT. MY SIBLINGS WERE THERE, AND ALL MY EXTENDED FAMILY. EVERYONE WAS SAD.

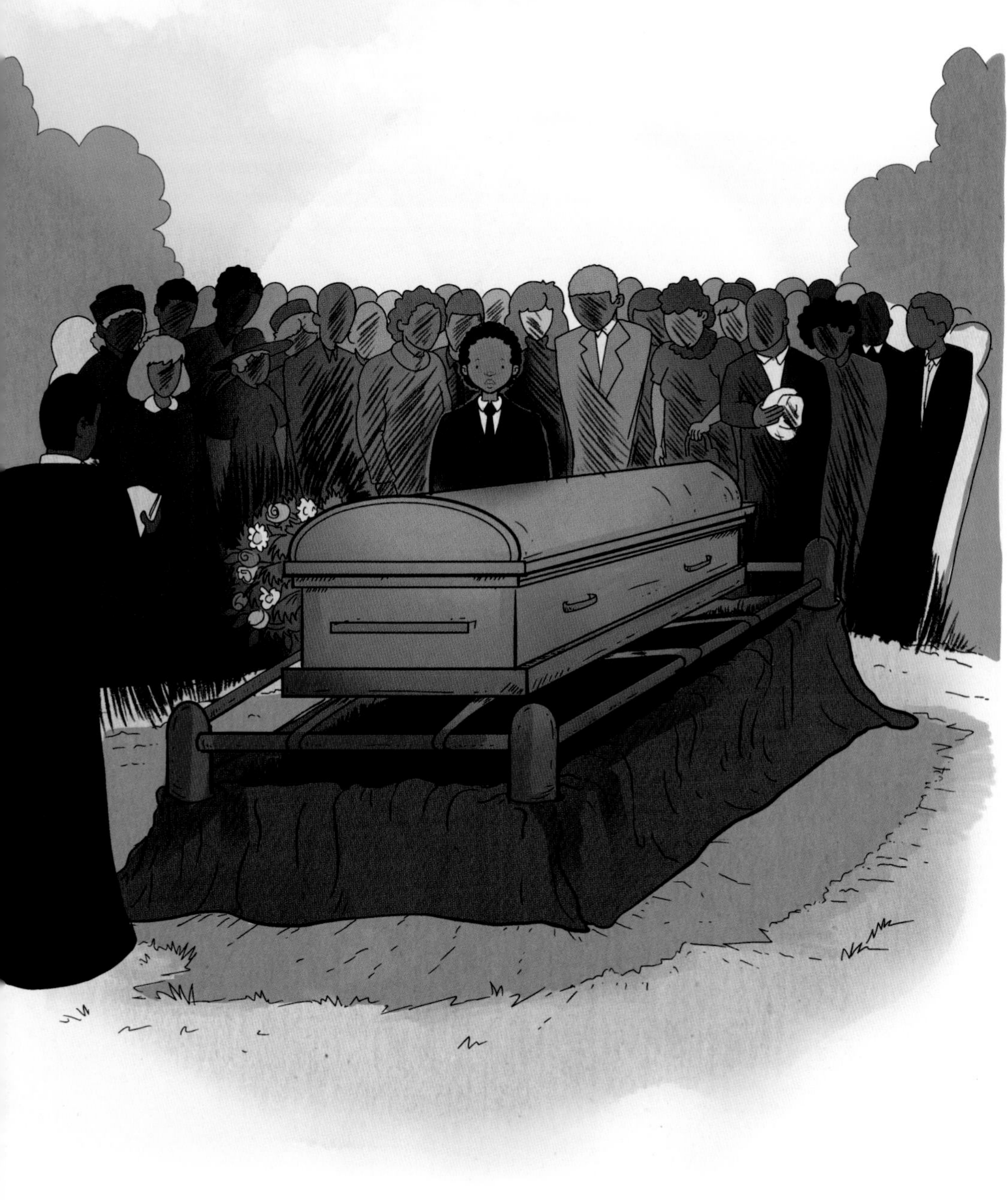

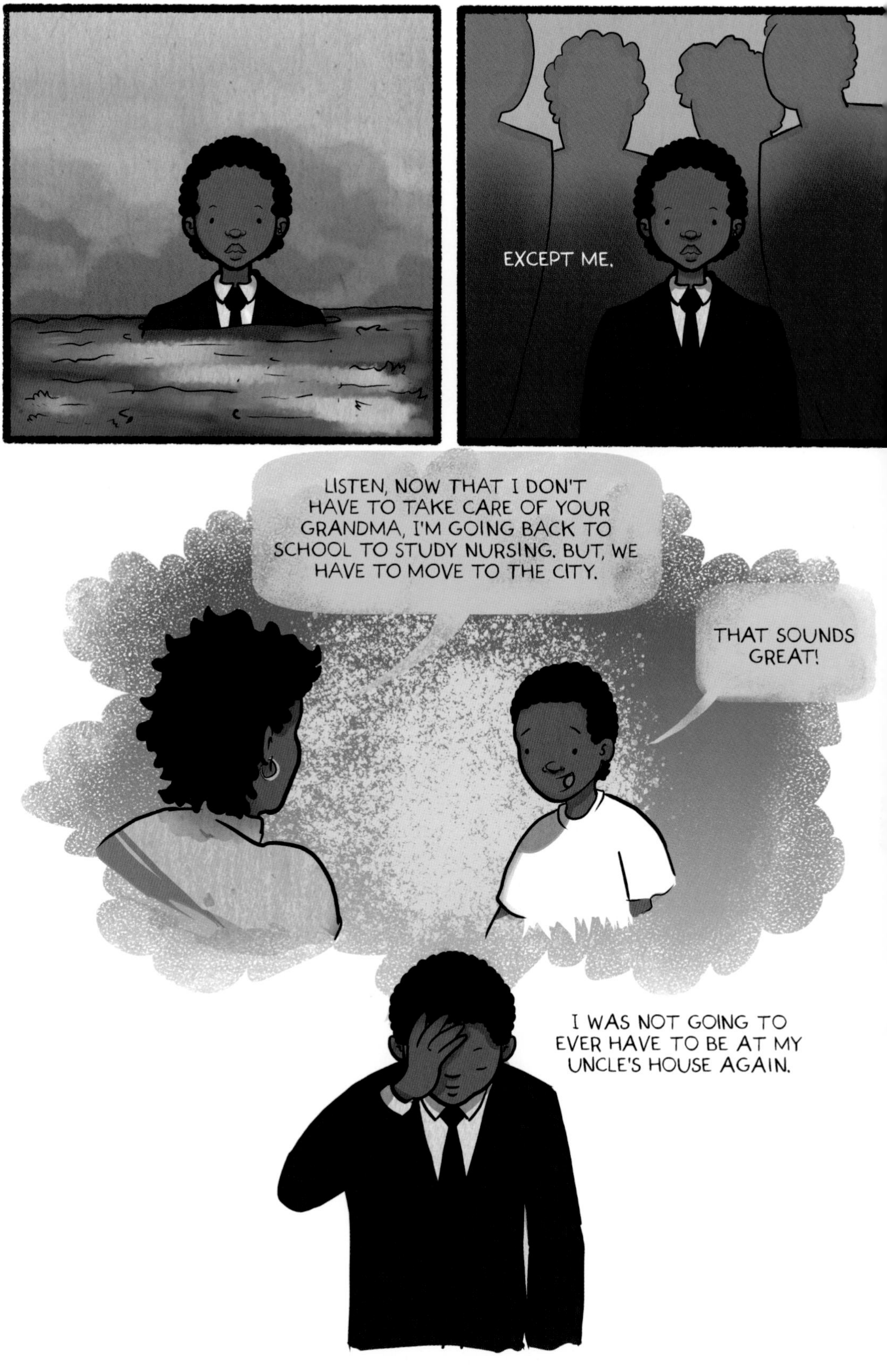
EXCEPT ME.
LISTEN, NOW THAT I DON'T HAVE TO TAKE CARE OF YOUR GRANDMA, I'M GOING BACK TO SCHOOL TO STUDY NURSING. BUT, WE HAVE TO MOVE TO THE CITY.
THAT SOUNDS GREAT!
I WAS NOT GOING TO EVER HAVE TO BE AT MY UNCLE'S HOUSE AGAIN.

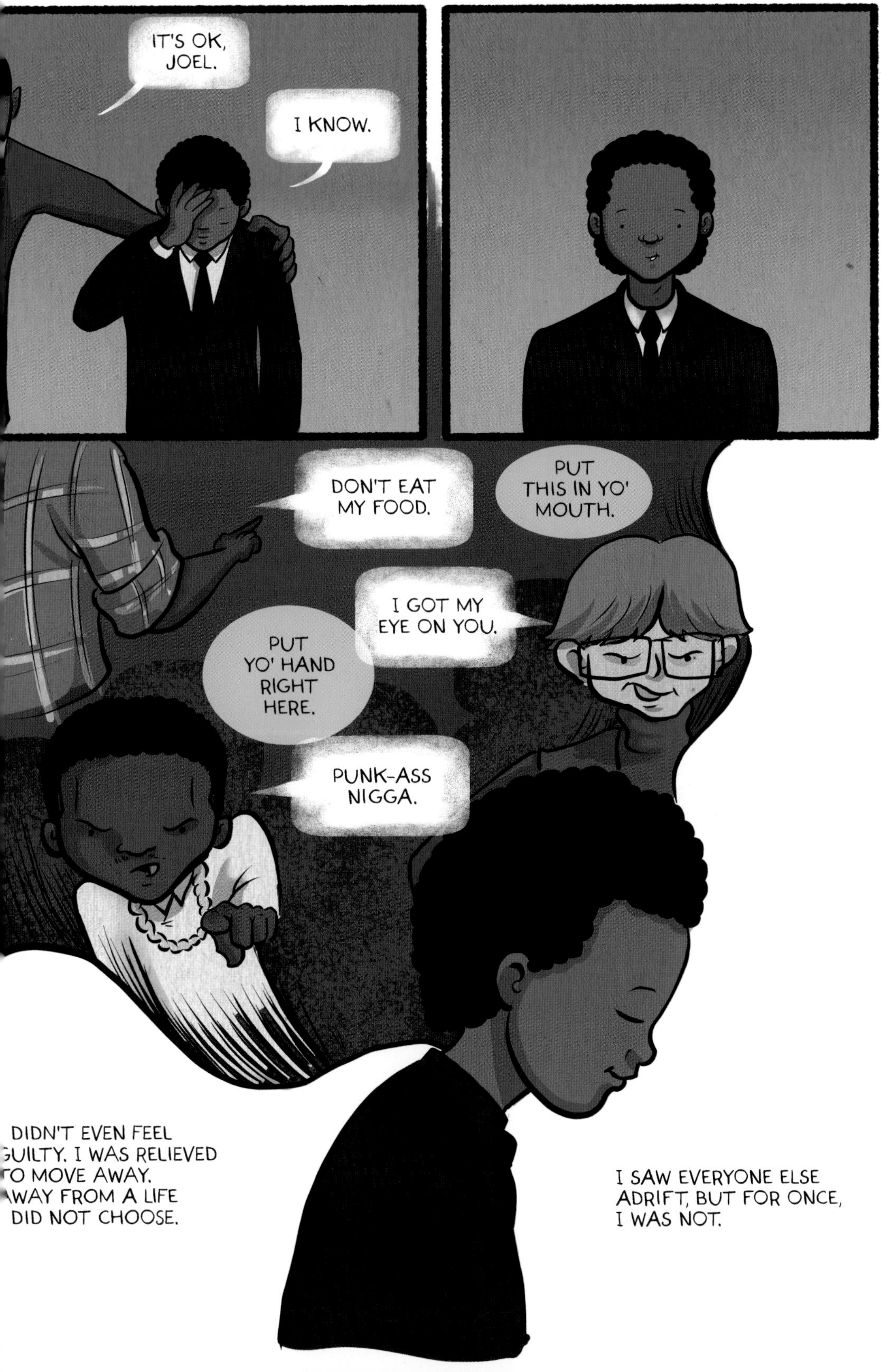
IT'S OK, JOEL.
I KNOW.
DON'T EAT MY FOOD.
PUT THIS IN YO' MOUTH.
I GOT MY EYE ON YOU.
PUT YO' HAND RIGHT HERE.
PUNK-ASS NIGGA.
DIDN'T EVEN FEEL
UILTY. I WAS RELIEVED
O MOVE AWAY.
WAY FROM A LIFE
DID NOT CHOOSE.
I SAW EVERYONE ELSE ADRIFT, BUT FOR ONCE, I WAS NOT.

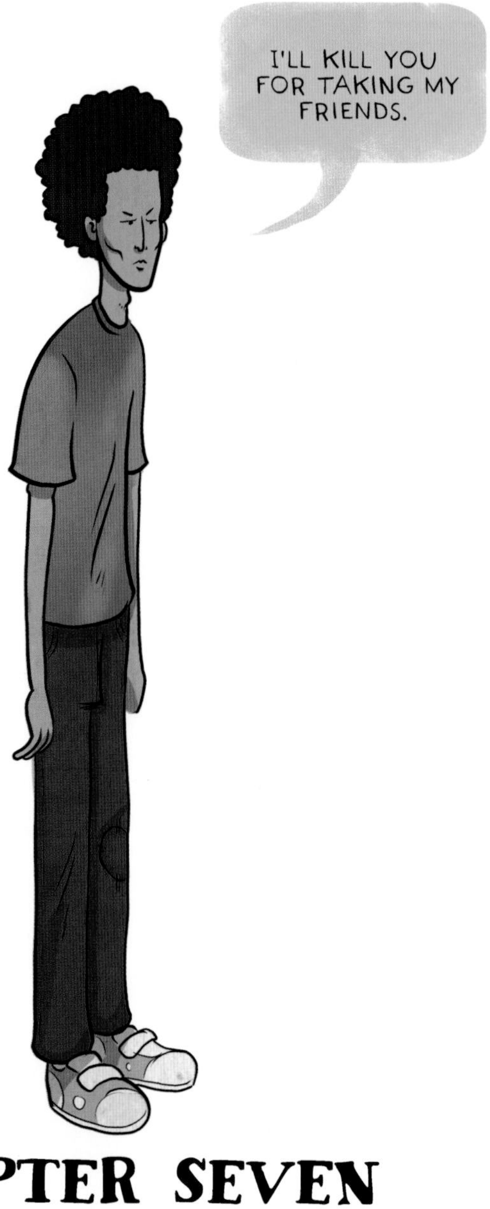
I'LL KILL YOU FOR TAKING MY FRIENDS.

CHAPTER SEVEN

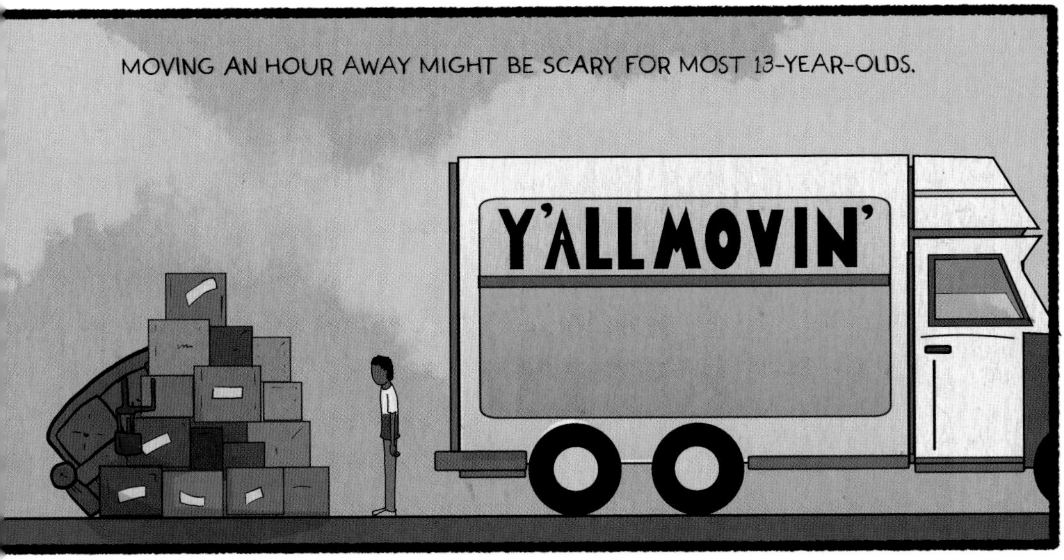
MOVING AN HOUR AWAY MIGHT BE SCARY FOR MOST 13-YEAR-OLDS.
Y'ALL MOVIN'
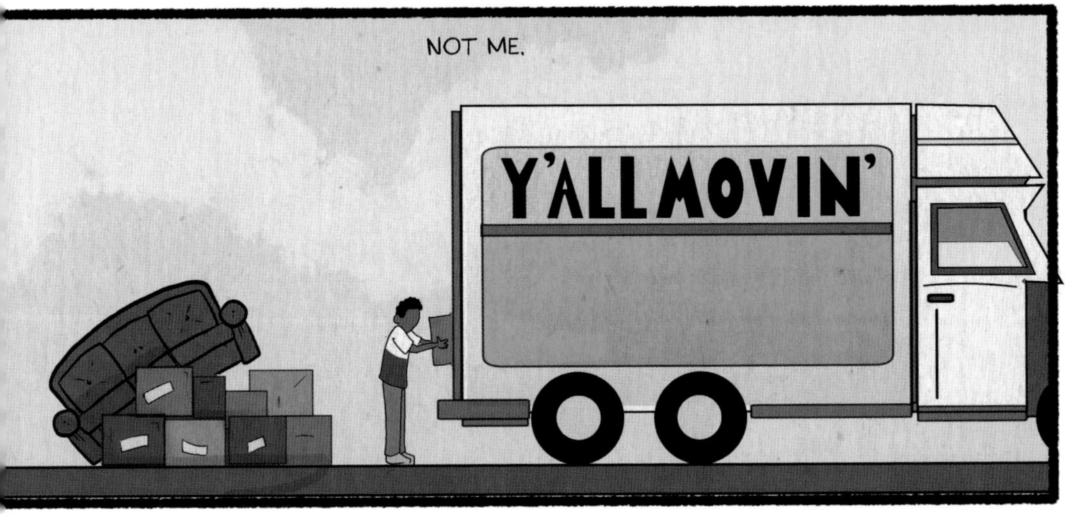
NOT ME.
Y'ALL MOVIN'
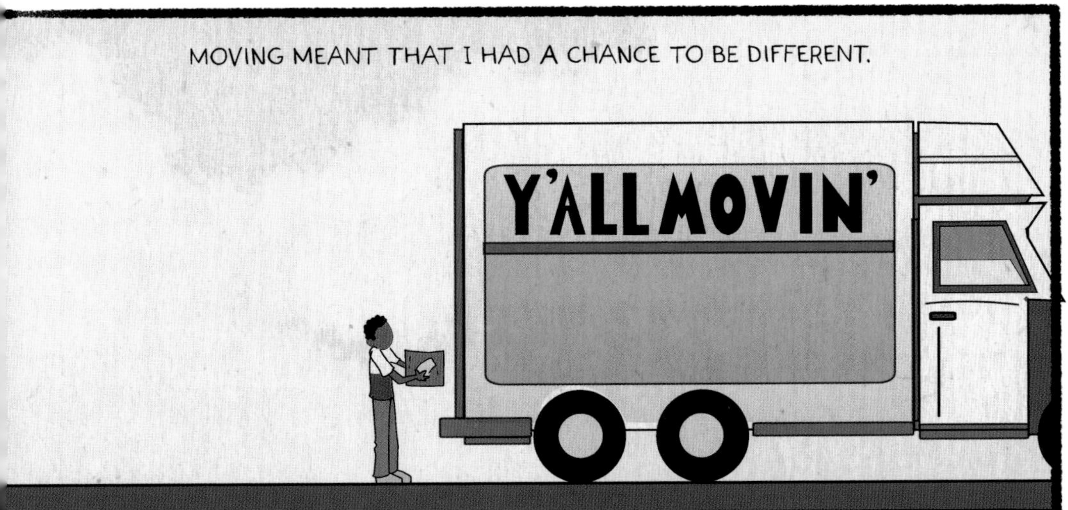
MOVING MEANT THAT I HAD A CHANCE TO BE DIFFERENT.
Y'ALL MOVIN'

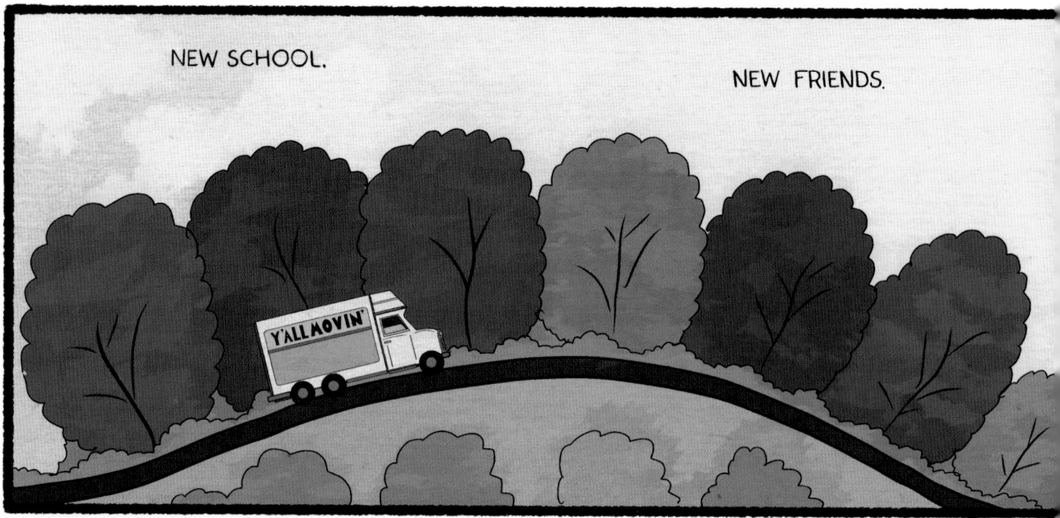
NEW SCHOOL.
NEW FRIENDS.
Y'ALL MOVIN'

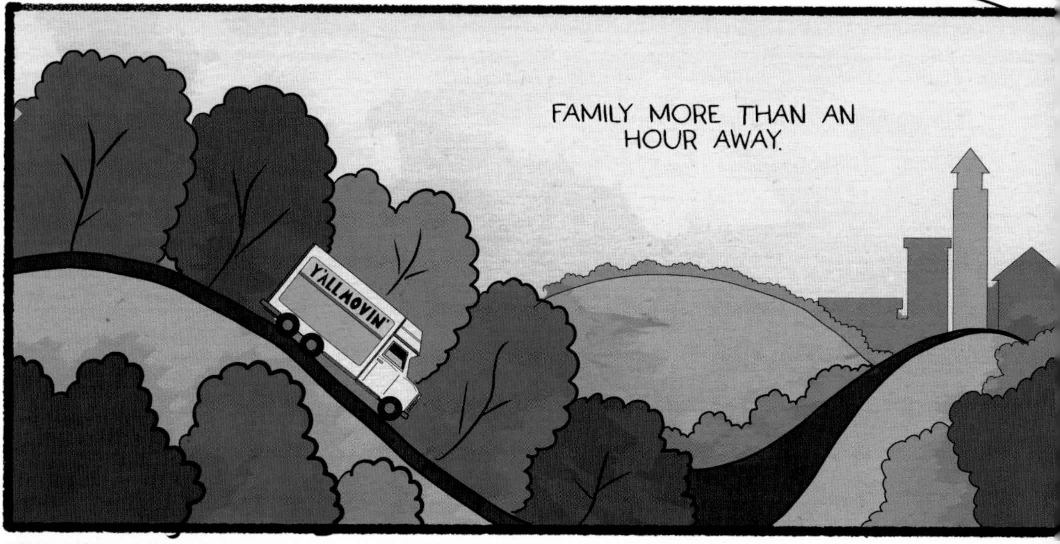
FAMILY MORE THAN AN HOUR AWAY.
Y'ALL MOVIN'

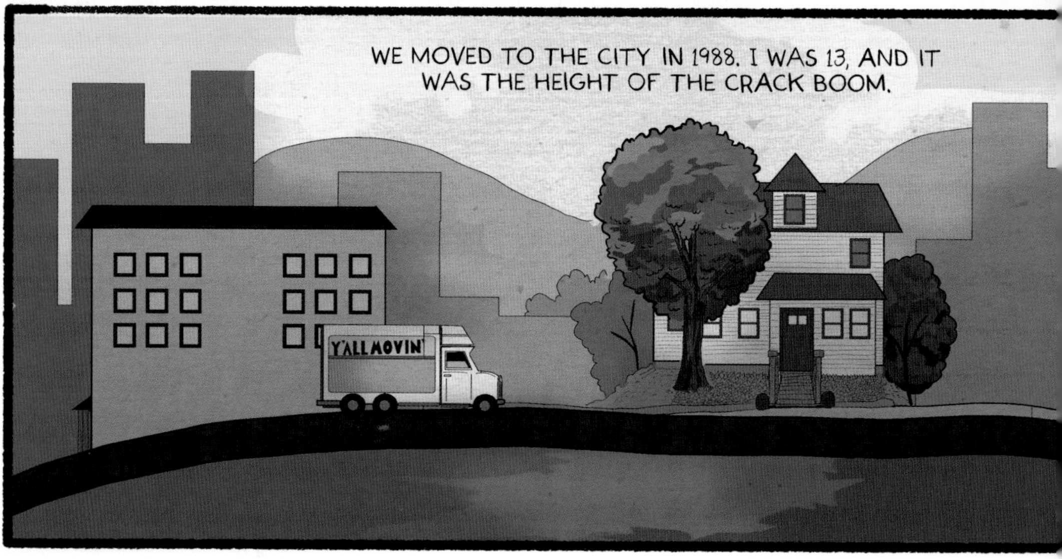
WE MOVED TO THE CITY IN 1988. I WAS 13, AND IT WAS THE HEIGHT OF THE CRACK BOOM.
Y'ALL MOVIN'

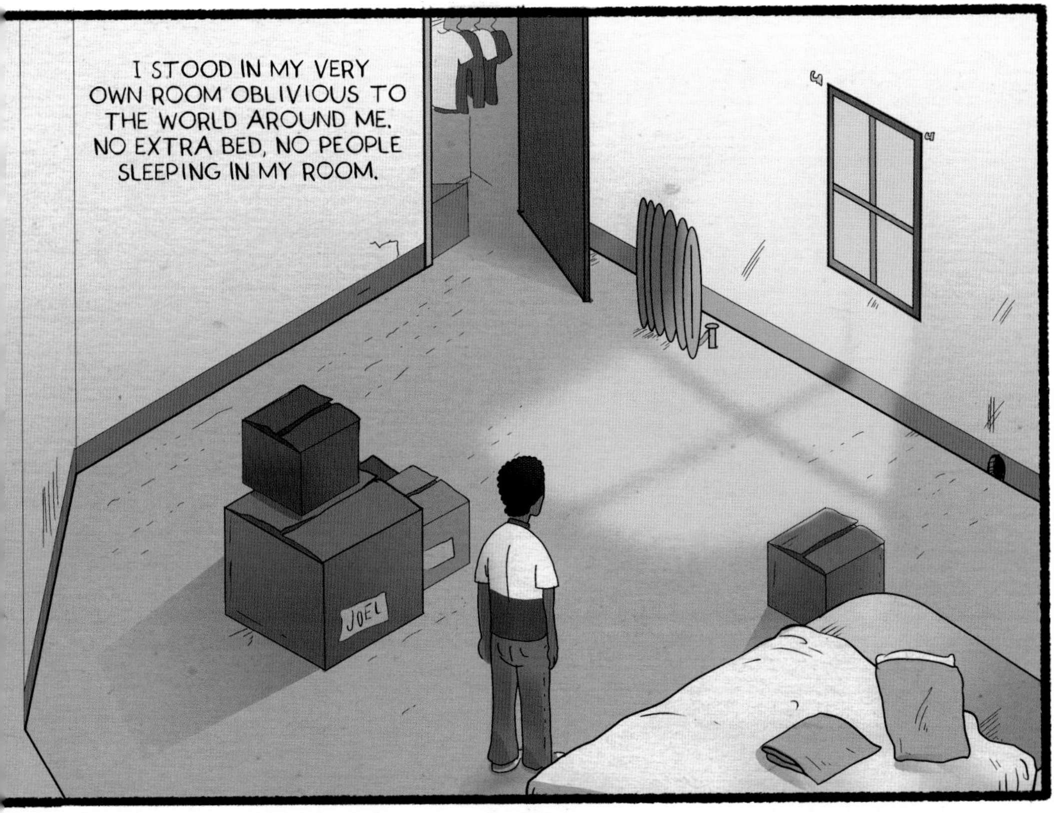
I STOOD IN MY VERY OWN ROOM OBLIVIOUS TO THE WORLD AROUND ME. NO EXTRA BED, NO PEOPLE SLEEPING IN MY ROOM.
JOEL

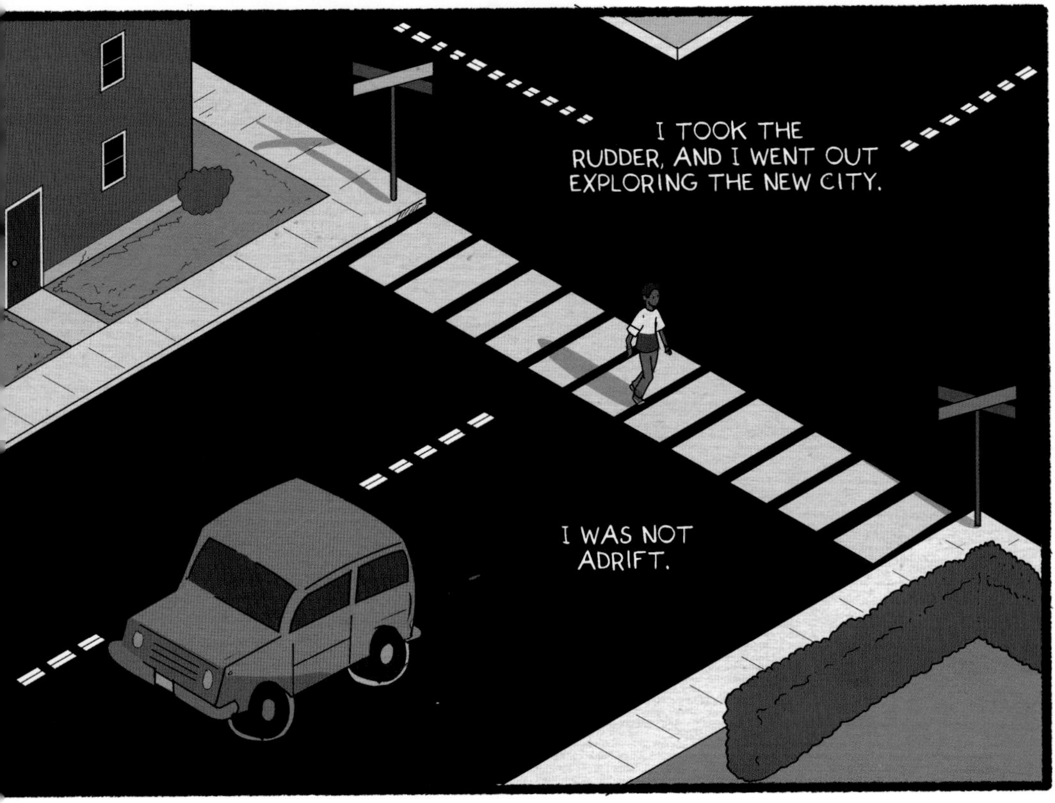
I TOOK THE RUDDER, AND I WENT OUT EXPLORING THE NEW CITY.
I WAS NOT ADRIFT.

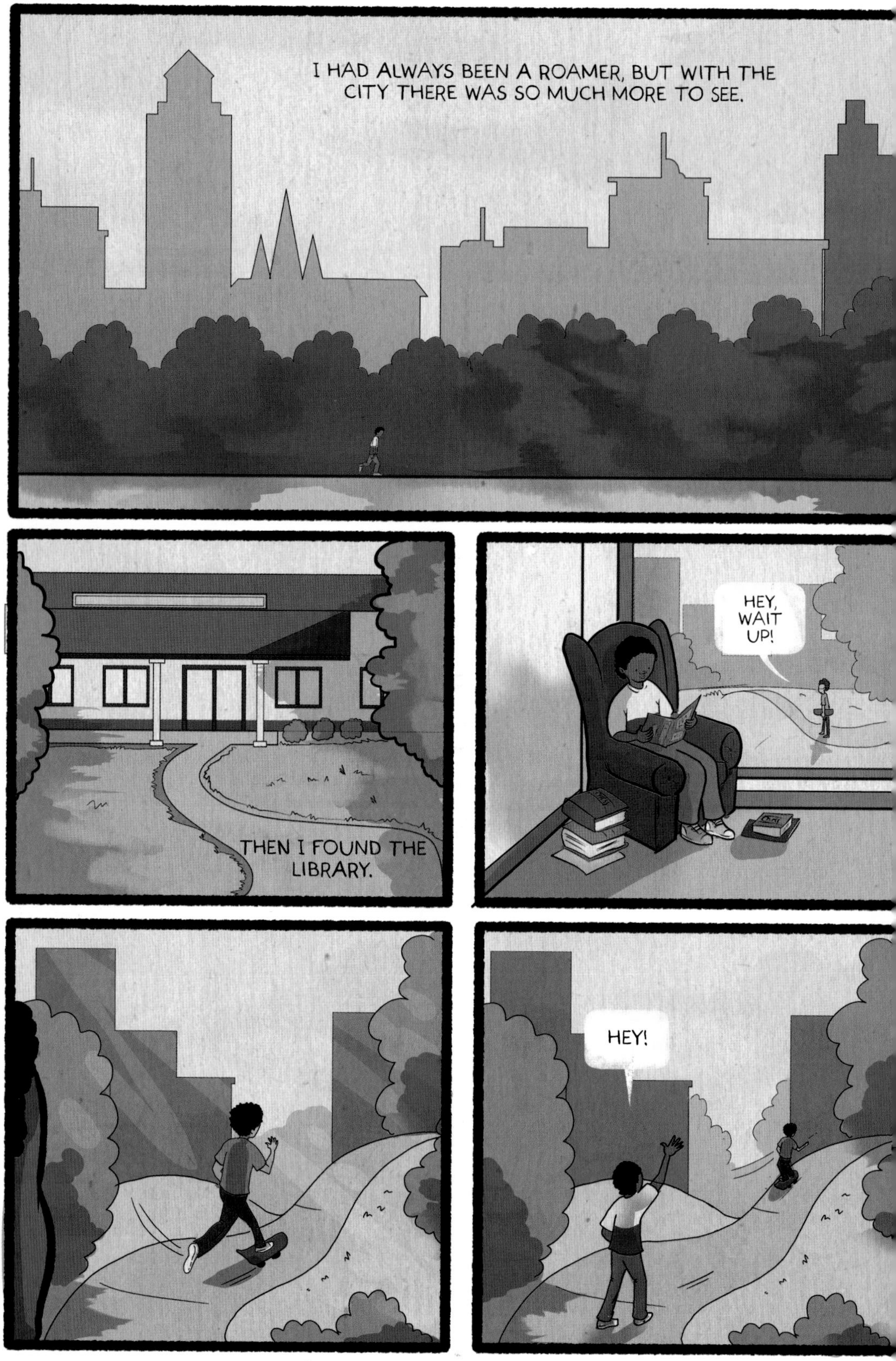
I HAD ALWAYS BEEN A ROAMER, BUT WITH THE CITY THERE WAS SO MUCH MORE TO SEE.
THEN I FOUND THE LIBRARY.
HEY, WAIT UP!
HEY!

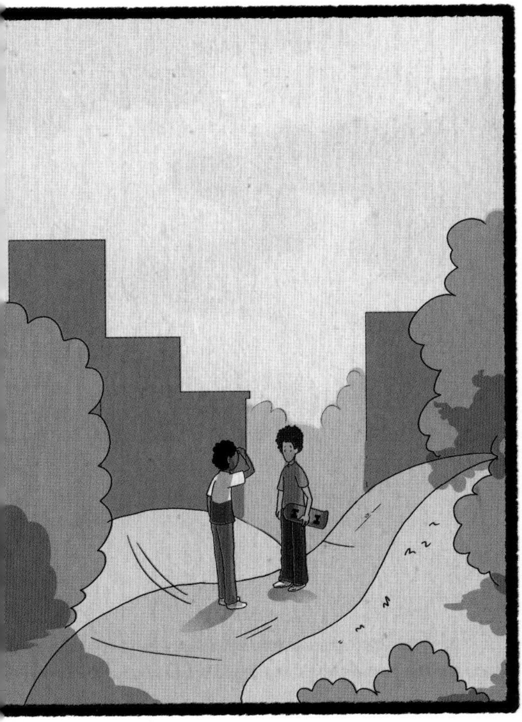

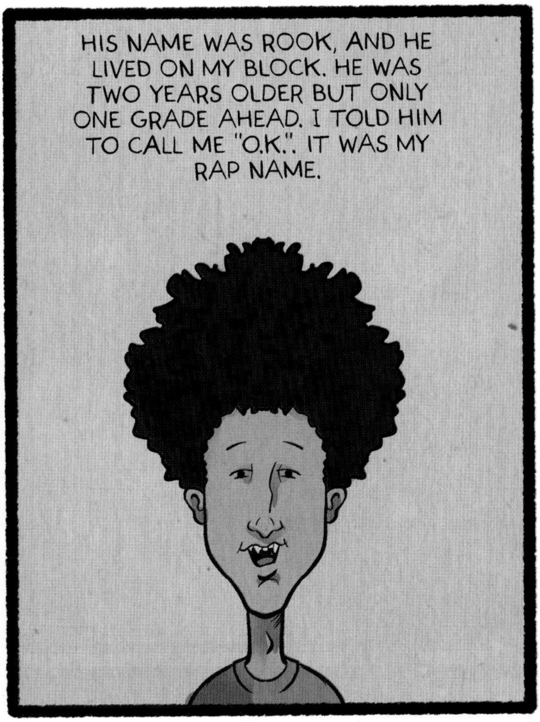
HIS NAME WAS ROOK, AND HE LIVED ON MY BLOCK. HE WAS TWO YEARS OLDER BUT ONLY ONE GRADE AHEAD. I TOLD HIM TO CALL ME "O.K.". IT WAS MY RAP NAME.

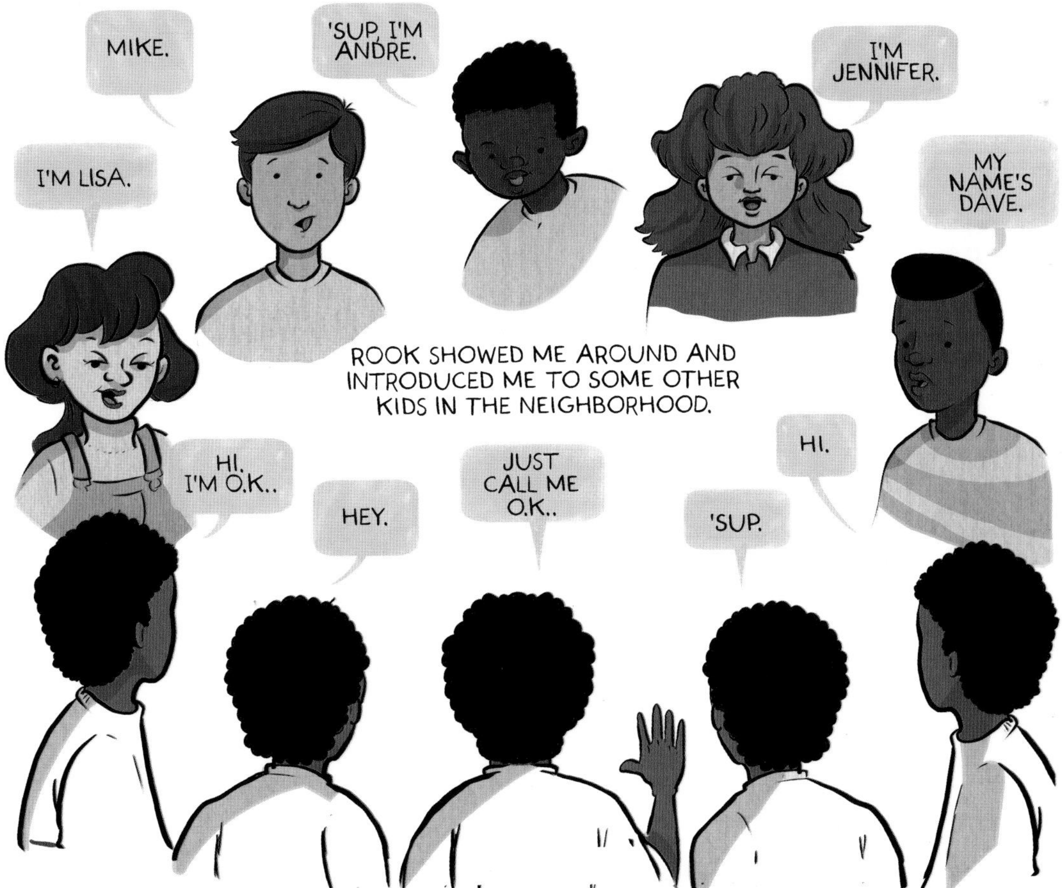
MIKE.
'SUP, I'M ANDRE.
I'M JENNIFER.
I'M LISA.
MY NAME'S DAVE.
ROOK SHOWED ME AROUND AND INTRODUCED ME TO SOME OTHER KIDS IN THE NEIGHBORHOOD.
HI. I'M O.K..
HEY.
JUST CALL ME O.K..
'SUP.
HI.

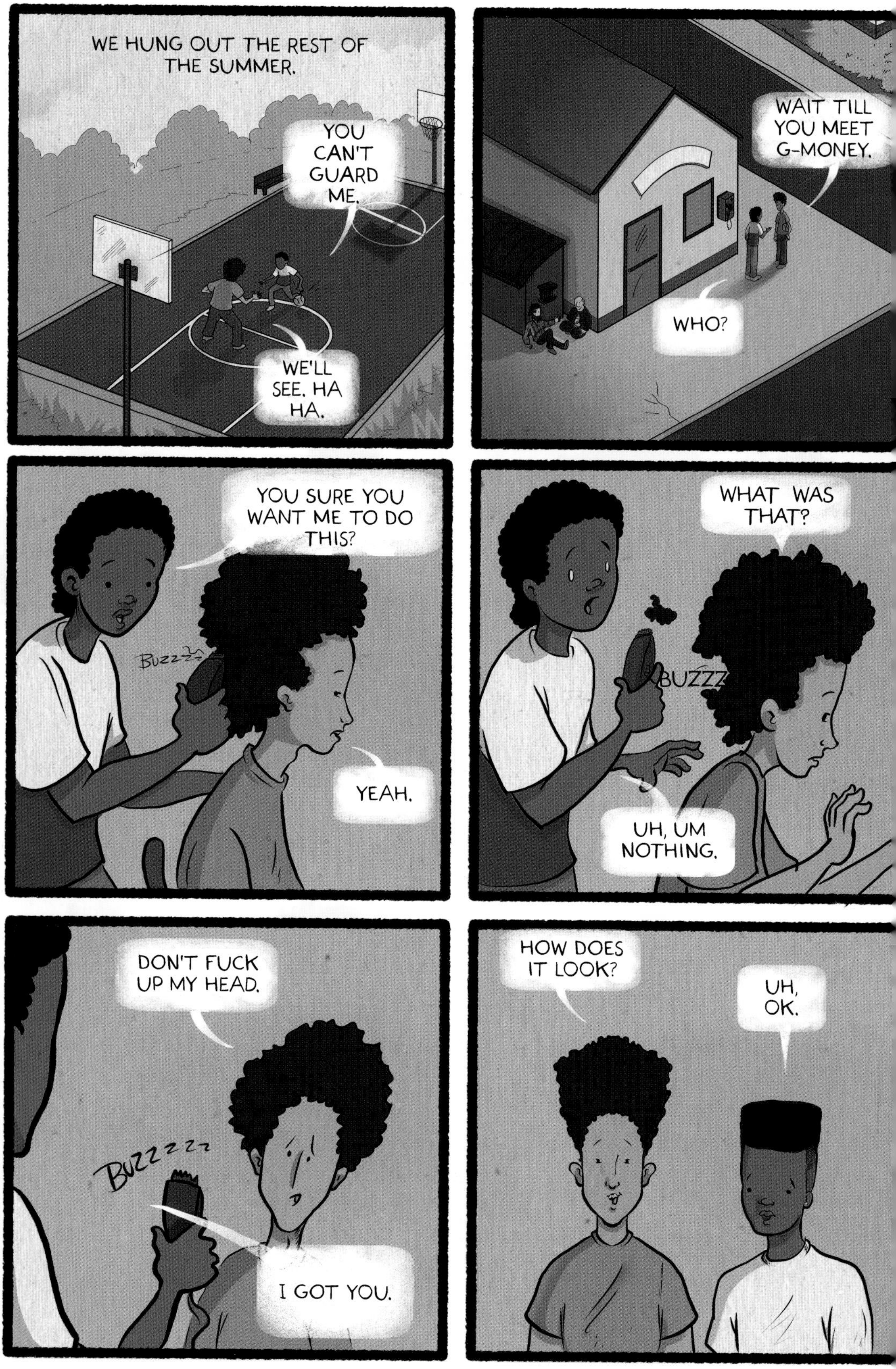
WE HUNG OUT THE REST OF THE SUMMER.
YOU CAN'T GUARD ME.
WE'LL SEE. HA HA.
WAIT TILL YOU MEET G-MONEY.
WHO?
YOU SURE YOU WANT ME TO DO THIS?
BUZZZZ
YEAH.
WHAT WAS THAT?
BUZZZ
UH, UM NOTHING.
DON'T FUCK UP MY HEAD.
BUZZZZZ
I GOT YOU.
HOW DOES IT LOOK?
UH, OK.

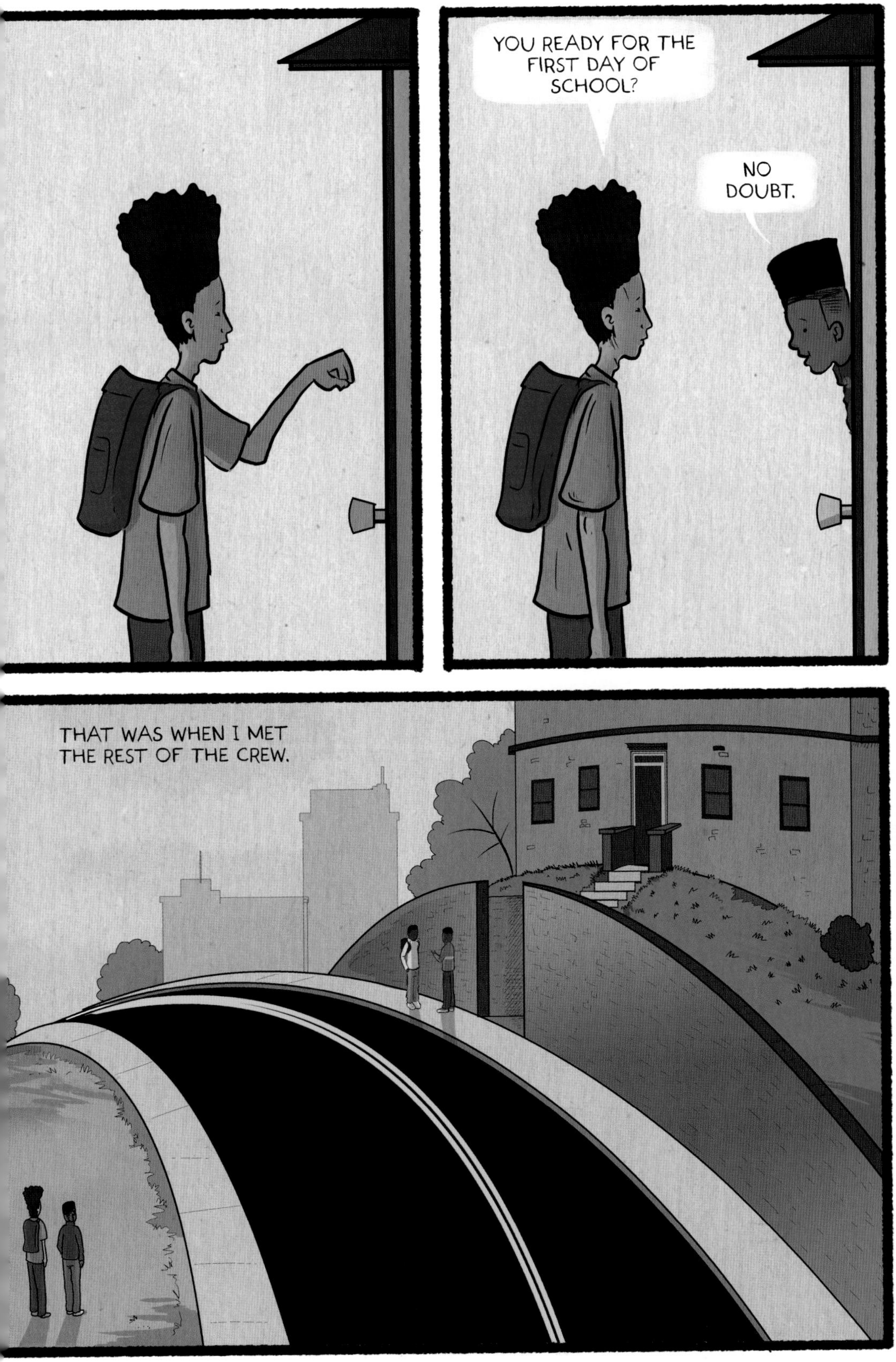
YOU READY FOR THE FIRST DAY OF SCHOOL?
NO DOUBT.
THAT WAS WHEN I MET THE REST OF THE CREW.

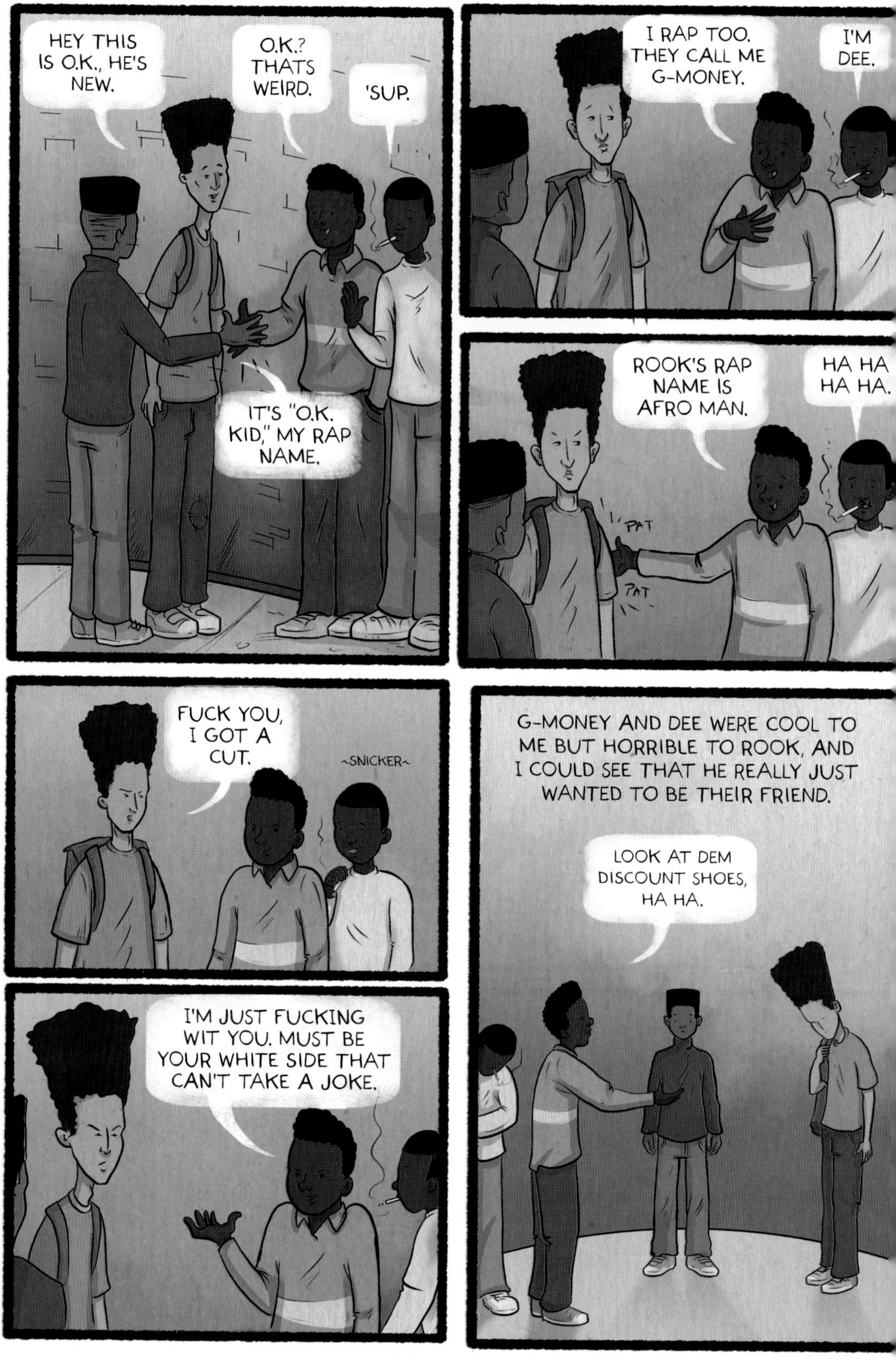
HEY THIS IS O.K., HE'S NEW.
O.K.? THATS WEIRD.
'SUP.
IT'S "O.K. KID," MY RAP NAME.
I RAP TOO. THEY CALL ME G-MONEY.
I'M DEE.
ROOK'S RAP NAME IS AFRO MAN.
HA HA HA HA.
PAT
PAT
FUCK YOU, I GOT A CUT.
~SNICKER~
I'M JUST FUCKING WIT YOU. MUST BE YOUR WHITE SIDE THAT CAN'T TAKE A JOKE.
G-MONEY AND DEE WERE COOL TO ME BUT HORRIBLE TO ROOK, AND I COULD SEE THAT HE REALLY JUST WANTED TO BE THEIR FRIEND.
LOOK AT DEM DISCOUNT SHOES, HA HA.

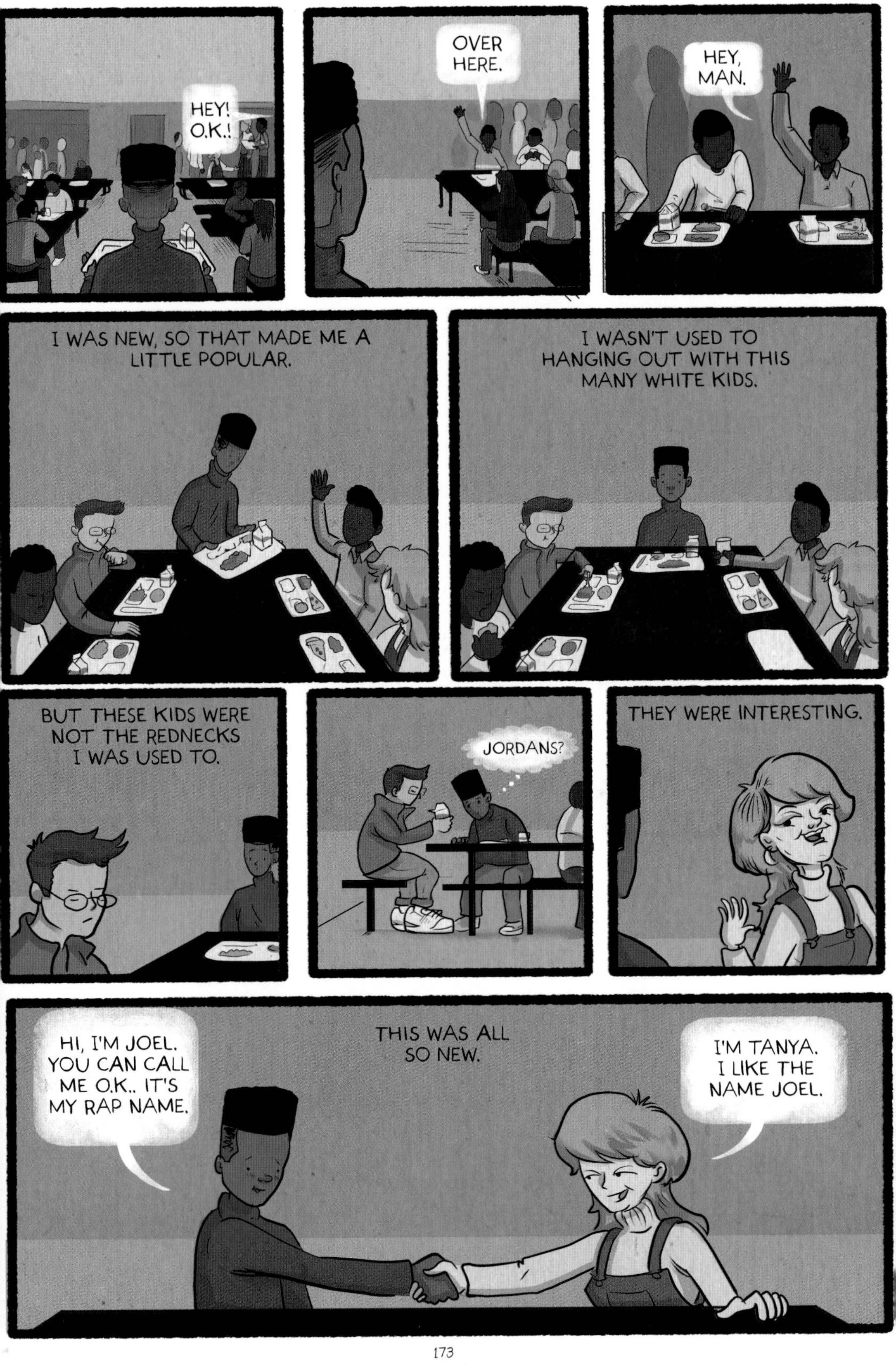
HEY! O.K.!
OVER HERE.
HEY, MAN.
I WAS NEW, SO THAT MADE ME A LITTLE POPULAR.
I WASN'T USED TO HANGING OUT WITH THIS MANY WHITE KIDS.
BUT THESE KIDS WERE NOT THE REDNECKS I WAS USED TO.
JORDANS?
THEY WERE INTERESTING.
HI, I'M JOEL. YOU CAN CALL ME O.K.. IT'S MY RAP NAME.
THIS WAS ALL SO NEW.
I'M TANYA. I LIKE THE NAME JOEL.

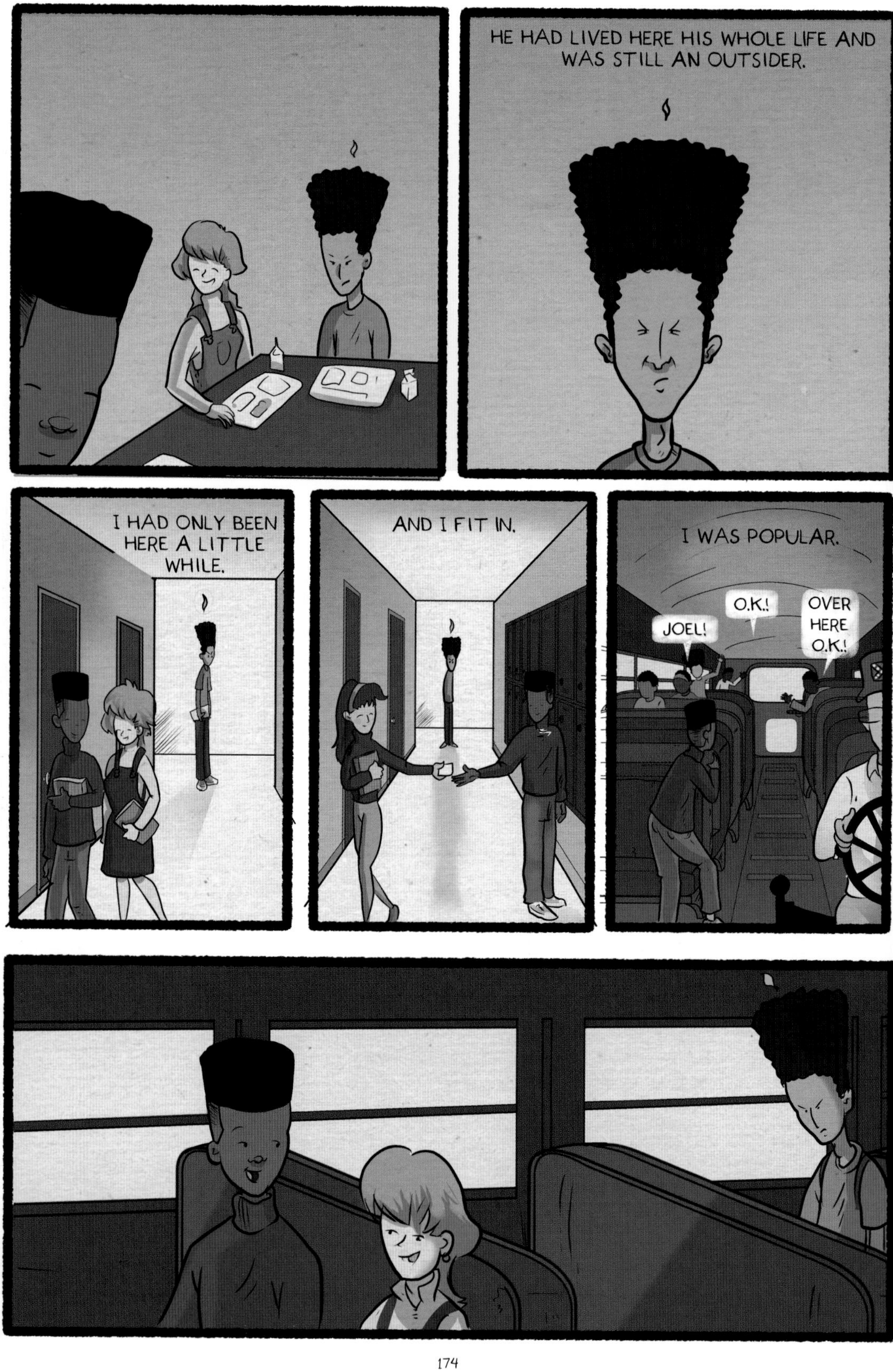
HE HAD LIVED HERE HIS WHOLE LIFE AND WAS STILL AN OUTSIDER.
I HAD ONLY BEEN HERE A LITTLE WHILE.
AND I FIT IN.
I WAS POPULAR.
JOEL!
O.K.!
OVER HERE O.K.!

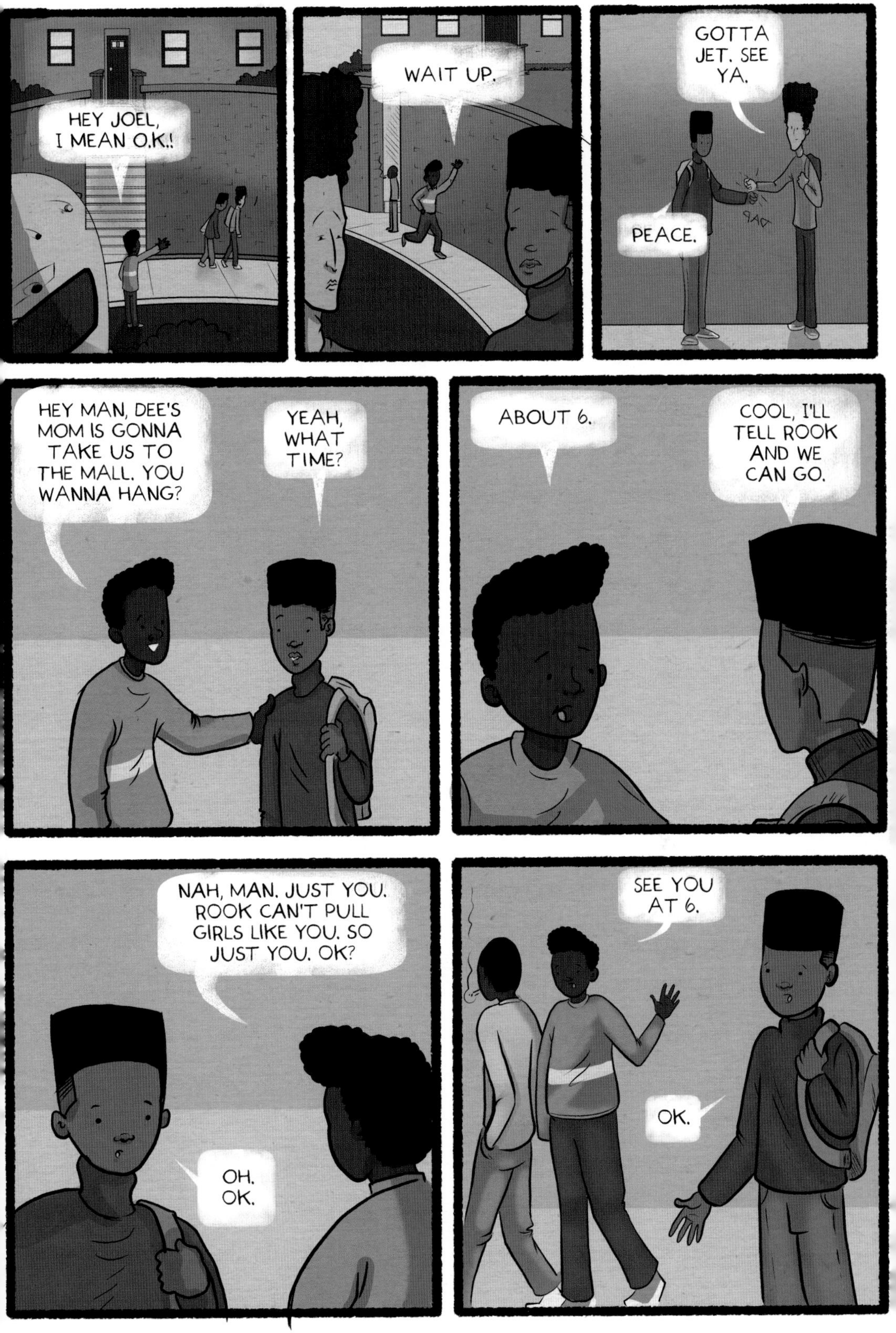
HEY JOEL, I MEAN O.K.!
WAIT UP.
GOTTA JET. SEE YA.
PEACE.
DAP
HEY MAN, DEE'S MOM IS GONNA TAKE US TO THE MALL. YOU WANNA HANG?
YEAH, WHAT TIME?
ABOUT 6.
COOL, I'LL TELL ROOK AND WE CAN GO.
NAH, MAN. JUST YOU. ROOK CAN'T PULL GIRLS LIKE YOU. SO JUST YOU. OK?
OH. OK.
SEE YOU AT 6.
OK.

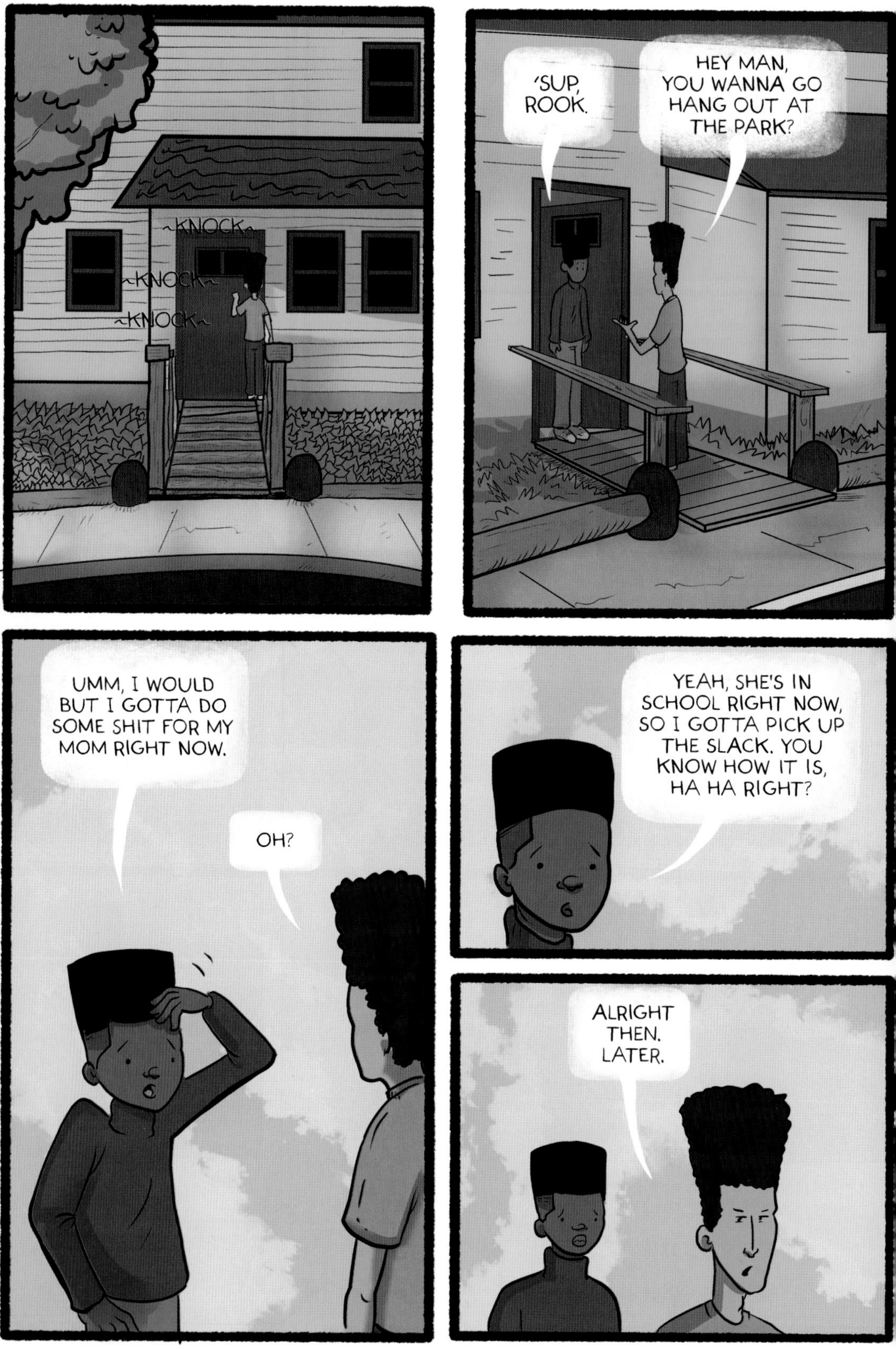
KNOCK
KNOCK
KNOCK
'SUP, ROOK.
HEY MAN, YOU WANNA GO HANG OUT AT THE PARK?
UMM, I WOULD BUT I GOTTA DO SOME SHIT FOR MY MOM RIGHT NOW.
OH?
YEAH, SHE'S IN SCHOOL RIGHT NOW, SO I GOTTA PICK UP THE SLACK. YOU KNOW HOW IT IS, HA HA RIGHT?
ALRIGHT THEN. LATER.

BY DITCHING ONE FRIEND I GAINED A FEW MORE.

I BECAME ONE OF THE GROUP.

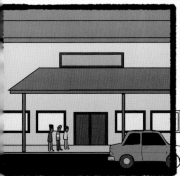

IT WAS GREAT!

IT WAS EASY TO EXCLUDE ROOK.

GIRLS WERE THE ONLY REASON TO DO ANYTHING.

EVENTUALLY, I REMEMBERED.

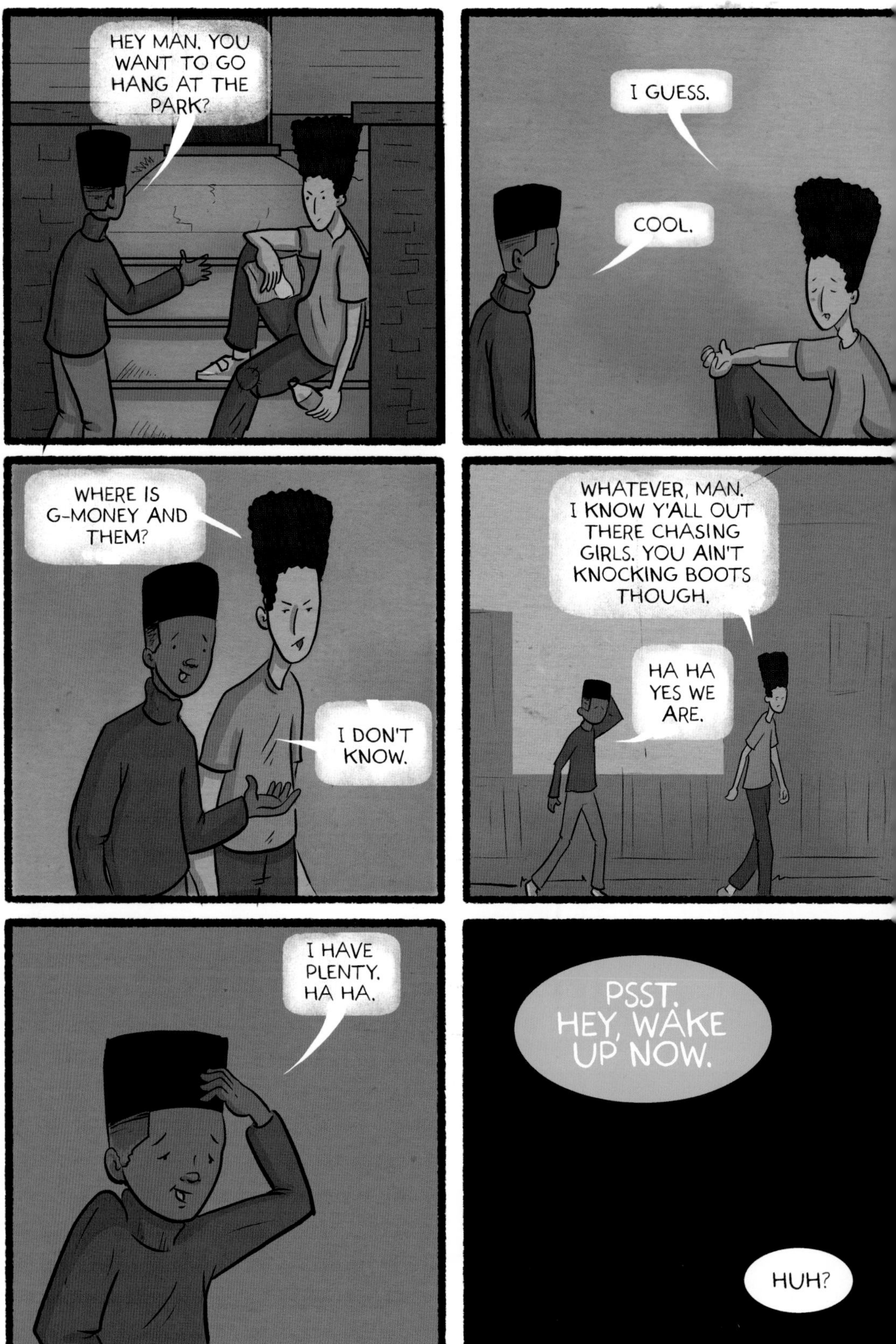
HEY MAN. YOU WANT TO GO HANG AT THE PARK?
I GUESS.
COOL.
WHERE IS G-MONEY AND THEM?
I DON'T KNOW.
WHATEVER, MAN. I KNOW Y'ALL OUT THERE CHASING GIRLS. YOU AIN'T KNOCKING BOOTS THOUGH.
HA HA YES WE ARE.
I HAVE PLENTY. HA HA.
PSST. HEY, WAKE UP NOW.
HUH?

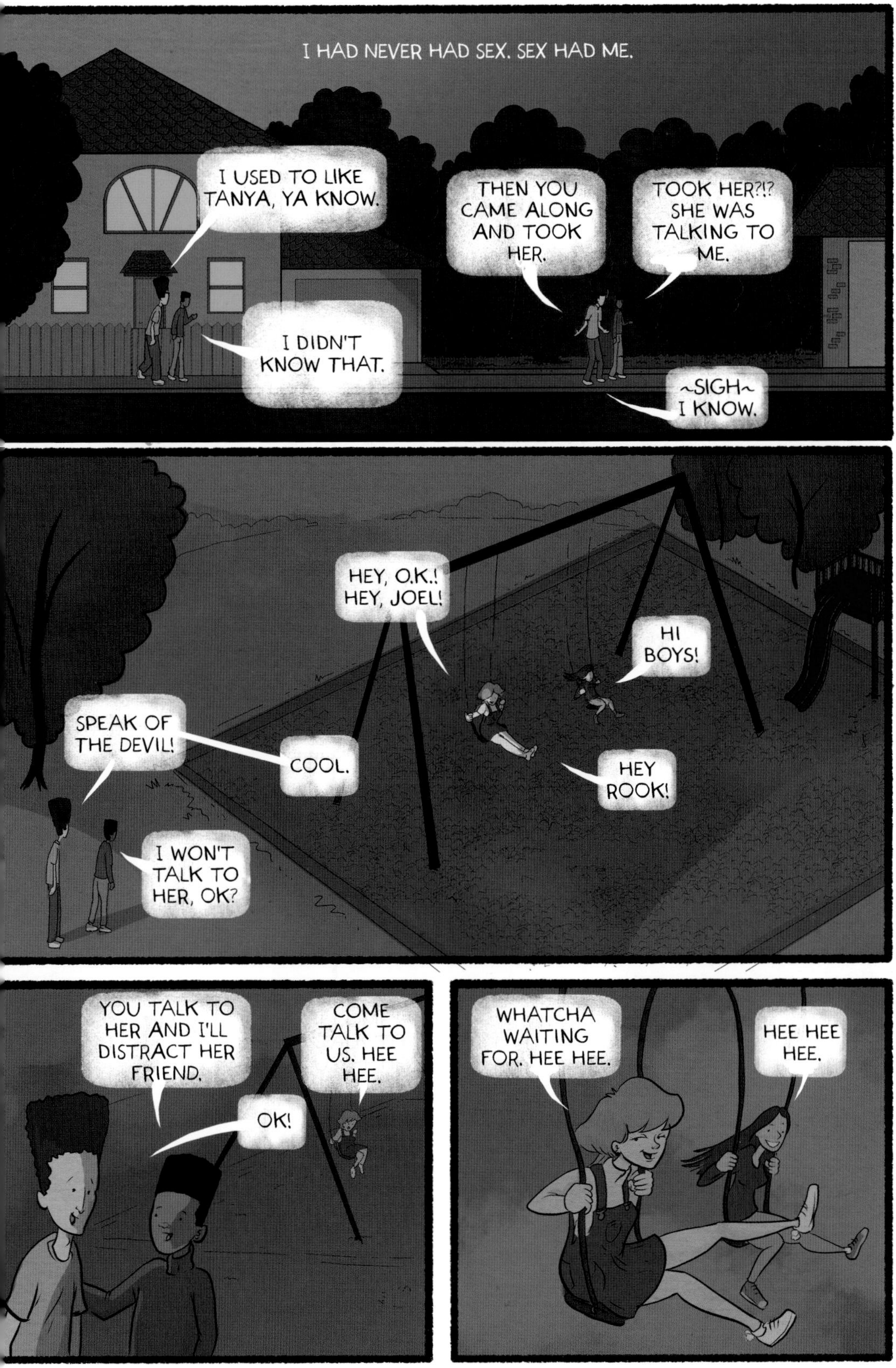
I HAD NEVER HAD SEX. SEX HAD ME.
I USED TO LIKE TANYA, YA KNOW.
I DIDN'T KNOW THAT.
THEN YOU CAME ALONG AND TOOK HER.
TOOK HER?!? SHE WAS TALKING TO ME.
~SIGH~ I KNOW.
HEY, O.K.! HEY, JOEL!
HI BOYS!
SPEAK OF THE DEVIL!
COOL.
HEY ROOK!
I WON'T TALK TO HER, OK?
YOU TALK TO HER AND I'LL DISTRACT HER FRIEND.
COME TALK TO US. HEE HEE.
OK!
WHATCHA WAITING FOR. HEE HEE.
HEE HEE HEE.

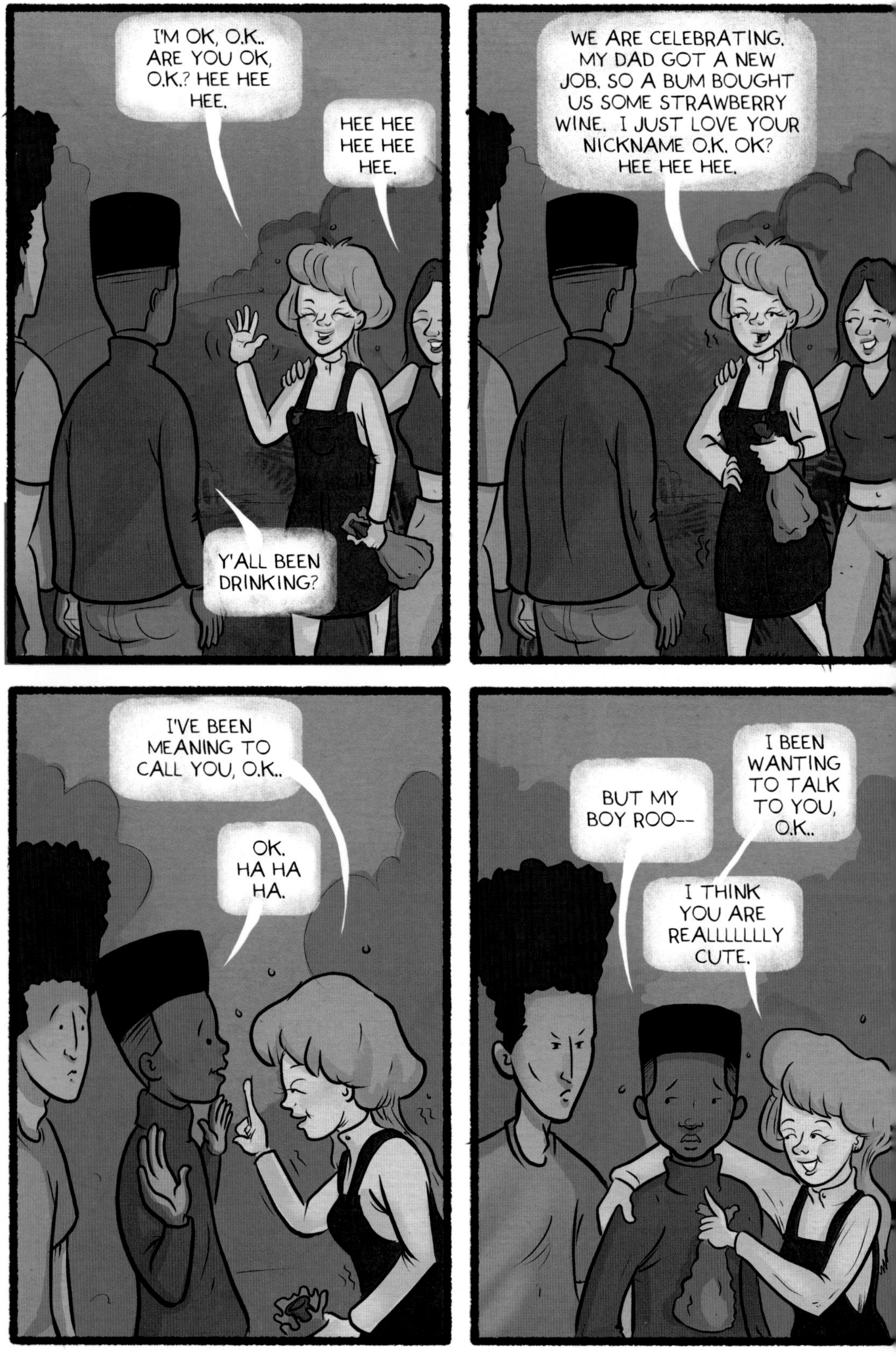
I'M OK, O.K.. ARE YOU OK, O.K.? HEE HEE HEE.
HEE HEE HEE HEE HEE.
Y'ALL BEEN DRINKING?
WE ARE CELEBRATING. MY DAD GOT A NEW JOB. SO A BUM BOUGHT US SOME STRAWBERRY WINE. I JUST LOVE YOUR NICKNAME O.K. OK? HEE HEE HEE.
I'VE BEEN MEANING TO CALL YOU, O.K..
OK. HA HA HA.
BUT MY BOY ROO--
I BEEN WANTING TO TALK TO YOU, O.K..
I THINK YOU ARE REALLLLLLLY CUTE.

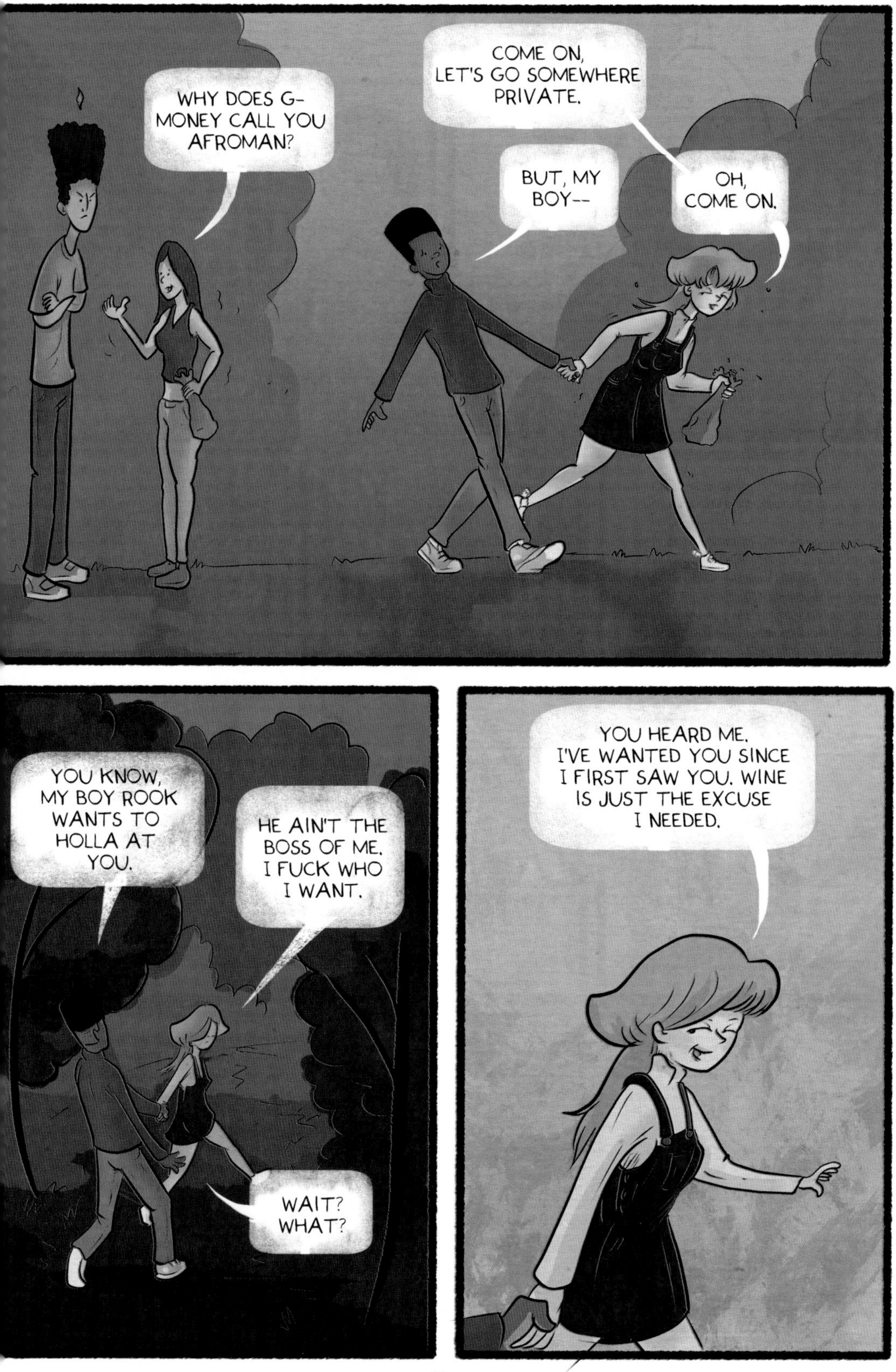
WHY DOES G-MONEY CALL YOU AFROMAN?
COME ON, LET'S GO SOMEWHERE PRIVATE.
BUT, MY BOY--
OH, COME ON.
YOU KNOW, MY BOY ROOK WANTS TO HOLLA AT YOU.
HE AIN'T THE BOSS OF ME. I FUCK WHO I WANT.
WAIT? WHAT?
YOU HEARD ME. I'VE WANTED YOU SINCE I FIRST SAW YOU. WINE IS JUST THE EXCUSE I NEEDED.

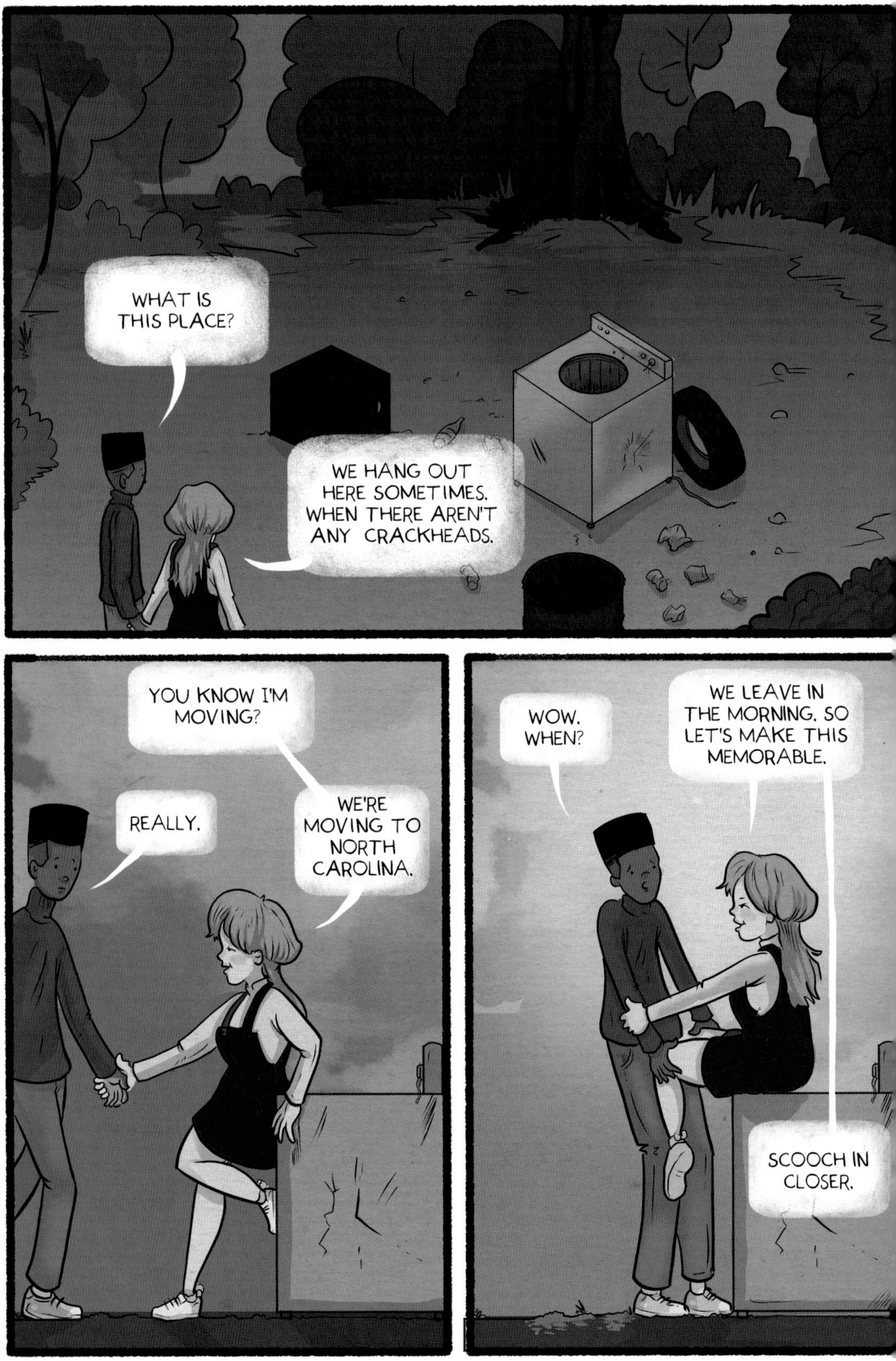
WHAT IS THIS PLACE?
WE HANG OUT HERE SOMETIMES. WHEN THERE AREN'T ANY CRACKHEADS.
YOU KNOW I'M MOVING?
REALLY.
WE'RE MOVING TO NORTH CAROLINA.
WOW. WHEN?
WE LEAVE IN THE MORNING. SO LET'S MAKE THIS MEMORABLE.
SCOOCH IN CLOSER.

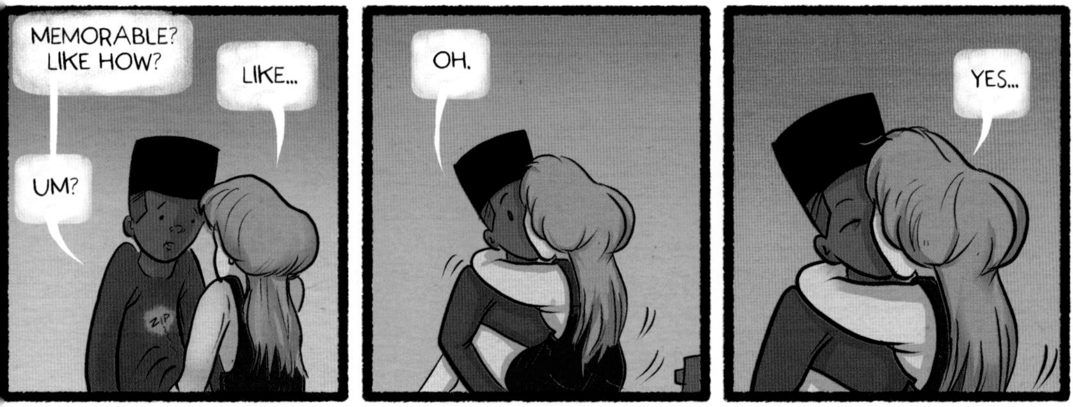
MEMORABLE? LIKE HOW?
UM?
ZIP
LIKE...
OH.
YES...

STRAWBERRY WINE, HAIRSPRAY, AND THE SMELL OF DIRT AND TREES. IT WAS AMAZING, PERFECT, INCREDIBLE, AND HORRIFYING.

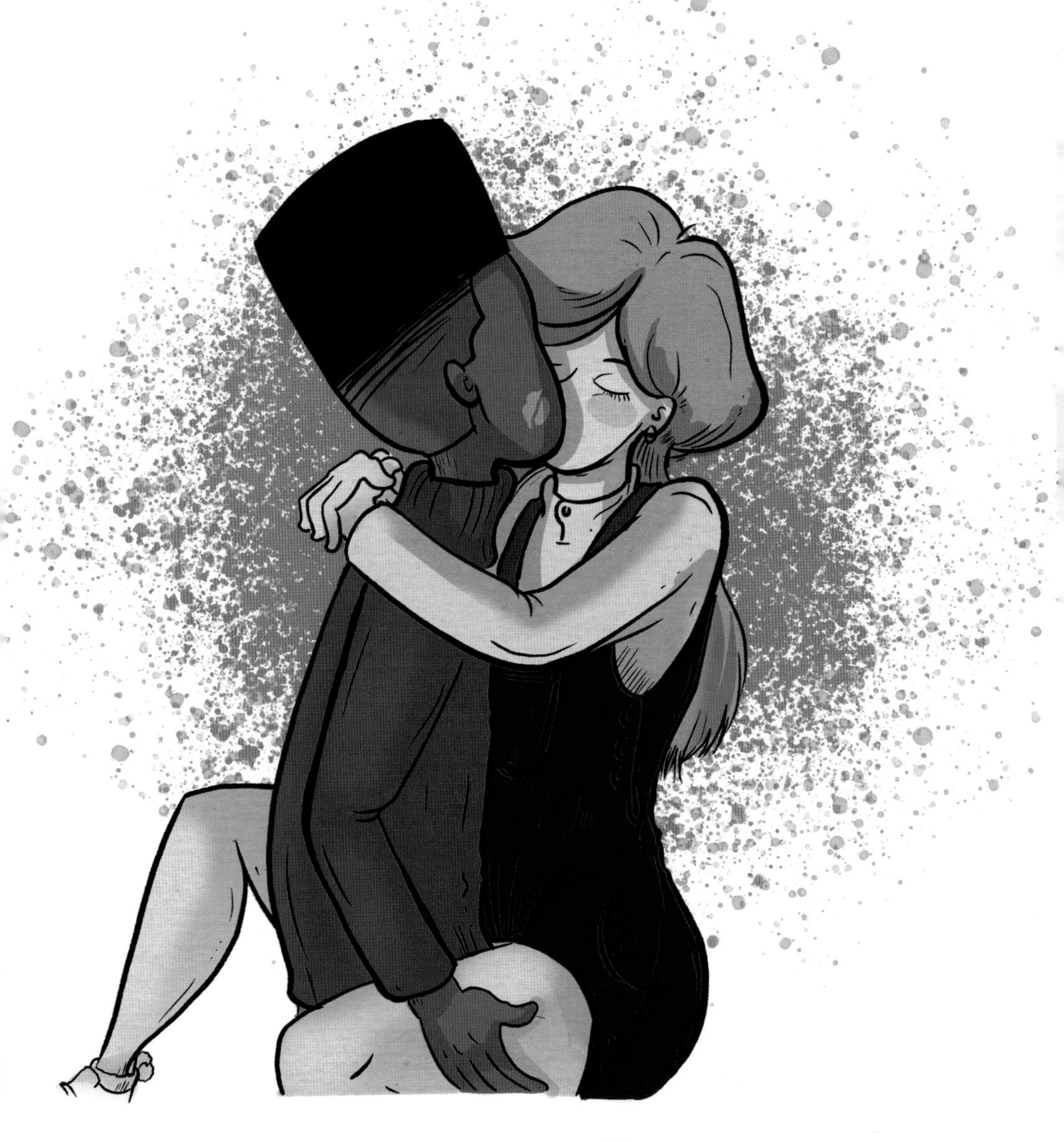

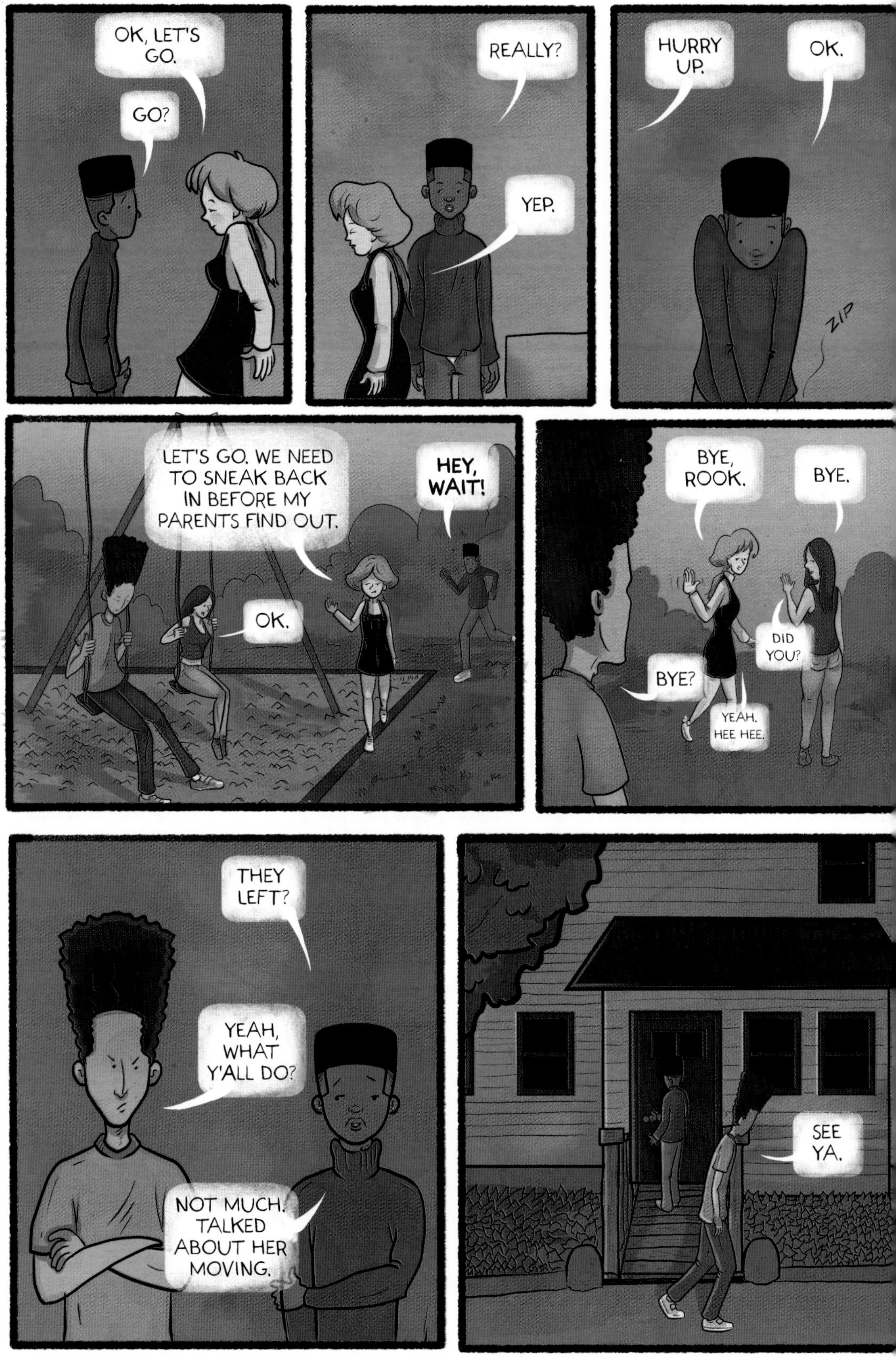
OK, LET'S GO.
GO?
REALLY?
YEP.
HURRY UP.
OK.
ZIP
LET'S GO. WE NEED TO SNEAK BACK IN BEFORE MY PARENTS FIND OUT.
HEY, WAIT!
OK.
BYE, ROOK.
BYE.
DID YOU?
BYE?
YEAH. HEE HEE.
THEY LEFT?
YEAH, WHAT Y'ALL DO?
NOT MUCH. TALKED ABOUT HER MOVING.
SEE YA.

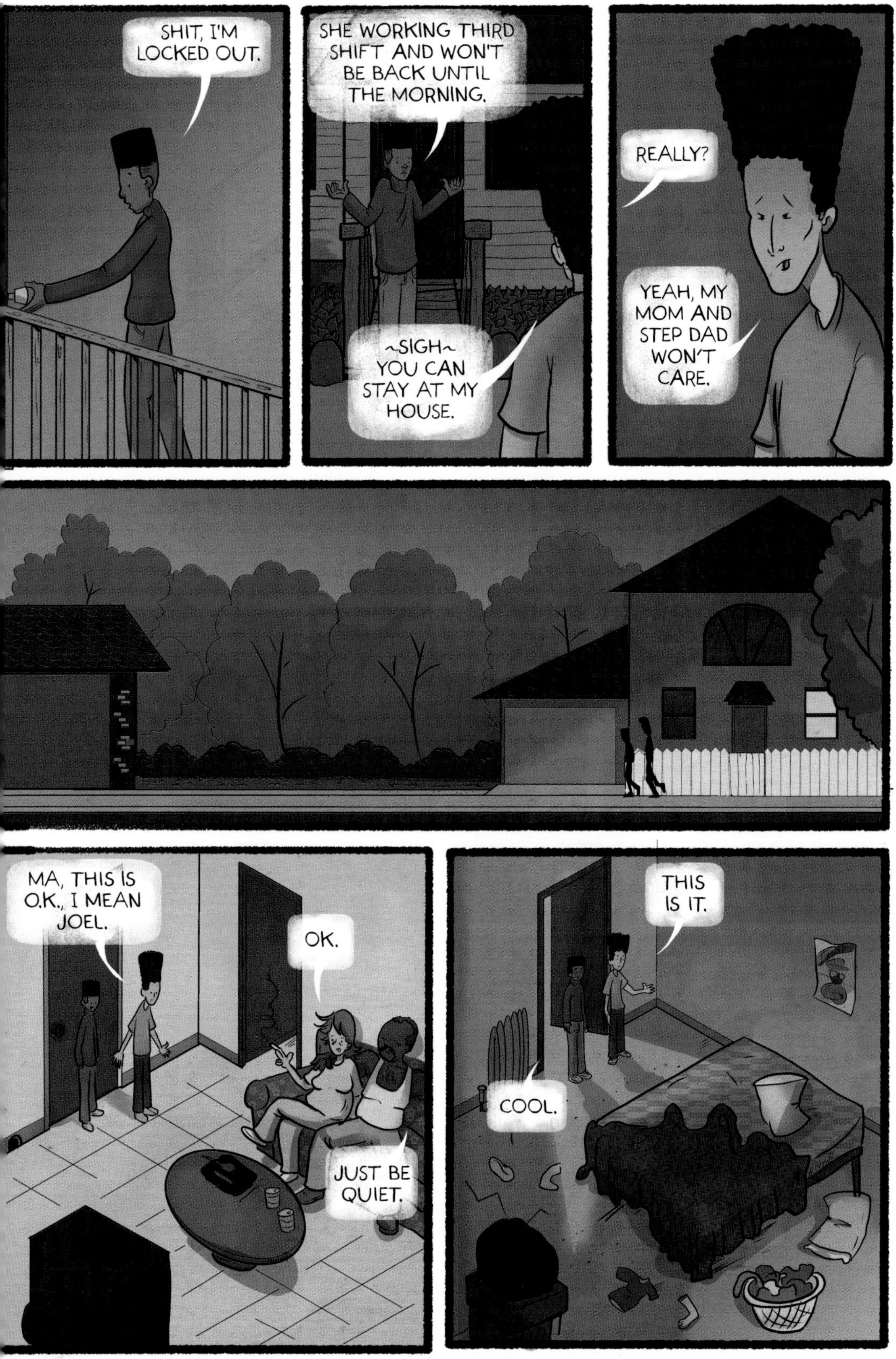
SHIT, I'M LOCKED OUT.
SHE WORKING THIRD SHIFT AND WON'T BE BACK UNTIL THE MORNING.
~SIGH~ YOU CAN STAY AT MY HOUSE.
REALLY?
YEAH, MY MOM AND STEP DAD WON'T CARE.
MA, THIS IS O.K., I MEAN JOEL.
OK.
JUST BE QUIET.
THIS IS IT.
COOL.

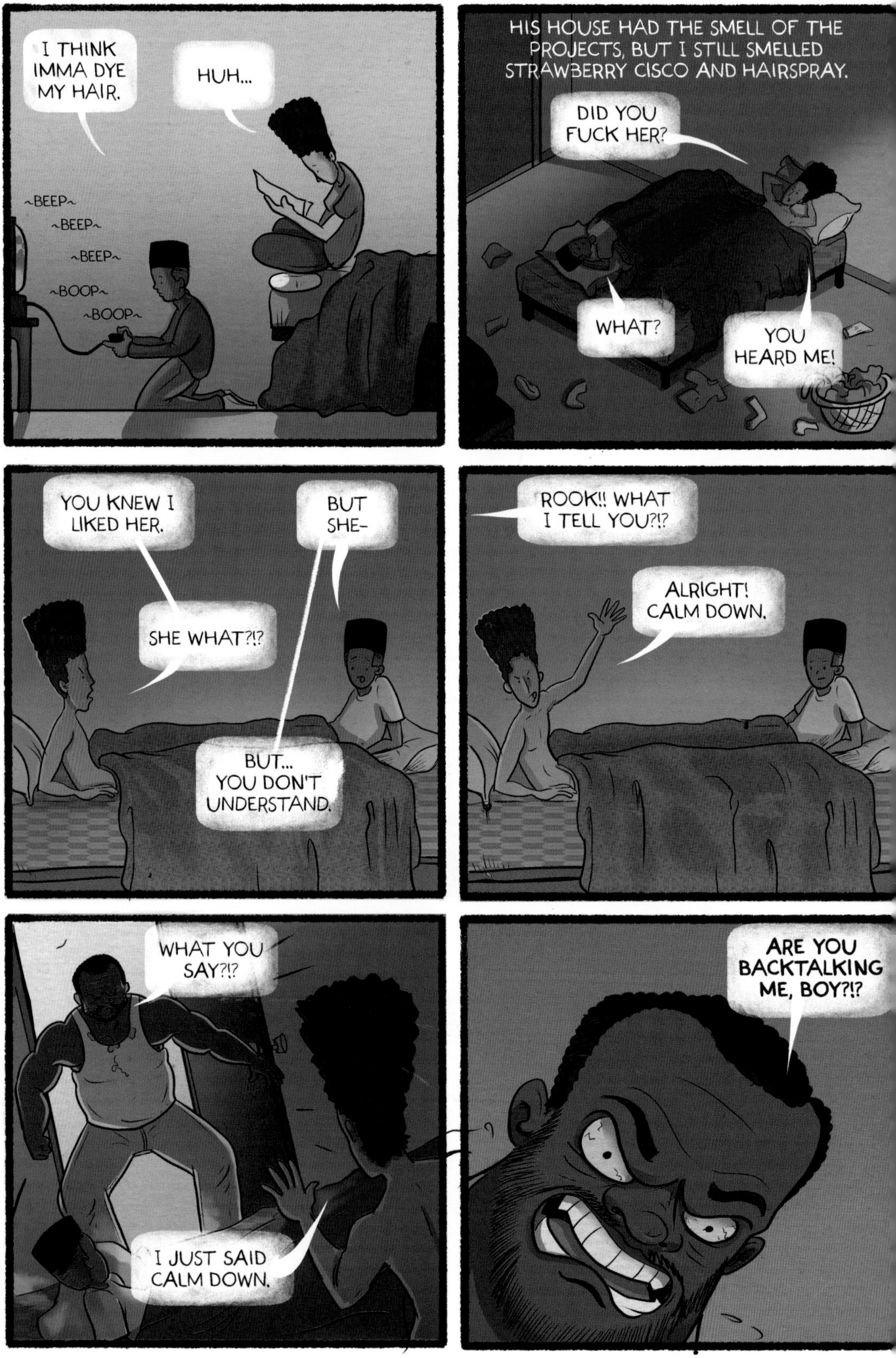
I THINK IMMA DYE MY HAIR.
HUH...
~BEEP~
~BEEP~
~BEEP~
~BOOP~
~BOOP~
HIS HOUSE HAD THE SMELL OF THE PROJECTS, BUT I STILL SMELLED STRAWBERRY CISCO AND HAIRSPRAY.
DID YOU FUCK HER?
WHAT?
YOU HEARD ME!
YOU KNEW I LIKED HER.
BUT SHE-
SHE WHAT?!?
BUT... YOU DON'T UNDERSTAND.
ROOK!! WHAT I TELL YOU?!?
ALRIGHT! CALM DOWN.
WHAT YOU SAY?!?
I JUST SAID CALM DOWN.
ARE YOU BACKTALKING ME, BOY?!?

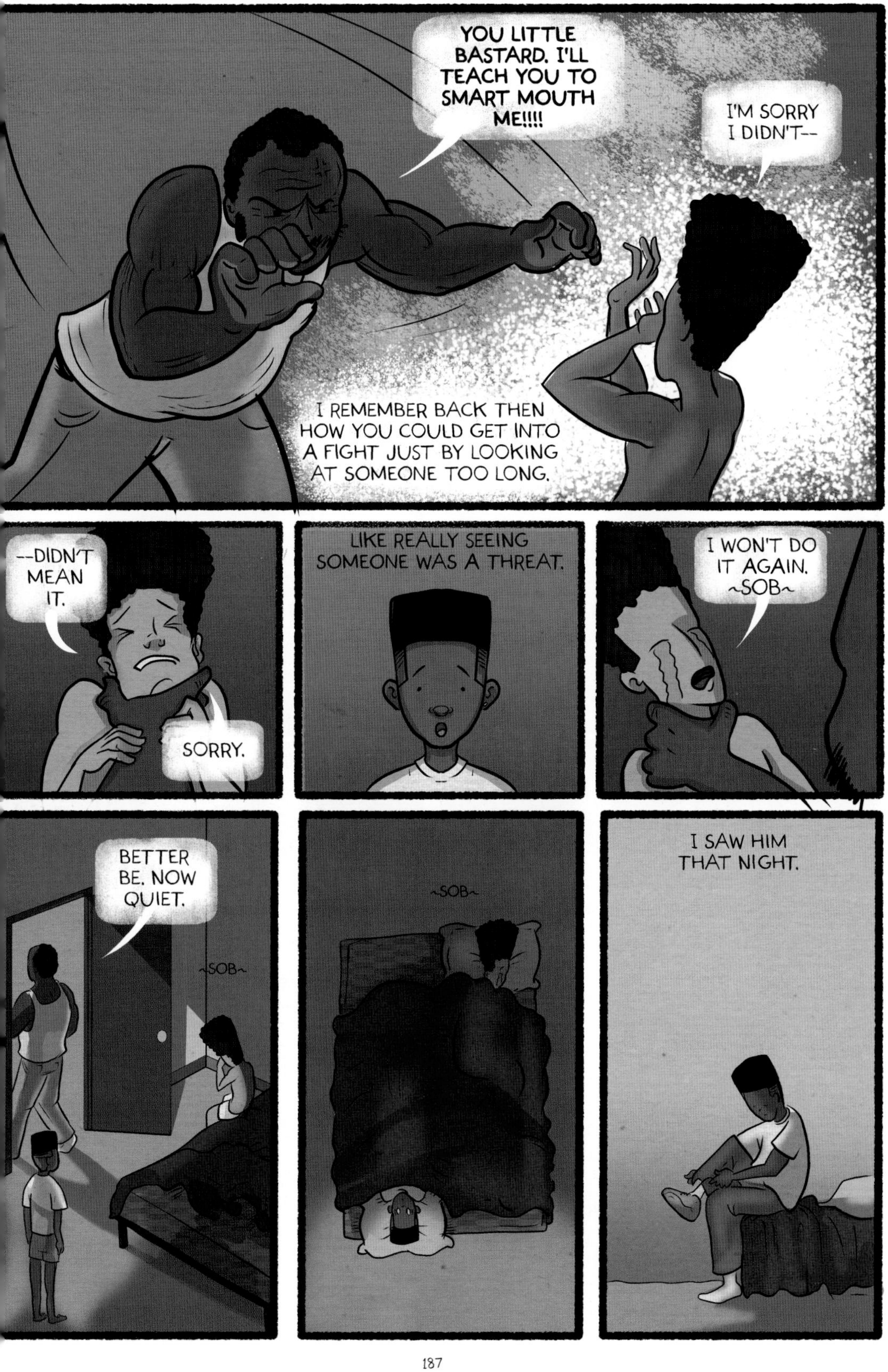
YOU LITTLE BASTARD. I'LL TEACH YOU TO SMART MOUTH ME!!!!
I'M SORRY I DIDN'T--
I REMEMBER BACK THEN HOW YOU COULD GET INTO A FIGHT JUST BY LOOKING AT SOMEONE TOO LONG.
--DIDN'T MEAN IT.
SORRY.
LIKE REALLY SEEING SOMEONE WAS A THREAT.
I WON'T DO IT AGAIN. ~SOB~
BETTER BE. NOW QUIET.
~SOB~
~SOB~
I SAW HIM THAT NIGHT.

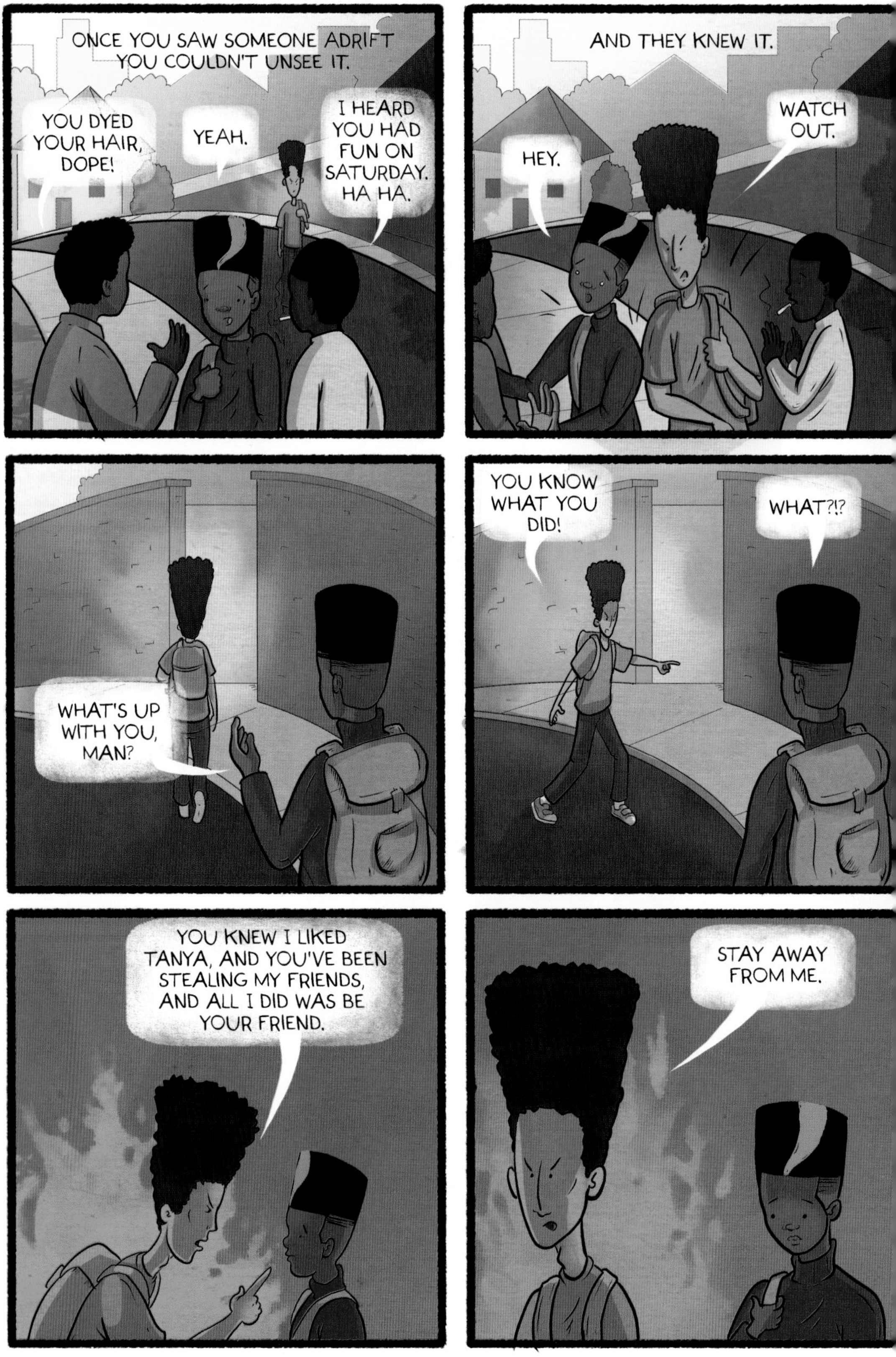
ONCE YOU SAW SOMEONE ADRIFT YOU COULDN'T UNSEE IT.
YOU DYED YOUR HAIR, DOPE!
YEAH.
I HEARD YOU HAD FUN ON SATURDAY. HA HA.
AND THEY KNEW IT.
HEY.
WATCH OUT.
WHAT'S UP WITH YOU, MAN?
YOU KNOW WHAT YOU DID!
WHAT?!?
YOU KNEW I LIKED TANYA, AND YOU'VE BEEN STEALING MY FRIENDS, AND ALL I DID WAS BE YOUR FRIEND.
STAY AWAY FROM ME.

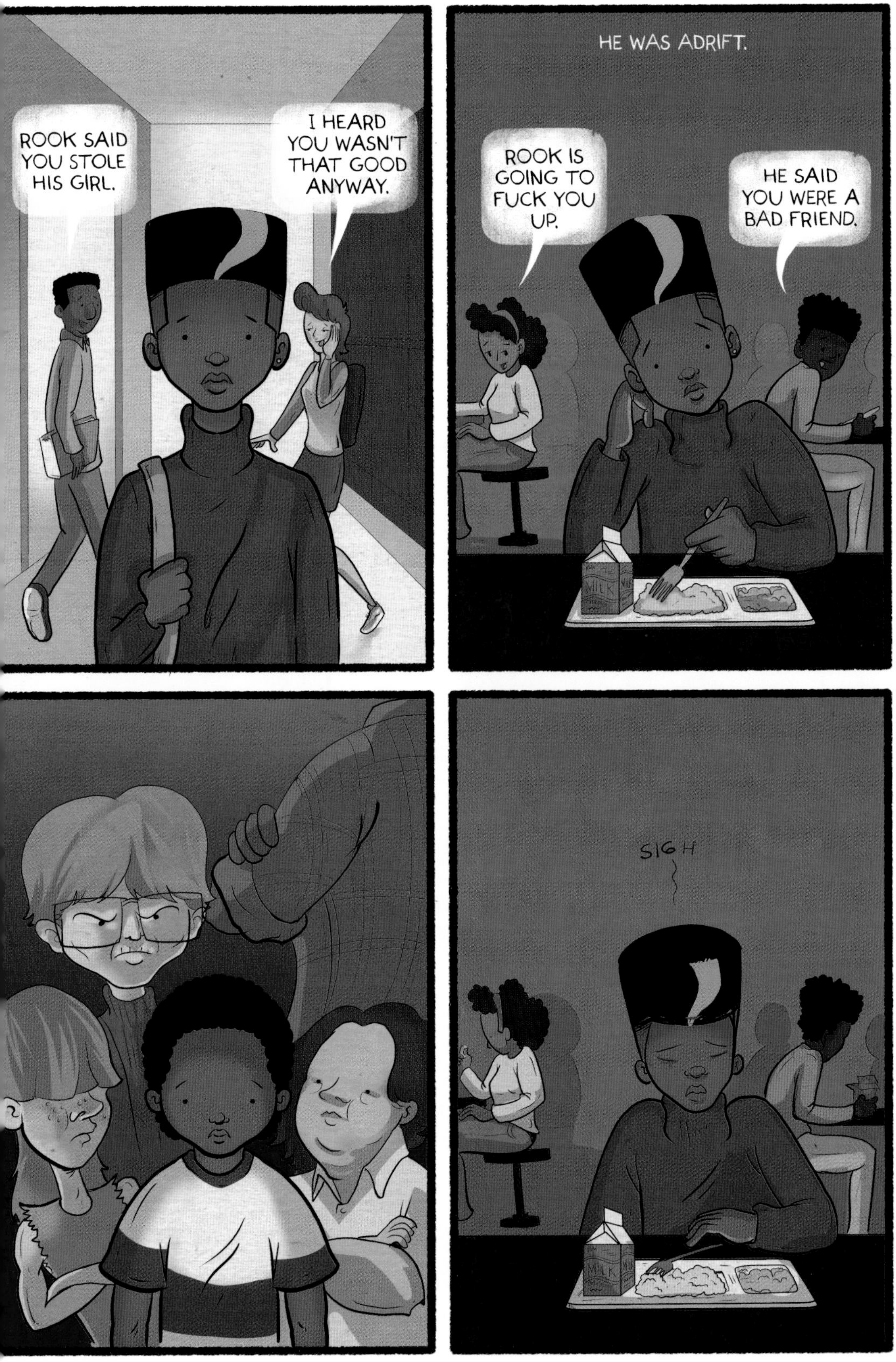
ROOK SAID YOU STOLE HIS GIRL.
I HEARD YOU WASN'T THAT GOOD ANYWAY.
HE WAS ADRIFT.
ROOK IS GOING TO FUCK YOU UP.
HE SAID YOU WERE A BAD FRIEND.
MILK
SIGH
MILK

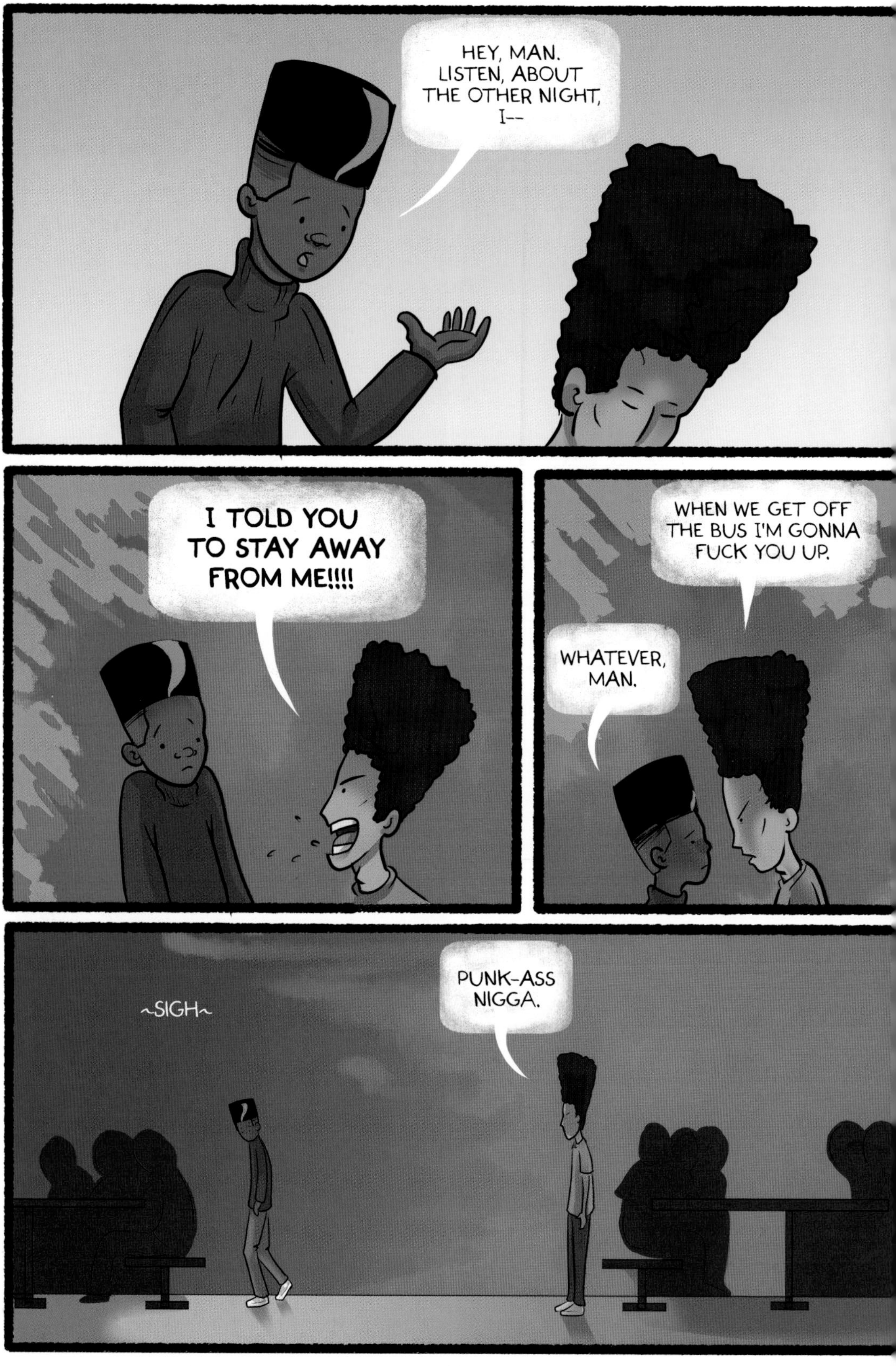
HEY, MAN. LISTEN, ABOUT THE OTHER NIGHT, I--
I TOLD YOU TO STAY AWAY FROM ME!!!!
WHEN WE GET OFF THE BUS I'M GONNA FUCK YOU UP.
WHATEVER, MAN.
~SIGH~
PUNK-ASS NIGGA.

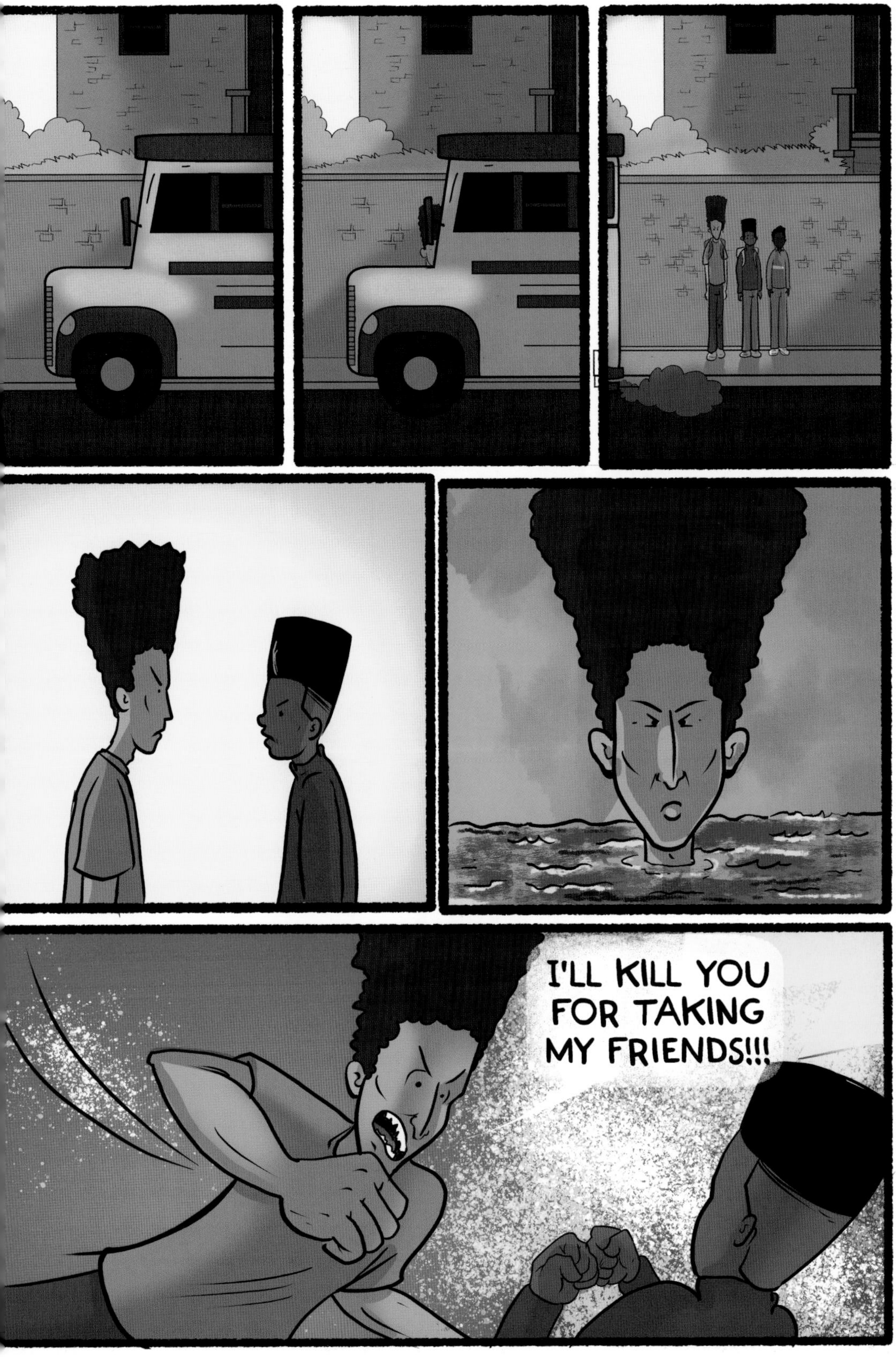
I'LL KILL YOU FOR TAKING MY FRIENDS!!!

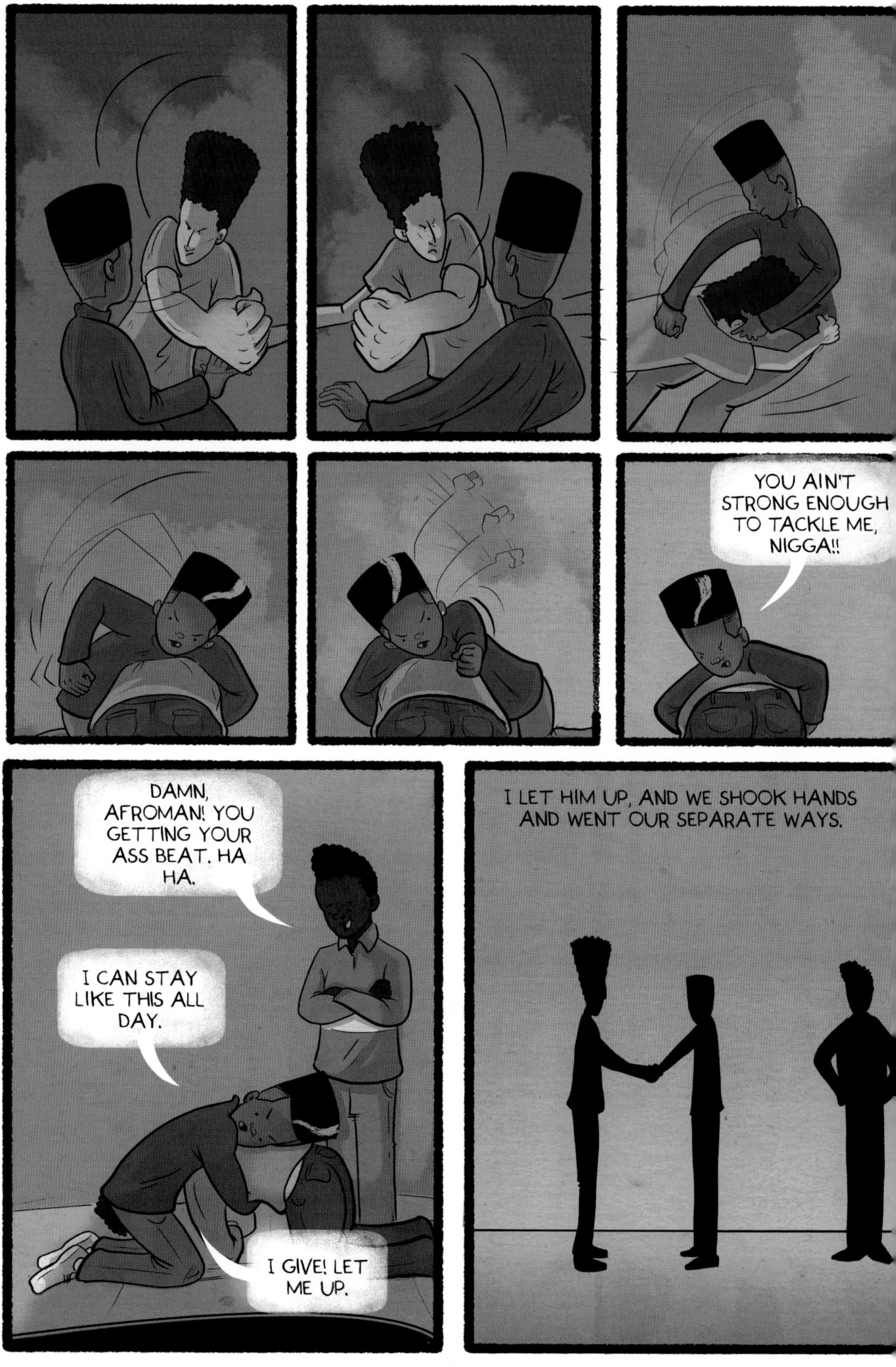
YOU AIN'T STRONG ENOUGH TO TACKLE ME, NIGGA!!
DAMN, AFROMAN! YOU GETTING YOUR ASS BEAT. HA HA.
I CAN STAY LIKE THIS ALL DAY.
I GIVE! LET ME UP.
I LET HIM UP, AND WE SHOOK HANDS AND WENT OUR SEPARATE WAYS.

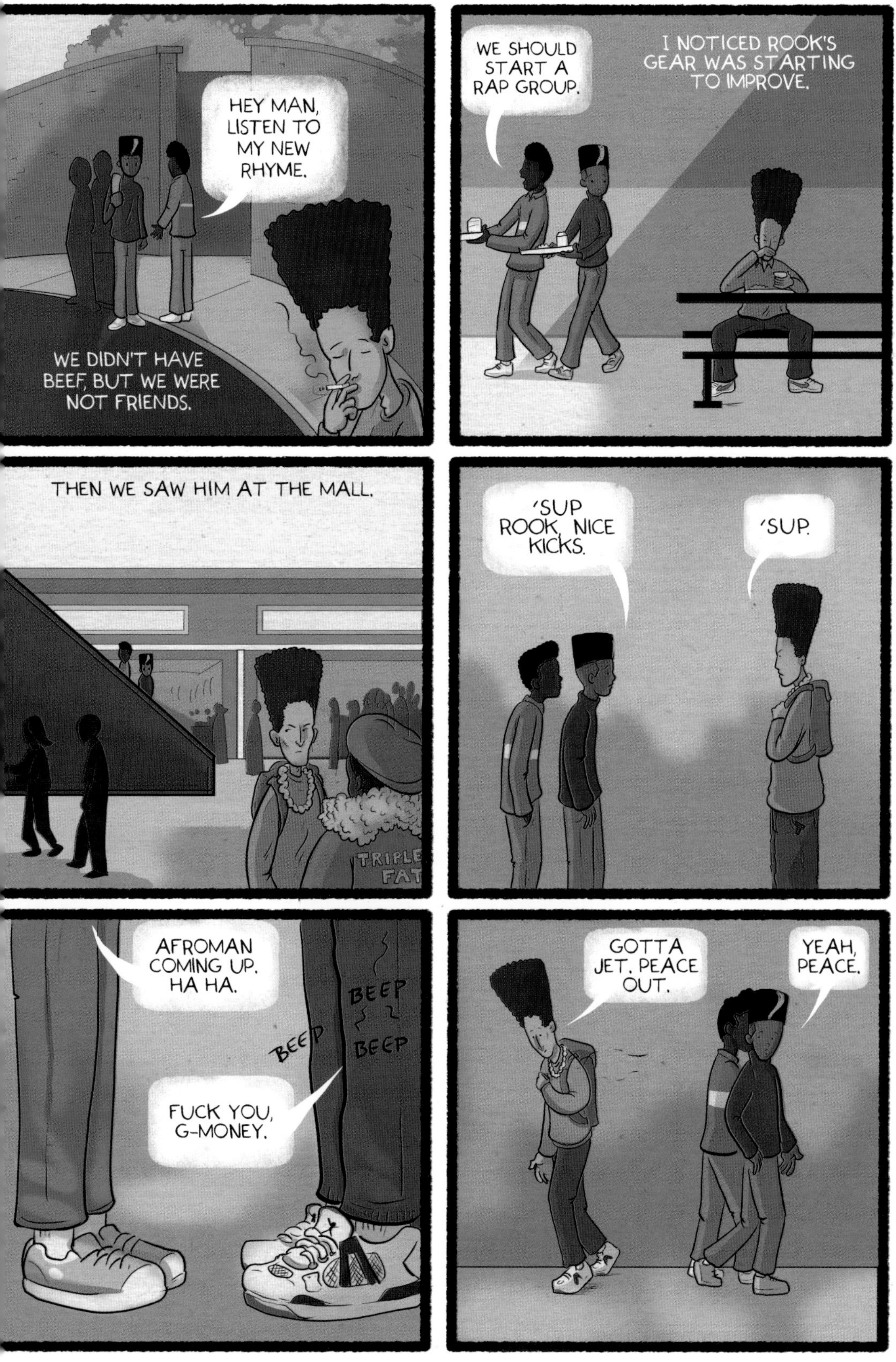
HEY MAN, LISTEN TO MY NEW RHYME.
WE DIDN'T HAVE BEEF, BUT WE WERE NOT FRIENDS.
WE SHOULD START A RAP GROUP.
I NOTICED ROOK'S GEAR WAS STARTING TO IMPROVE.
THEN WE SAW HIM AT THE MALL.
TRIPLE FAT
'SUP ROOK, NICE KICKS.
'SUP.
AFROMAN COMING UP. HA HA.
BEEP BEEP BEEP
FUCK YOU, G-MONEY.
GOTTA JET. PEACE OUT.
YEAH, PEACE.

ROOK WASN'T ON THE BUS ANYMORE. I DIDN'T BLAME HIM. I ALWAYS HATED RIDING THE BUS. ALL THESE PEOPLE RIDING AROUND IN CIRCLES.

SOME PEOPLE WAITING FOR THEIR STOP.

WHAT'S UP, HOMIE?

IT'S ALL GOOD.

'SUP, MY NIGGA?

HOW MANY POINTS?

YOU KEEP TWO POINTS.

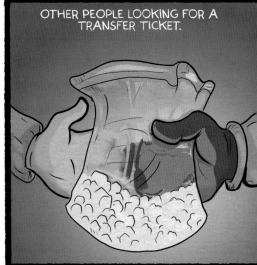

OTHER PEOPLE LOOKING FOR A TRANSFER TICKET.

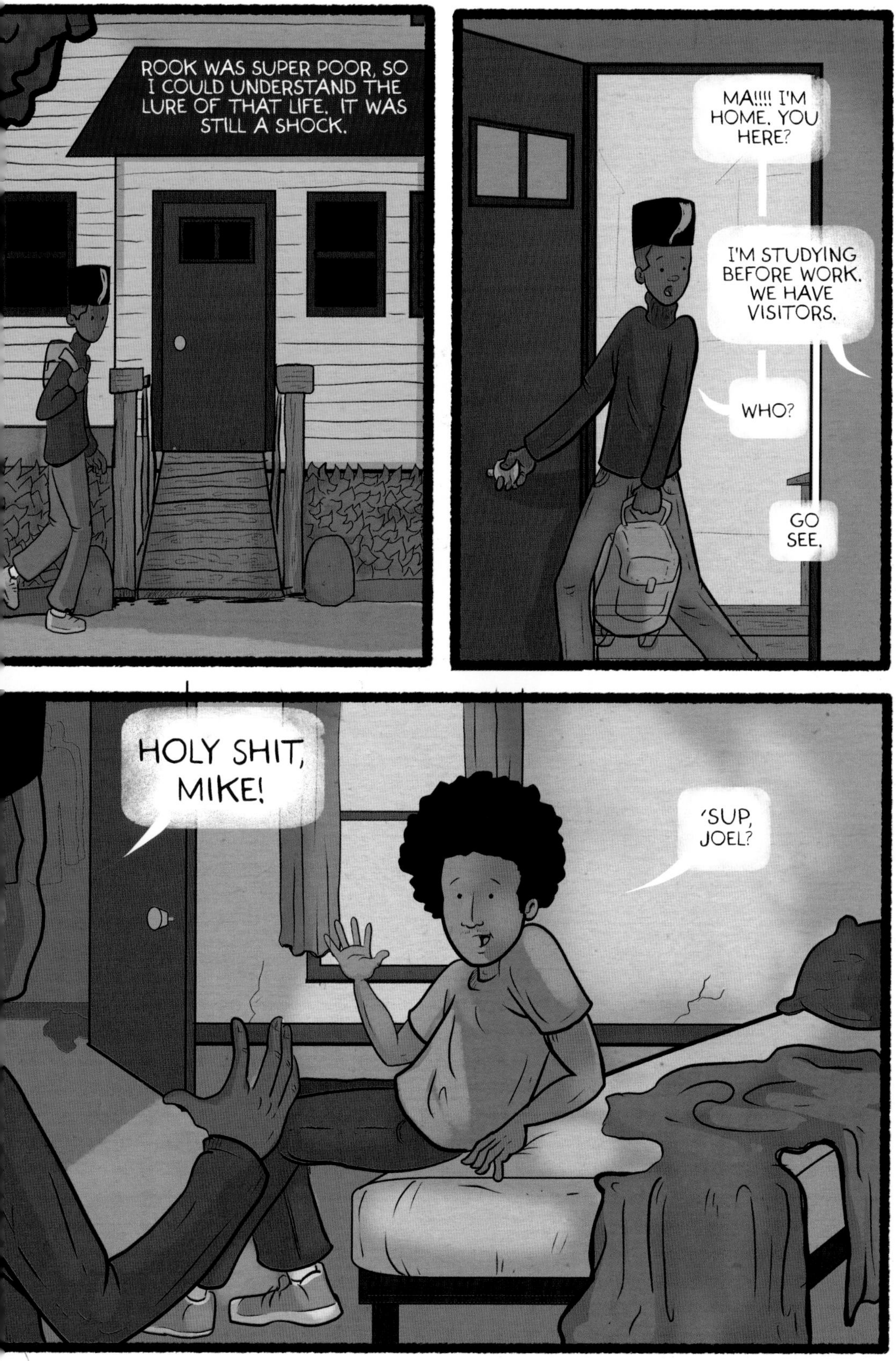
ROOK WAS SUPER POOR, SO I COULD UNDERSTAND THE LURE OF THAT LIFE. IT WAS STILL A SHOCK.
MA!!!! I'M HOME. YOU HERE?
I'M STUDYING BEFORE WORK. WE HAVE VISITORS.
WHO?
GO SEE.
HOLY SHIT, MIKE!
'SUP, JOEL?

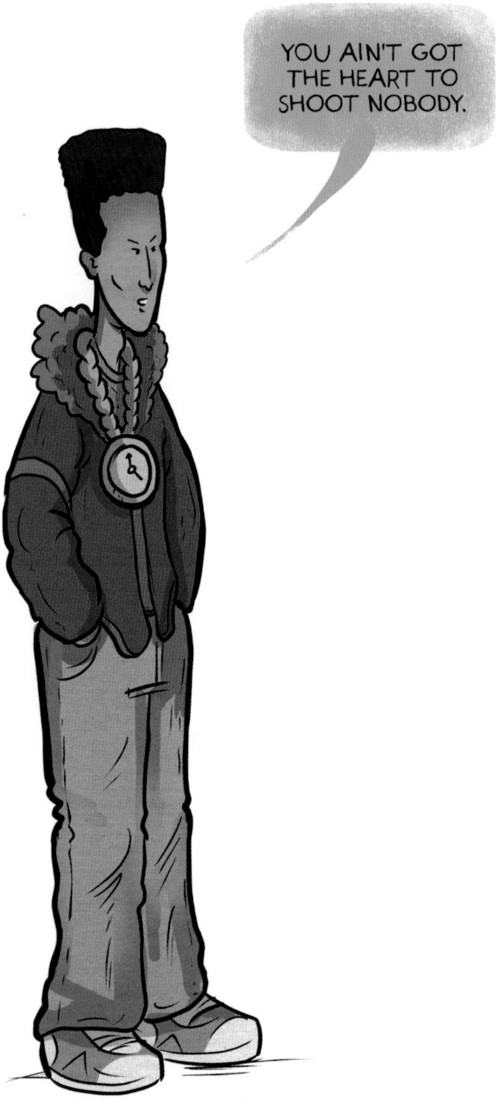
YOU AIN'T GOT THE HEART TO SHOOT NOBODY.

CHAPTER EIGHT

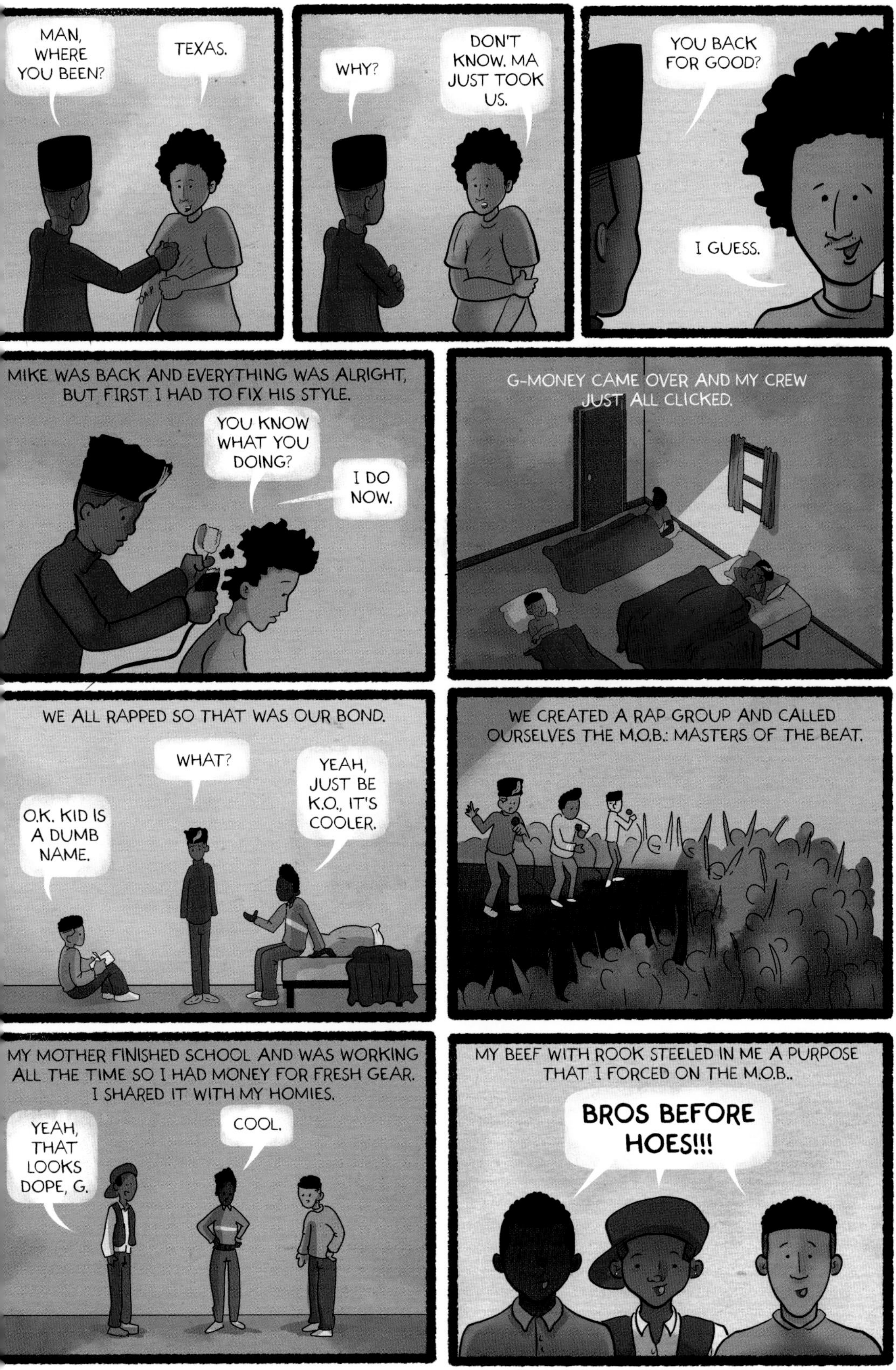
MAN, WHERE YOU BEEN?
TEXAS.
WHY?
DON'T KNOW. MA JUST TOOK US.
YOU BACK FOR GOOD?
I GUESS.
MIKE WAS BACK AND EVERYTHING WAS ALRIGHT, BUT FIRST I HAD TO FIX HIS STYLE.
YOU KNOW WHAT YOU DOING?
I DO NOW.
G-MONEY CAME OVER AND MY CREW JUST ALL CLICKED.
WE ALL RAPPED SO THAT WAS OUR BOND.
O.K. KID IS A DUMB NAME.
WHAT?
YEAH, JUST BE K.O., IT'S COOLER.
WE CREATED A RAP GROUP AND CALLED OURSELVES THE M.O.B.: MASTERS OF THE BEAT.
MY MOTHER FINISHED SCHOOL AND WAS WORKING ALL THE TIME SO I HAD MONEY FOR FRESH GEAR. I SHARED IT WITH MY HOMIES.
YEAH, THAT LOOKS DOPE, G.
COOL.
MY BEEF WITH ROOK STEELED IN ME A PURPOSE THAT I FORCED ON THE M.O.B..
BROS BEFORE HOES!!!

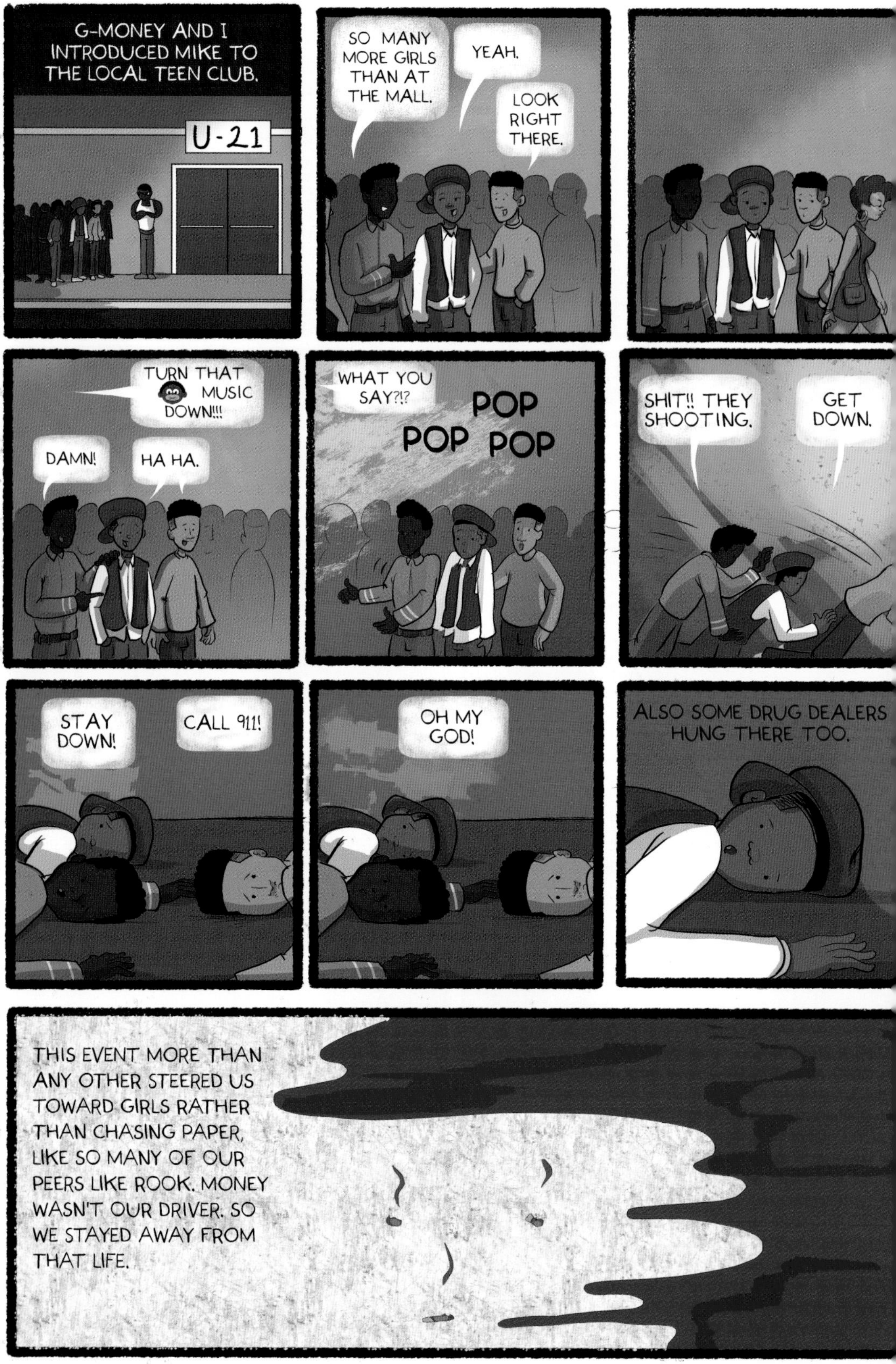
G-MONEY AND I INTRODUCED MIKE TO THE LOCAL TEEN CLUB.
U-21
SO MANY MORE GIRLS THAN AT THE MALL.
YEAH.
LOOK RIGHT THERE.
TURN THAT MUSIC DOWN!!!
DAMN!
HA HA.
WHAT YOU SAY?!?
POP
POP POP
SHIT!! THEY SHOOTING.
GET DOWN.
STAY DOWN!
CALL 911!
OH MY GOD!
ALSO SOME DRUG DEALERS HUNG THERE TOO.
THIS EVENT MORE THAN ANY OTHER STEERED US TOWARD GIRLS RATHER THAN CHASING PAPER, LIKE SO MANY OF OUR PEERS LIKE ROOK. MONEY WASN'T OUR DRIVER, SO WE STAYED AWAY FROM THAT LIFE.

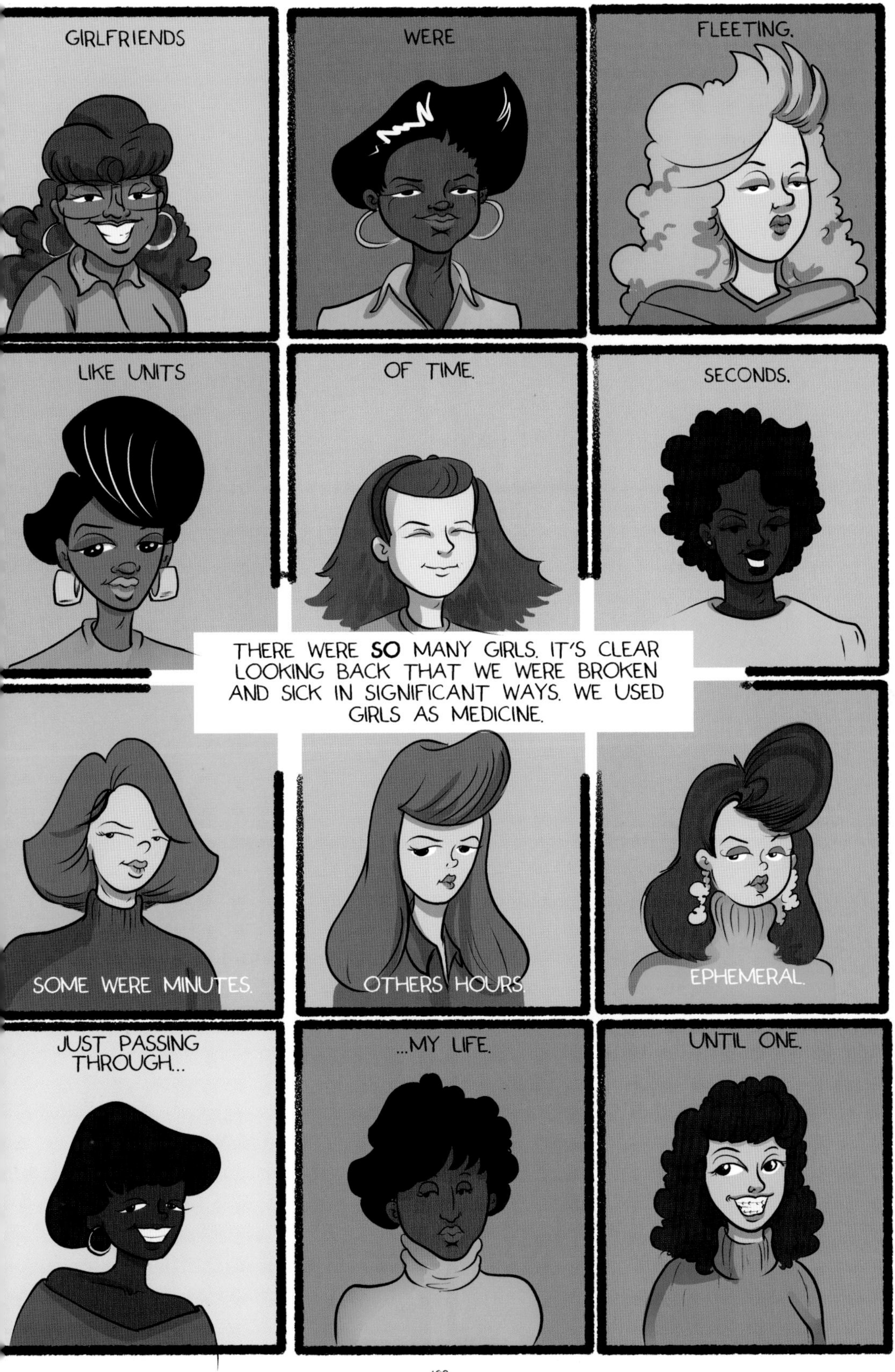
GIRLFRIENDS
WERE
FLEETING.
LIKE UNITS
OF TIME.
SECONDS.
THERE WERE **SO** MANY GIRLS. IT'S CLEAR LOOKING BACK THAT WE WERE BROKEN AND SICK IN SIGNIFICANT WAYS. WE USED GIRLS AS MEDICINE.
SOME WERE MINUTES.
OTHERS HOURS.
EPHEMERAL.
JUST PASSING THROUGH...
...MY LIFE.
UNTIL ONE.

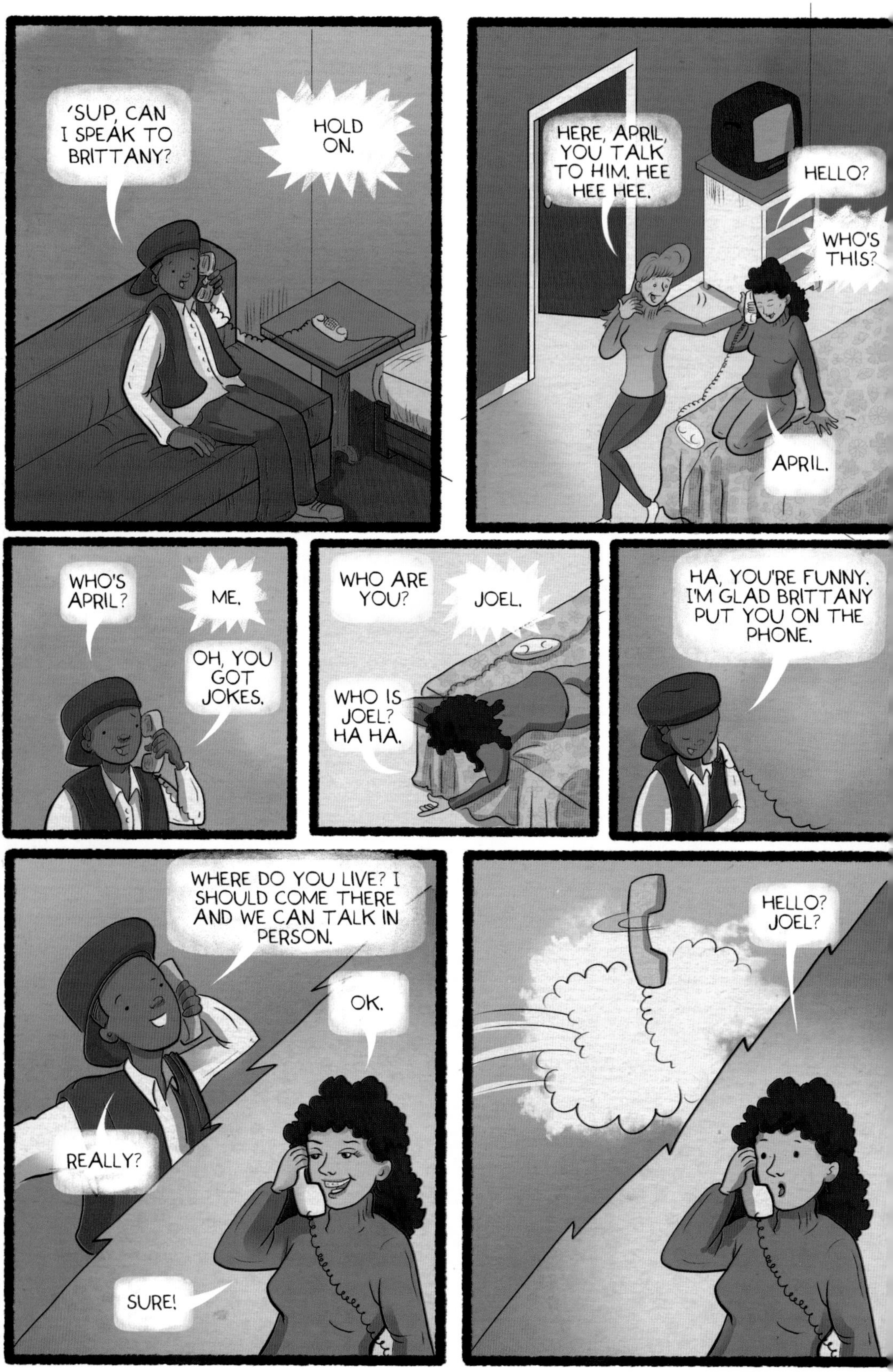
'SUP, CAN I SPEAK TO BRITTANY?
HOLD ON.
HERE, APRIL, YOU TALK TO HIM. HEE HEE HEE.
HELLO?
WHO'S THIS?
APRIL.
WHO'S APRIL?
ME.
OH, YOU GOT JOKES.
WHO ARE YOU?
JOEL.
WHO IS JOEL? HA HA.
HA, YOU'RE FUNNY. I'M GLAD BRITTANY PUT YOU ON THE PHONE.
WHERE DO YOU LIVE? I SHOULD COME THERE AND WE CAN TALK IN PERSON.
OK.
REALLY?
SURE!
HELLO? JOEL?

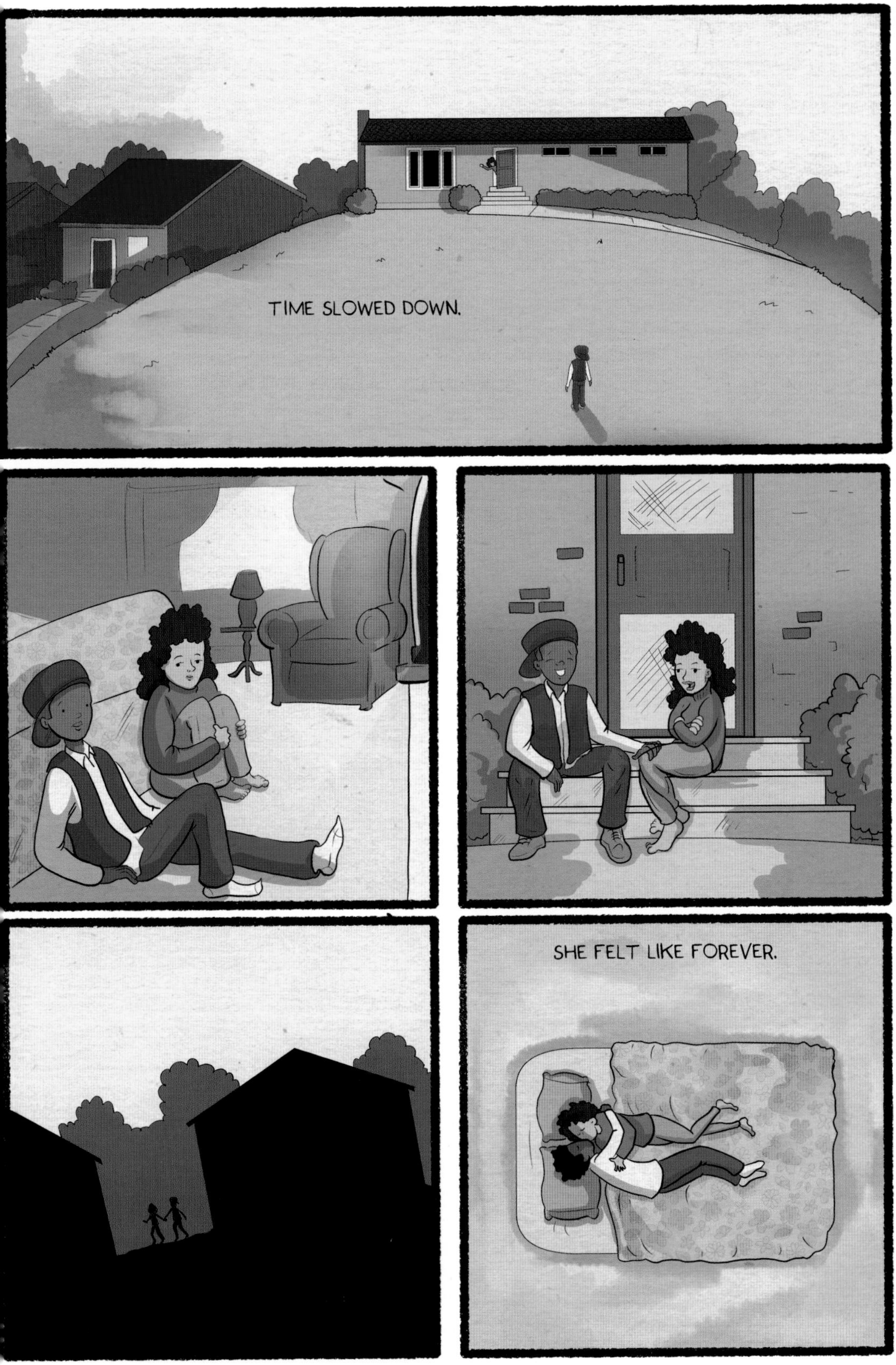
TIME SLOWED DOWN.
SHE FELT LIKE FOREVER.

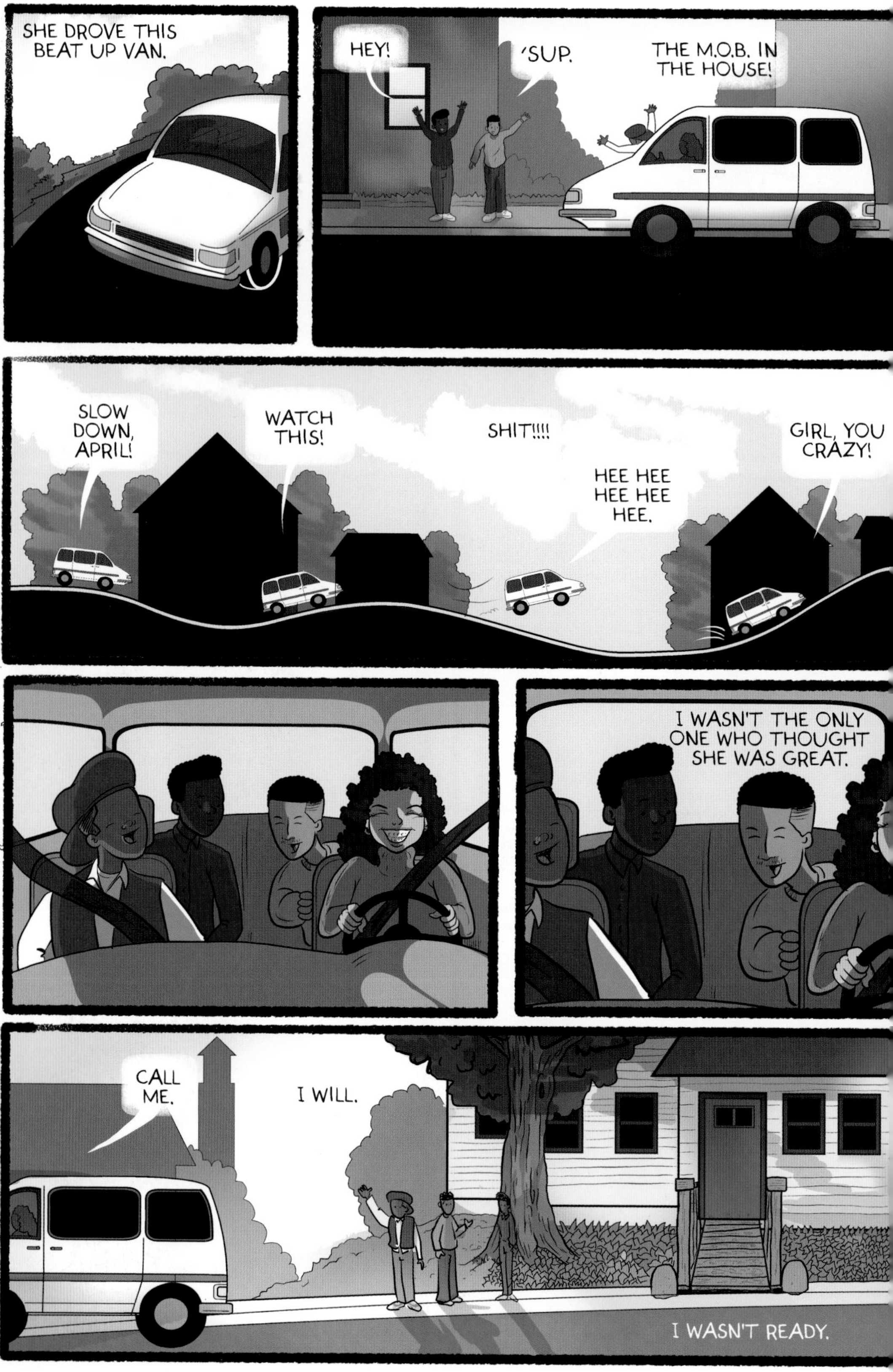
SHE DROVE THIS BEAT UP VAN.
HEY!
'SUP.
THE M.O.B. IN THE HOUSE!
SLOW DOWN, APRIL!
WATCH THIS!
SHIT!!!!
HEE HEE HEE HEE HEE.
GIRL, YOU CRAZY!
I WASN'T THE ONLY ONE WHO THOUGHT SHE WAS GREAT.
CALL ME.
I WILL.
I WASN'T READY.

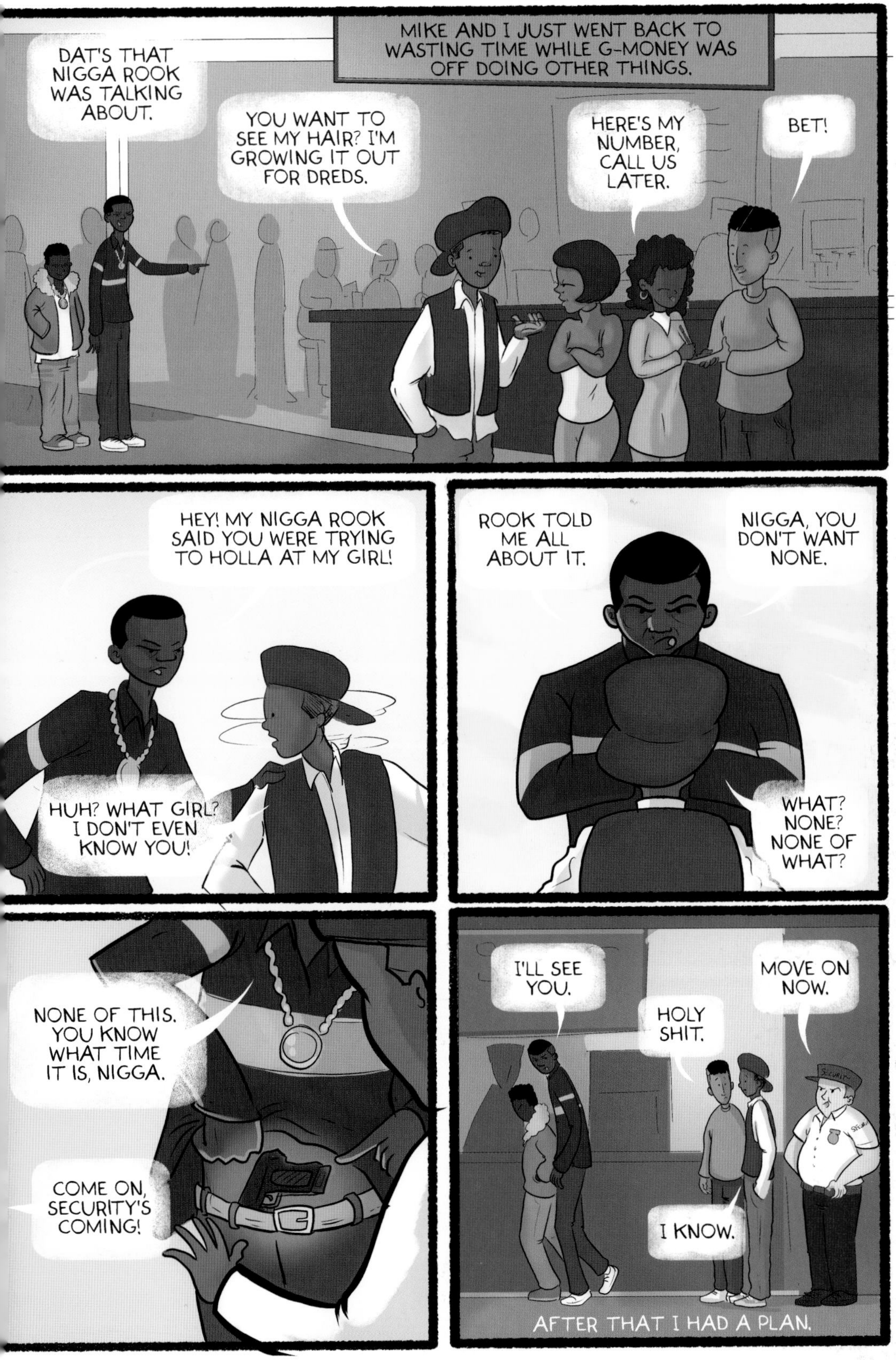
MIKE AND I JUST WENT BACK TO WASTING TIME WHILE G-MONEY WAS OFF DOING OTHER THINGS.
DAT'S THAT NIGGA ROOK WAS TALKING ABOUT.
YOU WANT TO SEE MY HAIR? I'M GROWING IT OUT FOR DREDS.
HERE'S MY NUMBER, CALL US LATER.
BET!
HEY! MY NIGGA ROOK SAID YOU WERE TRYING TO HOLLA AT MY GIRL!
HUH? WHAT GIRL? I DON'T EVEN KNOW YOU!
ROOK TOLD ME ALL ABOUT IT.
NIGGA, YOU DON'T WANT NONE.
WHAT? NONE? NONE OF WHAT?
NONE OF THIS. YOU KNOW WHAT TIME IT IS, NIGGA.
COME ON, SECURITY'S COMING!
I'LL SEE YOU.
HOLY SHIT.
MOVE ON NOW.
I KNOW.
AFTER THAT I HAD A PLAN.

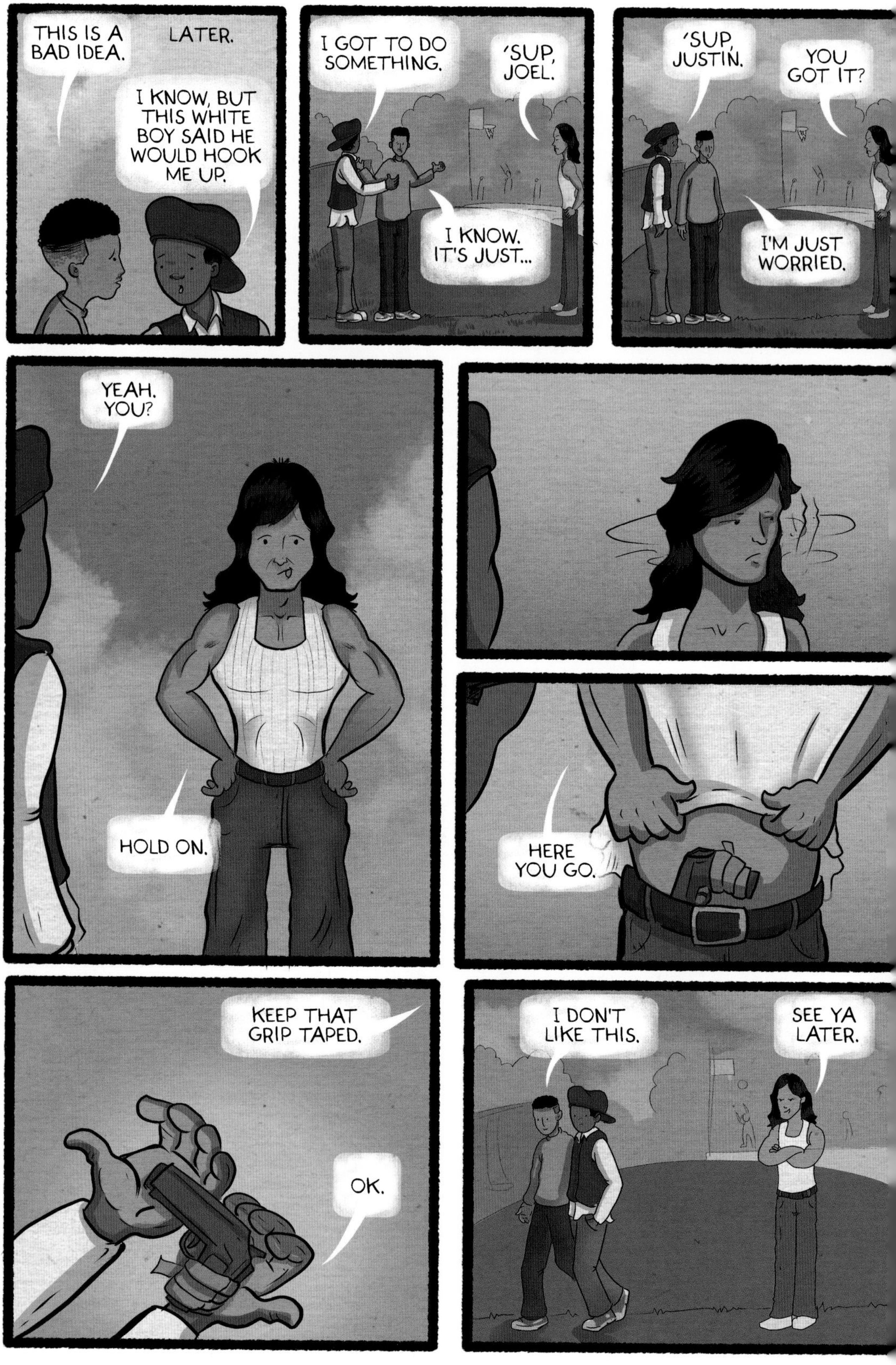
THIS IS A BAD IDEA.
LATER.
I KNOW, BUT THIS WHITE BOY SAID HE WOULD HOOK ME UP.
I GOT TO DO SOMETHING.
'SUP, JOEL.
I KNOW. IT'S JUST...
'SUP, JUSTIN.
YOU GOT IT?
I'M JUST WORRIED.
YEAH. YOU?
HOLD ON.
HERE YOU GO.
KEEP THAT GRIP TAPED.
OK.
I DON'T LIKE THIS.
SEE YA LATER.

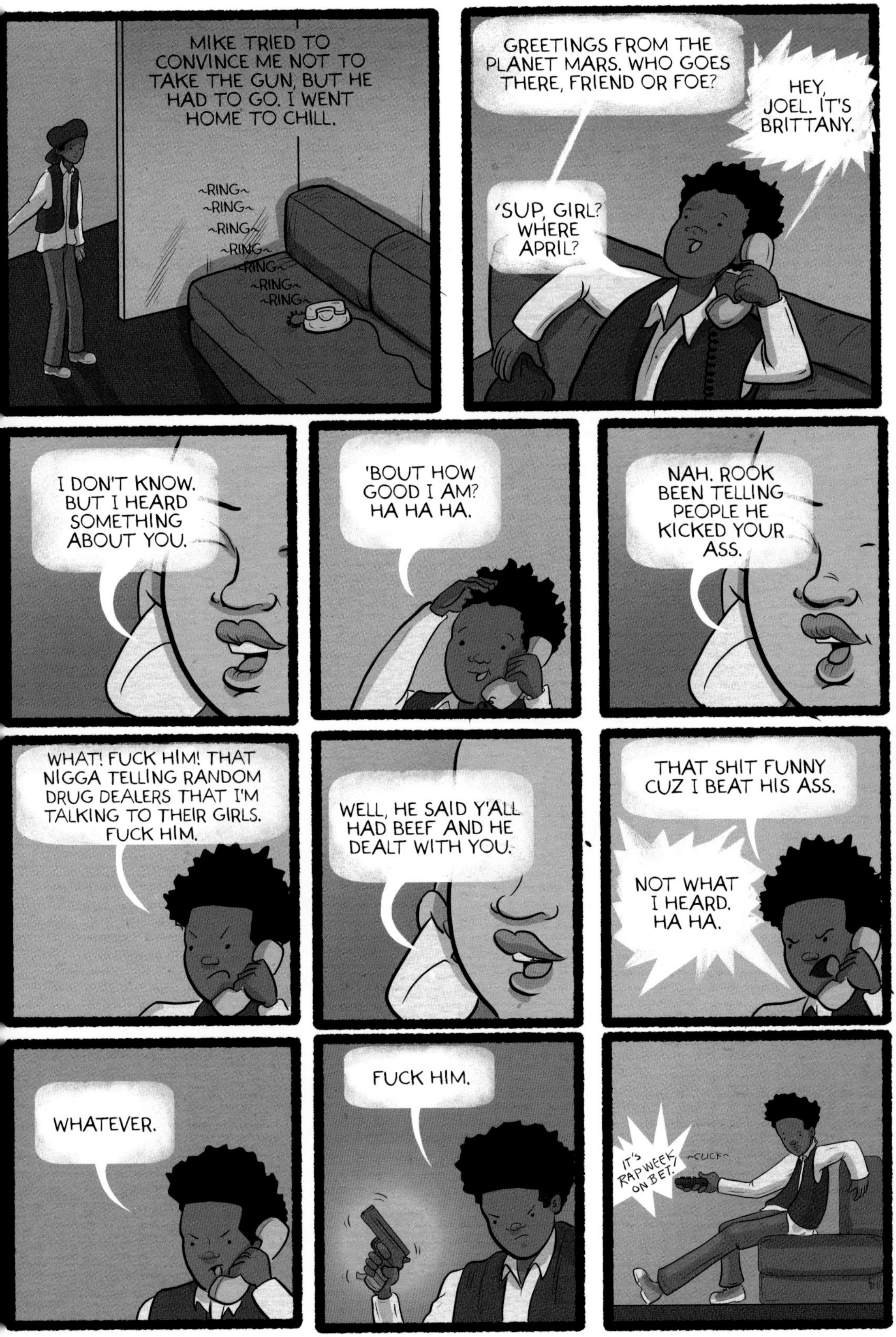
MIKE TRIED TO CONVINCE ME NOT TO TAKE THE GUN, BUT HE HAD TO GO. I WENT HOME TO CHILL.
~RING~
~RING~
~RING~
~RING~
~RING~
~RING~
~RING~
GREETINGS FROM THE PLANET MARS. WHO GOES THERE, FRIEND OR FOE?
HEY, JOEL. IT'S BRITTANY.
'SUP, GIRL? WHERE APRIL?
I DON'T KNOW. BUT I HEARD SOMETHING ABOUT YOU.
'BOUT HOW GOOD I AM? HA HA HA.
NAH. ROOK BEEN TELLING PEOPLE HE KICKED YOUR ASS.
WHAT! FUCK HIM! THAT NIGGA TELLING RANDOM DRUG DEALERS THAT I'M TALKING TO THEIR GIRLS. FUCK HIM.
WELL, HE SAID Y'ALL HAD BEEF AND HE DEALT WITH YOU.
THAT SHIT FUNNY CUZ I BEAT HIS ASS.
NOT WHAT I HEARD. HA HA.
WHATEVER.
FUCK HIM.
IT'S RAP WEEK ON BET!
~CLICK~

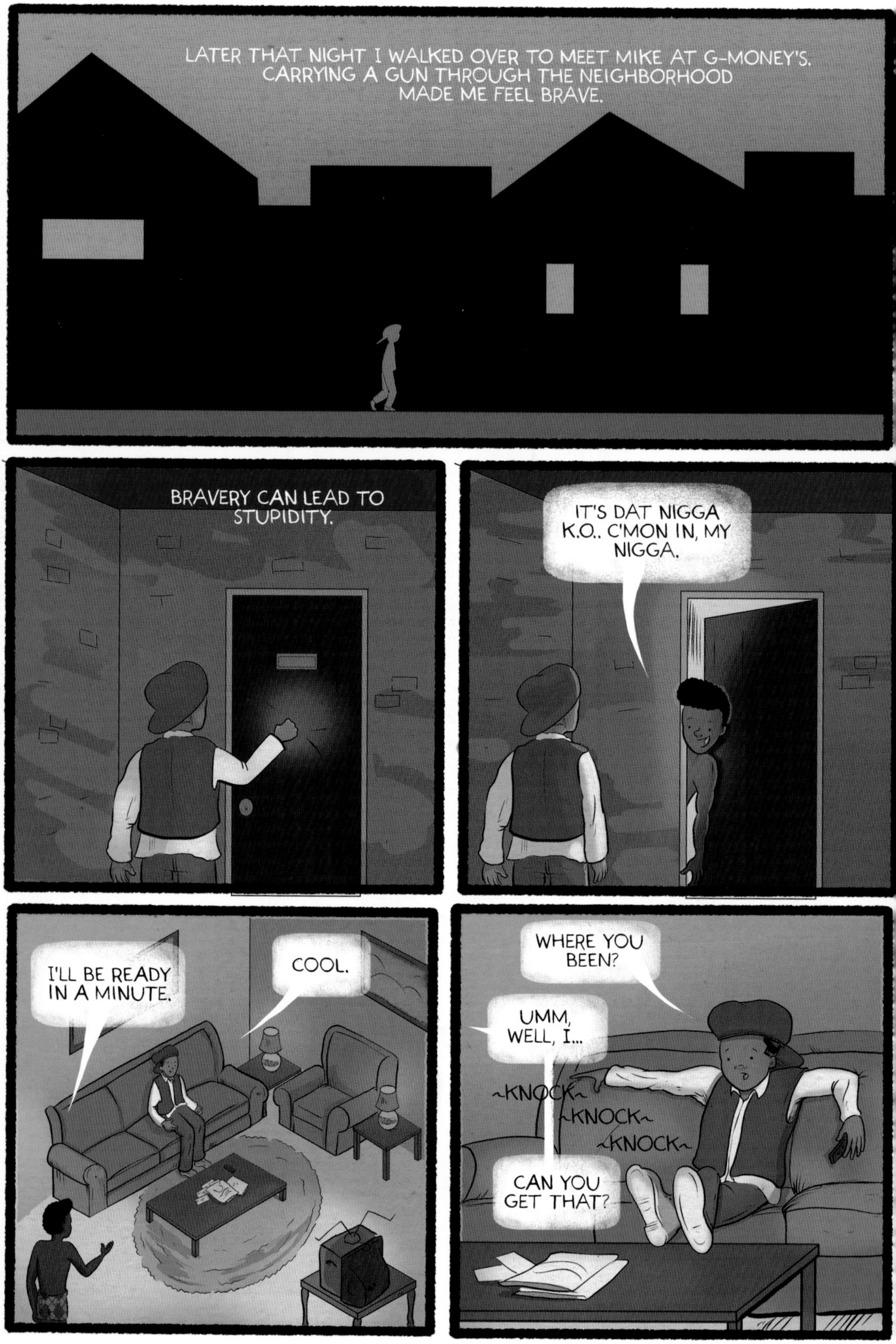

LATER THAT NIGHT I WALKED OVER TO MEET MIKE AT G-MONEY'S. CARRYING A GUN THROUGH THE NEIGHBORHOOD MADE ME FEEL BRAVE.
BRAVERY CAN LEAD TO STUPIDITY.
IT'S DAT NIGGA K.O.. C'MON IN, MY NIGGA.
I'LL BE READY IN A MINUTE.
COOL.
WHERE YOU BEEN?
UMM, WELL, I...
KNOCK
KNOCK
KNOCK
CAN YOU GET THAT?

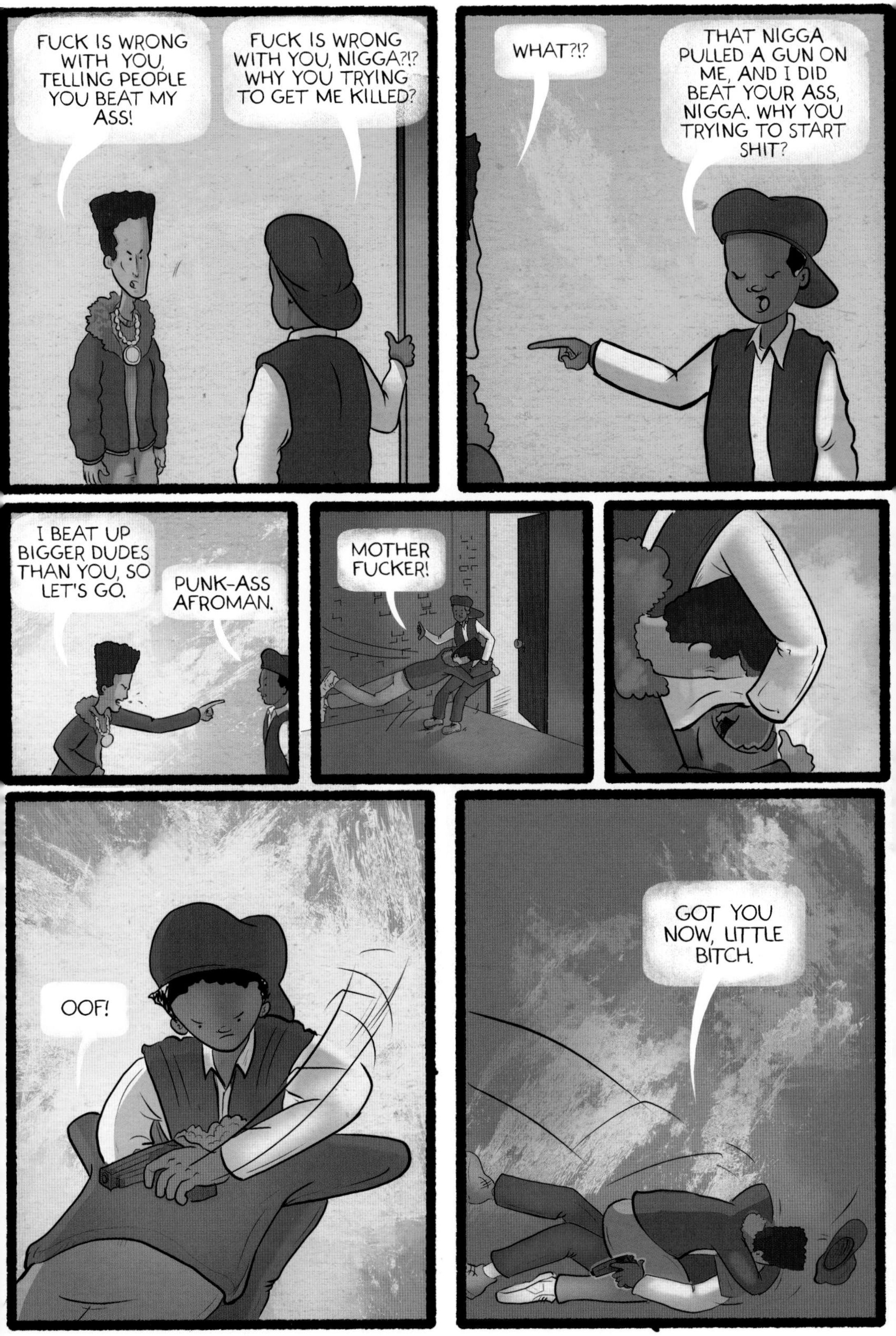
FUCK IS WRONG WITH YOU, TELLING PEOPLE YOU BEAT MY ASS!
FUCK IS WRONG WITH YOU, NIGGA?!? WHY YOU TRYING TO GET ME KILLED?
WHAT?!?
THAT NIGGA PULLED A GUN ON ME, AND I DID BEAT YOUR ASS, NIGGA. WHY YOU TRYING TO START SHIT?
I BEAT UP BIGGER DUDES THAN YOU, SO LET'S GO.
PUNK-ASS AFROMAN.
MOTHER FUCKER!
OOF!
GOT YOU NOW, LITTLE BITCH.

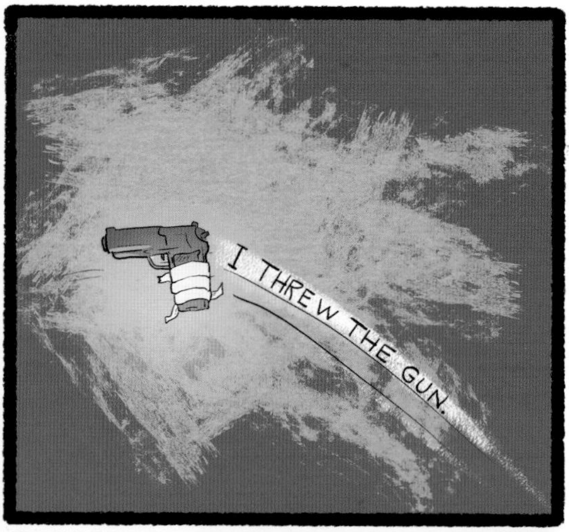
I THREW THE GUN.
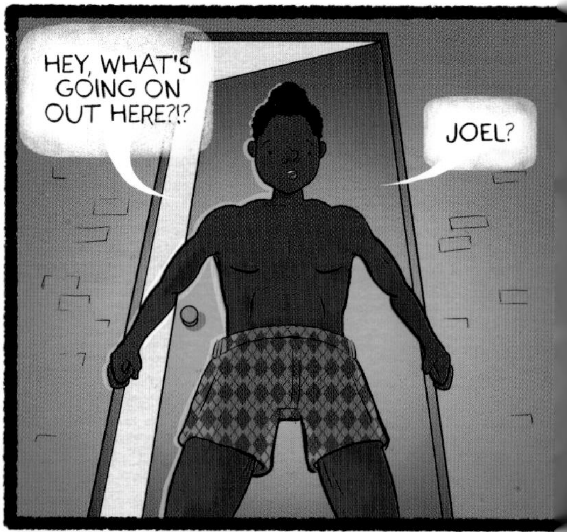
HEY, WHAT'S GOING ON OUT HERE?!?
JOEL?
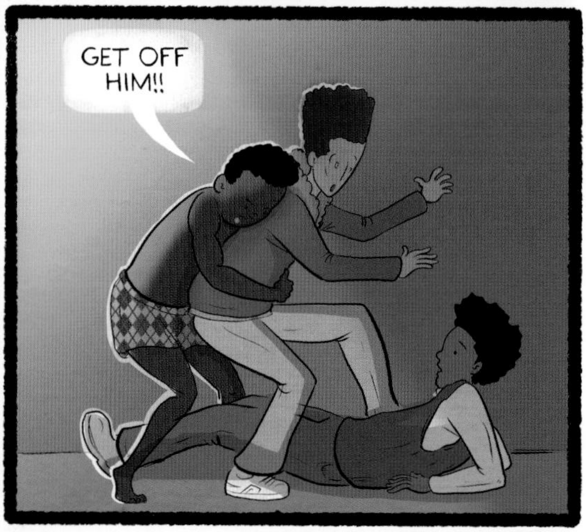
GET OFF HIM!!
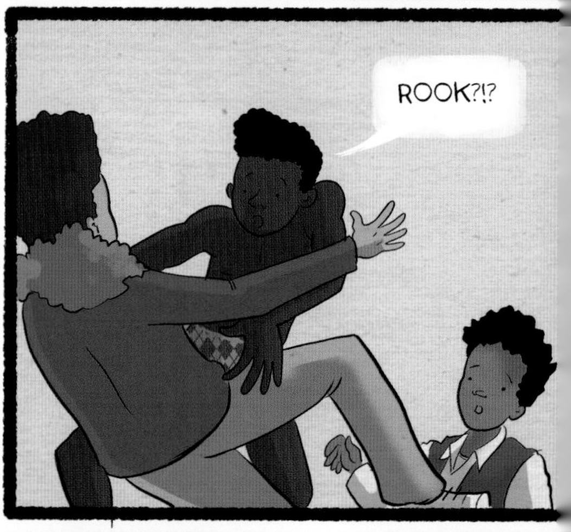
ROOK?!?
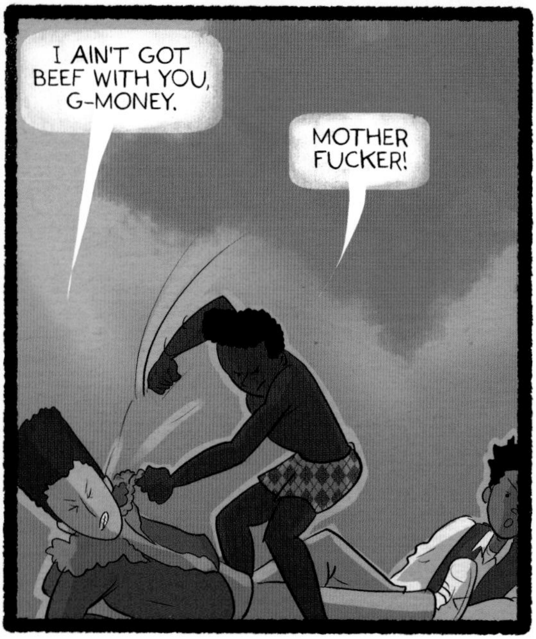
I AIN'T GOT BEEF WITH YOU, G-MONEY.
MOTHER FUCKER!
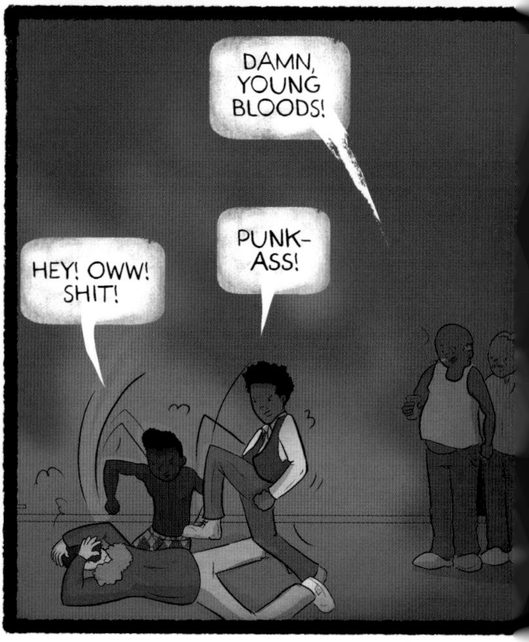
DAMN, YOUNG BLOODS!
PUNK-ASS!
HEY! OWW! SHIT!

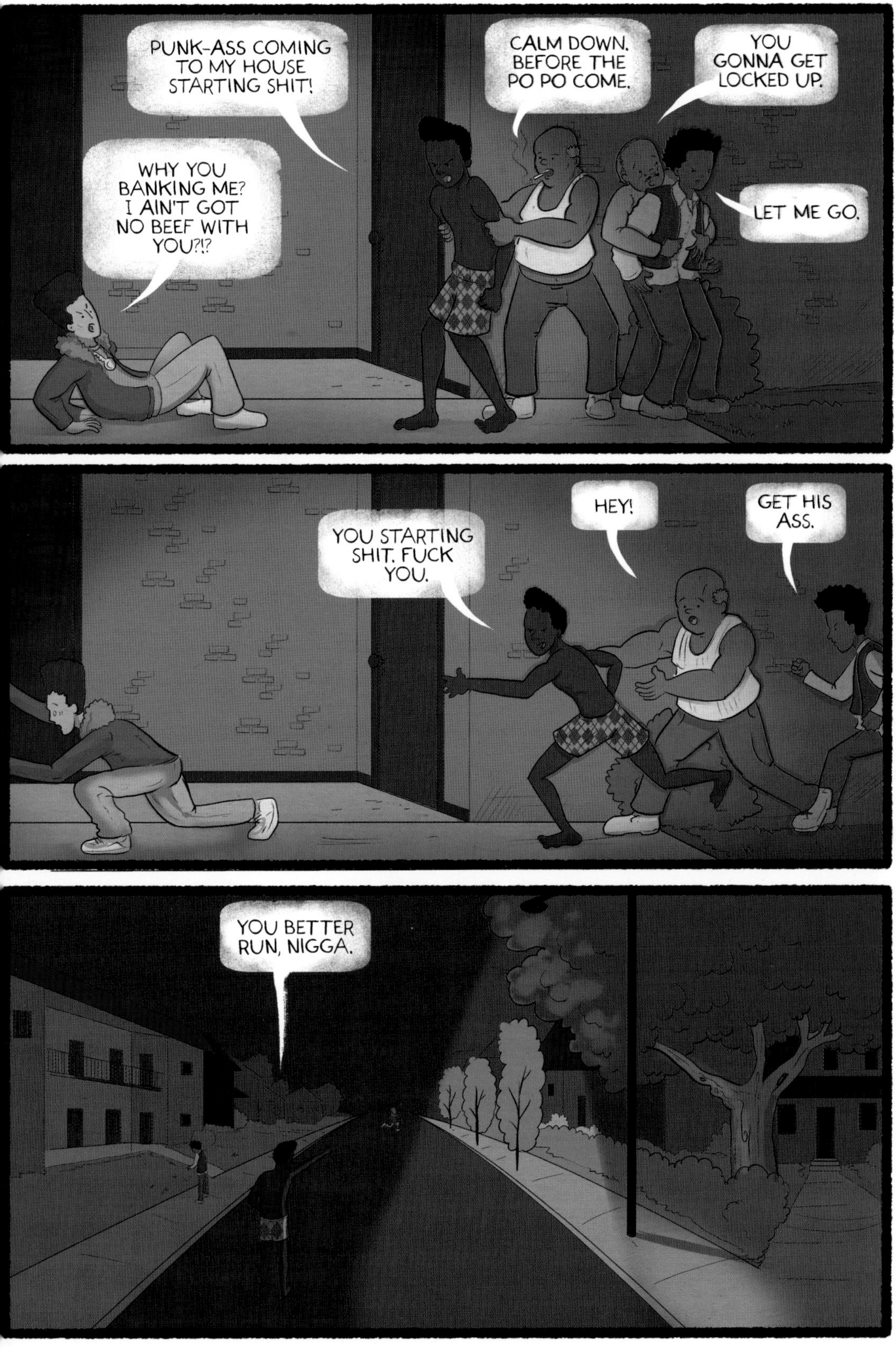
PUNK-ASS COMING TO MY HOUSE STARTING SHIT!
WHY YOU BANKING ME? I AIN'T GOT NO BEEF WITH YOU?!?
CALM DOWN. BEFORE THE PO PO COME.
YOU GONNA GET LOCKED UP.
LET ME GO.
YOU STARTING SHIT. FUCK YOU.
HEY!
GET HIS ASS.
YOU BETTER RUN, NIGGA.

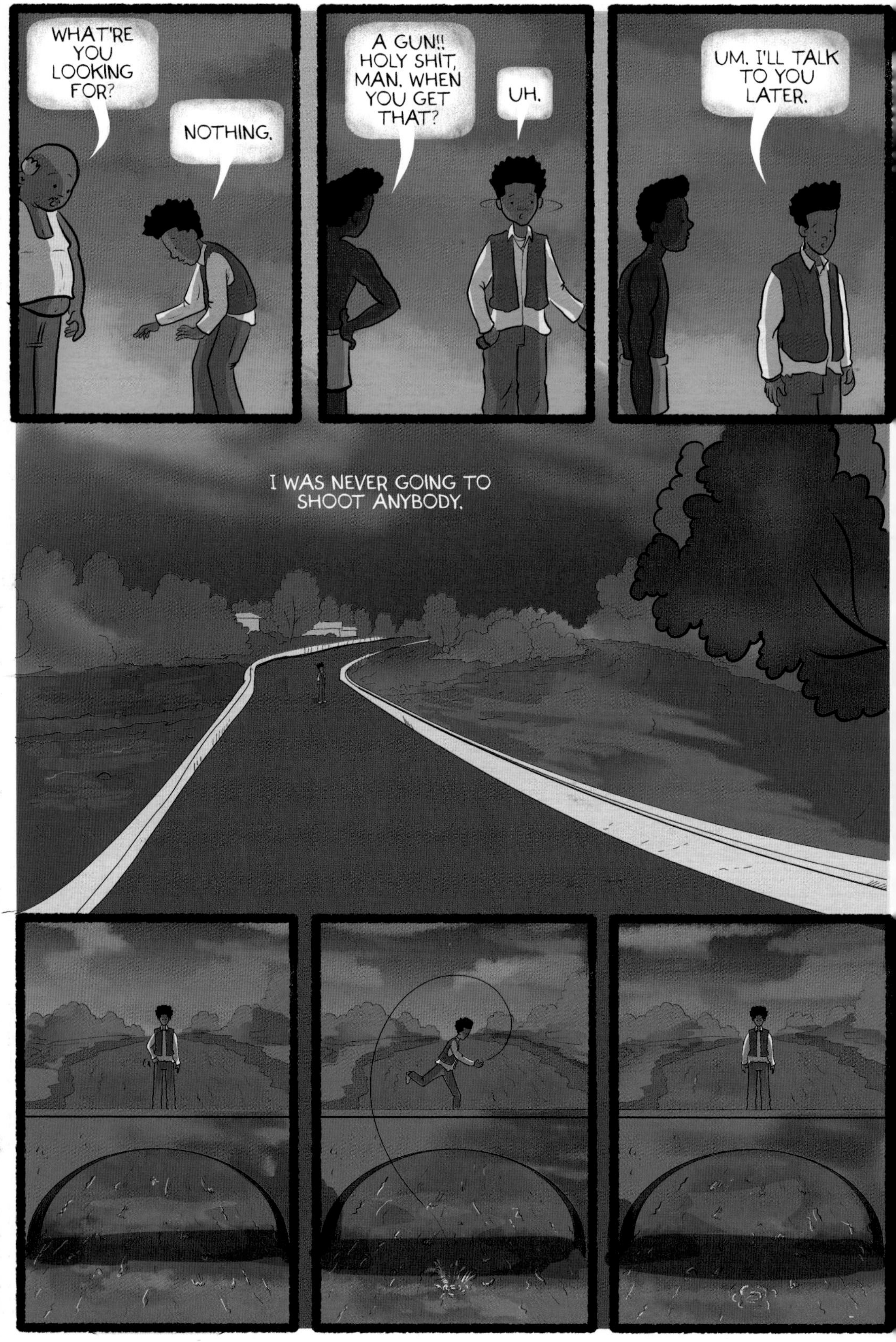
WHAT'RE YOU LOOKING FOR?
NOTHING.
A GUN!! HOLY SHIT, MAN. WHEN YOU GET THAT?
UH.
UM. I'LL TALK TO YOU LATER.
I WAS NEVER GOING TO SHOOT ANYBODY.

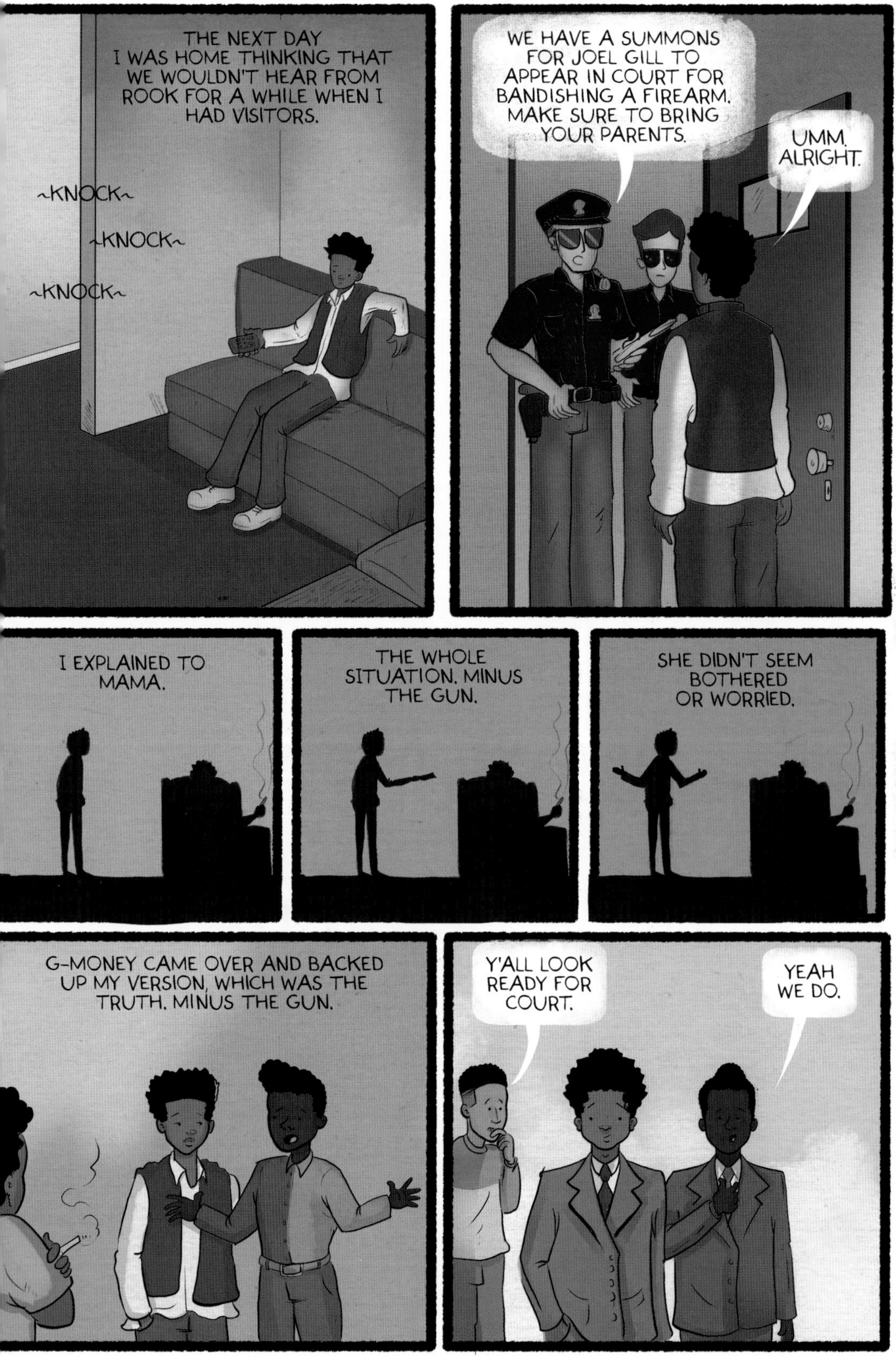
THE NEXT DAY I WAS HOME THINKING THAT WE WOULDN'T HEAR FROM ROOK FOR A WHILE WHEN I HAD VISITORS.
~KNOCK~
~KNOCK~
~KNOCK~
WE HAVE A SUMMONS FOR JOEL GILL TO APPEAR IN COURT FOR BANDISHING A FIREARM. MAKE SURE TO BRING YOUR PARENTS.
UMM. ALRIGHT.
I EXPLAINED TO MAMA.
THE WHOLE SITUATION. MINUS THE GUN.
SHE DIDN'T SEEM BOTHERED OR WORRIED.
G-MONEY CAME OVER AND BACKED UP MY VERSION, WHICH WAS THE TRUTH. MINUS THE GUN.
Y'ALL LOOK READY FOR COURT.
YEAH WE DO.

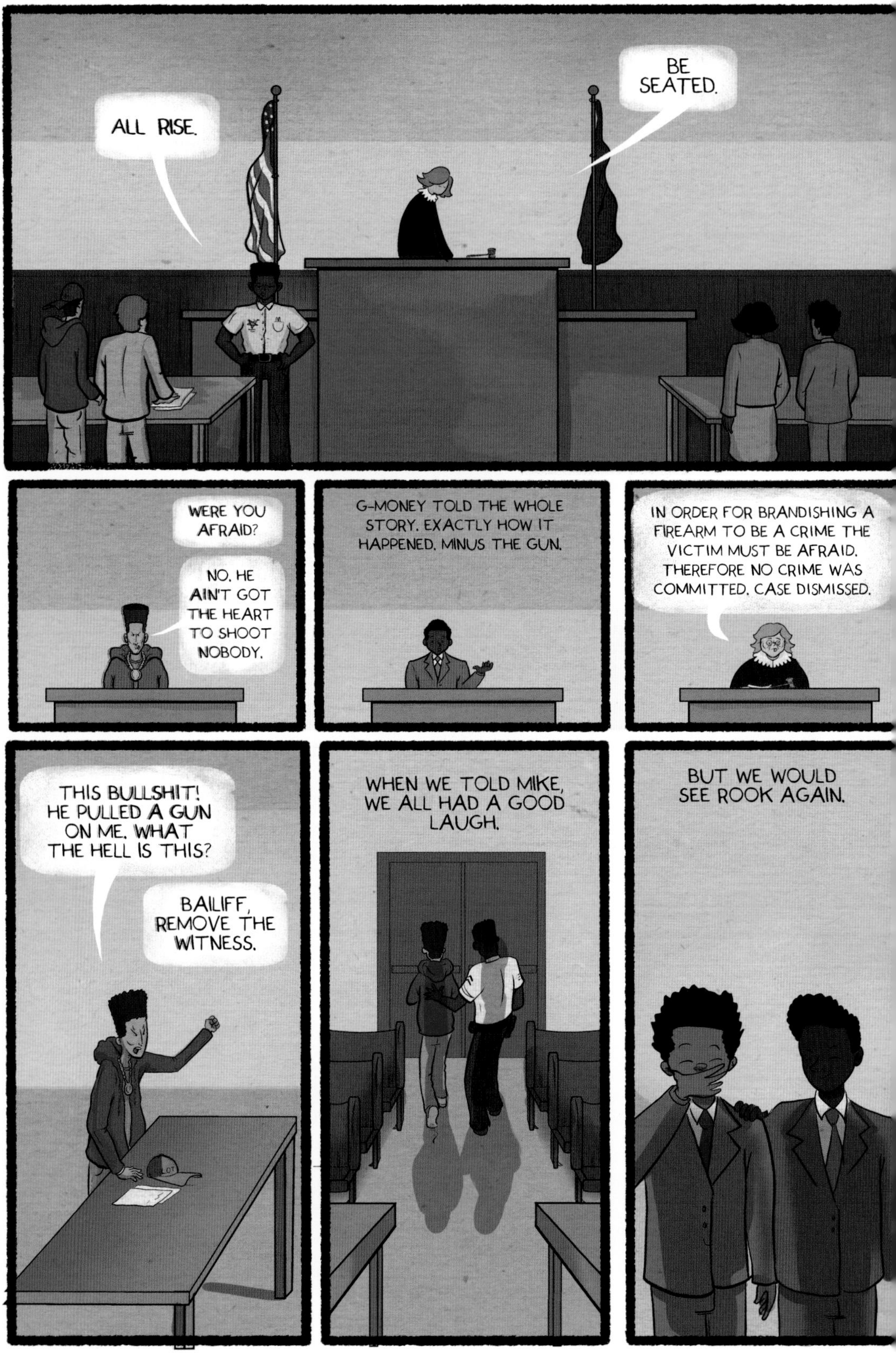
ALL RISE.
BE SEATED.
WERE YOU AFRAID?
NO, HE AIN'T GOT THE HEART TO SHOOT NOBODY.
G-MONEY TOLD THE WHOLE STORY. EXACTLY HOW IT HAPPENED. MINUS THE GUN.
IN ORDER FOR BRANDISHING A FIREARM TO BE A CRIME THE VICTIM MUST BE AFRAID. THEREFORE NO CRIME WAS COMMITTED. CASE DISMISSED.
THIS BULLSHIT! HE PULLED A GUN ON ME. WHAT THE HELL IS THIS?
BAILIFF, REMOVE THE WITNESS.
WHEN WE TOLD MIKE, WE ALL HAD A GOOD LAUGH.
BUT WE WOULD SEE ROOK AGAIN.

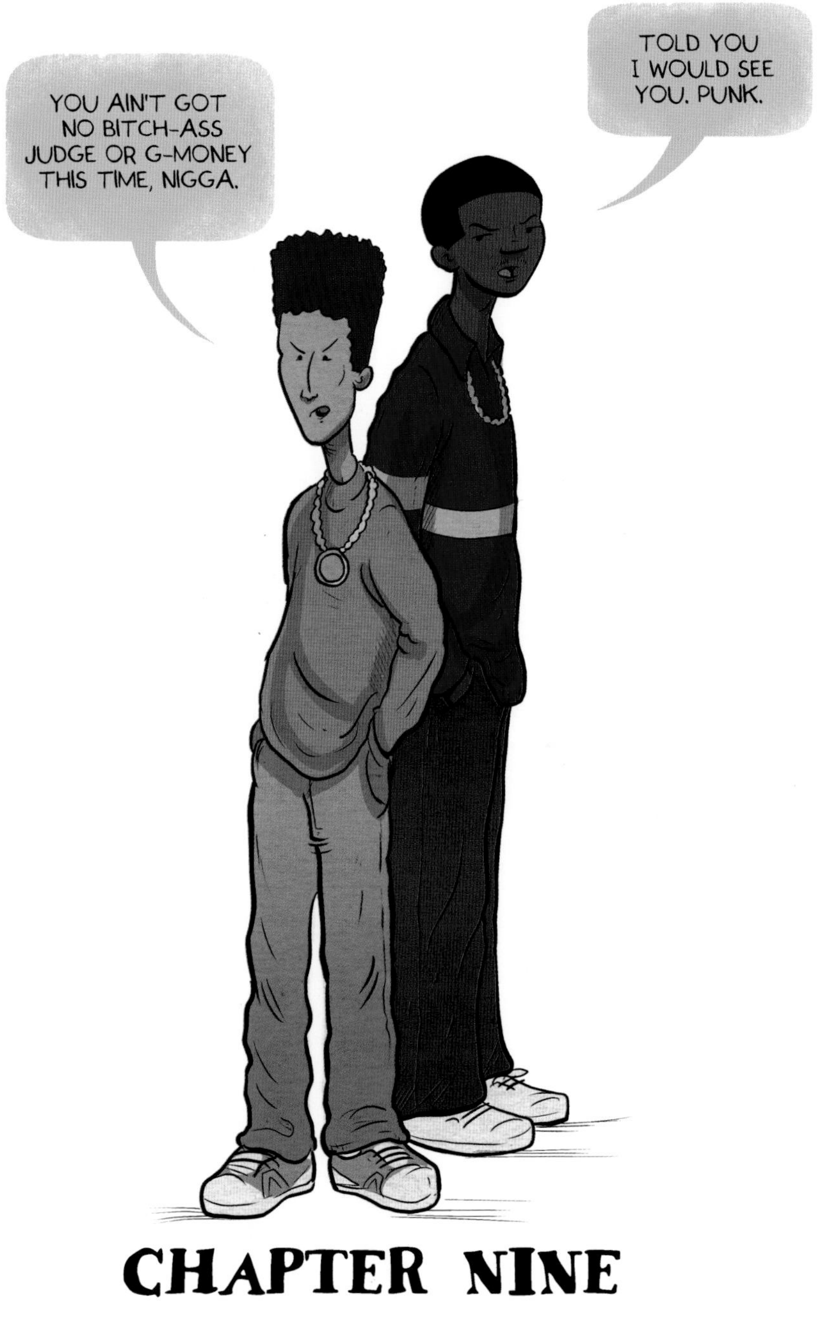
YOU AIN'T GOT NO BITCH-ASS JUDGE OR G-MONEY THIS TIME, NIGGA.
TOLD YOU I WOULD SEE YOU. PUNK.

CHAPTER NINE

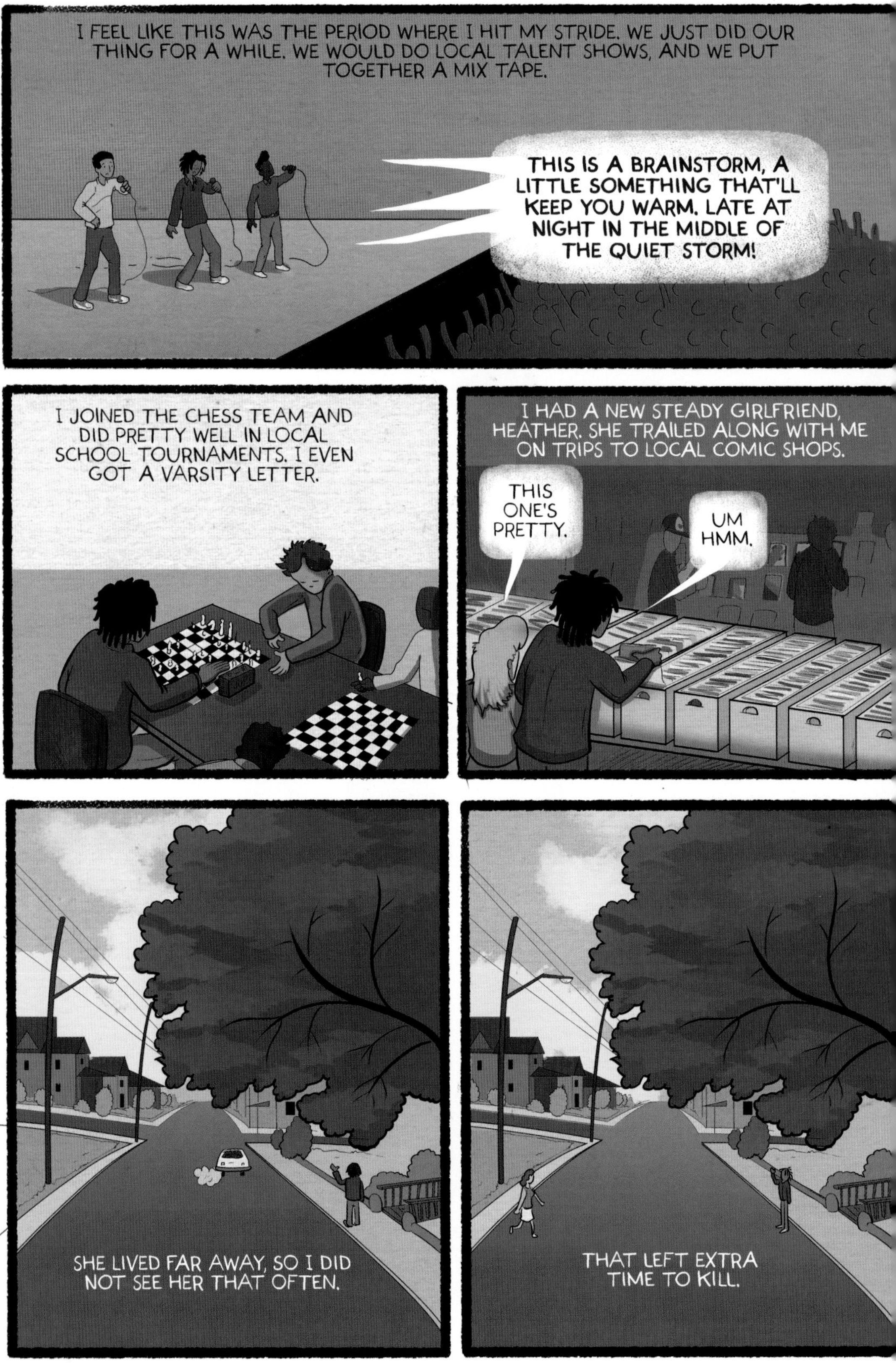
I FEEL LIKE THIS WAS THE PERIOD WHERE I HIT MY STRIDE. WE JUST DID OUR THING FOR A WHILE. WE WOULD DO LOCAL TALENT SHOWS, AND WE PUT TOGETHER A MIX TAPE.
THIS IS A BRAINSTORM, A LITTLE SOMETHING THAT'LL KEEP YOU WARM. LATE AT NIGHT IN THE MIDDLE OF THE QUIET STORM!
I JOINED THE CHESS TEAM AND DID PRETTY WELL IN LOCAL SCHOOL TOURNAMENTS. I EVEN GOT A VARSITY LETTER.
I HAD A NEW STEADY GIRLFRIEND, HEATHER. SHE TRAILED ALONG WITH ME ON TRIPS TO LOCAL COMIC SHOPS.
THIS ONE'S PRETTY.
UM HMM.
SHE LIVED FAR AWAY, SO I DID NOT SEE HER THAT OFTEN.
THAT LEFT EXTRA TIME TO KILL.

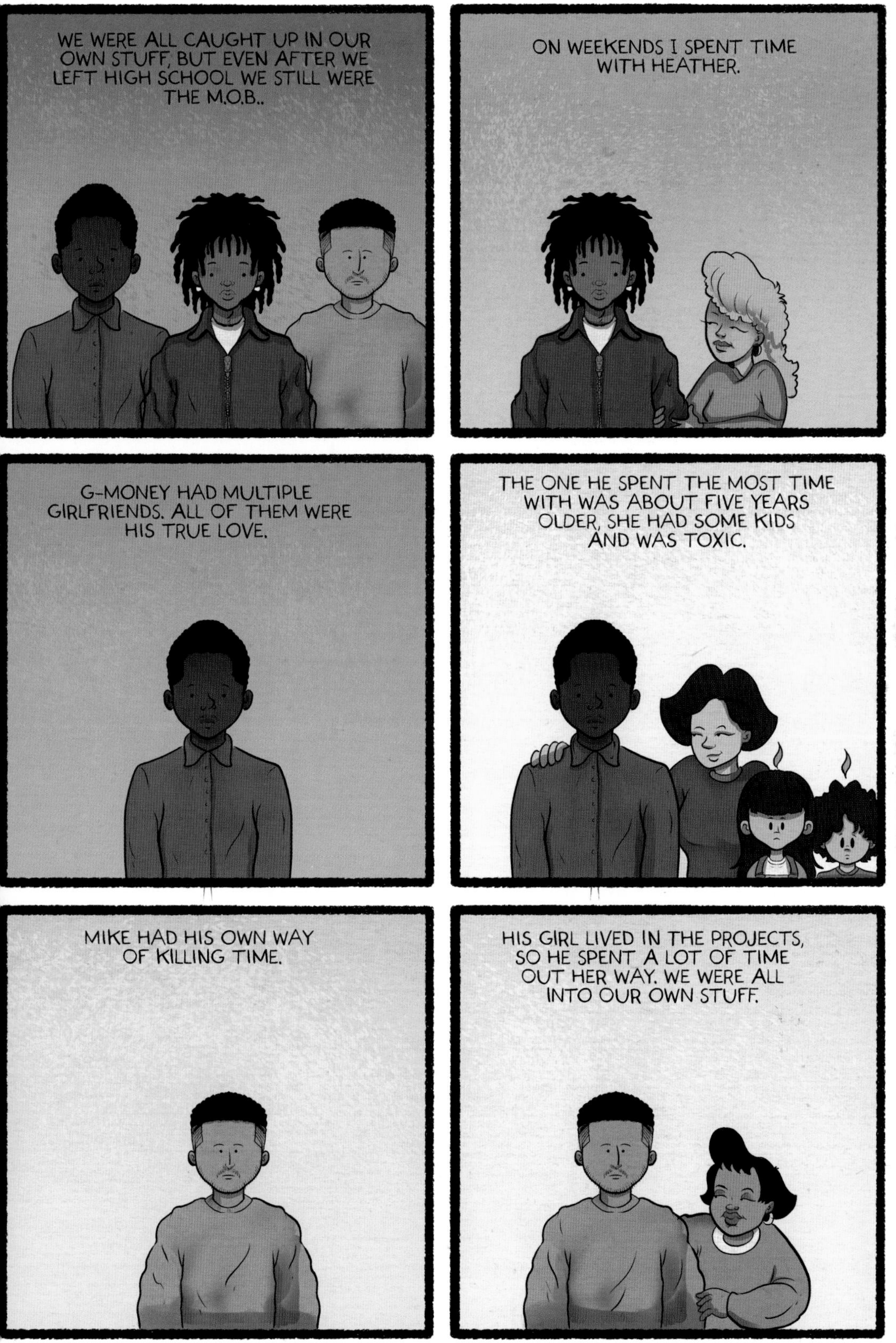
WE WERE ALL CAUGHT UP IN OUR OWN STUFF, BUT EVEN AFTER WE LEFT HIGH SCHOOL WE STILL WERE THE M.O.B..
ON WEEKENDS I SPENT TIME WITH HEATHER.
G-MONEY HAD MULTIPLE GIRLFRIENDS. ALL OF THEM WERE HIS TRUE LOVE.
THE ONE HE SPENT THE MOST TIME WITH WAS ABOUT FIVE YEARS OLDER, SHE HAD SOME KIDS AND WAS TOXIC.
MIKE HAD HIS OWN WAY OF KILLING TIME.
HIS GIRL LIVED IN THE PROJECTS, SO HE SPENT A LOT OF TIME OUT HER WAY. WE WERE ALL INTO OUR OWN STUFF.

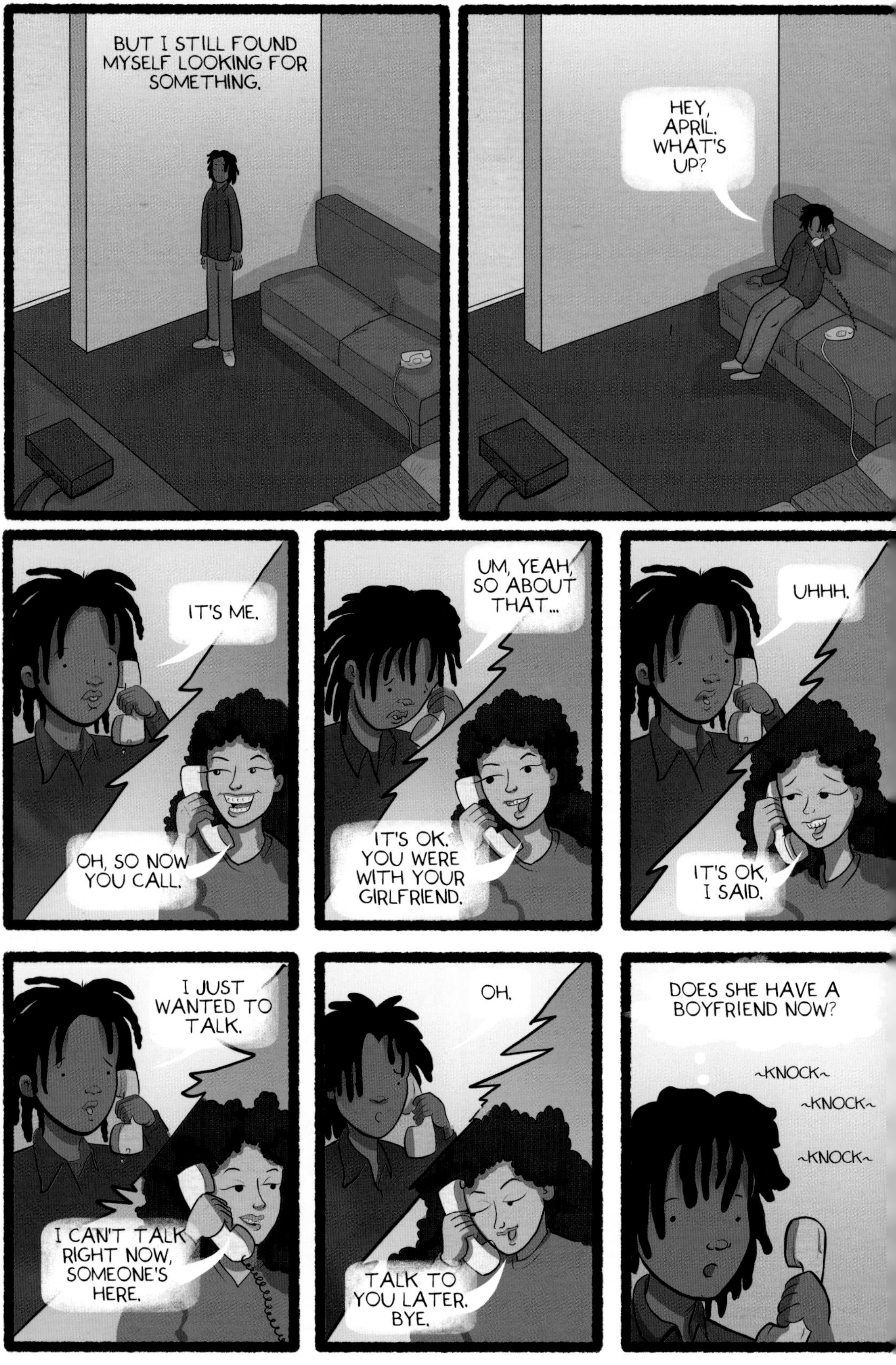
BUT I STILL FOUND MYSELF LOOKING FOR SOMETHING.
HEY, APRIL. WHAT'S UP?
IT'S ME.
OH, SO NOW YOU CALL.
UM, YEAH, SO ABOUT THAT...
IT'S OK. YOU WERE WITH YOUR GIRLFRIEND.
UHHH.
IT'S OK, I SAID.
I JUST WANTED TO TALK.
I CAN'T TALK RIGHT NOW, SOMEONE'S HERE.
OH.
TALK TO YOU LATER. BYE.
DOES SHE HAVE A BOYFRIEND NOW?
~KNOCK~
~KNOCK~
~KNOCK~

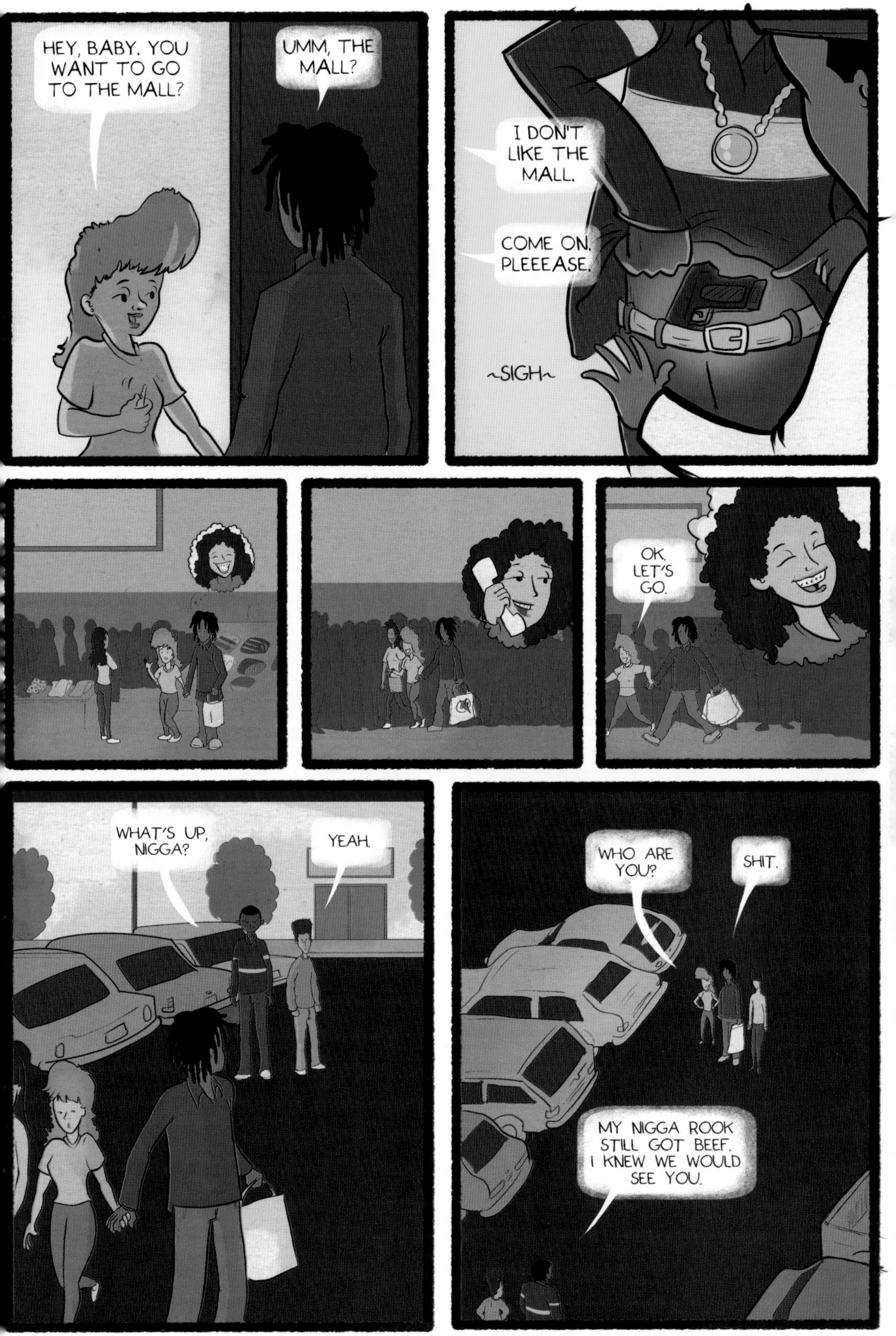
HEY, BABY. YOU WANT TO GO TO THE MALL?
UMM, THE MALL?
I DON'T LIKE THE MALL.
COME ON. PLEEEASE.
~SIGH~
OK. LET'S GO.
WHAT'S UP, NIGGA?
YEAH.
WHO ARE YOU?
SHIT.
MY NIGGA ROOK STILL GOT BEEF. I KNEW WE WOULD SEE YOU.

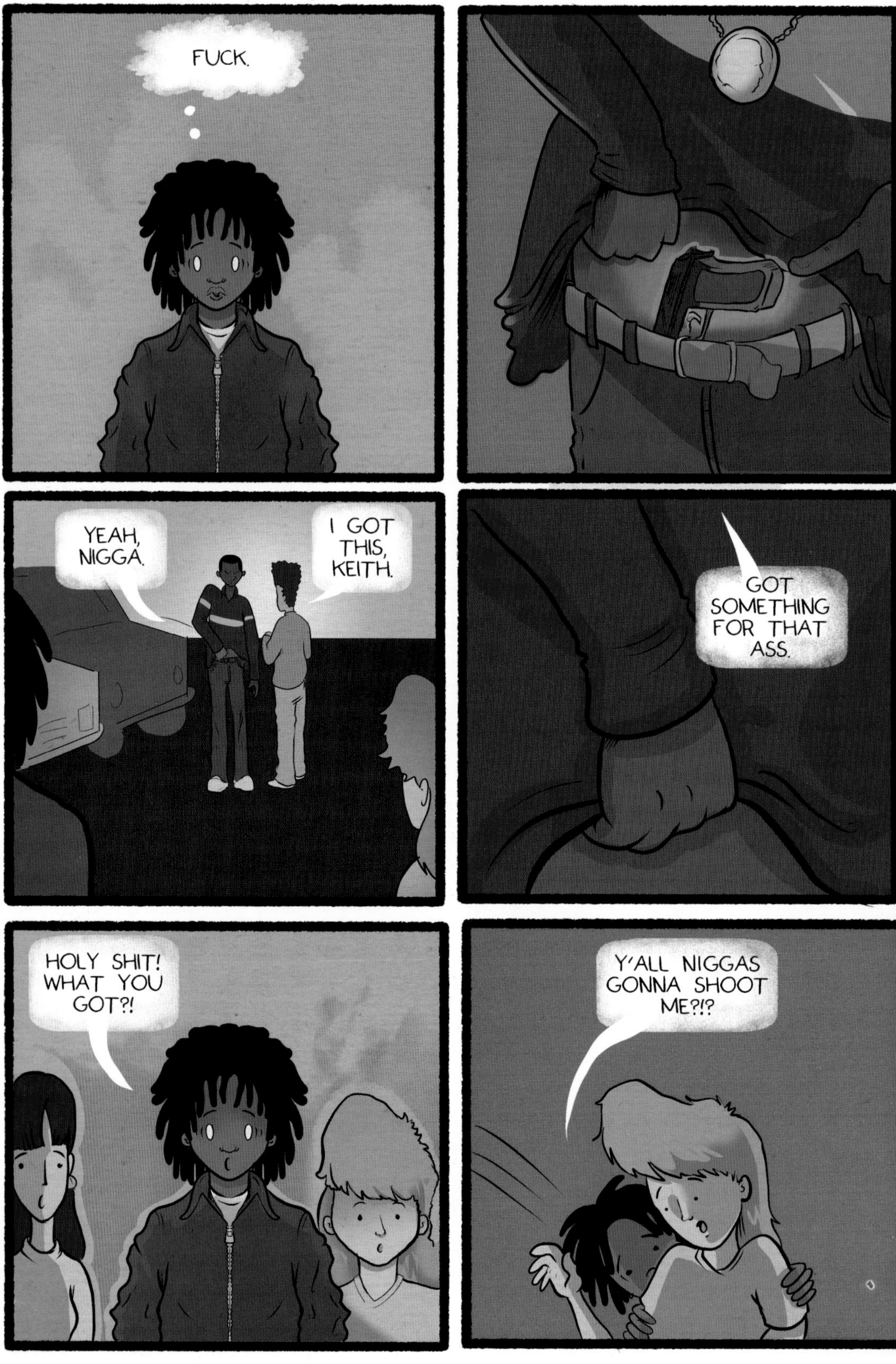
FUCK.
YEAH, NIGGA.
I GOT THIS, KEITH.
GOT SOMETHING FOR THAT ASS.
HOLY SHIT! WHAT YOU GOT?!
Y'ALL NIGGAS GONNA SHOOT ME?!?

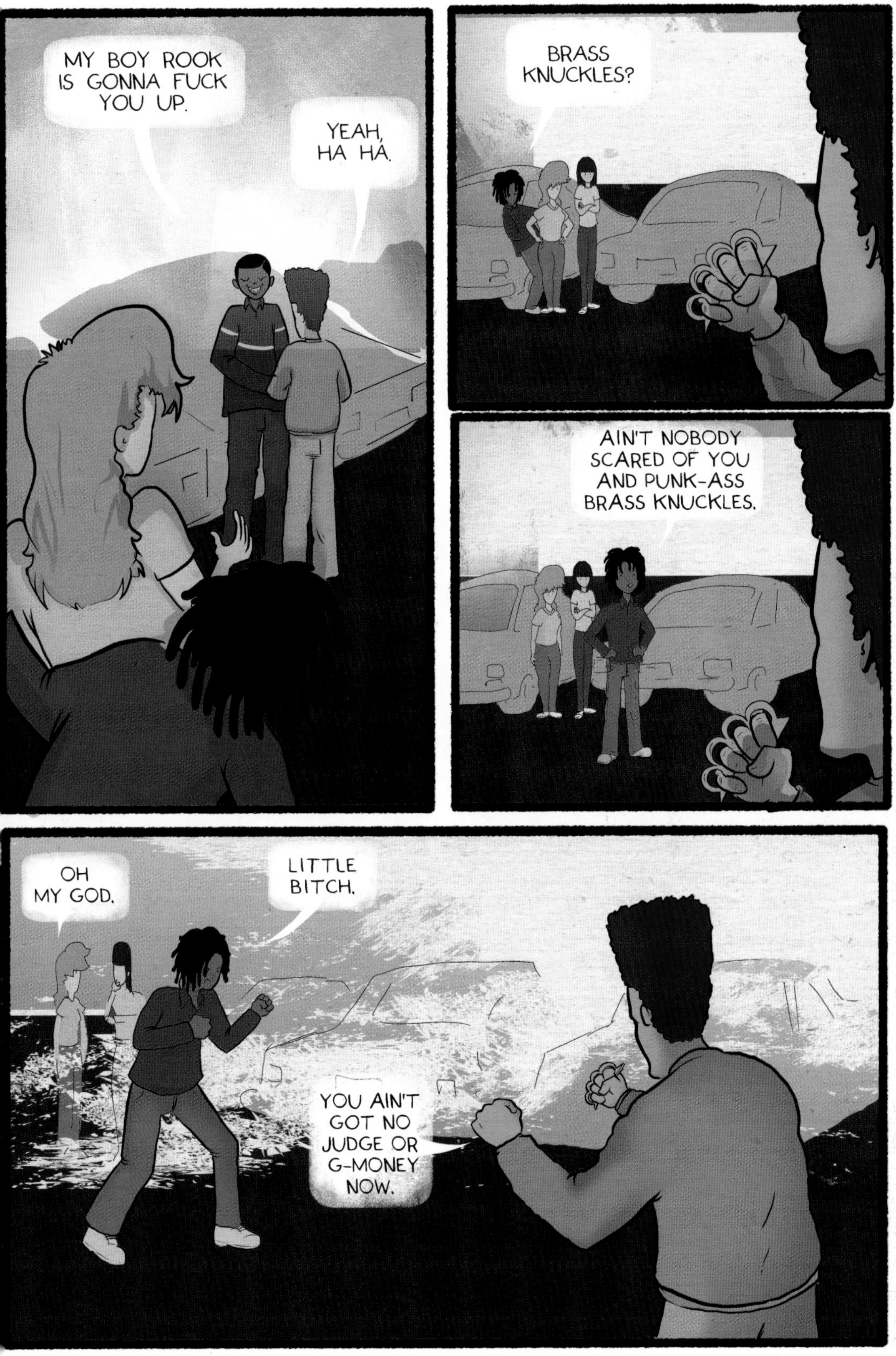
MY BOY ROOK IS GONNA FUCK YOU UP.
YEAH, HA HA.
BRASS KNUCKLES?
AIN'T NOBODY SCARED OF YOU AND PUNK-ASS BRASS KNUCKLES.
OH MY GOD.
LITTLE BITCH.
YOU AIN'T GOT NO JUDGE OR G-MONEY NOW.

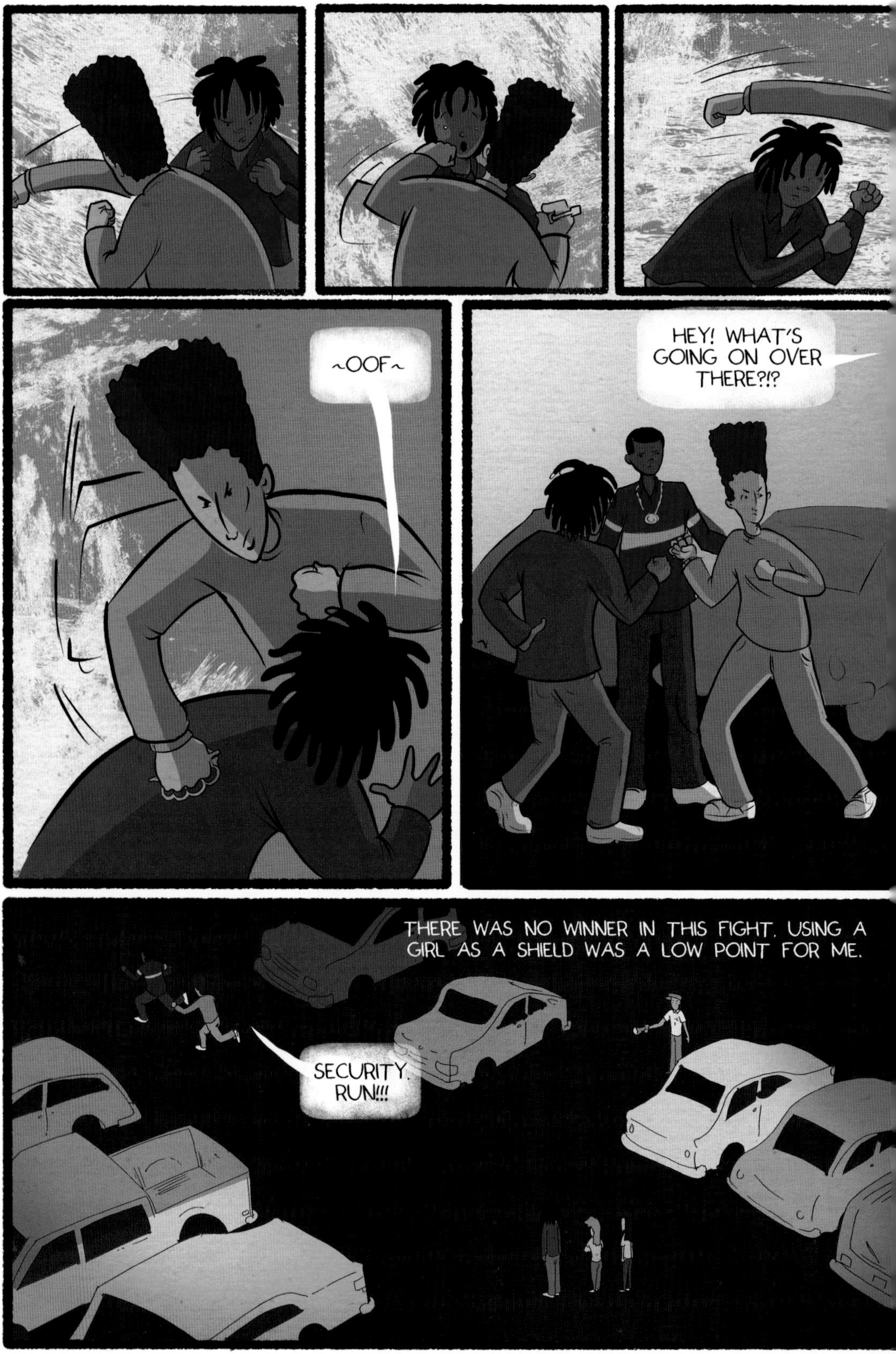
~OOF~
HEY! WHAT'S GOING ON OVER THERE?!?
THERE WAS NO WINNER IN THIS FIGHT. USING A GIRL AS A SHIELD WAS A LOW POINT FOR ME.
SECURITY. RUN!!!

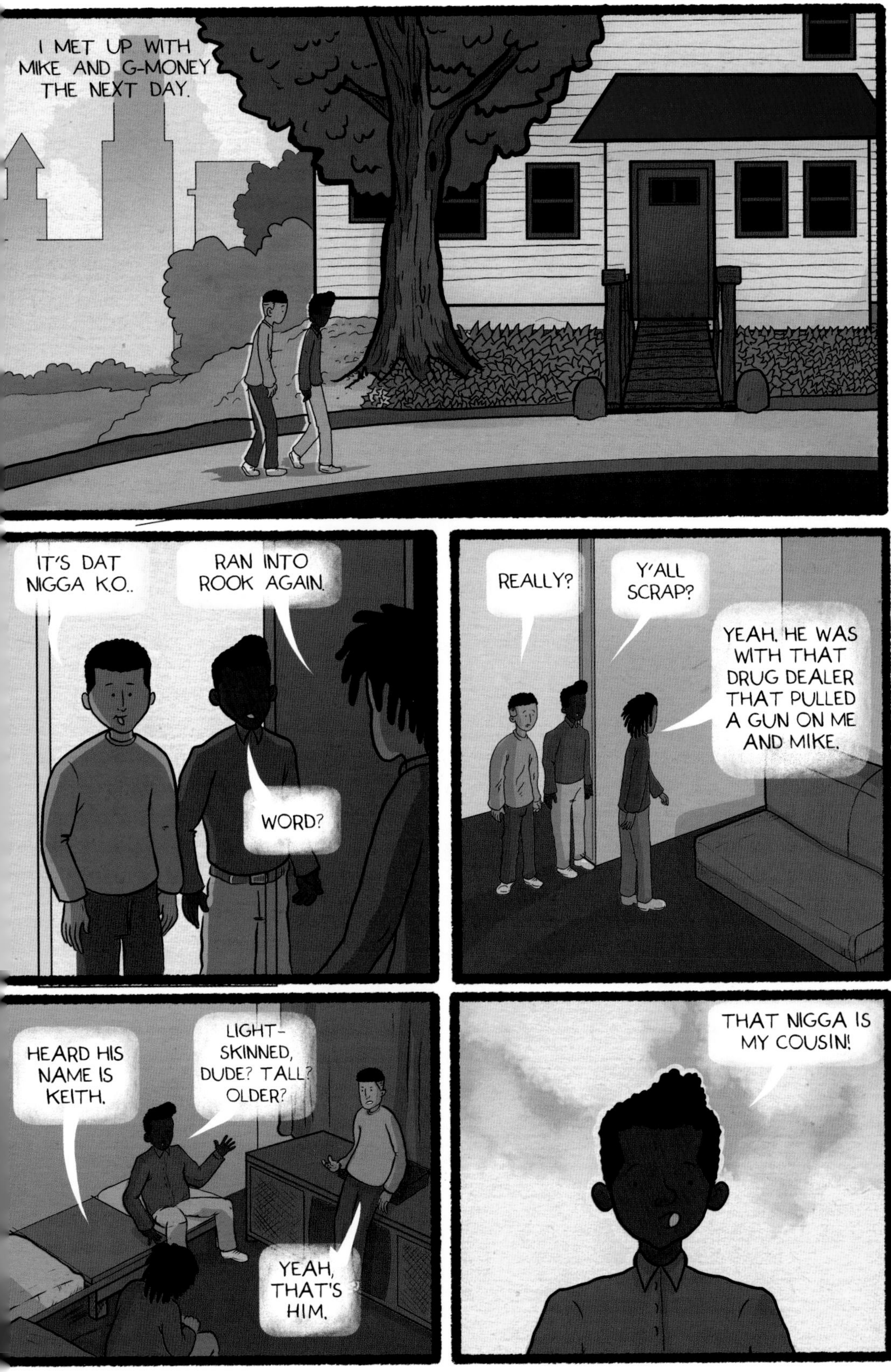
I MET UP WITH MIKE AND G-MONEY THE NEXT DAY.
IT'S DAT NIGGA K.O..
RAN INTO ROOK AGAIN.
WORD?
REALLY?
Y'ALL SCRAP?
YEAH. HE WAS WITH THAT DRUG DEALER THAT PULLED A GUN ON ME AND MIKE.
HEARD HIS NAME IS KEITH.
LIGHT-SKINNED, DUDE? TALL? OLDER?
YEAH, THAT'S HIM.
THAT NIGGA IS MY COUSIN!

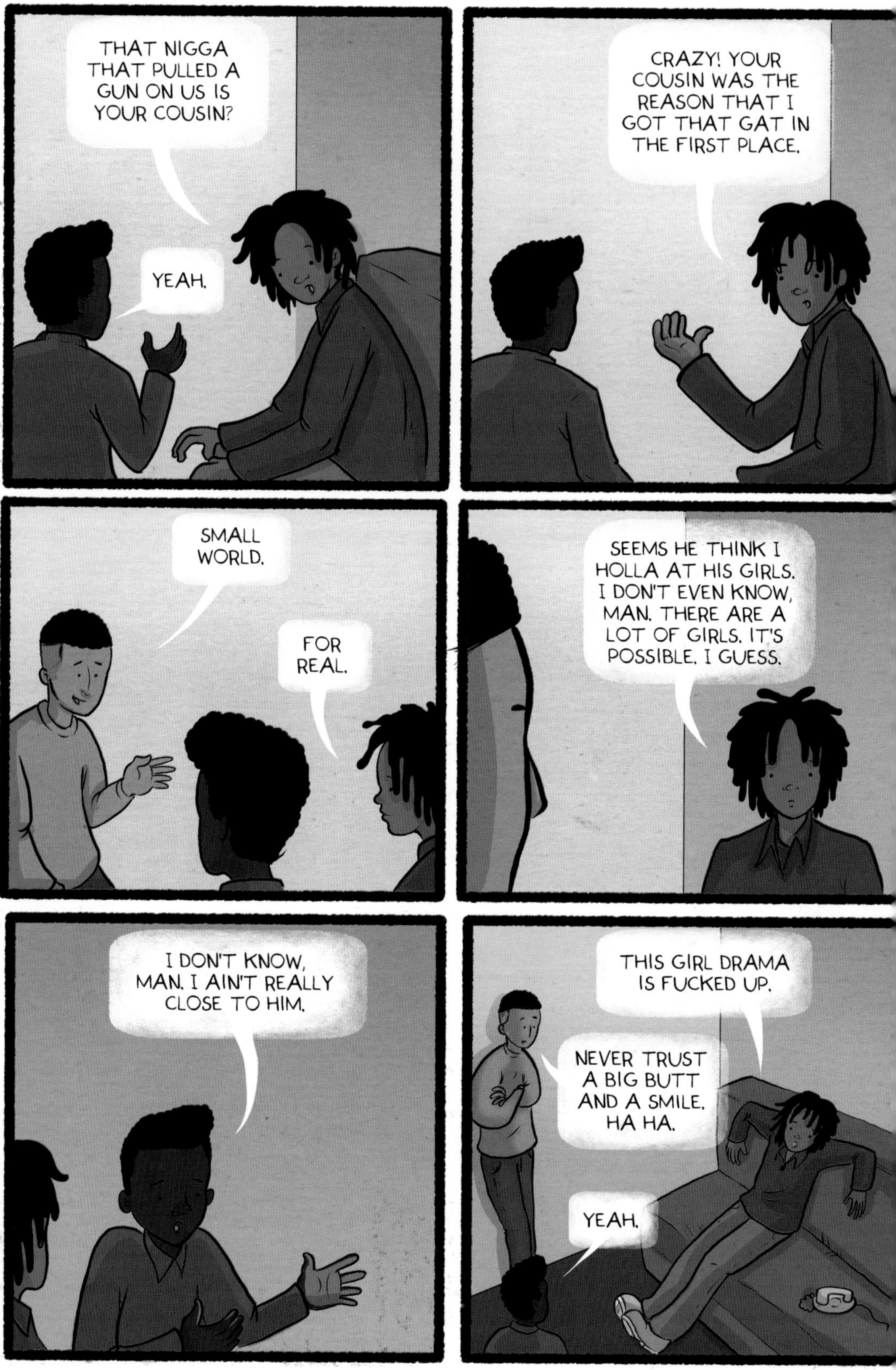
THAT NIGGA THAT PULLED A GUN ON US IS YOUR COUSIN?
YEAH.
CRAZY! YOUR COUSIN WAS THE REASON THAT I GOT THAT GAT IN THE FIRST PLACE.
SMALL WORLD.
FOR REAL.
SEEMS HE THINK I HOLLA AT HIS GIRLS. I DON'T EVEN KNOW, MAN. THERE ARE A LOT OF GIRLS. IT'S POSSIBLE, I GUESS.
I DON'T KNOW, MAN. I AIN'T REALLY CLOSE TO HIM.
THIS GIRL DRAMA IS FUCKED UP.
NEVER TRUST A BIG BUTT AND A SMILE. HA HA.
YEAH.

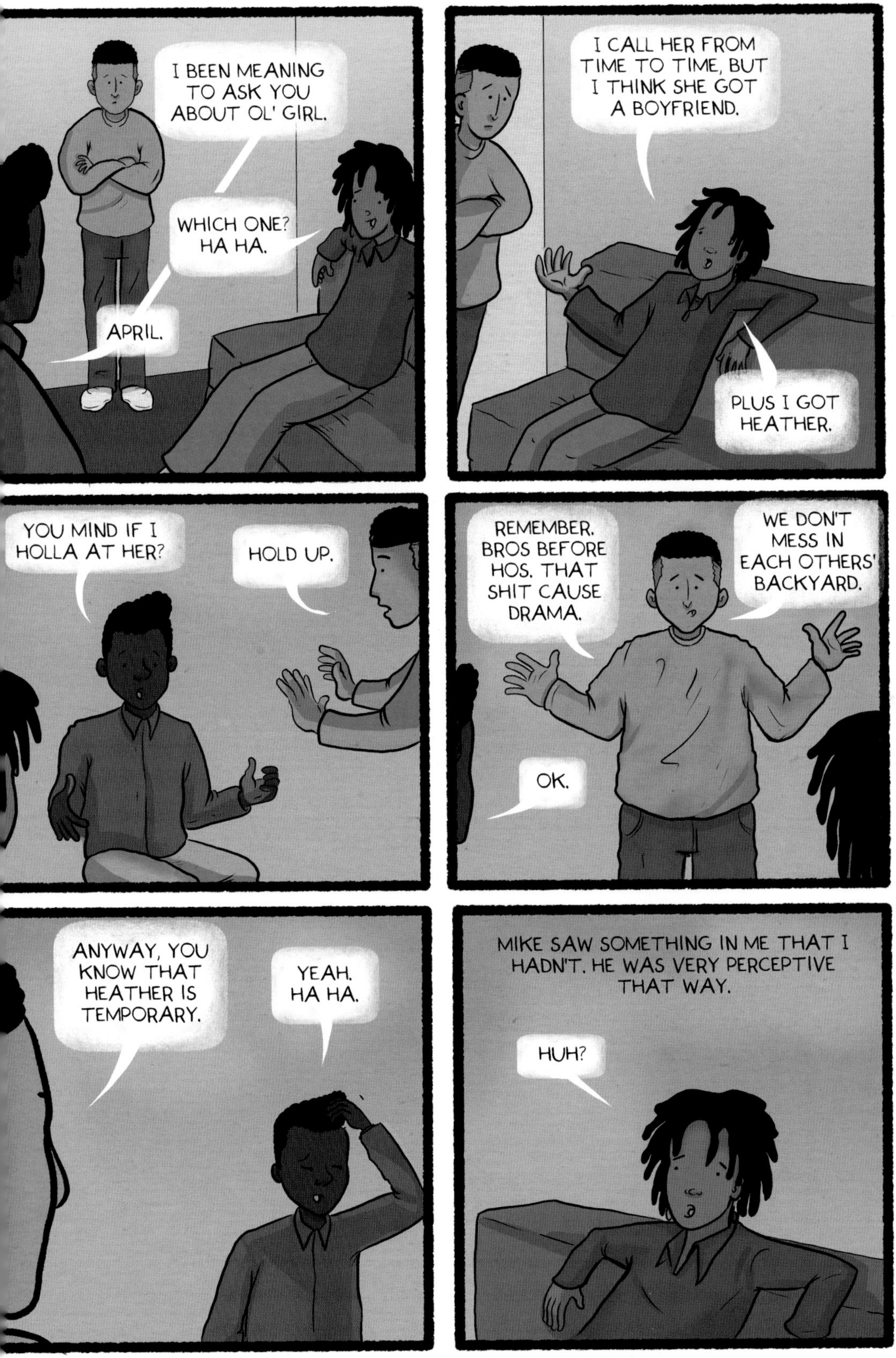
I BEEN MEANING TO ASK YOU ABOUT OL' GIRL.
WHICH ONE? HA HA.
APRIL.
I CALL HER FROM TIME TO TIME, BUT I THINK SHE GOT A BOYFRIEND.
PLUS I GOT HEATHER.
YOU MIND IF I HOLLA AT HER?
HOLD UP.
REMEMBER. BROS BEFORE HOS. THAT SHIT CAUSE DRAMA.
WE DON'T MESS IN EACH OTHERS' BACKYARD.
OK.
ANYWAY, YOU KNOW THAT HEATHER IS TEMPORARY.
YEAH. HA HA.
MIKE SAW SOMETHING IN ME THAT I HADN'T. HE WAS VERY PERCEPTIVE THAT WAY.
HUH?

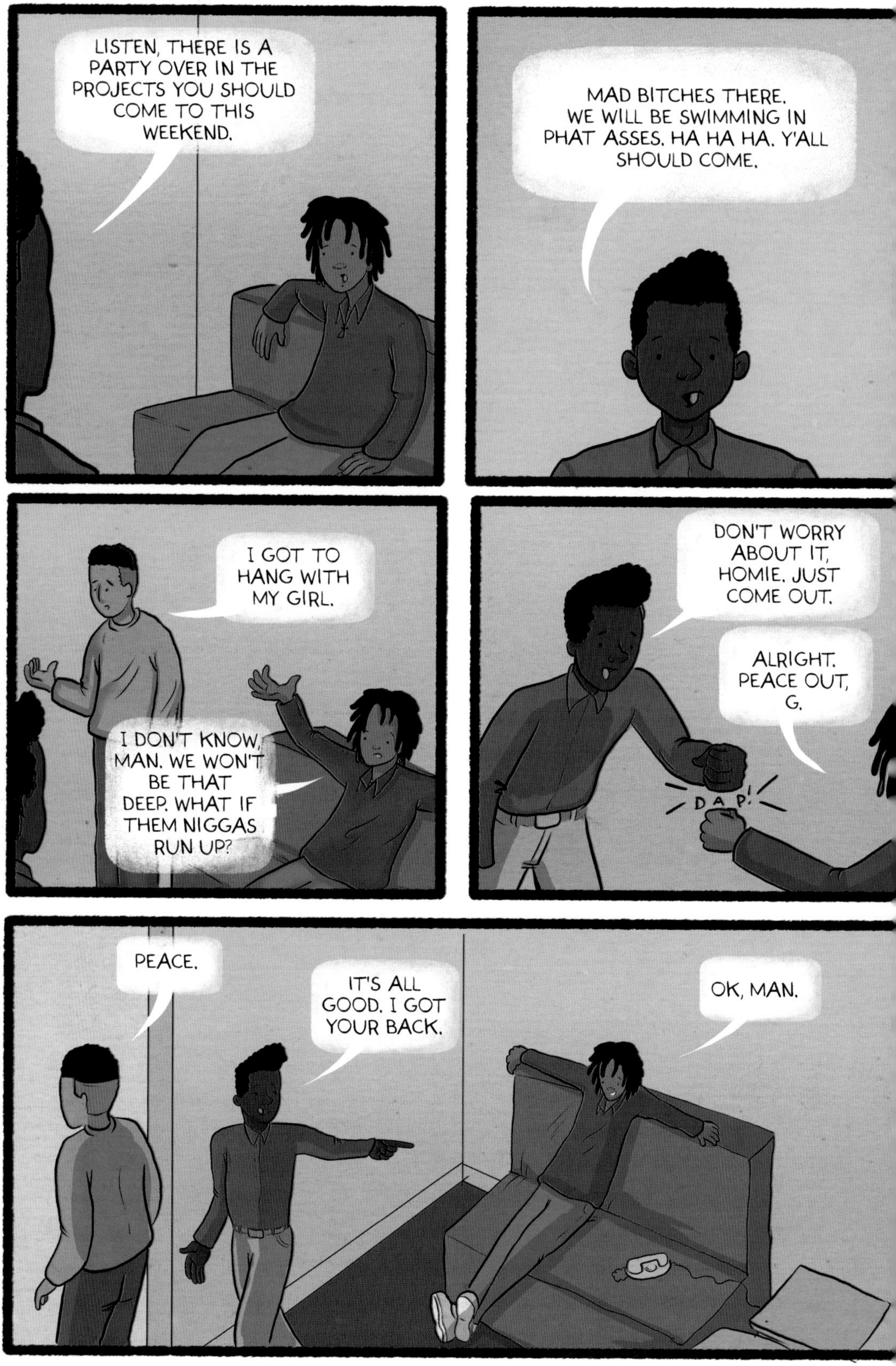
LISTEN, THERE IS A PARTY OVER IN THE PROJECTS YOU SHOULD COME TO THIS WEEKEND.
MAD BITCHES THERE. WE WILL BE SWIMMING IN PHAT ASSES. HA HA HA. Y'ALL SHOULD COME.
I GOT TO HANG WITH MY GIRL.
I DON'T KNOW, MAN. WE WON'T BE THAT DEEP. WHAT IF THEM NIGGAS RUN UP?
DON'T WORRY ABOUT IT, HOMIE. JUST COME OUT.
ALRIGHT. PEACE OUT, G.
DAP!
PEACE.
IT'S ALL GOOD. I GOT YOUR BACK.
OK, MAN.

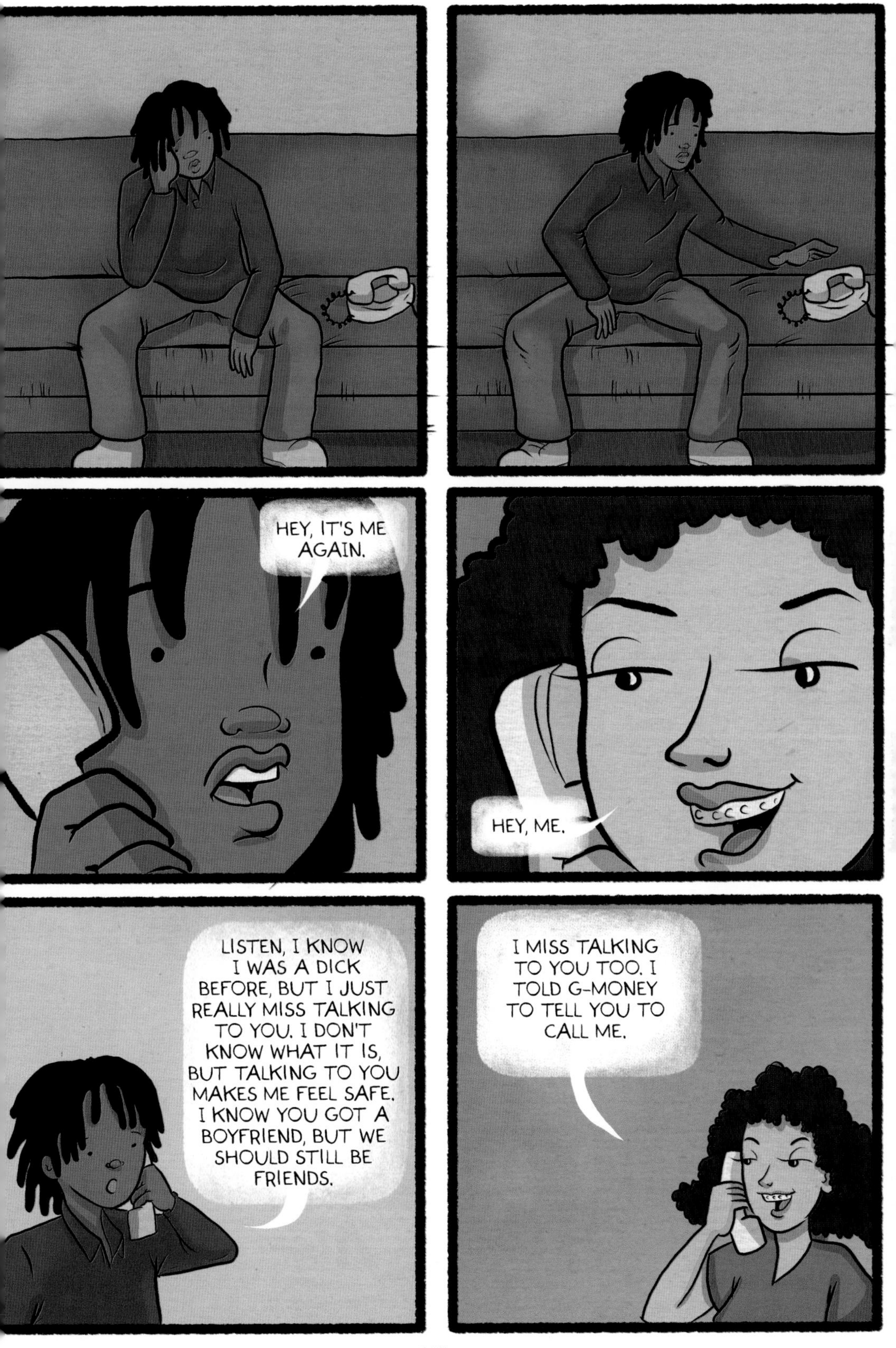
HEY, IT'S ME AGAIN.
HEY, ME.
LISTEN, I KNOW I WAS A DICK BEFORE, BUT I JUST REALLY MISS TALKING TO YOU. I DON'T KNOW WHAT IT IS, BUT TALKING TO YOU MAKES ME FEEL SAFE. I KNOW YOU GOT A BOYFRIEND, BUT WE SHOULD STILL BE FRIENDS.
I MISS TALKING TO YOU TOO. I TOLD G-MONEY TO TELL YOU TO CALL ME.

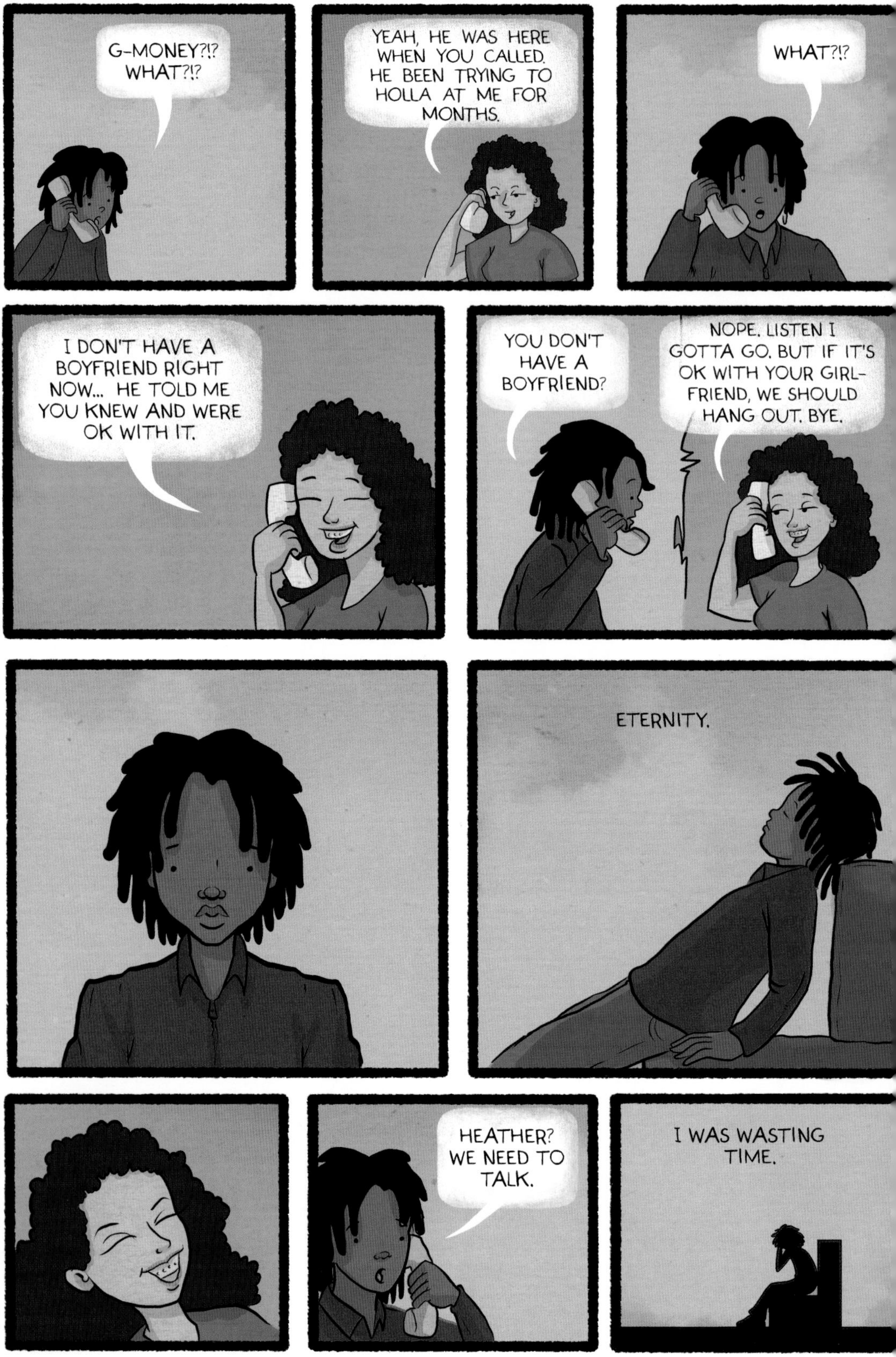
G-MONEY?!? WHAT?!?
YEAH, HE WAS HERE WHEN YOU CALLED. HE BEEN TRYING TO HOLLA AT ME FOR MONTHS.
WHAT?!?
I DON'T HAVE A BOYFRIEND RIGHT NOW... HE TOLD ME YOU KNEW AND WERE OK WITH IT.
YOU DON'T HAVE A BOYFRIEND?
NOPE. LISTEN I GOTTA GO. BUT IF IT'S OK WITH YOUR GIRL-FRIEND, WE SHOULD HANG OUT. BYE.
ETERNITY.
HEATHER? WE NEED TO TALK.
I WAS WASTING TIME.

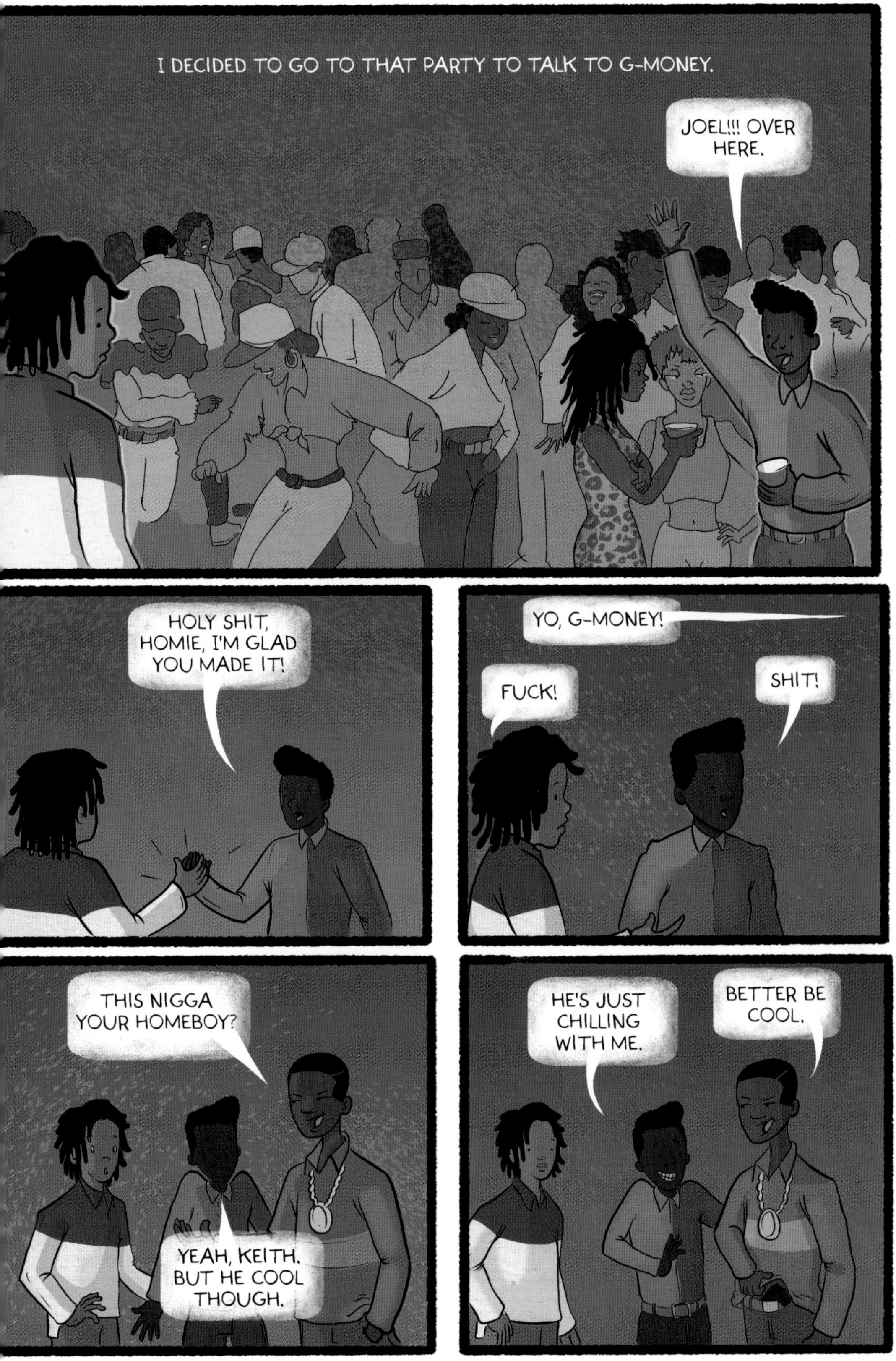
I DECIDED TO GO TO THAT PARTY TO TALK TO G-MONEY.
JOEL!!! OVER HERE.
HOLY SHIT, HOMIE, I'M GLAD YOU MADE IT!
YO, G-MONEY!
FUCK!
SHIT!
THIS NIGGA YOUR HOMEBOY?
YEAH, KEITH. BUT HE COOL THOUGH.
HE'S JUST CHILLING WITH ME.
BETTER BE COOL.

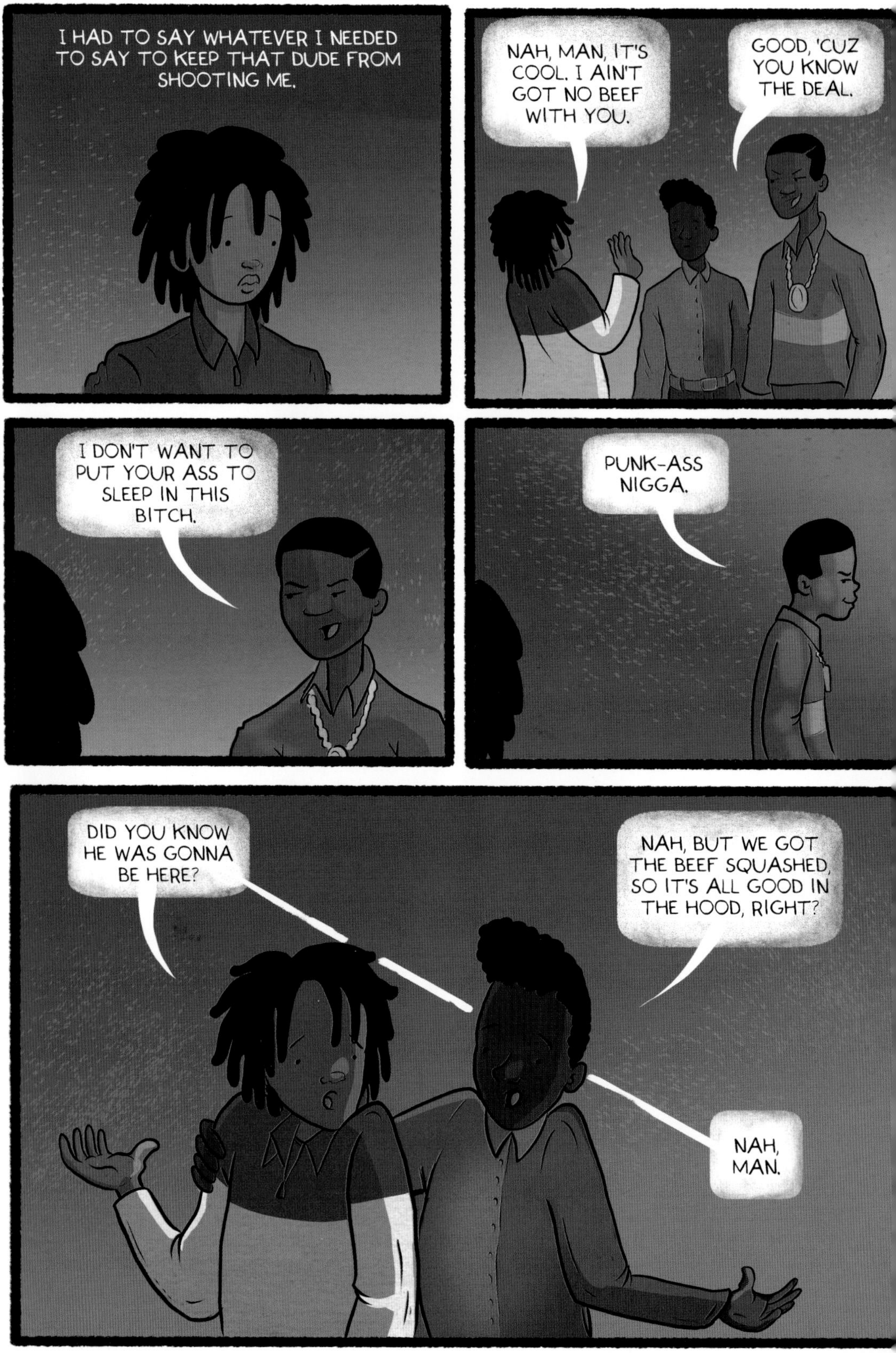
I HAD TO SAY WHATEVER I NEEDED TO SAY TO KEEP THAT DUDE FROM SHOOTING ME.
NAH, MAN, IT'S COOL. I AIN'T GOT NO BEEF WITH YOU.
GOOD, 'CUZ YOU KNOW THE DEAL.
I DON'T WANT TO PUT YOUR ASS TO SLEEP IN THIS BITCH.
PUNK-ASS NIGGA.
DID YOU KNOW HE WAS GONNA BE HERE?
NAH, BUT WE GOT THE BEEF SQUASHED, SO IT'S ALL GOOD IN THE HOOD, RIGHT?
NAH, MAN.

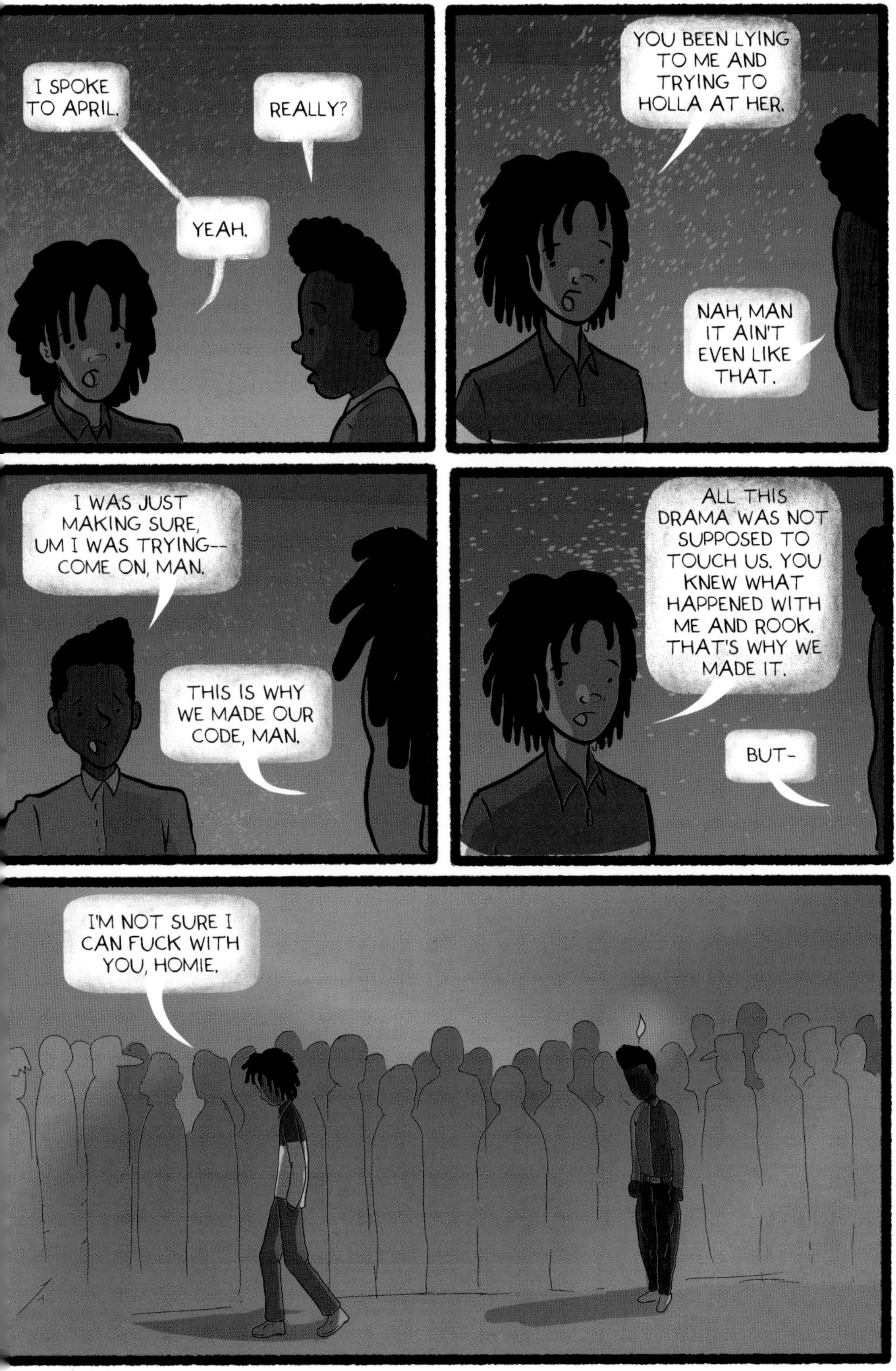
I SPOKE TO APRIL.
REALLY?
YEAH.
YOU BEEN LYING TO ME AND TRYING TO HOLLA AT HER.
NAH, MAN IT AIN'T EVEN LIKE THAT.
I WAS JUST MAKING SURE, UM I WAS TRYING-- COME ON, MAN.
THIS IS WHY WE MADE OUR CODE, MAN.
ALL THIS DRAMA WAS NOT SUPPOSED TO TOUCH US. YOU KNEW WHAT HAPPENED WITH ME AND ROOK. THAT'S WHY WE MADE IT.
BUT-
I'M NOT SURE I CAN FUCK WITH YOU, HOMIE.

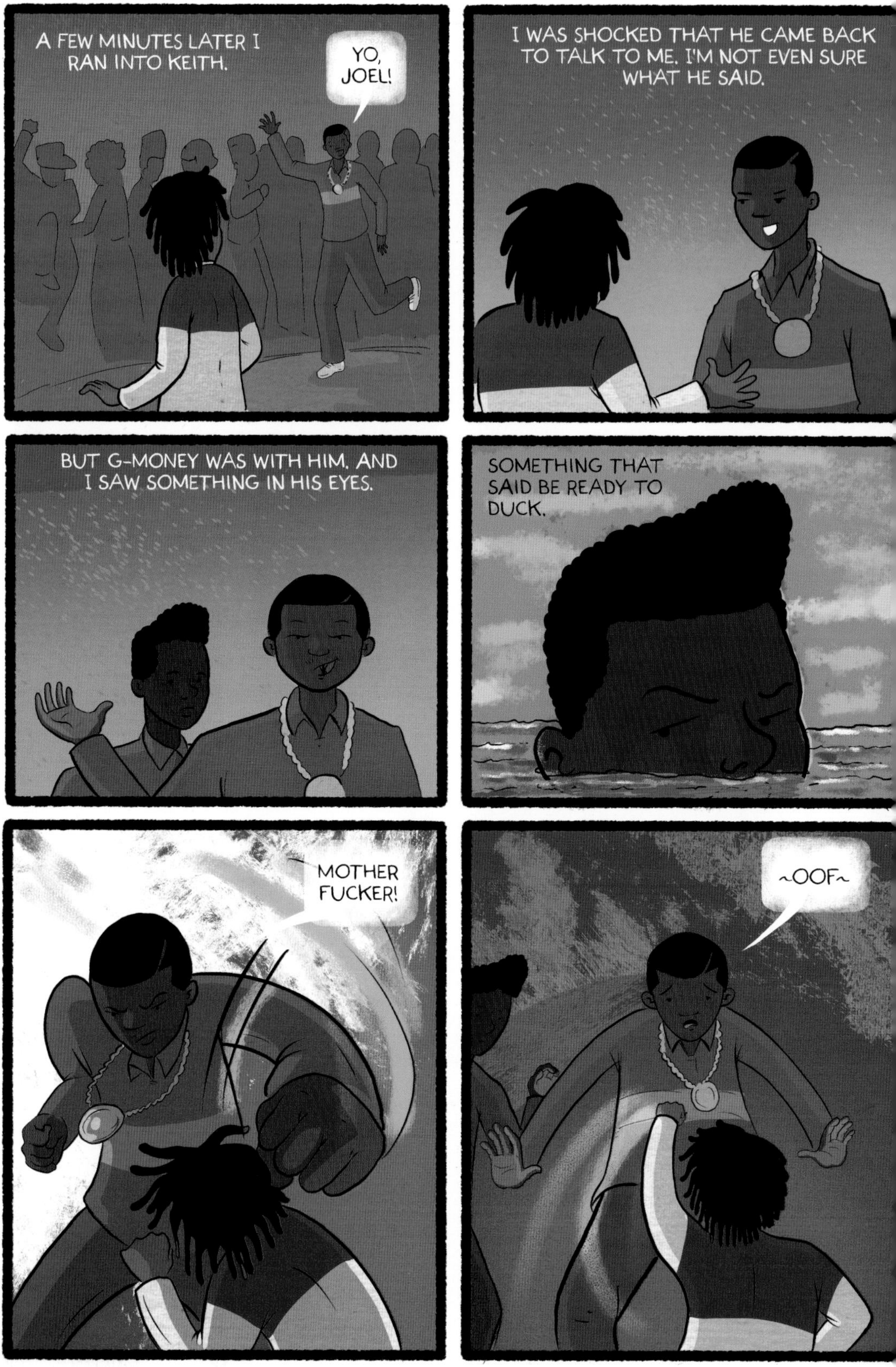

A FEW MINUTES LATER I RAN INTO KEITH.
YO, JOEL!
I WAS SHOCKED THAT HE CAME BACK TO TALK TO ME. I'M NOT EVEN SURE WHAT HE SAID.
BUT G-MONEY WAS WITH HIM. AND I SAW SOMETHING IN HIS EYES.
SOMETHING THAT SAID BE READY TO DUCK.
MOTHER FUCKER!
~OOF~

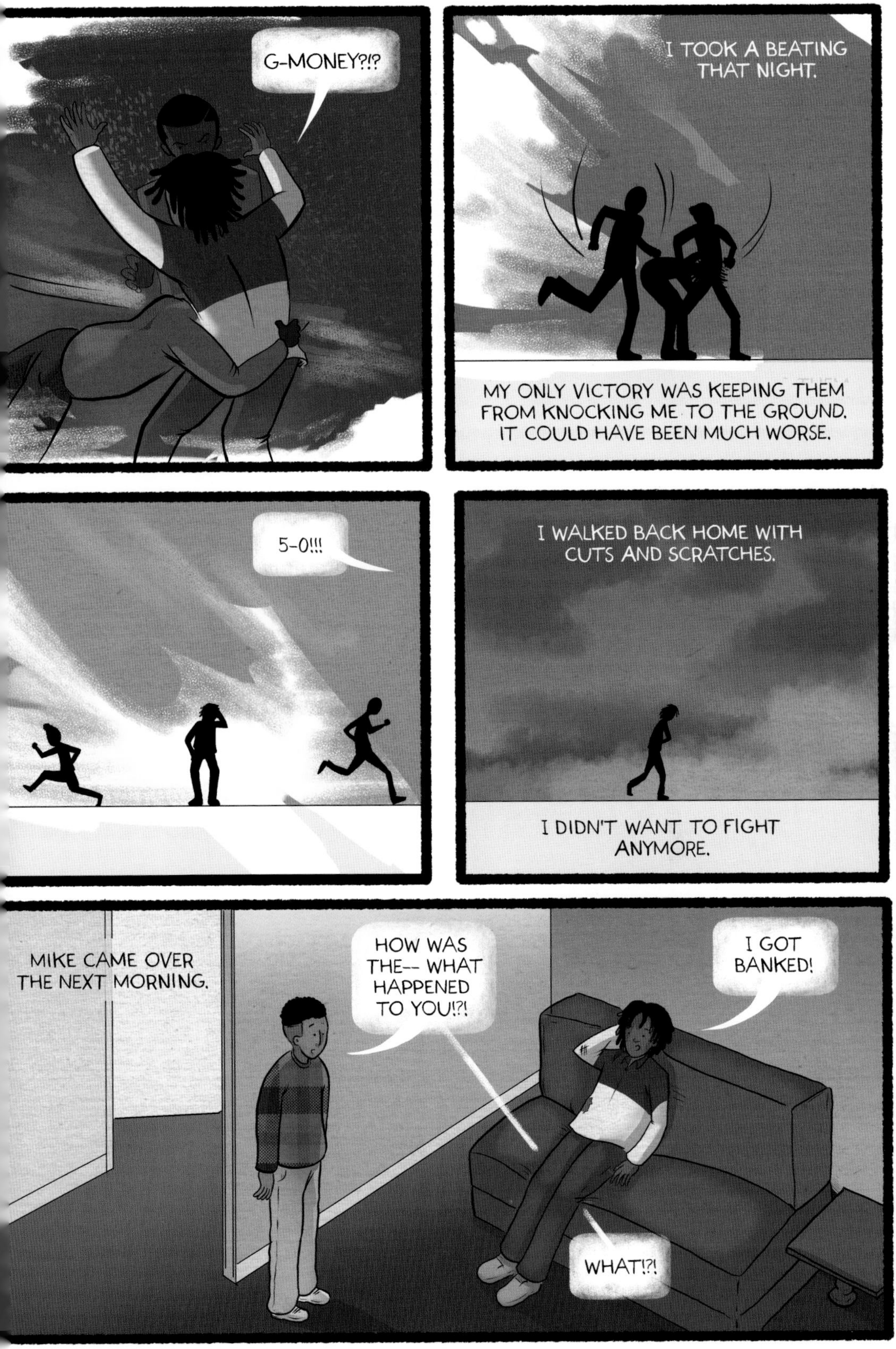
G-MONEY?!?
I TOOK A BEATING THAT NIGHT.
MY ONLY VICTORY WAS KEEPING THEM FROM KNOCKING ME TO THE GROUND. IT COULD HAVE BEEN MUCH WORSE.
5-0!!!
I WALKED BACK HOME WITH CUTS AND SCRATCHES.
I DIDN'T WANT TO FIGHT ANYMORE.
MIKE CAME OVER THE NEXT MORNING.
HOW WAS THE-- WHAT HAPPENED TO YOU!?!
I GOT BANKED!
WHAT!?!

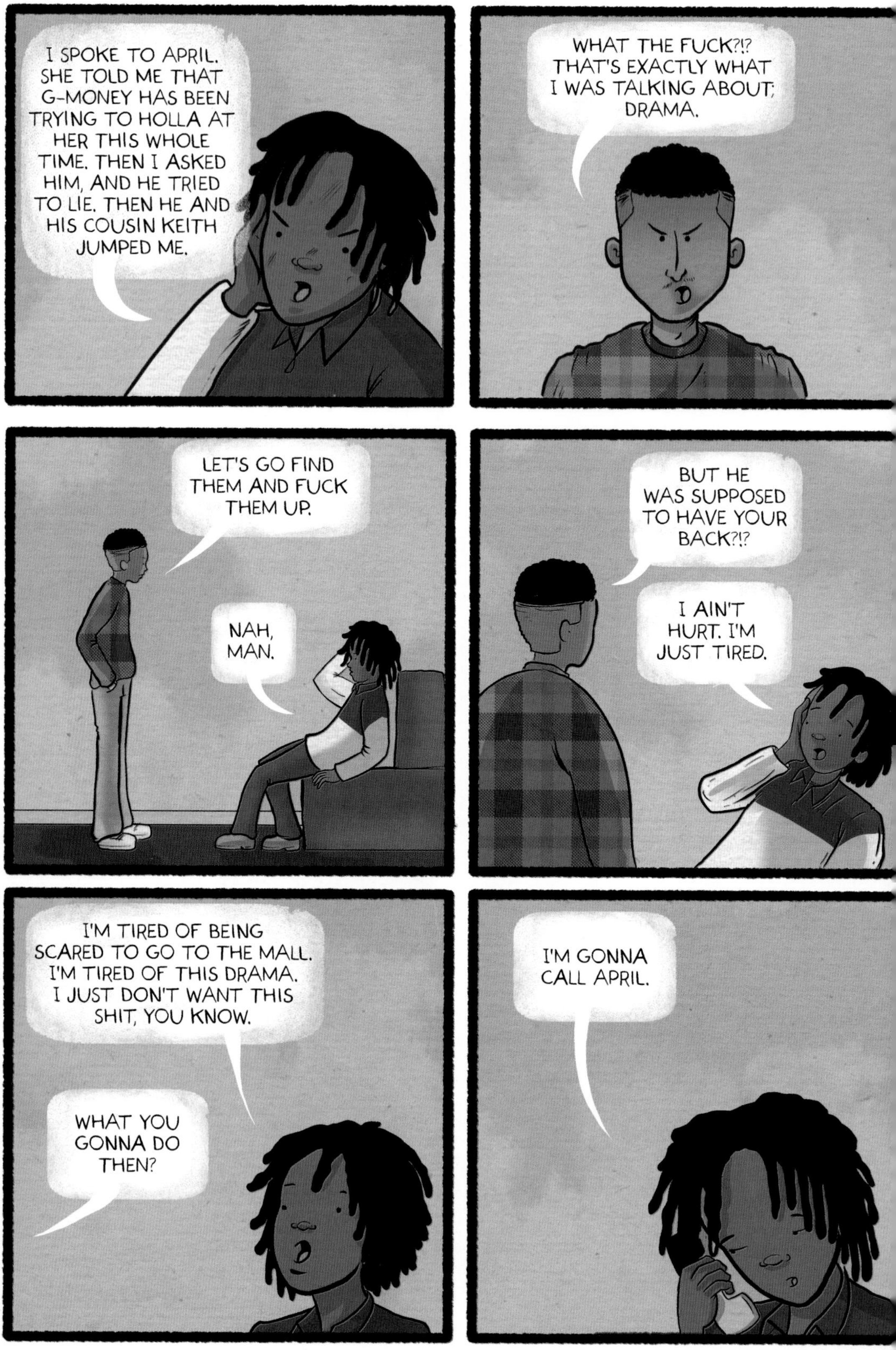
I SPOKE TO APRIL. SHE TOLD ME THAT G-MONEY HAS BEEN TRYING TO HOLLA AT HER THIS WHOLE TIME. THEN I ASKED HIM, AND HE TRIED TO LIE. THEN HE AND HIS COUSIN KEITH JUMPED ME.
WHAT THE FUCK?!? THAT'S EXACTLY WHAT I WAS TALKING ABOUT; DRAMA.
LET'S GO FIND THEM AND FUCK THEM UP.
NAH, MAN.
BUT HE WAS SUPPOSED TO HAVE YOUR BACK?!?
I AIN'T HURT. I'M JUST TIRED.
I'M TIRED OF BEING SCARED TO GO TO THE MALL. I'M TIRED OF THIS DRAMA. I JUST DON'T WANT THIS SHIT, YOU KNOW.
WHAT YOU GONNA DO THEN?
I'M GONNA CALL APRIL.

TIME SLOWED DOWN AGAIN.

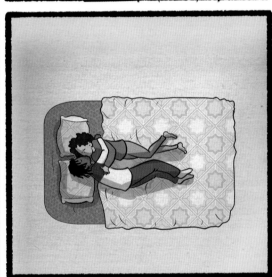

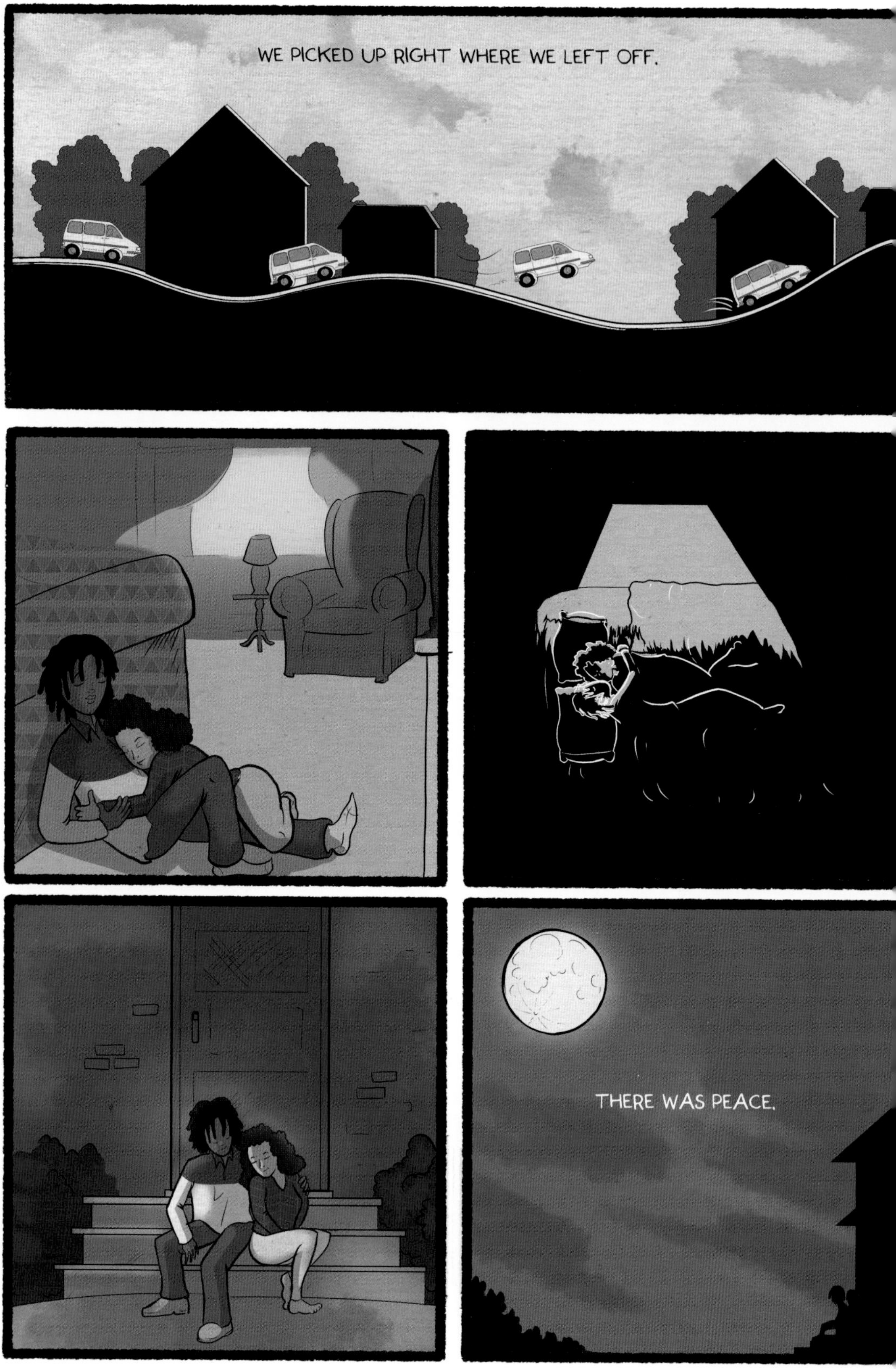
WE PICKED UP RIGHT WHERE WE LEFT OFF.
THERE WAS PEACE.

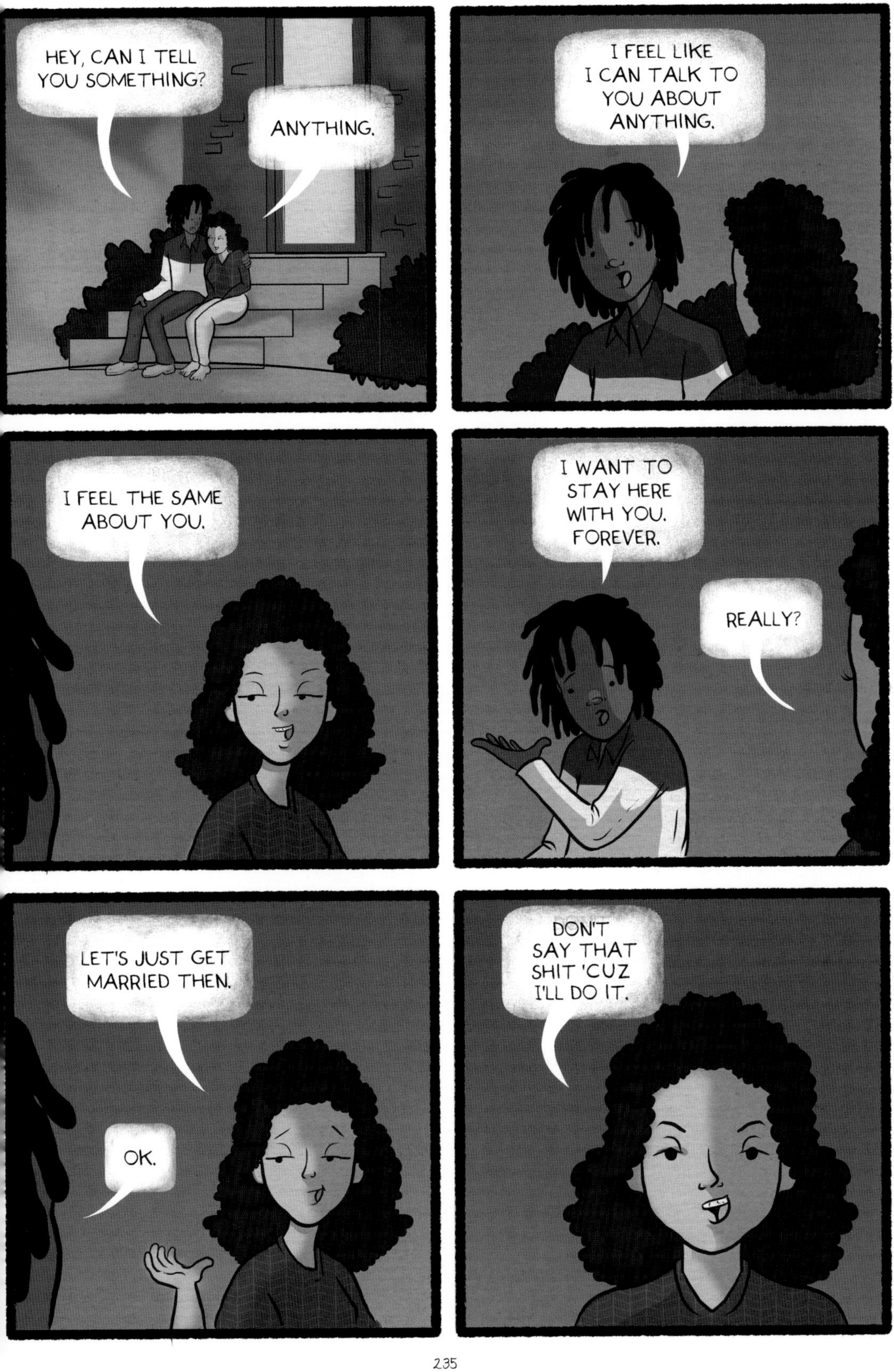
HEY, CAN I TELL YOU SOMETHING?
ANYTHING.
I FEEL LIKE I CAN TALK TO YOU ABOUT ANYTHING.
I FEEL THE SAME ABOUT YOU.
I WANT TO STAY HERE WITH YOU. FOREVER.
REALLY?
LET'S JUST GET MARRIED THEN.
OK.
DON'T SAY THAT SHIT 'CUZ I'LL DO IT.

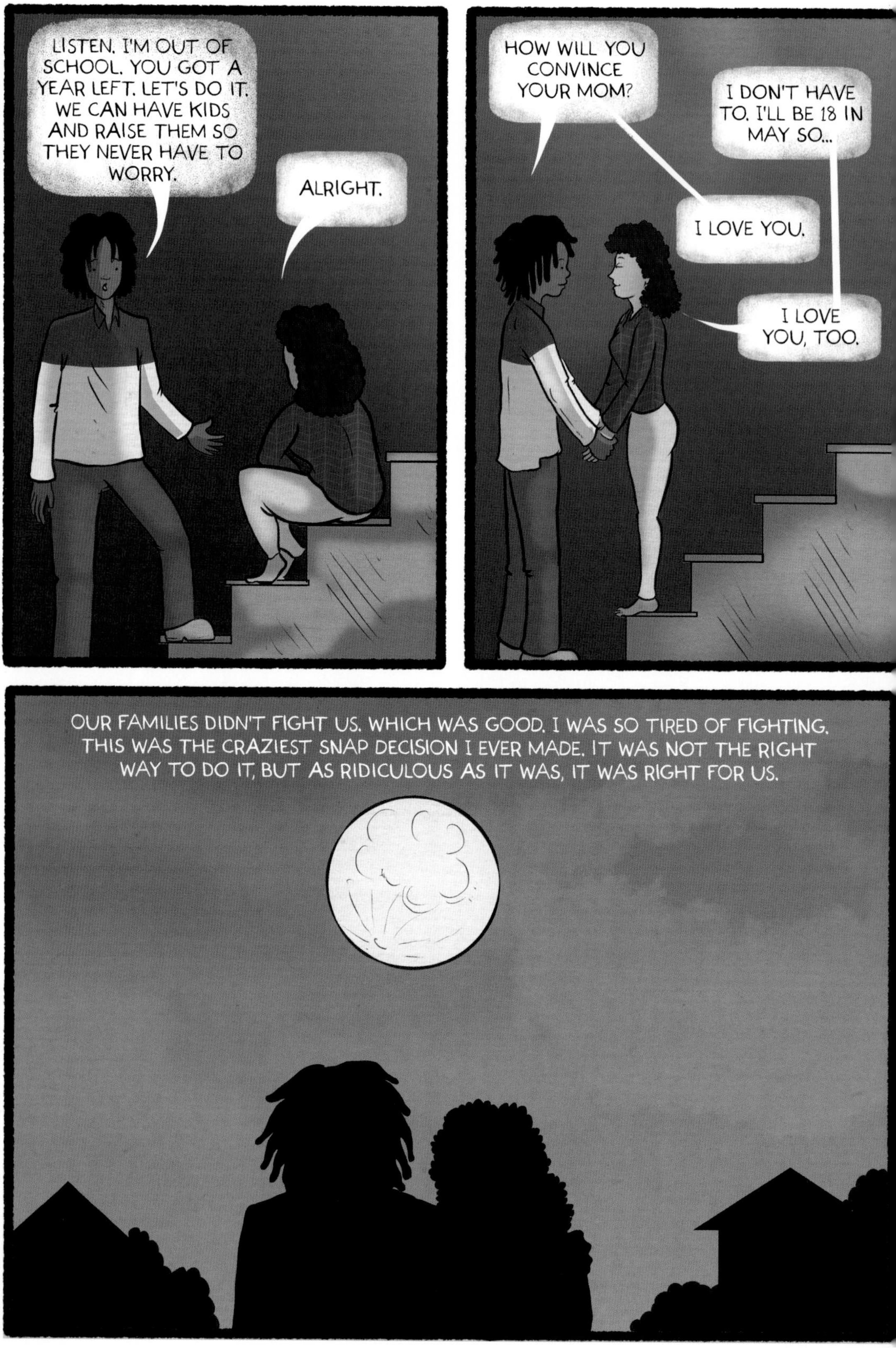

LISTEN. I'M OUT OF SCHOOL. YOU GOT A YEAR LEFT. LET'S DO IT. WE CAN HAVE KIDS AND RAISE THEM SO THEY NEVER HAVE TO WORRY.
ALRIGHT.
HOW WILL YOU CONVINCE YOUR MOM?
I DON'T HAVE TO. I'LL BE 18 IN MAY SO...
I LOVE YOU.
I LOVE YOU, TOO.
OUR FAMILIES DIDN'T FIGHT US. WHICH WAS GOOD. I WAS SO TIRED OF FIGHTING. THIS WAS THE CRAZIEST SNAP DECISION I EVER MADE. IT WAS NOT THE RIGHT WAY TO DO IT, BUT AS RIDICULOUS AS IT WAS, IT WAS RIGHT FOR US.

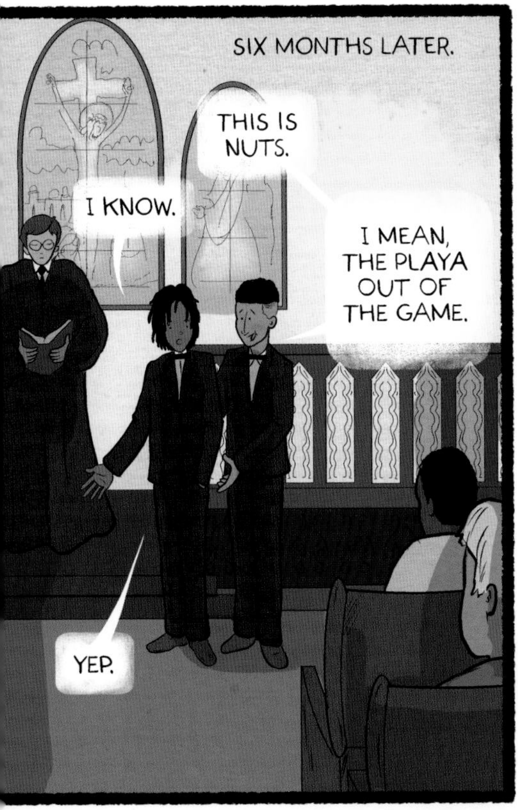
SIX MONTHS LATER.
THIS IS NUTS.
I KNOW.
I MEAN, THE PLAYA OUT OF THE GAME.
YEP.
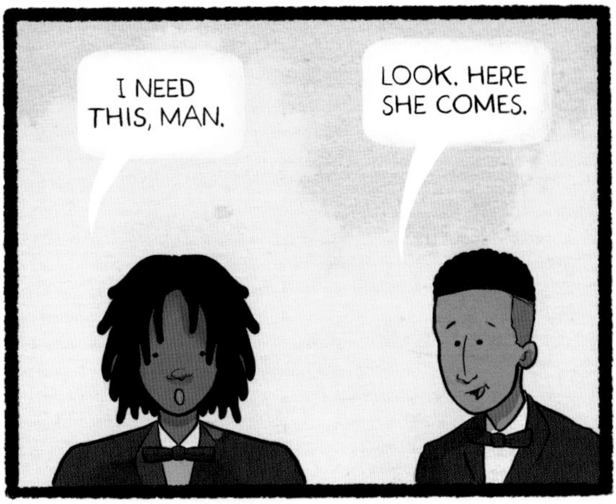
I NEED THIS, MAN.
LOOK. HERE SHE COMES.
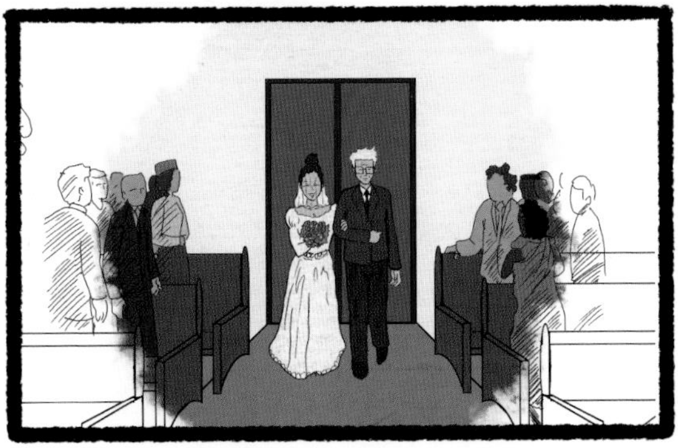
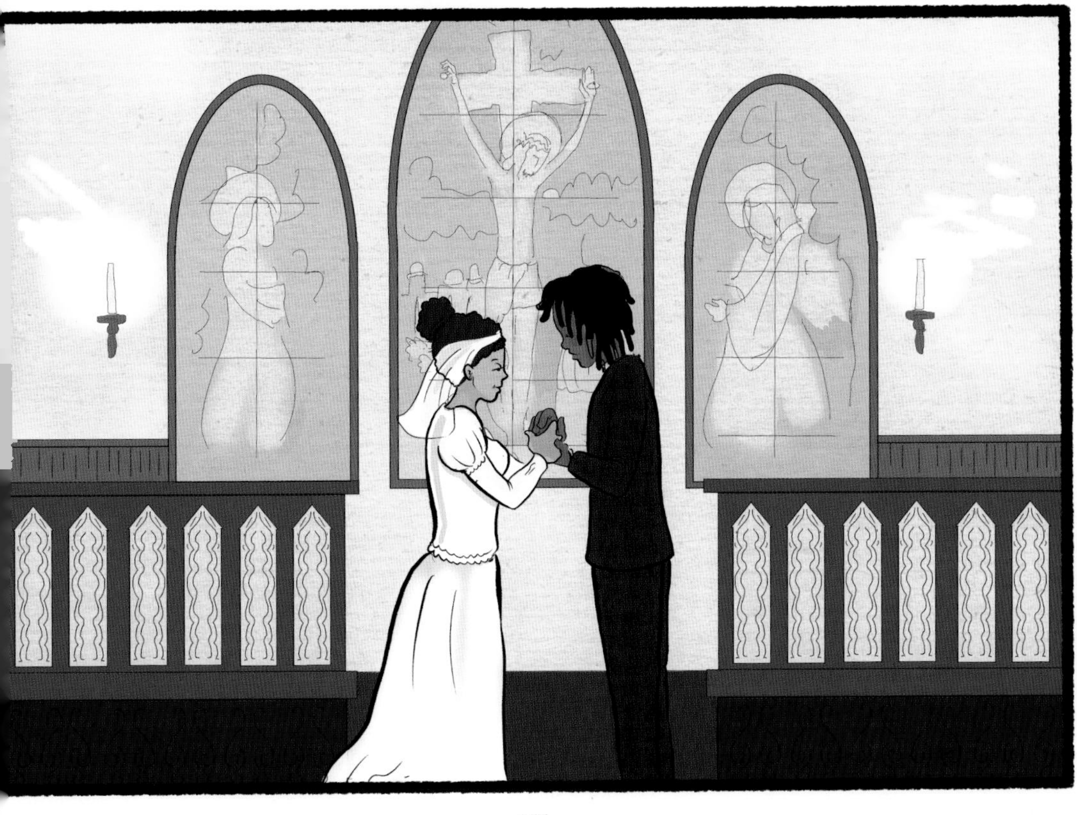

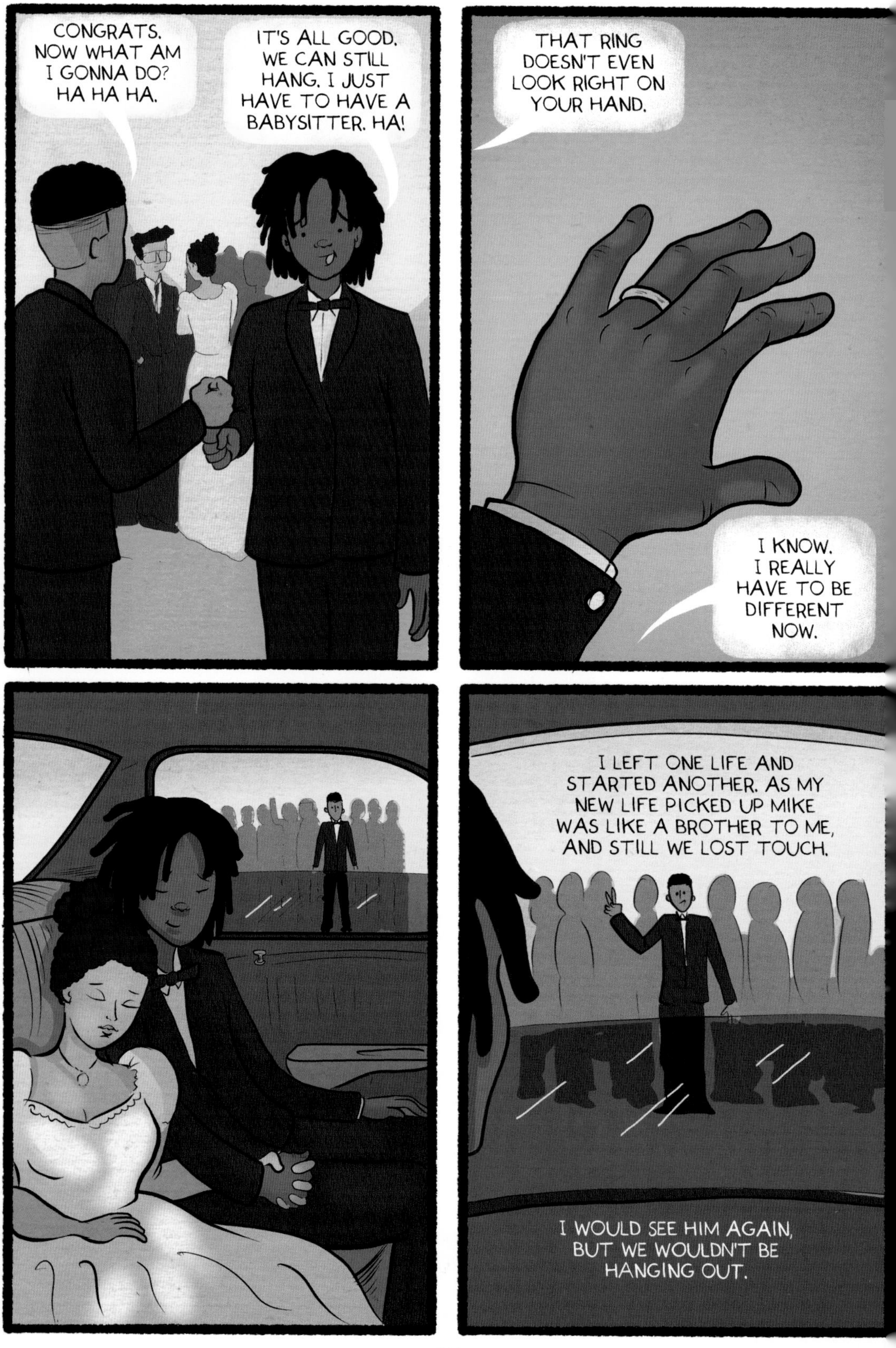
CONGRATS. NOW WHAT AM I GONNA DO? HA HA HA.
IT'S ALL GOOD. WE CAN STILL HANG. I JUST HAVE TO HAVE A BABYSITTER. HA!
THAT RING DOESN'T EVEN LOOK RIGHT ON YOUR HAND.
I KNOW. I REALLY HAVE TO BE DIFFERENT NOW.
I LEFT ONE LIFE AND STARTED ANOTHER. AS MY NEW LIFE PICKED UP MIKE WAS LIKE A BROTHER TO ME, AND STILL WE LOST TOUCH.
I WOULD SEE HIM AGAIN, BUT WE WOULDN'T BE HANGING OUT.

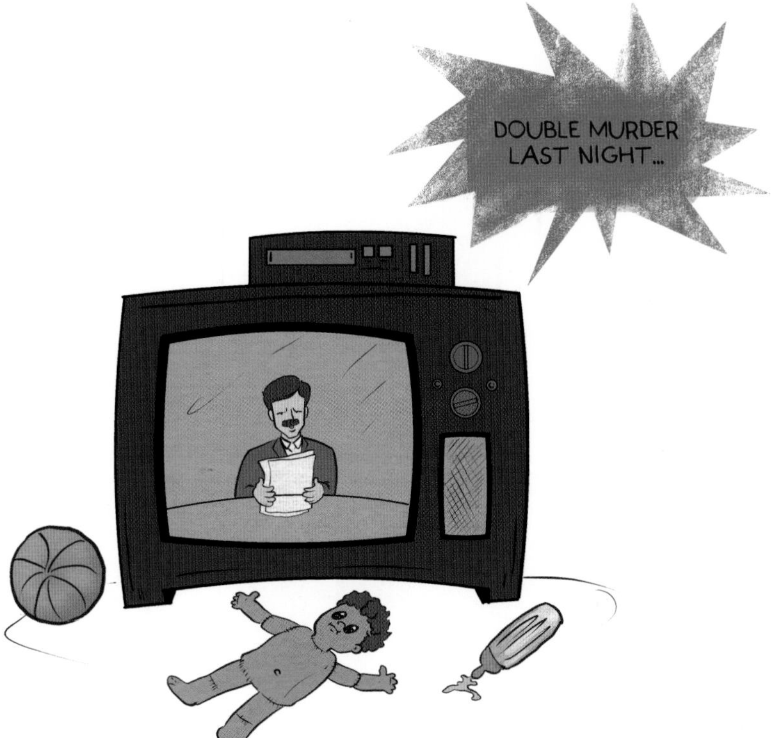
DOUBLE MURDER
LAST NIGHT...

TWO YEARS LATER...

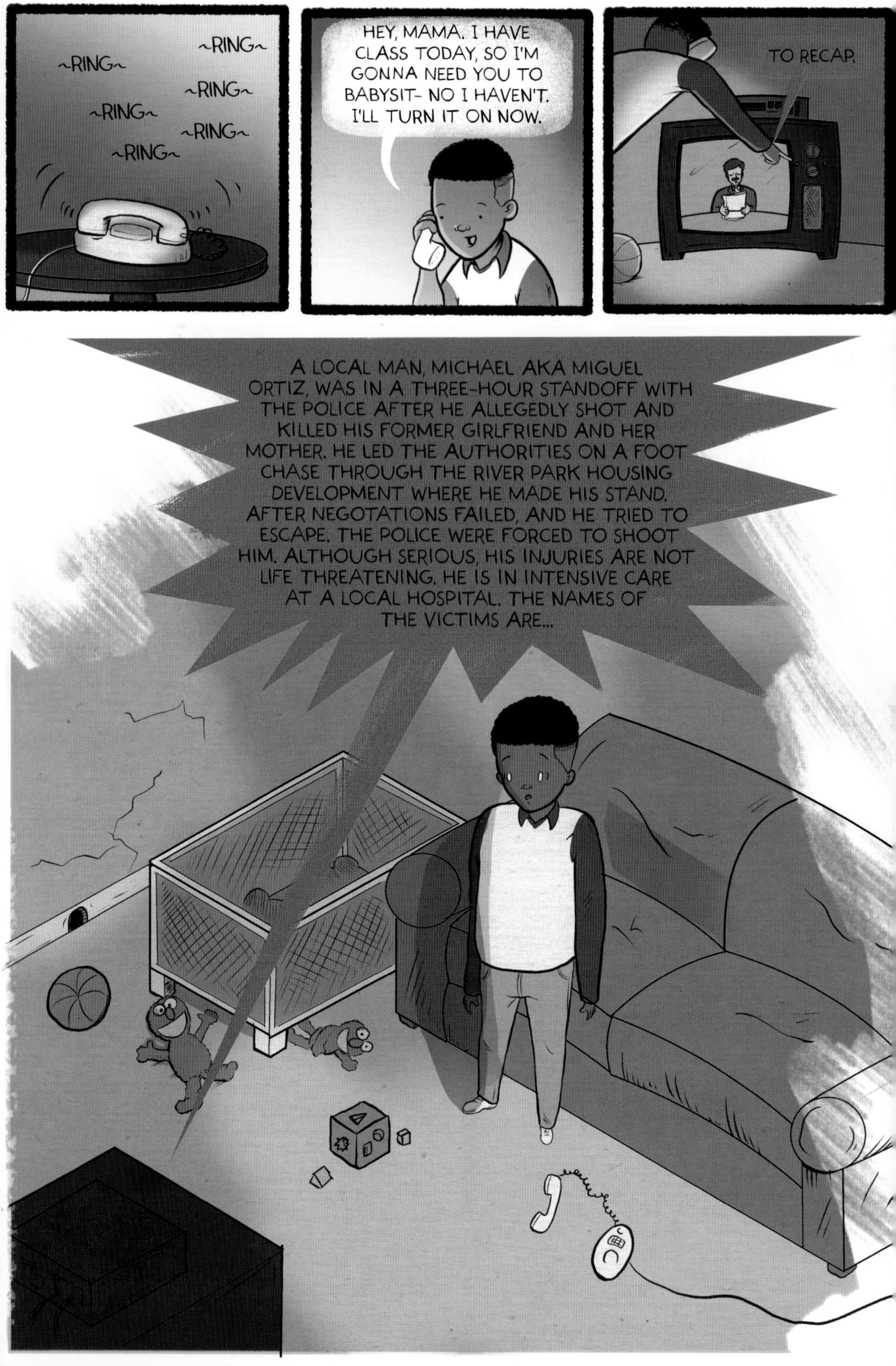
~RING~
~RING~
~RING~
~RING~
~RING~
~RING~
HEY, MAMA. I HAVE CLASS TODAY, SO I'M GONNA NEED YOU TO BABYSIT- NO I HAVEN'T. I'LL TURN IT ON NOW.
TO RECAP.
A LOCAL MAN, MICHAEL AKA MIGUEL ORTIZ, WAS IN A THREE-HOUR STANDOFF WITH THE POLICE AFTER HE ALLEGEDLY SHOT AND KILLED HIS FORMER GIRLFRIEND AND HER MOTHER. HE LED THE AUTHORITIES ON A FOOT CHASE THROUGH THE RIVER PARK HOUSING DEVELOPMENT WHERE HE MADE HIS STAND. AFTER NEGOTATIONS FAILED, AND HE TRIED TO ESCAPE. THE POLICE WERE FORCED TO SHOOT HIM. ALTHOUGH SERIOUS, HIS INJURIES ARE NOT LIFE THREATENING. HE IS IN INTENSIVE CARE AT A LOCAL HOSPITAL. THE NAMES OF THE VICTIMS ARE...

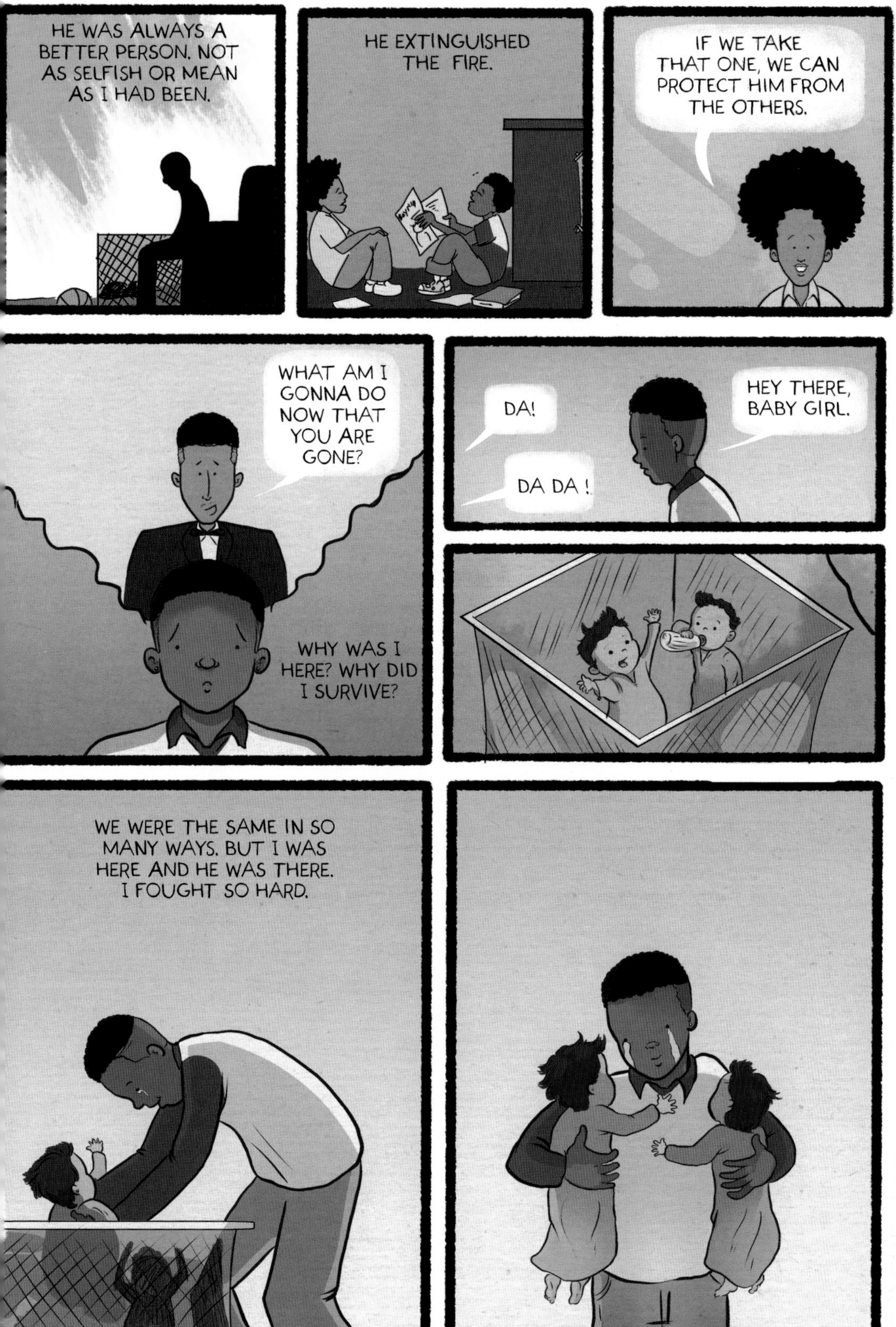
HE WAS ALWAYS A BETTER PERSON. NOT AS SELFISH OR MEAN AS I HAD BEEN.
HE EXTINGUISHED THE FIRE.
IF WE TAKE THAT ONE, WE CAN PROTECT HIM FROM THE OTHERS.
WHAT AM I GONNA DO NOW THAT YOU ARE GONE?
WHY WAS I HERE? WHY DID I SURVIVE?
DA!
HEY THERE, BABY GIRL.
DA DA!
WE WERE THE SAME IN SO MANY WAYS. BUT I WAS HERE AND HE WAS THERE. I FOUGHT SO HARD.

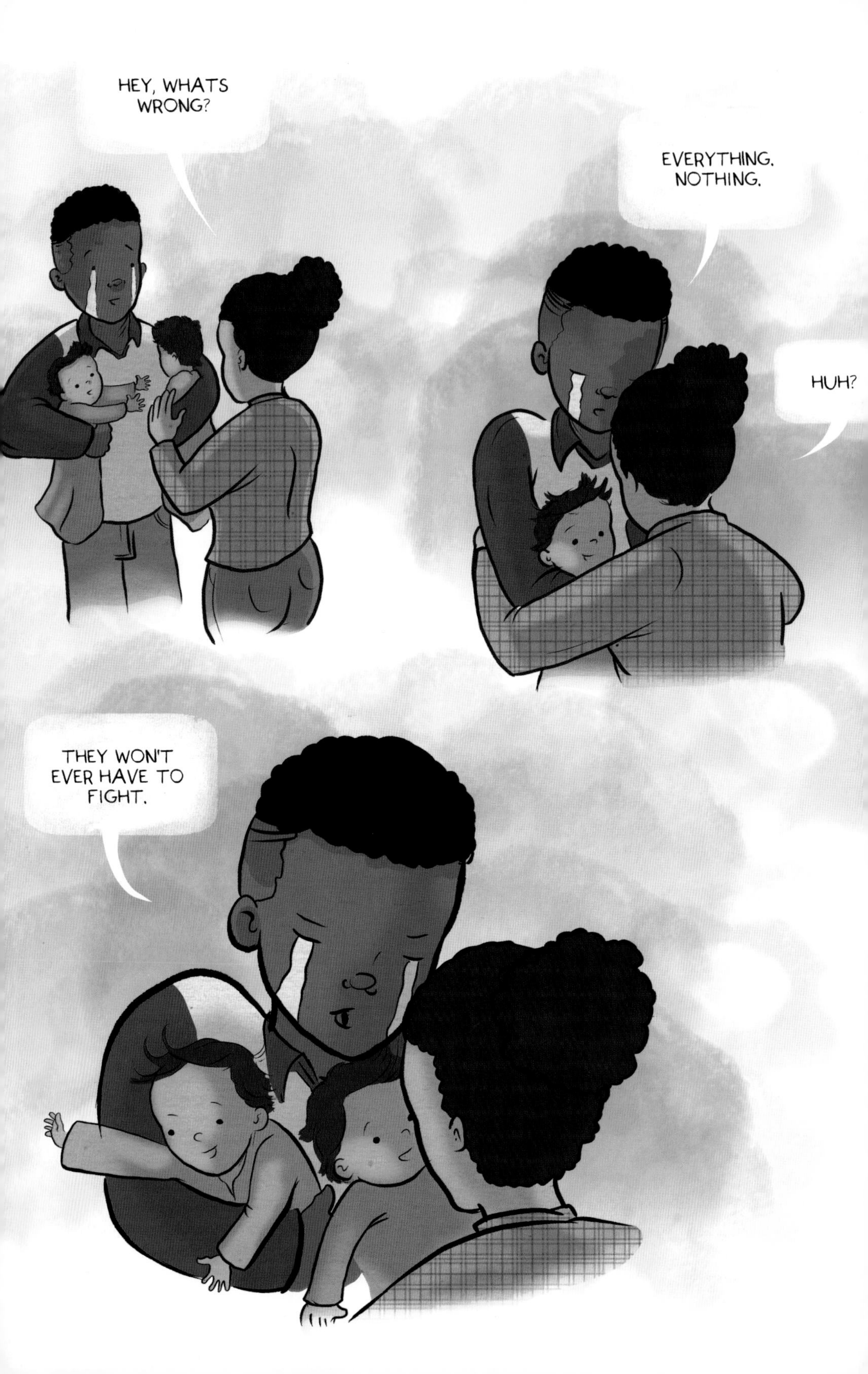
HEY, WHATS WRONG?
EVERYTHING. NOTHING.
HUH?
THEY WON'T EVER HAVE TO FIGHT.

EPILOGUE

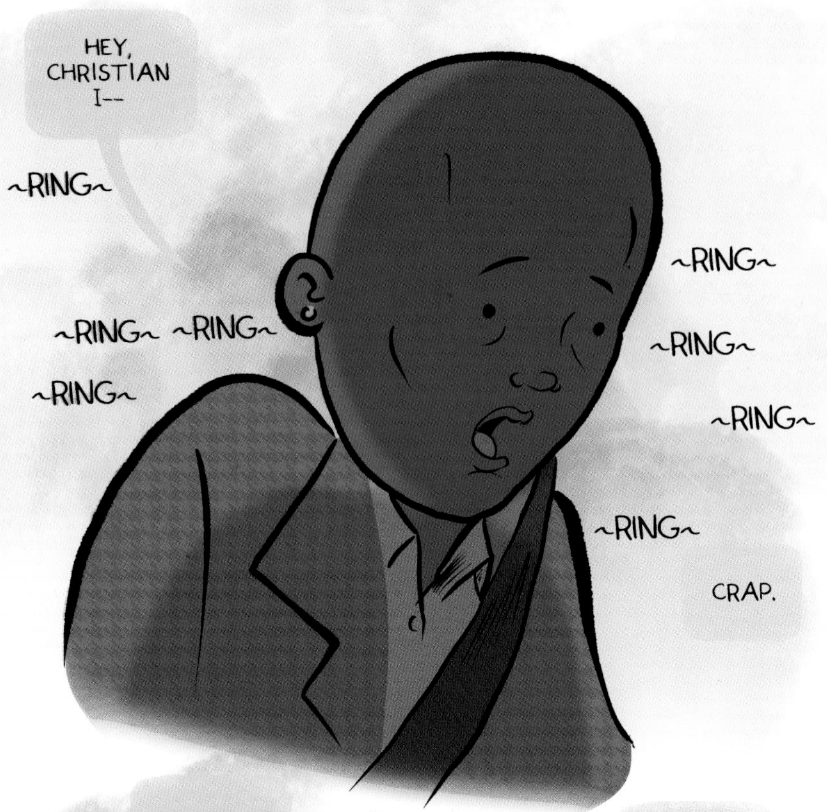
HEY, CHRISTIAN I--
~RING~
~RING~
~RING~ ~RING~
~RING~
~RING~
~RING~
~RING~
CRAP.
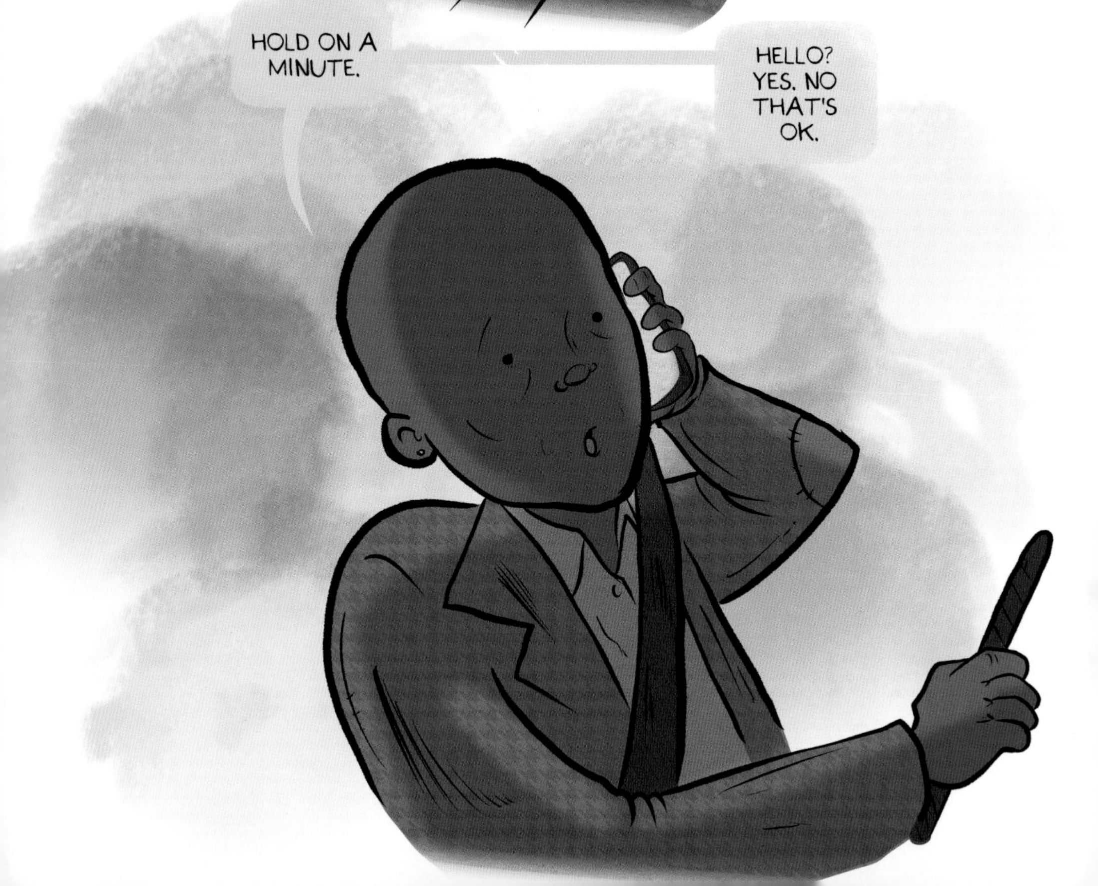
HOLD ON A MINUTE.
HELLO? YES. NO THAT'S OK.

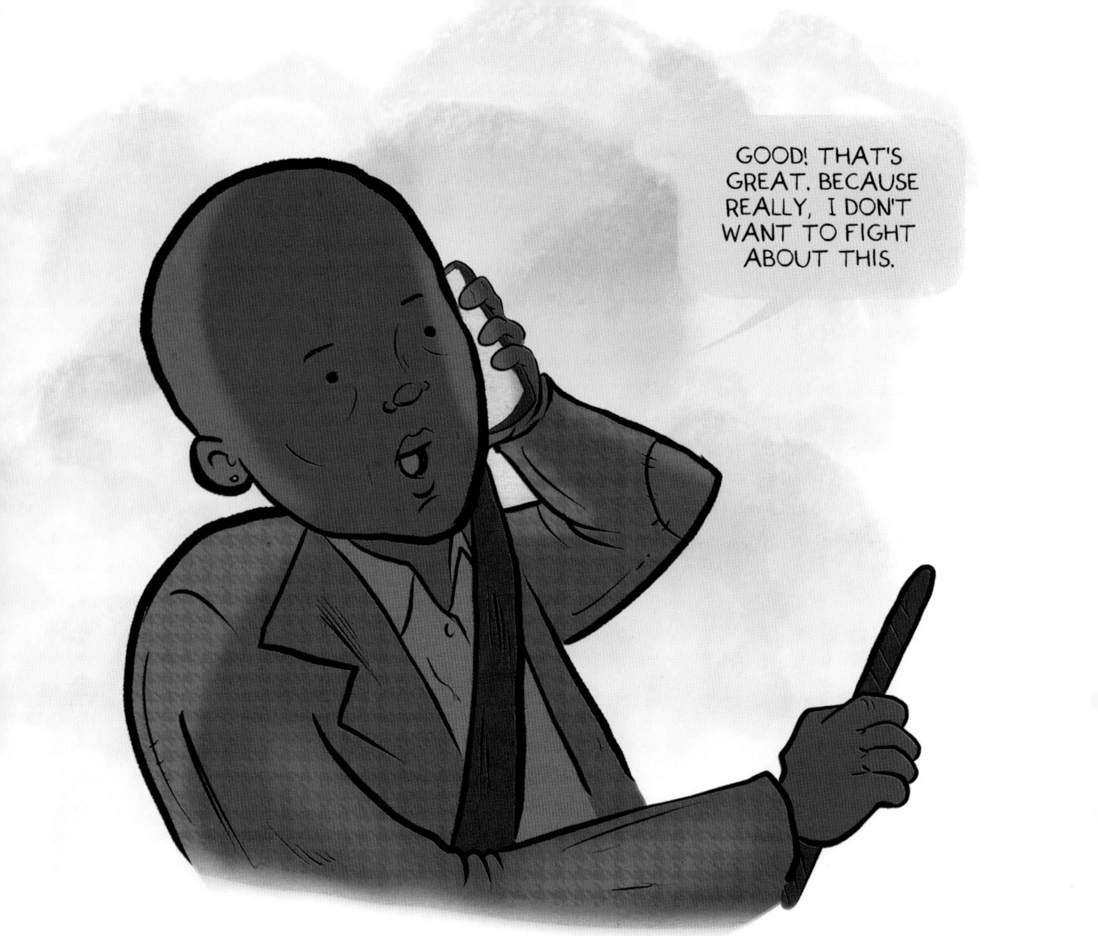
GOOD! THAT'S GREAT. BECAUSE REALLY, I DON'T WANT TO FIGHT ABOUT THIS.
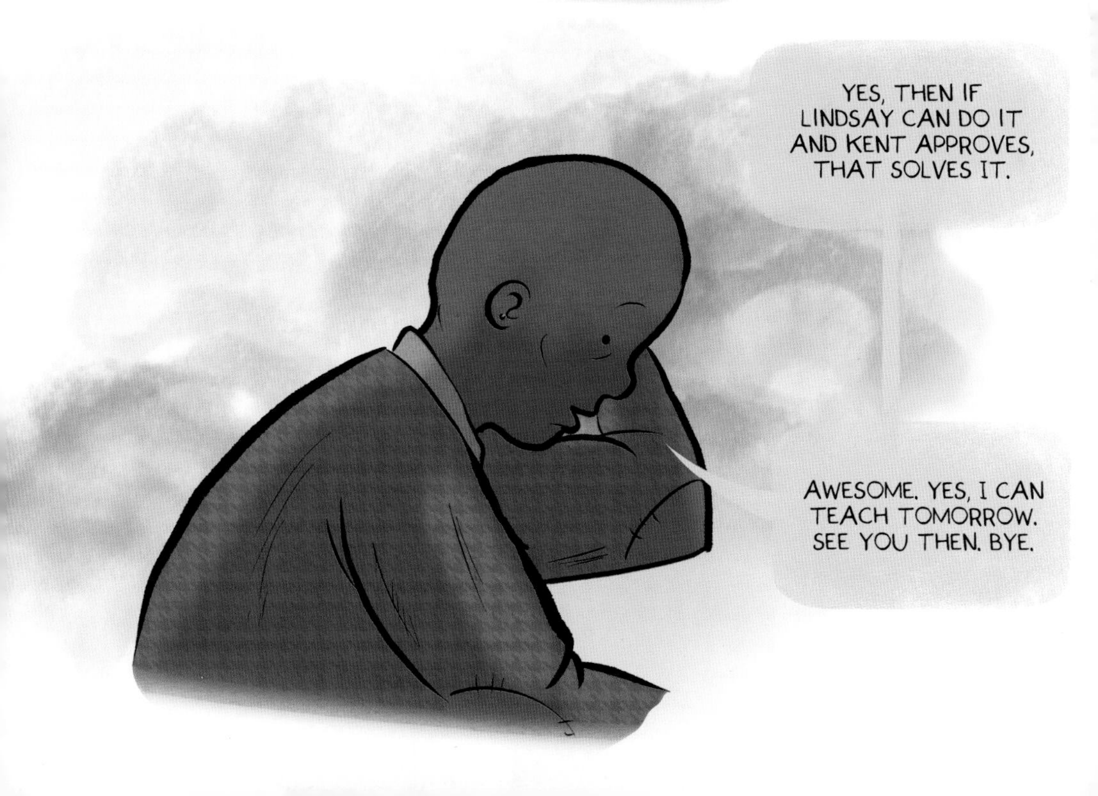
YES, THEN IF LINDSAY CAN DO IT AND KENT APPROVES, THAT SOLVES IT.
AWESOME. YES, I CAN TEACH TOMORROW. SEE YOU THEN. BYE.

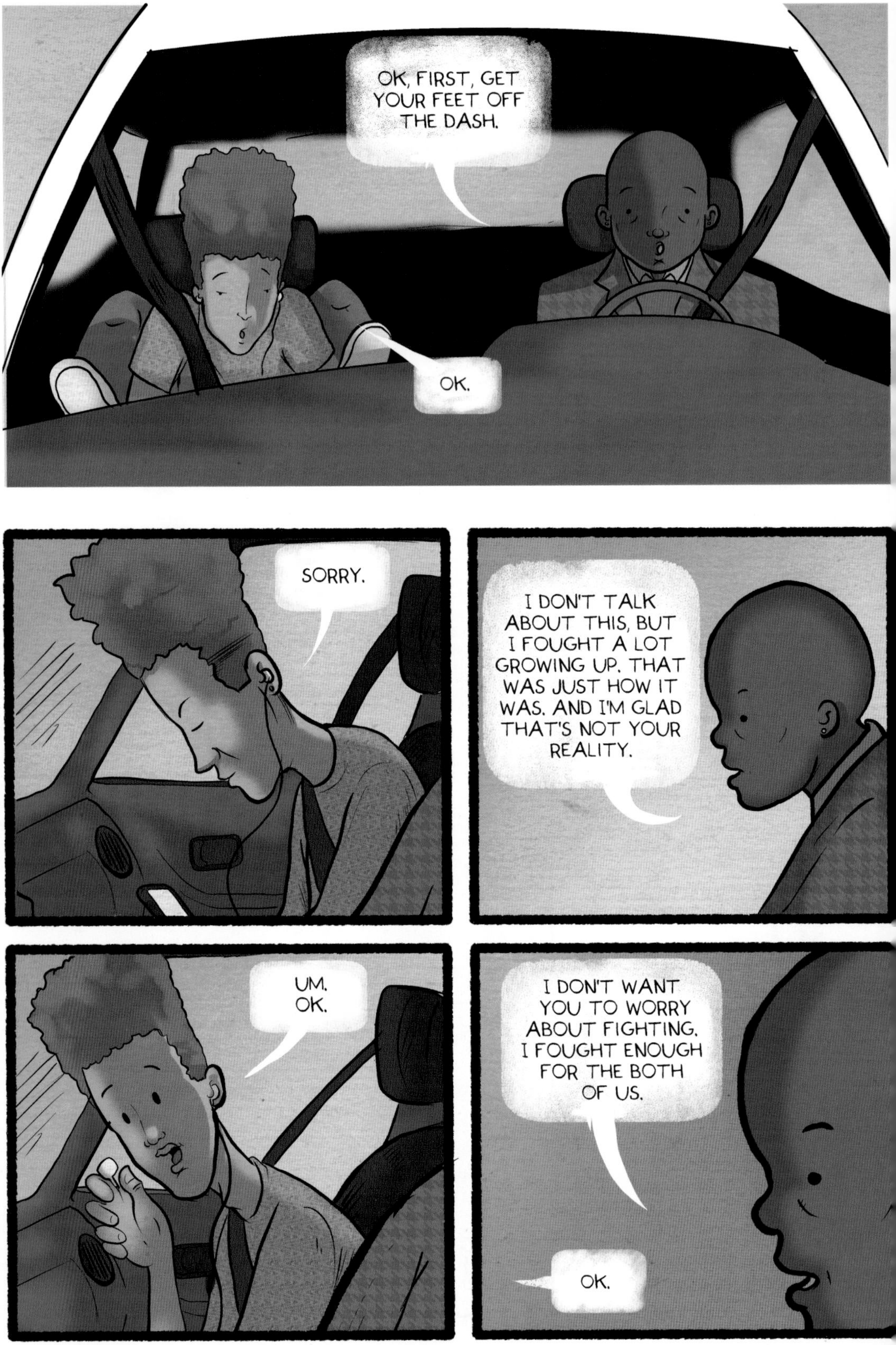

OK, FIRST, GET YOUR FEET OFF THE DASH.
OK.
SORRY.
I DON'T TALK ABOUT THIS, BUT I FOUGHT A LOT GROWING UP. THAT WAS JUST HOW IT WAS. AND I'M GLAD THAT'S NOT YOUR REALITY.
UM. OK.
I DON'T WANT YOU TO WORRY ABOUT FIGHTING. I FOUGHT ENOUGH FOR THE BOTH OF US.
OK.

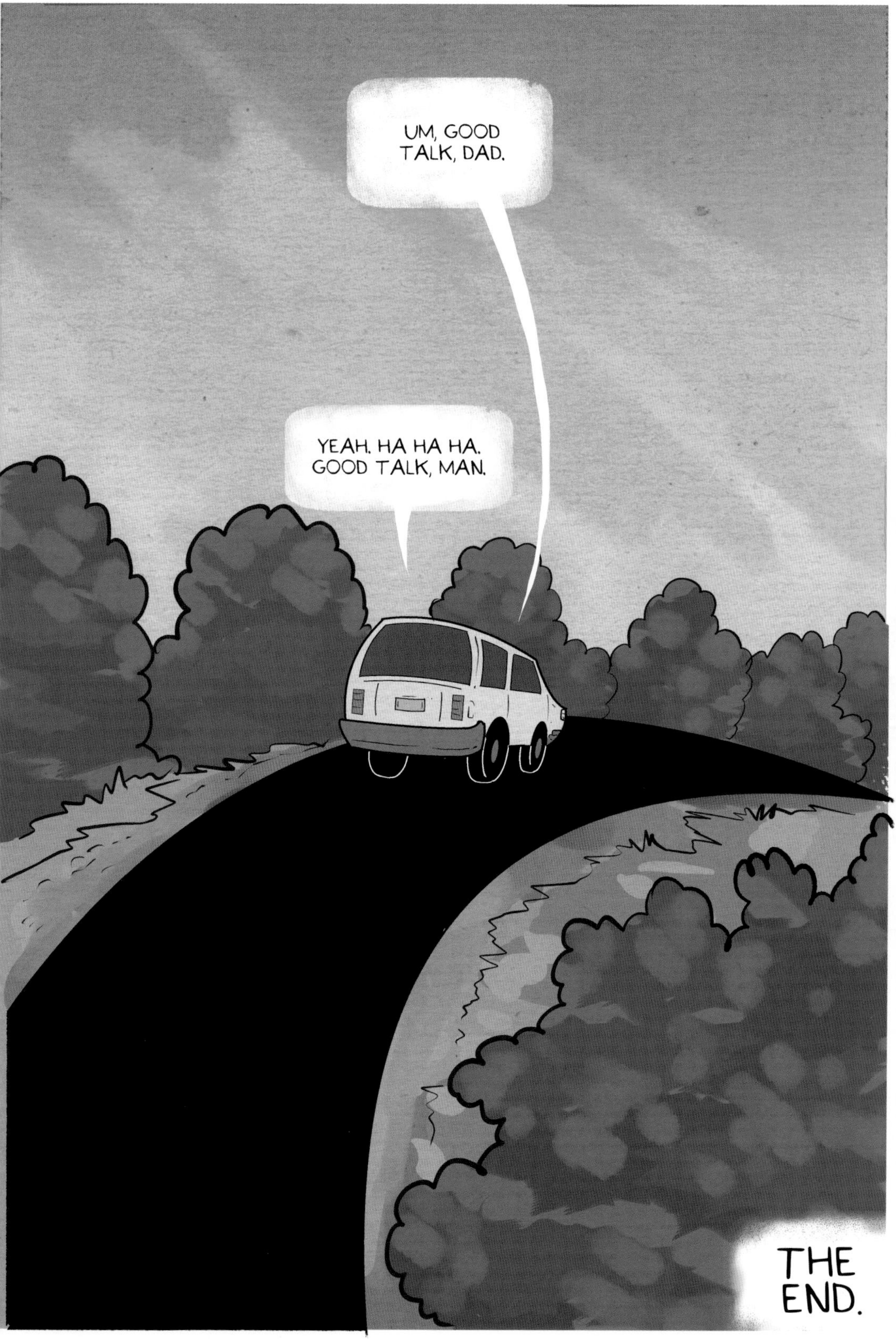
UM, GOOD TALK, DAD.
YEAH. HA HA HA. GOOD TALK, MAN.
THE END.

Memoirs are not biography—

—they're more like a recollection of past events. Recollections are different than reports. The stories in this book represent very real events in my life, however I have combined some events and people for the purposes of the narrative. These things happened, but not all of them happened exactly as they're shown in this book.

In many cases, I have combined people or aspects of people into characters that represent the actual individuals who played a part in my young life. For instance, my uncle and aunt in this book are not real and neither is Rook; they are amalgams of real people and real experiences. I have two brothers and two sisters whom I have chosen to leave out. This is mostly because they lived with their father for the majority of my early life, and they do not figure in the events that move the story along.

Elements of this book may be shocking to some people close to me because I have kept a lot of these details to myself, only sharing them with my wife and various therapists over the years. However, I did not write and draw this book as a cathartic exercise for myself. This book is for all those who feel trapped in similar circumstances.

It's bad enough to have to deal with trauma, violence, and bullies as a child, but when there are teachers and adults in your life who fill that same space, it can become unbearable and lead to all kinds of acting out and other problems.

If you are a young person and you read this story, it is my hope that you will see that even as bad as things became for me, it was possible for me to think for myself and choose to behave differently than I'd been taught to. If you are older and read this book, I hope that when you see children acting out in ways that I acted out, this will help you understand that they might be in situations similar—or even worse—than what I experienced. This insight, I hope, will encourage you to try and learn their story.

It is that story that will give you insight and empathy. It's that story that will help you understand that kid. Our stories make us human. Understanding our stories makes us better. Understand someone's story. It will make things better.

Take care,
Joel Christian Gill

There are a number of people to whom I owe a great deal of thanks.

James Sturm was probably the first person I showed *Fights* to. He told me that memoir was not biography—that it sat someplace between memory and recollection—and that stuck with me throughout the creation of this book. Among others who gave feedback and advice (in no particular order): John Jennings, Dan Mazur, Heide Solbrig, Steve Bissette, Monica Bilson, Erin Sweeney, BethAnne Miller, Jesse Lonergan, Cory Levine, and Whit Taylor. I would also like to thank Judy Hansen and Andrea Colvin for believing in my story. The amazing color work in this book is by Shannon Scott—she is the best. And Jade Rodriguez was fast and efficient with her first-ever job flatting the colors for Shannon.

Finally, I want to thank my wonderfully supportive wife April. No success I have would have been possible without her. Thanks to her, most of all.

c. 1975

JOEL CHRISTIAN GILL wrote the words and drew the pictures in *Fast Enough: Bessie Stringfield's First Ride* (published by Lion Forge, 2019) and the award-winning graphic novel series *Strange Fruit: Uncelebrated Narratives from Black History,* as well as, *Tales of The Talented Tenth* from Fulcrum Publishing. In Fall of 2019, he accepted an appointment as Associate Professor of Illustration at Massachusetts College of Art and Design. Gill has dedicated his life to creating stories to build connections with readers through empathy, compassion, and ultimately humanity. He received his MFA from Boston University and his BA from Roanoke College.

Me and Mama

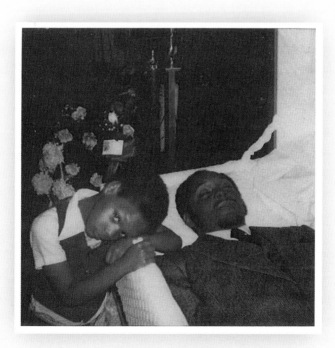

Me and Dad

—1985—

—1990—

—1994—

April

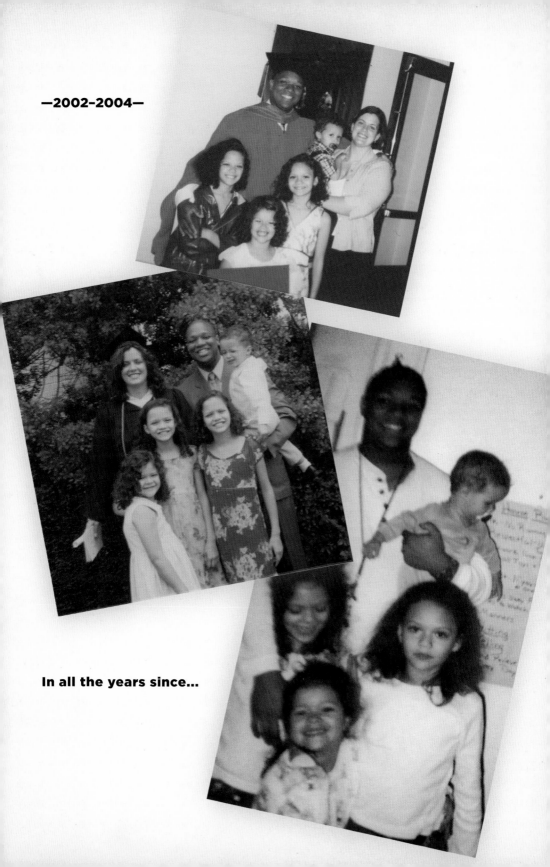

—2002–2004—

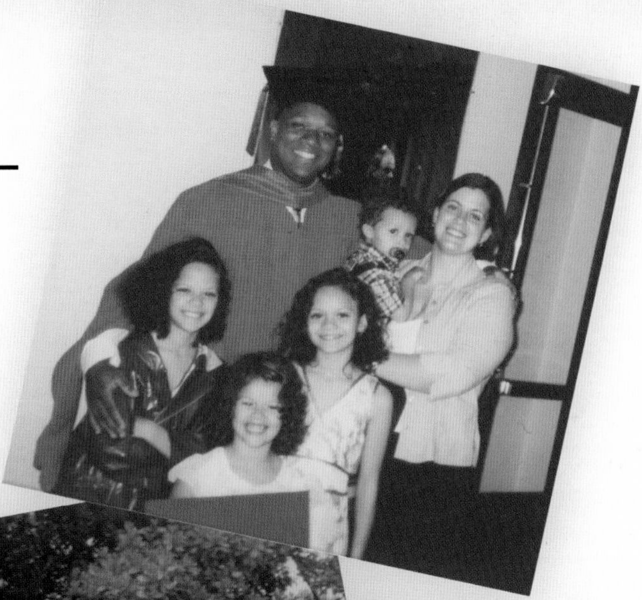

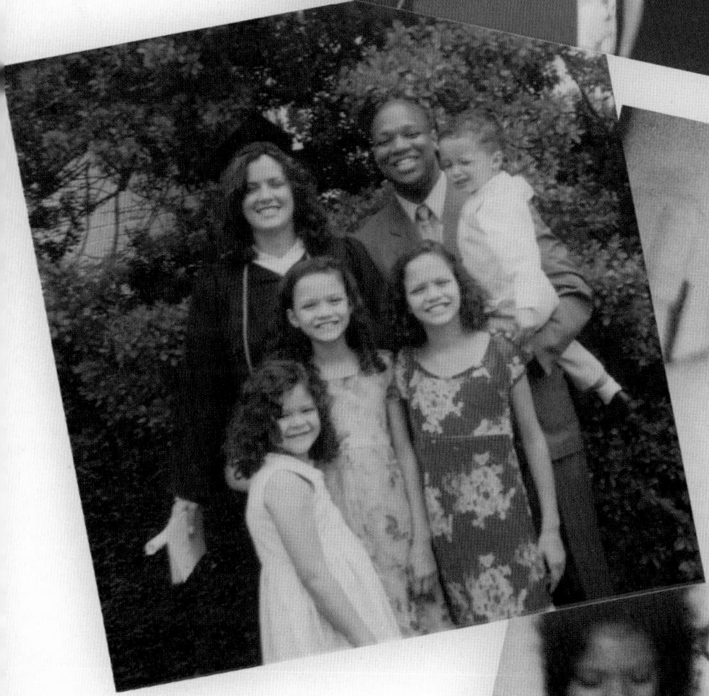

In all the years since...

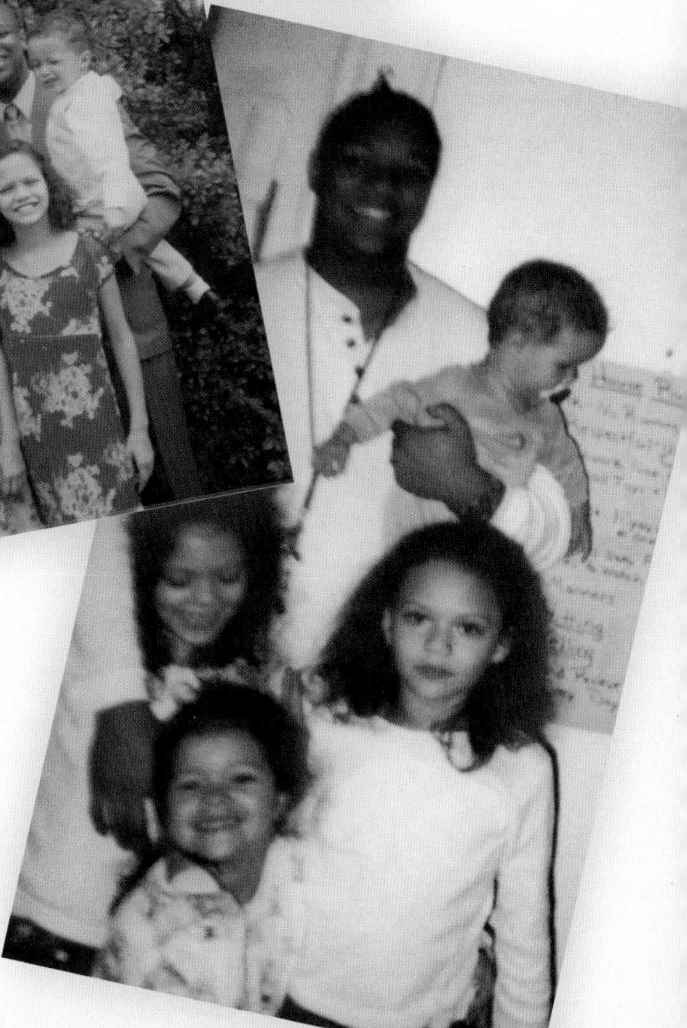

—2017—

...they never got into fights.

Also available from
Joel Christian Gill

FAST ENOUGH: Bessie Stringfield's First Ride • By Joel Christian Gill
40 pages • Hardcover • $17.99 • ISBN 978-1549303142

Bessie dreams of riding her bike with the boys
after school, but they tell her she is not fast enough. When
she finally gets a chance to race, she proves that
she is not only fast enough—she's faster!